Aileen F. Labuche 1/83
5°°

NAKED
TO MINE ENEMIES

The Life of Cardinal Wolsey

WOLSEY AT ABOUT THE AGE OF FORTY

The original of this drawing, quite possibly by a Flemish artist, was probably painted about the time of Wolsey's visit to Flanders in 1513, two years before he became Cardinal. It bears a contemporary inscription: *Thomas Vulsey Cardinal dyork* and (in a later hand) *autheur du schisme*.

NAKED TO MINE ENEMIES

The Life of Cardinal Wolsey

by

CHARLES W. FERGUSON

BOSTON · Little, Brown and Company · TORONTO

Published simultaneously in Canada
by Little, Brown & Company (Canada) Limited

PRINTED IN THE UNITED STATES OF AMERICA

Had I but served my God with half the zeal
I served my king, He would not in mine age
Have left me naked to mine enemies.

— SHAKESPEARE, *King Henry VIII*, Act III, Scene 2
(Based on words spoken by Wolsey
immediately before his death.)

Contents

NAKED
TO MINE ENEMIES

The Life of Cardinal Wolsey

The End as Prologue

It was Saturday night — the last Saturday night of November in the troubled year of our Lord 1530.

A chill mist from the River Soar crept in over the walls surrounding the Abbey of St. Mary of the Meadows, half a mile northward of the town of Leicester, and nestled around its massive hulk, making it look in the gloom of a winter's evening all the more reassuring and hospitable.

Lying near the center of England, known to dukes and beggars alike as a place of certain hospice on the road that led from the north to London, the Abbey would receive to its bounty tonight one who in his person was at once a prince and a pauper — Thomas Cardinal Wolsey, Archbishop of York, returning to London under the King's guard to stand trial for his life.

In the late afternoon a messenger had brought to the Abbot word of the Cardinal's slow progress from Nottingham. Sick with a coldness in his stomach, deterred and weakened by the flux, the Cardinal was said to be scarce able to sit on his mule. He would reach the Abbey grounds near nightfall and enter by the gate that opened off the main traveled road.

In the tower rising high above the Abbey church, a giant bell announced in cadent code to the surrounding countryside the approach of the broken prelate, suspending the stately routine of the black-robed Canons Regular of the Order of St. Augustine and summoning the whole convent to join the Abbot at the gate. Great tapers were lighted. The hounds, which some said were so numerous that they overran the Abbey, caught the itch of excitement and began to dash about and bark their thoughts and inquiries. All through the Abbey expectancy was punctuated by sounds of preparation. Men and beasts both seemed alert to the momentous.

A year before — and for fourteen years before that — Wolsey had ruled England in the name of the King. He had shown Henry VIII what a state was good for and how it could be made to do a man's will better than a man could do it himself. This Ipswich boy had grown up to teach a monarch — and a Tudor monarch at that — the arts and artifices of

3

statecraft. Legend mixed with fact and woven into envy covered him at the height of his glory with vestments richer than the sumptuous robes of his office. He was the most talked-of man in England. Many quaked before his baritone wrath. Few but his servants, and possibly at one time the King, loved him. Not a few hated him lavishly. Yet among all he excited unending curiosity. The pageantry of his living and the shocking power that he wielded at home and among the crowned and mitered heads of Europe combined to leave his contemporaries bewildered. For he was of the people and lowly, yet he consorted with rulers and bent them to his stubborn will and made them seek his favor.

The essence of tragedy is to know the end. The end was now in sight. With Cardinal Wolsey an age was dying, too, and the end could not be casual. The death of one who had lived on such a scale as the Cardinal, and through such thunderous years of change, was not to be treated lightly. And the Cardinal would make an event of it, whether he died before ravenous enemies among the nobility on the Tower green or in the vaulted halls of a great abbey where he could play out the last scenes with inspired eloquence born of courage, for he was now free of the fear cast by the shadow of hope.

His life had been a tumultuous interlude between his christening fifty-nine years before and the moment when, now, broken in health and deprived of all the accouterments of power, he approached the Abbey.

The occasion of his death would be the occasion on which he and those about him relived the days of his years. . . .

Book One

(1471-1509)

In which is pictured the early life of Thomas Wolsey and the world of which he was a part; his years at Oxford; his unhappy activities as a young priest; his various employments at Canterbury and Calais; and his acceptance at the court of Henry VII.

CHAPTER I

SEVENTY miles northeast of London in the county of Suffolk lies the venerable town of Ipswich. Situated where the River Gipping meets the sea, introduced by a deep and ample estuary, Ipswich in 1471 was a sheltered port through which thousands of fat and sturdy woolsacks passed to the English-held port of Calais on the coast of France. There the wool was sold to merchants on the Continent. And back into Ipswich came the cloth, so that the English had a way of saying that they sold the Flemings a fox for a farthing and bought the tail back for a guilder.

Here in this busy and hospitable port and market town lived a man and his wife by the names of Robert and Joan Wolsey. The name, spelled *Wulcy* until the spelling was modernized, was not uncommon in the region, being Teutonic in origin and signifying an island owned by a man named Wulf or Ulf.

Suffolk was a county made up of many people out of many lands, the beneficiary of many invasions. Evidences of Roman influence were all around. Colchester had been a Roman city of high importance. To the north some fifty miles away stood the indestructible fortress of Burgh Castle, one of the main points in the Roman defense against the savage Saxons. Inside walls built fifteen feet thick of rubble and stone, Roman legions had drilled and farmed and taken to wife women of the countryside until, in A.D. 47, they had suddenly been summoned back to the Eternal City as auxiliary troops to help crush a rebellion there. These legions had never returned, but they had left as an undying reminder of the glory that was Rome their massive fortress on the hills above the sea. And they had left other imperishable and sustaining reminders as well: for the Roman legions were not Roman at all but made up of soldiers from Egypt, Macedonia, and Spain; they were Tartars and Germans and Bohemians; and they had left in Suffolk veins the mixed blood of the known world.[1]

In Saxon times the town had got its name of Gyppeswyk from the small River Gyppes that flowed down from the north. It had enjoyed prosperity even in those days and aroused the covetous interest of the Danes, who

7

made forays and sallies against it across the sea. Twice—in 991 and 1000 —Danes had invaded the town, broken down its ramparts, and set it on fire.

To Robert and Joan Wolsey in the year 1471 a son was born. The day of his birth remains uncertain, for there were no parish registers then. Antiquaries who reckon such matters, however, set the month as March, and they believe that St. Thomas of Aquino, whose feast day is celebrated on March 7, may have marked the natal day and given the child his name of Thomas.

There had been harbingers from the sky. Three years before, a blazing star had appeared in the west "and so endured for five or six weeks." The next year there was a second comet, "the flame thereof like a spear-head." In January of 1471 there appeared the most marvelous blazing star that had been seen. It arose in the south "at two of the clock at midnight and continued twelve nights; and it arose easter and easter til it rose full east." It was marked by "white flame of fire fervently burning . . ." Sometimes it would seem quenched out and suddenly it would burn fervently again. In March of 1471 there were "great storms, winds and tempests from the sea." [2]

The year 1471 was a sorry time to bring forth a child. For one thing, the bubonic plague, dubbed the Black Death when in 1349 its clammy hand had claimed nearly half the population of England, returned to waste the land. There was in this year an attack of "the most universal death that ever I wist in England," Sir John Paston wrote to his mother, who resided in a county north of Suffolk. His inquiries of travelers failed to elicit the name of a single town that was not infected. [3]

The disease "took men generally in the head and stomach, appearing first in the groin," says Villani, "or under the armpits, as little knobs and swellings called kernels, boils, blains, pimples or plague-sores; being generally attended with devouring fever, with occasional spitting and vomiting of blood, whence, for the most part, they died presently or in half a day, or within a day or two at the most." [4] One friar tells of seeing penitent and confessor borne together to the same grave.

The unmeasured effects of the Black Death still lingered in 1471. For when the plague tumbled so many of the poor and lowly into swollen graves, it gave a new human worth to those it left. Survivors enjoyed a death benefit. Although of the commonest clay, they took on a strange and unpredictable value. The serf, formerly bound by the thongs of feudalism to the soil, found himself eligible for release. There was no longer an indefinite supply of men whom the lord could make do his bidding.

8

The serf suddenly and unexpectedly became a laborer. And labor, being hard to get, became a commodity. If my lord's bailiff sought to press a serf into compulsory service, the man might desert the manor and flee into the forest. Then later he could emerge on the other side of the forest and find himself hired for good wages. Meanwhile my lord had a field on his hands with none left to till it, and if he were to get aught for it, he would have to find some enterprising fellow who would rent it rather than farm it as a villein.[5]

A spiral of respectability had thus been started by the commotion attending the Black Death. For those who had once been content to be serfs became laborers and forgot their place. It was noised in Parliament that laborers did keep greyhounds and other dogs, "and on the holy days when good Christian people be at church, hearing divine service, they go hunting in parks, warrens and coneyries of lords and others, to the very great destruction of the same."[6]

Land values fell as farms were abandoned by serfs and the gentry confronted demands for higher wages. To meet this frustration there had been enacted by Parliament a series of Statutes of Laborers, fixing in detail the pay of all manner of workmen.

Yet somehow the lower classes would not remain in place, and the spiral could not be halted by the ceiling laws had made. Among those who had been serfs, some had become landless laborers who had sold their brawn; but others had become yeomen farmers, ranking only a little below gentlemen, men with independence and enterprise.

The men of Suffolk in 1471, then, were still at sea regarding the confusion and change wrought by the distant doings of the Black Death. It was a time of growing wealth and strange decay. The wealth came from the backs of sheep, and it settled in the hands of a limited if increasing number of yeomen who had not enjoyed wealth before and who were lusty for it. At the same time, the sheep multiplied out of hand and threatened to overrun and devour the land, upsetting all other types of agriculture. The sheep may have numbered eight million, Bindoff says. If so, this meant that there were three sheep to every human. "The 'golden hoof' turned moss-land into cotton-grass and heather moor into mat grass, and slowly destroyed the oak, the hazel and the birch."[7] And as the number of sheep grew, more and more of the village common lands and farming areas were firmly enclosed in hawthorn hedges to make room for more and more sheep.

"Commons to close and keep; Poor folk for bread to cry and weep;

9

towns pulled down to pasture sheep . . ." ran the lament. Another: "I have heard of an old prophecy that horn and thorn shall make England forlorn." [8]

Robert Wolsey was a man who in his small way rode the crest of the wave of change. He was a grazier who lived off sheep and cattle. A London merchant who visited Ipswich in the summer of 1483 spoke of "the fat cattle he saw feeding on the lands of Maister Wolci." Fetherstone, a learned monk who resided in Ipswich about 1480, told of a squire named Wolci who fattened cattle for butchers on his grass near the town.[9] This squire sold wool to the English market in Calais as well as meat in the market of the town. As merchant and grazier both he was in a fair way to be hated and envied, but he was also in a fair way to accumulate at least some of the tangible rewards and assurances that come from business success.

Under old arrangements a farmer might tend a few sheep and let them graze with the other cattle of the village on the common field. But as the demand for English wool increased abroad and the price rose, and as men of enterprise saw the advantages of sheep farming, the earlier system of open land stretching out from the village would no longer suffice. In order to run large bands of sheep and cattle, which could be cared for almost as cheaply and with as little labor as small ones, vast stretches of land had to be enclosed with hedges.

What happened to the farming villages under the increasing system of enclosure was sad and plain. In one case, Henry Smith, Gentleman, enclosed 640 acres of land, "whereby twelve messuages and four cottages fell to ruin, and eighty persons there inhabiting, being employed about tillage and husbandry, were constrained to depart thence and live miserably. By means whereof, the church grew to such ruin, that it was of no other use than for the shelter of cattle, being with the churchyard wretchedly profaned, to the evil example of others . . ." [10]

From the deserted villages the disinherited wandered about, seeking either work or relief as beggars. Beggars stood in the highway "whom ye be afraid to say nay unto, lest they take it away from you violently." [11] Loiterers lurked in alehouses, of which the towns had an abundance. They would sit "swilling, gulling and carousing all the day long, yea, all the night too . . ."

On the other side of the fence, those who stood to profit from the increasing number of sheepwalks relished and encouraged the transformation of England from a land of small farmers to a land of sheepmen with large holdings. One stapler, grown fat on wool, set in the stained-glass windows of his elegant new house this legend: "I thanke God and ever shall. It is the sheepe hath payed for all."[12]

Even if a wool merchant could not afford stained-glass windows, he might at least afford windows of plain glass. Windows were often covered with oiled linen or thin horn, but the use of glass windows was also becoming common. Sometimes the upper parts of the windows were glazed, while the lower ones were fitted with wooden shutters. Glass was available but the price was high; among fines listed for servants the penalty for "toying with a maid" was fourpence, whereas the fine for breaking a glass was twelvepence.[13]

The growing class of merchants and yeomen were now able to afford chimneys for their houses. Chimneys were looked upon with some scorn and some concern, it being pointed out that in the old days, when the smoke was allowed to escape as best it could, the children suffered from fewer rheums and colds and wheezes.[14] The chimneys and now some of the houses were beginning to be made of brick. At the port towns bricks from Denmark were coming into use. The growing use of brick was only another sign of the prosperity to be had from sheep and of the way men might rise from one class to another on the backs of sheep and cattle.

In the days surrounding 1471, England was bled from the effects of the Hundred Years' War. In this war she had sought to make good her claim to France. There had been moments which carried the promise of success, as at Agincourt, but then England had lost by gradual amputations the territories she had gained in France until only the port of Calais remained as a place for the shipment of her wool to the Continent.

Not only had that dismal war failed in its purpose; its failure had gravely affected the realm. As it staggered to its inglorious end in 1453, more and more soldiers skilled in brutality were loosed upon England, ready to pillage for pay, eager to sell to any lord the only talent they had. Knights and archers, to whom plunder and brawling were a habit, roamed about until they fell into the hands of some shrewd paymaster who would hire them for his lordship's private army and sometimes for his private war. And if they were not hired for some nefarious end by the nobles, they were left with a free lance to fend as best they could, derelict and restless.

With these recruits had begun, fifteen years before Wolsey was born, the bitter and internecine battles known in the poetry of history as the Wars of the Roses. Chivalrously the rival claimants to the Crown accepted as symbols of their bloody contentions the rose — white for the House of York, red for the House of Lancaster. Each thorny faction took unto itself ruffians home from the war in France, ready to wear the rose of

11

any lord for pay; and the gentry that might be drawn into the conflict kept changing their badges as the fortunes of strife brought one or the other contender to the fore.

In the early months of 1471, England was a headless realm. For years her wretched and shadowy King, the sixth Henry, had been held captive in the Tower. Earlier the noble Houses of Lancaster and York had played his image like a card — now in, now out; now dealt, now discarded. Of late the Earl of Warwick, he who was called the Kingmaker, had taken the aging Henry from the Tower, dusted him off, and, after parading him around London on a white charger, had propped him on the throne again.

It was plain, however, that this feeble rulership could not last. For the Yorkist King, Edward IV, who had fled to Europe six months before, was even now preparing to return in force and recover the throne, Warwick and his flabby puppet Henry notwithstanding.

It was a period of suspense in government, when the King's writ ran hardly at all; a period, as it were, between reigns, and it invited riot and civil commotion. Murderers and thieves crept out of sanctuary.

Uneasily the people watched and were right queasy. The English had temporarily deprived of power nearly half the kings who had reigned over them since 1066. The office of king was sacred; the person of any particular king was subject to hazard, often to contempt. It was the idea of king that mattered; his person mattered only if it served the interests of the nobles in power to maintain it. "In the 280 years before Henry VII established the Tudor dynasty, England was ruled by twelve monarchs, beginning with John and ending with Richard III. Of these 12, only three were permitted to reign until death overtook them. Of the remaining nine, seven were stripped of their powers, five lost their lives by violence, two were insane." [15]

The pathetic Henry VI had inherited the throne of England while in his cradle, and at the age of two had been proclaimed King of France as well. He was never in fact King of either country. But all his life he was made ceremoniously to act the role. He had toddled in processions of state at the age of five. At eight he had endured his coronation. At nine he had been carted with pomp and circumstance across the Channel to be crowned in France also.

He was not made to be a king, this Henry; not a ruler, this gentle, feckless, devout fellow. When the times cried for swords and treachery, his pride was to found a school for poor scholars at Eton and the King's College, Cambridge. He wore from his youth square boots like a farmer

12

and a long cloak and hood like a burgess. Nor had he any of the pious cruelty that was common to his day. Once he saw a quarter of a man set over Cripplegate in London and asked what it was. "A traitor false to the King's majesty," was the reply. "Take it away," Henry ordered. "I will not that any Christian man be so cruelly used for me."

In the midst of tumult and change, the sixth Henry remained at inward peace. He gaped not after conquest, took no part in the war abroad, though his countrymen refused to surrender his French claims; those who continued the French war used pretensions made in his behalf to espouse their plunder.

His marriage to a relentless young Frenchwoman, Margaret of Anjou, had done nothing to ease his distracted life. On the contrary, he was constantly harassed by the events which her ambition and quarrelsomeness stirred within the kingdom. After eight fruitless years of marriage, Margaret bore Henry a son and heir. Both the people and the King were astonished, Henry declaring through a glaze of incredulity that the child must have been fathered by the Holy Ghost. Shortly after the birth of his son, Henry lost even the semblance of interest in his office and retreated into amiable madness. There was no violence about him, even when he was deprived of his reason. He merely stared into space, his mind a fugitive for a season from the problems it confronted.

In the pageant of disease, disorder, and mischief, Henry remained an idea, however weak his person. Nobles sought to control him, not to abolish him. He was the national emblem. Weak as a ruler, preoccupied with heavenly matters, impoverished by his own charity, and incapable of rich display, Henry the son of the hero of Agincourt, where the flower of French chivalry had been destroyed, was still the King.

He was still the King, that is, until Edward defeated his troops mercilessly at the battle of Towton, fought on Palm Sunday, 1461, in the north of England, hard by the city of York. Aided by a snowstorm that blinded the Lancastrian archers and a wind that made their arrows fall short, the Yorkists and Edward gained a great slaughter. The Lancastrians were killed as they ran, and the snow all the way to York was colored with blood.[16] Henry had taken refuge in Scotland, then had returned to England, wandering about the west of his whilom Kingdom disguised as a bumpkin (it was not difficult) until agents of Edward found him in a farmer's cottage and brought him to London and lodged him in the Tower. There he remained until, through the maneuvering of Warwick, Edward was forced to flee the kingdom and the ineffectual Henry, he of so many fits and starts and in and outs, was put on England's throne

13

again. It was like a game of musical chairs: when the noise of battle stopped, the player nearest the throne dashed and sat.

Shortly after Thomas Wolsey was born in Ipswich, Edward returned from Europe, where he had fled when Warwick seized the reins of government. He had a few men with him, and he hoped to recruit thousands more as he marched toward London.

A country still suffering from the wastes of a hundred years of costly bloodshed abroad, smitten by the recurrent plague, overrun by thieves and robbers and vagabonds, ruled by a king listless and unhinged, with a foreign harridan for a queen, shaken by the rise of the lower classes to create a new and unexpected class of traders and yeomen farmers and merchants with emerging impudence and arrogance — this distraught land was now to be subjected again to the bloodletting of continued civil war.

During these parlous times the problems that concerned the people of Ipswich were strictly local, and the record of the town's activities showed a sturdy indifference toward matters beyond the walls. With the landing of Edward a gossiped fact, the annals of Ipswich reported only that Ingell Bolton was fined "for nuisance done to the highway at Cole Dunghill, by laying muck therein." Later, with no mention of the fact that meanwhile Edward had defeated the Lancastrians at Barnet, it was solemnly stated: "Such as suffer their hogs to go at large within this Town shall pay for the first offence, for every foot 1d, for the second offence 2d, and for the 3rd offence shall forfeit the hogs so wandering." Whatever happened to kings and princes on blood-soaked fields, what mattered in Ipswich was this: "All the Inhabitants of the Town shall grind their corn at the Town mills under forfeiture of half a bushel of corn ground elsewhere."

Robert Wolsey had come to Ipswich from his native Combes, near Stowmarket, ten miles away. In Ipswich he was therefore an alien, and the plight of the alien there was severe. It was provided "that no stranger being inhabitant in this Towne shall harbor in his house as guests or otherwise any strangers, merchants, mariners or others, under peril of forfeiture of 6s8d for every person so harbored, and imprisoned." [17]

There was a detailed and scrupulous regulation of trade, it being decreed, for example, that "all victuals and fish shall be sold by the owners thereof, and not by retail by the inhabitants of this Town, under peril of seizure." And: "No butcher within this Town or liberties thereof shall sell any flesh of Beasts within this Town, but only in the Butchery, on

14

Mondays, Tuesdays, Thursdays and Saturdays, under forfeiture of 12 pence for each offense." [18]

As an alien from ten miles away, possibly unfamiliar with details of regulations and under ubiquitous suspicion besides, Robert Wolsey was often in trouble with the town authorities. The first notice in the rolls of Edward IV marks his appearance in court for keeping an "hospicium" whereat he sold victuals for excessive gain. Again he was also in the same court, "in company with another Stowmarket butcher, one John Wood, fined for selling bad meat at the Ipswich market and for not exhibiting the skins of beasts which they had slain."

The offenses for which Robert Wolsey was haled before the authorities commenced before the son was born, and by the time his son was nine he was the "greatest offender before the leet. He brewed ale and sold it in illegal measures; he provided horse provender for excessive gain; he did not maintain the street gutter in front of his house in good repair; he permitted his pigs to wander about at large within the borough precincts; and he defiled the highway with filth from his stables instead of placing it within the public pits." [19] Among the charges made against Robert Wolsey was one that he allowed his house to be used for immoral purposes. Precisely what the immoral purposes were is not clear. Under the stern ordinances of the town the charge might have meant that he allowed his house to be used as a place of assignation — or it might have meant that he allowed Dutchmen to stay there.

Preoccupation with local concerns proved sound for Ipswich. By the time the year 1471 was half over, the Kings had settled their affair of honor, and the succession, and the whole realm was to enter upon fourteen warless years. Accompanied by his brother Richard, Duke of Gloucester, Edward had landed at Ravenspur, seventy miles to the north of Ipswich. He had defeated and demolished Warwick's army at Barnet, ten miles north of London. Warwick, unhorsed and unable to flee in his heavy armor, had been killed — a kingmaker dead and turned to clay at the age of forty-four. Weeks later Edward had defeated the Lancastrian forces under Margaret and her eighteen-year-old son in the shambles of the battle of Tewksbury. It was the lad's first battle and he would not fight another. Overtaken after the battle and cut from his horse, he had his head bashed in like any common knight's. Some said it was Edward's faithful brother Richard who cut him down.

There was no rival heir apparent now. Edward returned to London with Margaret as his prisoner. And the night of his return the unfortunate and bewildered Henry VI found rest at last, murdered in the Tower. History would not impose on him again.

Ipswich could now settle down to the business of shipping wool and to the graver concerns of local government. It made little difference to the citizens in their concerns with wool and hogs and laws that Henry, as Warkworth chronicled, was murdered "on a Tuesday night 21 May between 11 and 12 of the clock." Or that "on the morrow he was chested and brought to St. Paul's, and his face was open that everyone might see him. And in his lying he bled on the pavement there; and afterwards at the Black Friars was brought, and there bled new and fresh; and from thence he was carried to Chertsey Abbey in a boat and buried there in Our Lady's Chapel." [20]

So the sad event stood in the chronicles of the realm, but there is no mention of it in the annals of Ipswich. There we find, in the midst of the stern and stirring events of the day, space given to more immediate local concerns — as, for example: "The Town millers are, at their peril, to take no excessive toll." Apparently a miller was a greater threat than a king, new or old, for the town was in many respects autonomous and must discipline its own, whereas a king could hardly do more than molest the inhabitants occasionally.

Still and all, Edward was back on the throne and he was the King who had said, "Hang the rich by the purse and the others by the neck." It would be well to keep on durable terms with him.

CHAPTER II

IT WAS a period when rulers sought to control restlessness by laws and keep the lower members of society in the proper and ill-fitting uniforms of their class. It had been decided that "because the Commons of this Realm do daily wear excessive and inordinate array to the great displeasure of God," no knight or his wife under a lord's estate might wear cloth of gold or fur of sable.[1] Laced sleeves, stuffed with wool or cotton and known as bolsters, were fashionable among the nobility, and the same statutes marked bolsters as a special privilege of the upper class and forbade any yeoman or person under that degree to wear these full-padded sleeves.

The consignment of certain men and women to certain kinds of labor

16

was construed to be religiously ordained. It was almost mythological in its significance. As one writer depicted it, Mother Eve hid the least favored of her children, "but such as were fair and well made she wisely and cunningly kept with her." God in due course came to call upon her and asked to see her children so that He might promote them in their different degrees. He choose the eldest to be an emperor, the second a king, the third a duke; all the rest he made earls, lords, barons, squires, knights, judges, mayors, and so on down the respectable line. Then Eve produced her other children from their hiding places. They were dirty, rough, and covered with cobwebs, misshapen in stature. God did not conceal His disgust. "None," He said, "can make a vessel of silver out of an earthen pitcher . . . or a bright sword out of a cow's tail." He then went on to pronounce sentence: "You shall all be ploughmen and tillers of the ground, to keep oxen and hogs, to dig and delve, and hedge and dike, and in this wise shall ye live in endless servitude . . . Some of you shall be allowed to dwell in cities . . . butchers, cobblers, tinkers, costard-mongers, hostlers or daubers . . ." [2]

The fashion of seeing human history thus cast up in terms of the *status quo* lent a comfortable sense of permanence to the existing order, a species of eternality, as though social distinctions inhered in the very nature of the heavens. Thus interpreted, the spade of Adam was seen to be the first shield in heraldry. Cain was the first churl. Society, in brief, had been ordered from the beginning to remain fixed. It behooved a man to recognize this fact and to stay where he belonged.

In such a society as prevailed at the time of Thomas Wolsey's birth, the lot of children was low. Manifestly the best way to teach a person his place and station in life was to begin with the child. There was in force a statute that any boy or girl who had served at husbandry, at the plow or cart, until the age of twelve "from henceforth shall abide at the same labor without being put to any mystery or handicraft." The only release from this onerous provision lay in the permission of the parent to withdraw the child from labor for schooling. For the statute added: "Provided Always that every Man and Woman, of what Estate or Condition that he be, shall be free to set their Son or Daughter to take learning at any School that pleaseth them within the Realme." [3]

Moreover, a child's work was needed to help win the family bread, or he must be sent elsewhere to make one less mouth to feed. "Poor people," said Thomas Deloney, "whom God lightly blessed with most children, did by meanes of this occupation so order them, that by the time they were come to be six or seven years of age, they were able to get their own bread." [4] In some cases the age might be older, but usually the child was looked upon as a source of revenue, not as a responsibility. Mrs. Green tells us that children came into the towns constantly as young as seven; that they were never older than twelve when they came. And it was said in the letters of the Paston family that "every poor man that hath brought up children to the age of twelve year waiteth then to be holp and profited by his children." [5]

Being important in the economy, children were received with rejoicing and swaddled and coddled in their early years by their parents, just as spring lambs are tenderly cared for by a good sheepman. A child was kept tightly swathed until it was necessary to teach him the use of his limbs. Christina Hole points out that rattles were provided and that there were corals with bells. These helped the baby cut his teeth and were generally believed to have some value in warding off witches and preventing the falling sickness.

Because education was the means by which a child might escape the grim routine society had plotted for him, instruction began early and severely. If a child in his prattle and brightness showed aptitude, he was pushed. If he proved sluggish and inept, he was beaten. In either case he suffered torment along with learning. "Boys and girls alike were frequently beaten for childish faults, and tutors were not only permitted to but expected to underline their instruction with a liberal use of the rod." A parent's word was law and filial piety the chief of infant virtues. Any lapse from prompt obedience or respectful bearing was met with swift punishment, and there were no fancy ideas about self-expression or the danger of inhibitions. "Children addressed their parents as Sir or Madam and stood bareheaded in their presence; on special occasions they knelt before them to ask their blessing." [6] A dictum of the day put the matter plainly: "Never have the rod off a boy's back; specially the daughter should be handled without any cherishing. For cherishing marreth sons, but it utterly destroyeth daughters." [7]

In spite of all the severity and solemnity, there was still time for play. One picture shows a child blowing soap bubbles. The children of rich parents had many toys: whipping tops, dolls, toy windmills, and wooden knights on horseback to play at tilting. The games played by groups of children had the range and vigor of children's games everywhere. In Suffolk, blind man's buff was played as "Blind Hob." Another was a cheery version of "Here Comes One Duke A-Riding." One Ipswich game had the lilt that goes with swinging arms and showed the awareness even at that time of the importance of London town:

18

How many miles to London?
Three score and ten.
Can I get there by candlelight?
Yes, and back again.
Open the gate and let me through,
Here's my black and here's my blue.
Not unless you're black and blue.
Here's my black and here's my blue,
Open the gate and let me through.
Dan, Dan, thread the needle; Dan, Dan, sew.[8]

Sometimes the games were surrounded with a religious atmosphere. One of these had to do with the custom of electing boy bishops and then giving each boy elected wide scope throughout his town and diocese, providing them with all the accouterments of pomp and circumstance.

"After his election, being completely appareled in the episcopal vestments, with a mitre and crozier, he bore the title and state of a bishop and exacted ceremonial obedience from his fellows, who were dressed like priests. Strange as it may appear, they took possession of the church and performed all the ceremonies and offices save Mass." [9]

Clearly the vestments and panoply of the Church afforded children marvelous opportunity for dress and parade, for the kind of matchless play that would, at such times as on St. Nicholas' Day, give their imagination and histrionic bent full scope. The Church was solemn and serious in many aspects, but it prompted play and it aroused the fancy of the child, as these ceremonies surrounding the boy bishops show.

The Ipswich Grammar School had been founded by the burgesses a few years before Thomas Wolsey's birth, and the fee was fixed by the Bishop of Norwich at tenpence a quarter. (One penny would buy that ineluctable luxury, a pound of black soap.) Later the fee was reduced to eightpence. It was reasonable for the students, but it left the master somewhat underpaid, and to supplement his income he was given a monopoly in the town on the sale of quarry stone.

It is recorded in the annals of Ipswich that the master of the grammar school was to have "the government of all scholars within the liberty of this Town (excepting little ones called Apes Eyes) taking such salary as the Bishop of Norwich has appointed." Later it was provided that "every Burgess inhabitant shall pay to the Master of the Grammar School, for a boy 8d per quarter and no more." [10]

The town had begun to awaken, to see the need of contact with the great world beyond. Men wanted to learn to read and write, "to learn the

19

languages used in countries about us, that we might write our minds to them and they to us." Grammar schools had begun to be established by mayors and by merchants. It was specified that masters should teach "all manner of persons, children and other, the Science of Grammar," although the provision wisely added, "as far as lieth in him for to do." [11]

Over and beyond the curriculum of the schools a new educational interest appeared. It was manners. This interest did not make itself felt primarily in the schools for a long while; but it gained currency in the parishes and in the books of the day, and gradually an aim of education came to be the sweetening of life, the cultivation of behavior and civility, the gradual improvement of conduct among the common people.

This was new indeed. In Italy the movement had begun much earlier, and England was coming more and more under the Italian influence. Circumstances in England, too, greatly aided both the wish of those in the upper classes to improve the manners of those in the lower classes and the desire of those in the lower orders to learn the tricks and stratagems of courtesy which were the hallmarks of breeding. As the two orders of society came closer and closer together, and on occasion intermingled, it became important for those to whom manners were formerly a luxury to learn to make them a daily practice. No longer was it convenient for a select few in society to have a monopoly on good behavior. In a word, the movement up from serfdom continued on all fronts, and the etiquette of the lords and ladies was but one further area to be invaded by the poor.

Those who served at the squire's or lord's table often proved to be unruly and rude. Fresh from the barnyard and swilltub, brash and uncouth, they cared little for the elegance of the tables they waited upon; and if they did, they had no training to assure their acting in a seemly manner. Many times they were quarrelsome and corrupt, given to fights and lewd remarks — in general, sloppy and in no regard fitted to the services they were called upon to perform. Particularly was this true as new men rose to wealth and the demand for servants increased.

To meet the new requirements, servants must be trained, not only in the niceties of placing dishes but in the decencies that would keep a household from being corrupted by its servants. One writer said of the serving-men of the period: "Their company, their talk, their over-great experience in mischief, doth easily corrupt the best natures and best brought up wits . . ."

How sore the need for manners was may be seen from some of the early written instructions: "Don't spit or snot at table . . . Don't fire your stern guns or expose your codware . . . Don't pick your teeth with your knife . . . Don't claw your back as if after a flea; or your head as if after a louse . . . Don't pick your nose or let it drip or blow it too loud . . . Don't claw your cods, pick your ears, retch, or spit too far . . . Don't squirt with your mouth, gape, pout or put your tongue in a dish to pick dust out . . . If you blow your nose, clean your hand. Wipe it with your skirt or put it through your tippet . . . Don't pare your nails at table or pick your teeth with a knife." [12]

Functions of the various officers of a large household appeared in detail in the books of the day, together with pointed and detailed instructions on how the carrying out of these instructions might be improved. The almoner, for example, said grace and put down the alms dish at the beginning of every meal. The carver put the first loaf of bread into it. The almoner had a staff in his hand. He kept the broken food and wine left after the meal for the poor men at the gate, and he was sworn to give it all to them. What was left in the lord's cup went into the alms dish, and in some cases a piece of everything served went into the dish. Also the almoner distributed silver as he rode with his lord or master.[13]

Books prescribed and regulated the management of a house. Fires were to be kept from November 1 to February 2. It was specified, too, that the lord's privy must be kept sweet and clean. "Cover the boards with green cloth, so that no wood showeth at the hole; put a cushion there." Routine smooth and gentle marked giving m'lord a bath: "Hang round the roof sheets full of sweet herbs, have five or six sponges to sit or lean on, and one great sponge to sit on, with a sheet over and a sponge under his feet. Mind the door's shut. With a basin full of hot herbs, wash him with a soft sponge, throw rose water on him . . . Stand him on his foot-sheet, wipe him dry, put his socks and slippers on, take him to bed to cure his troubles." [14]

Deference ran through it all like a refrain, and the arts encouraged and the skills bestowed were all designed to please masters or betters. This rigid insistence upon deference to rank is carried over into the manners of the home. The advice runs: "Don't mock old men . . . Bow to all before you leave . . . Give the wall side to all you meet, and let your better enter first . . . Let your better choose which side of the bed he will lie on . . . Don't go to bed first until he asks you to, and first pull off his hose, shoes. When you're both in bed, lie straight and say 'Good night' when you've done your chat. Next morning wish your fellow 'Good morrow' tho' he's asleep." [15]

There are also household hints now and then, such as the intelligence

21

that cheese is the best cement for broken pots. Occasionally the books go so far as to suggest methods for improving health and the state of mind: "Don't take cream, strawberries or junket unless you eat hard cheese with them. Hard cheese keeps your bowels open." [16] One is advised after dinner to keep standing against a cupboard until the food has had a chance to digest. In sleeping one should have a hole in the top of the nightcap through which the vapors may go out. As for the technique of sleeping: "Shut your windows, lie first on your left side, to sleep grovelling on the belly is bad, on the back upright is worse." Indeed, to "lie upright on the back is to be utterly abhorred." [17]

CHAPTER III

As THOMAS WOLSEY grew up, his father improved in station and came to be a fixture in the community. In 1479 he purchased for eight pounds and a certain amount of land a house just down from the Cornhill, past Rosemary Lane and Dog's Head Street. It was a good address in the heart of things. Nearby rose the massive Church of St. Peter and back of that the Ipswich Grammar School. The house was in the parish of St. Nicholas, and Robert Wolsey was a member of this parish; and in the shadow of the church, which was solid and substantial rather than imposing, Thomas Wolsey lived as a boy. On either side of the door of the church, and at the height of a child's head, were two grimacing griffins, fixed there in stone as if to guard the portals against uglier spirits.

Not far from the Wolsey house stood the town shambles. Here customs made of iron held the merchants to rigid habits. It was an offense to sell the flesh of a bull that had not been baited for at least an hour. The bull was tied to a stake, with its horns guarded, and worried to exhaustion or death by dogs. This savage and noisy practice was said to add to the flavor of the meat, and it provided a daily spectacle as well. If the animal was not dead from mutilation by the end of an hour, it was finished off by the butcher. There was a balcony around the shambles, and the town often used the arena of the shambles as a place for pageants and cere-monies.[1]

In the midst of the pealing of the bells of the fourteen churches of Ipswich and of the bellowing of harried bulls in the town shambles, young Thomas Wolsey played. By the time he was eleven, he had exhausted the

22

local educational facilities. Although Cambridge was in the next shire, he went to Oxford, which was then recovering from the ravages wrought by the heresies of Wycliffe and was still, in spite of the ill repute it had gained, first in the hearts of the countrymen. And a lad so lingual and so intense in application, so eager to advance in learning, deserved the best. The Wolsey boy was set on his way to Oxford a good three years ahead of the age usually chosen in that time for sending boys there.

At Oxford Thomas Wolsey entered the College of St. Mary Magdalen. The College of St. Mary Magdalen was still abuilding when the young Wolsey arrived to take up residence there. It was the handiwork of the pious Bishop William Waynflete and was one of the early efforts to control the rampant students of the day by herding them into sheepcotes called colleges. Up to the time colleges came into being, the students at Oxford had been free to roam the streets, and they could not be compelled to live in any one place. "They might spend their evenings in the tavern and drink as much as they pleased. Drunkenness is rarely treated as a university offense at all." [2]

With the coming of the colleges came discipline, practically unheard of in university circles up to that time. The founding of these colleges marked a change from the period in which students, callow and irresponsible though they were, nonetheless enjoyed treatment as men. The student had been, as Rashdall has called him, a gentleman at large. He came now to be treated in the university as a schoolboy who must be disciplined and held in check. This change had as its accompaniment a new view of the university — as a place of custodial care, not only of the student but of learning, a giant repository or treasury where men must go if they were to enjoy the fruits of education. The university became fixed as a kind of fortress, hard to get into and hard to get out of; a guardian of the realm; a protection in the view of the prelates against the invasion of alien forces.

There had once been a hospital named for St. John the Baptist on the site of Magdalen. The buildings of the hospital were granted by Henry VI to William of Wainfleet with the thought that they be put to educational uses. The foundation stone of the college had been laid only two years after Thomas Wolsey was born, and the first building of the great quadrangle was completed three years before he arrived. Built of heavy stone, the college had a huge door that could be barred against hostile mobs and could hold the student back from the taverns. It was closed at a certain hour, and it stood always as a sign that the Magdalen scholar belonged not to the outside world but to the world within the gates. He was no longer living in a rickety tenement where he could do as he pleased and discipline himself only if he chose. He was no longer free to leave one set of lectures and walk across the street to another set given by a rival lecturer. Rules hard as the stone walls began to curb his impulses. He gradually became accustomed to the birch "at the discretion of the college lecturer for unprepared lessons, playing, laughing or talking in a lecture, making odious comparisons, speaking English, as well as for unpunctuality or non-attendance at chapel." [3]

Statutes enacted at the time Thomas Wolsey entered Oxford forbade swearing, games of chance, "unhonest garrulities," being out after eight in the winter and nine in the summer, entering another man's chamber without his consent, speaking English except at a feast. All were required to attend Mass daily and to hear sermons. Clothes were regulated; inordinate hair was condemned. Card playing was prohibited but chess allowed,[4] being a game in which kings and queens and bishops and knights were maneuvered to advantage.

Poorer students were licensed to beg by the chancellor of the university. There were some known as "battelers" who were required to wait on the others before sitting down to the table. Nor did menial service of this sort constitute any disgrace or set the students apart from their fellows. Rashdall says that there were very few traces of fires in any of the college chambers and that in "the mediaeval lecture room there was no warmth but what was supplied by the straw or rushes upon the floor . . . The cheerless picture created by the fireless studies is completed by the wooden window-shutters, the clay or tile floors either bare or strewn with straw . . ." The cost of candles put "reading by candlelight beyond the means of the poorest students. This meant disputations and repetitions as evening employments, at which a candle might suffice for the whole company." [5]

The senior enjoyed a bedstead, also certain coverlets and perhaps now and then hanging linen and curtains. The juniors often slept in beds which could be put away under ordinary bedsteads. Each room had a "study," which was movable, being treated as a part of the furniture. Gradually the studies came to have doors and were made into cubicles where a lad might withdraw and concentrate, away from all the commotion that went on outside.

The stern attempt to make angels suddenly out of the medieval students brought in its train a succession of failures. Indeed, it provoked and fostered wild indulgences. On the roads round about "were to be met parties of scholars — many of them expelled or banished for previous transgressions — who had turned highwaymen and now waylaid the more peaceful student approaching the University with his purse equipped for a nine months' residence." Rarely is the report of such a case varied by the statement that the accused was obliged to take sanctuary. "In the majority of cases nothing worse happened to the offender than being compelled to go to Cambridge."[6]

With all the hell-raising, both inside and outside the bounds of the university, a large core of the students applied themselves sedulously to learning. It was clear to the thoughtful that the only careers of distinction which were not in the hands of ecclesiastics were those of the soldier, the lawyer, the physician. The hold of the Church was notable in the line of diplomacy and administration. Thus the young men of Oxford might not always aim at holy orders for holy purposes. They might take the cloth if they were to perform any number of tasks in any number of good administrative positions which might be performed only by those who had been ordained.

The regimen of the colleges was too severe to be endured unless it led to some ultimate surcease. Lectures began at six in the morning, and "often . . . in the dark without artificial light . . ." The first morning lecture might last three hours. As a maximum, the student attended three lectures a day. His schedule during the day and evening was filled near to overflowing, as it was a plan of the authorities that little time should remain either for mischief or the exercise of choice. There was a very early breakfast for some of the more fortunate students, but both the hard and the economical student would omit this meal. Dinner was usually at ten o'clock. This would be followed by a disputation, carried on in impeccable Latin, dealing with matters of ethics or morals. There was some time allowed for relaxation then; but regular schoolwork resumed at noon, and the student either studied or attended other lectures until supper at five.

After supper the student took his postponed pleasure. He was free until eight or nine o'clock. Homemade amusements were encouraged. The disciplinarians of the college allowed storytelling and carol singing or the reading of "poems, chronicles of the realm, or wonders of the world." Assemblies to hear such performances took place around the one fire in the college hall. Much of the recreation was saturated with religion. There are records in the college register during the time Wolsey was in Magdalen of the election of boy bishops. Elections were followed by elaborate ceremonies and processions, so that the elected bishop and his attendants, together with the whole college, had for a day a sense of taking part in the great dignities of the Church.[7]

25

In 1483, while Thomas Wolsey resided in Magdalen and moved forward to his bachelor's degree, Edward IV died. He died in bed, which was no small feat for an English king. His son, Edward V, was destined not to reign. Instead Richard, Duke of Gloucester, lodged the thirteen-year-old heir and his brother in the Tower (lest a boy king set off again the Wars of the Roses) and had himself proclaimed Richard III.

To extend himself in public favor, Richard chose the device of kings, a royal progress, paying visits at the expense of the people to the several parts of his kingdom and receiving the petitions and obeisance of his subjects. One of Richard's first stops was at Oxford — in July 1483. Magdalen College was required by the statutes of its founding to entertain the kings of England and their eldest sons whenever they came to Oxford. In line with this requirement, Richard was honorably received there, and Magdalen was his headquarters and the center in Oxford from which the royal radius ran. The visit called for vast preparations, for clearing the halls, for laying in extra food. It provided, too, the chance to observe royalty in action, to note at first hand the customs and practices of the court, the deference accorded the royal person, and the manners proper to those attending upon great stations. Here were the world and the kingdom brought through the great gates and displayed before the eyes of the scholars.

The King for his part entered heartily if briefly into the academic life. The day after his arrival the authorities held for his benefit and possible instruction solemn disputations on moral philosophy and divinity. The brightest scholars were trotted out for the royal pleasure. To those who made orations or engaged brilliantly in the disputes, King Richard scattered his benevolences liberally. Next day he visited several colleges of the university and some of the schools attached to these colleges. In these he listened to more learned disputations.

On the occasion of his visit the two contrasting worlds of nobles and scholars were brought sharply together to the information and benefit of each. A scholar could look at a king; and a king could get, through the disputations and orations, some faint idea of a world he would never know.

In this stirring mixture of worlds, the profligate and the ascetic, the young and impressionable Thomas Wolsey began his career at Oxford, beholding the dramatic pomp of a royal progress and the rewards and royal esteem bestowed upon the glib tongues of those who had mastered the art of philosophical fluency.

Four years were required to attain the degree of Bachelor of Arts at

Oxford. According to Wolsey's testimony in later life, he received this degree at the age of fifteen — "a rare thing and seldom seen," the usual age being not less than seventeen. The ceremony by which the degree was attained, known as determination, was both elaborate and hazardous. The candidate was known as a determiner. Under the supervision of a Master of Arts the determiner took his stand for nine days, fully prepared, he hoped, to demonstrate his learning. For at least seven days he stood at a desk from nine to twelve in the morning and from one to five in the afternoon, ready to defend certain propositions against all comers. As Lyte describes the process, "an ambitious determiner could court attack by raising a knotty point, while conversely an unskilled disputant could almost as surely escape discomfiture by laying down some proposition that could hardly be impugned."[8]

In a word, the successful candidate engaged in the theatrics of learning. His aim was to impress, and the system under which he labored made the occasion of his determination one of vital importance to his future. It was an individual performance, not merely a matter of meeting set requirements. It was the high point of a young man's college career. Unless he took his Bachelor of Arts by determination, he would have to have an extra year beyond the seven required to get the degree of Master of Arts. If he did well in his determination, he might attract students for his future lectures, enlist worthy and wealthy patrons. And he would, of course, gain the plaudits of his classmates and impress himself on the body of the college. So important was the occasion that friends would "stand outside the door and forcibly compel passersby to come in and witness the proceedings."[9] It was an arrangement that encouraged ostentation of mind and put a premium upon a man's resourcefulness under stress and upon his ability to joust with words.

There were, of course, unearned degrees. The Convocation of Canterbury had to deal with this problem in 1486. Boys of ten and twelve might receive a Master's degree after a year's study at Oxford or Cambridge, and, according to one report, they might become venerable archdeacons before they knew how to sing Matins.[10]

That Wolsey was not one of the beneficiaries of this system of indulgence may be seen from the fact that he remained at Oxford for further study and later became a Fellow of Magdalen. He won his degree in the competitive system of the university and became known round about by the sobriquet of the Boy Bachelor. The degree brought to the boy who achieved it a good deal more personal liberty than was accorded the younger boys, and certain privileges; and the accolade bestowed after a

27

dramatic test of wits upon a boy of fifteen singled him out from among the other Bachelors and lifted him to special heights in the college community. Here was a student who, if his health held and his development continued would sit high in the councils of the godly.

There would be need of strong men in days to come. Times were still unsettled and the people queasy. With all the dignity that attended his station and with all the royal robes draped about him, Richard wore his crown warily. The princes remained in the Tower, and gossip stained the beards of men in the taverns and alehouses and went from ear to ear among the solid womenfolk. Anxiety marked the mood of men, and signs of it showed on every hand. Forces visible and invisible worked behind the pageantry of kings, both at home and on the Continent, and some of these forces took the form of men and some of machines.

William Caxton had brought the printing press to England in 1471. The first book in English had appeared in 1477 — *The Dictes and Sayings of the Philosophers,* translated from the French by Lord Rivers. There was no title page, the pages were not numbered, the lines were uneven, and the letters were a close imitation of the handwriting of the period. The sayings which made up the book had been compiled in Latin about 1350 and had been translated into French about 1410. This first book was followed by others, among them Chaucer's *Canterbury Tales.* England became conscious of her language and of its richness. Wandering German printers in other countries had used Latin. England's first printer issued his books in English — in the vernacular. There was now a way by which people could know the language and the ideas of the day without the laborious and tedious business of having scriveners in a monastery copy out the words. Something new had been added, if only barely added, to the blood and mind of a people.

Ideas that once crawled could now walk. In times past, the written word could be speeded in the scriptorium of a monastery only by having one monk dictate from a high stool while scriveners took down his words and turned out identical copies. Now a hundred copies of a page could be printed within a short period. Men's words could speed across the country as fast as roads would permit, and a thousand people might be reading the same words at once, whereas in times but recently past only a few monks could take down what one man said. A thousand men might, so to say, take down what one man said.

But it was too early for the printing press to aid appreciably the circumstances which would quietly alter the face of society, seaming it with

28

new problems men had not even begun to anticipate. Men acted as if they lived in a world immutable, made up entirely of a present formed in the womb of the past. The aristocracy and landed gentry went on cutting each other's throats as if they would enjoy that privilege for years to come.

The system of livery and maintenance still held sway in the days when the lad Wolsey held forth precociously in disputation on subjects of moral philosophy in the walled College of St. Mary Magdalen. A lord had men who were sworn to his service, bound by oath to execute his wishes, however monstrous. These hirelings would terrorize, capture, ransom, beat, or maim upon command. They wore the livery or badge of the noble thug who paid them, and in exchange for their reckless devotion he stood pledged to aid them if they stood trial by jury or fell afoul of the law on any personal matter.

The system kept the land in turmoil and the nobles in a passion and under the illusion of the importance and permanence of their own position. They seemed to be making history as always or as before, yet the formative forces of history were gathering to pass them by. Society appeared still to consist of King and lords, the Church and yeomen and laborers beneath. But, as Gretton puts it, "somewhere hovering on the flanks of these good men is a mysterious, generally dishonest, sly person who stretches cloth or lends money upon usury. He is not regarded as belonging to any class, but appears as a kind of unexplained renegade from uprightness." [11] He is the emerging businessman. In the center of the sound and fury of the old medieval world he goes right on making money and establishing himself firmly in the presence of, and under the stimulus of, confusion — yet he is hardly noticed, save as an annoyance.

Back in Ipswich, Robert Wolsey continued his varied pursuits with vigor while his son was at Oxford. He was able to buy a new house in the south ward of the town. He continued also to fall afoul of the regulations of the town, but apparently they did his progress no great harm. With the grace and help of a substantial income, he achieved an increasing measure of respectability in the parish of St. Nicholas. He was of the new and as yet unnamed class — businessmen — who had no standing by virtue of birth or position but had a larger and larger measure of control because they were able to finance enterprises, including the wars of kings.

Plenty of opportunities for wealth, a lot of them new, showed up close at hand. Chief among these was the manufacture of cloth at home in England and the export of this finished cloth instead of raw wool. And the merchant who had the shrewdness to manage all phases of the manufacture of cloth developed a high degree of business intelligence. It was a new kind of intelligence, that had nothing to do with the succession of kings or with the wars fought to settle that succession. It moved on a different plane entirely, but it would come in handy one day to kings. For it began to be clear that war could no longer be fought casually by independent soldiers but must be organized around the supply and the assembly of all of an army's diverse needs.

To an uneasy King busy with the pageant of royalty, however, imperceptible changes that might one day affect the government did not greatly matter. Richard had much that was immediate and pressing to reckon with, and in his reckonings he made the land as uneasy as himself.

Vague dissatisfaction flared into open rebellion. There was another Henry in the offing, a young man named Henry Tudor. He had been a lad of fourteen when the sixth Henry was restored to the throne for that brief and piteous season in the year of Thomas Wolsey's birth. Then they had brought him up to London from Wales and presented him to the old Henry, who, it was said, being much struck with the boy's "wit and likely towardness," remarked, "Lo, surely, this is he to whom both we and our adversaries shall hereafter give place." [12] For safe keeping, the young man was later sent to France.

The year Thomas Wolsey became a Bachelor of Arts at fifteen, with all the perquisites of privilege attached to that status, this Henry Tudor became King of England at the age of twenty-eight, inheriting the problems of a realm that had been weakened by generations of strife and quarrels, that was without status in the family of nations and without stability, or prospect of stability, at home.

The world of 1485 was like the streets of Oxford, given to quarrels and strife. There was nothing in the affairs of kings to lure a young man who lived in a maze of words. It was a period of dreadful night. The prospect just before Henry became King appeared to be one of endless contention, of continued battles for the succession, though why anyone would want to be king of beasts in a jungle like England was an increasing mystery to the merchants and traders and printers and graziers and all who drew their wealth and prestige from the handling of goods. The vast tournaments of the nobles to decide which man should sit on the throne had become a matter of less and less interest as long as the man who sat there was firm and kept the nobles at peace.

The Wars of the Roses, long a tragedy, had become a bore. Even so, Richard could not last. He moved almost constantly about his kingdom. In 1484 when Parliament broke up, he left London early in March and went to Cambridge. He tarried but a while at Cambridge and went on to Stamford and Nottingham. Here he stayed more than a month. It was the center of England, and here he could poise prepared if Henry Tudor landed on England's shores, as he was sure to do, to claim the throne.

It was while he was yet at Nottingham that the King received tidings of the death of his only legitimate son. The news threw him and his queen into the most violent grief, and it removed another of the strands by which he held his hope. There was now no direct heir. He was forced to name a successor, and this act would in itself make the whole matter of the succession fair game. First he named young Edward, Earl of Warwick, but later he changed his mind and nominated John de la Pole, Earl of Lincoln.

Again Richard began to pace about with his throne on his back. He moved to York and then to Durham and then turned south and came to Scarborough; returned to York and was next at Pomfret. During June and July of that year — 1484 — he moved about from Pomfret to York to Scarborough, and on July 30 he was back at Nottingham, where he remained until August, returning in that month to Westminster. It was at Nottingham that he could best be posted for the invasion. For the news grew bigger with the passing of the months that Henry Tudor would land in England. All along the principal roads, Gairdner tells us, horses were stationed at every twenty miles, "ready to mount and carry messages at a moment's warning. Important news could thus be conveyed by letter transmitted from hand to hand two hundred miles within two days." [13]

But the invasion did not come that summer, and the winter was quiet. In spring and in March, but a year after his son and heir had died, his wife Queen Anne died. She had been visibly declining. On the day of her death there was a great eclipse of the sun. The heavens seemed to be in on the event, and rumor ran that the sun had hid its face because King Richard had poisoned his queen. This rumor was followed by another still more bitter, to wit, that he would now wed Edward's daughter, Elizabeth, his own niece, to make more certain of his throne. Richard did what he could to allay public suspicion. He called a meeting of the mayor and citizens of London at the great hall of the Knights of St. John at Clerkenwell, "and before them all with a loud voice proclaimed that the design imputed to him was a fiction." [14]

From now on his time would be spent in protest and defense. Toward summer he learned that Henry Tudor had assembled a huge fleet at the mouth of the Seine and was ready to set sail for England. On August 11, Richard heard of the actual landing of his enemies. Yet with all his forethought, he had no proper sense of his real danger. He trusted men who turned against him, who were never really in his camp. He had thought that Sir Walter Hebert and Rhys Ap Thomas would oppose Henry Tudor's march into Wales. The Welsh rebel had landed at Milford Haven. But Richard heard nothing from the system of posts he had put up the year before. Either the sentinels were not provided this year or else they failed him, as did so many others. He knew nothing of the whereabouts of Henry, it appears, until Henry had reached Shrewsbury.

Then Richard sent immediately for the nobles to join him with all their forces. They came. Among them was the Duke of Norfolk, he who had been Sir John Howard of Norfolk, created Duke for his sturdy services to the Yorkist cause. Among the noblemen, too, was Norfolk's son, the Earl of Surrey; also the Earl of Northumberland. Not among them was Lord Stanley, who was joined in marriage to Henry Tudor's mother. His brother, Sir William Stanley, was chamberlain of North Wales, and he had done nothing to stay Henry Tudor's progress toward the center of England. He had already been declared a traitor. Richard held Lord Stanley's son as a hostage, a fact which showed how definitely he suspected this nobleman's loyalty.

Yet whatever Richard thought or suspected, there was nothing he could do but take at once a position where his military skill and experience might turn the tide against an opponent who had never been in battle before. The King moved from Nottingham to Leicester, and on Sunday morning, August 21, he left Leicester with a goodly army, "wearing his crown upon his head that all might see him." A march of about twelve miles westward brought him to the village of Sutton Cheney, two miles south of the town of Market Bosworth. There Richard pitched camp for the night. His scurriers told him that the army of Henry Tudor was but three miles away.

The battle for England was joined the next day. The actual fighting lasted hardly more than an hour.[15] When it was over, Richard was dead and Henry Tudor had been proclaimed upon the field Henry VII. Nobles on whom Richard had counted for support had turned against him at the height of the battle. The battle had not been won. It had been lost. Henry Tudor, an upstart Welshman, who had spent most of his life abroad, had shown no generalship. He displayed no bravery. Treachery and deceit had been his allies. Without the disaffection of the nobles — nobles Henry did not know until the final hour that he could trust to desert Richard — his claim upon the throne would have miscarried.

England was still, as it had been for seventy years, in the hands of powerful houses of lords. There could be no stability in the kingdom until some king became king in fact and put the nobles, outdated by the course of history, in their proper place: subordinate to the Crown.

There seemed little prospect that an untried Welshman, who was now King by the grace of God and the wager of battle, could accomplish this any more than his tragic predecessors. Yet he set to work almost at once to fashion a nation. To make fast his title, Henry summoned Parliament to meet on November 9. He let it be known that he would, as he had promised, marry Elizabeth of York, daughter of Edward IV, and thus bring together in one plant the rival roses of Lancaster and York. But he made it clear that the time of the nuptials must be of his own choosing: if he married her before his coronation and before Parliament had acknowledged his sovereignty, it would appear that he claimed the throne partly in her right.

Next he gave signs that he might unseat nobles as he had unseated a King. At his coronation he bestowed but few honors. He made his uncle Jasper a duke and he acknowledged his debt to Lord Stanley, who had deserted Richard, by making him Earl of Derby. But these honors were as events wagged them, and they had not the disadvantage of loading the nobility with new heads and thus encumbering the kingdom where it already had too much weight. The ends sought were plainly those designed to give strength to the idea of kingship as well as to his person. He appointed a body of yeomen of the guard to secure the King's person — to attend him and all Kings in the future. And the men who made up his Council were in themselves another kind of yeomen, for they were not lords of exalted rank but men who had shown, through law or architecture or some of the other professions, that they knew something about business and administration. He chose those who could use a pen as well as draw a sword.

Having established the character of his reign in these subtle and pointed ways, Henry pressed forward on two other important matters. One was to touch to the quick the pride of the nobles: it dealt openly with the menace of livery and maintenance. All members of the King's household and later the House of Lords and the Commons were made to swear that they would not receive or shelter any known felon, retain any man by indenture or oath, give liveries contrary to the law, or assent to riots or unlawful assemblies. All the lords swore observance, each of the lords spiritual laying his hand upon his breast and each of the lords temporal laying his hand upon the Gospels.

There was much murmuring amongst the lords over the King's exaction, but though they bridled at the thought, they nonetheless took their solemn oath in the presence of the new ruler, and a principle was raised on a standard for all to see.

Not less to the satisfaction of the people was the sound of their own voices and echoes made possible by the meeting of the Parliament. For one of the great pleasures of the people was the pleasure of grievance, the right to petition for the righting of wrongs. Protest was raised against the practice of allowing the royal household to raid the provisions of the citizens of the realm. The Commons pointed out that "food and cattle were constantly requisitioned for the use of the royal household, for which the owners received no adequate compensation." Henry saw the injustice of this casual robbery and devised an arrangement which was accepted. "A sum of £14,000 derived from land and customs dues was to be allocated each year to the king's household and an annual assignment of £2,105 19s. and 11d. was made to the wardrobe." [16] By this settlement of an issue which had nettled the English people for generations the King showed not only a novel sense of justice but an administrative precision which sounded a new note in the music of a monarchy. The new note, almost dissonant in its surprise, was a prudent regard for law.

For all the worth of Henry's measures, Richard's ghost cried out from his grave in the monastery of the Gray Friars in Leicester. Richard still had friends, particularly in the north of England, where he had always been high in the hearts of his countrymen. After Bosworth the corporation of York entered in their records that through the great treason of many who had turned against him Richard had been "piteously slain and murdered to the great heaviness of this city." [17] Soon Henry deemed it wise to forsake the security of London and move out into the northern shires and still the restlessness that lingered against him. It was well that he did. By an admixture of clemency and the threat of force, he quelled a double rebellion in the north and in the west of England. When he returned to London four months later, he had not only shown his royal person and the determination of his countenance to the people on a journey of some five hundred miles, but he had also listened heartily to the people and learned their grievances.

Henry's position as King now appeared tenable if not wholly secure. There had meanwhile been added papal sanction in the form of a bull which threatened with excommunication any who should rebel against Henry. It carried, further, the proviso that in case of Elizabeth's death, his children from any other marriage should still possess unrestricted

34

hereditary right to the crown. This bull was read and proclaimed by the bishops in all the cities. Also Henry had it printed — the first time a king had used the printing press for a proclamation.[18] Everything would be up-to-date in Henry's reign.

In September of 1486, the Queen bore Henry his first child — a son. The boy who seemed destined to be a King was given the name of Arthur, "in honor of the British race." There would be another King Arthur, or so the confident Henry planned in his dreams, perhaps one in whom fact and fable would be incarnate.

Whatever his ultimate fame, the infant son offered Henry immediately a coin with which he could do business abroad and lift his eyes from the pressing problems at home. The young prince was hardly a year old, says Gairdner, when a proposal was made by Henry to Ferdinand and Isabella of Spain and Castile for the marriage of Arthur to their infant daughter Catherine, who was just nine months older. Special envoys came from Spain to consider the matter, and "Henry opened his eyes wide with joy and broke into a *Te Deum Laudamus* when he found that they were armed with powers to conclude the alliance . . . He seemed entirely the servant of the Spanish sovereigns, whose names he never mentioned without taking off his bonnet, with conventional courtesy, in the presence of their representatives."[19]

In the time of these events, Thomas Wolsey remained secure in the citadel of learning. To young men gifted in language and cultivated in casuistry, Oxford was the world and the College of St. Mary Magdalen was a world within. A king might fall; another rise and face revolt. The whole structure of government might change, but Oxford remained intact. Knowledge was endless, at least in the sight of those who were its custodians. There was no use to speed the process of education and face the jolt of a non-Oxford world any sooner than was necessary or customary. There were two places on earth — Oxford and elsewhere. Why hurry?

So the Boy Bachelor settled down and followed his studies diligently and hard. Yet in spite of his burrowing, a mist of occurrences seeped in. A young priest in Oxford had groomed and put forward an impostor who claimed to be the Earl of Warwick, son of the Duke of Clarence, brother to the late King Edward and Richard. The Earl of Warwick at the age of ten had been confined to the Tower by Richard, lest discontented elements gather round him. There were abroad now ugly rumors that Henry had put the young prince to death, Warwick being a likely contender for the throne, his strength of lineage being all the greater for Henry's weakness. Later the rumors changed their character: it was said that the young Earl had escaped from the Tower and was intent upon raising a rebellion.

With these restless rumors the priest, by name Richard Simon, showed a close acquaintance in the scheme he laid. For he craftily found the son of an Oxford artisan, a lad called Lambert Simnel, the same being well mannered and bearing a likely resemblance to the young Earl of Warwick. So it was that the priest, seeing the resemblance and the designs that might be made on it, felt that the Oxford boy might impersonate the Earl, who was well known among Yorkist champions, and do it with such vividness that he might seize the throne.[20]

The better to circumvent any early frustration of his plot, Simon took the impostor to Ireland and played the prologue there, trying out the full effect of his cunning conception on the Irish lords, who were favorable to the Yorkist cause. And as Simnel walked like a well-trained peacock among the Irish and convinced them of the qualities of his person, there grew up and took shape a design that might well put this lad on Henry's throne.

So successful was the plot that Henry had to raise an army to meet the rebels, Henry who only two years before had been a rebel himself. The battle took place at Stoke, three miles from the city of Newark on the Trent. It endured three noisy hours, and when it was over, four thousand lay dead on the soggy meadows round about. As a rebellion, the affair had come to nought and had ended in a bog of blood. But there was more to it than would meet the eye of the historian. The rise and fall of Lambert Simnel had demonstrated an idea before the gaze of the rich and poor, the highborn and the low. One from the artisan class could walk with princes and wear the paraphernalia of royalty and occupy a lofty position, indeed be crowned King of England, if he had a proper tongue and stance. He could, that is, provided his rise and performance were to the advantage and service of his betters.

It was after the decision at Stoke that Henry came on a royal progress to Oxford, accompanied by a right noble train. In the course of the ceremonies attending his reception he was presented with a pair of gloves (costing fourpence) as a token of the esteem in which he was held and possibly with the suggestion that gloves might be needed, seeing all he had to handle.

The College of St. Mary Magdalen entertained him officially by virtue

36

of its charter and the obligation therein to be host to royal persons. There were eight solemn processions among the colleges as the King's train made its way and the King sampled the intellectual wares of the university. There was also another chance in this round of activity for the scholars to mingle with attendants of the court, to see the royal household in operation, and to gather from those stationed with the King an account of this young man, not yet thirty, who held with both hands the crown of his country firmly on his brow and promised to remain steadfast in his claims, albeit there were still rumblings against him and probably new treacheries afoot.

Already he had put to rout two rebellions, one by strategic clemency — this one in the very center of the Yorkist hotbed — and another by force of arms followed by clemency and his favorite practice of exacting fines from the survivors instead of their heads, of drawing their purses instead of their veins. He had a further feather in his cap in that he had exposed to high ridicule an impostor who had fooled not only a vast concourse of Irish, which was easy enough, but also the English who had shown willingness to die for him.

It was an auspicious moment for a visit, a lull between conspiracies, and one could assess with some accuracy and at close range the measure of the man who was now England's ruler. The lads of Oxford could turn from their abstractions and disputations for a holiday in the present.

Yet even at close range they could not be sure of the King, for Henry left men in a quandary. He looked old beyond his years and wore a cowl of gravity which he did not remove even in repose. Yet he was wondrously aware of appearances and of walking always before the gaze of his courtiers and subjects, so that his demeanor when on display was often one of gaiety and cheer; his eyes lighted up when he made speech, and his smile was quick when he engaged in riposte and rejoinder, as was his wont.

No one said he was handsome either of face or body, but he showed that he was supple from riding and hunting and the exercises of the chase; and if his hair was thin and his look quizzical, there was still and all about him the implacable confidence of one born to rule and to serve as father to his countrymen.

In deed and gesture, in proclamation and counsel, he set about to make himself patriarch despite his years. His appearance, which was not distinguished, and his bearing, which was not regal, somehow achieved a combined aspect that was both distinguished and royal: he showed in all that he did that his prime aim was to put the affairs of his house in order and have his national family well in hand before he was through. He was a sovereign, and it is not surprising that in his reign the King of England began to be referred to as His Majesty.

The indulgence Henry showed traitors was as a father pitieth his children. He was a graven image wrought by his own acts and chiseled by his own imagination to serve as father to a people orphaned by the death of many kings and now waiting a steady hand and a solemn face at the head of the table and a firm voice that would bring order and let little men get on with business and commerce. Henry was young, yes, but ages old — old as the Old Testament — in his way with the children of men and with men who were children.

These things were patent and to be seen by one who would see. And to add a cubit to the royal stature, whatever the animadversions and conspiracies raised against him, was the fact that he was a man of many Masses and pious practices, much given to praise and religious observance. He acknowledged with fitting humility the spiritual authority of the Holy Father of Christendom, and he had found it fortunate that some of his decrees had been reinforced with bulls that came without any apparent solicitation from Rome. Whatever the plan of his day, it always left room for God, and no man of the court had more intimate access to the King of England than the priests who served him as chaplains. There was an unction to all his serious acts, and the heady atmosphere of religion which surrounded his person and court made for mystery and enigma and drew a veil across the temple. "On my faith" was Henry's favorite oath.

As the King moved in eight processions around Oxford, news of his accomplishments moved with him. There were many jesters but not many dandies with the court; for the King had seen fit to encourage new men in his train, and these new men were to be judged not so much by family and forebears as by ability to serve their country. Three of these men stood out and lighted signal fires for the rest — Morton, Bray, and Fox. All were men whose loyalty to the King had been tested and burned of dross in past controversies, and none of them had claim to greatness by lineage. They stood on their own recognizance.

John Morton was now Lord Chancellor of England and Archbishop of Canterbury, in which latter position he ranked as head of the Church in the kingdom, and he worthily set about to remedy some of the grossest errors of the clergy. He noted well the laxness of the period and insisted that priests should reside in their own benefices, or, if they had more than one, that they reside in each for a season. He noted with dismay how widely the clergy had grown slack in dress and given up the tonsure. It was his order that they be shorn, and that right early, enough to reveal their ears; and further that no swords or daggers be carried by priests. Only graduates of universities, he ruled, should be allowed fur on their garments.

In the vigor with which he began to prosecute these measures he revealed his devotion to the King's cause and his desire to bring order out of the chaos created by earlier reigns. But what distinguished him, apart from all his specific aims, was an ability that had nothing to do with the cloth he wore: while Bishop of Ely, Morton had proved himself an engineer of high and notable talents, having supervised a great cut, or drain, through the fens from Wisbech to Peterborough. Such a man of practical skill and proven competence in handling tangibles, Henry had made his Lord Chancellor.

The other two of the three most cordially seated in the Council were of a like stripe. Richard Fox, Bishop of Exeter, was the son of a Lancashire yeoman, a priest and a doctor of canon law, versed to the King's liking in secular as well as sacred matters. Sir Reginald Bray was an architect, a diplomatist and a soldier, not a noble either. Bray was Lord Treasurer and his position in the new government was one of yeasty importance. That Henry had bestowed the custody of funds upon one not of the nobility, a plain man who had risen by sheer force of ability and by tasks competently performed, showed the King's firm intent to use men who could aid his hands in the fashioning of a new state and a stable one. There might well be a sprinkling of peers, especially if the King could create new ones to his liking. But there was serious business at hand to be done, and Oxford scholars could note that the King's choice of men to do this work of government would fall on thoughtful and not necessarily noble heads.

The new nobles created tended to be of the rural class, men who had made their wealth and position by the fruits of agriculture and the sale of wool and the produce of herds. They were men of substantial wealth, not merely men who enjoyed suzerainty over great domains through the accident of inheritance. The new nobles had risen out of rather than come down from. Any honest yeoman of good repute and tangible wealth and a knack for management might become a baron — and a useful one at that. The commonalty of men might still be imprisoned in the class and station which God had assigned them by birth. This they demurely knew. But all around now there were signs too unmistakable to miss that men of talent and usefulness could pass from one station to another. They might in a

39

sense serve an apprenticeship to respectability and later be accepted into the guild of the nobility or the higher clergy. Wars and confiscations had plucked many a lord from the ranks of the nobles and left spaces to be filled.

One could note still another reason why new faces appeared at the court. The King was lonely and suffered much from the tortures of suspicion. This Henry, whose garb on occasions of state was adorned with a most rich collar full of great pearls and many other jewels set in four rows, and who in his bonnet wore a pear-shaped pearl — this Henry lived as if in fear of ambush. And well he might, for the times had been out of joint for thirty years. The nation was full of discontent, of unemployed soldiers and turbulent men without livelihood, men ousted from their holdings by the munching enroachment of sheep, ever more menacing.

Even if no other leader arose to foment rebellion among the dissatisfied and the disinherited, there was still plenty to twist the King's head in sidelong glances. "Under the custom of livery and maintenance and the stress of civil war the old judicial and police system of England had broken down," Fisher tells us. "The judges indeed still went on circuit, but the juries were intimidated by the local landlords and could not be relied upon to do their duty. The justices of the peace still held their petty and quarter sessions but they neglected their administrative duties and failed to enforce law and order." [21] Complaint ran that the coroners would in divers places omit to view the body of a slain man, there being no fee or emolument attached to this duty. In these circumstances of negligence a murder might pass unnoticed. And if it were noticed, it might go unpunished. Small wonder that murder was treated as a pastime, following the ravages of a protracted civil war in which the slaying of Englishmen by Englishmen had become a sanctified habit.

By the time of his progress to Oxford Henry had established a new method of dealing with crime and lawlessness. He had turned his Council into a court, a court which met in a room of Westminster Palace known as the Star Chamber. Here was a study indeed for young scholars who would observe the law in action and see it change to meet the iridescent times. For if local authorities would not make the bad behave, the Council would richly see to it that they did. The members of the Court of the Star Chamber were chosen by the King to dispense decisions that others dared not make. Those who still kept large bands of retainers, those who bribed or threatened sheriffs or jurymen, those who took part in riots or upheavals — those who would have escaped scot-free in the days before the sitting of the Court of the Star Chamber — were haled before the King's appointees to give an account of their acts in due season.

These were the cases that were tried without benefit of privilege, and the enormity of their acts was measured against the picture which Henry wanted to paint for his people. The justices of the peace in the shires were in turn urged to refer hard cases to the Star Chamber. In this way the Council and the Court established central control of behavior by forthrightness and by the absence of awkward procedures and safeguards that attended trials in ordinary courts. The justices operating as agents of the Star Chamber enabled this new juridical body to reach out in all directions and fasten on any offender who might think he could with impunity breach the King's peace. Thus not merely such hefty offenses as treason came within the purview of the Court of the Star Chamber but also such offenses as housebreaking, horse stealing, the carrying off of cattle, and assault.

Matters momentous and trifling paraded before the Court of the Star Chamber and there drew a rough and positive justice that by degrees began to get the land on the way to order. With its twenty or thirty men sitting at the hub of affairs, the Court was the busiest and most formidable in the kingdom, what with the six or seven hundred justices throughout the realm supplying grist all the time and the commoners feeling gradually that they had through the King's Council a ready access for their grievances and for airing the injustices they were wont to suffer in humble silence or contentious frustration.

What Henry had fashioned in the room of Westminster Palace decked with stars in the ceiling was in effect a new class — an official class made up of men who gave time daily to the business of governance, whose role it was to spread equity and to regulate from the pivotal point of London the affairs of society on a national scale. Through the justices of the peace this grim arm of the King could reach out into every hamlet and make felt the strength of the central government. The Council was now a place of work, and through its operations the King's eyes peered into every manor and hut to fetch out what was amiss.

CHAPTER IV

For twelve shapeless years there is no record to tell us what Thomas Wolsey did or thought or felt. From the week in 1485 when he held his elders at bay and won his first degree until the day in 1497 when his name adorns the college rolls, only fancy can fill the gap and backward reasoning give us some surmise. We can merely guess how much the shouts of men and the eddy of events touched his growing mind; we can only measure what we know of all else against the youth and man of whom we know nothing.

What affected him? What passed him by? What stirred some sharp incentive to goad him later on? What in this period when the government of England changed before men's eyes and men changed their views when new forces expanded the mind and sent men out to find new worlds — what if aught of this had its bearing on the Boy Bachelor?

A violence of mind and weather swirled around the walls of Magdalen. Men were on edge, their spirits either restless or defensive, for there came to be an awareness, in spite of walls, of what lay beyond the narrow Thames and even beyond the Channel and the North Sea. The whispers of distant lands came symbolically in a new language. Frowned upon as pagan and of devilish consequence, Greek had suffered for years exclusion from doughty England, where Latin held court and enjoyed obeisance in every school. Then came a man bearing the gift of Greek, William Grocyn by name and a native of Wiltshire, who had traveled in Italy and fallen there to the charms of an ancient literature encased in another language. Thus Greek made its way, smuggled in under the guise of respectability, to Magdalen, bringing with it scents of spices from other climes, as a summer wind carries memories and is laden with traces of treasure from some indefinable country far away.

Greek was more than a language or a new course or an addendum to the curriculum. It was a new culture and a new way of thinking and a new body of literature which might, unbeknownst to those who were steeped in Latin, bring all manner of infectious ideas that could produce vapors, agues, and plagues and might people the atmosphere of a college with apparitions. Why endure the risk? Latin sufficed for all ideas a man could comfortably entertain, and it served a solid and useful purpose besides.

42

It aided the priest, the diplomat, the lawyer, the civil servant, the physician. Like the old Roman roads, Latin led everywhere, and if one wanted his thoughts to travel or the thoughts of others to come to him, Latin was the means. Books on all kinds of subjects were written in Latin; it was the means of communication, real as trade routes, between the scholars of all nations. Besides, it had become firmly entrenched in the schools. Here it was a language required and no other language was allowed. To enforce the use of the language, a spy was paid, the good Trevelyan says, to sneak among his playmates and "report if any of them used an English word in their play." [1]

Manifestly, then, a language so firm in the fortress of education could not regard with equanimity an invader which might usurp its place. Grenadiers of the Latin tongue leaped to battle as the warriors of a reigning king might leap to repel a rebel. Grave doctors preached against the study of Greek. The issue was down, and there were jousts and tilts and, at a later time, trial by street battle. It needed finally a royal edict to quiet the matter. Later in Bishop Fox's College of Corpus Christi the new language found hospice and was "allowed as an alternative to Latin in ordinary talk in hall and chambers and lectures in theology." [2]

Which of these two schools of language that ultimately came to contention with clubs among the scholars had its hold on the mind of the emerging Wolsey? Back of the High Street and the fights, deep in the recesses of the reflective apparatus, lay a war between resistance and awareness. It was more than a language brawl in an intellectual tavern. It was a play, a mystery play, an allegory in which Greek and Latin wore the masks of other forces and men as actors knew inwardly but would not admit the disguise. The question at stake was whether a society furnished with and carpeted by one set of ideas would admit another set of ideas alien and strange of tongue.

Yet the conflict between stability and awareness would not remain a drama of the educational stage to be acted out conveniently in symbols. Men were beginning to sail the roiling seas, and there were signs aplenty of islands and great land masses which might intrude upon the firmly fixed and comfortably known world of England. For in these same days Bartholomew Columbus came before King Henry of the English and with maps and compass persuaded him that the unknown not only might become known but might become England's as well. Bartholomew thought in water, not on land. Men said he was uncouth, but under the gust of his enthusiasm the King's fancy set sail. Let him bring his brother Christophorus, the King ordered, and let an expedition be arranged, that India

43

might be found by sailing north by west. But Bartholomew had fallen among pirates on his journey to England; and he had suffered much delay. Nor had it been easy for an unknown Genoese mariner to arrange an audience with the King. So by the time Bartholomew returned to his brother, he found that Christophorus had already settled with Ferdinand and Isabella. The ships which would launch him on his quest would bear the flag of Spain.

Henry had missed the boats. But his meeting with Bartholomew and his maps, together with the experience Christophorus enjoyed on the crossing, released something like a spring in the practical, matter-of-fact, notebook-carrying Henry. The prospect of gain based on chance touched off the gambler in him. Enormous dice to roll upon the sea, with — who knows? — continents for stakes!

It was common talk that the King looked with longing beyond the rim of the seas and that he was willing to shell out some of the gold that had begun to fatten his coffers if he could find men who would enrich the holdings of England, as the expedition of Christophorus Columbus might have enriched them. It was an odd twist and the subject of much wonder in the realm, this preoccupation of a solemn, precise, and businesslike King (whose favorite gesture was to rub his palms together like a shopkeeper) with distant isles and shores shrouded in the mists of uncertainty. Nothing could so unsettle the mind, especially if it happened to be of a conservative bent and steeped in Latin, as the suspicion that the world was bigger than all its parts and that all parts of it were closer than one had previously thought.

It might be possible to keep Greek out and set the mind and tongue against alien forces. But men could not be chained to the land, particularly if the King encouraged them with his support and sanction and letters patent to wander to and fro upon the waters. Here was a King who by firm measures and stern command had brought a modicum of peace to a shattered society and had put its affairs in order — only to look now beyond the watery borders that kept it safe from molestation and to look, as it were, for new troubles abroad. Better, was it not, to stay at home and improve each shining hour and each shining shilling? Would it be Greek or Latin? New worlds with new problems, or a stable homeland? Europe or the Seven Seas? Where should a young man's mind center if he looked to the future?

To the King, of course; but in this case the royal head looked both ways, one face being grave toward his subjects and the other one light and expectant toward the west. It was plain enough that England now possessed a ruler who possessed the kingdom, a man at its head who, because his claims were dim, meant to make up for any lack of security in lineage by the security of careful government. And the outlook thus became bright for young men of talent and smart operating ability who could adorn routine with energy. But the matter was not as simple and amiable as that, if the resources of England were to be deployed over the whole face of the earth and if the comfort of a self-sufficient and Europe-focused society were to be disturbed by the pulls of distant magnets. This promised for the moment to be the case.

With all his painful problems at home and at the calculating courts of Europe combined, Henry could not keep his eyes off far horizons. He could not forgive himself for the twist of fate that had cheated him from backing Columbus.

So he would back others.

In particular he gave ear to the restless whisperings in Bristol. On his very first royal progress he had paid a visit to this hospitable and enterprising port in the west of England, looking to the wild west of the sea beyond. Bristol was a meeting mart for those who sailed to Iceland and those who came from the warmer climes as well. It was a gossip chamber in which all the tales that stirred men's minds to vast physical speculations were exchanged.

To this port in 1490 came another man of Genoa, by name John Cabot. In his early manhood he had become a citizen of Venice. Now, after seeking vainly some support from both Spain and Portugal for venturesome voyages he wished to make, he came with his entire family to take up residence in Bristol. And in due course he laid his far-flung hopes and plans before the King, having first inspired other mariners to cast off in search of mythical lands and islands under the financing of Bristol merchants.

To the dreams of John Cabot, fashioned of mist like the rainbow, Henry lent a ready ear. So it came about that John Cabot, together with his three sons, set sail on substantial waters, trusting themselves to the assistance of the sea. They sailed as an adventure, but they carried an adequate ballast of royal approval, for the letters patent granted by the King gave them permission to seek out "regions or provinces of the heathens and infidels which before that time had been unknown to all Christians." It was further the order of the letters that no other English subject might even visit any of the territories discovered by the Cabots without express license and permission of the said John and his sons or their deputies.

45

The Pope had already divided the new world between the kingdoms of Spain and Portugal, but this stupendous fact Henry piously overlooked under the assumption that the Pope's edict applied only to the south and that Cabot might take a northwest passage and hence find new territory beyond the papal fold. It was odd, all the same, for one who so carefully cultivated the Church and attended her Masses to set Church rulings aside on a matter so important. It simply went to show how strong were the new currents that were passing through the minds of men.

When the Cabots returned in the first week of August in 1497, they brought no myrrh or spices, no tangibles of any kind from their bourn. But they brought further information of the great beyond. They had sailed north and had found land. And though they had not seen inhabitants, they had seen the signs of men; and they had found the waters near the distant shore temperate and heavy with fish, so much so that the fish could be caught up in a weighted basket. In these beneficent waters the Cabots had drifted far to the south, and everything they saw was good. And what they told upon their return refreshed again the imagination of the people who stayed home, and the tidings of these lands stirred the people from the languor of their thinking. There was something of the pull of the tides in these vast new movements of men and ships — and mind was bound to follow.

These tides were a part of the time of the hidden years of Thomas Wolsey, or Master Thomas Wolsey now, whilom Boy Bachelor and by way of becoming a Fellow of Magdalen College and a priest of the Church. There were pulls and tugs on the shores of his mind. Whatever he did in later years, he was now a votary of known wisdom, with Latin as a base, to be sure, but with Greek on his horizons. He pursued his studies of divinity in the cubbyhole of piety, but he could not escape the distractions of discoveries that now sounded loud enough to penetrate the Oxford quiet.

Meanwhile, he was of time and space and a solid citizen of Magdalen, where men of the world and of learning came and went with more frequency than ever and where the elements beat down. Wood tells us that in 1490 the predictions of Thomas Kent and other Oxonian astronomers concerning a great frost and scarcity of grain came to pass. Frost continued until January 29 and "became at length so hard and vehement that carts and horses could pass over the river near Oxford." [3] Game and fish were destroyed in great numbers by the merciless angry weather. Nature, being ever in those days given to violent extremes, as if to set

46

the uncertainty of the times to music, next withdrew her bounty altogether, and the frost was followed by a dearth of rain which endured until the time of the harvest the same year. As a result, wheat and barley were sold in Oxford at a usurious price which brought great grief and trouble to the scholars.

The college, for all its walls, was in these periods of severity becoming an inescapable part of the great outside, and the poor scholars, being without fire, "were fain to walk and run up and down half an hour to get heat in their feet when they went to bed." [4] And the already dismal fare was worsened as the simplest food became dear.

Visitors made for festive occasions, and the ceremony with which they were treated adjourned from time to time the tedium of lectures and the savage pastime of disputations. There had been the royal call paid by Henry shortly after his coronation when he left a characteristically frugal offering on the altar in the chapel. The president of the college, Richard Mayhew, stood high in the royal favor. He had gone to London to attend Henry's coronation. The account books indicate that the president fared well in the disbursements made for various details of administration. In 1484 bed and bedclothes were bought for his lodgings in London and one ell of linen for his shaving cloths. Later a new case was provided "for carrying the college arrows when the president went on progress." [5]

Enough went on to give the College of St. Mary Magdalen touches of convulsive gaiety, but there was always the weather, some grim reminder of the raw. And if it was not tempest or drouth or relentless frost or overabundant snows or a great water upon the land, there was pestilence. In one instance hardly had the scholars returned to Magdalen after having fled from fear of one disease than they were forced to flee again from another that had seeped into the confines of the College. All activities were suspended when a plague took up residence, and the scholars found refuge in the houses beyond Oxford. Wood tells us that "so frequent were the pestilences in these and after times that they gave a great blow to learning, and caused it much to decrease and lose its vigor . . . It was consulted by great personages of annulling the University." [6]

In this quarrelsome atmosphere of tempest, disease, and insecurity young Master Wolsey pursued his education at Magdalen during the years that the college forgot him. Education went forward somehow and constructive forces worked with steady vitality to keep things in a kind of balance. The physical buildings, the externalization of inward drives, the increase of tangible properties, seemed to be one answer to the confusion and turmoil all around. In one period 139 cart loads of stone were brought in for a wall in the grove. It was in this time that the first corner-stone of the new Tower of Magdalen was laid with fitting ritual by the chancellor of the university. The south cloister was rebuilt and the great gate erected. There were lodgings put up for the president of the college and a school for choristers. Bishop Waynflete, the founder, died and willed all his goods to the college, these being hauled in three fat carts. In one year eighty volumes were given the library by two Fellows, and expenses for chains to hold them were duly noted. In the hall at this time were figures of angels, and in the record there is entered a payment for washing the angels and for saffron for coloring their faces. [7]

There was a policy of progress and upkeep in spite of all difficulties. Gradually the institution grew in substance and tangibles and gave thus some answer to the world and some assurance to its occupants. The Tower of Magdalen rose steadily as if by right and as a symbol that might stand through the centuries. It was evidence in stone of both stability and aspiration. Architecture gathered up and said and amplified what men could not say with words. There might be bloody flux and bubonic plague and the sweat; there might be riot and civil commotion and the intrusion of Greek and foreign bodies of culture. But as long as there were massive edifices a-building, the university would not be annulled. The tower and the great gate and the cloisters and the new buildings — these were permanence in a world rife with change and uncertainty. If a man would make himself felt, let it be in stone.

Robert Wolsey of Ipswich died respectably in the autumn of 1496. Shortly after his death, the name of Thomas Wolsey began to appear in the records of his college.

In any attempt to reckon the cause and course of events it would be too much to say that the death of the father sired the son or that the interment of the elder signaled the birth of the younger. But by any reckoning it is plain that the son beheld in the father's attainments a sign of what the times required. By the simple acquisition of property, by the ownership of a house and the accumulation of moneys, the elder Wolsey had risen from the rank of an alien butcher to a position of at least moderate local eminence. It was an achievement not to be despised in those days, for the man was not many generations removed from serf-dom.

In 1493 Robert Wolsey had become a churchwarden in the parish of St. Nicholas. At his death he was able to bequeath not only funds for the

48

painting of the archangel above the altar of his parish church but other moneys as well to provide that a Mass be sung for him and his friends for the space of one year and at a worthy stipend.

This was the sort of provision that a man of wealth could make. It showed that, whatever the complaints raised against him earlier, he had established himself now in the eyes of the Church. It was a kind of posthumous sanctuary for one who had fled the law, showing in a right convincing way — which is to say, through the hiring of prayers — that the charges of the past were no longer valid.

On every hand now was to be seen the growth of wealth and with it the emergence of new comforts — more, a standard of comfort. Wealth became a criterion, even among the nobles. "The peers were expected to remain as a class the greatest of landowners. Indeed, those who fell below the required standard risked their titles or privileges. In 1477 and again in 1493 a duke was 'demoted' for lack of a sufficiency of land and 'decayed peers' were sometimes not summoned to the House of Lords." [8]

Not only wealth but the appearance of wealth was important. Men of money aimed at splendor, at a conspicuous evidence of wealth, at a display of their possessions. Noble birth had now to be accompanied by signs of commerce. If a man was noble, he had to be wealthy to maintain his nobility — and, by the same token, if a man amassed enough property or fixed upon himself and his heirs and assigns enough wealth, he might even be created a noble. In a word, the measure of a man had begun to change. It had shifted from birth to possessions. Naturally this change affected the whole populace, both in judgments and practices.

In former times the Merchants of the Staple gathered wool and shipped it abroad for refinement and manufacture into cloth. These merchants enjoyed a monopoly of the wool trade and held this monopoly in a grim grip. Then gradually wool began to be sold at home for the manufacture of cloth. "Instead of the 30,000 sacks which they yearly counted in the fourteenth century, they could not at the close of the fifteenth century collect more than 8,624 sacks. England was turned from being a country whose chief business was exporting wool into a country whose chief business was exporting cloth . . ."[9] At the close of the century the English Merchant Adventurers exported 60,000 pieces of cloth yearly."

Under this remarkable change there was a great stirring of trade within the realm, and more and more of the lowly found profitable means of latching on to coin and exchanging their services to advantage. "Great religious corporations and landowners who had once provided on their own estates for local wants recognized the new condition of things and

49

. . . sent every year far and wide across the country to great clothing centers to buy material for their household liveries."

It was upon a world teeming with trade and quickened by the interchange of goods and services, rife with an increasing number of contacts and with people moving hither and yon in the business of buying and selling, that young Thomas Wolsey looked out in 1497. It was a world in which England had discovered how to use her own resources. Bell foundries, cooperworks, brickmaking, the production of glass and stained-glass windows, the brewing of beer and the weaving of linen, the work of lacemakers and ribbon weavers — all contributed to the change in men's habits and men's minds. A man now could step from one class to another on stones of fortune. It was a time of opportunity, of new worlds to conquer close at hand.

The first mention of Thomas Wolsey in the records of the College of St. Mary Magdalen occurs in the year 1497. Then he appears as a Master of Arts and "fourteenth on the list of Fellows." Fellows formed the governing body of the college, members of the inner circle which administratively guided the policies and plans of Magdalen. The honor, it was said, had been conferred upon him for his brilliance and percipience as a scholar. And by now, too, he had had a grounding in the classics and some experience as a teacher.

Indeed, at this stage of his life Thomas Wolsey seemed set and destined for the life of a schoolmaster. The degree of Master of Arts at Oxford disposed him strongly to that career — practically committed him. It was presumed in the very nature of things, and written into the college requirements besides, that a man who learned enough to be a Master would relay his learning to others. The university would "not recognize as a Master anyone who had not already actually undertaken the duties of a teacher in the schools. Great importance was accordingly attached to the occasion on which the licentiate began to teach with authority, or, in technical language, to his 'inception' or 'commencement.' A licentiate who omitted to incept within the year prescribed by his oath was required to pay a heavy fine, and the fine was doubled if he held any lucrative post at the time. His license to teach was also cancelled." [10]

Some reports have it that Thomas Wolsey attained the degree of Master of Arts in two years instead of the seven commonly required. Whatever the speed, he did attain it and with it its dignities. As was befitting the bestowal of a degree so elevated, the ceremony surrounding its completion was a lay ordination, an admission into mysteries and fellowship. The matter was not to be taken lightly and one who entered into the company of Masters had much to remind him of his importance. It was for a young and impressionable man an introduction to the pageantry of superiority.

"On the day of an inception," Lyte tells us, "all lectures and disputations were suspended, in order that members of the different faculties might be present. After the solemn celebration of the mass, every one went to his appointed place in St. Mary's Church, and, at a signal given by one of the Proctors, the proceedings began. First the Father stepping forward delivered a book into the hands of the inceptor, placed a cap — the emblem of magisterial authority — on his head, and greeted him with the kiss of peace . . . Later as he knelt down and placed his hand on a volume of Holy Writ the Proctor, addressing him for the first time as 'Master', made him swear that he would respect the statutes and privileges of the University, that he would not foment discord, that he would not recognize any University in England save Oxford and Cambridge." [11]

In this time-honored, leafy, and almost Druidic manner had the Ipswich boy been inducted into the sacred cult of the learned, the guild of scholars sworn to an institution which, along with Cambridge, enjoyed a monopoly on wisdom. He was by this act, too and likewise, given the crest of authority — to teach other men's minds, to lecture and to pass to lesser men the fruits of his own erudition. He had been vested with authority and clothed with the raiment of learning, he of a sensitive and ambitious nature, in the years that were teeming with new industry and the promise of wealth on every hand, when the severe seventh Henry was putting the nation's house in order and men were in quest of new lands and Oxford was shaken by the invasion of a new language with its threat of a new culture.

From the time Thomas Wolsey's name began to appear in the records of Magdalen, his rise was rapid and conspicuous. His father's will provided that if the son should become a priest within a year of the father's death the son should receive the fee named in the will for the singing of Masses for the father and his friends. Wolsey was not a priest in the prescribed time. He was busy with college affairs. He traveled about on college business, among other things buying cloth for choristers' clothes and developing habits of management and assiduity.[12] He had already gone beyond the academic life. He had become third bursar — one of the treasurers and managers of the property of Magdalen; later he was made second bursar, then chief bursar. And he came for a time to be school-master at the grammar school connected with the college.

In the course of his tutoring and teaching he had under his care three of the sons of Thomas Grey, Marquis of Dorset, a man of parts and wealth who stood in these days close to the throne, even if at the time of the Lambert Simnel affair there had been spread abroad venomous ru-mors of his disloyalty and Henry had clapped him in the Tower until the rumors — and the rebellion — passed. Since then he had received various tokens of the royal confidence. He had been present at the chris-tening of Arthur, Henry's first-born and heir. In 1492 the Marquis had taken part in an expedition to extricate from one of his perennial diffi-culties the Emperor Maximilian of the Holy Roman Empire in a bootless foray against the French. In 1497 he held a commission in the forces Henry assembled to suppress an ominous rebellion fomented and formed against the King by the men of Cornwall.

In the stations of the nobility, a young man needed hardly to be re-minded, a marquis ranks immediately below a duke. Commonly the favored sons of men of such rank enjoyed release from the college grind, being right well educated by the standards of the day if they learned aptly the manners and trickeries of the chase and if they knew the proper use of courtly manners at the houses of other great and wealthy worthies. Certainly it was not ordinary for the sons of nobles, and especially high nobles, to be among the canaille in colleges.

It stands plainly to reason, then, that the presence of three of the seven sons of the mighty Marquis (he had eight daughters) in the sacred precincts of Magdalen created lusty attention among the young Fellows seeking patrons.

Nor was Wolsey's tutoring and special attention bestowed in vain. For it came about at the glad season of Christmas in 1499 that it pleased the Marquis to summon the schoolmaster to accompany his three sons on their visit home for the holidays and to enjoy with the considerable family there sports and festivities befitting the season.[13]

The family seat of the Greys was a mansion called Bradgate Park, which lay seven miles west of Leicester, not far from the scene of the battle of Bosworth. It was one of the important mansions of the day, pleasantly regarded then and destined to be famous later as the birth-place of the hapless Lady Jane Grey.

The journey to Bradgate Park from Oxford involved a trip of over fifty miles each way — a trip not without hazards, of course, and the presence of a schoolmaster as a guide and guard was a plain convenience to the Marquis. But if it was a convenience to the Marquis it was a joy to the schoolmaster. Here was a chance for a young man of rising dignity — by now he had become chief bursar of Magdalen and responsible for disbursements touching its many activities, including the completion of Magdalen Tower — to meet the family of one of the highest lords of the land in one of the most finely appointed houses of the realm. It was a full-scale chance for the young scholar and university official to get formally and for a convenient season out of the atmosphere — nay, miasma — of Oxford scholasticism. He would visit one of the great houses of the kingdom; but, great though it was, it might prove to be but the gatehouse to something vaster.

There were changes going on in such houses in these days — all in the direction of luxury and privacy. The hall, which at one time was the center and focus of the life of the manor, had become only a passageway. Important members of the household no longer ate with the servants but in rooms withdrawn — some of these rooms having chimneys and other new appointments. Still the hall remained the most spacious apartment in the house, "open to all who were admitted within the precincts." Distinctions in rank and age were apparent and emphasized at every turn. Seats or benches with backs were reserved for "the superior members of the family." In other rooms "one chair . . . was considered enough for a room and was no doubt reserved for the person of most dignity." Fancy cushions "called bankers and dorsers to be placed over the benches and backs of the seats of the better persons at the table were now also in general use." [14]

The movement toward privacy was to be noted in the use of parlors for meals. Cupboards "stood high on long legs and were used to keep bread and cheese or sweetmeats to which you helped yourself between the two main meals of the day." The female members of the family began to use these parlors as sitting rooms, and bedchambers, which in former times had been meeting places, now became much more private. The beds "were large and elaborately upholstered and canopied, and remade as couches by day." [15]

It was an education in itself to see the details of a large and well-managed household. There was an astonishing amount of linen used, much of it woven in England, for underwear, sheets, tablecloths, towels, room hangings. "Torches were made of wood resin and tallow. Flambeaux or iron holders for the flaming wood hung against the stone walls where there was sufficient draught. Candles were made of mutton fat and beeswax with flax, or rarely cotton wicks brought from Sicily." [16] The increase in the use of candles was one of the signs to show how products from many lands were flowing into England to enrich and absorb the new wealth.

Thomas Wolsey was a hearty and talkative young man, full of zest for living and in good fettle with the three sons he had in his charge. In the liveliness of his eloquence he made such good use of his time that the Marquis was delighted with him and with the solid learning he apparently had instilled in the sons.

Here, obviously, was a young man of great talent and promise who deserved a future. And so, obedient to a practice that belongs to no age and an irony that belongs to all ages, the Marquis saw that the schoolmaster must be rewarded for his good teaching by not teaching at all, by being withdrawn from teaching. There was no future in teaching. Education was to fit a man for something else.

The only portal open was the Church. In the Church a man might advance, might get into government, aided by a long English tradition. The priesthood was the ladder, and a man of Thomas Wolsey's promise, having done his work so well and being of an eloquent turn, should get into the priesthood.

It chanced that the Marquis had in his possession a parish church in a town one hundred and fifty miles away — at Limington, near Ilchester in the shire of Somerset. What he had was the right to bestow the income and emoluments of the parish on whom he should choose, the parish being vacant of a rector at that time.

He chose Thomas Wolsey.

A living was a living and not to be despised. If a man named rector of a parish did not relish the idea of ministering there, it was simple for him to use part of the revenues of the place to engage a curé or vicar to say Masses and perform the duties while he went abroad or sought out some other gainful pursuit. Indeed, it was rather expected that the rector would follow this casual course. But whether he stayed or served in absence, the main thing was to have an assured income and get established in the precincts of the Church. For, once this was done, there would, especially in the case of an exceptional fellow, be every chance of advancement.

CHAPTER V

THE ancient shire of Somerset, which contains the placid village of Limington, is a basin formed on one side by the Bristol Channel and protected on the other three sides by forbidding hills. In the north are the Mendip Hills, penetrated only by deep coombs, among them the Cheddar Gorge.

Partly because of the surrounding hills, Somerset was removed from the main preoccupations of England. It had taken little or no part in the venomous quarrels of the nobility during the Wars of the Roses, and its only sign of real interest in events arose in 1497 when some of its sons championed, to their later remorse, the cause of a pretender to the throne, by name Perkin Warbeck, a fabulous young European who had passed himself off, first in Ireland, of course, and later before the courts of Europe, as a son of Edward IV. The pretender had finally made his bid at arms by trying to seize the city of Exeter in the neighboring county of Devon. His effort failed, and Henry fetched him out of sanctuary and carted him conspicuously back to London.

Otherwise the royal authority seemed vague and distant. Somerset was well contained and sufficient unto itself. Since the eleventh century it had grown grain enough to export, and the quality of its cattle was known then and to be confirmed later when Cheddar came to be celebrated for its cheese. The region had that sort of contentment that comes from isolation. It was a great and well-filled pocket, with plenty of resources in minerals besides the produce of its land.

In a broad valley within the basin, Limington was a village that drew its sustenance from the soil. The village was oddly placed, for it lay only a mile and a half from the ancient Roman town of Ilchester, one of the stations on the old Roman road from Bath to Exeter, the station of Ilchester (the suffix *chester* indicating a walled town or a place where Roman roads crossed) being at a point where the road passed over the River Yeo. It was as if there were little excuse for the town and then, a short distance away, less for the village, save that Limington had been from the time of the Saxons a place where farmers lived and from which they had gone out to work their fertile fields.

Today the houses of the village are strung out like beads on either

55

side of the road. Halfway along among the houses stands the Church of St. Mary. It is a work of the thirteenth century, constructed of sturdy stone, with a nave eighty-seven by twenty-four feet and a chantry on the north. To the west a perpendicular tower rises — a tower big and unwieldy in proportion to the church, which for all its charm looks like a miniature imitation of something vast and important. Although the whole churchyard is encased in ancient cedars, as though they had been grown in the Bible, early pictures indicate that the church stood out above the meadows, and there is a faint suggestion of an alert turtle about it.

To this quiet church in a small rural village in a remote part of the kingdom, Thomas Wolsey came to be instituted as priest on October 10, 1500.[1] It was at first blush an odd choice for a young man who had just wound up his job as bursar of Magdalen. With all the remoteness and the inconveniences and the small scale of the operations at Limington, there had to be reasons for Wolsey's accepting the appointment there. Some of these reasons are not far to seek.

It was a good time to get away from Magdalen. Wolsey had stood well with the president of the college, Richard Mayhew. He had championed the cause of the president while Mayhew was absent from the college and had taken his side against detractors and in a dispute between the Colleges of Magdalen and Morton over the ownership of a mill.[2] But Mayhew's administration had ended in confusion and disorder. There had been controversies; charges and countercharges. There were claims, although they were never supported by evidence, that Wolsey had diverted college funds to the completion of the tower — funds that should have been spent on other causes. Later, after Wolsey and Mayhew left, Magdalen continued in ways unbecoming to the intent of its founder. In 1507 there was a visitation to the college, and some of its members were admonished and told to reform; others suffered penalties for breaches of statutes, especially in respect to card playing. Complaints against members included charges of adultery, of receiving stolen goods, of concealing a thief. One member was charged with having baptized a cat.[3]

Wolsey exchanged the uncertainties and quarrels of Oxford for the patronage of one of the great nobles. Thomas Grey, while he was merely Lord Ferrers of Groby, back in 1471, had been on the Yorkist side. His mother was Elizabeth Woodville, who later, to the consternation of the Earl of Warwick, who was accustomed to selecting queens as well as kings, married Edward IV. Grey as a stepson of Edward fought with the King at Tewkesbury. Four years later he was created the first Marquis of Dorset, and by family and loyalty he stood high in the royal favor under

Edward. Then Edward died, and the Marquis championed the cause of the young King Edward V, his half brother. When Richard III won the throne, the Marquis was suddenly a rebel and attainted. He took vigorous part in the Duke of Buckingham's rebellion against Richard. When this failed, he fled to France and joined the conspiracy formed by Henry Tudor. Of late his honors had been high, and he enjoyed the firmest confidence the King could repose in him — a royal commission to have troops under his command.

Wolsey had been ordained a priest in Lent of 1498.[4] From the moment Bishop Augustine Church (his very name could not escape notice) laid his hands on the young schoolmaster in the parish of St. Peter in Marlborough, the man who had hitherto been ordained a Master in a lesser fraternity of teachers became a vital part of something vast and organized. This sense of belonging to the Church brought the doubly comforting assurance of being a part of the Body of Christ and at the same time on the road to success.

But the ways of the world are wondrous and its caprices hard to calculate. Hardly had young Father Wolsey begun his labors in the parish of Limington than he somehow ran afoul of a custodian of the law. There was in these parts at that year of 1501 a shining and zealous knight by the name of Sir Amias Paulet, a very energetic gentleman who had often been sweaty in good causes. He had been a Lancastrian in the intermittent Wars of the Roses, and after Buckingham's rebellion, at the beginning of the reign of Richard III, Paulet had been attainted by the Yorkists. After the triumph of Henry over the Yorkists at Bosworth, he had been appointed sheriff of both Dorset and Somerset, which meant that his suzerainty extended over an area of 2617 square miles — a territory that should have been adequate even for a man of his nosy talents. Following the battle of Stoke, Amias Paulet had been knighted, and the scope of his operations given an even more loyal tinge. For now Henry, with an ever-open eye for painless income, sent Sir Amias to levy fines upon those who had dared espouse the cause of Perkin Warbeck.

Revenue gained from Somerset and four adjoining counties equaled an amount sufficient to run the royal household for well over half a year. Thus the rebellion was made to pay in cash. More to the point, however, was the fact that the collections were punitive, and those who might yield moneys for their transgressions in the Warbeck war were hunted down and haled before the King's collectors.

One of the staunchest of those on this errand without mercy was Sir Amias Paulet. He had the run of the King's highways and enjoyed an almost unbearable sense of virtue from prowling the country and poking into the problems of loyalty and ferreting out those who, by any connection with plots against the King, might be susceptible of rough treatment.

In this sort of activity he was busy in the years before Wolsey arrived at Limington. But apparently this activity was not enough to engage all his time or his faculties. His family home was at Hinton St. George, a few miles to the southwest of Limington, and Sir Amias appears to have found time for an interest in local affairs. He and young Father Wolsey clashed head-on. Wolsey, fresh from Oxford, protégé of a marquis and a member of the privileged clergy, was nonetheless seized by the knight-errant and made a public spectacle. He was put in stocks — laid by the heels in a public place for his parishioners and all to gape upon.[5]

What provoked the knight to visit this humiliation upon the priest, no one knows. Rumor still holds that Wolsey was guilty of excessive gaiety; that he grew drunk and disorderly at a country fair and, in the course of his pastimes there, pinched maidenly bottoms. The story, once told, would not down. One hears it to this day in Limington. But in point of fact it gained currency only in later Elizabethan times, and there is no shred of record to support it and little or nothing to lend it plausibility.[6] Rather, the incident of Wolsey's arrest bears all the marks of an officious and vindictive act beyond the line of any duty Sir Amias might have had to perform. The priest was not in the jurisdiction of a secular officer, and the fastening of a man or woman in stocks was a form of punishment meted out to scolds, vagabonds, beggars, petty offenders — persons to be held up to ridicule and scorn.

The Church had full means and procedures for the discipline of the clergy, and the knight had no right to handle a priest. A group of parishes formed a rural deanery. The function of the rural dean "was both administrative and disciplinary. His chief duty seems to have been to report serious cases of clerical or lay incontinence to the bishop's or archdeacon's court. The bishop's consistory court concerned itself with the property, dress and conduct of the clergy from the gravest moral offenses to small breaches of discipline, such as asserting oneself to be as learned as the bishop of London."[7]

In addition to the pain and exposure of public ridicule, then, Wolsey suffered the indignity of having the secular arm reach out and take him from the protective fraternity of which he had recently become an official member. The Church had failed to protect him — and in a quarrel with a lay official associated with the nobility. Possibly the incident showed how the civil authorities were getting out of hand.

In this year and about the time of these sobering events, Thomas Grey, first Marquis of Dorset, died at the age of forty-nine. Plainly it was time for the young priest to shake the dust of Limington off his feet and find another patron.

Although Father Thomas Wolsey departed Limington in the latter part of the year 1501 to become chaplain to Henry Deane, Archbishop of Canterbury and Primate of All England, he did not cut himself off from the revenues of his Limington parish. Indeed, he had already begun that clerical kleptomania which was to mark his career — the sedulous collection of income from appointments which carried emoluments but required no distasteful chores. Already he had influential friends who could recommend him. He obeyed a rewarding custom of his day, but, even in his youth, he obeyed it with unaccustomed zest. While yet at Limington, Father Wolsey had applied for and received permission to hold certain other parishes which he never saw.

The mystery, of course, lies not in the fact that the young priest left his small parish for the immense security of Canterbury but in the fact that, in spite of certain advantages, he had gone to Limington at all. The duties of a parish priest held hardly enough lure to attract a young man of his bounding imagination. A properly organized parish, Gasquet tells us, was a corporation. No lords of the manor or political personages were supposed to have any power or authority over it. In times of change, however, and in local situations, principles long honored were subject to violence, as the clash with Sir Amias Paulet plainly showed. The Church as a massive institution still held sway in theory, but men of the cloth in its outposts might not always be treated with the same deference accorded a prelate. The lords of the Church might be secure, but assaults were often made on unpopular local clergymen.

Added to the vulnerable and exposed position of the parish priest was the soggy tedium of his routine. He preached, and administered the sacraments, as any clergyman must; taught children and adults the Lord's Prayer, Hail Mary, the Ten Commandments; taught people how to cross themselves properly; farmed the glebe and often other land as well; sometimes acted as a tradesman. Also he was expected by the State to act "as a kind of Sunday newspaper and read out from the pulpit official bulletins of victory or other intelligence." [8]

It was no life for a Wolsey. Far better to accept the prevailing rubric of the day — farm the actual work out to a poorly paid priest known as a perpetual vicar and go on to larger fields of service. Under this arrangement the appointed priest would receive the full pay of the rector but leave the duties of the parish in the hands of one who might be known as a chaplain but who would actually be a curate; this unhappy and often wretched mortal would be engaged at the lowest possible wage — from one third to even less of the rector's regular salary — and in some cases he would be sworn not to ask for a larger stipend during his tenure. The scroll in the little Church of St. Mary at Limington proudly displays the name of Wolsey as rector there until 1509, but during the last eight years he held the living he was nowhere near the place.

This arrangement did not make for a contented clergy, but it did provide a smooth and speedy means by which a young man with an eye to the top could get on with his career. For the system had among other things the aim of cultivating the talented, of grooming them for responsible posts which the relatively uneducated and unpromising stipendiaries could not fill. There were classes within the Church as well as within lay society. The Church might offer through its ascending hierarchy the road by which a young man could climb out of his almost destined station; but the ascent of any who did this was based upon the help and work of a whole body of carriers and pack-horse priests who did yeoman service while those of gilded promise and shining eyes went on to the heights. It took a host of yeomen to make a lord, even in the Church. It was in the order of events, then, that Wolsey should go to Canterbury, leaving the custodial care of Limington and his other parishes to lesser men.

Administratively Canterbury ranked supreme. The archiepiscopal province of York contained but three dioceses — York, Durham, and Carlisle. The others — sixteen in all — came under the jurisdiction of the Archbishop of Canterbury. And, as if this were not enough, it had been by long custom appointed that the Archbishop of Canterbury should serve ex officio as Lord Chancellor of England, the Keeper of the Great Seal of England, the man in whose person was summed up both Church and State.

One who served on the staff of such a man in environs rife with ritual and tradition would have every chance to observe the methods by which the business of the Church and the kingdom went forward; and he would be in a position where he must feel, were he sensitive or not, the weight and power of the great institutions of his day. Here he would become, if his mind were alert and open, an apprentice to power.

The occupant of the Archbishop's chair at the time Wolsey was made one of the two chaplains at Canterbury left something to be desired, it is true. Henry Deane was about seventy years of age, and he had grown infirm through a long period of service — distinguished more by its fidelity than its drama. No one was precise about his background, although it was claimed that he was a member of the ancient family of Dene in the Forest of Dean. He was without special flair or assertiveness. Appointed to the archbishopric by Henry VII in 1500, he assumed the office but was never installed, either because he lacked the necessary funds to meet the huge expense or because he accepted the fact that he was not long for this world and thought the elaborate ceremony a waste of labor considering how little time he had to stay. He seemed preoccupied with his own demise and prepared minute stage directions for his funeral, as though resolved that it would be one of the big events of his life. He seemed to prefer it to his installation at Canterbury.

Henry Deane had delighted in building and in repairing. He rebuilt the manor house at Otford, and under his jurisdiction the great bridge at Rochester was put in order again. Whatever he did he did slowly, prudently, and well, and the King rejoiced at so true a man and rewarded him with the highest honors.

At Lambeth Palace, the Archbishop's house near Westminster, he entertained Catherine of Aragon on her way to London after her stormy passage from Spain to marry Prince Arthur. And it was Henry Deane who conducted the marriage ceremony of Catherine and Arthur in November of 1501, thus joining together the royal houses of England and Spain in what Henry had thought to fashion as a shrewd and indestructible alliance.

Where great ceremonies of state were called for, the Archbishop of Canterbury was present. In his person moved the Church. And at the cathedral and monastery of Canterbury, not only could Thomas Wolsey study the chief minister of the Church and the Crown, but he could also feel and experience that long gathering of forces that had made Canterbury more than an administrative post. It was a shrine.

The shrine commemorated the blood and bones of another archbishop, who had been murdered and mutilated in the north transept of the cathedral over three hundred years before. It was the tomb of Thomas Becket, who had defied King Henry II and asserted the supremacy of the Church over secular rulers.

Pilgrims of all classes and quarters came to the shrine in bands. Geoffrey Chaucer, a justice of the peace and commissioner of the riverbank between Greenwich and Woolwich, had watched these pilgrims and celebrated them in a collection of tales. This collection had been among the early books published by William Caxton, and the tales lent interest to the pilgrimages and increased them in the days Wolsey spent at Canterbury. Miraculous cures had been accomplished, and many persons came in great penance and devotion; but not a few came for the ride, and the term *Canterbury gallop*, denoting the leisurely and pleasant pace of the horses of the pilgrims, had begun to take its place in the language, later to be reduced to the word *canter*.[9]

The shrine was one of the sights of the world. An Italian visitor to England noted that the tomb of St. Thomas surpassed all belief. "This, notwithstanding its great size," he wrote, "is entirely covered with plates of pure gold; but the gold is scarcely visible from the variety of precious stones with which it is studded . . . and these beauties of nature are enhanced by human skill, for the gold is carved and engraved in beautiful designs . . ."[10]

What would the shrine signify to a young priest?

Certainly a nimble imagination would see in it a story as rich as the jewels and gold that adorned it, for the tomb held the body of a man who in his life and death and immortality played out the whole drama of the Church and the State, the priest and the king. Here was a man kings and pilgrims alike reckoned with, centuries after his blood and brains had been strewn by assassins around the sacred precincts. In his martyrdom and canonization the person of the priest had been elevated to its highest eminence. One who sought preferment in the Church and advancement in the kingdom would find in him a subject fit for endless reflection.

Once made Archbishop of Canterbury, Becket refused to accept the principles Henry had set forth to curtail rights previously enjoyed by the Church. On Christmas Day, 1170, he lashed his enemies from the pulpit of the cathedral. "When the rights of the Church are violated," he said, "I shall await no man's permission to avenge them." In a voice of thunder he excommunicated from the pulpit in the cathedral men who had offended him and dashed the candle to the pavement in token of the extinction of his enemies.[11]

Four days later Thomas Becket had been done to death, and gruesomely, by courtiers of the King. Few believed that the King was directly responsible for the murder, but that he was indirectly to blame could not be gainsaid. He had declared, it was reported: "What cowards have I brought up in my court, who care nothing for their allegiance to their master! Not one will deliver me from this low-born priest!"[12]

Well, he had been delivered from the Archbishop but into hands of greater evils. The King fell into instant and wide disfavor with his subjects when the report spread that he had laid his hands even indirectly upon the head of the Church in England. At Avranches, France, where he was at the time, Henry swore on the Gospels that he had not ordered or wished the Archbishop's murder.

Still people muttered. Two years later Becket had been canonized, and the kingdom of England was in general revolt. The Scots had crossed the border under their King; Yorkshire had rebelled and the midland counties, too. All hostile movements were fomented and sustained by the belief that Henry had been privy to the murder of the saint.

Penance at Avranches was not enough. The King must come to Canterbury. There followed a scene which history in time would gloss over and forget, aided by the incredible nature of events. But another Thomas at Canterbury, himself geared for greatness, could not miss or ignore the dramatic humiliation of an English King. Here was the stuff dreams are made of, and cardinals too. If there was any precedent on which a man's thinking might rest when he came to consider the ascendancy of the Church over the State, it was to be found in the story of Henry II at Canterbury.

In the summer of 1174 Henry started from France to England. His passage was marked by a gale that troubled the waters. He landed, however, at Southampton on July 8. "From that moment he began to live on a penitential diet of bread and water. He approached the sacred city of Canterbury on the 12th of July. At the first sight of the Cathedral he leaped from his horse and went on foot to the outskirts of the town. Here at St. Dunstan's Church he paused and stripped his royal robes from him and walked from there on through the city in the guise of a penitent pilgrim. He was barefoot and the rough stones of the streets were marked with blood that started from his feet."

This man was King of England.

Straight to the scene of the murder in the north transept he went. "Here he knelt again and kissed the sacred stone on which the Archbishop had fallen, the prelates standing around to receive his confession. Thence he was conducted to the crypt, where he again knelt, and with groans and tears kissed the tomb and remained long in prayer." The King requested absolution and received the kiss of reconciliation from the prior.

Even now the King had not done with his groveling before the minions of the Church. He removed his clothes, placed his head and shoulders in the tomb, and then received five strokes from each bishop and each abbot who was present, the stroke being laid on with a monastic

63

rod. Then he submitted to three punitive strokes from each of the eighty monks who were there.

It was to be noted that Henry's penance had almost as clear and measurable effect as the murder. For suddenly matters stood better around the land. The Scots were soundly defeated in battle, and the tensions which had laid hold upon the nation subsided. If further proof of the value of the King's acknowledged humiliation had been needed, it could have been found in the favorable turn of national events.[13]

When Thomas Wolsey began his chaplainship in 1501, pilgrims came daily to pay tribute to Thomas Becket, the tribute of memory. And when they came they celebrated the transcendent worth of a prelate backed by the power of the Church and the moral sanction of the ages.

The young priest did not remain long in the most sacred spot of England. The year 1503 was a year when death stalked in high places. Henry's good queen Elizabeth died nine days after the birth of a daughter. She was thirty-seven years of age and had borne Henry seven children, three of whom died in infancy. Her first-born, Arthur, had died the year before and only a few months after his marriage to Catherine of Aragon.

The King was stricken in his grief, and he made up in her funeral and interment for much he had failed to give her when she was alive. All the streets along which the cortege passed were filled with torches. The whole number was hard to reckon, but the chronicler was much impressed with the display and mentioned the two hundred that went with the corpse, adding quaintly, and still impressed, that these were at the King's cost. The bearers of the torches were arrayed in white gowns.

It was a funeral worthy of a queen. But the next week Henry Deane, Archbishop of Canterbury, died; and in ground and water covered his funeral outdid the Queen's. He had seen death ahead and had written a play to go with it. He managed to die in London at Lambeth Palace, which was fitting and proper for the Archbishop, that being his official residence. But it was part of the drama too, for Wolsey and another chaplain had instructions to transport the body by water, in a bedecked and appropriately solemn barge, to Faversham and there to put it in a hearse and convey it to Canterbury, accompanied by thirty-three sailors arrayed in black.[14]

Following hard upon the heels of the Queen's funeral, this one called for surpassing skill in management. Wolsey conducted his part well. Here was a task worthy of his energies and the biblical stretch of his imagination. It called at once for solemnity and for pomp.

CHAPTER VI

FROM his Canterbury experience Wolsey got a taste of the tradition and ceremony of the Church. But it was not likely that he would be satisfied with righteousness and ritual. He was meant for government, and he took on now a less pious patron, one to whom he could prove his skill in the handling of the hundred and one details that attended the regulation of men and trade. By this means, seeing that the man to whom he was attached stood well as a servant of the King, Wolsey would be commended to court.

The man who next became his patron was Sir Richard Nanfan, Lord Deputy of the port of Calais. The Deputy of Calais was in a sense the gatekeeper of the kingdom of England, for this seaport of Calais lay twenty-two miles east by south of Dover. Edward III had wrested the old town and the spacious harbor from the French following the battle of Crécy in 1346. The town had fallen after a siege that lasted a year. Being now a possession, an outpost, it was fiercely English; and having been captured and stubbornly held, the port had to be used, whether it was useful or not, and made to seem important. It was a center of business and the point of all coming and going. A man or a shipment was not out of England until past Calais.

No matter was so minor that it could be allowed to escape official attention. The Deputy was ordered in one case to assist the movement of ambassadors to and from England, from France, Spain, and Germany, and at the same time to arrange for two stags and two does to be brought along under diplomatic privileges if the Archduke of Austria might have them to spare. There were remonstrances against tolls levied by the captain of Gravelines on all boats passing from Calais to Flanders and from Flanders to Calais. A close supervision had to be kept over strangers lodging in the town, "the different keepers of lodging houses being sworn to report daily on the number of guests and quality." [1]

Calais was a fortified town. A fort commanded the only road across the "marishes" by which Calais was approached from the south and southwest. It was a fort "possessed of sluice gates to the sea which enabled the holders to flood the surrounding country at will." The gates of the city were closely tended. "The lord deputy himself received the keys

65

every night and gave them to the night-porter at his 'lodge' in the morning, specifying the number of gates he appointed to be opened for the day." [2]

There was plenty of color and pageantry in all the daily doings of Calais. It was a place of movement, a crossroads in water. But back of the pageantry and the official performance was a vast amount of complicated paper work to be done, and it was here that the priest Wolsey came to the aid of the aging Nanfan. For every lordly display of power there were a hundred pieces of paper to be filled out and tucked away. That was the lesson of Calais. Wolsey learned it well and his scrivening diligence did not go unrewarded.

When in 1505 Sir Richard made ready to leave his exacting post and return to England, "intending to live more at quiet," he commended Wolsey for his incessant labor to the special favor of the King. Wolsey was promoted to the King's service and made his chaplain.

So Wolsey came at last to court — and under an arrangement that appeared to have been well worth waiting for. His position, while minor, entitled him to be often in the royal presence. A scrupulous observance of the rituals of the Church had long been the practice of Henry VII. The monarch's health was not good — some said he coughed with every breath — and one might reasonably expect him to show more of a disposition to see his chaplain than his ministers. Wolsey might become on intimate terms with the King.

In one respect, however, the chaplain's arrival at court was marred by disappointment. There was a good deal of severity, if not downright drabness, about the court of the parsimonious Henry. In these days there was little that was gay and less that was convenient to one who had enjoyed the ceremonious living at Calais. The court followed the King, and often there were not adequate sleeping quarters. Wolsey occupied a bed with Lord Darcy of Templehurst, an older man and a Privy Councilor. Darcy wrote Wolsey later to remind him of those grim days, recalling the long hours they had spent revealing their minds and ambitions to each other, talking over their frustrations, each promising to help the other later if he could.[3]

It was hard to know how a resolute and determined man, forward-looking and full of energy, could advance himself in the crowded court of an ailing king who kept everything under his firm control. Wolsey was in the vigor of his middle thirties. The force of his personality may be measured by the fact that he had commended himself to, and had been recommended by, a series of worthy patrons. There is good reason to

66

believe that Sir Reginald Bray, high in the Council of the King, had recommended him to Sir Richard Nanfan; and Nanfan not only had recommended him to Henry VII but had shown further confidence in him by making Wolsey his own executor. His ambition had been encouraged by the Marquis of Dorset and the Archbishop of Canterbury. He impressed the people he dealt with and served. The court was his aim, essential to his fullest success, and he had some justification for thinking, as one biographer reports, that if he could "but set one foot in the court he did not doubt but to obtain anything he could wish for."

Casual accounts of Wolsey's life leave the impression that not much of importance had happened to him before he reached the court of Henry Tudor. Actually he had lived more than half his life, and all the forces that bent and shaped his ambition and oiled his abilities had already worked their effect. In a fixed society he had seen his father change from a rebel to a churchwarden, accepted for his property where he had been rejected as an alien. Thomas Wolsey had proved the power of words when he determined for his degree at Oxford. He had shown his ability for something besides the scholar's life by engaging in the intrigues of the administration of his college. He had run head-on into the civil authorities, and to his sorrow, in his first parish. He had sampled the sweetness of patronage. At Calais he had shown that he knew how to do the world's work.

But what made the arrival of Wolsey at the court of Henry VII significant was the nature of Henry's reign. He was a businessman King who believed in the tidy management of the affairs of the kingdom. There was now a market for competence just as much as there was a market for wool. Henry rated ability higher than nobility. An unusual prince and an extraordinary commoner had met at a given point in history.

At the time of Wolsey's arrival at court, however, Henry was in no mood to make immediate use of the new chaplain's proven abilities. Rather Henry was concerned with the whole question of the succession, of guaranteeing the future of the Tudor line he had established.

Considering the constant threat from dissident elements, the fewness of Henry's executions might be looked upon as a study in Christian forbearance. He had been selective and judicial in his killings. He had even spared Perkin Warbeck as long as he could, although Perkin had dealt him handsome misery for almost ten years. After his capture at Exeter in 1496 Perkin had been brought back to London, fully con-

67

fessing his perfidy, and had suffered but a token imprisonment, escaping now and then, only to be hauled back each time to genial confinement. It was three years later, after he had been put into the Tower and had been detected in communication with the Earl of Warwick there, that Henry had him disposed of — along with the Earl of Warwick.

Here the case had been legally conclusive. There had been a trial, though there was no record kept of the proceedings. The young Earl had admitted the charges of conspiracy against him. It is true that his wits had been dimmed by fifteen years of close confinement; and the Earl and Perkin had been placed in cells one above the other where they could be caught communicating. But the court adjudged him guilty according to his confession, and he, along with Warbeck, had in November of 1499 been hanged, disemboweled, and quartered.

The execution of the young Earl had not been popular. In the same month a dreadful plague had broken out in London, and the people "on the highway coldly stated that the scourge was sent by heaven for the murder of Warwick." [4] But the disposal of Warwick had been the most necessary execution of all. He was the son of the Duke of Clarence, brother of Edward IV, and as long as he lived there was a living and livid threat to the throne of Henry VII. Warwick was unmistakably of royal blood, and his lineage and claims would stand up under test better than those of Henry Tudor. Henry Tudor, whatever his lineage, had brought peace and unmeasured prosperity to England. It would not do to wreck this peace and squander this prosperity by letting the nation be plunged again into internecine strife.

There was another reason why the hapless young Earl of Warwick could not be allowed to tarnish Tudor claims. This was the Spanish alliance based on the marriage of Catherine of Aragon and the King's son who had been given the name of Arthur after England's king of legendary greatness. Arthur was the hope as well as the son of Henry Tudor. His marriage to Catherine of Aragon had been designed to bring Spain and England indissolubly together; it would be the means of putting the stamp of approval of the most powerful nation of Europe on the validity and soundness of the Tudor dynasty. The Princess Catherine was a descendant of John of Gaunt, and hence of Edward III. Thus she had the royal blood of the Plantagenets. Her descent was "not like the Tudors through a dubious left-hand marriage, but through an undoubted line of royal kings." [5]

The Spanish ambassadors, haggling over the amount of the prospective bride's dowry "did not hesitate to hint at the insecurity of such an upstart dynasty as that of the Tudors. 'Bearing in mind what happens every day to the kings of England,' they declared, 'it is surprising that Ferdinand and Isabella should dare to give their daughter at all.' " [6]

This remark had been passed when Arthur was only two years old. But on January 11, 1500, the same ambassadors wrote to their sovereigns: "England has never been so tranquil as at present. There have always been pretenders to the crown of England, but now that Perkin Warbeck and the son of the Duke of Clarence (the Earl of Warwick) have been executed, there does not remain a drop of doubtful royal blood, the only royal blood being the blood of the King, the Queen, and above all, the Prince of Wales." [7]

The wedding had seemed to put the seal of finality on what had been so devoutly hoped for. Yet the marriage, so full of promise, had not endured. Its failure and the events that followed made it seem that there might be some curse of blood upon it. For Arthur had sickened and died at Ludlow five months after the ceremony, leaving the young Catherine in widow's weeds and in a strange land. For Arthur, death was a sleep and a forgetting; for Henry VII, the loss of his son was an awakening from a dream. The death of the Prince, proud hope of a new England, threatened the very structure of the future. The solidity of the Tudor dynasty, to which Henry had given such devious thought and persistent energy, rested on the marriage. Catherine must not be allowed to return to Spain. Not only would her return weaken claims which the fruits of her marriage would make secure; there was the possibility also that the first instalment of her dowry, duly paid by Ferdinand and Isabella, might return with her.

Henry faced a predicament which he could not hack his way out of with the executioner's axe. Yet he must move at once to save both the dynasty and the dowry. There was still his second son, five years younger than Catherine, but a sturdy lad and tall and full of the seeds of promise. Catherine had never herself been well in drafty, damp, and gloomy England; but if she survived, it might be possible to get the consent of her bargaining parents for her marriage to young Henry. Then it would be necessary to solicit a dispensation from the Pope. The Pope alone could grant permission for a man — even a prince — to marry his brother's widow, seeing that the Levitical code expressly forbade such a marriage.

Appropriate petitions were addressed to the Pope, but Alexander VI died inconsiderately while the matter was before him. His successor, Pius III, died a month later — in the summer of 1503. Julius II was not elected until November of that year, but he made it his early business to entertain the singular request from England, and on November 26, 1503, a bull was issued allowing the young Henry to marry his brother's widow, provided he himself agreed to the arrangement when he reached the canonical age of consent.

It had been a period of suspense and waiting. Henry VII waited ten months after Arthur's death before he named his younger son Prince of Wales; by then it was decently obvious that there would be no issue from the marriage of Catherine and Arthur. The King waited another four months before he allowed the younger Henry to enter into a contract to marry his brother's widow. When the younger Henry reached the age of thirteen, the same being the canonical age of consent, he immediately renounced the contract. And the elder Henry, having by now developed chilly qualms about the marriage, gave his royal sanction to the renunciation. Catherine meanwhile remained in England, her status undecided, her life a coin in the hands of kings, her comfort neglected. There was some talk that the bald, widowed, and aging Henry might marry her himself, rather than let the dowry and alliance go; but the rumor probably arose from Spanish sources, and if it was more than a rumor Isabella put a prompt end to it when the matter came to her shocked attention.

With all his royal prerogatives, Henry VII could not decide Catherine's fate alone: it was endlessly hashed over in his Council. And if Wolsey found the King preoccupied in his devotions and worries and little inclined to notice him, the Council proved to be a place where his talents as a talker could command an audience. Cardinal Morton was dead, likewise Reginald Bray. And there were those who said that the character of the King had changed with the passing of these men and the death of his wife, Elizabeth of York. He was more severe, less tempered in his judgments. But there were others who remained near him and were staunch and were able to influence him.

One of these was Richard Fox, now Bishop of Winchester, and to him Wolsey commended and attached himself. Fox enjoyed the full confidence of his royal master, and through him rather than through contact at the altar did Wolsey make his approach to Henry.

Instead of idling his time or spending it on books and scrivening, Wolsey at this period sought the company of men who would be seen by other men, following the path of advancement by association. If the

King would not notice him, he would impress his presence upon men whom the King would notice.

In this way it came about that, when the King wanted a mission accomplished, there were those who could recommend Wolsey for his ability to talk and to act as a negotiator. To Henry there was nothing more important than negotiation. He had been busy all his royal life with embassies. Following the death of the Queen in 1503, Henry's mind turned to marriage schemes. Hardly more than a year after Elizabeth of York was laid away he thought of marrying the young Queen of Naples, a widow. To find out whether she might prove a suitable match for him he sent three gentlemen from his court on a confidential mission.

There were twenty-four items to be investigated. Item sixteen required that they "mark her breasts or paps, whether they be big or small." The ambassadors reported: "The said queen's breasts be somewhat great and full, and inasmuch as they are trussed somewhat high, after the manner of the country, the which causeth her grace to seem much fuller and her neck to be shorter." Item 24 was decisive: "The said King's servants, by the wisest ways that they can use, shall make inquisition and ensearch what land or livelihood the said Queen hath or shall have after the decease of her mother." There was, alas, no satisfactory answer to this question. The embassy ended in failure. Henry would not make overtures to a person if she could not contribute visibly to his coffers.[8]

Besides, there were other queens in the pack. There was Margaret of Angoulême, a creature to toy with in his multifarious negotiations, just to keep notice before Europe that Henry was in the market for a bride and the competition was sprightly. The person he really had his beady eye upon was Margaret of Savoy, regent of the Netherlands, daughter of Maximilian of Austria, impecunious and evasive Emperor of the Holy Roman Empire. She was likewise the sister of Philip, Archduke of Flanders, and in 1506 the Archduke, having been driven upon English shores by an adverse wind while he was seeking passage to Spain, found that he could not escape his polite confinement unless he signed a treaty with the King of England. This treaty was full of provisions, many of them concerned with trade and allowing English goods to be imported advantageously into the Netherlands. It also provided that the hand of Philip's sister Margaret of Savoy would be given in marriage to the King of England, and a marriage portion of 300,000 crowns was fixed, each crown to be worth four shillings.

It was a neat arrangement on paper, but the lady Margaret had a will of her own. She had also had two husbands before and she was in no hurry to take on the ailing Henry VII. Some pressure would be needed to bring the marriage off, and in the spring of 1508 it was found that the Emperor Maximilian lay in the Netherlands for a season and an embassy should be sent to urge him that he might expedite the marriage. The man needed to perform the task must be eloquent, persuasive, and able to impress the wily Emperor with the advantages of pushing the marriage forward.

Richard Fox and Sir Thomas Lovell, trusted advisers to the King, hit upon the idea of sending Wolsey. They went straight to the King with the matter, and he consented to see the priest and to render judgment as to his fitness. Having separate eyes and compartments for his religion and for his policy, he had paid no heed to Wolsey as a chaplain; but he looked upon him with favor as a messenger, seeing that he was so highly recommended to his attention and finding him smooth and personable in his discourse.

Accordingly it was settled that one of the King's chaplains should set off on the King's business to the Low Countries. Cautious arrangements would have to be made, of course, and there would be many meetings of the Council to discuss odd ends of the mission. Meanwhile the King, never too sure of anything, felt it expedient to trust Wolsey with a lesser mission to Scotland. Henry had complained to James IV of Scotland that Scotsmen, "among them men of high rank, traveled through England in disguise and without passports, and even took with them the envoys of foreign powers." Wolsey went to Scotland to protest, but he confessed to Henry that, "according to the information he had gathered, the offenses of Englishmen were to those of Scotsmen as four to one." [9] Wolsey had thus shown that he could make an honest report even if it involved telling the King facts he did not expect to encounter. He also had a constructive suggestion to make, not content merely to be an errand runner. He suggested that the Kings of England and Scotland meet and talk matters over between them. The idea seems to have found favor with James, but there was no enthusiasm for it among his Council.

In his mission to Scotland Wolsey demonstrated his diplomatic skill and confirmed the prophecies and recommendations of his friends. Men said that the peace of the two kingdoms was assured by his mission. He should now go to the Netherlands and to the Emperor. During the time the letter was being prepared and he was receiving instructions from the King, commending himself to the royal presence with every appearance,

Wolsey had obviously prepared a plan for the speedy execution of his mission. He knew the King and had taken his measure; he understood the importance of carrying out the assignment with dexterity and singleness of mind. It was not a job for a courtier but a runner. It was business; and a plain chaplain, if he put his tempered mind to it, could do it better than a prince given to ceremony and dawdling politeness.

Wolsey had his final audience of leave with the King at four in the afternoon at Richmond. He took a barge immediately for Gravesend, having seen to it that the barge was ready for immediate departure. By virtue of the time of departure he had the aid of the wind and especially of the tide on the Thames, and he reached Gravesend in hardly more than three hours. Post horses had been arranged at Gravesend for the passage to Dover, where he would take ship for the Continent. With such planning and with more post horses prepared in relay, he reached Dover the next morning at the very moment when the packet across the Channel got under way. By noon he was at Calais, and by late afternoon, riding hard, he was at the residence of the Emperor.

When the Emperor heard that a messenger from Henry had arrived, he gave orders that the man be brought at once to his imperial closet, for, as he explained, "his affection to the king of England was such, that he was glad of any opportunitie to doe him a curtesie." Wolsey stated his mission and his requests promptly and asked the Emperor for a decision within the briefest compass consistent with his royal pleasure. Evidently he did his job well, for he had his answers early the next morning — all of them favorable. Whether the Emperor meant Yes or would do what he said was not a part of Wolsey's responsibility, and he need not tarry in meditation on this point. Rather he left immediately for Calais, accompanied by a splendid train of nobles from the Emperor's court to do him honor. From Calais he took packet after an uneventful night's rest and was back at Dover by ten the next morning. That night he was at Richmond. The whole mission had taken less than seventy hours.

Wolsey was up at daybreak — ahead of the King. He stood outside the royal bedchamber as the King left for early Mass. Seeing him there and thinking him remiss in his embassy, the King said, "Why have you not passed on your journey?"

To which Wolsey replied, "Sire, if it may stand with your Highness's pleasure, I have already been with the Emperor and dispatched your affairs, I trust to your Grace's liking."

Then the King inquired about a messenger he had sent after Wolsey with further instructions. "I encountered him, Sire," said Wolsey. "And I made bold, your Grace, upon my own discretion, to despatch the same. And for as much as I have exceeded your Grace's commission, I most humbly crave your gracious remission and pardon."

To this Henry blinked and replied, "We do not only pardon you thereof, but also give you our princely thanks, and also for your good and speedy exploit." [10]

The story of the mission comes from Wolsey's own recollections of it years later. It may not be true or accurate in every detail, but it could be true; and whatever the detail, it bears the test of history, for from the moment of the visit to Maximilian dates Wolsey's favor with Henry VII. He had proved himself able and fast, and that he could gird his priestly robes about him when the occasion demanded. Such a man the King needed.

Of course a good man must needs be rewarded in some coin that betokens the true measure of his worth, and here again the King's cunning found the energetic Wolsey to his satisfaction. This eager fellow ranked only as a humble priest, one of a stable of royal chaplains: it would not be necessary to give him a slice of the King's lands or to dole out to him precious and husbanded funds from the royal coffers.

Rome could pay his wages, and England could enjoy his talents.

It was an honored custom that the man who wore the crown could appoint his royal servants to posts in the Church and have his actions sanctioned by the man who wore the tiara. Henry had taken Richard Mayhew, he who had been President of Magdalen College, and, in exchange for his counsel and services as Almoner, had named him Bishop of Hereford in 1504. It was logical, then, that he should take this other Magdalen product, the priest who had proved himself such a swift harbinger on his mission to Maximilian, and make him Dean of Lincoln.

The system had its conveniences all around. It reduced government costs, a matter of importance to the acquisitive Henry; and it gave the Church a host of men habitually at court and close to the King's presence. It was a highly dignified way in which the King and the Pope could scratch each other's backs across the intervening miles between London and Rome.

At this moment the circumstances required, however, that Wolsey should have income and offices consonant with his high position at court. There must be badges and honors appropriate to his station. One could not expect a man who was privy to the King to continue living off

74

such parishes as Limington and the few others that had been doled out to him. He still held Limington in his grasp, nor would he let go of it until he had full assurance of other honors. These came thick and fast. Not only was he made Dean of Lincoln on February 3, 1508, but a few days later he was presented with a prebend in the same cathedral, which too he held until he managed to exchange it for one more valuable in another cathedral. It was not contemplated that he should actually serve Lincoln. He was installed by proxy and did not take possession, and then only formally, until two years later. He was also given the Vicarage of Lydd in Kent by the Cistercian Abbot of Tintern. And to cap his honors in the Church, he next achieved sufficient status at court to be made Royal Almoner — on November 3, 1508. Through his rise in the Church he now had enough stature to occupy a dignified position in the royal household. Now he was willing to hand over the rectorship of Limington to another priest. This he did some time before July 2, 1509.[11]

Around the court it was plainly understood that Wolsey had high honors in his destiny. He was under the care and tutelage of Richard Fox, who, along with William Warham, Archbishop of Canterbury in succession to Henry Deane, represented the Church at court and stood for its honors and influence there. Henry's piety and genuflections gave the churchmen some ascendancy, but there were remnants of the old nobility still around the edges, and it was just as well to keep these remnants in their place. Their spokesman was Thomas Howard, Earl of Surrey, Lord High Treasurer of England, and the fact that he was there at all served notice upon all who attended the King that Henry would place his stamp on loyalty and ability and not weight his Council to the full with any single element of the realm.

Howard's father, the first Duke of Norfolk, had been killed with Richard at Bosworth. The title had been attainted and the son deprived of his lands and his freedom and confined to the Tower of London after the battle. A year later, however, he was pardoned and given an honorable office in the north of England. After a steadfast performance there, he had been brought back to court and restored to the earldom of Surrey.

Thomas Howard was in the best tradition of the English nobility. His loyalty was not to be questioned, and Henry knew it. When Henry talked with him after Bosworth, Howard made it plain that he had fought for his King, and that he would have died willingly if Henry had been his King. Henry liked the mettle of that. He liked also the sense of identification with the great of the past, a kind of connection between the nobility and his own throne. The nobles were to be kept in their place and not allowed to thrash the land again with their wars. But they were not to be eliminated. Rather they were to be represented; for they were one of the priceless ingredients in English life, and Henry knew it.

Fox as a churchman could be expected to have different ideas. To stand against the old nobility and the great landowners who remained, he thought it well to groom Wolsey and see that he had the King's favor. With rumbles of anticlericalism abroad in the land and signs to be seen at every turn of hostility toward the wealth of the Church, and with threats to deprive the clergy of their privileges, the first order of business ought to be to see that the Church had a friend at court — preferably a young friend who would grow up with the government, whose power would increase within the Church and the State at one and the same time.

For this ultimate purpose a priest who came inconspicuously to the service of the King, and grew through royal favor, was ideal. Especially if he showed that he had the kind of managerial ability that the reign of Henry VII placed approval on. Government had ceased to be a matter of conduct in wars and had become a very high order of humdrum, of keeping accounts, of administering justice, of collecting revenues, of maintaining peace on the King's highway, of promoting trade, of rolling up revenues and guarantees against adversity. The King had become a housekeeper, and for all the details connected with this kind of national housekeeping, he needed worthy assistants.

Continuity was all the more urgent as the health of the King worsened and a new and more vigorous reign impended. Catherine was still in the kingdom and the Council still meditated her status, but Henry VII in his fits of conscience still forbade the young Prince, now taller than his father, to marry the Princess.

But Henry's preoccupation with his own marriage was intense. As Bacon put it later, if he "had been young, a man would have judged him to be amorous." One could see in all his moves in the midst of threats and disease and his own decline an incurable desire to perpetuate himself, to stake out many claims of blood against adverse fortune, to trust the future of the present he had created to no single reed.

Again in October of 1508, Wolsey was sent off to the Netherlands to hasten the marriage with Margaret. On his first mission he had succeeded, at least as far as one could succeed in dealing with the Emperor Maximilian and his kin. For early in October Margaret had executed the marriage treaty and agreed to fines that should be paid if the marriage did not take place. On the same mission Wolsey had been able to advance the proposed marriage between Archduke Charles and the daughter of the

King, the Princess Mary. Thus Henry had the prospect of another conquest by marriage. Even if the young Henry did not go through with his marriage to Catherine of Aragon, his sister Mary was now pledged to Charles, who upon the death of Ferdinand would rule Spain.

Still and all, Henry the elder must marry Margaret. In doing it he would wed the Netherlands, rich in trade. Wolsey stayed on the Continent from the beginning of October into November, trying to straighten out details to Henry's satisfaction — and Margaret's in particular. Henry tried to move Margaret by a letter addressed directly to her. There was a grand embassy headed by the Earl of Surrey. Yet the marriage was delayed. Events gradually closed in around Henry, while Margaret dallied with the idea of decision and the execution of her earlier decision. Henry's last cause became a lost cause.

His health, which would have killed a less determined man years before, now grew sharply worse under his frustrations. The doctors had long said that he ought to rest less and sleep more. He began to be troubled with gout, an irony considering the proper and diligent life he led.

In the spring of 1509 rumors of the King's illness spread all over Europe. Thomas Wolsey became less the priest who served as diplomatic messenger and more the King's Almoner, in charge of Henry's increasing charities — in charge, that is, as far as anybody could be in charge of anything touching Henry. The King gave daily alms to the poor and needy. He sent money for ten thousand Masses to be recited in his behalf. He had built the Savoy Hospital, near Charing Cross, in London, to afford shelter for one hundred poor persons; "and in the last year of his life he determined to erect at Bath a large hospital on the model of the one in Paris." [12] To accomplish this — and both Wolsey and the younger Henry might well have noted the act — he appropriated the revenues of ecclesiastical houses that were falling into decay. These houses were to be closed and their money spent for more useful purposes.

Henry could amply afford the lavish gifts he laid upon the altar of appeasement at the end of his life, whether out of remorse or zeal. His life had been a study in acquisitive thrift, and if it proved one thing above all things visible it was that a man in high position could lay up treasures on earth and still serve the general good. One need only think primarily in terms of money, not war.

Early in his reign there had been a threat of war with France. Say rather a prospect of it. Henry could ill afford not to press English claims in France, so long standing were these claims. Accordingly he assembled

Parliament and laid the matter before their deliberations. They readily granted funds for an invasion of France, and now Henry was under the necessity of making warlike moves. His elaborate and conspicuous preparations impressed both England and France. At last the King "actually crossed the Channel to take command of the army of invasion; and sat down before Boulogne. Then on a sudden the air cleared." It appeared that the French King did not want a war any more than Henry VII. But he must make a settlement to get rid of the English army. The settlement Henry gladly accepted and withdrew. Thus he "secured Peace with Honour and a solid cash equivalent for his expenditure." [13]

This was but an instance of the principle he had established: that any enterprise worth undertaking at all should be made to pay a handsome profit for the good of the realm. And in all cases he took the money personally and kept it in hiding under his own lock and key at his beloved Palace of Richmond. He would hold the purse and handle the coffers and dole out to his Almoner and Lord High Treasurer only what he decided should be given away or spent.

With all his charities, the King's conscience would not rest. It was as if he would make peace with his Maker as he had made peace with France — by a cash settlement, but in reverse. He gave abundantly, and in his last days he gave lenience — this time lavishly and on a wide scale and with no view to reward this side of heaven: he granted a general pardon to those who had offended against the King's laws, and the prisons and jails were emptied, and pilgrimages were organized among the wealthy and the dispossessed to pray for his recovery.

Nothing helped. On April 21, 1509, he died at Richmond. On May 10 he was buried. As the casket with his wasted remains was placed in the vault at Westminster by the side of the body of Elizabeth of York, "the heralds took their tabards from their shoulders, hung them on the railing round the catafalque, and cried out in French the lamentation, 'The noble King Henry VII is dead!' Then they put their tabards on again, and with loud voices uttered the joyful cry, 'Long live the noble King Henry VIII!' "

He who mounted the throne as the eighth Henry to reign over the English was not yet eighteen years of age.

Thomas Wolsey, firm in the Council and ascendant in the Church, was twenty years his senior.

Book Two

(*1509-1520*)

Setting forth the rise of Wolsey in the reign of Henry VIII; the stupendous failure and disgrace of his first venture for his King and the amazing accomplishments of his second; his roles as judge, as Church reformer, as educator, as builder of palaces, and as diplomat; the triumph of his policy of friendship with France at the Field of Cloth of Gold.

CHAPTER I

Thomas Wolsey had lost another patron.

In this case, however, he was fortunately circumstanced. He knew the lie of the royal household, and he held a position of responsibility, flanked by appointments within the Church, that gave him status. And since the young man who came to the throne was unversed in the day-to-day business of the court, Wolsey could become a patron himself, for his increasing command of court detail might enable the Almoner to shepherd the King through tasks for which the monarch was unprepared.

Apart from talks, often wearisome, occasionally stimulating, with men who populated his father's household, young Henry had had little contact with the world beyond the confines of a parsimonious court except in jousts and competitive games. He was a master at archery and could contend with the best when he drew the bow — long or short. Likewise in other sports. Giustiniani, the Venetian ambassador, wrote: "He is extremely fond of tennis, at which game it is the prettiest thing in the world to see him play, his fair skin glowing through a shirt of the finest texture." [1]

Too, young Henry had a proven skill at music. Even when Duke of York, he had had a band of minstrels apart from those of his father and his brother. "He became an expert performer on the lute, the organ and the harpsichord and all the cares of State could not divert him from practising these instruments both day and night." [2] In the years that formed him, when by his brother's seniority and his father's sternness he had been isolated from his times, he had grown fond of his mind. In music the spirit was free and eternal and richly above the humdrum of shallow courtiers and toothy men flitting busily about the court with airs of solemnity. Music belonged to religion, to the Mass, and it belonged to Maypoles, strolling minstrels, and the limbo where men withdraw from chores and exactions.

Upon the head of this versatile lad, brilliantly trained in many arts and pastimes but not in the art of governance, was placed the scratchy crown of his father, and into his good right hand was thrust the rusty scepter. A magic moment in an ancient ceremony attended by the mitered and caparisoned dignitaries of Church and State was supposed to turn this impetuous boy, this tennis player, this performer on the lute, instantly into a king. It was an old English custom to expect it, and often it worked: the metaphysics of change might touch with some wand the latent greatness of all men and give it special force in one man. But coronation was at best a magnificent experiment, a venture in confidence; and, on a plain and practical level, men of wisdom, whether in court or tavern, were never sure that the miracle would work.

In the case of the accession of young Henry VIII hopes were unfeignedly high, for the news of the passing of the old King had occasioned undisguised satisfaction. It was time for a change. The moment had struck when one could hear the swish of history as it turned a corner. An almost national sigh seemed to signal that a long period of boredom had come to an end. The joy was not only prompted by the comely and stalwart person of the young King; it also sprang from incurable expectations, from the feeling that, whatever happened, here would at least be a contrast and hence welcome.

The old King had left a fortune of £1,800,000. He had applied himself almost endlessly to the business of being King. He had not played upon the virginals. In all he did he wrapped the whole mantle of government firmly and securely about himself. It was therefore plain upon the accession of young Henry, with his love of music and sport and his addiction to personal pleasures, that someone would have to do, or see that the young King did, all the work that the old King had done. This was an item of great concern to the Council. The lad now on the throne might be very fit for a king in public and remain a dilettante in private, a lute player with a mountain of wearisome documents to be handled.

This serious question could be suspended in the first days of the new regime, for there were certain ceremonies that with the English must take precedence over all matters of state. The pageantry of kingship must be preserved. In this the Council could not have found a better actor. Henry's first royal decision was clear and unequivocal: he would marry Catherine of Aragon, put an end to the uncertainty of her status, keep the dowry beyond question, and seal the alliance with Spain.

On the wisdom of the marriage, the Council had been divided. William Warham, Archbishop of Canterbury and Primate of All England, had grave ecclesiastical doubts about the validity of the bull from Julius II. It had been slow in coming; its delivery had been postponed from time to time; and when the bull and the documents with it arrived, it evidently had not been satisfactory, for immediately thereafter the young Henry "on the eve of his fourteenth birthday made secret but formal protest against the validity of his marriage to Catherine." It was known that the old Henry, with all his eagerness for the alliance and the dowry, could not then bring his aching conscience to urge the marriage.

And even if the bull had been explicit and had satisfied lay and ecclesiastical minds, it did not take an archbishop to see that in the laws of the ancient Hebrews the Lord had spoken unto Moses, saying: "And if a man shall take his brother's wife, it is an unclean thing: he hath uncovered his brother's nakedness; they shall be childless." [3] The same law which forbade men to lie sexually with animals or other men forbade even a king to lie with his brother's wife. Nay, in the case of a king the matter was worse; for the law of the Lord said he would be childless.

The decision taken was momentous; and it was taken in part because Richard Fox — himself an ecclesiastic even more than Warham, for Warham had been a lawyer and had simply been given an ecclesiastical post — saw the marriage of Henry and Catherine as a practical matter, an affair of state. Besides, there was clearly no evidence that Catherine and the sickly Arthur had lived together as man and wife. Young Henry had imbibed piety from his father; he was alert to the laws of the Church and a dutiful son of the Church, for with all his many interests and affairs of culture he still found time for three Masses every day. His own reckoning of the law, therefore, and the beck of his own conscience, should be respected. If there had not been union between Arthur and Catherine, she had not been in fact but only in name and outward appearance his brother's wife.

Other considerations were put forward by the party in the Council headed by Wolsey's sponsor. Henry VII in his death agony had besought his son to carry out the marriage with Catherine. In his final insecurity he had seen the importance of the alliance. Moreover, the bride's father, Ferdinand, upon hearing of Henry's impending death, had sent forward representations to the English court that France and the other powers of Europe would endeavor to prevent the marriage and break off the alliance with Spain. To Catherine, Ferdinand wrote bluntly that she would get no other husband.

Fox, and by proxy Wolsey, prevailed. So in the excitement of the new reign Henry and Catherine were joined together in almost unseemly haste — scarcely six weeks after the death of Henry VII. As Burke puts it, the news was suddenly announced to the Council "that the King and Princess had gone early on a June morning to the chapel of the Observant

Friars at Greenwich and 'had a private marriage,' and were 'determined with God's assistance to abide by that contract to the death.' " [4]

Catherine of Aragon was at last, and with all her embarrassment, wed to a king. And it was to be noted that at the ceremony she had been conspicuously and pointedly dressed in white to show her virginity. Three weeks later, the coronation of the royal pair took place at Westminster, and Archbishop Warham placed the crowns upon their heads. Again Catherine appeared as a virgin. Londoners first saw her as Queen while she was borne from the Tower to Westminster, "sitting in a litter of cloth of gold slung between white palfreys, clad, herself, all in white satin, the costume of a virgin bride, with her gleaming hair 'hanging down her back, of a very great length, beautiful and goodly to behold.' " [5]

There would, at the outset of the new regime, continue to be a touch of sobriety and severity in the court of England. Not for long. The beginning of any reign is, in some respects, bound to be an interregnum in which the royal advisers square off to tilt for power; a period in which the King himself accustoms himself to the business of being king and decides which of a hundred white horses he will ride.

Wolsey kept his presence at court, which was the important thing for a man whose strength and power lay chiefly in the impressiveness of his personality. He aided in the disposition of the effects of the dead King. When after four months he was appointed Almoner to the new King, he began to operate on a more lavish scale, for there was a dash and color about the new regime lacking in the old. The kingship came out of hiding. Henry VIII made it a point to be seen on every occasion. He was given to display, and yet he felt himself at all times keenly identified with the people of the country he ruled. The affairs and ceremonies of his court, as a consequence, took on some of the thrust and zest of his person. The realm had endured penurious prosperity long enough. It would now enjoy a pageant.

In his moderate habits and dress Henry VII had tried to serve as a sober model for his people. With his furred gown and square cap, he had sought to make simplicity stylish. The nobility, however, being curtailed in many particulars, had stood regulation ill in matters of dress; extravagance would flare up among them on such occasions as funerals, and it had become necessary to control the expenditures allowed for mourning. Yet with all the rebellious outbursts of color there had been a tendency toward moderation. When Henry VII died, men of all classes "were wearing long hose or tights called stocks, low round-neck shirts, short jerkins or doublets and a longer gown or cloak for warmth. The doublet was usually like a waistcoat, with or without sleeves and reaching to the waist, and the stocks were tied to this garment with a sort of bootlace called 'points' . . . The hair was often worn long or just to the shoulders." There were ways, of course, by which even this somber attire could be made conspicuous. "Small hats or caps decorated with a feather gave a jaunty air to the young gallant. Excess of fashion was displayed by the tightness of the nether garments and the extreme brevity of the jerkins which in some cases finished with a frill at the waist. The more soberminded covered their thighs." [6]

When His Grace young Henry VIII came to the throne and to wide public gaze, dress blossomed, both because the desire had been pent up and because the treaties engaged in by his father had made goods available. Formerly the cloth needed for a fashionable jerkin had been only two yards. Now it was seven or eight. Other signs announced the assertive change. Garments were slashed "to show a contrasting undergarment of lining," so that by this token observers might behold layers of wealth beyond what first met the eye. "Sleeves, both for men and for women, were now separate articles of dress, and were of different colors and materials from the rest of the body-clothing. They were trussed at the shoulders by points." The hood, worn for so long a time, disappeared, "and the flat hats were cut and slashed, and edged or laden with feathers . . . The small, flat, round bonnet continued in general use; it lingered long with the apprentices, and was spoken of as 'the city flat cap.'" [7]

For all the change toward gaiety and extravagance, Henry VIII served as a new model, brandishing his love of dress wherever he went. He came to be known as "the best dressed sovereign in the world, for he put on new clothes every holy day." He could be seen in a black-and-gold-embroidered shirt of slashed velvet. His stocks or tights might be one color and his hose another, for stocks and hose had now become separate garments. Both descended into slashed, broad-toed shoes.

The whole emphasis on dress announced that parsimony had ceased to be a national standard; the vogue was now for the consumption of goods. Even the dressing of horses was made an art. Henry made dress and the display of goods a policy, a sign of the richness of the kingdom, a model for prelates and all of the upper classes. Clothes were assets, both in terms of station and of actual wealth, for there was little besides clothes and houses on which money could be spent. Indeed the right to dress in costly attire was, by being confined to the upper classes, made an incentive to wealth, and it became necessary to renew again the laws which confined sumptuous apparel to those of rank. In the first Parliament Henry called, it was enacted that no man under the rank of duke should wear any cloth of gold; "not any under the rank of an earl should wear any sables . . ." [8] The King, on the other hand, might wear what he pleased, and he had the right to license the wearing of special apparel among those who deserved the royal favor. The clothes of the class above might be a reward or a perquisite.

While the office of almoner in the royal household carried no great prestige, it could be executed with competitive aplomb if the man who occupied it put his mind to the task and calculated with proper histrionics what effect the bestowal of gifts could make. It was an honorable and customary office in all grand houses, secular and religious — a part of the courtly condescension of the rich and mighty to the poor and needy. At the Abbey of St. Augustine at Canterbury and at Westminster Abbey "twice a week the Almoner distributed food to all the poor who came to the dole house . . ." No one went away without a share. "It was the duty of the Almoner to find out the sick and the poor in the neighborhood, to visit them with his servants and to take them food and drink." [9]

There were more lofty offices in the staff of a great house and in the court, but the office of almoner brought with it the privilege of contact with the outside world. The Almoner represented the King's graciousness and wealth in public; if he doled well, he extended the King's public relations and burrowed into the hearts of the people. The way he passed out alms afforded one of those vast intangibles by which the royal person became manifest and vivid.

Wolsey showed himself a good and faithful servant in the few things early entrusted to him. Less than seven months after Henry VIII came to the throne, Wolsey received a notable mark of the royal favor which showed that his labors and learnings would not go without reward: he was given a grant of one of the houses forfeited by the attainder of Sir Richard Empson. The house lay at Bridewell. In a grant dated January 10, 1510, it was called "La Maison curiale, with twelve gardens and orchards between the Thames and St. Bride's gardens in Fleetstreet." Here Wolsey lived in a "noncanonical" marriage with a woman called Joan Larke. The edict that priests, regardless of their functions or the character of their work, should remain celibate had not been wholeheartedly accepted in England. Hence the rule of celibacy was not uncommonly honored in the breach and the offense forgiven by regular fines, which, in some places, constituted a source of episcopal revenues. "There were many ecclesiastics, from the popes downward, who had wives . . . Warham is said by Erasmus to have had a wife who was not secluded from the knowledge and society of his friends." [10]

Wolsey's views of marriage may not have been exemplary in his chosen profession, but they were forthright, open, and strenuously aired, a circumstance shown by the fact that he later made himself responsible (in the Parliament of 1523) for an act which relieved six clerical priests employed as clerks in Chancery from taking vows of celibacy. A vast number of clergy in England were engaged in clerical work, the term "clerical" deriving from the fact that many of the services of society were under the hand of the Church. It did not seem essential that such men, engaged in secular work, be asked to avoid marriage.

There is no indication that Wolsey was married but once. Although records are obscure, the woman he married appears to have been the daughter of one Peter Larke, "gentleman of Huntingdonshire." In 1463, members of a Larke family were associated with the town of Thetford, not far from Ipswich, and a man named Peter Larke was twice mayor of that town. He is described as a farmer and a grazier and as the grandfather of Joan Larke. A kinsman of Joan's father was Thomas Larke, who became "surveyor of the King's works" and later was Wolsey's confessor. Erasmus said that of all the men he had known in England, Larke was the most cultured and sincere; and the Latin secretary to the King wrote that he was "omnipotent with the Cardinal." [11]

Obviously the connections of the marriage were good, and the union was in its odd way respectable. Wolsey seems to have remained faithful to his wife and later to have given her in marriage as a father might — even fixing upon her a dowry — when she was wed publicly and formally to George Legh of Aldington, a wealthy landowner in the county of Cheshire.[12] Wolsey continued his friendship with the Larke family and gave tokens of it from time to time: Joan's brother Thomas was instituted by him to the rich living of Winwick in Lancashire and was entrusted with the education of the future Earl of Derby; likewise he remained on close family terms with George Legh after the marriage of his noncanonical wife to that young gentleman.

Two children were born from Wolsey's marriage with Joan Larke. One, a daughter named Dorothy, was later consigned to a nunnery in the fashion of the day; but the son was given all the emoluments of affection any lavish and preoccupied father might bestow upon his heir in lieu of companionship. He was known as Thomas Wynter; and he was spoken of sometimes by his father and by others as Wolsey's son, "sometimes, according to the euphemism of the time, as his nephew." He was "brought up carefully as a wealthy man's son and educated by private tutors in England and at the universities of Louvain, Padua, and Paris." When the boy was scarcely ten years old he was given the revenues of a parish. The scandalous way in which Wolsey managed to make the Church provide this comfortable, if not ruinous, allowance afforded his enemies with some of their best reasons for their final vituperative attack. As a father, Wolsey made the mistakes of other fathers, all growing out of overstuffed privilege and a lack of close personal relationship with his son.

With his house and his family and all the accouterments of respectability, Wolsey was now part of the ruling fraternity in terms of property as well as status. This time he had been rewarded out of the royal coffers, directly and well, and not simply with another benefice in the Church. He did not relinquish his religious honors or permit himself to be identified wholly with the throne. The King ruled the homeland, but Rome ruled the world. There was no need for one to surrender the larger scope of the Church, especially if this scope could be turned to good account in the homeland. One might be a lawgiver but still remain a prophet.

The new King summoned Parliament to meet on January 10, 1510 — the first time it had met in six years. Members of the Commons — squires and burgesses all — came reluctantly. Parliament was a bore. The scant wages of the members of the lower House were paid by local constituencies, and a man lost touch with his private business and his family when he came to London and spent forty or sixty days sitting around drafty halls, hearing wise men talk as if they were wiser, and carrying out the haughty instructions of the Lords. Most of the bills originated with the Lords and were often written in the Council. The Commons felt that its chief business was to ratify the labors of its betters, though occasionally there were conferences designed to compromise moot matters.

This Parliament lasted only twenty-nine days. Its achievements were not weighty, but the fact that it had met and that the Commons had asserted themselves showed the ripple of a trend which men with a proper sense of society might well mark.

But Wolsey was too busy with the King and the Council to see much of anything. By 1511, while still officially only the Royal Almoner, he was engaged in circumventing the normal procedures of the King's officers and expressing himself freely and cozily on affairs of the court. One of his earliest private letters extant was written on September 30, 1511, to tell Fox that Thomas Howard, Earl of Surrey and the chief of the nobility around the King, had met with a cool reception at court and had gone home the next day. Wolsey then proceeded to observe "that with a little help he might be 'utterly excluded' therefrom, 'whereof in my poor judgment no little good should ensue.' " [13] It was big talk from the son of an Ipswich commoner, whose native county had long stood cap in hand to the Howards of Norfolk. But the Ipswich boy had been transformed by his closeness to the King.

Already he enjoyed the confidence of the young King to an astonishing extent, and he showed that he was resolved to use this confidence to the full. A few months earlier he had side-stepped and by-passed all official procedure. There was an established method of giving legal effect to the royal will. The King would sign a bill or petition presented to him and pass it to his secretary. The secretary would in turn write a letter under the King's signet to the Lord Privy Seal, keeping the bill signed by the King. The Lord Privy Seal would then write under that seal to the Lord Chancellor as Keeper of the Great Seal, holding the secretary's letter as his warrant; and the Lord Chancellor would issue paper orders. On May 26, 1511, "Wolsey produced for the chancellor a signed bill which had gone through none of this official routine; and the chancellor acted without his proper warrant, safeguarding himself by the singular entry on his record that he had expedited the matter because Wolsey had given him the letters by the king's command, *ut asseruit dictus dominus Wulcy*." [14] To trespass thus on prerogatives, ignoring all channels of procedure, was a highhanded act for a lowborn cleric. And the fact that the Lord Chancellor of England accepted the act without question showed how close the Almoner stood to the King.

He stood close on religious as well as secular grounds. Wolsey wrote to Fox about the illness of Pope Julius II, who was said to be dead or dying. He reported to Fox that the day before at Mass he "brake with the King in this matter and showed unto his grace how much honour and also furtherance of all his affairs in time to come should issue to him if that by his commendation some Cardinal might attain to be Pope." [15]

But any report that Julius II was dead left a wholly false impression. He was much alive and full of schemes, "this swarthy and pugnacious Genoese," who let it be known that he had pulled a galley oar in his youth and who conducted the office of pontiff as if he were a sailor on leave. Julius II saw the world about him as one of conflict. He had a sharp sense of the physical, and he aggressively believed that the Pope, being the ruler of Christendom's spirit, should have a fair possession of Christendom's territory, a series of buffer and protective states so that the Holy Father would not be molested in his duties by quarreling kings.

To this estimable end he had in 1510 invited the Most Christian King of France (kings of France were so designated by a pontiff in the previous century) to put the Republic of Venice in its proper place. The Most Christian King, in this case Louis XII, had done the job better than the Pope bargained for. At the battle of Agnadello the French won a crushing victory. "In one day," wrote Machiavelli, "the Venetians lost all they had acquired during eight hundred years of strenuous effort." [16] The Most Christian King loomed now as a bulky threat to the Pope's peace of mind: he had advanced too far and too powerfully for comfort. More practically, an ally of the Most Christian King, the Duke of Ferrera, had begun with shocking impiety to produce salt at Commachio, "to the detriment of the papal monopoly at Cervia." [17]

The situation manifestly called for a realignment, and Julius, disregarding the treaty by which the Most Christian King had come to his aid, formed now a league to expel Louis from Italy. Julius made a treaty with the Swiss, who agreed to supply him with 6000 troops at a good export price. He absolved the Venetians and brought them back into the papal camp against Louis. Then the Pope took the field in person and with warlike mien led a combination of troops to two victories in the north of Italy. He enlisted also the aid of Ferdinand and called the coalition he had formed against France the Holy League.

When the Holy Father became warlike, the Most Christian King, as seems appropriate, became theological. Louis XII assembled the French clergy and secured from them a declaration that a general council of the Church should be held. From Milan on May 16, 1511, half a dozen dissident cardinals called for a council to be held at Pisa in September. They summoned the Pope to attend. Julius retorted by calling for a Lateran Council to be held in April 1512, excommunicated the cardinals who had rebelled against his authority, and created eight new ones, just to be on the safe side. One of those he named was Christopher Bainbridge, Archbishop of York, whom Henry VIII had sent as his ambassador to the Holy See. Bainbridge had actually gone to protest the investiture of Venice, which Henry had deplored. Knowing the English addiction to Venice, Julius had made it appear that he had forgiven the Venetians at Henry's behest. And as a token of his appreciation of Henry's splendid interference he sent the King of England on April 10, 1511, a golden rose. There was a not unreasonable hope nestled in the canny mind of Julius that the impetuous young King of England, son-in-law of the King of Spain, advised by a brilliant priest who had risen to strength through the good offices of the Church, might join the Holy League against the Most

Christian King, who had compounded his offense against the Holy See by outrageously daring to call a council of the Church without the Pope's consent.

CHAPTER I I

THIS is the way matters stood in distant Rome when Wolsey became a member of the King's Council and began to transact the King's business without recourse to the petty nonsense of protocol. With a persuasive tongue long trained in eloquent conversation, a commanding figure with the grace of quick movements, a manner attentive and deferential to those who rated his deference, he moved about the court earnestly and diligently. Accustomed to advancement through the simple and unfailing expedient of pleasing his superiors by doing their work, he made a perfect companion for the young King. And it was natural that for a time as king Henry VIII should follow the practices in which he had been reared and be satisfied to have servitors following after him, tidying up, while he changed his attire and showed himself like a jewel. Members of the Council urged that he attend the deliberations in which important decisions were made; but by the testimony of some Wolsey gave the opposite advice, saying, according to Godwin, that the King should "hawk and hunt and not intermeddle with old men's cares." [1]

His gentleman-usher testifies that older advisers of the young King would persuade him to spend some time at the Council table, but this pleased the King not at all: "he loved nothing worse than to be constrained to do anything contrary to his royal will and pleasure." This Wolsey understood, says Cavendish, "and so fast as the other counsellors advised the king to leave his pleasure, and to attend to the affairs of his realm, so busily did the almoner persuade him to the contrary; which delighted him much, and caused him to have the greater affection to the almoner." [2]

But if the bustling Wolsey protected the lute-player from the distractions and tedium of governing a people, he could do little but admire the King in his jousts and tilts and games. These jousts were not to be taken lightly; the aggressive side of Henry's nature must find an outlet, as it had in childhood, and it was plain that to him the sport of fighting was more than a commodity for home consumption. After all, war was

91

hardly more than a tourney on a large scale. Early in his career Henry VIII showed that he was not likely to follow the cautious and plodding footsteps of his progenitor, who had settled for cash the only war he undertook.

The new reign would be a new regime in more ways than one. The elder Henry had even made peace with the Scots, though the act was considered unnatural for an English King. Now young Henry would set a fiercer face to the north, and he began by refusing to hand over to Margaret the jewels bequeathed to her, as wife of the Scottish King, by her father. Border incidents increased. Then Sir Edward Howard in the summer of 1511 killed Andrew Barton in a body of water known as The Downs and captured his ships. Barton was a favorite of the Scottish King, James IV. He had in the past committed depredations on English ships, but there was no evidence that he had attacked the Howards before the slaughter in The Downs. Henry was pledged by treaty to consider Scottish grievances, but in this case he replied to the protest haughtily that "kings do not concern themselves with the affairs of pirates." [3] By this supercilious act he broke with a spit of contempt the alliance which his father had so methodically put together.

The temperament of the young Henry had begun to reveal itself. He would make himself felt beyond his borders. He would have trial by wager of battle and not by the dullness of jury. He would have some part in the world of affairs — but it would be the known world, the world he could tilt at and ride horseback on, the visible world near at hand. His father had shown a keen interest in the world to the west beyond the seas, where rewards might be ultimate and rich. Spain had already shrewdly won an empire there. Even Portugal, not fit for the better quarrels of Europe, had established itself in India. There were those in the Council who pointed enviously to these achievements and felt that the energies of the nation should be directed to the west. They suggested that "when we enlarge ourselves, let it be in that way we can and to which it seems the eternal providence hath destined us, which is by the sea." [4]

But Henry turned his back on the willowy worlds that might one day develop across the seas and entered the lists of Europe with a comfortable horse under him and a trusty sword in his youthful hand. The decision was his, and it expressed his nature. But the credit for it went, in the judgment of the day, to Thomas Wolsey of Ipswich, still the King's Almoner. Because the war that followed was known as Wolsey's War; and for the fiasco that ended the first phase of it — a fiasco unparalleled in the annals of English history — the upstart from Ipswich got the blame.

By encouraging the ambitions of a boy-king, by relying on a nation untrained in the arts and cruelties of war and unprepared for foreign enterprise, and by depending on an ally who had no intention of keeping his solemn word, the priest brought disgrace on England and made his sovereign the laughingstock of Europe.

Wolsey's venture of 1512 was a case of ingenious theory applied to slippery facts. The theory was to aid the Pope against his savage enemy, the Most Christian King, who was at once a menace to the peace of the world and an offender against the Holy See in the schismatic scheme for a council at Pisa. To this end on November 13, 1511, Henry joined the Holy League the Pope had formed. Ferdinand had joined it in October. Four days after Henry joined the League, he made a solemn treaty with Ferdinand to attack France before April 1512. That Henry had renewed the treaty of peace his father had made with France did not seem to matter greatly; this treaty would simply serve the better to disguise his preparations. The theory further held that Ferdinand and Henry would attack France together, Ferdinand through his own borders and Henry across the Channel.

Ferdinand's solemn treaty promise to Henry, his son-in-law, provided the fulcrum on which the whole plan rested. It was a noble plan and satisfied the aspirations of all concerned, providing Henry with an early chance to assert the manly qualities of his reign and of his countrymen and affording the Dean of Lincoln a chance to show the Pope where England and its ministers stood on matters touching the Church. It also afforded Ferdinand some proper notion of the fact that the marriage alliance would be an alliance in fact.

In England there was every good reason to believe that Ferdinand would behave according to plan. Certainly the man seemed harmless and amiable enough. And to give further assurance, his daughter, the wife of the King of England, was his ambassador. She had been the means of a close and informal contact between the two sovereigns. On November 1, 1509, Henry had informed Ferdinand that Catherine was pregnant and that the child had quickened. On January 31, 1510, after days of labor, she had given birth to a daughter, but the child was stillborn. In the May following she wrote to her father to say that the stillbirth had been considered an evil omen in England "but that Henry took it cheerfully and she thanked God for having given her such a husband." On January 1, 1511, she had been delivered of her first-born son. "A tourney was held to celebrate the joyous event and the heralds received a handsome largesse at the christening. The child was named Henry, styled Prince of Wales

. . . Three days later he was dead; he was buried at the cost of some ten thousand pounds in Westminster Abbey." [5] He had lived but seven weeks.

At the death of his son, Henry had been so grief-stricken that "ambassadors dared not even offer their condolences." [6] But he had recovered with that resilience which was in him, and in spite of haunting prospects suggested by the Levitical code, he continued demonstrative toward Catherine. He was heard frequently to say, "This will please the Queen," or, "The Queen must hear this." [7]

With Catherine cozy to the King of England and at the same time representing her father's interests, it was possible to make the impending war seem like a family affair as well as a crusade against the enemy of the Pope. All three of the principals in England — Catherine, Henry, and Wolsey — had strong motives, diverse but easily unified. Henry was spoiling to show his manliness on a stage bigger than the tourney field; Catherine was a dutiful daughter and devout in her father's cause; Wolsey knew the importance of the Pope as the arbiter of Christendom and his value in future moves that England might make on the Continent.

Thus the decision gathered force. There was little opposition. Only William Warham, forlorn Archbishop of Canterbury, held out. When Parliament was assembled on February 4, 1511, to consider ways and means of financing the war against the Most Christian King, Warham opened it with an address on the theme, "Justice and peace have kissed." [8] He reminded the assembled lawgivers sternly that God permitted war only because of the sins of princes and peoples.

But Parliament paid the solemn voice of the prelate scant heed. The Archbishop of Canterbury was the Primate of All England, but he was less than Pope. A papal brief in English translation was read to Lords and communicated to Commons. It recounted the "wrongs done to the Holy See by the impiety of the French king." The Parliament was also told of the Scottish outrages and of the threat of invasion from France. It was said that Bretons knew every landing place in Cornwall and that the whole area from Plymouth to Land's End would have to be fortified. "A statute was passed to promote the use of the long-bow and to enforce the acts against unlawful games which were supposed to compete with the practise of archery . . . Justices, mayors and constables in the maritime counties were empowered to impress labor for the construction of fortresses." [9]

Evidently the King thought the best defense was to attack France while the fortifications were being built. England made no declaration of war, but the plan of attack was worked out in handsome detail and

94

showed the beginning of Wolsey's easy-chair strategy in the affairs of Europe. The command of the invading army was placed under the second Marquis of Dorset, son of Wolsey's first patron.

Why the King and his Almoner chose to put the young Marquis in charge of a far-flung operation involving the navy as well as the army is not clear. During the older Henry's life the Marquis had fallen under royal suspicion, and in 1508 he had been imprisoned in the Tower and later sent to Calais. But he was dear to the heart of the new King because he was a great jouster, and Henry could not rid himself of the notion that if a man had unseated his opponents on the field of play he might surely unseat the enemy on the field of battle. For this reason, if for no other, a courtier of thirty-five, with no more administrative experience than the King himself, was chosen to command an expedition involving the transport and care of the largest English army an English king had ever set across the Channel.

The whole strategy of the attack was conceived in the crafty mind of Ferdinand and accepted by Henry. Dorset "was to land at Feunterrabia, a town on the southern border of Guienne, with a force of 10,000 men; there he would be met by an equal force provided by the King of Aragon, one half of which was to be mounted." [10]

Only a small part of the operation went according to plan. While the young Marquis and his ships tarried at Southampton for a fair wind, news came that the papal forces in Italy had been soundly defeated at Ravenna, a town near the sea east of Bologna. Undaunted by the news, Henry sent forward the attack. The Marquis set out with his expedition, landing June 7 at St. Sebastián on the coast of Spain, where the English army would take up its position for the attack on Guienne. It advanced twelve miles to Feunterrabia, and there waited for the promised transport and reinforcements. The English continued to wait throughout the summer. Ferdinand never came; nor did he make a move of his royal muscles toward aiding the English. He left them without cavalry or transport. To the protestations of the Marquis he answered with excuses for delay. To John Stile, Henry's ambassador to Ferdinand, he said, according to Stile's report, that he would yet "perform everything unto your grace, and that all the delays of time hath been for the best advantage for your enterprize of Guienne, that Navarre should be first put in a surety." And Stile concluded: "It is evidently seen and known, by his policy and long drifts he attaineth many things to other men's pains." [11]

It took the English three unendurable months of inaction and demoralization in the Spanish sun to believe that Ferdinand had no intention of carrying out his part of the agreement. Gradually it became clear that he had merely used the English force to guard his flank while he busied himself with the conquest of Navarre, adding this landlocked and petty kingdom to his possessions while the Marquis of Dorset and ten thousand men lay sweltering without transport on the shore of Spain in the pious hope that he would join them in their attack on France.

The treachery, so successfully executed, was a damaging enough blow to the King of England. It revealed the stark innocence of this boy who occupied the throne of his country and fancied himself a warrior worthy of a decisive role in the military intrigues of an old Continent where kings survived only by a brutal respect for their own advantage. Yet the unfolding perfidy, so familiar to all the other crowned heads and yet so shocking to the beardless Henry, was not the worst of the damage done. For to complete the disgrace to the King and his Almoner who fashioned this war, the English troops, at least those who survived the pestilential summer, revolted against the plan, mutinied against their officers, defied the King's command, and sailed for home.

The priest had reckoned without the flesh. Men do not behave on paper but on earth. The troops sent with the young Marquis, while impressive in number, were shire levies, which meant that they were country bumpkins without any training in the automatic responses of military discipline, hastily assembled at the King's command, and sent, much against the inclination of their home-loving bowels, to fight on foreign soil for a cause that was as vague as Rome was distant.

Even so, they might have stayed in line and acquitted themselves with honor if there had been a staunch and visible enemy. There was nothing to fight but the Spanish weather. It was a season of almost incessant rains, and the troops were without proper tents. There were no musters or drills to maintain the appearance of army order. Worse still, and disastrous, was the want of beer — the allowance for an English fighting man being a gallon a day. The men drank Spanish wine instead, which made their "blood to boil in their bellies that 3000 of them fell ill of the flux and thereof 1800 died." Lacking proper provisions, they raided the commissariat, and, being bored and idle and hungry, found that their money would not serve their needs. So they struck for more pay — eightpence instead of sixpence a day.[12]

All of this was duly and disgracefully reported to Wolsey. All the correspondence from Spain was addressed to him. As summer wore on, conditions grew steadily more alarming in the ranks. Without a proper enemy, the character of the English yeoman soldier, a farmer with a bow, asserted itself; what seemed to the court at Westminster rank indiscipline became a form of discipline characteristically English — a twitch toward self-government. Officers as well as men formed a council of war and planned a campaign of their own: its object was to return to England the last of September, and they announced that they would abide in Spain after Michaelmas "for no man."

A letter to Wolsey from Dr. Knight told of the council of war and of the plans to return. A herald was sent to tell the whole army they must winter in Spain. This advertisement of the King's orders met with shouts of defiance. The men "crowded round their leaders, crying 'Home! Home!'"[13] The Marquis of Dorset, with scant choice, acceded to the demands of his officers and troops. By the time the news reached the court, the recalcitrant army had provisioned its ships and, early in October, baked its biscuit for the voyage home. Ferdinand, all indignation, protested the move, and Henry showed his royal temper and kingly fury. He wrote Ferdinand to stop the return of the army and to cut every man's throat who refused obedience. But this request of an English king to a foreign monarch to cut the throats of English troops, futile and rhetorical anyway, came too late. The bedraggled and defiant army was already on the sea.

In this humiliating manner ended Henry's first foray into the maze of Europe. The expedition had wasted two hundred thousand ducats and it had lost nearly two thousand English lives, without striking a single organized military blow. Its failure confirmed indelibly every low impression the old heads of the Continent had of this upstart young King who would dare to take an honorable part in their experienced quarrels. And it made plain, too — this failure of Homeric proportions — that the King of England was in the toils of bad advice. There were no secrets kept in Europe. In England the resentment was concentrated on "this Ipswich fellow" who was deemed to be the author of all the mischief. By an extension of the arm of blame, Wolsey was held responsible not only for the war but for the outcome and for the triumphant treachery of Ferdinand, who had outfoxed his English ally and killed his own prey while the English masked the French for him.

In his first effort beyond the comfortable confines of the court, where he could use his eloquence and his favor to silence opposition, Wolsey had failed. His failure had been lavish in scale, shameless in detail. As a priest who enjoyed no higher rank than Almoner, he had arrogated to himself the role of chief councilor and executive. He had been the means, through the lack of thoroughness with which the Spanish campaign was planned, of bringing disgrace upon his King and country. And the country which had suffered knew his intimate part in the affair.

What could be the future of such a priest?

It was part of the temperament of Thomas Wolsey that he met failure by a magnificent scheme for success. The mistakes of the Spanish campaign were plain for all to see, and in their remedy might well lie the secret of victory where defeat had followed before. Obviously the best arrangement would be to invade France again, this time thoroughly prepared in all particulars, especially beer, and with the person of the King as the commander who could hold the troops to their course.

Such an invasion was, in fact, a national necessity. There was no other way in which to escape the disgrace which the Spanish fiasco had fastened on the throne of England. Wolsey may have taken the blame at home for this failure, but the King knew that he himself shared it. Among kings and rulers Henry and not the priest would be the object of laughter and scorn. He was thus in the odd position of having to rescue Wolsey from the low esteem into which his minister had fallen.

There were other reasons, of course, and other forces steadily at work. The best way to cover the embarrassment of a mutiny was to plan another war. Henry had wanted to bring the Marquis of Dorset to trial, along with his subordinates. But it was generally reasoned in the Council that it would be hard to fix degrees of blame where all were responsible for the withdrawal of the army. So the disaffection was treated quietly, and as the voices of the other kings and rulers of Europe reached the English court, Henry instructed his ambassadors formally to state that he and Ferdinand had mutually agreed "upon the return of the troops in consequence of the rainy weather." [14] It was a charitable statement and it covered a multitude of sins.

As early as November, after the return of the recalcitrant army in October, it was reported in London that the King and Queen were bent on continuing the war. At first the Council demurred. The patent reasons which led to the launching of the attack the year before had disappeared. The Most Christian King could not longer be adjudged a threat to Christendom. By one of those curious reversals of fortune, and with no thanks to the sterling efforts of the King of England, France had suddenly fallen into weakness. She had been driven out of Lombardy only a few months after her victory at Ravenna. Moreover, the threat to the spiritual rights of the Holy See as forecast in the Council of Pisa had failed to materialize, and the schismatic cardinals had come to terms with the Pope.

There was no reason to argue or believe that the palladium of the Church suffered threat any longer from France or her king, whose fortunes had sadly ebbed and who was now depressed, aging, and gouty besides.

Yet the war must go on, even if the reason for it had changed. Ferdinand professed himself to be outraged at English perfidy and was loud in his comment on the weakness of his son-in-law for letting his troops desert en masse. Catherine was his dutiful and devout daughter. Most of all, an impression had to be corrected. This impression, which shook and riled the soul of the young Henry, was best expressed by Margaret, who told the English ambassador that Englishmen had "so long abstained from war, they lack experience from disuse, and, as it is reported, they now be almost weary of it." [15] Henry had no choice, if he were not to retire from being a respectable and competitive monarch, but to redeem the failure of 1512. The war changed from a crusade to a demonstration of national might, and preparations for it were undertaken accordingly so that no man could henceforth taunt Henry.

In January 1513 the bellicose Julius II, whose trumpet of war had first aroused the nations against France, died and was succeeded by Cardinal Giovanni de' Medici, who took the title of Leo X. He was a man of artistic rather than military or political concerns, but he had enough stamina and interest to continue the Holy League against the Most Christian King. After due and proper negotiations among its members this League, now slightly changed in its membership, drew up a covenant to attack France. It was signed on April 3, 1513, by envoys representing Leo, Ferdinand, Margaret of Burgundy, and Henry. Four days before the agreement was signed, Ferdinand had signed a year's truce with France.

If the war now afforded an opportunity for the English King to redeem himself in the eyes of Europe, it afforded no less of an opportunity for Thomas Wolsey to redeem himself in the eyes of his master. For the entire burden of equipping and victualing an army of 40,000 men and transporting it across the Channel for the invasion of France was placed firmly and exclusively upon the shoulders of the Royal Almoner. No English army remotely comparable in numbers or arms had been sent to foreign shores before. There being no precedent for it, there was likewise no organization, no departments of government, to carry out the project. The King and his Almoner were the high command and the whole command. The two were identified again, this time in a colossal enterprise. On its success, in their estimation, would the future of England depend. If England succeeded, she must be reckoned with by all the nations of her world. If Wolsey succeeded, he would prove himself indispensable to the King.

The stubborn confidence of Henry VIII in the lowborn Thomas Wolsey, a confidence which endured for fifteen years in the face of all outcries and criticisms and astonished the diplomats of Europe and the upper classes of English society, dates from this feat in preparing for the invasion of France during the early months of 1513. Henry found in Wolsey a servitor who not only would but could do anything he was told. The priest wrought with the energy of a demon. No plan was too large and no detail too small to engage his fanatically patient attention.

He was forty-two years old at the time, still in abundant health, and he needed every bit of it for the long, solid days and infinite number of nights spent haggling over prices, scurrying for provisions, corresponding with ambassadors and purveyors and admirals and lords. Since the disaffection and ill-content of the English soldiers in Spain had been due to lack of beer, this item was made of first order of importance. The English soldier's habits and hankerings must be respected; there was no use taking any chances with human nature. If beer was to be stored on the transports in good supply, there must be casks for the beer — called foists. Of these, pursers on board the ships of the King's navy were very careless, and Wolsey was forced to write in protest that he could not properly provision the ships if foists continued to be burned or broken. Fox declared that the pursers deserved hanging for their carelessness with the King's equipment. And Wolsey warned the Admiral, Sir Edward Howard, that if the wasting and burning of foists did not stop the King's whole enterprise would be endangered. "Orders should at once be given," said the Almoner to the Admiral, "that the offenders be punished." [16]

Every single phase of his task led sooner or later to a firmament thick with detail that came like stars out of the darkness. For once the casks for beer were secured, and at as fair a price as the purveyors could be brought to offer in view of the demand, he had to have assurance that they were sound and firm and that the beer would not go bad once it was on board, or stored at Calais for use in the campaign. It was one thing to see that the standard allowance of a gallon a day was met on paper and another to follow through and see that the purveyors did not cheat on their casks. There must not be another mutiny for lack of beer.

The same thoroughness, the same capacity for seeing a transaction entire and looking to the King's economy, was to be noted in his purchase of victuals. He ordered the slaughter of 25,000 oxen, and when he contracted for "oxen for salting, he would have only the finest beasts from Lincolnshire and Holland; and he insisted on securing rebates for the hides and the tallow. The prices of flitches of bacon are also submitted to him, likewise those of biscuits, cheese, dry cod, ling, beef; also of cauldrons to seethe meat in." [17]

There had never been an enterprise like this in the history of any man living. First it was calculated that 30,000 men would be set across the Channel. Then the number was raised to 40,000, these troops to be joined there by an additional 10,000 mercenaries from Germany. The full movement of these troops must be allowed for, and their supply must be reckoned sagely at every turn. But Wolsey went further. He even allowed and made definite plans for the return of the King's forces, and his calculations included schemes for meeting any contingency that might arise if the return of the army should be delayed by adverse winds even a few days beyond the time set provisionally for its return.

Nothing must be overlooked, least of all those things which in the test of battle and conflict would add to the striking power of the good right arm of the King. Henry must have not only men and provisions but arms — great arms, new weapons. Up to now England had relied on foreign countries for such cannon as it employed. Now it would make these in its own bailiwick. The attaché of the Venetian embassy, much impressed with the preoccupying preparations he saw on every hand, wrote: "These English go a good pace, I can tell you . . . Night and day and on all festivals the cannon founders are at work." [18] Heavy guns were coming into use for the first time, and Henry would outstrip his rivals in their manufacture and use. Besides, he would make great use of them as a threat, and he let gossip of the monsters be spread abroad by his ambassadors. The feature of his arsenal for the attack on France was to be a collection of a dozen great guns "bigger than any ever cast before, each named after one of the Apostles and furnished with an effigy of the Saint; so that throughout Europe was bruited the fame of the King of England's 'Twelve Apostles,' who were to preach in tones of thunder and with tongues of fire, Henry's new crusade in defense of the Church of God and the Christian faith." [19]

But with the recollections of the Spanish campaign fresh upon the royal mind, the main scurrying of the King's Almoner turned to day and night supplies for the soldiers who would represent the kingdom abroad. Soldiers must be well cared for by the government, so drastically had times changed since the days when a man went to battle under the aegis of his lord or squire. For this enterprise carried with it the name of England; performance must be above reproach. Thus item by item the Almoner checked his list, and in checking it he came to tents. The lack of tents, what with men ill clad and undernourished, sleeping under bushes or the open sky, exposed to rains and a merciless sun, had been one of the bitterest complaints that had led to the return of the mutinous army from Spain. Wolsey set as his standard that all of the 40,000 men the King took to France would be under canvas. There was at least a department of the government for this undertaking; but the supply was short, and it was necessary for workers to mend old tents as well as fashion new ones. The supervision of this department alone was enough work for a dozen sturdy men in high places, but Wolsey studiously kept all control and responsibility in his hands, being accountable only to the King.

His fierce sense of responsibility had advantages, which his calculating eye well saw. If he succeeded, the King succeeded. That was meat and drink for the morrow and honors heaped beyond even his own febrile imagining. But it also had its drawbacks, for murmurs and complaints among the people, strained by so huge an enterprise, would be directed toward him. Prices rose. As stores poured into Calais during January, February, and March, including such items as 1000 lambs to supplement the diet promised by the slaughter of the 25,000 oxen, the price of meat more than doubled. The price of bread rose, too. There was a public clamor inevitably, and it was the Almoner who got the blame. Merchants from abroad complained that business was at a standstill, that the English had no use for goods that did not help the King's immediate cause. The Venetians were bitter, and their letters are full of the lament that England in these days was no longer a market.

More serious and painful than the discontent over the rising prices of meat and bread were the prospect of financing a gigantic war and the criticism voiced of the King's Almoner because of the mounting national budget. During the first three years of the young Henry's reign, crown expenditures did not exceed £65,000 a year. At this pace the resources Henry VII had husbanded — the fortune of £1,800,000 which he is reckoned to have left — would have run the regime comfortably for years on end, and taxgatherers would not have needed to molest the land. But in 1512, the year of Henry's decision to rescue the Pope from the Most Christian King, crown expenditures bounded to £270,000. And as the people paled before this figure, the King's Almoner, busy with foists and fodder, beef and bacon and bread and beer, totaled up the costs of the war and reckoned that the invasion of France on the scale contemplated would come to £64,000 a year; and this was above and beyond the amount the lords of the manors and those in high places would be expected to spend in the care and maintenance of their own retinues. An obedient Parliament, still under the spell of the King's bidding, granted the amount in theory; but £64,000 was easier to say than to raise, and the process of separating it from the fists of nobles and clergy and farmers and artisans had many of the aspects of wholesale amputations, with nothing but the heat of indignation against Wolsey to cauterize the wounds.

Wolsey wangled the best prices he could, and his Ipswich eye scrutinized all values. He investigated "the wages of the servitors on board his Majesty's ships; the cost of masters' and pilots' coats . . . the cost of anchors and cables for the fleet." There is in the Record Office a letter telling how he had bargained for the carrying of the King's two great siege guns with twenty-eight mares at tenpence a day for each mare. The son of Suffolk, academician though he was in the days of his training, knew the cost of everything; and the bursar who had been in charge at Magdalen when the Tower was completed came now to apply bursaring on a stupendous scale.

Yet with all his shopping and bargaining and shrewd handling of a per diem for mares, the total costs of the impending war rose like a great wind, and the people were aware of it and of the man who, at the King's behest, sat in the countinghouse and counted out the money. Assessments were levied on the basis of a man's wealth, and the King's commissioners visited victims with searching inquiries. They examined a man's property, his books and records, talked with his neighbors and servants, fingered his coins, pawed at his tapestries and clothing, nosed about his house, ran appraising eyes over his stock and lands. These roving commissioners were empowered to evaluate on the spot and to make assessments at once. No man of any means or property escaped. There was no way to assure passover, for the King's men were everywhere. Empson and Dudley had been publicly disposed of and a lesson made of them, and the new Henry was precisely legal and most orderly in his depredations. The levies hurt just the same, and the gossip that went with them told on every estate and in every hamlet of the new priest at the court who was sitting on the money bags.

Wolsey still had no rank beyond the smile of the King's countenance. He was still officially the Royal Almoner. He had accumulated offices within the Church, but only gradually and always at the King's hand or the hands of the King's councilors. On January 16, 1512, he had been made a prebendary in York Cathedral. This had been at the instigation of Christopher Bainbridge, Archbishop of York, whom Henry had sent as his ambassador to the Holy See; the Pope had seen it wise to make Bainbridge a cardinal and Bainbridge, knowing through his whispering agents the importance of Wolsey in the King's practical plans, had recommended the York appointment. A year later, and in the midst of the confusing purchases and preparations for the defeat of France, Wolsey had been made Dean of York. He was a man of growing stature, yes, but still he was no tower within the Church, and the work of the assessors in the King's enterprise fell upon the clergy as well as upon the laity: the same humiliation of inspection of means and the same crushing assessments for the King's war, with the money going straight into the hands of a man who was not even a bishop.

. With all the grumbling at prices and taxes, the work of readying the army and the navy went forward like an unfolding drama before the incredulous eyes of the nation. The King meant business, and he had a style and an imagination made to the scale of his enterprise. He had learned his lesson. War was not a casual affair, at least not on foreign soil. It might be a tourney, but the setting and the arrangements had to be complete before it started. This he knew, and he had in Wolsey a manager of detail who would let nothing amiss come to pass.

So it seemed. So much stress and emphasis had been put on intense preparedness that the King and his Almoner were ill prepared for the blow that struck them when the actual fighting began; being prepared had seemed to offer a guarantee, to provide a kind of charm for success. But the navy, in which the King took as much personal pride as he did in the Twelve Apostles, met with disaster when it made its first sally at the coast of France. It returned to port mutinous and disheartened, having lost its doughty Admiral, its failure due, of all things, to lack of victuals. Impatience was the real enemy in this case, and there was no occasion save by indirection to blame the plan. But the incident showed again that the best of plans must reckon with human impulse and frailty.

The Admiral of the fleet of twenty-three English and five borrowed ships was Sir Edward Howard, second son of Thomas Howard, Earl of Surrey. In the Spanish war the year before, he had redeemed in some respects the degree of English disgrace by his prey upon French vessels. Now his assignment had been to rid the Channel of the French fleet so that the King's army could pass across the Strait of Dover unmolested. On April 20, 1513, he set sail from Plymouth with plenty of guns and confidence and men, but short of beer and biscuit and patience. He believed he could dispose of the French in swift engagements and return later for supplies if they happened to be needed. "Such a fleet," he wrote to the King, "was never seen in Christendom." [20] It was a sight to put the French to fear, and fifteen of the French vessels fled to port before its majestic approach. "Sir," wrote the Admiral, "we have them at the greatest advantage that man ever had. The first wind that ever cometh they shall have broken heads that all the world shall speak of it." [21] The Admiral in his cheer at the thought of victory again reckoned without the new French strategy.

Pregent de Bidoux, Admiral of the Mediterranean, had been sent to take command of the French defenses of the Channel. "He knew his business. He had laid his hands on 24 huge hulks to launch as fireships upon an English attack. It was clearly Pregent's plan to entice the Admiral into the shallow water of the harbor, where the French galleys could easily overpower any English row-boats which could be sent against them, and at the same time be out of reach of the enemy's ships of line." In the harbor the French galleys were protected by bulwarks on both sides. These bulwarks were planted thick with guns and crossbows that shot square iron bolts known as quarrels. In the face of any attack the "quarrels and gunstones came together as thick as hailstones." [22]

Now Admiral Howard needed nothing so much as victuals. With beer and biscuit aboard his bulky fleet he could have contained the French ships by blockade until the King and his grand army had passed safely across to France. Without victuals to keep his sailors nourished and beer to keep them happy and warlike, a blockade was out of the question. His rashness had led him into a serious predicament, and Howard now decided that he would attempt to deliver himself by still greater rashness. Against the prudent advice of his captains, the Admiral decided to attack the French fleet in four small rowboats. The scheme was to board the main vessel and take possession of it by force of arms. The Admiral went in person on this foolhardy and tactless tactic. He succeeded in boarding Pregent's ship but, doing battle fiercely to the last in the manner of the best of knights, he was thrust overboard by morris-pikes.

Likewise in this act ended the heroic plan to free the seas of the French before the great invasion. The English fleet, with its leader lost, sailed home in disorder; nothing but exceptionally vile weather on the Channel prevented the French from pursuing. Lord Thomas Howard, first son of the Earl of Surrey, was sent down to take up his brother's office as head of the fleet. He reported that it was "the worst ordered army and furtherest out of rule" that he had ever seen.

It was scarcely a month before the main host of the King's army was scheduled to cross the Channel. What else might be wrong? The preparations were pushed with tense earnestness, all the greater because of the new disaster, and with increasing attention to the problem of coordinating the diverse strands that would pull the enterprise together. It would do little good to have provisions and troops if the two could not be assembled; all the salted oxen on earth would avail the King's cause scantily if they were not in the proper place at the proper time. Still the Almoner had not given up.

Meanwhile the defiant death of Sir Edward Howard at Brest proved a boon and a blessing to the King's cause. Careful planners could not have anticipated its sharp effect upon the English mind. Up to now the English had been engaged in packing beef and paying taxes and spinning tents and brewing beer. Preparation had been a commercial enterprise, beneficial to some, annoying to others, but a cold affair at best. The Admiral's death suddenly gave the war meaning, for it was a display of personal courage of the sort Englishmen and Europeans had understood and admired throughout the epic of the past. Working day and night to mold great cannons or to stitch tents was one thing; to hear of a Howard who mounted a French galley from a rowboat, called to his men to follow him, and met death personally and not abstractly in the Spanish sun — this was quite another. War was suddenly no longer a business enterprise but a tournament in which brave men, brave Englishmen, did great deeds of valor.

CHAPTER III

UNDER the spell cast by the news of Howard's bravery the English nation became at last a cohesive mass, more than a combination of plans and procedures. By the time Henry got ready to cross the Channel the fleet was able to throw a threatening cordon about the whole unprecedented spectacle and carry out the transport besides.

On June 30, 1513, Henry arrived at Calais with the main body of his troops. The vanguard had already crossed under the command of Charles Brandon, now Viscount Lisle, a commoner by birth. His father, plain William Brandon, had been Henry Tudor's standard-bearer at Bosworth and had been killed defending the future King — some said in personal encounter with Richard III. His son Charles was "a bluff Englishman after the King's own heart. He shared, as none else did, in Henry's love of the joust and tourney." In the hierarchy of England's nobility he had been given the title and rights of a viscount, a rank above a baron and below an earl. In manner and heartiness he was dear to the King, standing for the healthy overtness that Henry identified with the Englishman at his best. With the King on the expedition there were said to be "two obstinate men who governed everything." One was Wolsey, unforgettably a commoner, and the other was Brandon, emblem of the new nobility. And in the invasion of France in 1513, designed to display a nation's might, England's nobility, new and old, was on display along with all else that might impress the French.

In intent and purpose the army of the King went to invade; but first and foremost it went to parade. Or so it seemed, for here was a rich and tapestried pageant of the old and new England for all of Europe to see. The Earl of Northumberland carried with him a feather bed and mattress for his pavilion, "with cushions of silk, hangings of worsted, twelve dishes, six saucers, twelve silver spoons, two or three folding stools, a folding table, a close carriage with seven horses, two chariots each with eight horses, four carts each with seven horses, not to speak of a steward, a chamberlain, and a treasurer of the household, a treasurer of wars, two chaplains, a gentleman usher of the chamber, a master of the horse, carvers and cupbearers, a herald and a pursuivant." [1]

Northumberland's accouterment was but a sample of the costly encumbrances which, without regard for military aim, were transported across the Channel. And Northumberland merely brought up the rear. First into Calais came the King's household to the number of three hundred. Next came England's only Duke, the Duke of Buckingham. His banner was followed by Mr. Almoner with two hundred in his train; Ruthal, Bishop of Durham, with one hundred; Fox, Bishop of Winchester, with the same number. "Next came the King and his banner and guard of 600 men, the priests and singers of the chapel to the number of 115, secretaries, clerks, sewers, grooms and pages of the chamber, with Peter Marmelanius, his lutanist," and the most important members of the Council. Henry had 14 fine horses "with housings of the richest cloth of gold and crimson velvet with silver gilt bells of great value." [2] He had brought with him his Master of the Jewel-house; also a "house of timber went about with him in fourteen wagons." [3]

Wolsey not only rode high in the procession; he was also in close attendance upon the King despite his paltry rank. For once the great body of all the King's horses and all the King's men was safely across the Channel and on the hostile soil of France, it was clear that he had left nothing undone. He had managed the beer and the biscuits and the mares and the tents (for all the host was snugly under cover); his genius lay in the fact that he had thought too of the artistic touches and the aesthetic fillips that gave the whole display its proper opulence. He had even chosen "the shade of the colour of the satin for the King's doublet." And three months before the King crossed to Calais, Mr. Almoner had given instructions to Sir Gilbert Talbot, deputy at the port, "to have a tun of a certain wine ready against the King's coming at the house where he is to lodge." [4]

The war must be a clean and courtly affair, carried on with aplomb and under the highest rules of chivalry. To this end Mr. Almoner displayed his greatest refinement in the preparations, for he caused to be printed 1600 copies of *The Statutes of War*, done in a proper manner by the King's printer, Richard Pynson, and at a cost of £16 13s. 4d. In this book was set forth the manly and sportsmanlike code of arms which must not be violated any more than the rules of a tourney. The war would be played by rules, and here was the book with the provisions plain for all to see. "Murmurs or Grudges against the King or the Officers of his Host" are of course strictly forbidden. "Everyone, except he be a Bishop, is to bear a Cross of St. George, 'suffysaunt and large.'" There follow stern injunctions against such acts of unknightly warfare as "sacrilege, robbery, pillage, violence toward the inhabitants of the invaded country, firing of houses . . . all of which offences are punishable with death." There are rules against dicing, card playing, and other games of chance. And finally with a thought to morale and the rivalries of unruly men from all parts of the kingdom, it is stated that "no man is to give reproach to another, because of the country he is of, that is to say, English, Northern, Welsh or Irish." [5]

Considering all the grains of detail Mr. Almoner had winnowed out for the care of the King's men and the comfort of the King's person, small wonder that he enjoyed in the procession at Calais a position far above his rank, or that in the consultations he was, along with Viscount Lisle, hard by the King's side. He stood ready to remedy any error in the line of march, to dispatch messengers who were needed to do the King's immediate bidding, to prompt the actors if they faltered in their appointed parts. He was present to give feet as well as wings to Henry's conception of conquest, to execute faithfully the dreams of a young King.

Henry arrived at Calais about an hour and a half before sunset. According to John Taylor, one of the King's chaplains, who did a chronicle of the whole campaign, Wolsey, as became his station and as a stratagem of his priestly humility, rode in plain cassock — and on a mule, not on a richly caparisoned horse. The cavalcade moved from the quay to the Lantern Gate of the fortress, the gate with a beacon marking the port from the sea. For weeks soldiers in Tudor white and green had been pouring into Calais. Now Henry was here in person to give the inhabitants of the portside city some sense of English might and color. The inhabitants were descendants of the English colonists planted there 160 years before, mostly from County Kent. Their contacts had been only with English merchants and traders, and this was to be their first sight of the stupendous pageant which marked the pomp and circumstance of the homeland.

Henry bore their homage well. He received the plaudits and respectful tokens from maidens and men at the windows of houses that overhung the streets, the greetings of the Merchants of the Staple and the mayor, well appareled, at the Staple Hall. But he moved with the grim intent of a true crusader to the Church of St. Nicholas in St. Nicholas Street, which he entered just as the day was waning. There he made offerings to the church and its clergy and "prayers to God and His Saints — for the safe passage of himself and his armies across the perilous seas, dedicating both to the services of the Almighty and of His Church, in the great enterprise he was entering on in vindication of the rights of the Holy See against the sacrilegious insolence of Louis XII." [6] The King and the priest were at one in pageant and in prayer. Thomas Wolsey had at last become the fleshly shadow of the King.

Henry kept his portly character as an armed apostle bent on the Lord's work in the nondescript engagements which followed. When some German soldiers in his hire burned some churches at Ardres, "the king, mindful of the sacred character of his expedition, had three of them hanged." [7] His exemplary personal conduct — in such matters as practicing archery with his archers and surpassing them all and in refusing one rainy night to undress, insisting instead upon riding about camp encouraging the watch — all was calculated to impress his soldiers and the people of France.

It was a lofty and chaste performance, all told, in which the business of bashing men's heads seemed out of place. There was, of course, a certain amount of fighting, all conducted according to *The Statutes of War*, but not much. In skirmishes around Thérouanne, French chevaliers and English knights challenged each other to single combat, their followers looking on.

War began with this crusade, however, to change subtly in character. The use of great cannon, which would belch and fume at one place and destroy men and property at a distance, was part of this change. Fighting was beginning to be industrialized. It was a convenience to be able to set off a great gun and have the gun do the work of destruction. War was taking on a faintly impersonal character. The obsession with its preparation and financing showed among other things that the design was not so much to conquer the enemy as to intimidate him.

In the case of this war Henry had so advertised his might abroad that he expected France to quail before his coming. He was not disappointed. Weakened by the series of disasters of the year before, France had no heart for the affair and seemed merely to go through the motions of defense. When Henry decamped from Calais on July 21 and arrived before Thérouanne August 1, Louis XII — he who had seemed such a ferocious threat to Christendom a year before — drove out from Paris in a carriage, but he was ill and feeble and lacking in heart and he took no part in the action to defend Thérouanne. In common with almost everyone else, he seemed but a spectator at a war that never quite came off.

Thérouanne fell August 22, the first French city to be captured by English arms since the days of Jeanne d'Arc. And before it fell, the English had accomplished a disastrous rout of French cavalry sent to supply the town. This engagement, in which the French unceremoniously took to their horses' heels, first at a trot and then at a canter and then at a gallop, came in English lore to be known as the Battle of the Spurs. Henry was mounted for this fray, but his staff kept him at a safe distance until the French cavalry had been thoroughly routed. Then "he had the delightful experience of chasing a defeated enemy as long as his horse would go, and of capturing dukes and counts and the Chevalier Bayard himself. He never forgot this exhilarating afternoon — but he had no chance of repeating its joys in all his life." [8]

Protected from actual encounters, Henry had all the glory of war and none of the gore, a circumstance which colored his views of Europe for years to come. He was the man on horseback, the strong deliverer. At Lille he received all the honors of a conquering hero simply by riding through the town, riding "with as much pomp," to quote from Taylor's diary, "as ever he did at Westminster with his crown on." The people, Taylor continues, "crowded out of the town to meet him in such numbers you would have thought that none could have been left behind; girls offered crowns, sceptres, and garlands; outlaws and malefactors with white rods in their hands sought pardon. Between the gate of the town and the palace the way was lined with burning torches, although it was bright day, and there was scarce room for the riders to pass. Tapestries were hung from the houses, and tents erected at frequent intervals, where histories of the Old and New Testament and of the poets were acted." [9]

But if the burly and puffing Henry played only a supernumerary role in the engagement, he managed to be on hand for the official ceremonies of surrender, and he got the credit for the behavior of his troops. It was plain that the French now had no desire to engage the English troops directly. Henry was full of confidence. And when Thérouanne fell and the walls by his order were destroyed, foreigners began "talking respectfully of the renewal of English might. Ferdinand, who had sent only regretful messages in answer to Henry's appeal for help, now sent a special envoy to draft plans for a grand joint invasion the next year." [10]

The campaign served to show Henry that as a sovereign ruler he rated with the best. And to complete the picture, Emperor Maximilian of the Holy Roman Empire showed up one day in his camp in the guise of a common soldier and volunteered his services and those of his troops — for pay, of course. Taylor described the Emperor as "of middle height, with open and manly countenance and pale complexion. He has a snub nose and a grey beard; is affable, frugal, and an enemy of pomp. His attendants are dressed in black silk or woolen." [11]

It was a touching scene, this homage paid by the Emperor to the King. True, he was Emperor in title only and not quite that, for he had never been crowned, having been refused passage through the territories of Venice when he set out to Rome for his coronation. His empire, which ostensibly embraced the German states under the Hapsburgs, Switzerland, the Netherlands, and Burgundy, was tenuous and scattered, stitched together by marriages, a coat of many colors and endless seams. Known as "the man of few pence," Maximilian never stayed long enough in any one part of his putative dominion to govern, being forever occupied with ambitious intrigues, all designed to bring him ready money. He exported his services. He found it easier to raise money by large-scale chicanery than by attending to the grubby business of taxation. He was full of ideas for reforms, many of them good, but never carried out; the task of actually governing his empire or any part of it seemed to be beneath his dignity.

But still and all he was the Emperor of the Romans, in line of succession with Charlemagne, a genial and likable fellow in all his personal dealings, which were many, and it was no small tribute to the young and virtuous King of England when the great man appeared in his camp and offered to serve as a common soldier. Besides, Maximilian, whatever his cash balance at any one time, was well connected, and one could never tell when one of his relatives might stand a King in good stead. His daughter Margaret was regent of the Netherlands, and she had in her tender care the upbringing of the Emperor's grandson, Charles, who in turn was the son of Joanna, ruler of Castile; and Charles, when he reached beyond the age of puberty and old Ferdinand died, would become King of Castile and Aragon. Joanna was mad, to be sure, having been inconsolable since the death of Maximilian's son and her husband, Philip, who had ruled the Netherlands until his death a few years before. Still she was head of Castile all the same.

To him Europe was more or less a family affair. He was in his vague way a good man to know and to cultivate. And while Henry was in France and the Emperor was in his hire, he visited Margaret to arrange for the marriage of this young and potential Charles to his sister the Princess Mary.

After the fall of Thérouanne, Henry turned next to Tournai, then held by the French, "the wealthiest city," writes Tuke, the clerk of the signet, "in all Flanders, and the most populous of any on this side of Paris . . . The gates were of iron, the towers of stone, and the heavy guns of Lille were requisitioned for the siege."

In the fall of Tournai on September 24, well ahead of schedule, Henry marked up the greatest triumph of his campaign. Tournai was a city of carpetmakers and a place of wealth, with the legend THE UNSULLIED MAIDEN inscribed over its great gate. And in its fall, too, Master Almoner displayed the crowning genius of his thoroughness. Indeed his preparation proved to be too thorough, as far as practical needs were concerned, but it shone all the more spectacularly in the galaxy of English commercial grandeur because it was not necessary. He had prepared for a long and strenuous siege. Knowing from the days he had visited Maximilian something of the vagaries and unpleasantness of Flanders weather, he was not content to trust the army of the King to canvas. Instead he had ordered the building of an immense number of wooden huts, "of which a great part had chimneys" — huts "sufficient to shelter the whole English army of 40,000 men. They were so numerous and ample that they covered a space around the walls of Tournay as extensive as the area covered by the town itself, which . . . harboured no less than 80,000 inhabitants." [12]

It was a fanciful scheme. The town capitulated quickly; there was hardly time to put up the huts. They were in practical terms a costly military waste. But they left an impression of English skill that was not only immediate but durable. For they were standing long after the English army returned to its native land, and they served as suburban homes for laborers engaged in the industries of the city.

In the fall of Tournai the French campaign ended, and, leaving a garrison of 6000 men to hold the city, the English army slipped safely home before the rigors of winter set in. Everything had gone according to plan, and since the war had been nine-tenths preparedness and one-tenth fighting, it was Thomas Wolsey who got the credit with the King. He had confirmed at every turn his master's faith — a faith all the more remarkable because of his signal failure in the Spanish campaign the year before. Here was a man whose worth to the kingdom must be reckoned in thousands of pounds.

There was a tide running now in the destiny of this Ipswich fellow. For the moment when his powers were fully recognized by the King was also the moment when the fortunes of England in the realm of war and national might and prestige turned triumphantly for the better. Thomas Wolsey and the King and England at one and the same time had arrived at the moment of ascendancy. Their images assumed a strange identity, molded by a oneness of purpose — the assertion of might. England would no longer be the laughingstock of older nations in Europe, or her King regarded as a cherub who might best attend his lute, or his new councilor a paltry and officious priest.

To make matters firmer than the campaign in France had made them, the English, while Henry was jousting in Flanders fields, had gained a decisive victory over the Scots at the battle of Flodden. There was nothing polite or courtly about this affair. It was bloody, attended by frightful slaughter. In the bitter scheme of things it supplemented the pageant in France and the display there of the nation's wares of war, for it demonstrated that in the hard tasks of war the English soldier was not to be counted glibly out as a military man. Upon the carnage wrought at Flodden, no less than on the elaborate and pretentious siege of Tournai, England's new reputation rested. And by one of those odd twists of circumstance that bring greatness by association, Henry and Wolsey found themselves enhanced by Scotland's slithering downfall. Its defeat contributed to the notion of the greatness of England and by indirection to the power of the young King and his ubiquitous aid.

The Scottish invasion of England while Henry was in France vaunting his supremacy and his wardrobe came as no surprise, in spite of the habitual English effort to make every move of the Scots appear to be an act of treachery. Wolsey had been bound to admit to the seventh Henry that in the matter of border raids the English had given the Scots more provocation than the Scots had given the English. At least, the solemn old Henry had set up diplomatic means by which the traditional differences between the two countries could be made into talks, if not altogether amicably settled. He had even given his daughter Margaret as a hostage to the future relations of the two countries. The young King Henry had changed all that, or if he had not changed it he had notably neglected to carry forward his father's efforts. He had studiously ignored a proud land of six hundred thousand people to the north. Bent on the assertion of his own manliness and regality before the audience of the Holy See and the rulers of Europe, he had been at no pains to develop friendship with his estimable brother-in-law, King James IV of Scotland. To Henry, Scotland was not a country but a quarrel. A quarrel he could understand and handle. But a country which was hospitable to foreigners, even partial to influences from abroad, a country having chimneys and windows when these items were by no means common in England, yet a country not given to manufacture and industry — this sort of country, or any country other than the one he inherited, Henry could not understand and did not aim to try. It was easier to fight a problem than solve it.

The Earl of Surrey had been appointed Lord Lieutenant of the North and left behind when the main force of Henry's army crossed to France. Preparations against the Scots had even been calculated in Wolsey's plans for the invasion of France, and if they were less showy they were more practical and thorough; for by September 1, the Earl of Surrey, old Thomas Howard, now in his seventieth year, who had fought with Richard at Bosworth but had been loyal these twenty-eight years to the Tudors, was able to assemble an army of 26,000 men — and within a week after James had delivered his ultimatum to Henry in France. The levies, tough men all from the northern counties, "were given conduct money from their homes and taken into the king's pay as from 1 September." [13] Wolsey had made his plans big enough to include provisioning the army that would be needed to guard the Scottish border. Everything was in readiness for the surprise. Even the royal artillery had been sent north and was at Newcastle ready for use when the troops arrived there.

During the summer of 1513 Catherine the Queen had kept up a lively and resilient correspondence with Mr. Almoner. "She arranged to write once a week and to have every courtier bring back a letter, at least from Wolsey if Henry was too preoccupied with war. She worried about Henry's rashness in battle, and his tendency to get overheated and catch cold . . . She pestered Wolsey about her husband's health and remembered to send fresh supplies of linen for him." Her letters were labored in language but full of solicitude on personal matters and vocative with detail on matters of state, particularly touching the impending Scottish invasion and the last-minute preparations for it.[14]

She had been left as Henry's regent in England, and as such she was responsible officially for the defense of her adopted country. But her devotion was to Henry, and if she wrote confidently of the defense against Scotland and the busyness of the people with it, it was more to set Henry's royal mind at rest than anything else. She was a woman and wife before she was a ruler, and her feminine mind knew that through the King's Almoner and steady companion she could keep in touch on those daily trifles that have such vast significance to a solicitous female. She wrote Wolsey on July 26, 1513, begging him "to take the (pains) with every of my messengers to write to me of the King's health, and (what) he intendeth to do, for when ye be so near our enemies I shall never (rest) till I see often letters from you . . ." [15] Again she writes to Wolsey on August 13: "Ye may think when I put (you to) this labour that I forget the great business that ye have in hand, but if ye (remember) in what case I am that is without any comfort or pleasure unless I hear, ye will not blame me to desire you (though it be a short letter) to let me know from you tidings as often as may be . . ." [16]

Apparently Wolsey performed his task well, for on August 25 she wrote again: "Master Almoner, for the pain ye take remembering to write me so often, I thank you for it with all my heart . . ." [17]

Even her personal letters to Wolsey and Henry offer picturesque information to ease the royal mind about affairs at home. She wrote Wolsey to tell the King that "all his subjects be very glad, I thank God, to be busy with the Scots, for they take it (for a) pastime. My heart is very good to it, and I am horribly busy with making standards, banners, and badges." [18] There is no doubt that the Scottish war was Catherine's war. She was "the soul of the enterprize. She quieted Henry's dangers by occupying herself with warlike occupations." [19] When the Scottish invasion struck, it was Catherine who by virtue of the authority vested in her summoned 40,000 men from the south to meet in London, while Surrey collected his men according to plan in the north.

James crossed the Tweed into England with a large Scottish army, strong in artillery and adequate in provisions. It was said that a token from the French Queen, "who besought James as her true knight to advance three feet into English ground and to strike a blow for her honour," swayed the King at the last moment of indecision. Wise men in his council sought to stay the step, but gallantry prevailed over wisdom. James was not a man to let an impulse pass or to let a lady down. He was not a man, as James Gairdner puts it, "to think lightly of any provocation he received." Well educated, a good Latin scholar, he could not only "talk Gaelic with the

Highlanders as well as lowland Scotch, but he (also) had the command of all the leading European languages." [20]

With all his accomplishments of the mind and his amiable temperament in dealing with his people, he was essentially a volatile Scotsman who loved a fight and whose measure of personal bravery was the willingness to die against odds. The main course of his life, however, had been to forge Scotland into some semblance of a nation. He had given his country status, so that it had diplomatic dealings with other nations and a voice that was coming to be respected in the courts of Europe; it sent accredited representatives hither and yon and played at the game of diplomacy as well as at the games of war. More, he had given the Scots some measure of unity, as great a measure as anyone could hope for.

In scope and extent the Scottish move into England had all the aspects of a diversionary move made to divide English energies and take the pressure off France. With all his vast army, James spent the first few precious days of his campaign destroying castles, including one owned by his episcopal highness the Bishop of Durham. But beyond this the King of Scotland did not go; his tactics were the tactics of endless years of border raids, and on or near September 1 he drew up his army in a strong position on a hill facing south at a place ten miles west of Wooler. The hill was called Flodden Edge. There he awaited developments, the plan apparently being to draw Surrey and his army as far north of London as possible. Whatever his plan or motives, and no one knows, the fact remains that he did not move more than fifteen miles into English territory.

It was far enough to provoke a battle. On September 9 the battle was joined.[21] By nightfall it was mercifully over, and the victor had begun stripping the dead, which numbered 10,000 Scots and by all accounts only 1500 Englishmen. Effective artillery fire from the English had maddened the Scots, so that they forsook their commanding position on Branxton Hill. At first the fury of undisciplined border fighters swept the English before it, but the King's men, holding the center of the line, were also lured down the slope. His men carried spears fifteen feet long and marched in a solid phalanx, so that the effect was like a porcupine. But the spears proved of no use at close quarters, where English broadswords won the day. By an expert maneuver, Howard swept to the rear of the King and his men while they were fighting at close quarters with the English. Attacked on all sides and "forced to fight in a ring," the Scots went down, resisting to the last man. James fell "not a spear's length from Surrey's standard, riddled with arrows and gashed with swords and bills." Godwin tells us that "his necke was opened to the midst with a wide wound, his left hand almost cut off in two places did scarce hang to his arme." [22] With him there died his natural son, "the youth of twenty who had been a pupil of Erasmus, a bishop, two abbots, twelve earls, fourteen lords and representatives of most of the families of consequence in Scotland." [23]

When Henry heard the word from Flodden he shook his head and said with pompous magnanimity that James had paid a higher price for his perfidy "than we would have wished." But another dragon had been slain, even if he had not been there in person to attend the matter. It was his queen, the daughter of Ferdinand, who had accomplished this feat, and she let him know the significance of the victory when she wrote: "But to my thinking, this battle hath been to your grace and all your realm the greatest honour that could be, and more than if ye should win all the crown of France." [24]

It was a tactless thing to tell a husband, much less a King — and one who was still puffing from the pursuit of the fleeing flower of French chivalry, but Henry had a great capacity for enfolding honors, for absorbing credit. It was part of being a King to construe what happened under a reign to be an evidence of God's favor, what with one's fighting solidly on God's side. A woman may have been as regent technically responsible for the victory, but the effect was something that Henry could gather to his growing bosom and meditate on. In a single year Henry had emerged from the chrysalis of obscurity and failure to be feared throughout Christendom. It was this that mattered; all else was detail.

Except the succession, of course. In September of the eventful year 1513 the Venetian ambassador announced the birth of another son. But it was a son Henry never saw. Either it was stillborn or it died immediately after birth. Henry went home from his triumph in France to a Queen who had not borne him an heir.

CHAPTER IV

How rapidly Wolsey rose to acknowledged power after the ponderous invasion of France and the repulse of Scotland may be seen from the fact that three bishoprics were bestowed upon him in a single year. It is said that Erasmus decided to dedicate a book to the ascendant Wolsey, but before the book could be readied for the printer he was forced to change the salutation three times. The priest who had hitherto borne such petty titles as bursar, chaplain, and almoner now went about the business of collecting titles and tokens of esteem like a man starved for recognition.

First, and in direct and open acknowledgment of his administration of the French war, Wolsey was made Bishop of Tournai. Henry had captured the city in a holy war, and he considered it within his royal prerogative to take the bishopric, vacant at the time the city fell, and bestow it as he chose. Then the diocese of Lincoln fell conveniently vacant through the death of its occupant. Wolsey being already dean of the cathedral there, it was within the logic of the text "To him that hath shall be given" that the zealous servant of the King should now be elevated to the bishopric of Lincoln. There followed some spirited correspondence between Wolsey and Sylvester de Giglis, the English agent at Rome, about reducing the fee to be paid the Pope for the rights to the see, but Rome replied that the church at Lincoln was rich and must pay the tax. De Giglis did say, however, that the Pope would forgo the customary annates expected from another honor conferred on Wolsey, the deanery of the Church of St. Stephen, which stood hard by Westminster. There would also be a reduced fee for expediting the bulls to this deanery, due to the insistence of the Pope, though, de Giglis adds, "the officials are angry with him for having brought it down so low." [1]

Within a few months Cardinal Bainbridge died in Rome, his death attended by more than a suspicion of poison, and Thomas Wolsey succeeded him as Archbishop of York.

All of the honors that had befallen Wolsey up to this point had been granted by the authority of the King and sanctioned by the power of the Pope. From the very beginning of his service at the court, but particularly now in this period of the enhancement of his honors, there was duality, a double recognition and a double leverage at every move. Theoretically, bishops were elected by the clergy of their dioceses. In practice bishops were named by the Crown. If a bishopric fell vacant, a writ was immediately issued to vest its temporalities in the Crown; the property connected with it, in a word, became the property of the Crown for the time being. Then a candidate for the bishopric was proposed by the King. If the candidate was acceptable to the Holy See, he was then consecrated and invested in the episcopal see, having first been required to take an oath of allegiance to the Pope and the Holy Catholic Church. This oath of obedience to the Pope contained clauses "not easily reconcilable to the duty of a subject or the rights of secular princes." [2] Hence in this situation the bishop, duly consecrated and invested by the Holy Father, must next apply to the King for the restoration of his temporalities. And before the temporalities of any archbishop or bishop could be restored "he was obliged to disclaim and renounce all clauses in the Pope's bull prejudicial to the rights of the crown or the King's prerogative." [3]

It was a double deal, a system that rested on contradictory oaths solemnly taken and ceremoniously denied. To become a shepherd of the Lord's work in England a man who should have stood as an exemplar of morality and honesty in office was by his very induction disqualified for any but the temporal care of his flock and see. He served two masters and was sworn publicly to do so. This followed hallowed custom, and Wolsey was not one to question procedure or depart from order; his genius lay in the extraordinary energy with which he carried out what was expected, and there is no indication that a ripple of concern over the curious relation between Rome and England ever rolled across his mind at this stage. He had above all else a sense of the immediate; and he had a sense of the Pope. To serve both the King and the Pope became his chief concern — to use both when needed, to play upon the favor of one to gain favors of the other, to identify himself subtly with the interest of both, to choose to see their interests as at all times identical and his own interests as supreme. This policy he continued indefatigably for years until at last his own interests could be served by neither and he was compelled to make a bitter choice between the two oaths he had taken.

From the very moment of his ascendancy, Wolsey began to press for honors beyond those that the King had the power to bestow. Shortly after his consecration as Bishop of Lincoln, he sent Polydore Vergil to Rome. The ostensible purpose of the trip was to let a man who had been resident in England for twelve years "visit his old home and kiss the feet of the new pope." [4] But the real mission was confidential. Wolsey had already set in motion the forces which were designed to make him a cardinal, not unmindful that the word derives from the Latin word meaning *hinge*, on which the door of the Church and other important matters turn. As a cardinal he would be technically a member, if not in residence, of the governing body of the Church, and a visible — nay, conspicuous — representative of the Church in England.

The stratagem suggested by Wolsey called for Vergil to pay his respects to Cardinal Hadrian, a man Wolsey had in 1511 recommended for the papacy at a time when to all appearances Julius II might give up the ghost. Julius had lived two more years, and there had been no occasion to elect a new Pope. But Vergil was to refresh Hadrian's mind of events not long past, and, if Hadrian showed himself disposed to recall gratefully Wolsey's recommendation, then and then only was Vergil to broach the matter of Wolsey's own election to the College of Cardinals.

The flanking attack for the cardinalate went well, for Hadrian broached the matter to Leo X, who thought not ill of it, seeing how by this time the Archbishop of York stood with the King of the English. England was regarded in Rome, in the words of one of the popes, as "our storehouse of delights, a very inexhaustible well; and where much abounds, much can be extorted from many." [5] The question, as Pollard phrases it, was not whether Wolsey was worthy of the cardinal's hat but whether he was worth it. When the time that suited best the circumstances at Rome dictated it, Hadrian was to write to Wolsey and Wolsey was then to secure the royal assent. Meanwhile, not a word was to be said, "and the affair was to be so managed as to appear the spontaneous offer of Leo X, 'as,' remarks Vergil to Wolsey, 'your reverend lordship told me it was to be done.'" [6]

Nor was this sufficient unto the day. An archbishop might be made a cardinal and still he would not enjoy plenary powers befitting the good right arm of the King. There still remained the Archbishop of Canterbury, dry and dull perhaps, but in the residue of his vigor nonetheless Primate of All England. Wolsey foresaw that if his own position were to be safeguarded by the proper bastions of power within and without the realm, he must be made a papal legate in England. Not a nuncio, for such an official had but temporary powers deriving from a special mission; and not simply a legate either, for Warham by virtue of his rank was already legate *natus*. What Wolsey would have to become was legate *a latere* — and for life. This position would make him the Pope's permanent representative in the kingdom of England, invest him with the right to reform the Church, which obviously needed attention in view of the undercurrent of criticism that had been mounting for the past fifty years, and give him the right to make judicial decisions on religious matters without forever referring these matters by laborious correspondence and slow messenger to Rome.

Wolsey had not trusted the request for the legateship to Vergil but had routed it through Sylvester de Giglis. It was better to have two agents than one and to exercise pressure through a squeeze. De Giglis wrote to Wolsey that His Holiness had the matter under favorable advisement and that, with certain conditions accepted by the Archbishop of York, he might be made legate *a latere* — if not for life, at least legate *a latere* for successive periods, the matter to be renewed each few years.

Thus tentatively assured how matters stood at Rome, Wolsey now thought it propitious to send forward the King's letter of request that he be made a cardinal. The letter was drawn on August 12, 1514. It sang in eloquence the worth of Wolsey, adding from the royal hand the remarkable statement that Henry could do nothing of the least importance without Wolsey and referring to him as "our most secret counsellor." [7]

This letter was a secular request made by the secular power. There is no reference in it to the spiritual qualifications of Wolsey for the high office in store. These qualifications are assumed or ignored. The King wants his "counsellor" honored and supported by the Church. And if it was true that the King could do nothing of the least importance without Wolsey, it was doubly true that Wolsey could do nothing without both the King and the Pope. His advancement and maintenance under the system of his time depended upon their joint will and approval. With the power vested in him by them both he could do what he chose.

The Pope in his deliberations delayed a full year, and if there was any doubt in Wolsey's mind as to whether the King or the Pope was the greater in power to grant his wishes, this year, a sobering one, must have resolved the doubt. With all the King's approval, he could not win the hat. But that he won it in the end assured him more profoundly than ever of his ability to manipulate even the greatest person in Christendom. If there was any power stronger than that derived from a Pope, it was the power to influence a Pope and make him do one's bidding. The year of waiting and maneuvering for the hat, whatever else its effect, fixed his mind more than ever on Rome as the primal center of his authority; and certainly his success in wresting the hat from the obstinate Leo left in his thinking the lingering impression that by proper blandishments and stratagems he could do all things through the Holy Father.

Leo's reluctance was partly due to the atmosphere of scandal in which the enemies of Wolsey linked his name with the murder of Cardinal Bainbridge, but it rested on other foundations besides. Grave understanding of Wolsey's aggressiveness and ambition underlay much of the reluctance. "Men say an English cardinal ought not to be created lightly, because the English behave themselves so insolently in their dignity," wrote in his diary de Grassis, papal master of ceremonies at this time, adding, "as was shown in the case of Cardinal Bainbridge, just dead. Moreover, as Wolsey is the intimate friend of the King, he will not be content with the cardinalate alone, but, as is the custom for those barbarians, will wish to have the office of Legate over all England." [8]

Meanwhile, and during the course of his strenuous negotiations for the hat, Wolsey faced exacting problems in England. One was the increasing hostility toward the Church. In handling this problem there is no indication that the Archbishop, busy with the new dignities he enjoyed, was stirred to thought or driven to perception. Wolsey's life was a round of activities that left little time for reflection and deadened him to the vital forces moving in the current of his day. Wolsey thought like a knight in a joust, his mind a lance to use in unseating his opponent or in preventing himself from being unhorsed; and in the sweat and urgency which attended all his designs he never seems to have paused to inquire whether jousts were necessary or wise or an essential part of the divine nature of things. His was not to reason why, to raise abstract questions for which there was no practical answer.

Since history bears small trace of his introspections, it is not possible to tell whether his incessant concern with the practical was invoked consciously or unconsciously to protect him against matters deeply disturbing. Whatever the reason, we do know that the man whose most distinguishing mark was that he came from the common people did upon his accession to power surround himself with all the paraphernalia of success and did sever in his daily manner of living all connections with the commonalty and did cushion himself extravagantly against the abrasive cares that made up the life of the average Englishman. He who was a rebel and in revolt against the nobility took on all the manners of the nobility as if eager to establish his worth beyond dispute by the outward station of his living.

His duties as a man of influence, of course, took an ever larger measure of his time. He began to charge fees for professional services rendered. As early as June 11, 1513, he received a substantial annuity from a Lady Margaret Pole for such counsel as he might give in handling money matters for her ladyship. It was said that more than ever, after the affray in France was over, he encouraged Henry to entertain and pleasure himself with jousts and the hunt and his beloved lute and to leave "old men's work" to his servant's willing hands.

In this business, with its infinite shuffling of papers, Wolsey was diligent beyond compare. George Cavendish, who in later life became his gentleman-usher, tells of one occasion which illustrates his power of preoccupation and his capacity for sustained application. Cavendish says that the Archbishop rose one morning about four of the clock and sat down to write letters, "commanding one of his chaplains to prepare him to mass, insomuch that his said chaplain stood revested until four of the clock at afternoon; all which season my lord never rose once to —— , nor yet to eat any meat, but continually wrote his letters with his own hands, having all that time his nightcap and keverchief on his head. And about the hour of four of the clock, at afternoon, he made an end of writing, commanding one Christopher Gunner, the king's servant, to prepare him without delay to ride empost . . . with his letters, whom he dispatched away or ever he drank." [9]

Here was diligence fit to serve a King. "Writing," admitted Henry, "is to me somewhat tedious and painful." When Wolsey thought it "essential that letters in Henry's hand should be sent to other crowned heads, he composed the letters and sent them to Henry to copy out." [10] He was the one, an enemy admitted, "who knew more and could do more than all the rest of the King's council put together." [11] Leo, who by all tokens had good intelligence at the court of England, said that Wolsey had the King so much under his influence that Henry would sign state papers without knowing their contents.

With manifold duties in high places, a private practice in canon law, and his sees to supervise, the Archbishop was as busy as the forces of evil. Earlier it had been his duty to conduct the preparations of war, not to sit around and think whether the war was justified in the sight of God or ethics. And now when he confronted his first great problem as Archbishop, he met it on practical grounds. He had no time and he was in no position to feel the impulses of the people of England or to understand the assertiveness of a mass of laymen in revolt against the clergy; he had time only to hear the clamor and to treat it as a watchman might.

On the early morning of December 4, 1514, the body of a well-to-do merchant-tailor, by name Richard Hunne, was found hanging from a beam in the prison of the Bishop of London, a place known as the Lollards' Tower in St. Paul's. It was announced by Richard FitzJames, Bishop of London, and by his chancellor Dr. Horsey that Hunne had died of his own hand while being detained in the prison to stand trial for heresy.

The announcement of Hunne's suicide met with no favor or credence among the laity, for the deceased was known as a man who held strong views on the privileges and pretensions of the clergy; who had read the New Testament in English and had referred to priests and bishops as Scribes and Pharisees. Stories began rapidly to circulate and to gather flame as they went. It was said that Hunne had refused to give the priest who buried his infant son the child's bearing-sheet as a mortuary. Under the custom of mortuaries the Church claimed the best article belonging to the deceased as a burial fee. Hunne had resisted on the ground that his son, being only a few weeks old, "had no property in the bearing sheet which the parson claimed." [12] It was further rumored where men congregated and reviewed the case, which gained daily in common interest, that the priest had sued Hunne for the fee in a spiritual court and that Hunne had countered with a suit in the Court of the King's Bench, charging that the spiritual court in which the priest's suit had been entered was a foreign tribunal and that those who sat in it were guilty of a breach of praemunire.

The use of the term "praemunire" excited the greatest antagonism among both the laity and the clergy, but more particularly among the latter: loosely it meant treason, but it also meant a peculiar kind of legal treason instituted by the allegiance of the Church in England to the Church at Rome. The term came from the first word of the summons issued to the defendant to answer the charge, a harmless Latin word but colored and poisoned by years of painful use. An act of Parliament had been passed in 1353 called the Statute of Praemunire. It enacted specifically that all who appealed abroad any plea which might properly be tried in the King's courts were in danger of being guilty of offense against the King.

The clergy were sensitive and touchy on any charge that hinted an action of praemunire, and it was said bitterly in London that Hunne had been haled into prison for his audacity and arrogance in charging the spiritual court with foreign origins and thus invoking praemunire; that the Bishop of London and his officials had examined him for heresy and imprisoned him on the basis of preliminary evidence and, once he was jailed, had done him to death.

So the stories ran. And they were given some fuel when a coroner's jury examined the body of Hunne, ruled out the official announcement of death due to suicide, charged Dr. Horsey and two of his servants with murder, and ordered them to stand trial. "The text of the inquest, with subsequent additions, was circulated in pamphlet form, and the air was full of inaccurate and untested surmises." [13]

The jailer, Charles Joseph, had fled the day after the coroner's jury was impaneled. He first had taken sanctuary in Westminster and then had escaped to a secluded village in Essex. This escape made the task before the coroner's jury, "24 right honest men," as Thomas More described them, all the more difficult and heightened the feeling of those who were already convinced that Hunne had been murdered.

The officials of the see of London, seeing how things stood in the matter, now faced the question of whether Richard Hunne should be given

Christian burial. To accord him this privilege would be tantamount to admitting that he was not a heretic and that he had been unjustly held for trial. Thus on the Sunday following Hunne's death a fresh list of charges was read out against the deceased, all pointing to heresy. On December 16 the corpse "was solemnly tried in the presence of the mayor and aldermen by an ecclesiastical court, the bishop of London presiding with the assistance of three other bishops." [14] The dead man was "pronounced a heretic, and his body handed over to the secular power to be burned; and burned it was at Smithfield on December 20, to the grief and indignation of the people." [15]

The Church had triumphed again over heresy, but still the coroner's jury patiently continued to sift the evidence. Joseph, the escaped jailer, when finally brought back to London from Essex, sought to establish an alibi for himself, saying that he had spent the night on which the murder was alleged to have been committed in a house of prostitution; and in support of his claim he brought two whores before the coroner's jury, one being the madam of the house. But other witnesses, less disreputable, swore that they had seen him making his way from the Lollards' Tower in the twilight of the December morning when the body was discovered. "He then made a confession in which he accused Dr. Horsey, the bishop's chancellor, and Spalding, the bell-ringer, as his accomplices." [16] The three were ordered by the jury to stand trial for murder at the next assizes or in the King's Bench.

It was at this point that FitzJames turned in desperation to the Archbishop of York who had the ear of the King, and it was the royal ear that FitzJames felt he must have. It would be futile, he said, to expect a London jury to do justice in the case, "so set were they on heretical depravity." [17] His plea and his appeal put the whole question at issue plainly. He was concerned for Horsey alone, who held orders in the Church. It would not do for Horsey to be tried by a secular court and before a jury. Even if he were convicted, he would not be hanged but could claim benefit of clergy and be handed over to Warham of Canterbury for custody. But what FitzJames sought was to avoid the indignity of having his chancellor tried for murder by a lay court. He concluded his plea to Wolsey with the plaintive words, as if Wolsey were Pope: "Help our infirmities, blessed father, and we shall be bound to you forever." [18]

Meanwhile, however, Parliament, which had been summoned before the Hunne episode, met at Westminster, and the ground swell of interest had become so marked that the King made no move to intervene. Here was a chance to study the forces at work in the whole controversy over clerical immunity, involving as they did a definition of the rights of the Crown. And it was to this problem that the Parliament inevitably addressed itself — the upper House, with the lords spiritual being slightly in a majority over the lords temporal, seeking to preserve the rights of the clergy against civil molestation; and the Commons, made up of knights of the shires, squires, and burgesses, boldly asserting that these rights must be curtailed. Summonses had been sent to twenty-one bishops, twenty-seven abbots and the Prior of Coventry. There were thus forty-nine spiritual lords and forty-two laymen in the upper House, the laymen comprising three dukes, one marquis, ten earls and twenty-eight barons.

Agitation for revoking the special privileges accorded the clergy in criminal cases had long plagued the Church in England, and Wolsey knew it. The issue had come to be a perennial source of bitterness. It flared up threateningly now and then, but as an old complaint and a worn theme for orators of discontent; it was not to be taken too seriously. The problem simply needed to be dealt with administratively. It was only one of the problems Wolsey faced, including that of gaining the cardinal's hat and the powers of a papal legate. If he garnered those powers, he would be able to work matters out to the satisfaction of all. It was important that an institution as powerful and permeating as the Church, which owned one fifth of all the land in England, should regulate questions pertaining to its rights and not have these questions the subject of irritating public discussion among civil authorities. The Church could look after itself. The right of the Church to self-reform was the heart and kernel of its sacred prerogatives; and the contention that religious practices and decisions should be regulated by laymen acting through a lawmaking body must be resisted at all costs.

Yet the Parliament meeting in 1512, assembled essentially for the purpose of granting the new King funds by which he could rush to the rescue of the fiery Pope Julius from his enemies the French, had passed a law which denied benefit of clergy "to all those clergy who murdered people in their own homes, in hallowed places or on the king's highway." A clergyman who did murder, being duly convicted in a civil court, could no longer escape the penalty imposed in civil law. He would be sentenced like any other criminal; not merely placed, if he successfully pleaded benefit of clergy, in a bishop's prison from which he might easily escape.[19]

In all cases the civil court had to convict the holy man of murder; what the act of 1512 did was simply to remove the benefits deriving from his sacerdotal character after his conviction. It seemed not un-reasonable to Parliament to do this, seeing the daily increase in robberies, murders, and felonies. But although Parliament had passed this legislation, it had seen fit to qualify it. The act was to be in force only until Parliament met again and must be renewed then. Furthermore, it withdrew privileges only from those in lower orders and left all the old benefits in force among clergy who enjoyed the rank of priest, deacon, or subdeacon.

Now so shortly after the death of Richard Hunne, and with a man high in holy orders held for his murder, Parliament met again. Plainly an old controversy would this time take on new force and meaning, and both sides to it were arrayed for battle. The Lords, with a majority of bishops and abbots and priors over the dukes and marquises and barons, fired the opening shot of the battle before Parliament assembled. They did not use one of Henry's Twelve Apostles, nor yet a canon, but they did choose an abbot who could thunder. He was the Abbot of Winchcombe, and he rejoiced in the name of Richard Kidderminster. He was to preach at St. Paul's Cross on the Sunday, February 4, 1515, before Parliament opened and set the tone of the deliberations. Meanwhile Pope Leo X in the previous May had declared that, "according to the law of God as well as the law of man," laymen had no jurisdiction over churchmen. The good Abbot of Winchcombe followed the same high line, but he came down to earth enough to apply it to the troubled situation in England. "He denied the distinction drawn by that act [of 1512] between holy and lesser orders: all orders, he said, were holy orders, and any clerk in any order was immune from punishment by lay tribunals for criminal offenses. His doctrine was that it was for the church and not for parliament or the crown to determine the limits of criminal and coercive jurisdiction." [20]

The Abbot's sermon may have lacked some qualities, but it did not lack clarity. It stated the case for the Church, but it overlooked the deep basis of popular complaint: there were no corresponding privileges accorded laymen. A priest could murder, but a layman could not think for himself. A man in orders might commit crimes of violence against his fellows and not incur the punishment prescribed by the law; but a man outside of orders could not even read what he pleased or think the way he chose without incurring the censure of the Church, and, if this censure was strict enough, without paying for his thoughts with his life.

The question of clerical privilege was indissolubly tied up with the corresponding question of lay privilege. All other matters left aside, the rankling fact remained to give overtones of bitterness to the whole controversy that Richard Hunne, a man in charity with his neighbors and respected as a freeman of the city of London, had been brought to heel for heresy, and, after he had met death while in the custody of the Church, his body had been ceremoniously burned for heresy. And full many other bodies had been burned before they were dead, and full many others might be burned any day.

There had been no need of a warrant to arrest Hunne for heresy. An act of 1401 "had authorised any diocesan synod, which meant the bishop and (or) his officials, to condemn heretics without appeal, and had made it part of the routine duty of sheriffs to carry out the sentence without recourse to chancery or the King's council for any special warrant." [21] Nor was there any clear or statutory definition of heresy. What was heresy rested on local judgment, and the threat of heresy and its penalties was always present to disturb the citizen. It might be used as a pretense to cover the anger of Church officials on some other cause, as so many believed it to be in the case of Hunne; for it was still a bruit far and wide that he had been lodged in the bishop's prison on trumped up charges of heresy merely because he had seen fit to charge the officials of the bishop with acting in behalf of a foreign power.

In the face of the fact that the civil rights of laymen could be invaded at any time by officials of the Church, the claim of the Abbot of Winchcombe that the clergy had privileges which could be invaded at no time had a hollow sound and made music only to the ears of those who had put him up to preach. The course of their action in the convening Parliament was easy to see anyway. On February 10 the Lords considered the statute of 1512 and, by letting it drop after a single reading, made it be known that they would not renew it. Even so the Commons were not daunted. They spiritedly passed a bill to renew the act which the Lords above had dropped.

The two Houses being at loggerheads over the issue of extended clerical privilege, it came about that the scene of the controversy shifted to the presence of the King. For the rights of the Crown as well as the rights of Parliament were at stake. Besides, the idea of a public debate in the royal presence pleased and flattered Henry. He was not averse, as Fisher puts it, to presiding over a tournament of learning. It would be well to have the whole matter, raised by the act of 1512 and given fresh significance by the case of Richard Hunne, aired and propounded by advocates of both sides of the issue. Hence the King acted with favor on a proposal made by Sir Robert Sheffield, who had been Speaker of the Parliament of 1512 in which the act against clerical privilege had passed, and ordered the learned men of the land to appear before him and his councilors in the great hall at the Abbey of the Blackfriars.

Being busy with the King's affairs, Wolsey could not give the full weight of his attention to the controversy set off by the death of Hunne. He was a diplomatist as well as a churchman, and hardly had Parliament assembled than he faced a crisis in the Council that might upset the delicate balance of Europe. Louis XII of France died and was succeeded by his nephew, who took the throne as Francis I. Francis was a youth of twenty-one and of unknown qualities, although it was generally believed that he was reckless and might play havoc.

The death of Louis was a personal blow to Wolsey, for in the months following Henry's invasion of France the Most Christian King had become an ally. And to seal the matter, Mary, the sister of Henry and one of the most beautiful women of her day, had become the wife of Louis and the Queen of France. The match had been a turn of fortune little to be expected, a great diplomatic feat. And if only Louis had died with issue planted and quickening in the body of the Queen, England and France might have been forever joined in blood and even united later in kingship. Instead, the marriage had killed off the doddering Louis, old and worn-out at fifty-three, and now the hopes so patiently fashioned were set at nought.

To compound the complications, Mary, soon after the death of Louis, had married Charles Brandon, who had gone to the French war as Viscount Lisle and had been made Duke of Suffolk by Henry after the war was over. Henry had sent him back to Paris to offer Francis I formal congratulations at the beginning of his reign. While there Suffolk had married Henry's sister, secretly, without the royal consent.

Nor was this neglect of the royal consent the only bad feature of the marriage. It removed from the list of those eligible to form other profitable alliances two persons of immense value. Mary might, as long as she remained single, serve as a queen in the hole to win England some other worthy ally. Charles Brandon, Duke of Suffolk, had been hopefully groomed by Henry for a marriage with Margaret, regent of the Netherlands. There was widespread disgust among wiseacres around the court that so beautiful a princess as Mary "should be wasted on a mere love match when she might have purchased a substantial political alliance; and the council was full of men who clamored for Suffolk's ruin." [22]

The King himself was furious. Charles Brandon, according to Godwin, had been "rather a companion than a servant to the young Prince of whose household he was." He was a commoner made noble by Henry and a close personal friend. There was no assurance that Henry would ever forgive Suffolk's presumption or Mary's offense.

Wolsey placed himself boldly on the side of Suffolk; became his only advocate and friend at court. Here was a chance to pit his mind and might against the arrayed hauteur of the nobility of England. It is not singular that he chose to defend the romantic right of Charles Brandon, Duke of Suffolk, who held the highest rank in the hierarchy of the nobility but was the son of a commoner. For my lord of York, so close to the King that the King had written the Pope that it was impossible to do anything without him, was the son of a commoner, too. And if he won the King's approval of the outrageous marriage, he would give a further intimate and convincing sign of his hold on his master's favor.

Also Wolsey had been closely connected with the arrangements for the marriage of Louis and Mary, and it was natural that she as well as Suffolk would turn to him in their extremity. After the triumphant invasion of France in 1513, Henry had planned with both Ferdinand and Maximilian to invade France again the next year. But both had treacherously and secretly formed an alliance with France. Henry had learned of the deceit, and Catherine, in piety and devotion as well as in fact still the daughter of Ferdinand, had borne some of the brunt of Henry's rage. The King had reproached her with her father's abandoned faith, and some attributed the premature death of Catherine's fourth son to the brutality Henry displayed toward her at this period.

Henry had decided to make a firmer peace with France than the peace made by the sovereigns he had counted on as allies against France. When in January of 1514 Louis's queen died, Henry had proposed that Mary, a gay and graceful girl of seventeen, be pledged to the French King. But it had not been reasonable to base an alliance upon a matter as insubstantial as the life of Louis. "Being of an amorous disposition, which his advanced age had not entirely cooled," says Hume, "he was seduced into such a course of gaiety and pleasure, as proved very unsuitable to his declining state of health." [23] Reports from France told how Louis "loved to observe the good old French custom of dining at 8 of the clock in the morning; and going to bed at 6 in the evening; but now it suited his young Queen that he should dine at noon, and not go to bed till midnight." [24] The physicians had warned that this change in his mode of life would cause his death. Whether because of the change in his way of living or the strenuous effort to repeat his youth, Louis had inconsiderately lived less than three months. And his death had left Mary, the beauty of the house of Tudor, with her rich belongings, stranded in France; and it had left Henry, pride of the house of Tudor, with all his ambitions and schemes, stranded in England.

Wolsey had been the father and confessor of Mary in the affair of the marriage and in the confusing events that followed its dissolution by death. Hardly was the wedding over when Mary found her English servants dismissed. This dismissal she attributed to the Duke of Norfolk, who had been sent along to look after her household. Mary wrote: "Would God my Lord of York had come with me in the room of my Lord of Norfolk; for then I am sure I would have been more at my heart's ease than I am now." [25] It had been made plain also in a letter from Suffolk that Norfolk had dismissed Mary's servants because they were of Wolsey's choosing.

In the bitter aftermath of the marriage, Wolsey had continued to act as Mary's father and confessor. Immediately following the death of Louis, Wolsey had written her stern advice. "And if any motions of marriage or other fortune be made unto you, in no wise give hearing to them," he had said. But the counsel of the prelate could not prevail with an impulsive girl freed by death from a marriage she detested and at the same time romantically inclined to the manly Suffolk. Nothing would deter her — not even a proposal from the new King of France. At first flip and flirtatious, Francis I had suggested that he might free himself from other commitments and marry her. But Mary had merely written to her brother Henry to tell him of "the extreme pain and annoyance I was in by reason of such suit as the French king made unto me not according to mine honour." She feared he would "take courage to renew his suits unto me." And she said to her brother again that, having obeyed him in marrying the old King, "now I trust you will suffer me to marry as me liketh for to do."

She had not waited for an answer. She had gone ahead in the manner of a headstrong woman and married Suffolk. And one of the weighty problems before the Council in the spring of 1515, when Richard Kidderminster was thundering against the plea of laymen that criminous clerks be tried and sentenced in secular courts, was the acceptance or dissolution of the marriage Mary had made.

Wolsey's position as a go-between in a royal family quarrel called for judicious juggling at every turn. He must keep the lines of communication free and open, but there must be no doubt, even when he winked, about the chief object of his loyalty. This was ever the King. In reply to the early letters of entreaty which Mary and Suffolk sent him, he could only counsel patience and report to them how matters stood with the royal will. He wrote to Suffolk to say that the King had called him apart after sittings of the Council and had bade him "use all effort to obtain from Francis Mary's gold plate and jewels; until this was accomplished, Suffolk and the Queen would not obtain license to return." In his letter to Suffolk he continues: "I assure you the hope that the King hath to obtain the said plate and jewels is the thing that most stayeth his grace constantly to assent that ye should marry his sister; the lack whereof, I fear me, might make him cold and remiss and cause some alteration, whereof *all men here,* except his grace and myself, would be right glad." 26

The negotiations dragged on, and tempers grew warm, and Suffolk bumbled and failed lamentably to get from the French what Henry sought. Meanwhile, no reply or assurance was given by the King of England to the repeated requests of the lovers that their marriage be approved. Suffolk's letters to Wolsey, along with those of Mary, are full of lamentations and bewilderment that the suit of the great matter within their hearts is brushed aside disdainfully by the King. One finds no trace in Henry's acts and no hint in his words to indicate any disposition to believe that the passion of a man and a woman and the desire for marriage should be reckoned with in affairs of state. Thus did bluff King Hal behave in the spring of 1515. Love was one thing and government was another. If there was a conflict between the two, love could wait.

It was up to Wolsey, when he received the intelligence of the secret marriage, to explain as best he could the King's mind to Suffolk. The King, he said, had taken the news "grievously and displeasantly." He is careful to remind Suffolk of his origins and of his dependence on the King for his station, bewailing that "ye hath failed to him which hath brought you up of low degree to be of this great honor." The sign of the importance of this point in the mind of my lord of York may be seen from the fact that the words "low degree" were inserted in the place of "nothing" — the only editing Wolsey did in the letter.27

Having wagged his head and clucked his tongue in the first part of the letter, Wolsey gets down to business: if there is anything that will soothe the outraged sentiments of the King, it will be an obligation to assume an annual payment to the royal household. He closes with the warning to Suffolk that "ye put yourself in the greatest danger that ever man was in."

Henry's policy, if it was policy rather than stubborn inaction, seems to have been to keep the couple dangling and enlist their uncertainty for whatever it was worth in the procurement of money and jewels. Mary finally received permission to return home the week after Easter. Even then the way was hard and the reception uncertain. From Calais Mary wrote to Henry. Her letter is preserved in the form it was carefully revised by Wolsey. "I am now comen out of the realm of France," she writes, "and have put myself within your jurisdiction, in this your good town of Calais, where I intend to remain till such time as I shall have answer from you of your good and loving mind herein; which I would not have done but upon the faithful trust I have in your said promise." She then promises to give him "all such plate and gold as I shall have of my said late husband's. Over and besides this I shall, rather than fail, give you as much yearly part of my dower to as great a sum as shall stand with your will and pleasure." [28]

Possibly the letter had some effect. Mary and Suffolk were openly married at the palace at Greenwich in the presence of the King and Queen on May 13, 1515. But Henry took her plate and jewels and obliged her to repay the expenses of her former marriage with Louis in yearly installments of one thousand pounds for twenty-four years, and to give up her dowry, if ever recovered, to the full amount. The terms were firmly made and rigidly enforced.

For Suffolk, it was a triumph discolored by lasting debt. But he still had his neck and his bride, and he could easily have lost them both if it had not been for the good offices of Wolsey, who had managed to circumvent the Council. It was a pretty good indication that in negotiations Wolsey could do anything he chose. Both as a servant and a friend he had been tested and shown his worth.

CHAPTER V

In the odd ways of history, it was Francis I and not Henry VIII who created the circumstances that made Thomas Wolsey Cardinal.

Neither Henry nor Wolsey properly anticipated the turn events would take in 1515. They knew only that Francis was an untrustworthy ally and that he might cause mischief. He spent much time dawdling in his mother's salon, little time at the council table, and talked volubly about what he would do — so volubly, in fact, that Henry and Wolsey thought he was not likely to do anything. Henry was still redolent with confidence after his own triumphs in France, and he refused steadfastly to believe that Francis would make a move that might incur Tudor displeasure. Even after the Venetian ambassador told Henry that Francis had left Lyons and was on his way to Italy, Henry replied: "The French king will not go into Italy this year. I believe he is afraid of me, and that will prevent him from crossing the Alps." [1]

Nothing, least of all the fear of Henry, prevented Francis from crossing the Alps. Not only were preparations, both diplomatic and military, conducted with such secrecy that the English, under a renewed alliance with France, learned of them always indirectly and always late, but the passage of the Alps itself was carried out with such heroic stealth and fortitude that neither the Italians and their Swiss defenders nor the English could believe it had happened.

Francis started from Lyons for Grenoble in July, 1515. The regular passes in Italy were firmly guarded by the Swiss. The French must employ one of these passes or else plan to abandon their artillery. In this perplexity Francis accepted the counsel of one of his aides and decided that his army and artillery would cross the unguarded and unsuspected Cottian Alps leading to the plains of Saluzzo. It was a masterful suggestion; but there was no road, and the enterprise would be attended by certain losses of men and equipment and by the gravest hazards at all times. Albeit, the French made the passage. They fenced dangerous slopes and dragged their guns with incredible toil to the top of the mountains.

The descent was even worse. As Brewer puts it: "Men in armour fell headlong into the abyss; horses plunged and struggled in vain with their unmanageable burthens, lost their footing, and rolled thundering over the precipice with guns, carriages and drivers. But the French troops, with wonderful spirits and alacrity . . . were not to be baffled. They dropped their artillery by cables from steep to steep; down one range of mountains and up another, until five days had been spent in this perilous enterprise, and they found themselves safe in the plains of Saluzzo." [2] Meanwhile the men-at-arms had followed various passages as best they could, and the Swiss, who had never imagined that such a passage was possible, were caught entirely by surprise and were so dismayed by this display of French bravery and tenacity that, though they fought with their usual vicious skill at the battle of Marignano, the French, with Francis the dawdler performing marvelous feats of individual bravery, won the day.

Europe was topsy-turvy again and the hated French were again in command of Italy. With this situation before him, Leo acted on the request that Wolsey had so long kept before him, a request he had resisted on moral grounds and against royal pressure. Events had come to his aid, but Wolsey left nothing to the course of events. He warned Leo pointedly, saying that he wanted a cardinal's hat mainly "to make the king fast to the pope." [3] Henry, he explained, wanted the hat more for Wolsey than Wolsey wanted it for himself. He warned Leo that if Henry forsook him Leo would "be in greater danger on this day two year than ever was Pope Julius." And as Francis descended into Italy, Wolsey had reminded Leo that he as Archbishop and friend of the King, "no earthly man helping thereto," had prevailed upon Henry to consent to the league with the papacy "on the red hat being sent." [4]

Leo showed signs now that he would yield. Indeed he swung full circle, and word came early in September that he would insist on the promotion of the Archbishop in spite of all the cardinals, hastily summoned from their vacations for a consistory to deal with the threat to Rome. At last, on September 10, "Leo X notified Wolsey that the creation had taken place; and in ten days a royal courier arrived in London with the important document." [5]

There had not been a cardinal resident in the realm of England since the death of Morton fifteen years before. Meanwhile the color of the court had enhanced, and opportunities for display were increased a hundredfold. The splendor of the court and the nobility was to less fortunate mortals one of the entertainments of the time. Government, with all its exactions, was still a pageant, and a fully bedecked cardinal and his train would embellish the pageant and give the people a little more for their tax money in the way of public show.

The arrival of the hat, then, was not to be treated casually. Here was an opportunity for drama, and from the days when he superintended the interment of Archbishop Deane, Wolsey had never missed seeing the force of drama. Well ahead of the invasion of France, he had sent to the Deputy Collector of the port of Calais and had asked him to procure "some French black for his own wearing," that he might be dressed in a garb appropriate to the position of the King's Almoner. Now he sent at once to Rome "for a pattern of the exact texture and shade of red of the cloth worn by the Cardinals in the Eternal City." [6] He was not one to overlook a detail.

There was another reason why the arrival of the hat must be treated with the fullest dignity. The hat formally signified the promotion of this

Ipswich fellow in rank above all the nobility of the realm. It was the position and not the man who filled it that carried the honor. Wolsey did not create the system or arrange the order of precedence. He simply benefited by it. He saw that the same man who six years before had been a mere chaplain to the King was now, by virtue of the authoritative position he occupied, only slightly less than King. Society stood on ceremony and by custom was compelled to acknowledge rank. By the good offices of the Church, the lad from Ipswich had bested the whole nobility.

It was something to celebrate. The ceremony of Wolsey's transcendence over the nobility would be turned on the arrival of the Cardinal's hat. He received word that the hat, together with a valuable ring bearing the affection of the reluctant Pope, was on its way in the care of Boniface Collis, secretary to Sylvester de Giglis. But it was the hat that mattered. The hat mattered more than the man who would walk under it. The Cardinal's hat was distinct.[7] Other ecclesiastics wore a hat of the same shape, but the Cardinal's hat was scarlet, and it was distinguished by the series of fringed tassels that adorned it. It was a kind of crown, having inherent and continuing virtue in itself, and it was not without significance that a proper ceremony for its reception would be known as an enthronement.

Apparently the protonotary of the papal court who carried the precious symbol did not fully perceive its worth. He arrived at Dover, according to some reports, carrying the hat under his cloak and made ready to push on to London like an ordinary courier. But Wolsey intercepted his casual passage, "clothed the ruffian in rich array and sent him back to Dover again." When the hat reached the gates of the city, "the mayor and aldermen of London on horseback and the city gilds on foot were turned out to do reverence as it was borne through the city on Thursday 15 November; and there it reposed on the high altar until the following Sunday."[8] A chronicle of the day tells us that tapers were set about it, "so that the greatest duke in the land must curtsie thereto; yea, and to his empty seat, he being away."

On the Sunday morning after the hat had been ensconced on the high altar of Westminster Abbey and treated with proper deference by the world and the Church alike, a procession formed at Wolsey's palace, York Place. Mounted on horseback were knights, barons, bishops, earls, dukes, and archbishops. In due order all proceeded "from his place betwixt eight and nine of the clock to the Abbey; and at the door aforesaid his grace with all the noblemen descended from their horses and went to the high altar; where in the south side was ordained a goodly traverse for My

Lord Cardinal. And when his grace was come to it immediately began the mass of the Holy Ghost, sung by the Archbishop of Canterbury." [9]

Two other archbishops from distant sees had been summoned to attend the ceremonies — the Archbishop of Armagh and the Archbishop of Dublin. The high and the mighty were all there, arrayed in the magnificent trappings and habiliments of their stations or offices, all witnesses now to the ceremonious recognition of Wolsey as Cardinal of Rome bearing the title of St. Cecilia Beyond the Tiber. It was an occasion such "as I have not see the like," says Cavendish, "unless it hath bin at the coronation of a mighty prince." The hour of glory had struck in the clashing cymbals of Church and State. London should be astonied and reminded by this display of sanction and power that the Church was here to stay and not to be trifled with through legislative meddling.

Yet there was one somber figure in all the splendor, and he rose now to sound a minor and dissonant, if not actually discordant, note, in the thundering paean of acceptance. And if my lord Cardinal sought to awe London and remind its citizens of the magnificence of the Church, the man who preached the sermon in the Abbey that day reminded the assembled lords spiritual and temporal that there was more to the Church than cardinals and that the Church arrayed in all its glory might to its grief overlook the simple requirements of Christian virtue.

The man who preached was John Colet, Dean of St. Paul's. He was the son of a London merchant, and he had been sent early to Oxford, being there at the time Wolsey was completing his own work. He had left Oxford, probably in 1494, for several years of travel in Europe. In Italy he had spent some time in the study of the Scriptures, always with a view to an analysis of their meaning and of ways by which that meaning could be made plain to plain men as well as to the learned. He had been in Italy during the pontificate of Alexander VI, when dissoluteness and scandal blackened the system of the papacy and showed that the man mattered as much as the office. He had returned to England sobered in outlook and with a strong ethical message. He had gone straight to Oxford and there delivered a course of lectures on St. Paul's Epistles. Later he had been advanced through the favor of the seventh Henry to be Dean of St. Paul's.

There the common people heard him gladly. "Instead of assuming the purple garments which were customary, he still wore his plain black robe . . . For years he abstained from suppers, and there were no nightly revels in his house. His table was neatly spread but neither costly nor excessive . . . Somehow or other he contrived so to exert his influence as to send his guests away better than they came." [10]

This is the man who, high in the ranks of the Church and exemplary in habits and conduct, stood forth before my lord Cardinal to preach the Gospel. He chose as his theme the doctrine of Christian humility, and in expounding this doctrine he chose to stress the spiritual side of the cardinalate. He acknowledged the honor that had come to Wolsey, but he went on to say — directly to my lord Cardinal: "Remember that our Savior in his own person said to his disciples that he came not to be ministered unto but to minister; and he had said also that he that is greatest among you shall be your servant. And whosoever shall exalt himself shall be abased; and he that humble himself shall be exalted." The exhortation rolled forth across the heads of the nobility and clergy in sonorous and cadent Latin: *Et qui se exaltat humiliabitur, et qui se humiliat exaltabitur.* Then as if the Scripture were not enough, Colet closed with these words: "My Lord Cardinal, be glad, and enforce yourself always to do and execute righteousness to rich and poor, and mercy with truth." [11]

It was straight talk, simply made, carrying the authority of a good life. In pointed terms it suggested to the Cardinal that there was more to his jurisdiction than the administration of the temporal affairs of the Church; and to those present it served notice that, whatever the just criticism of the Church for excessive privileges, there were still among the clergy men of moral fiber and stern will who dared assert on the enthronement of a cardinal the revolutionary precepts of the Carpenter of Galilee.

It was noted that as William Warham, Archbishop of Canterbury and still Primate of All England, passed down the nave of Westminster Abbey after the ceremonies were over, no cross of gold to herald his rank was borne before him. What went on inside Wolsey during Colet's sermon he never made a matter of record. But as he passed down the nave, two great crosses of gold were borne before him by comely priests, one cross signifying that he was Archbishop and the other that he was now Cardinal. These crosses would precede him hereafter wherever he went. None was ever borne again before Warham in the presence of Wolsey.

Wolsey's hour had come. Crowned with the red hat, he was the leading Church dignitary of the kingdom, and even though the Pope had not seen fit to make him legate *a latere,* he had by his rank lordship over the nobility. After the ceremony he was conducted back to York Place by eighteen temporal lords. And the procession of state was led by the Dukes of Norfolk and Suffolk. Not bad for the son of an innkeeper of Ipswich.

It had been a part of the cunning of Wolsey's program for the arrival of the hat that the event would distract public attention from the debate over the rights of the clergy which still raged, indeed with greater vehemence than ever, in the fall of 1515. A massive display of the Church's power manifest in England and now vested in the person of a common son of the kingdom might also be hoped to overawe the aroused laity. The hat arrived and the enthronement took place just as Parliament convened from an adjourned session in the spring and just as Convocation, the term given to a separate meeting of the ruling body of the clergy, assembled also. The question before both bodies — the question on everyone's mind — was that raised by Richard Hunne's death: the rights of secular courts to have jurisdiction over men in orders.

It was a question too deep and vital to be shunted, and, from the standpoint of public interest, the vast ado over the hat and the enthronement proved actually to be only a sideshow to the main events. The Commons met and promptly passed again the bill limiting the benefits extended to criminous clerks, but the Lords cavalierly took no action on it. The Commons presented another and more pointed bill making it a matter of record that "clergymen declined to bury their parishioners unless they were rewarded by the most precious jewel, suit of clothes, or other possession of the deceased person; and it prayed that every incumbent should be compelled to bury the dead or administer the sacrament to the sick upon penalty of £40." [12] Again there was no action in the Lords. Nor was there any when the Commons impatiently passed the benefit of clergy bill a second time and sent it to the upper House.

The Houses were obviously deadlocked over the issue. Frequent adjournments were necessary among the Lords in order that the bishops and abbots might attend sessions of their own order separately in Convocation. Moreover, the scene of action had now been transferred significantly to the presence of the King again. The matter was to be laid before the throne again as it had been in the spring. But this time the issues would be more sharply drawn, and the meetings before the King would be more than splendid tournaments of learning. The young Henry, greatly instructed by the debates and sensitive as Tudors always were to the currents of popular feeling, showed that he was beginning to know his own mind and see his own future.

In the spring the Abbot of Winchcombe had appeared before Henry at Blackfriars to state the case for the clergy. The interests of the State had been represented by Dr. Henry Standish, warden of the Grayfriars in London. He was a favorite preacher at the court of Henry, and in these circumstances and with the King's protection he felt free to speak his mind and to offer the case against a strict and unreasoning interpretation of the Church's position. The Abbot of Winchcombe urged the sanctity of a papal decree which forbade calling criminous clerks before a secular tribunal, but Standish pointed out that the decree had never been accepted in England.

The joust between Standish and the Abbot had been so unequal that some of the members of the Commons had sought to have the Abbot offer a public recantation for his sermon. At this point, however, Parliament had been adjourned until the fall. During the interim Dr. Standish had continued to advance his views in a series of public lectures, all of them distasteful to the lords spiritual and all inclined to give aid and encouragement to the members of the Commons who sought to bring clerks within the jurisdiction of the regular courts. Thus when Convocation met again at the time of the arrival of the hat, the lords spiritual haled Standish before them and began meticulously to inquire into his views. What he had said in the presence of Henry was protected, but what he had said publicly might be made the basis of procedure against him. He had said in effect that "a papal decree could not stand against the continuous usage of a country."

Serious and searching questions were propounded to Standish at the convocational inquiry. Can a secular court convent clergy before it? Are minor orders holy or not? Can a temporal ruler restrain a bishop? These were questions which, if answered to the displeasure of the lords spiritual, might lead Standish into something resembling the fate of Hunne. But he answered them in favor of the State by refusing to plead his answers at all and by appealing to the King for protection. By this very act and by the acceptance of responsibility by the King under his coronation oath, the direction of events could be clearly seen. For Henry now summoned Standish to Blackfriars again "to plead before his majesty in the presence of the judges, the king's counsel, the temporal and spiritual lords, and some members of the lower house." [13]

Here again Dr. Standish acquitted himself to the full satisfaction of those who agreed with him anyway. His answers to the charges brought against him in Convocation exalted the rights of the Crown and Parliament. So enthusiastic were the judges present that they eventually declared the clergy present at the Convocation which had cited Standish before them to be guilty of praemunire. It was an opinion expressed to the King and not a judgment rendered by the benches in session, but it served notice of the temper of the temporal authorities, this charge that the Convocation had acted under the influence if not the bidding of a foreign power.

It was a strange and unscheduled reversal of events. The clergy had placed Standish before their tribunal in Convocation to answer for his views. He had refused to state his views for their inspection but had in turn appealed to the King who called Convocation to stand before him. And, supported by the strong arm of his judiciary, the King had heard the Standish case in its fullness, and the judiciary had subsequently declared the clergy guilty of what was tantamount to treason. The declaration had a chastening effect on the actions of the lords spiritual if it did not change their views. They had better seek an audience with the King.

Flanked by the lords temporal and led by my lord Cardinal, the lords spiritual appeared in the presence of the King at Baynard's Castle. There was a sprinkling of commoners there, too. Here was the first official appearance of my lord Cardinal after his elevation. And his first official act as Cardinal was to kneel before Henry in the presence of the assembly and offer the explanations and apologies of the clergy. In his dual role as friend and adviser of the King and as representative of Rome by virtue of the cardinalate, he could do the job as no one else could. He explained humbly that the clergy had not intended to do anything which might reflect on the prerogatives of the Crown. Far from it. At the same time he declared that the conventing of "clerks before temporal judges seemed to all the clergy contrary to the laws of God and to the liberties of the church, which they were bound by their oaths to maintain." [14] Then my lord Cardinal followed this repetition of the stated beliefs of the lords spiritual with the astonishing suggestion that Henry — to avoid the censures of the Church — let the whole question be referred to the Pope and his counsel in Rome.

Henry shook his royal head. "It seems to us," he said in reply, "that Dr. Standish and others of his spiritual counsel have answered you on all points." There was an outcry from Fox and Warham, but Henry closed the proceedings with prophetic vigor and firmness. "Kings of England have never had any superior but God alone. By the Providence of God, we are King of England . . . and I would have you take notice that we are resolved to maintain the rights of our crown and temporal jurisdiction in as ample a manner as any of our progenitors." [15]

Clearly Dr. Standish would not have his case remitted to the dubious mercies of Convocation. And the decision on matters of clerical and temporal authority would not be referred to Rome. Kings of England had no superior but God alone.

My lord Cardinal made a poor spokesman for the clergy that dreary November day in the drafty reaches of Baynard's Castle. He stated the clerical case clearly and well, beating a kind of refrain to what had been said before. To no avail. Henry addressed him like a child: "It seems to us that Dr. Standish and his spiritual advisers have answered you . . ."

With all his red robes and gold crosses and tasseled hat, he had failed, for he spoke as a Roman and not as a subject of the King. He encountered that duality which was to prove his doom. His position as Cardinal exalted him above the nobility, but when he displayed himself as a churchman he ran head-on into Henry's imperious will. Whether his plea that the question before the nation be referred to Rome came from his own initiative, or whether he was prompted by Convocation to advance it, we do not know. In either case, the plea was incredibly misguided and tactless, and it fell upon ears that were already listening to the sounds of the future.

The humiliation of the Cardinal, a commoner beneath his vestments, had in it many lessons. The role Wolsey played best was not the role of a debater. There is no record that he accomplished anything by means of public speech. He bore the talent but not the will of an orator. His voice had the ring of authority, and his sentences had the rhythmic breathing of eloquence; there was in his style a melody that comes from the love of words as music. But in pleading publicly he was out of character. The matter before the kingdom was too important now to be left to a forum. It would be well to deal privately with the King in this matter — to dispense with forensics.

Although my lord Cardinal failed in his address to the King at Baynard's Castle, he persuaded the King soon after the meeting to dissolve Parliament. The session came to an end on December 22, in time for the holidays, and with no action taken on the bill for limiting benefit of clergy. The act of 1512 was not renewed. Both Houses had been in session six weeks and had accomplished little. The chief item they were called to consider had been referred to the King. If the court was to be the scene of action and the King the source of authority, why keep Parliament around? If the Church was not to guide England's legislative program, why should the Commons? Let Henry, now so assertive of his rights, take control; let the government be centered firmly in him. And let Wolsey be his aide.

Three days after the dissolution of Parliament, William Warham, who as Archbishop of Canterbury held the Great Seal of England by long tradition, surrendered this emblem of authority to the King, who conveyed it at once to Wolsey. Warham had advocated the frequent meeting of Par-

142

liament. The change meant, among other things, that from now on the King would reign. And on Christmas Eve, 1515, Thomas Cardinal Wolsey became his prime minister, succeeding Warham as Lord Chancellor of England.

CHAPTER VI

THERE was something meet and fitting about Thomas Wolsey of Ipswich seated on a sack stuffed with wool. The woolsack was the throne, so to say, of the Lord Chancellor of England, and now the Chancellor was the son of a man of sheep in a land of sheep which owed its wealth and daily living to sheep, with sheep outnumbering humans three to one. Dealing in cloth occupied men's thoughts daily. Many figures of speech came directly from it. One spun a yarn, carried a thread of discourse, unraveled a mystery. A thing was fine-drawn or homespun. Unmarried women were spinsters. The government concerned itself gravely with every detail of the trade in cloth: the import of foreign-made hats and caps was forbidden; the prices of articles produced at home were fixed; the export of more expensive kinds of cloth was not to be allowed unless the cloth was fully finished.[1]

The woolsack was a healthy and solid reminder of an ancient fact. It survived ceremonially out of a time when woolsacks had been occupied in Parliament by high dignitaries of the Crown. Now the highest councilor of the Crown still occupied it. With all his glory, and though a Cardinal, the Chancellor of the realm accepted as his symbol a sack stuffed with wool and covered with rich and appropriately red cloth. It gave him, this emblematic sack, some kinship with the common people and some basis for concern with their daily problems. The connection might be tenuous, as it is in any ritual, but it was there just the same. The King existed above and beyond the commonalty; the Lord Chancellor was of it: an audience for the complaints and aspirations and pleas of the lowborn and the bedraggled. The Chancellor stood between the throne and the people, and the woolsack signified that he was of the people.

Wolsey took his woolsack seriously. It is true that he had little or nothing to do with the actual symbol of his office, for the woolsack was the seat of the Chancellor in Parliament, not outside of it, and Parliament sat but once during the fourteen years he occupied the office. But if Parliament was not to meet for its endless snarling and backbiting, there must still be hearings for grievances, and there must be some machinery by which the law could be put into force.

The Parliament of 1515 had passed an act to restrain the rise in the cost of labor. The first draft of this act was in the handwriting of Wolsey. Humbler artisans and traders were beginning to demand some voice in the organization of trade and in the conditions under which they worked. This situation was highly irregular and would of course, if not restrained, lead to riot and civil commotion. In London there were strikes among the shearmen, the saddlers, the shoemakers, and the tailors. There was implicit in all this unrest the threat of government by mobs.

Persons of low degree might by severity of punishment be kept in their places; but there was to be noted also a restlessness and eagerness for betterment to be found among the slightly more privileged classes. These classes showed a tendency to dress and eat beyond their appointed station. The whole question of dress needed to be reviewed; and the Parliament of 1515 passed an Act of Apparel, fathered and furthered by Wolsey, which restricted the burgesses to their appropriate homespun and defined in more precise terms than did the earlier laws what men of the several classes would be permitted to wear.

The Act of Apparel went further. It set up regulations in another area where the tendencies of persons of low order to ape their betters had begun to show themselves — the area of food. Those who stood in the ranks of gentlemen were permitted to have three dishes at a meal; lords of Parliament, Lord Mayors, and Knights of the Garter could have six. In the proclamation issued by my lord Cardinal to make this law known, it was pointed out that, since a cardinal ranked above the nobility and even above princes of the realm, he himself would be entitled to nine dishes; and it was further made a matter of record in the same proclamation that the number of dishes allowed would be "determined by the rank of the most distinguished guest." [2]

It was plain from this Act and from the proclamation accompanying it, that Wolsey as Lord Chancellor intended to inspect and oversee every detail of the common life of the people of England. Regulation had become an established Tudor principle; it was a part of the heritage of the seventh Henry, who had set the land in order after chaos, that government in its essence meant making people behave according to the wisdom of those charged with the responsibility of governance. The English were quarrelsome and unruly, wild and restless, addicted to factions and fighting, assertive and independent. They needed a strong ruler, who would

144

hold them firmly in check and exact obedience. Their society was based fully upon the principle of rank and authority by rank. The King stood above all ranks — that much Henry VII had made painfully clear. And as he had brought law and order to the profit of one and all, so his successor must continue that government by law and edict lest the land fall again into weakness and decay. And the King being busy with many matters and with the ceremonies of the throne, it would devolve of necessity upon his chief aide to see that orders from the throne for the good of all be severely enforced.

The office provided my lord Cardinal with all the appurtenances of authority. Theoretically he had scant connection with the law courts, save that he was entitled to name the justices of the peace in the shires and could in this wise keep a finger on their conduct. But the personality of Thomas Wolsey overflowed any polite bounds of tradition. The King must be made the center and focus of the whole life of the people, and the royal prerogative must be exalted above royal factions, "and even above the law, if necessary."

There was, of course, an elaborate web of courts spread across the kingdom. These courts were under the sitting of men of rank, as a rule, for it was part of the English tradition that the privileged and the titled should condescend to administer justice. For example, it was provided that there should be a court held in every market. It was composed of merchants, but it was deemed best that it be presided over by the mayor. This was the Court of Piepowder or *Piepoudre* — "dusty feet" — so called because "the chapmen or merchants came straight in without ceremony to have their differences adjusted on the day on which they happened, and to have offenders punished without delay." [3] Any notice of a fair always carried with it the announcement of a Piepowder Court, with the assurance of swift adjudication.

It was a court of dusty feet, with its rough-and-ready decisions of equity arrived at promptly and without haggling over the technicalities of the law, that Thomas Wolsey of Ipswich now instituted on a large and lordly scale. The place of its sitting was the Star Chamber in the palace at Westminster, where a court had commenced to sit in the early and turbulent days of the seventh Henry, designed to bring recalcitrant lords to heel and obedience. It kept its purpose and tradition; all Wolsey did was to extend the purpose and amplify its jurisdiction in line with his high intent of disciplining the people.

The Star Chamber had long been a place where the King's Council sat in judgment. It withdrew there to resolve itself into a judicial body.

But its meeting had been only occasional before the time of the seventh Henry. Parliament "authorized the king to establish a court of judges chosen from the Privy Council to relieve the Council of its judicial duties. The particular function of these judges was to seek out offenders among the barons, to summon those to trial and to punish those whom they found guilty . . . The activities of the new tribunal were gradually extended. In 1495 it was given jurisdiction over 'heinous riots', perjury, and appeals in criminal cases. Still later such unrelated subjects as usury, enclosures, and quarrels between merchants trading beyond the sea came within its competence." [4]

Over this Court of the Star Chamber Wolsey, by virtue of his office as Chancellor, now came to preside; and it was this court which, by virtue of his personal capacity and his great disposition for official meddling, he converted into an instrument that brought him in touch with every quarter of life of England. He stretched out his judicial hand and drew into his venue every conceivable kind of dispute, settling it without the embarrassment of recourse to the awkward procedures of law. In the awkward procedures of law my lord Cardinal had never had a whit of training, neither in canon nor civil law. His training had been in the sturdy principles of philosophy, and to these, as he pontifically sat, he had recourse. His court was a court of equity and a court of conscience, and his dual role as the King's chief minister and as a high official of the Church vested his decisions with no small measure of sanctity among his countrymen, accustomed as they were to bow before princes and to accept the edicts of those who stood above them. In effect, the court over which Wolsey presided was the court in which the King was judge, and if the King cavalierly delegated his authority and prerogative to the richly robed Cardinal, it did not lessen the honor of appearing before a tribunal in which the sovereign with his inherited wisdom was the supreme symbol of justice among his subjects.

Precedent aplenty could be found in the attic of the past for the use Wolsey made of the Star Chamber as a court of conscience. In his own thinking he drew a sharp line between law and conscience, a line so sharp that the two would appear to be antithetical. He had no odd moments during his frantic administration to formulate his principles, but he acted them out every day, and after his fall he wrote his sentiments to Mr. Justice Shelley. In giving advice to one of the King's advisers, he says: ". . . for when ye tell him this is the law, it were well done ye should tell him also that although *this* be the law, yet *this* is conscience; for law without conscience is not meet to be given to a king by his counsel to be ministered by him nor by respect to conscience before the rigour of the law . . . The king ought for his royal dignity and prerogative to mitigate the rigour of the law, where conscience hath the more force; and therefore in his princely place he has constituted a chancellor to order for him the same . . ." [5]

With such a philosophy and with abounding confidence in his own conscience, Wolsey provided a court that was welcome to the hearts of the people. Actions were prompt, delays at first rare. Counsel fees were moderate and, in the case of the poor, dispensed with entirely. A poor man who because of his poverty found it difficult to engage in litigation could come before the Star Chamber at will. Here was a court open to one and all, superior in rank and dignity to all the old-fashioned and creaky courts of common law. And it was a court where, as Pollard puts it, justice "was rarely denied merely because it might happen to be illegal."

In no other phase of Wolsey's life does one find such a daily, sustained, unrelenting interest as he showed in sitting as a judge of other people's problems. He taught that decision should at all times be vested in a person and not in a procedure or a rule of conduct. His court, and those that broke off from it with delegated authority when the docket grew too heavy even for Wolsey to handle, established plainly in men's minds that conscience was king, that supreme authority lay within a man, or at least within a man of rank.

In this respect the Chancellor never forsook the woolsack. With all his pomp and glory and his insatiable appetite for position and the emblems of authority, he remained seated on his origin: a local wiseacre with a talkative mind, full of opinions of right and wrong, sharing them fully with his fellows in a moment of respite while waiting for the pack train to come.

It was an odd twist in the character of a Cardinal. Wolsey had risen above princes in a society where princes ruled by right of inheritance. Yet somehow he could not rise above his station; there was too much ancestry in him. He would remain until the day of his fall from the King's grace, until the day of his reversion to nothingness when he would walk about in empty robes, a bright and meddlesome mind ceaselessly at work where people congregated to air their grievances; a man who knew it all and could solve any problem other than his own; a bumpkin with a vocabulary and a fluency far beyond his station, always seated on a sack stuffed with wool and able to prate the solution to any difficulty, however complex, or offer the government free advice on any policy, however great the crisis.

Whatever Wolsey did, he could not do simply. He was incapable of simplicity or directness. If he remained inwardly a peasant, the fact was disguised better from himself than from any of his associates. He overlaid his personality with vestments, with layers of assurance, and he could never get enough to be sure that his nakedness was covered or that the body of the man would not be detected by others or by himself. The elaborate manners of the day aided and abetted him in this and sanctioned his behavior as well. He could not perform a commonplace act such as going from one place to another; if he went anywhere his going became a procession; he was flanked and escorted by priests bearing maces and poleaxes and the ubiquitous hat.

Thus, however much he might descend into the market place to hear men's disputes from all over the King's realm, he made his attendance upon the Court of the Star Chamber an act of regal condescension. Wolsey was usually ready to set forth from his house about eight in the morning. Cavendish, his gentleman-usher, describes Wolsey's procedure of getting to the scene of equity, taking pains to tell us first how my lord Cardinal was attired:

"His upper garment was of either fine scarlet, or taffety, but most commonly of fine crimson satin engrained; his pillion of fine scarlet, with a neck set in the inner side with black velvet, and a tippet of sables about his neck; holding in his hand an orange whereof the meat or substance within was taken out, and filled up again with part of a sponge, wherein was vinegar and other confections against the pestilent airs; the which he most commonly held to his nose when he came among any press, or else that he was pestered with any suitors."

Thus fortified against the smells of the common people, my lord of York, late of Ipswich, moved forward to his chamber of presence. "And before him was borne first the broad seal of England, and his Cardinal's hat by a lord or some gentleman of worship, right solemnly. And as soon as he was entered into his chamber of presence, where there was daily attending upon him, as well noble men of this realm, and other worthy gentlemen, as gentlemen of his own family, his two great crosses were there attending to be borne before him; then cried the gentlemen ushers, going before him bare-headed, and said, 'On before my lordes and masters, on before, and make way for my lord cardinal.'"

In this lofty manner did my lord Cardinal fare forth from his dwelling to hear disputes and dispense justice and equity in behalf of the common man. He rode, as became the Christian humility which Dean Colet had urged upon him at the time of his enthronement, a mule, a lowly commoner among beasts of burden and one with long and honored traditions of simplicity. Yet the mule which bore the Cardinal's festooned carcass was disguised out of all recognition in crimson velvet, and, lest there be some discomfort to the posterior of the Cardinal, the saddle was of like material. The stirrups for my lord Cardinal's feet were of gold, no less.

"Then marched he forward," Cavendish reports proudly, "with a train of noble men and gentlemen, having each his footmen, fewer in number about him, bearing each of them a gilt poleaxe in his hands; and thus passed he forth until he came to Westminster Hall door. And there he alighted, and went after this manner up into the chancery." Usually he would stay a while "at the bar, made for him, beneath the chancery, on the right hand, and there commune sometimes with the judges, and sometimes with other persons; and that done, he would repair into the chancery, sitting there until eleven of the clock, hearing suits and determining of other matters." [6]

This stately procession to the Court of the Star Chamber was Wolsey's routine every Monday, Tuesday, Thursday, and Saturday.[7] The court itself was as public as his going to it. It met in the outer Star Chamber as distinct from the inner chamber where the King's Council sat to discuss matters of policy. Any who wished could come in off the street and watch the great Cardinal perform his acrobatic feats of judgment and throw his conscience around. In the early days of his administration, Henry himself occasionally attended. Wolsey was always sure of an audience. Indeed the attendance at the Court of the Star Chamber was so great that the King complained at times of the scanty attendance at his own regal court. It was quite a show, and Wolsey was so much the center of it that the people gained the impression that the Cardinal himself had created this majestic court. He had a talent for doing a thing as if it had never been done before, even though the practice was hoary with custom and precedent.

That Wolsey's efforts in the Star Chamber met with popular favor and filled a current need is the common testimony of his day. Giustiniani, the Venetian ambassador who was no admirer of Wolsey in the area of diplomacy, spoke eloquently of his role as a judge, reporting that he had the "reputation of being extremely just; he favors the people exceedingly, especially the poor, hearing their wants and seeking to dispatch them instantly." [8] He also noted the Lord Chancellor's policy of making lawyers plead gratis for all paupers. Edward Fox, Bishop of Hereford, said that he had never known so painstaking a judge, adding that he was "always on the side of the poor man when opposed by the rich or unscrupulous." And when he decided against the claims of a poor man, he gave assistance to the poor man in money or employment. Sir Thomas More declared that no Chancellor of England ever acted with greater impartiality, deeper penetration of judgment, or a more enlarged knowledge of law or equity.[9]

Dealing as he did with all manner of problems and quarrels, Wolsey naturally made enemies. Sir Robert Sheffield, who had been Speaker of the Commons in the Parliament of 1512, was sent to the Tower "on a charge of having said that, if the temporal lords had only been of one mind in the last parliament, they might have made Wolsey's body as red as his cardinal's hat." And rumors were spread among vulgar folk that Wolsey "had threatened to burn all common beggars in a barn, that Henry had refused without Warham's consent, and that Warham would consent only if Wolsey were put in the barn and burned as well." [10]

Wolsey's ignorance of the law made him in popular fancy a superior judge, enabling him to arrive at common notions of justice without circumlocution, by rule of thumb and rule of tongue. He had a natural penetration which enabled him to discern false from true evidence and to select the most practical mode of judging a case. Wolsey made his own opinion the law and enforced it by the King's writ. And it was not only in thus setting up his conscience as the arbiter of moral action, but also in arrogating to his court all manner of disputes, that he revealed the temper and bent of his mind and the nature of his procedure. His court had validity for the simple reason that the common law was in decay; yet there is no indication whatever that he taught to reform common law courts. His method was rather to show that he personally, sitting in London, could handle cases better than all the legal population of the realm.

The nature of his court, being as it was a part of the King's household, freed it from the common afflictions of perjury and bribery. Local trials throughout the country often ended in travesty because judges and juries were corrupt and could be bribed or bullied by the more powerful party to a suit. Trial by jury was often "a contest in perjury, which itself was hardly an offense at common law." [11] Bribery occupied a public part in community life. "The whole complicated system of local administration had long been kept in working order by a generous system of bribes — bribes given largely and openly, registered in the public accounts and granted indifferently to any official, great or small, who might be induced by a timely gift to 'show his friendship' . . . At the appearance of the King's harbinger the first thought was to collect a sum which might induce their formidable guest to limit the number of troops billeted on the town, or even to march them away altogether. Counted among the usual incidents of government, and reckoned in the ordinary expenditure of the municipality, the payment of such bribes was to all concerned merely the customary mode of defraying some of the expenses of administration." [12]

With bribery an official practice sanctioned by long tradition, court procedure might be made a farce if the two litigants were of unequal station and one could outbid the other for the favor of the court. Added to bribery and perjury was the delay encountered in the common law courts, making litigation hopeless among men of few farthings, who needed its benefits most. Changes which had been irresistibly in process since the end of serfdom some two hundred years before had brought into prominence and into the courts a whole new range of crimes and mischiefs that were not even contemplated in the common law. For the law of the land was the law of land lords; it was not common at all. An accused person was tried by "a jury of his peers." The presumptions and procedures of the law were ill suited to adjudicating the claims of those in the lower orders of society, especially if these claims were urged against the upper classes for which the law was originally intended. It was the right of serfs and villeins to appeal above manorial courts directly to the King that had begun to change the law. The serfs, in a word, had begun to achieve legal status in manorial courts of equity presided over by men of common sense, not in courts of common law.

Wolsey took this fact and this tradition of manorial justice and with his usual vigor extended it to a series of courts around the King, all under the close supervision of himself. What he did was to assist and amplify a trend, not to start one. The plain man could not get what he called justice in his dealings with the high and the mighty as long as he sought it in a series of common-law courts designed for the nobles and the gentry. He could and did get it in the Star Chamber, in the King's court of equity. Wolsey's sense of history was sufficient to see the role he might play in speeding up "the halting process by which the law for the gentry slowly broadened down into the law for all." [13]

Common plea might be moved from the common bench into the Star Chamber "on the ground that the plaintiff was too poor or weak and the defendant was too rich or strong for justice to be had at the common law." The Duke of Suffolk even appealed to Wolsey on behalf of a servant on the ground that the poor man "is not able to sue against Lord Dacre or abide the long process of the law." [14]

Once haled before Wolsey in the Star Chamber, a lord or gentleman found himself on the defensive, and Wolsey showed delight in finding some fault with his case. As a noble ex officio he acted against the nobles by birth and weighted what he called justice heavily on the side of the poor. He went further and began actually to make effective the laws which had been set upon the statute books sternly in the reign of the seventh Henry and then in many cases blithely ignored. The plowing under of special privileges among those who exalted themselves above the King was the central means by which the Tudors sought to cultivate a new land for England.

In a like manner Wolsey dealt with survival of livery and maintenance, those twin practices that had cohabited to make the Wars of the Roses possible. Even in the middle classes the number of idle servants impressed foreign visitors unfavorably. "Owing their existence to the ostentation of their masters, they aped the vices and extravagances of those above them, gambling, swearing and living riotously. Even in their dress, they aimed at show rather than use, wearing long coats that were nothing but a nuisance when they had to ride and doublets with such pleatings and puffings of sleeves that if they had to defend their masters or themselves they must throw off their garments before they could draw a bow." [15]

Men of distinction were judged by the number of servants they kept. And as long as great households were required by the King and custom to be attended by hangers-on who served mainly as emblems of rank, it was but a step to the employment of the coterie of servants for private wars or for the intimidation of lesser men. This was the threat of livery and maintenance. The Duke of Buckingham was one of those who maintained a lavish establishment. In November of 1520, Buckingham instructed his agent to tell the Cardinal that it would be necessary to take three or four hundred armed men with him on a trip to Wales.[16]

To humble such men and exalt the King became one of the Chancellor's games. The last Parliament of Henry VII had complained that little was being done by way of punishment for giving liveries and keeping great bands of retainers. Wolsey of Ipswich would set that matter right. Here in the Court of the Star Chamber he had both the law and conscience at his disposal. Edward Hall, one of the chroniclers of the times, writes: "He punished also lords, knights and men of all sorts for riots, bearing and maintenance in their countries, that the poor men lived quietly." [17] None could escape the wrath of the man of the red hat as it was expressed in behalf of both the King and the common man, directed as it was toward the maintenance of peace in the realm and the maintenance of the King's supremacy over all his nobles. This was the only kind of maintenance that Wolsey would allow. In 1516 when he began his vigorous execution of the law, the Earl of Northumberland was examined before the King in the Star Chamber and sent to the prison known as the

Fleet. The Marquis of Dorset, the Earl of Surrey, son and heir of the Duke of Norfolk, hero of Flodden, together with many others of rank, were called before the Star Chamber for keeping retainers.

Wolsey reveled in the role of one who to poverty born had wealth as his habit. That he overplayed his part, as if to ridicule his rivals, there is abundant evidence. During the fourteen lavish years he served the King as aide and Chancellor, he did not unbend in public or take off his mask of arrogance or show a trace of modesty in the presence of any but the King. He was without the confidence that makes condescension possible. He was unwilling to release his hold for one moment upon the amulet of office and the properties of his role. He had both the imagination and the histrionic bent to outdo the nobles at their own game of ostentation and needless pageantry. Yet he lacked the security of self that would enable him for a season to relax his insistence that he was as good as any man save the King and the Pope. He had the pride of a man who is afraid other men will forget his worth.

Giustiniani, the talkative Venetian ambassador long resident in London, sized up Wolsey's determination to be recognized at every turn and in every deal and remarked: "Were it a question of neglecting His Majesty or His Right Reverend Lordship, the least injurious course would be to pass over the former." Even Fox, who had discovered Wolsey's shining talent and done much to deliver it to the throne, once said of a matter: "We shall have to deal with the Cardinal, who is not Cardinal, but King; and no one in the realm dares attempt aught in opposition to his interests." [18]

The painful consciousness of station and position allied to grandeur never deserted my lord Cardinal. During the visit of the Emperor of the Holy Roman Empire to England in 1520, "Wolsey alone sat down to dinner with the royal party, while peers like the Dukes of Suffolk and Buckingham performed menial duties for the Cardinal, as well as for Emperor, King and Queen." [19] When he performed Mass at a great meeting of the Kings of England and France at a place that came to be known as the Field of Cloth of Gold, "bishops invested him with his robes and put sandals on his feet, and 'some of the chief noblemen in England' brought him water to wash his hands." A year later, at his meeting with the Emperor at Bruges, "he treated the Emperor as an equal. He did not dismount from his mule but merely doffed his cap, and embraced as a brother the temporal head of Christendom." [20]

Wolsey set a new mode for elaborateness of dress among the clergy, arraying himself in dainty silken garments and requiring that bishops and lesser clergy in attendance upon him do likewise if they were to enjoy the richness of his favor. The appropriateness of the attire required of his minions or the implications of that attire in a time of the increasing unpopularity of the clergy did not seem for one moment to trouble his conscious mind. He was the great imitator, a conformist who excelled, who broke the mold only to make it larger and fill it richer again. No one would say that he did not behave and dress as well as the best.

CHAPTER VII

THE hostility toward the nobility which the Cardinal showed at every twist of the screw of his power was far from abstract: it was also personal, directed openly against the most powerful. And the resentment he aroused among the nobles in turn showed itself not merely in gossip but in insult. Those who looked upon him as a wanton upstart, a Wat Tyler in silks and velvets, did not quibble to say so. In particular, the loftiest lord of the land looked with icy scorn upon this worm the King had made his Chancellor. The Duke of Buckingham, Edward Stafford, could afford to show his spleen even to the King's favorite councilor. Ensconced as Lord High Constable of England, he boasted royal blood among his forebears, being descended through his father from Thomas Woodstock, sixth son of Edward III. A man of prudent wealth, lending employment to a wide host of retainers, he appeared to be hedged with security. His father had rebelled against Richard III and had lost his head for his pains. The young son Edward, now the haughty duke, had merely had his own head shaved by his protectors and had been spirited from place to place in disguise and in the hands of a kindly farm woman until distracted Richard lost interest in the chase.

When Henry Tudor came to the throne as Henry VII, Edward Stafford was restored to the dukedom and ranked high in the esteem of the King. The young Duke had been brought up "almost as a member of the royal family." He became a companion of the young Henry, and he was in the procession which had set out to meet Catherine of Aragon when she came to wed Arthur. At that time he had been the only duke in the realm. He was a smooth and captivating courtier — "handsome, charming, extravagant, a little rattle-brained, a little stupid, with an exalted idea of the privileges and security of his position, but a great gentleman, none the less." [1] And later, when Henry and Catherine were married, he was close to them as a friend. Particularly did Catherine cherish him, for he had been one who had sent her fruit and venison in the days of her adversity after Arthur's death.

Being born to the purple, Edward Stafford, third Duke of Buckingham, showed by many acts that he could not tolerate with equanimity the person of Thomas Wolsey of Ipswich, merely elevated to the red. Wolsey stood in his arrogance as a threat to the whole social structure with which Buckingham was unconsciously familiar and in which he was comfortably fixed. It was a world that, with all its turmoil, had stood obediently still for the nobles during the past hundreds of years. It had its postulates and standards and shibboleths. One of these was that a man was born to what he was destined to become; he had no control over it, any more than he had over his birth. There were certain things a nobleman did; and there were certain things a plain man did not do. Into this fixed preserve now came the Cardinal, a man who, stripped of his vestments and the position to which these entitled him, was a plain Ipswich fellow, whose father was a butcher and grazier and innkeeper and whose grandfather, if the truth were known, was probably a serf.

Collision was inevitable. The Duke took no pains to conceal his disdain, and there began a rivalry in snobbery. In due course the two descended to childish rebuffs which, had they taken place among schoolboys, would have been punished by Latin verses or the cane. Chroniclers report that on one occasion the Duke of Buckingham was holding a ewer of water for the King to wash his hands in. The story goes that into this basin Wolsey had the effrontery to dip his hands after the King had finished. The Duke, outraged at the presumption, "shed the water in his shoos." [2] Wolsey, in turn outraged, said in a burst of eloquence to the Duke that he would "sit upon his skirts." The next day Buckingham came to court without the skirts of his doublet, thinking thus to put a jest upon the Cardinal. When the King asked him why he appeared at court in a short coat without skirts, he replied that he was resolved to disappoint the malice of Wolsey.

Thus continued the prattle and peevish scuffling between England's haughtiest nobleman and proudest churchman. It is likely that the stories of the "fumes and displeasures" between the Duke and the Cardinal were exaggerated in retrospect, seeing what happened later and how people often reach back and put a bold interpretation on incidents that had not even been noted in the first place. But whether this antagonism had any relation to the event, nonetheless it came to pass that reports of rash and treasonable utterances by the Duke reached the sensitive ears of Henry, son of another Henry whose main concern had been the security of the throne. These reports now in the light of history appear signs of indiscretion rather than treason, but the King displayed toward them a close and attentive interest and, after examining those who bore the reports, gave grave credence to what he had heard. It was the King and not the Cardinal who closeted himself with the bearers of the news, and it was the King who sent letters to the Duke at his pleasant estate in the west of England, summoning him to come instantly to London.

The Duke's diary shows that he had no suspicion of the royal displeasure as he started toward London. He had for the past few months been puttering in his garden, and otherwise engaged in wholly domestic matters. He kept a faithful and careful account as he moved toward London of his expenditures along the way. It was like any other journey until he approached Windsor. Then he began to note that armed men were watching his movements. "They seemed to hover in the distance: at every winding of the road, as if to cut off all hope of escape, real or imaginary, they drew more closely upon him." [3] Still the Duke did not suspect, but toward Windsor some twenty miles from London, some of the men he had seen even went so far as to take up lodgings in the same hostelries as the Duke. This seemed an impertinence to the lofty nobleman and aroused his anger. The morning after he arrived at Windsor, as he was sitting down to breakfast, he noted a royal messenger loitering about and demanded what he did there. "The messenger replied that his office lay there, by the King's commandment." Then for the first time the Duke discovered that he was a prisoner. "The news fell on him with the abruptness of the headsman's axe. He turned ashy pale, the untasted morsel dropped from his lips, death was before him, escape was impossible." [4]

The indictment the Duke faced was based on the testimony of discontented servants. One, Robert Gilbert, "deposed that he had heard the duke say that my lord cardinal was an idolater, 'taking counsel of the spirit how he might continue to have the king's favor,' and that he had ministered to the king's vices . . . The duke had complained in Gilbert's hearing that he had done as good service as any man and was not rewarded, and that the king gave offices and fees to boys rather than to noblemen . . ." [5]

On May 13, 1521, Buckingham was brought into Westminster Hall to be tried. The Duke of Norfolk was the chief judge. As Buckingham was led into the Hall the axe of the Tower was carried before him. The indictment was read, and he vehemently pronounced it untrue and forged to bring him to death. He was allowed no counsel save his own eloquence, which weighed little against the testimony of the witnesses. Their depositions over, "the duke was allowed to retire to a house called Paradise, to consider his defense." [6] Later he was brought back to the bar, and the Duke of Norfolk, as chief judge, pronounced the sentence of death for treason: "To be drawn upon a hurdle to the place of execution, there to be hanged, cut down alive, your members to be cut off and cast into the fire, your bowels burnt before your eyes, your head smitten off, your body to be quartered and divided at the King's will, and God have mercy on your soul." Norfolk had demurred at reaching the verdict, and now his voice broke down and he wept as he pronounced the sentence upon an intimate friend and one of the great noblemen of his day.

When Norfolk had finished, Buckingham spoke: "My Lord of Norfolk, you have said unto me as a traitor, but I was never none; but my lords I nothing laigne for that you have done to me; the eternal God forgive you my death as I do; I shall never sue the king for life; however, he is a gracious prince, and more grace may come from him than I desire. I desire you, my lords, and all my fellows, to pray for me." [7] After he had spoken thus to his peers and judges, the axe of the Tower was turned significantly toward him to show the edge of death, and he was conducted from the Hall. As he passed through the city, there were great lamentations among the people that he should die, and in a comely manner the Duke with dignity asked that the common people pray for him. This made a great impression and added to the wonder of the populace that so upright a man should be sent to his death by his peers.

It was said that if he would but seek the royal mercy he might escape death, but Buckingham refused to pray to any but God and not to the King for mercy. He expressed no regret save for the manner in which he was to die, this being so far beneath the dignity of a duke that he marveled at it, and before his death, four days after his condemnation, the King relented and graciously consented that the Duke not have his bowels burnt before his eyes but that he be merely decapitated. So he was, on May 17, 1521, to the astonishment and sympathy of the people far and wide.

Catherine had entreated the King to spare the Duke, her oldest and closest friend in England. But Henry was in no mood to listen. The words laid to Buckingham that rankled him were that God would not suffer his issue to prosper. For now there appeared to be many signs that this was so. Not less than five children borne him by Catherine had died. Only one, a puny child born in 1516, five years before Buckingham was disposed of, now lived. And she was a girl, a girl named Mary, after Catherine's affection for the King's sister, the Queen Dowager of France. A girl. Henry of the House of Tudor and the hope of England — all that stood between stability and the chaos of a repetition of the Wars of the Roses — had no son. It would not do for any whisper in behalf of a rival to find its way to the ears of the people. Now was the time to assert, with all the eloquence of a swinging axe, that this Henry would brook no pretender.

The part that my lord Cardinal played in the proceedings against Buckingham was far from conspicuous. It was certain that he did not intercede with the King, for it was the King's interest that was at stake and in the cultivation of this interest Wolsey always showed himself blameless and sedulous. But the lesson of the sequence of events was plain for all to read. Buckingham had been an enemy of the Cardinal, had resented him, had spoken against him, had taunted and insulted him. This same Duke was now dead, and though he had been Lord High Constable of England, he was dead all the same, his goods attainted, and the very office which he had held abolished as a token of the obliteration of his line and memory.

So fully and anxiously had the Cardinal allied himself with the King and so subtly were the two identified that an attack upon one was now an attack upon the other. Or so it did appear: barbs thrust at Wolsey would seem to be arrows intended for His Majesty. It was a warning to the nobles. Not merely in functions had he, my lord of York, taken on the position of King and left the King free for pleasures. More insidiously, he had made the King's interests identical with his own, so that when one was offended, the interests of the other might be offended too.

It was said that the Cardinal had bewitched his royal master, that he exercised over Henry some power of necromancy and held devilish fellowship with the spirits to maintain it. That he had some strange hold over the King to be explained only in terms of his communication with evil spirits was a view that persisted long and found wide currency. As late as 1532 there is record that the supposition so ran. In that year a dabbler in the black art said that Sir William Neville had asked him if it were not possible "to have a ring made that should bring a man favour with his Prince; seeing my lord Cardinal had such a ring, that whatsoever he asked of the King's Grace, that he had." In another and earlier case a man sought to summon up a spirit, but the spirit refused to speak because "he was bound unto my lord Cardinal." [8]

There had been nothing like it seen in all the realm, this man who ruled the ruler and seemed to make him do his bidding. Earlier kings had had great advisers and men who at the council table or by whispers in the King's closet had doubtless swayed them, but in the case of Wolsey and Henry it appeared that the two were but parts of the same person.

The explanation need not have been sought in the world of spirits. There were evident grounds for the King's confidence — and many of them must have been plain to rational observers. Thomas Wolsey had no thought as minister but to serve his King, to fashion the realm to the King's liking, to make the King supreme, to keep the nobles in an enclosure where they could not dispute his prestige or threaten his succession with their quarrels. That was all. There was no mystery about it, for Wolsey's purpose ran like a thread as conspicuous as his Cardinal's robes through all he said and did. His decisions in the Court of the Star Chamber, subtly and elaborately reasoned and supported by learned garrulity, weighted justice on the side of the Crown and against the ever-present threat of the ascendancy of great families and aggregates of wealth.

In matters of policy Wolsey sought to determine but one point: what was the royal will? If this could be found, and finding it was not difficult, then the policy of the Lord Chancellor was fixed. By habit under the seventh Henry and by appointment under the eighth Henry, the man who had received part of his training as chaplain to the Archbishop of Canterbury plied a course that aimed to show that the King of England could run his country like a monarch and not merely be suffered by the nobles to reign. Wolsey was born to make a king see what he was fit for and capable of.

Nothing could distract Wolsey from the labors that must attend the onerous execution of the King's business — not even the mysterious return of the dread disease known as the sweating sickness two years after he became Lord Chancellor. This dire epidemic had fallen upon the people first in the autumn of 1485, soon after the battle of Bosworth. Nor was its return a coincidence. It had come into the country with Henry Tudor and his French mercenaries. Known among the French as the Picardy Sweat, it had long persisted on the Continent in mild and somnolent forms; but once loose in England, where there was no immunity to it, it had taken on a violent and virulent character. In its first visitation just before the coronation of Henry VII it had lasted only a month, but in that time it had boiled the blood of those afflicted and made the blood run cold among those who saw its effects. The sweating sickness fell upon victims with the suddenness of a beast of prey. One chronicler, Forrestier, a doctor of medicine and a native of Normandy who tarried for a while in London, said that many died while walking in the streets, without being confessed. Dr. Gaius, a physician of the day who recorded the devastation of the disease, wrote of the victims: "As it found them, so it took them; some in sleep, some in wake, some in mirth, some in care, some fasting and some full, some busy and some idle; and in one house, sometime three, sometime five; sometime all; of the which if the half in every town escaped, it was thought a great favor." [9]

So shattering were effects of the sweat that accounts of it doubtless took on some of the panic of the disease itself. It is hard to believe with Gaius that it "immediately killed some in opening their windows." But the exaggeration with which the disease is reported tells more than accurate statistics. There was a sly malevolence about the way in which it pointed the finger of God at the realm of the Henrys, for "it followed Englishmen as the shadow does the body" into other countries. In Calais and Antwerp "it generally singled out English residents and visitors, whilst the native population were unaffected." [10] It raged throughout the greater part of England, yet it stopped short of the Scottish border and it did not spread to Ireland. And to cap the mystery, it seemed always to pick out persons who were in the prime of health, and, unlike the bubonic plague, it attacked the favored classes and the well-to-do rather than the impoverished.

The masquerade of the evil was all the more complete because there were no carbuncles to mark the disease, no purple spots to taint the body. As Bacon puts it: "Only a malign vapor flew to the heart and seized the vital spirits; which stirred nature to strive to send it forth in an extreme sweat . . ." [11] The course of it lasted from a few hours to twenty-four. "The attack began acutely, with high fever, palpitation, rapid pulse, difficult breathing, and a sudden, copious general sweating; nausea was common, vomiting rare. In nearly all cases there was delirium followed by an uncontrollable desire for sleep. Gaius says the poison 'moves the mind with madness and oppresses it with heavy sleep.'" [12]

After the first visitation in 1485 the sweating sickness disappeared from England almost as rapidly as it had descended. Then it returned stealthily in 1506 after an absence of twenty-one years — an absence as inexplicable as its return. Again it made its grim appearance in April of 1516, more of a feint this time than an attack, when it appeared that it might pass over without its full choking effect. What violence it showed subsided with the approach of winter, this tendency to retreat from winter being one of the few reliable traits of behavior it showed. But that winter was severe. The weather itself seemed to bear malice to man. A drouth bleached the country, beginning in September and continuing through a winter of shattering cold. On January 12, 1517, a freeze came upon London so severe that the Thames was thick with ice; men and horses could cross it. Then as the spring of 1517 came to bring some hope back to life and the earth seemed habitable again, the sweat returned, this time with silent and creeping fury. "Houses and villages were deserted. Where the sickness once appeared, precaution was unavailing; and flight afforded the only chance of security." Nor could plans of flight always be carried out. Ammonius, the Latin secretary to the King, was dining one day with an acquaintance. "They had arranged to meet the next day and ride to Merton to escape the infection. The next morning, before his friend had time to get out of bed and dress himself, a messenger arrived to announce the death of Ammonius. He was carried off in eight hours." [13]

London as a city suffered the suspense born of horror. This time the sweat continued off and on through the spring and summer and into November. During the winter, when the drouth was broken at last, it abated, as its custom was, hiding from cold; but early in 1518 it resumed like a ghost men thought had been laid, and its apparition stalked the roads, and its vapors seeped through the walls of houses. "Not only business but amusements ceased in a great measure; crowds and places of public resort were carefully avoided; the noblemen broke up their establishments and every one in dread of the infection hastened, as best he could, to isolate himself from his neighbours . . . No lord, except during his necessary attendance at court, was suffered to keep servant or staff in his chamber . . . Fairs were put down; and at Oxford, so long as the court resided at Abingdon, orders were given by Sir Thomas More in the King's name that the inhabitants of infected houses should keep in, hang out wisps of straw, and carry white rods in the same way that the king had ordered the Londoners." [14]

In the midst of the consternation the King moved from place to place, alarmed at every rumor and report of a disease that did not deign to spare the elite. Who knew that it might spare a King? And to the King's concern was added that of Catherine, who was not only solicitous of the health of her young husband but now had the worry of the Princess Mary, a child of two and a half and the only issue of the royal pair. Yet even movement and dodging and hiding did not suffice, for the disease, as if to tease, invaded the transient palaces established by the King. The pages that slept in the very bedchamber of the King died of this insidious plague. Henry further stripped his establishment, ridding himself of all his servants save three trusted gentlemen.

With the King in flight and the court stripped of suitors and attendants, the government might well have been at a standstill save for one man, and that was my Lord Chancellor, the one official who remained stead-fastly at his task during all the depredations of the disease. The King's business could not wait, and the duties he had taken unto himself could not be stayed or suspended or neglected. The Court of the Star Chamber could not meet, for presses of men were forbidden lest the contagion spread. But day after day Wolsey wielded the Great Seal of England, now like a club, now like a wand, and carried forward the business of the kingdom, administering personally the details of government. It was as though he had made the occasion of the disease but another occasion of his unflagging loyalty and devotion to the King.

For this he was abundantly rewarded in the esteem of his royal master, for Henry during this period of madness, which threatened the succession as no war had, put himself on the record of history. He said that "he was no less contented with the Cardinal's contentation than though he had been his own father." Here was a tribute from a young king to his middle-aged minister that might in future centuries explain more than could be guessed at that time of the unshakable hold that the Lord Chancellor had upon Henry. In 1517 Henry was twenty-six, and Wolsey was forty-six. A difference in age might make less difference later — and none at all when the King felt the full sinews of his power. Now it did. With steady application the older man stuck to business in the presence of danger and left the younger one free to move as he might in the fond hope that he could flee the affliction of the sweat.

To the lords Henry said "that there was no man living who pondered more the surety of his person and the common wealth of his realm." And as if this did not serve sufficient notice upon the lords to show the Cardinal what full confidence the King reposed in him, Henry addressed to Wolsey the following letter in his own hand:

"Mine own good Cardinal, I recommend me unto you with all my heart, and thank you for the great pain and labour that you do daily take in my business and matters, desiring you that when you have well established them to take some pastime and comfort, to the intent you may the longer endure to serve us; for always pain can not be endured. Surely you have so substancially ordered our matters, both on this side the sea and beyond, that in mine oppinion little or no thing can be added . . ."

He continues in this vein, touches with approval on certain specific items of business, and adds: "The Queen my wife hath desired me to make most hearty recommendations to you, as to him that she loveth very well, and both she and I would feign know when you will repair to us." [15]

The King knew well the value of his Chancellor, and he might well have been concerned for his health. With all his fidelity and bravado, Wolsey did not escape the sweat. The first severe attack came in June of 1517, and it was so harsh that his life was despaired of — to the undisguised delight of those who had been "compelled to pay their just debts to the Crown and submit to the impartial administration of the laws." In July of the same year he suffered from quinsy, and in August he had the sweating sickness again. This time many of his household died. Giustiniani reports that the affliction told heavily upon his appearance.

After the second attack the Cardinal felt that it would be necessary to find some surcease for a season, and he proposed a pilgrimage to Walsingham, hoping at the shrine of Our Lady for some aid of the spirit that might forfend other attacks. But even here he stuck to business, and in the course of his journey he went on to Norwich, "and settled a dispute between the citizens and the monks over a piece of ground in that city." The next year he suffered again from the sweat. Meanwhile the royal solicitude continued, not only in prose but in paste, for Henry was a great amateur medicine man and full of royal home remedies. One of these, designed for the sweating sickness, was called *Monus Christi*, made in part of coral and a half pound of some unidentified preventive, probably flour. But neither the sweat nor the King's remedies could kill the Cardinal.

All the while, Henry and his court and Queen and the Princess Mary moved restlessly about. Wolsey, when he was well enough to attend to business, and often when he was not, gave a certain stability and order to government, but not enough. London suffered when the court was not there, and its lawless elements and its discontented apprentices stirred with mischief as the court moved from Richmond to Reading, from Reading to Abingdon, to Woodstock, or Wallingford or Farnham.

Discontent in London had a focal point — one for which the King himself was held responsible — and it was natural that trouble would occur while he was away. For it was whispered, and later openly said, that Henry had been of aid to foreigners. In 1516 a statement had been posted on the door of St. Paul's "reflecting on the King and his council." It insinuated that strangers obtained money from the King "and bought wools to the undoing of Englishmen." The King had made foreign loans in order that merchants might do business in England, and his whole policy, like that of his father, had been to encourage foreign trade. He had lent money to Florentine merchants in particular. These and other foreign merchants in turn used the money lent by the King to buy goods and wools in

England, often competing sharply with their better bargaining power against Englishmen.

The whigmaleeries and involvements of foreign trade were no less a mystery to the overworked apprentices and workers of London than they would be to future generations, and the gossip of the King's doings caused grumbling and growling. What Londoners saw in the atmosphere of gossip was a band of overprivileged and often oversexed foreigners who infested the city, had no fellowship with the citizens, and took every advantage of their position.

Even under pleasant and moderate circumstances the English did not like aliens. Froissart had written a hundred years earlier that the English felt that foreigners "were neither on a level with them nor worthy of their society." A visiting Italian, who in this period accompanied the Italian ambassador on his rounds, said: "They have an antipathy to foreigners and imagine that they never come into their island but to make themselves masters of it, and to usurp their goods." [16] The matter was complicated further by the fact that English kings tended to favor aliens, either for the encouragement of trade or alliances or through a broadened sense of the world by means of international marriages.

Not so the ordinary English of the streets. The Italian observer wrote: "The English are great lovers of themselves and of everything belonging to them; they think that there are no other men than themselves, and no other world but England, and whenever they see a handsome foreigner they say that 'he looks like an Englishman,' and that 'it is a great pity that he should not be an Englishman'; and when they partake of any delicacy with a foreigner they ask him whether such a thing is made in his country." [17]

All of these natural antipathies toward foreigners were now brought to a focus like the sun's rays caught in a magnifying glass. The sweat had demoralized the watch commonly kept over the city. Business was depressed, English artificers being out of work while foreigners continued to flaunt their wares and parade their privileges. Even when the sweat subsided, its return was always a threat, and the King had withdrawn his court and suspended most of the activities connected with it. Trouble crouched ready to spring.

In the Easter season of 1517 a preacher was found and briefed who would stand before the people, the sweat having abated for the moment, and plead the plight of the artificers. He would report that even in that very season of Lent there had been seen no less than six hundred strangers shooting at the popinjay with crossbows and enjoying other hilarities and pastimes of a frivolous nature while honest Londoners suffered from the invasion of competition. Perhaps through a sermon reciting the enormities of the time the mayor and aldermen might be aroused "to take part with the commonalty against the strangers."

The sermon had its calculated effect — not on the mayor and aldermen but on the populace, who were urged by the preacher to defend their country against hordes of aliens as birds might defend their nests. May Day was at hand, and a rumor spread that on that day the Londoners would rise up and slay all who were aliens. The court had withdrawn to Richmond, but Wolsey took every precaution. He called the mayor and the corporation together. "We are informed," he said to them, "that your young and riotous people will rise up and distress the strangers. Hear ye of no such thing!" The mayor assured my lord Cardinal that all would be well. But to make doubly sure, the Cardinal called upon the old Duke of Norfolk and his son the Earl of Surrey. They brought thirteen hundred men "in harness into the city . . . 'Then proclamations were made that no women should come together to babble and talk and all men should keep their wives in their houses. All the streets that were notable stood full of harnessed men, which spake many opprobrious words to the citizens, which grieved them sore.' "

The precautions merely tightened the tensions. In one ward an alderman found a crowd of apprentices watching two playing at bucklers. He ordered them to disperse and they refused. He then made the tactical blunder of taking one of the apprentices by the arm. This was the incident upon which the event had been waiting. "Instantly the cry of *Clubs! Prentices!* was raised; and in a moment the streets were thronged with a motley crowd of watermen, serving-men, and apprentices, swaying hither and thither, bent on mischief . . ." The plan of attack, ill-organized but definite, followed the sermon and the threat. On the night of April 30, the rioters sacked the houses of the Flemish and French artificers. Then they swept on to the Italian quarter, but there the foreigners had fortified themselves with arms and artillery, and, facing real opposition, the apprentices withdrew and moved on to indiscriminate attacks upon stray foreigners less well defended.

The situation was now out of hand, being much greater in its dimensions than the mayor and aldermen had supposed it would be, and these officials were themselves overpowered and compelled to open the jails and release the prisoners. Now the Cardinal's second line of defense went into action, and Norfolk and his son seized the offending preacher, twelve of the ringleaders of the riot, and some seventy other persons that could be handily taken. The Earl of Surrey laid rough hands on all offenders, and he and his retainers showed in word and gesture their contempt for these lowborn rebels. Some were ordered hanged, drawn, and quartered, but the severity of the punishment had not the desired effect or the one which the upholders of law and order had anticipated. Not merely the apprentices but also the entire city of London was aroused.

Public sentiment was such that the whole matter was taken and laid before the King at Greenwich, where a body of aldermen attended him, they being arrayed in black, to ask his mercy on the offenders. He declined their petition and referred them to his Chancellor, "without whose counsel he would do nothing," as Stow, one of the chroniclers, observed.

Eleven days of suspense followed, and then, in spite of the momentary threat of the return of the sweat, there was staged in London a scene which beggars both description and understanding. The denouement would suggest that either Henry or Wolsey or both had resolved to use the occasion to show the power of the Cardinal. At any rate, the King, attended by the lords spiritual and temporal and by the Council, came to London and with great ceremony took up his position on a lofty dais in Westminster Hall to hear the matter reviewed. Not only were the lords and the chief citizens there. The King had also at hand three Queens — Catherine his own; Mary the Dowager Queen of France, now Duchess of Suffolk; and his rampant sister Margaret, Queen of Scotland. "The king commanded that all the prisoners be brought forth. Then came the poor younglings and the old false knaves, bound in ropes, all along one after another, in their shirts, and every one with a halter about his neck, to the number of 400 men and eleven women." It was noted that good Queen Catherine, "with her hair loosened in the traditional gesture of a suppliant, knelt before the King for the lives of the young men whose riot had spilled the blood of her Spanish countrymen." The other two Queens, long on their knees before the King, begged pardon for the rioters. Henry showed no signs of relenting.

Then the Cardinal besought His Majesty to grant them amnesty. Henry still refused, and the Cardinal turned to the wretches and announced the King's decision. Thereupon there arose great lamentations from the ranks of the prisoners, and those who scarce three weeks before had gone hither and yon about the city on errands of mischief, and fiercely and bravely, now fell upon their quaking knees and cried "Mercy! Mercy!" This appeared to be, as if by pre-arranged and carefully staged clemency, the signal for the Cardinal to fall in turn upon his knees and to entreat the King's compassion. The mercy was slow in coming, but it came at last and brought such gladness and rejoicing to those who were about to die that, as one witness put it, "it was a fine sight to see each man take the halter from his neck, and fling it in the air; and how they jumped for joy, making such signs of rejoicing as became people who had escaped from extreme peril." [18]

Even so, the Cardinal did not let the prisoners go without a stern and stately schoolmaster lecture on the importance of good conduct, enjoining them in his best manner to be obedient subjects, "and not to oppose the will of their Prince, who had resolved that all strangers should be well treated in his dominions."

It was well that the King and the Cardinal had made a stentorian uproar showing at once displeasure toward the culprits and a measured leniency to restore peace. For the whole occurrence dismayed the hearts of Londoners. The foreigners had gained the better part of the bargain, being in the last analysis championed by both the King and his favorite. Matters were not improved in the public mind, either, by the sight of festering parts of mutilated bodies around the city after the first vindictive executions. An eyewitness reports: "At the city gates one sees nothing but gibbets and the quarters of these wretches, so that it is horrible to pass near them." And there was talk where men gathered, talk that did not reach the ears of the King or the Cardinal but did reach the ears of history, talk against the way Surrey and his men had behaved toward the citizens of London.

Five months later the rebellion swelled again. This time the aldermen and the mayor were alert and it was quickly stayed, this rising against the aliens, with three of the ringleaders brought to heel. Outwardly the King and the nobility had triumphed over the citizen. But occurrences of this sort are not to be measured or reckoned in immediate effects. The resentment which had shown itself in the Richard Hunne case, a resentment against special privileges accorded representatives of a foreign power, now showed itself again. England did not propose to be tied up by cords of Church or finance to a foreign world across the waters. She was by God independent, sufficient unto herself, and she would be free of foreign entanglements. England was for Englishmen. The portmen of Ipswich, as shown by their annals, were no less resolute than the citizens of London. The time had come when England would be free. Those who could read the meaningful, angry glances and hear and interpret properly the murmurs in the streets and alehouses could see this as plainly as if they had been handwriting on the wall.

As FOR my lord Cardinal, he was too busy to see or read anything but documents thrust under his nose in the urgent business of running the kingdom for Henry. Busyness was his answer to every problem created by an old world shedding its skin. The kingdom would get justice, and men rising in the world would enjoy the blessings of their improvement and adjust themselves to the new order if he personally attended to these matters. He appeared to have, over and beyond his childlike devotion to Henry, a pathological sense of personal responsibility and a belief as strong as forged iron that he could discharge that responsibility by doing the job of ten ministers rolled into one.

Which he was. If a job was important, he was the man to do it. He set about to change England from a kingdom ruled by lords and whims into an orderly state. In this respect he extended and intensified the work which Henry VII had commenced. But he gave it a sense of detail and permanence. The very fact that he was a minister and not a king indicated that change had come about. For a king, with his might and tyranny, to order this or that was one thing; for Wolsey under the King's approval to set up accounts, investigate prices, supervise the coinage, look to export licenses, regulate wages and prices, monitor the diet and dress of the people, devise graduated taxes — this was quite another. The lines of a state which would have continuity were beginning to form.

In his zest for regulation of his contemporaries my lord of York committed many excesses. But he did establish and demonstrate a principle: the conduct of large masses of people within a country could no longer be left to local custom and practice but must be determined by central authority. Whatever his intentions, Wolsey's administration as Lord Chancellor suggested, if it did not fully demonstrate, that a people can be managed by their government.

To the end that affairs might be comely and fitting within his country, he spared no detail, even in dealing with the King's own household. Things must be done in decency and in order. He was meticulous in handling accounts, and he convinced Henry that the King himself ought for his own good to keep a record of where the royal money went. As a result, Henry's Privy Purse Expenses carry a record of his gambling losses and of the lavish gifts he made, including a black satin nightgown given to a favorite.[1] The King should be no less accountable in his handling of public funds. He was no longer above observation by virtue of his position.

Records were essential to supervision, and the extension of supervision was at all times Wolsey's aim. The treasury of the King's household was known as the chamber, and to this treasury funds for the King's use were withdrawn from the national exchequer. In 1515 payments made by the chamber amounted to £74,006. In 1518 and 1519 they had dropped to £50,000 a year. There were still leaks, and Wolsey complained of "the way the king's money goes out in every corner." Many items to ministers ordered by the King merely carried the explanation, "the king's business." In 1522 Wolsey proposed an extensive reform of the whole system of handling the accounts of the chamber and a systematic audit of the chamber accounts every quarter. One set of books was to be submitted to the King, while the other was to be kept in the chamber for reference and for auditing — to be available for inspection at all times. Wolsey's idea, says Richardson, "was to introduce the same regularity in chamber audit as in other departments of finance."[2]

Nothing around the court seems to have escaped Wolsey's eye. In 1526, "for the better avoiding of corruption and all uncleanness out of the King's house, which doth engender danger of infection, and is very noisome and displeasant unto all the noblemen and all the others repairing unto the same," it was ordained that "the three master cooks of the kitchen shall have every one of them by way of reward yearly twenty marks, to the intent that they shall provide and sufficiently furnish the said kitchens of such scullions as shall not go naked or in garments of such vileness as they now do, and have been accustomed to do, nor lie in the nights or days in the kitchens or ground by the fireside; but that they may be found with honest and whole coarse garments, without such uncleanness as may be the annoyance of those by whom they shall pass."[3]

All who were entrusted with the receipt of revenue were brought under strict audit. In this reform Wolsey gave offense to many, and it might be said that those he did not outrage in his decisions as a judge he humiliated in his demands as the King's minister of finance. One who felt the lash of these demands was the Duke of Suffolk, he whom Wolsey had befriended and defended when he married without permission the King's sister while she was Dowager Queen of France and yet on French soil. Suffolk owed the King heavily — and not merely in the continued payment of the moneys Henry had demanded of him upon his return with Mary to England; he also held certain public funds. These he could not pay, and he had to retire from court and lead a frugal existence until he could accumulate enough to cover his debt. By way of thanks Suffolk became a lasting enemy of the Cardinal. But nothing concerned Wolsey in the flush of his administrative efficiency but the orderly conduct of the King's affairs. The kingdom alone mattered. Let incidents fall where they might; his purpose was to bind the nation to its King with hoops of regulation.

These hoops were not in themselves sufficient. But they were the means by which the government began to pull the discordant elements of the kingdom together. Wolsey's steady and relentless insistence upon regulation and responsibility, while it was often misguided, established gradually the consciousness of nationhood. That consciousness was still dim when he came to power. Men were primarily loyal to their class or their locality, not to their country. Their loyalty lay naturally to what was close at hand. It was not that they were disloyal to the King either as a person or as a symbol of the larger weal; there was simply nothing in the range of their experience to encompass the land of England as a whole, save at times of crisis. A king in silken robes in far-off London who was still a laughing matter among the men of the border; the intense local loyalty which in the days of Wolsey's childhood could regard his father as an "alien" because he came from a village ten miles away — these attitudes showed what men felt and how limited was their sight. The State was an abstraction just beginning to emerge in men's minds, and it certainly had not yet the power to evoke strong emotion. To the King some feasible loyalty had in theory already been shown, so that the enlargement of the concept of the King was the easy and natural way of developing the lines of what was to become the State.

The State was still a person, and how much of current thought was draped around the State as a person may be seen from the publication of Niccolò Machiavelli's political cookbook, *The Prince*. This book was finished in 1513, and there is no evidence that Wolsey ever read it — or any analytical book, for that matter. He was first and last and day and night an administrator. But there is much in *The Prince* that adumbrated the work of Wolsey as Lord Chancellor of England. The book and the Cardinal were both part of the same drive to make a great body of people behave according to the will of those who were set to preside over them. Men were virtuous or lacked virtue as they contributed to the power of their Prince, emblem of government. Men were therefore viewed as political beings rather than as human creatures with inherent rights.

Equity and justice must prevail because these contributed to the wealth of the whole land. What Machiavelli wrote, Wolsey practiced. The aim and design of the ne'er-do-well of Florence and the pride of Ipswich were akin: to show how a whole country might be given cohesion and solidarity through an allegiance that transcended local obligations.

Wolsey the pragmatist, the man of deeds, was in a position to act out his ideas. His work lay in straight line with, and in continuity with, the startling attempts toward centralized government undertaken by Henry Tudor right after the battle of Bosworth. *Thomas Wolsey was in a sense the real Henry VIII, and the man who swaggers through history under that title was in effect Henry IX,* a king whose performance was made possible by the work of Wolsey, just as Wolsey's work had been prepared for and outlined by the seventh Henry. A valid judgment of Wolsey, or even a partial understanding of him, can be reached only through a due regard for the sequence of events and pageant of persons in his own day. In methods and intentions he stood in direct succession to Henry Tudor. Wolsey was the man who put the principles of control formulated and announced by Henry Tudor into telling effect, and a good deal of the support and confidence shown in him by the eighth Henry was due to the fact that Wolsey as Lord Chancellor carried forward ably and vigorously the work of the eighth Henry's father. By all the tokens of coronation and ceremony, the young Henry came to the throne on the death of his father. But in Thomas Wolsey, a man in the full vigor of maturity and twenty years older than Henry, the father-king lived on in the royal household until Henry, ever watchful and ever learning, saw that he could succeed the Cardinal-father.

Henry began his reign with an assembly of advisers called a Council, but it had no special form, and when Wolsey became Lord Chancellor it had no form at all. Affairs were delegated to an executive committee consisting of the Chancellor, of course, the Treasurer, and the Lord Privy Seal. The Treasurer was the Duke of Norfolk, who was content to look to the mending of his family fortunes and interfered very little with the business of the kingdom. The Lord Privy Seal was Ruthal, whose character was attested by his contemporaries in the statement that he sang treble to Wolsey's bass. Not until 1526, when it began to be clear that the days of the Cardinal might be numbered and the King might at last come of age, was a true Council formed. In that year Henry chose twenty councilors to attend his royal person. Of these, ten were to "give continual attendance in the causes of his said council, unto what place so ever his highness shall resort." [4] But even then the Council existed chiefly in proclamation form, its very existence still tenuous, and Wolsey managed to stave off the formation of a real Council for another few years. He was all the King needed.

Turn any corner in the maze of administration and there you would find the busy body of the Cardinal. All ministers incarnate, Wolsey subdivided himself for special tasks requiring special skills. His labors included even the admiralty. There he regulated the wages of seamen and investigated those paid to servitors on the King's ships. In 1526 a warrant was issued to Wolsey (and doubtless by Wolsey) authorizing him to supervise coinage. He was given full powers, and he acted on the advice not of members of the Council but of a committee of goldsmiths. The aim was to reduce the value of English money to the standard of foreign coins, since it was said that, "owing to the enhancement of value abroad, money was carried out of this realm by secret means."

Once he had his commission, he was not able to stop at ordering a new standard of twenty-two carats fine gold alloyed with two carats sterling silver (known as Crown gold). Rather he went on to imprint his Cardinal's hat under the King's arms on the coin known as a groat. This act gave great offense to those who were his enemies anyway, the groat being regarded as the King's special coin. He had transcended fitness, and while some signs of his arrogance might be considered transient, in this case he had stamped his excess permanently in metal. An archbishop's prerogative would allow his emblem to appear on a half-groat; but Wolsey had to do something better than custom allowed, and again and insidiously he now ranked himself co-equal with the King.

And why not? No problem, however complex, caused him more than executive hesitation. Before he had received the King's warrant and permission to reform the coinage, he had sent commissioners to the Low Countries "to require that all monies valued too highly should be reduced to a real rate." [5] He was not versed in economic theory any more than he was trained in law, either common or canon; but as he did not balk at sitting as the chief judge of the realm, so he did not think it unfitting that he should unravel the skein of trade.

Yet as his problems multiplied and their complexity increased and the interests of the kingdom grew more intersticed and gnarled, even Wolsey had to admit that he could not do it all. He would undertake any task unabashed, but he was compelled gradually to delegate parts of its performance and content himself with the role of supervisor. And while it was true that he started much that he did not finish — much that was not finished for generations — still he did have the initiative to pose a question and get it on the conscience of the kingdom. He made the people aware of difficulties he did not meet or solve. The very delegations and commissions which were named to carry out his purpose began to form the shoots of a government that was to grow and spread like ivy.

Jealous and disdainful though he was of any mind but his own if it threatened to be the equal of his own, he issued commissions right and left as his tasks increased. Some of these were to deal for him with passing matters; some with issues that affected the whole of the society of the day. And every time a commission was issued and a body of men went to work, it meant that through the tyrant's interest further interest was being stirred and men were gradually being trained in the practice of government. A commission of inquiry meant that at least a small body of men heard and entertained complaints and that those they touched by the inquiry began to have some idea on a scale larger than local that government was responsible for man's good.

Consider the attack my lord Cardinal made upon the growing practice of enclosing large bodies of arable land within hedges for purposes of sheep farming. This attack ran its course from sturdy initiative to ultimate failure. The situation could not be met by decree, and the King's wish was as a whim before the forces making for enclosure. Yet the vigor with which Wolsey faced the threat and the interest he stirred up over it asserted beyond doubt the fact that the central government in London would not look with equanimity upon the aggrandizement of lords and wealthy landowners. In his attempt to handle the practice he made a magnificent gesture toward government.

The hedging of land for pasture carried with it insults and grievances that touched every part of the population. Even London was outraged by the enclosure of land north of the city. In 1514 hedges and ditches had been erected where men were used to walking and hunting. The practice reached a point, says Grafton, where "neither the younge men of the city might shoot, nor the ancient persons might walk for their pleasure in the fields." [6] With urban indignation that open spaces nearby had not been left intact, Londoners murmured and prepared. One Sunday a mass of people assembled in the city, and a turner attired in a fool's coat ran among them crying, "Shovels and spades!" It was the signal for the attack on the offending hedges. People from the city swept beyond the walls, armed with implements to fill ditches and cut hedges. When the people returned to the city at night, they had left the fields open.

Elsewhere the rebellion was not as forthright. Among those dispossessed and thrown on the roads to become drifters and beggars, grievances festered. And the sad effects were plain on every hand. "Where forty men had their livings, now one man and his shepherd hath all." [7] So the lament ran. There was something merciless and unrelenting about the encroachments of the sheepmen. A picture of the process which had been insidiously at work for almost a hundred years is given by Barnard: "The arable land of England was mostly 'open field,' a mass of strips, scattered among various holders, each strip separated off by nothing but a balk of unploughed ground." [8]

Agitation had reached formidable heights when Parliament met in 1489 and two acts were passed with the hope and design that the enclosure of land would come to an end. The acts proved to be hardly more than expressions of social piety. Enforcement grew lax at best, largely because the men who were to carry out the orders of the authorities, when authorities existed, were themselves involved in the malevolence of enclosures. Thus the movement toward the hedging of more and more tillable land crept on and on. The sheepmen were like a band of grazing sheep, moving restlessly forward, ever moving.

When Henry VIII reached the throne, the threat had again thrown the country into turmoil. Great were the grievances laid before the King. Henry had issued in 1514 a proclamation against the "engrossers" of farms, "forbidding them to hold more farms than one and ordering that all the houses of husbandry decayed since his father's reign should be once more 'put to tillage' . . ." [9]

Enclosing went on as before. Henry might be King and a King might be worth fighting for or fighting over. But he had not the will to prevent the spread of sheep when the prices paid for the fleece they bore was good and men could fashion cloth and draw good wages from the business of harvesting it. Wool was everywhere, and most of all it was in men's minds and pockets.

Since the King's will did not suffice, Parliament was invoked in the cause. The Parliament of 1515 was persuaded to pass an act "directing the restoration to tillage of land enclosed since 1485." [10] But it neglected to authorize any means of carrying out the law. The letter of the law became a dead letter almost before it was scrawled on the statute books. The agents who under normal procedure would put it into effect were the justices of the peace, and these were often engaged in the rich profits of enclosing remnants of land. Also the law was so constructed that in many particulars it invited evasion. For example, it was enacted that no man could own more than two thousand sheep, but each member of a family, and even servants, might in theory and did in fact own that number of sheep. The destruction of farm buildings was forbidden; but the statute might be satisfied if a man kept a single room for the shepherd or the milkmaid. "A solitary furrow driven across newly laid pasture satisfied the law that it should be restored to tillage." [11] And if these tactics failed to comply with the requirements in the light of the justice who administered the law, exemptions might be purchased or breaches might be satisfied by light fines.

It was in this disheveled state of affairs that my lord Cardinal decided to intervene. He made a national campaign to defend the farmer, to hold the line against the invasion of great landlords and barons upon the small holdings of men who tilled the soil. What he did amounted to an attack by the national government upon a grievous social problem that could not be attacked piecemeal. The act of 1515 had been left to local administration. Wolsey stepped in now to make the matter a concern of the King. And the method by which he proposed to enforce the laws was characteristically vigorous, and it followed the pattern of his procedures in the Court of the Star Chamber: he would invoke and use the authority of the King instead of the authority of local justices of the peace.

The first step was to appoint on May 28, 1517, a commission of inquiry into all enclosures of land made since 1485. The commission was armed with more than rhetoric. It was directed to bring those who offended before the King and his Council in theory and before my lord Cardinal in fact. The Council was to have coercive power to enforce the decisions of the commission. This was a move strongly resented by those who troubled their minds over the delicacies of law and justice. But it was in this case effective, for the national government stepped in where the local government had failed or had proved itself too flexible. The next year Wolsey issued a decree ordering the destruction of all enclosures that had been made contrary to statutes. The Crown instituted proceedings against even great offenders, including some of Wolsey's friends, among them Bishop Fox, who had so lavishly commended him as a fair-haired boy to Henry VII.

In this and all other questions that had to do with a sense of wholeness in the kingdom Wolsey used authority to the discomfort of friend or foe. Spare the rod and spoil the nation.

CHAPTER IX

ONE whose soul was less feverish and tumultuous than Wolsey's might have been content to reign over the realm in the name of the King. But there was another kingdom in England: the kingdom of the Church, a transcendent realm with borders beyond England's shores, a superstructure of conscience to which kings and emperors made obeisance.

Of this vast state of the mind, this vision of spirit made flesh and mortar, Thomas Wolsey showed at all times and in all respects a guiding awareness. From the moment he stepped across the threshold from obscurity into power, the Church engaged his faculties and his concern. Not only did it serve as a vehicle of his progress; it proved also the magnet that drew into some focus and order the wild diversity of his thoughts and policies. Wolsey resided in Rome, although he never so much as visited the Eternal City. In the Church was some *mystique* which could never be fully comprehended and must never be ignored. The Church was shadow and substance combined; it gave architecture to a dream.

Consequently, Wolsey could not be satisfied merely with secular assignments. Once he became Lord Chancellor he set about restlessly to become also head of the Church in England, to gather unto himself the weapons of power in religion. And once he had made himself the chief churchman of England, superior in station to the Archbishop of Canterbury, he sought the papacy itself. In the midst of all his manipulations and circumlocutions one can get an occasional glimpse of an inward conscience. In all his petitions for power his avowed aim — however poorly carried out — was to reform the Church in the presence of its enemies. For such a task he firmly needed full papal authority, and it was for such a task that he sought the steady increase of his powers. As Archbishop of York, Wolsey was Primate of England. But as Archbishop of Canterbury, Warham was Primate of *All* England.

There was a mountain of difference in that one word. It is true that, as Cardinal, Wolsey trailed additional clouds of glory. The office of cardinal, however, gave him dignity rather than power. It signified hardly more than an umbilical connection with Rome. Considering the distance from Rome and his busy inability to take any part in the deliberations of the

Roman consistory, Wolsey was not a functioning Cardinal. He was Cardinal in name only, enjoying a deferential form of address made compulsory by tradition. Being Cardinal did not add one ounce of strength to his episcopal muscles. He was not, for all his flowing robes and sacred hat and costly ring and poetic title of St. Cecilia Beyond the Tiber, head of the Church in England.

Indeed the Archbishop of York was a country cousin within the Church. He had under his surveillance and jurisdiction only three dioceses which seemed remote from London, and the seat of the see was detached and far from London too. Various invidious details conspired to point up the difference between Canterbury and York and to keep the Archbishop of York in his place. Among these was the location of the residences of the two. The Archbishop of Canterbury resided at Lambeth Palace, hard by Westminster and the court and the King. He was near a teeming mass of perhaps five thousand people clustered around the court and the noble Abbey of the Benedictines at Westminster, a busy and thronging place. But York Palace, where the Archbishop of York officially resided when he came to London, was far down the river at Battersea. Such details were clear and significant to those who knew the hierarchy of the Church, and my lord Cardinal knew the facts perhaps better than anyone.

It was essential to my lord of York's avowed purpose of energetically reforming the Church that he make himself loftier in station than the Archbishop of Canterbury. With this aim in view he did two things. First, he built a better house in a more desirable location. He abandoned the decrepit and distant York Palace in Battersea and, with all his architectural talents, commenced a handsomely appointed abode near the King's palace at Westminster. The new house was not only more convenient; it was closer to the court than Lambeth Palace, and it was on the right side of the river. It was a palace fit for a king, but Wolsey modestly called it York Place in honor of his see and in the spirit of the kind of humility that made a Cardinal ride a mule. He had the right in building it to impress craftsmen, and in July of 1515 he spent as a matter of record fourpence "for ale given to the plumbers and others." [1] The house, when it was finished, contained vast libraries and picture galleries; its walls were hung with cloth of gold, and the tables were covered with "velvets, satins, damasks of various hues." [2]

Then, having assured himself that in the appointments of his living he would not, though only York, be outdone by Canterbury, he directed his efforts toward persuading the Pope to making him legate *a latere*. Only with the powers of a full legate would Wolsey have the right to accomplish the reformation of the English Church. And this reformation must be accomplished. The bitter and disquieting experience of the Richard Hunne case had sounded a new and ominous note in criticism: the Church might become subject to reform by outside forces, by government, by worldly legislators. The matter on which the Church stood most firm was the right to regulate its own affairs. Yet the state of the Church was such that it would invite increasing outside meddling and lay interference. Reform was in the air and in the minds of men. Strategically, the Church must order its house and its affairs in such a way that it would forfend parliamentary action.

Ample precedent existed to show that churchmen could offer sharp and improving criticism of the Church. Innocent VIII in 1489 had sent a bull to Cardinal Morton, then Archbishop of Canterbury, directing him "to admonish all abbots and priors in his province to reform themselves and those under them, with the threat of excommunication should they refuse to obey." [3] The Pope had heard that monks in some of the monasteries were leading dissolute and lascivious lives. Morton had charged the Abbot of the Abbey of St. Albans with having "laid aside the pleasant yoke of contemplation and all regular observances, alms, and other offices of piety." He accused the Abbot of having appointed as prioress of a neighboring and dependent nunnery "a woman who had already married, and who lived in adultery with the monks . . ." The brethren of the Abbey, Morton further charged, "live with harlots and mistresses publicly and continuously within the precincts of the monastery." [4] Conditions revealed at the priory of Norwich about this time were hardly better. These censures and disclosures had been pronounced by the Primate of All England a quarter of a century before Wolsey sought legatine powers to put the Church in order.

Morton had been as unsparing of the priests as of the monks. He had seen fit to forbid their having swords or daggers, or gold purses or other ornaments of gold, or wearing their hair in such a way as to conceal their tonsure. And above and beyond these strictures on what might have been considered details in which latitude could be allowed, he had remarked upon and reprobated the practice of clergymen failing to live in the benefices they held.

Here Morton had touched a nerve that was still exposed. Throughout the realm parish churches might be served by ignorant stipendiaries who mumbled Masses at stated intervals, little understanding the Latin they used and having no close or real interest in the people who came to the services. The parson who held the benefice, meanwhile, appropriated most of the income from the parish while he lolled in a university or traveled around Italy.

This situation, besides giving rise to an irresponsible body of clergy without stated functions or local roots, lent resonance to the voices of still other critics within the Church. These were the friars, who moved from village to village, preaching and bearing tidings of the outside world to persons who often never left the place where they had been born. Unlike the monks, who stayed customarily within their stately buildings and devoted themselves to piety, the friars identified religious zeal with evangelism. "In theory," Trevelyan says, "the friars . . . lived by begging alms, had no property of their own and preached the doctrine of evangelical poverty so dear to St. Francis. In practise they had now amassed wealth and treasure which they stored in their magnificent convents." [5] But their theory gave them latitude of utterance, and they were among those who protested the sloth of the clergy and the monks.

Notwithstanding the bulls of popes and the monitory letters of prelates, the Church had not substantially changed. While Wolsey had his agents busy in Rome seeking added powers for him, the Bishop of Ely visited a monastery in his diocese and found such disorder that he declared continuance of the monastery "would have been impossible but for his visitation." At Norwich Priory matters seemed worse. "Suspicious women were about, and there was dancing in the great hall by night. Sheep fed within the cloister, the brethren were neglected, there was no schoolmaster, and the number of monks had fallen short by ten." [6]

Apart from confidence born of conceit, my lord of York had small reason to suppose that he could succeed where other agents of the Pope had failed. His ambition was projected far beyond the practical, even beyond the bound of the possible. For all his eloquence, Wolsey often seemed to think in acts rather than words. He left no recorded plan of precisely how he hoped to go about the total job of reform; one step at a time was enough. It looked as if he had staked out a task of such dimensions that failure would be inevitable and yet magnificent in its very scope. He may have unconsciously courted failure, not the failure of inaction but of effort on a scale so extensive that men must admire his audacity in trying at all.

He faced a formidable array of obstructionists. The monastic establishments, for example, had numbers, wealth, and power. There were over seven hundred of them in England, and their wealth in terms of land showed that they had many ties and means of resistance in all parts of the kingdom. In Gloucestershire alone there were ninety monasteries, and they held an average of sixty-five thousand acres of land apiece. One had to reckon also with politics and the power of the abbots, for twenty-seven of the heads of great religious houses had seats as lords spiritual in Parliament. "The bishops could not control the monks, whose vows bound them to allegiance to their superiors, generally foreigners. They were directly connected with the Papacy, and the monastic orders came to be spoken of as the Pope's standing army . . ." [7]

The head of a monastery, usually an abbot but in some cases a prior, "was not only absolute ruler within his own domain, but also a person of great social weight outside it. He often had a house apart from the monks and a large staff of servants of his own." [8] In a day when dignity was advertised if not created by a conspicuous withdrawal from the common herd, the abbots set a haughty standard that left no doubt of their power. When the Abbot of St. Albans dined, it was in lordly state. "His table was raised fifteen steps above the rest of the hall, and in serving him the monks performed a hymn at every fifth step. He sat alone in the middle of his table, and when he received any guests of a very high rank they were only admitted to sit at the ends." How seriously would a prince of the Church with such a demeanor and notion of his own importance take the admonitions of a mere Archbishop of York, though he be a Cardinal?

While His Holiness delayed granting Wolsey the legateship, events kept their trend toward convulsive action. The ghost of Richard Hunne had not been laid; it still stalked in the recesses of controversy. The questions it posed had not been resolved but merely silenced for the moment, to be taken up again like an old quarrel. The threat which a man in Wolsey's position could easily detect was that criticism, now an antiphony in the Church and in the Commons, might unite in a deafening chorus of protest.

Reform had become a bone of contention beyond the Church, and it might at any moment become the chief business of those whose business it was not. Rebellion against ecclesiastical authority had slumbered through more than a hundred years of English life. Once before, the hostility had showed itself in Parliament, and only the timely and furious intervention of the King — in this case Richard II, called back from the bogs of Ireland by the alarmed bishops — had prevented the undermining by Parliament of the whole structure of the Church.

That earlier tempest of 1395 had been brewed by the Lollards, a name of derision bestowed upon the followers of John Wycliffe, denoting them as mutterers. Wycliffe himself was no mutterer. He was a man of strong views and trenchant utterance, and he advocated, among other preposterous reforms, the distribution of Church property among poor laymen. His disciples went about the country as Poor Priests, strenuously preaching his views of disendowment. Being of good demeanor and not ranting against lay property, the Lollards made friends among the gentry. In due course they had friends at court, and some of the members of the King's Council were loyal Lollards. It was these well-placed Lollards who sought in 1395 to lay the views of their co-religionists before Parliament.

At the time, King Richard was off on a long and bootless effort to tame the savage Irish with English swords. In his absence the Lollards of the Council wrote out in detail their beliefs, including an attack on "the riches and secular employments of the clergy." Their beliefs, eloquently stated, were not only presented to Parliament but, for good measure, nailed to the door of St. Paul's where the ordinary citizens of London might see and read.[9]

When Richard heard these tidings, he returned to London in haste, "vowing to hang all Lollards." Because of the prompt action of the King, the attempt to give heretical views respectability in Parliament had failed. And the repression was effective. Yet the memory of the views and of the day they had at court lingered on.

English memory lent urgency, then, to the petitions Wolsey presented to the Pope for the authority to institute reform. Both experience and perception showed that resentment might at any time break out like a fire in some unexpected quarter. It might be set off by a trifle, as news of occurrences in Germany at this time plainly told. There Martin Luther, a young friar attached to the monastery of the Augustinian Hermits at Wittenberg, had chosen to protest the sale of indulgences. Men of scratchy conscience had long objected to indulgences sold like wool in the marts of trade, but the practice of raising funds for an estimable cause by the sale of pardons did not stand at the top of abuses for which the Church had been criticized. And the commotion caused by the friar's protest seemed out of all proportion to the seriousness of the abuse criticized. For this reason the news from Germany was all the more instructive and merited observation and study. If an obscure and callow friar, with no status save that bestowed by his own eloquence, could write ninety-five defiant reasons for condemning a practice sanctioned by His Holiness, almost any insubordination might win popular support. Particularly was this so if the reasons were accepted with muttered approval by the laity.

It was as if the sound and fury had come back as an echo from events in England. In the whole affair were many elements spotted throughout English history.

The abuses which pinched the conscience of Luther were present in all countries where the Church held sway, and they were abundantly present in England. Occasionally a civic use was made of indulgences, by means of which Church authorities would remit penalties in exchange for work done to improve the community. In one case an archbishop granted a hundred days' pardon to all those "who contributed to the repair and to the building of new bridges at Oxnede." [10] Registers "abound with the details of indulgences granted for the repair or upkeep of bridges and bridge chapels." In many other cases, however, the sale of indulgences was put to less worthy use. An indulgence might reduce the severity of a punishment, and in some cases the punishments were "of long duration; fasting and mortification had to be carried on for months and years." Thus a sinner might for a consideration "exchange a year of penance against three hundred lashes, reciting a psalm at each hundred. Tables of such exchanges were drawn up by competent prelates." [11] Into this complex system pardoners stepped with offers of indulgences which might commute the punishment of the Church authorities when the Pardoner arrived "with his wallet 'bretful of pardons come from Rome all hot.'" [12] Exchanging penance for a money fee blunted the lingering moral perceptions of sinners. Chaucer told of the Summoner, sent to summon delinquents to Church courts, who would, according to Abram, "overlook an offense for a year for a quart of wine, and would warn 'a good felawe' not to fear the Archdeacon's curse, for he would be punished only in his purse." [13]

Ideas from the Continent were beginning to permeate England, and there was an audience not only for the fulminations of Luther but for other much less respectable outcries against the Church. There came to be circulated in England about this time a gross satire on the monks under the title of *Epistolae obscurorum virorum.* Its reception could not be accounted for by its worth or style, and the satisfaction which its vulgarity afforded the intellectuals who devoured it showed how sentiment drifted. "It is read everywhere," wrote Thomas More to Erasmus. [14]

Even if hostility toward the Church did not assume the proportions of a national revolt, it was still there to be reckoned with and guarded against as a threat of local violence. Thirty years before Wolsey set out on his tenuous program of reform, the clergy in Convocation had addressed to the throne a petition "complaining that churchmen were cruelly, grievously, and daily troubled, vexed, indicted and arrested; drawn out of church, and without due reverence, even from the altar, by malicious and evil-disposed persons, notwithstanding all the censures, anathematizations and curses, yearly promulgated and fulmined by the holy father the pope, and in all the churches of England; so that they could not be resident on their benefices, to execute duly and devoutly their office . . ." [15]

Gairdner points out the contempt which lay law officials had for the sanctuaries. Arrests were sometimes made by bailiffs in church, "leading to unseemly profanation of the House of God, and scuffles interrupted the parson even while he was saying mass." [16] The Pope cried out against these sacrileges, but the clergy were continually "drawn before secular judges and punished without ecclesiastical authority."

For three years Pope Leo resisted and evaded the importunities of Wolsey for the legateship. Nor is there any indication that he would ever have granted this barbarian Cardinal his request if events had not conveniently arranged themselves so that Wolsey was able to extort the appointment.

It chanced that in the same year that Martin Luther posted his Theses, Leo wrote to Warham as the Primate of All England to say that he planned shortly to send into the realm a legate of the Holy See for the purpose of raising funds to carry on an expedition against the Turks, who were moving closer and closer to the heart of Europe. It would be the purpose of this legate to aid in promoting a five-year truce among the princes of Europe, so that full Christian energy might be expended on the repulse. The letter went unanswered for months, being as studiously and conspicuously neglected as had been Wolsey's efforts to obtain the legateship. In Rome this neglect of the Pope's letter, especially seeing that the letter pertained to so important a matter as the union of Christendom and the protection of the civilized world against the inroads of Muslim hordes, occasioned great annoyance and astonishment. The English agent in Rome reported to England that the Pope "asked him ten times a day" when he might expect a reply.[17]

At last, although he had received no reply, the Pope announced that he was sending on his stated mission Cardinal Lorenzo Campeggio. This Cardinal had served the Holy Father well in other capacities, and he had been created Cardinal the year before. Campeggio set out for England, toward which place he came by slow stages, and finally reached Calais, where he sought admission into Henry's kingdom.

The admission was not granted, but at this time Wolsey, after consulting with his King, sent to Leo the reply so impatiently awaited. It was not the reply Leo expected to a routine request for assistance in the most noble of all causes. It stated imperiously that it was not customary in England "to admit any foreign cardinal to exercise legatine powers in the country." Still, the King was willing to release Campeggio from his detention at Calais and admit him on his mission provided the Cardinal of York be associated with him in the legatine commission and have equal legatine faculties. The dispatch concluded with the astonishing condition that if the Pope did not grant this concession "the King will in no wise allow Campeggio to enter England." [18]

The Pope had no choice but to bow to English stubbornness. It was in this wise, and with the known contrivance of the King, that Wolsey gained the legateship. Campeggio got the royal assent to cross to England. Once admitted, however, he was shown high deference, it being necessary for Wolsey to demonstrate the honors due a legate *a latere*. Hall in his *Chronicle* relates that Wolsey went to great lengths to help equip Campeggio with the splendor becoming his rank and mission. He says that the night before Campeggio entered London Wolsey sent him twelve mules bearing empty coffers trapped with scarlet; "and thus the cavalcade, with eight others belonging to the Legate, passed through the streets as if they had carried so much treasure." In Cheapside, however, "one of the mules turned restive, and upset the chests, out of which tumbled old hose, broken shoes, bread, meat, and eggs, with 'much vile baggage' at which the boys exclaimed, 'See, my lord Legate's treasure!'" Brewer considers the story more malicious than probable; but in any event Wolsey saw to it that Campeggio was lavishly treated and scrupulously honored on his way from Dover to London, that he was accompanied by a cavalcade of five hundred horse and received and dined along the way by the nobility of Church and State.[19]

Having established the importance of Campeggio as a legate, Wolsey next subordinated him and put himself forward in all their dealings, insisting that only his own cross should be borne before them. At their public reception Campeggio was given a seat raised three steps above the floor; but the seat on which my lord of York placed his own ample legatine frame was double that height.

With the legatine commission granted, Wolsey used Campeggio's presence in England to reinforce his demands on the Pope for powers of reform. He sought and secured a bull that empowered both of them to conduct visitations of the monasteries. But Campeggio had no stomach for a longer stay in England, and in March 1519 Wolsey asked that he alone be allowed to conduct the visitations, seeing that Campeggio would return to Rome. He asked at the same time for increased powers, "that I may be able to accomplish some good in the Lord's vineyard and be profitable to all christendom." [20] The powers to reform the monasteries after Campeggio left were granted by the Pope in due course. And at once Wolsey began beseeching the Pope to grant the legateship for life.

What Wolsey sought had at last come to pass, and the result left him with untrammeled power. "In the hand of one man," as Gasquet puts it, "were grasped the two swords of Church and State. One mind directed the policy of secular and ecclesiastical administration in England. Had that man been a saint, the danger of such a combination would have been considerable, but when he was a worldly and ambitious man like Wolsey, it was fatal." [21]

The legateship was granted on May 17, 1518. With all his impatience for it and his vast plans for its use and the continued urgency of reform, almost a year elapsed before the overworked Wolsey took steps toward turning a vague scheme of reform into action. And then his first move was hardly more than an unctuous exhortation of the sort that had been issued so many times and so vainly in the past, calling upon the men of the Church to lead a more pious life. Loftily ignoring the fact that his own personal life was far from exemplary, that he was an overlord and not a practicing priest in daily touch with religious needs, the legate issued statements that had the sound and sentiments of papal bulls. He urged the good to be better still, and he called severely upon the lax to mend their erring ways, talking to them like a schoolmaster full of inexhaustible impatience.

The move was without the advantages of tact, and, seeing that the independence of the bishops and abbots had the sanction of the Holy See, it was not calculated to endear the Cardinal to those he sought to reform. Later he summoned representatives of all the religious orders before him and, "after expressing his goodwill towards them, spoke very plainly of their defects, and of the desire he had to see them live according to their rules . . ." [22] The Cardinal further stressed his intention of attending to the business of reform personally.

At the time, he was busily engaged in the machinations of high diplomacy whereby he and not the Pope would be responsible for the union of the princes of Christendom. Likewise he was sitting in judgment and exercising his capacious conscience on the problems of the realm brought before his court; and he was dealing through a royal commission with such vast and complicated problems as enclosure, trying to hold back the stupendous changes that were going on in agriculture and in the tenure of land. Each of these activities was worth the total effort of a well-organized ministry, but Wolsey had to cover them all. And now he proposed to add to his labors a further task that might well absorb the energies of a generation of geniuses; and he assured the world that he would attend to the matter himself.

By the very nature of time and movement, his attempt to reform the Church with the part-time use of his left hand was doomed to futility. It would be marked at best by fits and starts. His schedule was such that the only visit he made during the year he secured the bull empowering him to reform the monasteries took him to Westminster Abbey, hardly a stone's throw from the busy scenes of the court and his residence at York Place. The Cardinal Legate treated the monks "with considerable rigour," for which there appeared to be no occasion. The monks of the Abbey enjoyed good repute; no question had been raised to suggest that they had violated religious proprieties. The Abbey's wealth might mark it for envy, for its holdings stretched out on all sides to embrace such areas as came to be known as Hyde Park, Pimlico, and Covent Garden. But nothing save covetousness could raise whispers against Westminster. Mainly the Legate's visit to the Abbey at Westminster was a household affair, a show of paternal authority over the Abbot and the monks.

Next he turned to the Order of St. Augustine; this and the Order of St. Benedict made up the great religious bodies of England. My lord Cardinal chose for his opening fanfare a bull issued by Benedict XII in 1334. In this he but called the attention of the Augustinians to previous admonitions, already accepted as worthy and accepted now as worthy of reiteration. At the same time he added some regulations of his own, the same to be kept in force from the moment they were pronounced, on March 19, 1519, until the Feast of the Holy Trinity two years later.

The didactic detail to be found in the regulations Wolsey visited upon this great Order reveals him as a preoccupied lecturer. He instructs them that the Office is to be said neither too quickly nor too slowly. He goes so far as to say that all of the monks are to be present at the services, especially Matins and Mass. And then, as if there were nothing else of more importance on the disturbed earth, my lord Cardinal and Legate proceeds to tell the monks of the Order of St. Augustine how to sing.[23]

Wolsey was a reformer by memorandum, setting forth stately thoughts to the clergy as he set forth devious and complicated directions to his agents in the courts of Europe and at the court of the Holy See. As Archbishop of York he issued resounding *statuta* for his province. In reckoning with the province he needed no legatine authority. In fact, he needed only an audience. Most of his injunctions and benedictions are drawn from the enactments (a term often used to suggest that the mere pronouncement of a Church official constituted a law) of his predecessors. His contribution was simply to draw up and edit these earlier pronouncements and issue them again as if to inaugurate a more vigorous policy. And in many cases he added the vigor of his own phrasing and a freshness of terms which would catch the eye even in a document of religious instruction. Four times every priest with the care of souls was to explain "in the vulgar tongue and without any subtlety or fantastic turning about of words," the fourteen Articles of faith, the Ten Commandments, the two evangelical precepts of charity, the seven works of mercy, the seven deadly sins, the seven opposing virtues, and the seven sacraments of grace.[24]

Enough high-sounding words, properly arranged for effect, were apparently supposed to jolt the whole Church into a newness of life. In the governing of his own province Wolsey ordered that all clerics must remain in their parishes unless they had papal dispensation or their bishop's permission to absent themselves — a measure that sounded good and struck the keynote of reform; but Wolsey himself knew that permission from the bishop could easily be arranged, and when he issued this edict he had not visited any of the livings which he himself held. The clergy of his province were forbidden to attend unlawful spectacles, "especially duels, tournaments and sports in which blood might be shed." [25] They were also urged to be different in dress and deportment from the laity to call the world's attention to the distinctiveness of the religious life. Yet he himself at the time paraded around London in competitive pomp and appeared to seek by his every act to show that the clergy could not only dress as well as the lords temporal but vastly better. Later the Cardinal ordered all bishops to be in attendance upon their cathedrals at the time of ordinations, yet in his own province of York the ordinations were held by his auxiliary bishop.

In all he said Wolsey seemed to regard himself as the appointed leader of reform; in all he did he appeared to look upon himself as an eloquent exception. He lived in his mind, and the fruits of his mind were schemes so vast that their mere entertainment gave him satisfaction and a feeling of accomplishment. He enjoyed his power and capacity more than his deeds, and in his dreams for the renovation of the whole Church in England he viewed the world from the icy heights of innocence. There was about him and those few who championed his efforts a touching naïveté, as well as a lordly disdain for practical difficulties and complexities.

The obstacles which confronted Wolsey when he turned from words to official action were thick and frustrating. The legatine powers he sought did not come all at once but by degrees, and only through his continued importunities in Rome. Before they were granted to the full, those who opposed "the great tyrant," as Warham's secretary called Wolsey, had prevailed upon the Archbishop of Canterbury to anticipate the Cardinal and make motions of reform ahead of him. Accordingly an official of the province of Canterbury prepared to conduct a visitation of the cathedral monastery in the diocese of Worcester. The visitation was refused admittance. The monks were excommunicated for their refusal, but they maintained that the power of visitation now rested with the Legate.

Incidents of this unhappy sort did little to prepare the way for Wolsey to carry out his commendable and highly commended designs. They represented the jurisdictional disputes which the Archbishop of York, a distinctly ecclesiastical underling, though vested now by the Holy Father with legatine strength, would encounter at all times. When he discovered that Warham had summoned his suffragans to hold a council at Lambeth for "the reformation of enormities," his remonstrance was prompt. If there was anything more important than the reformation of the Church, it was that this reformation should be conducted by the Pope's commissioned representative. To Warham, Wolsey wrote in dignified astonishment "that you should enterprise the said reformation to the express derogation of the said dignity of the See Apostolic and otherwise than the law will suffer you without mine advice, consent, and knowledge . . ." At this stage of his legateship, still amiable in his strength, and confident that there were larger rights yet to be bestowed by the Pope, Wolsey suggested to Warham that the two prelates meet and discuss the whole matter. He selected Richmond as a proper place for the meeting and added with a touch of politeness the hope that this "shall not be much incommodious" to Warham.

Then by way of official reply to the Archbishop of Canterbury and the mischief the provincial Convocation on reform might create, Wolsey summoned a legatine synod to meet at Westminster. The first session had to be postponed because of an outbreak of the sweating sickness, an affliction which upon its return always drove men to cover, whether kings or prelates. The synod finally assembled when the sweat had passed again, but its accomplishments are not a matter of record. The chances are that it was an exploratory meeting designed merely to make out problems, and that the problems which appeared were so many and fierce that they sobered the Cardinal in the matter of general reform through synods, convocations, or any other kind of clerical assembly. He did not understand or trust deliberative bodies, whether they were composed of those who wore the cloth or those who came together as squires and burgesses in the Commons. His idea of a legatine council henceforth was to assemble a few chosen bishops at his residence and deal with them as subalterns.

Four years after the first futile synod on reform met under Wolsey's jurisdiction, the King issued a writ to Warham to summon the bishops and clergy of his province to meet at St. Paul's in London, or wherever the Archbishop might deem it convenient to meet. The call was issued. At the same time a writ was issued to Wolsey to summon his clergy from his own province. But before the two writs were fairly cold, Wolsey moved to show that any assembly held would have to be under his auspices. As Hall puts it: "In this season the Cardinal by his power legatine dissolved the convocation at St. Paul's, called by the Archbishop of Canterbury, and called him and all the clergy to his convocation in Westminster, which was never seen before in England." [26] The Abbey of Westminster, where Wolsey ordered the assembly to meet, was exempt from the jurisdiction of the Archbishop of Canterbury.

After all the arrangements and counter-arrangements, nothing came of the Convocation that contributed to the reform of the Church. It marked the end of Wolsey's half-hearted efforts to institute reform by consent and reduced the government of the Church to what Pollard calls a legatine autocracy. The various divisions of government within the Church had the right to meet and enact through councils, but it was more of a right than a practice, and, as Sir Thomas More pointed out later, the weakness of the deliberative bodies within the Church had laid the way for their abandonment in the matter of reform. More deplores the fact that there had not been assemblies of the clergy in every province throughout all Christendom. Had this been so, he observes, "much more good might have grown thereof than the long disuse can suffer us now to perceive." He continues: "But of all my days, as far as I have heard, nor (I suppose) a good part of my father's neither, they came never together in convocation but at the request of the king, and at such their assemblies, concerning spiritual things, have very little done. Wherefore that they have been in that necessary part of their duty negligent . . ." [27]

IN 1524 Wolsey got the legateship for life. There was no remaining excuse now why he should not accomplish the high ends he had announced, save that he was already weary of the task and he had encountered enough difficulties to vex a saint. He had not touched the problem of priests in minor orders who did the clerical work of the kingdom — priests in name only whose privileges were deeply resented by the laity. He had done nought but preach to the general body of the active clergy, all of them under the jealous jurisdiction of their bishops. He had fitfully exhorted some of the monks. It took something more than authority to reform a body as amorphous as the Church.

When next he turned his attention to the friars, they met his advances with a stony eye; for all the good the Legate accomplished among them he might as well have remained only an archbishop. The friars were simply unavailable for reform; they wanted no legatine nose poked into their affairs. To begin with, they were vastly more than English: they were organized on a scale as big as the civilized world. Touched off by the Crusades, each order organized as "an ecclesiastical army with its general residing at Rome and with a cardinal designated there to give special protection to its interests." [1] The Dominicans (Black Friars) had been founded by the Spanish Dominic and had come to England in 1221. The Franciscans (Gray Friars) had come to England in 1224. Both these huge orders were well established, immured in English society, yet active in the whole life of the country and given to valorous independence of action. There were other orders of friars, less powerful but no less assertive.

No wonder Rome advised Wolsey to deal lightly with the body of friars. Before he could announce his intention to visit the Franciscans, representatives of that order had appealed to Rome in an attempt to prevent the visit. When the Observant Friars suspected that Wolsey would visit and reform them, they sent scurrying messengers to their cardinal-protector in Rome and asked him to lay their case at the feet of the Pope. As Hall put it in his *Chronicle,* the Cardinal "would have visited the Friars Observatines, but they in nowise would therein condescend." The appeal to the Pope was not without effect. His Holiness wrote Wolsey, calling attention to the good name the order enjoyed throughout the world and urging the Legate to "make use of gentleness and tact rather than severity in admonishing them." [2] The cardinal-protector also wrote the Legate, asking him to give up the visitation altogether. Both requests were polite and routine, but to reinforce a feeling the Pope could hardly express in an official communication His Holiness sent word the following month through one of Wolsey's agents in Rome that the Legate should "for God's sake use mercy with those Friars," seeing that "they be as desperate beasts, past shame, that can lose nothing by clamor." [3]

Another reason could be advanced for letting the friars go their unreformed way. They were popular with the rank and file, subject to criticism more by the bishops and the priests than by the laity. They identified the service of God with the service of man. Their convents were in or near the larger towns, signifying their mission to the masses, but they had a system of itineracy which sent friars two by two into villages and country districts and to the houses of the gentry and farmers. They heard confessions, and "there were many who chose to confess their misdoings to a comparative stranger, who did not live among them, rather than to their parish priests."

Mainly, however, they were preachers. They preached in churchyards and market places, wherever men and women would gather to listen. Their emphasis on preaching affected their architecture. Their churches had auditoriums where large congregations could hear sermons rather than witness liturgical processions. Their services were designed "to attract the sluggish and popularize religion." They encouraged and produced miracle plays to drive home religious lessons, and their preaching was calculated to influence men's daily lives. "The sermons were practical and moral rather than dogmatic, interspersed with anecdotes, often of a sensational type, and illustrations drawn from daily life . . . To go and hear a friar preach was one of the recognized forms of entertainment in the merry England of the Middle Ages." [4]

The favor enjoyed by the friars was not shared by the monks and nuns, and the houses of these great stationary orders continued to receive Wolsey's legatine attention. If the monastic establishments with their conspicuous display of wealth could be remodeled, the change might enhance in no small measure public good will toward the Church. The priests and bishops would rejoice to see the monks brought to heel. And the laity would nod with satisfaction too, for the monasteries were great landlords, and many of their dealings with people outside the walls were on the basis of business.

A new spirit of commerce in the towns made these institutions seem out of date, an obstruction to progress. They were "rentiers living on their revenues." [5] They stood to gain by keeping things fastened in place as they were. The problem that a reformer faced was not the morals but the immovability of the monasteries. Little concrete evidence came to light to show that the monasteries were dens of vice. Those rare cases in which charges were made were laid before the authorities of the Church by the members of some Church visiting body. This was true before Wolsey's day and in the visitations which he made or authorized. The reform of the monasteries could not be accomplished by an unsparing use of the rod on individual monks and nuns or by instructing them in a redoubled use of prayer and fasting or by a warning against such frivolous practices as the prick-song, which was fancy in its rhythms. Reform involved vastly more than private morals. The Legate was dealing with great corporations of power and wealth "faltering to decay, such as society has to reform out of existence from time to time." [6]

In times past, the monasteries had contributed to the vigor of the common life of the kingdom and had given stability when it was sorely needed. They had been pioneers. They had brought waste lands under cultivation and had set an example to the lay landowners by the use of enterprising methods in agriculture and horticulture, in the growth of food and the development of plants and trees. Cutts points out that they led the way in using streams for waterpower and for irrigation and sanitation. They developed the practice of bringing pure water long distances in conduits. And in all their practices they had worked pleasantly and well with the people who farmed or used their land. Not a few of the tenants of the monastic houses, "seated generation after generation" on their manors, grew into mighty and noble families.

Indeed it was the success of the monastic houses that engendered failure, as is the way with institutions. Their hospitality came to be accepted and then abused. The closeness of Church and State led to royal presumption upon their good offices. In the reign of Edward II the Queen left her pack of hounds at Canterbury for two full years. An Italian visitor writing in the days of the Legate observed that monasteries were obliged to defray the expenses of one, two, or three gentlemen, "and as many horses with their keep, at the pleasure of His Majesty. Because, whenever the King wishes to bestow an easy life upon one of his servants, he makes one of these monasteries pay his expenses." [7]

Abuse was not confined to royalty by any means. To those who visited the great monasteries hospitality was usually extended for two days, but many guests stayed longer. And it was one of the minor problems of administration that outside laymen looked upon the houses of the religious as hostels for their convenience. Often they paid for their keep, and the temptation to turn the houses into something other than places for meditation was great. Abram says that at one nunnery both men and women were received as paying guests, a practice that led to public criticism and, to put it mildly, a diversion of original purpose.

Plenty of provision also was made for the accommodation of wayfarers. Hospitality was regarded as a duty imposed by tradition as well as religious devotion, though it was of course exercised more freely by some houses than others; chiefly, according to Bernard, by the great Benedictine monasteries and some houses of Augustinian canons. At St. Albans's arrangements were made for the stabling of three hundred horses. Abingdon had "a special endowment to meet the cost of new shoes for the guests' horses." The hosteler of one monastery was reminded that "by showing cheerful hospitality to guests the reputation of the monastery is increased, friendships are multiplied, animosities are blunted, God is honored, charity is increased, and a plenteous reward in heaven is promised."

To these ends detailed duties were laid down for the hosteler, and the tastes and peculiarities of wealthy travelers were kept scrupulously in mind. The hosteler was ordered at the Augustinian monastery of Barnwell, near Cambridge, to see that guests had clean towels, "cups without flaws, spoons of silver, mattresses, blankets and sheets not merely clean but untorn, proper pillows; quilts to cover the beds of full length and width and pleasing to the eyes of those who enter the room." The guest house was to be kept clean of spider webs and supplied with "fire that does not smoke; writing materials; clean salt in saltcellars that have been well scrubbed." [8]

Less lavish attention was bestowed upon the comforts of the poor wayfarers who came to the monastery gate, but not less consideration of their needs. "The abbot of St. Albans's entertained every traveler that came to his gate for three days; at the priory of St. Thomas of Canterbury there was a hall 150 feet long and 40 broad, appropriated to the accommodation of poor pilgrims." [9] Monasteries in areas likely to be less traveled usually entertained the poor in the almonry near the gatehouse. Here charity as well as accommodation was dispensed. Often the volume of charity was not great in terms of money. Records indicate that one Benedictine monastery, having in it a community of twenty-two monks, gave only five shillings and eightpence in a year to the poor. The cash outlay was similarly slim in other monasteries, as at Abingdon Abbey. Yet the kindness bestowed probably went far beyond what shows in the cash disbursements. For example, when new clothes and shoes were given out "at regular times in the monastery, the old ones were handed to the Almoner for the poor. All that was left from meals in the refectory and guest-house was reserved for the Almoner." [10]

Those fortunate few who received bounty from the monasteries had some sense of the lingering kindness that came from the principles of their original foundations. But many others came to covet the privileges which the inmates enjoyed. For the comforts the monks bestowed upon visitors they likewise bestowed upon themselves. They lived well when many did not. They had, in the midst of their devotions and meditations and the exactions which their many administrative duties imposed, gradually abandoned manual labor and now maintained numerous servants to carry on the daily grind of their complicated establishments. At St. Peter's in Gloucester during these days there were thirty monks and eighty-six servants.

To those on the outside, the monastic life looked to be only one of comfort and of increasing uselessness in a world that was changing with the passage of each day. The monks "did too little and got too much." A writer of the day speaks of a body of "abbey lubbers, which are apt to do nothing only eat and drink." The Lord Mayor of London used as his reason for asking royal permission to have three hospitals put under his care the claim that the hospitals had been founded "for the aid of poor and impotent people, not to maintain canons, priests and monks to live in pleasure." [11]

By all accounts the flesh was weaker among the nuns than it was among the monks. Many of the nuns had been deposited in the houses by their families as good and fortunate riddance, and few of those who took the veil in this period seem to have been led or called by an intense religious experience. Most of the occupants of the one hundred and eleven nunneries in England during Wolsey's time were females unwanted at home, women who had not been married off. As Trevelyan points out: "It was rarely possible to become a nun without a dowry. In this way English nunneries were recruited and in part financed."

In general, the nunneries suffered the same faults as the monasteries. They had slipped gradually over to the side of the world. They were bogged down in comforts and had lost their alertness to moral distinctions. The cost of fur trimmings on the mantles of nuns came to be matters of competitive interest and a sign of status. Meetings of some of the chapters became, according to Gasquet, ecclesiastical pageants, occasions for the display of religious vestments in the latest style and in high degrees of sumptuousness. It is reported that "for more than six weary centuries the bishops waged a holy war against fashion in the cloister and in vain." [12]

What could Wolsey do as he faced the reform of the monasteries? The noticeable need, the one to which the Legate could address himself without undue perception of the deeper defects, was a tightened discipline that might call the orders back to their original intent. This course required that he should gird his own magnificent robes about him and lecture monks on the dangers of comfort. But he did not stick to do it. He addressed himself first to the startled monks of the Order of St. Benedict at Westminster Abbey, then to the Order of St. Augustine, with minute instructions on the betterment of their devotions. Next he returned to the Order of St. Benedict in a general chapter. Wolsey approached the Benedictines as he approached all other bodies and problems: with a flourish of authority and with written prescriptions for their ills. He merely told them what to do, what would be required of them by him.

The statutes laid down by Wolsey were accepted, but the monks took pains to point out that many were too severe. Their protest against the moral exactions and monastic severity imposed by the Legate told him what he as a practical man should have known already, namely, that the fierce monastic code adopted and practiced by such bodies as the Carthusians could not be applied to the Benedictines. Severity of this sort would lead to a depopulation of the monasteries; they were, whatever else, great institutions, and they needed numbers to maintain their standards as institutions. The monks besought the Legate to consider well this fact and the circumstances of the day, concluding: "For in these stormy times (as the world now decays towards its end) those who desire a life of austerity and regular observance are few, and indeed most rare." [13]

Having exercised his pen and his eloquence upon the monks with no evident sign that they would mend their ways at his bidding, Wolsey found a solution more in character with his understanding of the whole problem. Empowered by papal bulls for the express purpose, he began to suppress and dissolve the smaller houses, to dismember the Orders by cutting off their extremities, devoting the proceeds of his legatine transactions to the business of founding a college at Oxford University and a preparatory school for this college in his native Ipswich. All told, he and his agents visited and appropriated twenty-two monasteries and three nunneries. These houses which had their property diverted to other ends were all houses in which there were fewer than twelve surviving inmates. They were suffering conspicuously from what afflicted the whole monastic body: a paralysis of function.

Precedent existed for the move Wolsey made. The good Henry VI had dissolved ailing houses to set up King's College at Cambridge and Eton near Windsor. Henry VII had seen fit to replace monasteries with hospitals in London. And Bishop Alcock of Ely had founded Jesus College at Cambridge to replace the nunnery of St. Radegund.

There had been precedent for the acts of dissolution but none whatever for the scale on which the Legate now operated or the ferocious determination with which he went about the undertaking. It was a commentary that revealed much of his mind. Faced with a religious problem, he chose a businesslike solution. He evaded the problem by flying off into an abstraction. Hope lay in one word: education.

There was also the comforting assurance that the lofty end of founding colleges for the improvement of the clergy and the raising of the general level of the common life justified the means and the methods by which Wolsey and his agents acted. They met in many cases with sharp rebukes from the people of the communities where they suppressed monasteries. At Tunbridge in the province of Canterbury the inhabitants appealed to Archbishop Warham that he might cause the Legate to desist from the proposed dissolution of a small monastery of Austin Friars. Warham was asked by the Legate to go to the town and inform the people that it would be better to have "forty children of that country educated and after sent to Oxford" than to have six or seven canons living among them.[14] Warham's mission was in vain, and after discussing the matter five or six days the citizens again met with the Archbishop and let him know that they were of the same mind as before. Warham wrote to Wolsey to say that the murmurs were "very difficult to suppress."

In some places the resistance went beyond words. Wolsey commissioned the Bishop of Chichester to look into Beigham Abbey in Essex and report on certain scandals there. But the Abbey, according to Hall, was "very commodious to the country," and when the Legate started proceedings to dissolve the house the neighbors assembled in a "riotous company, disguised and unknown, with painted faces." They "turned out the agents engaged in the suppression and reinstated the canons. Before separating they begged the religious, if they were again molested, to ring their bell,

196

and they pledged themselves to come in force to their assistance." [15]

Hall paints a stormy picture of the way in which Wolsey as Legate acted toward the monasteries. As he tells it, the Cardinal "suddenly entered by his commissioners into the said houses, and put out the religious and took all their goods, moveables, and scarcely gave to the poor wretches anything except it were to the heads of the house." [16] Whether this statement is overdrawn or not, it is well attested that the two agents he chose for the bulk of the work acted with lack of grace in their dealings and were not averse, if the testimony of their own letters is to be trusted, to the taking of bribes and considerations for exempting houses which had been marked for their master.

These agents were John Allen and Thomas Cromwell. Fiddes portrays Allen as a man who, "accompanied with a great train, and riding in a kind of perpetual progress from one religious house to another, is said to have drawn very large sums for his master's service from them." [17] Brewer reports that "loud outcries reached the king's ears of the exactions and peculations of Wolsey's officers, in which the name of Cromwell was most frequently repeated." [18] More than once the King is said to have had to express his great displeasure at the conduct of the man.

Yet the Legate seemed deaf to all but his purpose. He had no ear for complaint or protest or for the resonant whispers raised against his agents. He was a man possessed of possessions, dealing with matters that he could understand, sure of his aim, and used to outcries stirred by his actions. Other views might differ, but the Legate had come to terms with the problem of reform. Both his sense of property values and the towering dream he had built of his colleges and must now reinforce with stone made him unmindful of the claws of criticism.

In this manner preoccupied, he neglected not only criticism but also all other aspects of Church reform. Education would be the answer. Beyond his stately plans for his colleges he showed no will or talent for the simpler reforms which might have extended the Church further into the good graces of the people — such as might well have come about, for example, by the use of English instead of Latin in its services.

And he turned his eyes also from the thorny problem which had been raised by the death of Richard Hunne. He took no pains to abate the hostility of the laity to religious bodies. He seems to have seen no connection between the laxity of the ecclesiastics and the system of benefit of clergy whereby "the bishops were able to demand from the civil authorities clerics who had been imprisoned by the king's justices for any crime." [19] Punishments by death and mutilation could not be inflicted by ecclesiastical courts. However bad the crime of the cleric, his punishment at the hands of his bishop would be light. Yet these same courts were able to arrogate to themselves cases in which laymen were involved, and if the crimes committed merited death by the laws of the Church the lay offenders were handed over to the secular arm of the government for burning or dismemberment.

What precise powers my lord Cardinal had as Legate, as distinct from those he claimed and flaunted, is a matter still lost in the mists of history. Still, he had plenty to deal with heresy. It is odd that, having gathered unto himself the powers of both Church and State, he did not grapple with the conflict between the courts Christian and the courts of the common law, except that he seemed always to see the world through stained glass. He was a Cardinal of Rome first and last, with all that the cardinalate implied; England was only a province of something larger and beyond, and to that larger thing men gave the name of Rome.

When Wolsey acted, then, it was in the manner in which he thought Rome might act. As Legate he paid no more attention to the betterment of the courts Christian than he did as Lord Chancellor to the reform of the courts of the common law. His answer in dealing with both courts was the same: he ignored existing courts, with all their ancient dignities and prerogatives, and created a system of his own. As Lord Chancellor he sat like Solomon on the bench of equity and, without any noticeable knowledge of his limitations, decided out of hand and with a godly nod every contention that his fellows brought or fetched before him. As Legate he created legatine courts that superseded in authority the other courts of the Church, and he had brought before these courts, which is to say before himself, whatever matter might trouble the heart or the conscience or whatever trifle — yea, even the fall of the sparrow — that might need the Lord's attention.

For a well-groomed tyrant he showed astonishing streaks of leniency, especially when his legatine courts dealt with heresy. During the dozen years when he controlled the religious jurisdiction of the kingdom, not one heretic was consigned to the flames. This is a fact all the more remarkable when one considers that his methods in every department of his activity were haughty and harsh and that he could, with public sanction and in the best tradition, have burned as many English heretics as he pleased. He did not change the courts or the practice which made this punishment possible; before the rise of his own power heretics had been condemned by the ecclesiastical courts and burned by the State; and after his fall the practice was punctually renewed and continued. The

198

whole system of courts and procedures which made the burning of heretics customary the Legate blithely ignored.

Being apparently ignorant of the intensity of conviction that makes men concern themselves with heresy, the Cardinal caused to be dismissed or let off with light ecclesiastical punishment those who were dragged before his legatine courts for this offense. He seemed confused rather than concerned. Toward the end of his days of power members of the college he had founded at Oxford were accused. One of them, a man named Taverner, the organist of the church there, was arrested. He was brought before Wolsey and charged with having hidden heretical books "under the boards in his school." It was a serious charge, all the more so because books were involved. But, as Godwin concludes the incident, "the Cardinal for his music excused him, saying, that he was but a Musician and so he escaped."

The power Wolsey exercised in his effort to reform the Church had Rome as its source. Here lay, in the long run, Wolsey's greatest disservice. He made Rome more and more distasteful to the English clergy as well as to a laity restive for freedom and feeling in its bones the stirring of nationhood. By bringing Rome to London and by making the power of Rome, once comfortably distant and ineffective by inconvenience, ubiquitous in the realm of the King, he held back the cause of reform until it could be achieved only by parliamentary action and royal violence.

Wolsey was, as Pollard phrases it, more papal than the Pope. And the plaintive and futile ambition he nurtured and pursued to become Pope was only a logical extension of his papal addiction and his subservient attitude toward reform by authority, showing both his faith in the power of the Pope and the power of himself and his boundless confidence in what might be achieved if the two could be conjoined.

He made two full-throated efforts to gain the papacy, each of which failed lamentably. The first was upon the death of Leo X, which occurred December 2, 1521. Thirty-nine cardinals assembled with due ceremony in the solemn conclave to select his successor. No communication was allowed between the penned cardinals and the outside world. Their food was passed through the walls "at a round turning wheel made in the wall." After a few days their dishes were "restricted to one kind of meat, with the prospect of further diminution if they failed to agree within a reasonable time." On the sixth day the food was diminished, though one sickly cardinal had been carried out almost dead from the conclave.

Meanwhile the Roman populace milled around the closely guarded quarters of the cardinals' convention or hung on tenterhooks for such news as might escape. Public interest in learning the name of the new pope was not altogether prompted by piety. It was a quaint custom that the cardinal chosen should have his house ransacked and pillaged before he could return to it, "an offense tolerated and overlooked in the general joy and license of the election." [20] Speculations had been rife long before the conclave commenced, and one of the men considered likely to succeed was Cardinal Farnese, a Roman, and one of the wealthiest and most influential of the cardinals. There were clamorous maneuverings in his behalf, and at one moment it appeared that he had triumphed, for a cardinal supporter cried out, *"Papam habemus!"* Those who opposed his election called for a test of the acclamation, and when a scrutiny was taken it was found that he had failed. But news of the first cry had crept through the guardians of secrecy surrounding the conclave. It was a sign for an attack on the house of Cardinal Farnese, which was duly plundered before the correct news could be spread abroad.

Fourteen disorderly days passed before the deadlock ended. When it had become likely that none of the sturdy contenders would draw enough votes in any scrutiny, a distant pedant, scarcely known and hence highly respected, was put forth. In the last scrutiny the choice fell on this man, Cardinal Tortosa, a Fleming, formerly the tutor of Emperor Charles V. No one in Christendom could have cared less for the papacy than the man who took the title of Adrian VI. He did not refuse it, but he accepted it with reluctance and announced that when he came to Rome he would rid the papal court of corruption.

In the bitter contest which thrust the tiara on the learned and unwilling head of Adrian VI, the Cardinal of York got only seven votes in one scrutiny. So ordinary accounts report the matter. He had been told by his agent in Rome that he had received votes in three scrutinies and that at one time the count had reached as high as nineteen votes. In any case and by either report he had not been elected any more than Cardinal Farnese.

Fortunately for Wolsey's aspirations, the pathetic tenure of Adrian VI lasted only eighteen months before death released the new pontiff and Rome from their joint miseries and earned him the epitaph: "Here lies Adrian VI, whose greatest misfortune was that he became Pope." He was elected in January of 1522 and did not reach the Holy City until August. Meanwhile the hangers-on had cleared out, among them four thousand papal officials and servants. "The Florentine traders who had swarmed into the city at Leo's accession packed and vanished. Commercial life languished, rents fell, banks closed. The artists migrated."

Adrian's arrival did nothing to allay the worst expectations of Rome. He proposed to abandon the great papal quarters in the Vatican and rent a small house. When he was finally persuaded to move into the Pope's palace, "he took up his quarters in a remote wing . . . His predecessor had kept a hundred grooms; he reduced them to four . . . He lived, not merely in retirement, but in hiding, inaccessible and almost undiscoverable among his books." It was the beginning of a strange interlude in the history of the papacy. "All Rome is horrified," wrote the Venetian ambassador, "at what the Pope has accomplished in one short week." [21]

His death brought not only relief to the Roman populace but also determination that another non-Italian must not ascend the chair of St. Peter. The inhabitants had foreseen clearly the mistake, and after the election of Adrian they had greeted the cardinals as they were leaving their unhappy conclave with "screams, whistling, and shouts of derision." So great had been the disappointment of the populace in the election of an outlander, a barbarian from beyond the mountains, that the lives of the offending cardinals had been in danger.

Plainly the cardinals of Rome would not at this stage accept another barbarian. Wolsey's hope, however, was such that it could not be deterred by precedent or by the ugly facts of the past. England had not had a Pope in Rome since the days of Nicholas Breakspear, who had ruled as Adrian IV in 1154. He had been English by birth, but he had spent only his boyhood in his native country, and his election had taken place before national rivalries had entered into the papal elections. Nor had this earlier Adrian's rule in Rome been much happier than the Adrian's just dead.

Steadfastly ignoring all these difficulties, Wolsey resolved to try again and began to lay his plans with his usual devious elaborateness. He was at The More, one of his great houses, when word of Adrian's death came. He wrote at once to the King, who was then at Woodstock, to announce the news and to say that, while he would rather continue in the King's service "than to be ten popes" and that he felt "unmeet and unable to so high and great a dignity," nevertheless he supposed that the King persisted in the same mind and intent as he had shown before. He notified the King that, on the basis of this assumption, he would draw up papers to be sent to his agent in Rome as before and that he would have these papers in the King's hands by the next post. In the same letter he points out that of course the King's interests will well be served if he goes to Rome.

My lord Cardinal and Legate followed through the next day, relieving the King of any onerous chore in connection with the representations to Rome. He had drawn up for him a letter to the Emperor. As he puts it, it was "a familiar letter in the King's name to the Emperor." The letter is already phrased to suit the purpose, but Wolsey expressed the hope that "it may please your Highness to take the pain for to write it with your own hand, putting thereunto your secret sign and mark . . ."

The letter from the King and in the King's own hand was designed to remind the Emperor of an earlier promise he had made to the King and the Cardinal that he would promote Wolsey's candidacy with all the imperial influence at Rome. Long after the election was over, the Emperor replied with apologies and excuses but in a tone most cordial and with every assurance that he had complied, saying "that you may be aware with what zeal and diligence we have taken up this affair in favor of the said lord Legate, we send you copies of our letters in his behalf, directed to the Duke of Sessa, our ambassador at Rome, written before the receipt of yours, as well as others afterwards sent to the Sacred College." [22]

It developed later that the Emperor had in fact written the letter to Sessa in Wolsey's behalf but that he had also taken the precaution of ordering the courier who took the dispatch to be detained, so that he reached Rome long after the election was over.

Meanwhile the Sacred College met and made its choice. The bitterness of feeling among the cardinals was as great as it had been in the previous election, when the Spanish ambassador had written to his master: "There cannot be so much hatred and so many devils in hell as among the cardinals." [23] A rumor spread that arms had actually been hidden in the conclave. A search was made, then the doors were walled up and the windows locked. For eight days there was no result and no prospect of a decision, though all indications pointed to the choice of Giulio de' Medici. Although a bastard, his name carried the weight of a great house. And he was an Italian. Then on the ninth day three French cardinals turned up, much to the consternation of the Romans. They presented themselves at the doors of the conclave in short coats, which, as Clerk writes to Wolsey, were considered very dissolute; and they came also in boots and spurs. One French cardinal wore a hat with feathers. The French were admitted amid laughter for their attire, and the conclave, after this high diversion and interruption, settled back into quarrelsome tedium that promised never to end.

Wolsey's agents waited anxiously and hopefully that the deadlock within might thrust their candidate into the papacy. It was not until the fiftieth day that the choice that had been anticipated all along was made. The Sacred College had chosen Giulio de' Medici who was to take the papal chair under the name of Clement VII. And in all the scrutinies that had taken place during those interminable fifty days my lord Cardinal and Legate had not received a single vote.

It would have seemed to be enough to crush ambition. But Wolsey kept his ignored hopes alive, always ready to thrust them forward and test them again by means of the apparatus of bribery and intrigue which he kept ready. Wolsey's obsessive effort to attain the papacy, an effort that never reckoned with the certainty of defeat or blushed after failure, went beyond the mere desire for high office. It revealed the defiant insecurity of his nature and his need as an Ipswich yokel to be constantly reassured and propped. He sought always the extension of personal authority, and he rested his claims on the good he could do the kingdom and the Church and by inference the human race if he were but vouchsafed the power.

It can be judged how he regarded himself when one notes the playacting he did whenever he received a fresh legatine commission from the Pope. He would absent himself from court, and then, having passed around the stage and changed his costume, so to say, he would reappear and be received in state as though he were really an ambassador fresh from Rome.[24] By such posturing of his soul he lived, wrapping his nakedness in rich symbols, masquerading among the lords towering above the clergy. If he could not be Pope at Rome he would be Pope at home.

CHAPTER XI

THERE was a corner in the capacious mind of Thomas Wolsey which was occupied by intellectual concerns. In this corner he acted not as Lord Chancellor or Cardinal or Legate but as one possessed of ideas, as a man named Wolsey and not as His Eminence. His lively and perceptive approach to the processes of education will bear the most critical examination. There were sober moments, hard come by, when he seemed to escape his showy public character and address himself to the inner spirit of his fellows and to consider well the means by which curiosity could be touched off and the pursuit of wisdom commenced. In these moments he was generations ahead of the prevailing views of his day and so far removed from the turgid presumptions of his official personality that something or someone hitherto unrecognized might be speaking through him. It is not without significance that the only book he wrote was an instructive essay on education. In this field his mind was often clean, unhampered by conceits, direct in its effort, free of irritations of insecurity that kept him driving and grasping for power.

Wolsey had even in his early days at the court a name to be noted in the field of education, and the deference shown him did not come wholly from his alma mater. In 1514, while he was yet only Bishop of Lincoln and not yet Archbishop of York, though a rising young man and obviously of great organizing talent, Cambridge University asked him to become its chancellor. Wolsey declined. The excuse he made to the delegation that brought him the invitation was "the multiplicity of public affairs wherewith he was taken up." He does say, however, that he is sensible of the honor conferred and that he will make it "his endeavor to show his gratitude by doing the University in general, and the several members of it, the best services in his power." [1]

That he was not without some use to Cambridge may be seen by the fact that that university later notified him by letter that because of the many favors he had conferred upon them they proposed "to appoint yearly and perpetual obsequies to be performed for him, which would be celebrated by all graduates with the greatest solemnity, and with every proper mark of honor, piety or religion . . ." [2] His own university doubled the deference Cambridge paid. It decreed in June 1515 that "all public preachers should pray openly for the good estate of the Archbishop of York, and after his death for his soul." [3]

Three years later Oxford University solemnly turned over to him its statutes and gave him a free hand in revising them. The surrender of the statutes into the hands of the Cardinal followed a state visit to Oxford in May 1518, when he accompanied the King and Queen on their progress to Abingdon. The Cardinal made a speech in which he declared how much he had the interests of the university at heart. He announced at the time that he proposed to found certain lectures, and out of the largeness of his heart he offered to "be intrusted with the care of reducing their statutes to some better form and order." [4]

The task of working some order out of the chaos of the statutes — "which were not only in much confusion, but in certain cases evidently repugnant to one another" — had been committed to other persons. However, the Cardinal said he would be glad to take the job in hand himself. His proposal met with solemn glee among the assembled officials, and

204

word was at once dispatched to Archbishop Warham, who was chancellor of the university, to acquaint him with the beneficence of the Cardinal's mind and heart.

Warham was decidedly less enthusiastic than the officials. He made bold to say that if the authority of such statutes should devolve upon any persons besides those who were vested with it, "the University, considered as a society, would be dissolved: a mere empty name or shadow of power would only remain to it, and the authority which it formerly exercised wholly terminate in the person to whom you may desire it may be transferred." Such was his judgment of the Cardinal's brash proposal and its placid acceptance by the university. He went on to say that it would be well to have the Cardinal's sentiments on the statutes and find out in what respects he would have them altered. These views could in due course be considered by, and decided by, the university.

Active administrators of the university took a different view, and Warham was "at last prevailed upon by their repeated instances and representations to depart from his former opinion." It came about shortly after that the university in full convocation passed "an ample and solemn decree" that the statutes be put into the hands of the Cardinal "to be corrected, reformed, changed, or expunged, as he in his discretion should think proper." All the rights, liberties, and privileges of the university — the rights and privileges of the separate colleges being sternly excepted, of course — were turned over wholly to Wolsey; "and he had full power of methodizing the public discipline, or of altering it, after what manner he judged most convenient." [5]

After the excitement of the decree was over, the Cardinal had in his lap another burdensome duty. This he accepted with his customary blithe disregard for the fact that he might never get around to the actual work. He was more interested in the corporate confidence conveyed than he was in the messy details of shaking down a wild mass of regulations designed to pull together an institution whose very genius lay in the fact that it was informal, casual, and amorphous. There is no sign that he ever reformed Oxford any more than he reformed the Church, but he added the honor of the request to his varied assortment of honors. And, on a practical basis, the request put him constantly in mind of the university, its corporate existence being now at his discretion, and he was inclined to bestow upon it favors and benefits which might not have crossed his thoughts if he had not been so officially cast into the role of its benefactor and proctor-at-large.

These favors were many and consistent and, seeing the sad state of

Oxford and of education in that day, not without some sharp value on the whole course of education in England. Wolsey's strategy was to secure the university against the town of Oxford and to gain for it exemption from taxes which the King visited upon his realm. He had gained for the university an exemption from the general tax levied for the support of the war against France in 1513. The custom of exempting the university from contributing to public wars the Cardinal had insisted upon to the King "as a matter of academical right." [6] The immunity was granted, and it was again granted when revenues were sought for a further war against France in 1522. The town of Oxford paid a subsidy but the university did not, and Wolsey was the instrument of the immunity.

If the university was exempt from the support of public wars, it was greatly aided in its unending private war with the town. The arsenal provided was a royal decree of unusual privileges. Wood, historian of early Oxford, reports that in 1523 "the King, at the influence of the noble cardinal, granted a large charter of liberties to the University." [7] It was part of the Cardinal's attempt to make the university "the most glorious in the learned universe." Wolsey caused the charter to be carried to the university by a special deputation. The deputation might well have been accompanied by the King's guard, for when the charter was promulgated, the townsmen were so incensed that they refused to submit to it. "Upon which account it was remitted to the King and proposed to be considered in Council."

In due course the charter was put in force. The mayor was obliged to take an oath at St. Mary's Church "to maintain the privileges and customs of the university." The charter did more, as Boase describes it, "than merely extend the powers of the chancellor and scholars, for it virtually placed the greater part of the city under their mercy." [8]

Despite its ample provisions, the charter did not cover all contingencies, and there was a spirited correspondence between the university and the Cardinal over details, quite as if he had nothing to bother about but the practical problems of Oxford. One letter touches on a matter full serious, for it tells of a pestilential distemper which had raged for months. The same distemper broke out again the next year and was so severe that many students had to retire from the university. The officials represent the colleges as reduced to a "most deplorable and disconsolate condition." There were various causes assigned to the pestilence. Wood notes that the contagion might have come from the fact that a vast concourse of students in a place "wanting both wholesome and convenient apartments" made the colleges like a city under siege. But the officials attributed the disease and its recurrence to the stagnation of waters in the adjacent fens, "and the noisome smells arising from them, occasioned by the want of a free current of water in the Thames, which their jurisdiction did not extend to open." [9] Wood claims that through the negligence of the citizens, the channel of the Cherwell and other currents near the university were choked with filth and dirt, which "occasioned a putrid and malignant air, replete with noxious vapors." More, the frequent floods overflowed the neighboring plains and "spread a slimy and vicious matter upon them, which, there being nothing to carry it off, did necessarily putrify and corrupt." The officials of the university prayed Wolsey, in this case as Lord Chancellor and an arm of the King, to help with some speedy remedy.

It was well that the higher learning had a friend at court, for the problems of both universities at this time were acute. Unsavory weather and noxious vapors had long been a feature of Oxford and its environs, and pestilence a tiger at the gates. Now there was another and more disturbing kind of distemper, and its symptoms were a falling off in the number of students who entered the colleges and a marked decline in public esteem. There was a crisis in education, and the nation, with its increased need of leadership and skills in government and commerce, might suffer if the crisis were not met. In 1523 the University of Oxford sent a jeremiad to Sir Thomas More to the effect that abbots had ceased to send their monks to the schools, nobles their sons, and clergy their parishioners. The halls were falling into ruin, the complaint ran, and only the endowed colleges showed any sign of prosperity.

The Oxford figures must be considered in the light of similarly pathetic conditions at Cambridge. Some years before, St. John Fisher as chancellor there had said: "Somehow, I know not how, whether it were continual strifes with the townsmen . . . or the long abiding of the fever . . . that carried off many of our learned men — or that there were few or no helpers and patrons of letters — whatever were the true causes, doubtless there had stolen over well-nigh all of us a weariness of learning and of study, so that not a few did take counsel in their own minds how they might get away from the university." [10]

In such a time and as matters stood, the universities needed staunch patrons of letters, advocates in high places who could by their influence help dispel the general contempt for education that had descended upon the public mind. Part of this contempt was traditional and of long standing. Richard Pace records a dinner incident that reveals the lingering attitude toward education among a certain segment of the population:

There happened to be present one of those whom we call gentlemen . . . and who always carry some horn hanging at their backs
as though they would hunt during dinner. He, hearing letters praised,
roused with sudden anger, burst out furiously with these words:
"Why do you talk nonsense, friend?" he said. "A curse on those
stupid letters! All learned men are beggars: even Erasmus, the most
learned of all, is a beggar (as I hear) and in a certain letter of his
complains that he cannot shake poverty off his shoulders . . . I swear
by God's body I'd rather that my son should hang than study letters.
For it becomes the sons of gentlemen to blow the horn nicely . . .
to hunt skillfully, and elegantly carry and train a hawk. But the study
of letters should be left to the sons of rustics." [11]

Changes wrought by such new forces as the spread of the printed word
affected public attitudes and made the old monkish learning of schools
and universities seem irrelevant to modern needs. "It was," says Abram,
"an epoch of commercial and industrial expansion, and a passion for trade
seized upon the nation." [12] Among the middle and lower classes, from
whose ranks most of the students seem to have come, the desire was for
"knowledge which would help them in their business life." The curricula
of the universities did not meet the changing needs of the day, and the
most eloquent statement of this fact and the most clear-cut criticism of the
universities lay in the fact of public neglect.

Another suspicion loomed, too, at this time; a suspicion that the universities were changing and not necessarily for the better. Ideas were
gathered for the convenience of public gossip into a bundle called the
New Learning. The term was, and is, an abstraction, the meaning of
which has changed with each use of it, but in general it then designated
views and impressions gained from Greek writers rather than Roman.
These views were perforce less influenced by the Church and more concerned with the development of the individual and society through human
energy than through divine guidance. Those who held or even entertained these views came to believe, unless watched and corrected, that
man might advance his station and improve his society without the aid of
priests or the instruments of the Christian religion as organized in the
Church.

There had been for a long time some dalliance with the materials of
the New Learning, but interest came during this period more definitely
into the open. In 1516 Bishop Fisher of Rochester arranged for Erasmus
to deliver a series of lectures on Greek at Cambridge. These seem to have
excited nothing approaching tumult, for Erasmus grumbled not only about

the low fees he got but also about "the poor attendance and inattention of the students, and the general lack of appreciation of his merits." In the same year, the statutes of Corpus Christi at Oxford provided that a public lecturer in Greek be among its principal officers.

To this overt change in the classics of education, in the way education had been formally and officially conducted, instant opposition arose, especially since the New Learning as taught at Corpus Christi found friends and enthusiasts among the students and spread a contagion of ideas as marked and noticeable as the pestilence that beset the university. Fox stood before the public as a man of pious bent and not to be blamed for self-seeking, having retired from the court to give the last years of his life to godliness and learning. He had spoken of "souls whereof I never see the bodies," and he had resolved that he would minister to individuals as well as preside over a vast diocese. There could be no suspicion, then, of Corpus Christi as arising out of alien or subversive sources. It was a sound place as far as auspices went. Yet there was no doubt that the establishment of a college with a body of teaching that revolved around Greek influence would stir men to questions.

In the midst of these doubts, and seeing the low estate to which education had fallen in the realm, Wolsey turned aside from his duties as Lord Chancellor and Legate and came forward as a patron of letters. His motives may have differed from act to act in the several moves he made, and no doubt these motives were at all times mixed. But at any rate he threw the weight of his public dignity and influence on the side of education and the New Learning. He provided at no expense to the university a foundation which should carry seven new lectureships. One was in Greek. And while he intended that these lectureships should in due time become the basis of a college he proposed to establish at Oxford, he instructed that they be read meanwhile in the halls of Corpus Christi College.

The continued attention to Greek was a signal for further commotion, which it took the weight of both the Cardinal and the King to still. Scholars at the university, "either in contempt of the literature of the Greeks . . . or out of idleness and a false taste for vain and trifling amusements," had formed a body known as the Trojans. The captain of the Trojans assumed the name of Priam, the second in command the name of Hector, the third Paris. The purpose was to "outbrave and ridicule those who addicted themselves to the study of Greek." It came about that one who knew Greek or employed his time in learning it "was not free at home or abroad from the insults and raillery of the adverse party, but was marked out, by one appointed signal or other, for the subject of their diversion."

Nor had the students been content with "wordy warfare." They had come "to open and public insult." The Trojans not only treated the Greeks "with opprobrious language but assaulted them in their persons." [13] Such incidents showed the way things might drift at Oxford and made it all the more important that the Cardinal continue his intervention on the side of enlightenment.

This he did in his usual way — by the use of authority from a high place. The King sent down a message to suggest that the students "would do well to devote themselves with energy and spirit to the study of Greek literature." In this way, as Erasmus puts it, "silence was imposed on these brawlers." By the open encouragement of Greek and by discountenancing the opposition, Wolsey had done much to promote the progress of the Greek tongue throughout the university. Soon after these events Greek was much encouraged in Cambridge, and the whole tapestry of the New Learning began gradually to be hung before the people.

In all his blandishments up to now, even to the founding of seven lectureships, the Cardinal had dealt with Oxford University as a unit. Yet he knew from his own experience at Magdalen that the university was at best a loose confederacy and that the real power lay in the several colleges. Each college was a separate entity with immutable prerogatives. A college owned its own property, managed its own affairs, set up its own program of instruction, and in general asserted itself as independent of the machinations of any higher body, such as the university, that might attempt control. To those who could read the map of learning, Oxford in essence meant *college* and not *university*. And if my lord Cardinal was to have an essential part in that center of enlightenment, he must add to the cluster of colleges one of his own. In this way he could have some substantial say in what was taught, selecting the subjects and the teachers and modulating the emphases the way he chose — at least, at the outset, and before the Fellows fiercely took control in the way of Oxford Fellows.

In a word, when Wolsey moved to found a college at Oxford he began to step out of the role of a contented patron of learning acting at a distance and signified that he wanted to have some direct part in the processes of education. Wolsey had seen Magdalen completed, seen the fruits of a founder's beneficence ripen into tangible beauty and useful substance. In a college ideas and stones could be joined, each rendering homage to the other. He could house learning, give it a better residence than it had ever had before because he knew, among many other matters, how to build. And seeing that my lord Cardinal was in other particulars not without envy, it must be said that the recent example of Bishop Fox, his early benefactor and discoverer, in building so successfully the College of Corpus Christi had a plausible bearing on his motives. For if a bishop could found and build a college that excited the whole university with sparks of new learning, what might not an archbishop and cardinal do?

Convenient to the Cardinal's purpose, there lay near the town of Oxford an ancient monastery of Austin Canons known roundabout as St. Frideswide's. Venerable in the countryside for services once rendered, it was now in a fortunate state of decay. It would make an excellent site for a college, for, while it was withdrawn from the other colleges which stood for the most part along the High Street of the town, it commanded a clear view of those colleges, and from the pinched windows of its cells the monks could look out across the meadows to the Tower of Magdalen. Its church might make an acceptable college chapel, and to the north lay enough solid land to afford a gracious spot for a stately dining hall and a magnificent quadrangle in thoughtful stone.

Early in 1524 Wolsey's agent in Rome wrote that he was "almost at a point with the pope about Wolsey's matters." Clement VII was "contented to confirm the legateship with all faculties for life, which was never heard before." [14] More to the point of the Cardinal's activities as educator, the agent wrote good news about the monastery which he would make into a college. Wolsey had sought its dissolution, and with the right to apply to his proposed college not only the property but any tangible proceeds that might result from the appropriation of its lands. Rome had been informed that the need for increased facilities for study was most pressing in England and that Oxford University "seemed likely to come to an end by reason of its slender revenues." The Pope had been persuaded to this effect, and the same letter which conveyed the intelligence that Clement would grant the legateship for life stated that "the ordering of Frideswide's in Oxford is also at Wolsey's pleasure." [15]

With the proceeds of St. Frideswide's and other monasteries which he had dissolved or had brought within the reach of his legatine arm, Wolsey was ready to set up his college at Oxford and to lay elaborate plans for the school to be founded at Ipswich. In attending the details of the dissolutions allowed, Wolsey showed his usual vigor and acted with a characteristically personal touch: instead of establishing a foundation or corporation for the receipt of the lands of the suppressed religious houses, he had instructed that the deeds be drawn to himself. These deeds "granted the lands to him and his heirs in fee simple forever, and no 'trust' or 'use' was expressed therein." [16] Wolsey would see to it that he owned every stick and stone of his colleges, just as much as he owned Hampton Court, York Place, and The More. These places would be residences for his person; his colleges would be residences for his ideas.

The Cardinal could do nothing, not even build a house of ideas, without trumpets. There were so many preliminaries and orations in connection with the beginning of the college that the marvel is he ever got beyond the stage of public talk. He sent the Bishop of London to Oxford in the quality of the Cardinal's orator to announce that he was ready to go ahead with the building of his college and to state that he hoped it would make Oxford "the most celebrated and flourishing seminary of learning in the whole world." The orator was further instructed to say that Wolsey promised to bring the King and Queen to Oxford about the beginning of Lent and at that time there would be further orations and entertainments fitting to the occasion and the founding of the college.

Preparations for the royal visit were busily set in motion, and it was considered what orations should be spoken and what exercises should be performed. But after all the arrangements had been made, and at not a little expense, and after particular attention had been paid to acts which might venerate the Cardinal, another pestilence struck, "which occasioned both the Court and the Members of the University to withdraw." [17] It was a frustrating experience, for no detail of preparation had been spared. To make a good appearance for the royal and legatine visit, orders had been issued for all the students who were absent in the country to hasten back and take up residence.

The vast ceremonies postponed by the pestilence never took place. Not long afterwards, however, the Bishop of London returned to Oxford. This time he came not as an orator but as an executioner, for he was empowered to eject the monks of St. Frideswide's, "that room might be made for introducing the scholars and lecturers of the Cardinal's Foundation, so that they might form a regular and independent body, whereas they had lived dispersed before in several halls and colleges." The foundation stone for the Cardinal's college was laid July 15, 1525. For one fortnight the Cardinal's accounts show that the numbers employed on construction included 122 freemasons, 25 handhewers, 47 roughlayers, 32 carpenters, 12 sawyers, and 228 laborers.[18]

In the bull granting the Legate powers to dissolve the Priory of St. Frideswide's and in the King's patent confirming to the Cardinal the powers of that bull, the new foundation was to be called The College of

Secular Priests. Indeed this name was one expressed condition of the grant of the lands and properties of the priory. But in some way not clear to historians and easily speculated on in the light of Wolsey's general tendency to draw all things around him like his robes, the name was authorized "by other powers from the king" to be changed from The College of Secular Priests to Cardinal College.

The new name had the advantage of being an honest description. Nearly every stone of the handsome halls Wolsey caused to be emblazoned with his Cardinal's arms. The design showed his grandeur as a builder. The spacious dining hall revealed his interest in talk as a method of education. The statutes which he sent down to Oxford under his hand and seal described with minute foresight how the scheme was to be worked out. There were to be two hundred scholars, and there must also be an elaborate superstructure of functionaries to give the college a magnificence others did not have. There were to be a dean and sub-dean, threescore canons of the first rank and forty of the second. There were to be no fewer than thirteen chaplains, twelve clerks, and sixteen choristers. Lecturers were happily not overlooked in the design, but the statutes go on to specify that there be four "censors of manners and examiners of the proficiency of the students." There were to be three treasurers — a stipulation indicating Wolsey's own background as well as his views of money and its importance — four stewards, and twenty "inferior servants." Out of the funds there was also provision made "for the entertainment of strangers, the relief of the poor, and the keeping of horses for college business." [19]

No wonder the officials of the university wrote Wolsey to say that they rejoiced that "your lordship's erudition is equal to your great dignities" and to add: "We no longer consider your new society as an additional college to other colleges but as a University super-added to a University." It is, they add, "as if Oxford, by such an extraordinary accession to it, were really founded anew . . ."

Such prose in praise of the founder's beneficence — a founder to whom letters began "To the Right Reverend Father in God, and my very singular good Lord my Lord Cardinal of York, and Legate a Latere" and ended "at your Grace's Commandment" — might well have lulled Wolsey into complacency; and the dazzling deference paid him by Oxford and Cambridge could well have blinded him to the genuine concerns of education. Yet the record shows that his interests went beyond staff and real estate. Bishop Fox said of him that he "gathered together into that college whatsoever thing there was in the whole realm — all such men as were found to excel in any kind of learning and knowledge."

213

In his search for teaching talent Wolsey turned even to "the other University." Some of his best men came from Cambridge, bringing with them ideas deeply tinged with Lutheranism. The results in some cases were not happy and confirmed the public suspicion of the dangers inherent in education. Unmindful of the criticism engendered by his choices, the Cardinal continued to search for scholars who would promote the spread of enlightenment. "On native scholars he heaped preferment, and the most eminent foreigners were invited by him to teach in the universities." [20]

His interest in teaching materials was no less personal or persistent. His agents posted at foreign courts were instructed to keep their unofficial eyes open for valuable manuscripts that could be borrowed for purposes of transcription. The same agent in Rome who was busy enlisting the necessary bulls for the suppression of the monasteries which would pay for Cardinal College was told to order copies made of Greek manuscripts in Italian libraries. Wolsey asked a Venetian envoy to ask the head of the Venetian Republic for "transcripts, for the college library, of the Greek manuscripts which had belonged to Cardinals Grimani and Bessarion." [21] One of his plans was to furnish the library of his college with the learning and curiosities of the Vatican, "and to have the Pope's manuscripts transcribed for that purpose." The Cardinal was never too busy in his official duties to use his position for the advancement of his project at Oxford or to beg from any source fresh materials that would fill the place with the spirit of the New Learning. To make sure of his purpose, "the great writers of antiquity were to be expounded daily and all conversation conducted in either Latin or Greek." Erasmus wrote: "Whoever was distinguished by any art or science paid court to the Cardinal and none paid court in vain." [22]

The best glimpses of the man beneath the red hat are to be seen, not in connection with Cardinal College at Oxford, but in the founding and attention Wolsey gave to his preparatory school, named the College of St. Mary, at Ipswich. Here boys would be properly started on the road to learning. The spirit of inquiry might be touched and the inner life quickened early so that time would not be lost but could be improved when the young scholar reached Cardinal College. And in his plans for arrangements for the educational care of tender youth, Wolsey showed his perception of education at its best.

The emphasis brought by the Ipswich school was sorely needed. The new quests which had begun to animate university education had not yet touched the lower schools. In these dismal places instruction often went forward by brutal rote and routine, the aim being to beat into the boy as many rules of grammar and as many submissive attitudes as possible in a given time. And the time given was often long. One boy at Winchester College wrote that he rose at five, "and after prayers at six, devoted himself to writing Latin verses with his fellow pupils, each one of them 'chained as closely to his desk as Prometheus to the crag on Caucasus.' " [23]

The headmasters of some of the schools were of course occasionally men of learning and of a sincere bent toward learning. But the status of the teacher was low and he enjoyed little esteem, as one Cambridge student revealed when he said to Erasmus: "Who would be a schoolmaster that could live in any other way?" The approach to lower education was, it appears, strictly in terms of conveying a given body of facts and rules to unreceptive minds. This approach made for dullness on the part of both the teacher and the pupil. Learning in school held a kind of physical terror, no doubt in part due to the fact that the dullness had to be relieved somehow. Thus the "best schoolmaster was held to be 'the greatest beater.' "

The observer from abroad saw the system with more sensitiveness and wrote of it sharply. Erasmus looked upon the schoolmasters he had seen as "a race of men most miserable, who grow old in penury and filth in their schools — schools, did I say? prisons, dungeons. I should have said — among their boys, deafened with din, poisoned by a foetid atmosphere, but, thanks to their folly, fully self-satisfied, so long as they can bawl and shout to their terrified boys, and box, and beat, and flog them, and so indulge in all kinds of ways their cruel disposition." [24] He tells of one cleric in charge of a school who would have nothing but flogging masters. Once when Erasmus was present at a meal the master called out a lad of about ten who had just come to the school from his mother, who had especially commended the boy to the master. "But he at once began to charge the boy with unruliness, since he could think of nothing else, and must find something to flog him for, and made signs to the proper official to flog him. Whereupon the poor boy was forthwith floored then and there, flogged as though he had committed sacrilege. The divine again and again interposed 'That will do — that will do'; but the inexorable executioner continued his cruelty till the boy almost fainted. By and by the divine turned round to me and said, 'He did nothing to deserve it, but the boys' spirits must be subdued!' " [25]

The degree of brutality exercised varied with the temperament of those who wielded the rod and doubtless with the circumstance and provocation. But the point to note is that flogging grew normally out of the dreary practices of the schools and the attitudes of the officials. It might or might not take place in the extreme degree which Erasmus describes, but it was always implicit in an approach to education which was essentially punitive. The child was severely threatened with learning and at the same time threatened with the consequences of not learning.

In beneficent contrast, Wolsey set forth the postulates and principles he wanted observed in his school at Ipswich. These he embodied in his only book. Vocal above his contemporaries, a man of many remarks, who met every crisis with a spate of words, nonetheless he had found no occasion to form his ideas into a system, this being the function of a book. His words were mortgaged to his business. But when it came to his views on education, only a book would suffice. Entitled *Rudimenta Grammatices*, it was published with the usual trumpets to herald the Cardinal's greatness. Its title page bore his hat and arms and his motto, *Dominus mihi adjutor*, which, being interpreted, means, "God my helper"; or being interpreted by some could mean, "God my assistant." There is a blubbering and fulsome Latin poem which extols the virtues of Thomas, the Cardinal, Our President, and voices the sempiternal gratitude of the scholars in terms of almost Oxonian deference. The preface is itself a brew of sentiments calculated for the palate of public esteem: "None, I apprehend, can be ignorant how earnestly, how zealously, and how assiduously we have directed our labours to the point of the good of our country, and of our countrymen, and not to that of our private concerns. In this single respect, we shall think ourselves to have reaped the fairest harvest of piety, if, through the blessing of God we shall have improved the minds of our fellow citizens . . ." [26]

Once the turgid front matter of the book is overpassed, however, the content reveals the other Wolsey, known to few and scarcely known to himself. He has the grace to see and to say that the school he has founded at Ipswich and around which the whole book centers is "the highest and noblest testimony of our love to our country." He is willing to rest his case on this act and not on all his other assorted dignities. Then he gets down to the heart of the book, which is to provide a series of inspirational instructions to those who are to teach. He observes: "It avails little to have built a school, however magnificent it might be, unless it be furnished with skilful masters." It is upon the masters of the College of St. Mary that he lays the burden of his argument.

"We admonish particularly," he stresses, "that tender youth be not effected by severe stripes or threatening countenance or by any species of tyranny." Wolsey warns the master against overworking the pupil. "It will be best if the boy is led to regard the school as a place of pleasure, a literary playground." In all studies pleasure "should be so intermingled that the lad may think them a sport, not a labor." The pupils should not be "wearied by too long reading, nor exhausted by immoderate competition." Most remarkable of all is the allowance Wolsey makes for play, which he recognizes as important and not merely frivolous, seeing in it a way to relax the mind.

Wolsey laid down in delightful detail how the masters should undertake each of the subjects in the eight forms. They were to encourage in one form a "pleasing elocution," little attention having been paid to that matter in the schools. For another form the books, "if any," are specified. A further form is to read "Aesop, who is wittier? Terence, who is more useful?" The cardinal idea of the Cardinal all the way through his plans and instructions is to make reading a pleasure and to encourage intelligent training through contact with good authors. The master should use only those devices which arouse the student's interest in the writer.

Both the emphasis on the sharing of knowledge and the usefulness of learning indicate the fatherly interest Wolsey took in his school at Ipswich. He felt free to express and reveal his mind without validating his views to an academic hierarchy. The College of St. Mary was even more of a personal affair, as seems appropriate, to the man from Ipswich than Cardinal College was to the Cardinal of York. Here he would be a teacher, an intimate in the whole mysterious process of learning. Here he would not have to pose as a chancellor or legate while actually being a schoolmaster; he could be a schoolmaster forthrightly. There need be no role, no masquerade, no mumming. It was a comforting and sincere return to his first love, a love of learning, from which the whole journey of success had been a costly detour. His interests postponed and thwarted by a meddlesome destiny, he had at last come back to Ipswich with a mind aware of riches beyond the world of wealth and pomp.

Directions to parents were clear and simple. They were to provide the scholars with clothes for winter wear; ". . . also ye shall find him convenient books to his learning." Admission was based on ability and willingness to learn and not on social status: "If your child can read and write Latin and English sufficiently so that he be able to read and write his own lessons then shall he be admitted into the school for a scholar." If the child, after a reasonable season, "be found here unapt and unable to learning, then ye, warned thereof, shall take him away." [27]

Rules and regulations, no matter how minute, were prepared by the moving hand of Wolsey. No detail was too small to escape him, either in building or operation of the school: "If your child be absent six days and show not a reasonable cause such as sickness then his room is to be void without he be admitted again and pay four pence. Also if he fall thrice into absence he shall be admitted no more."

Wolsey had large plans and hopes as well as personal pride wrapped up in his Ipswich project. His aim was to demonstrate the values of public education. He looked forward to "a great extension of local secondary schools, educating boys free of charge throughout an eight-year classical course." He would see to it "that the very best in school and university education, in the finest structural surroundings, should be provided free of all charge for the sons of the people." [28] He would, with the consent of the Holy See, convert the wealth and property of languishing monasteries, which had served another day, into schools where young men might be taught. It were better, as he had written to Warham, that children be brought up in learning than that a monastery be maintained for doddering canons.

First, he had to dissolve the necessary number of monasteries — eleven in all — to provide the money for a school which, of course, must be grander than Eton. In particular he needed to take over a religious house that would provide a proper site, as he had done at Oxford. Conveniently the Priory of St. Peter and St. Paul, hard by the parish Church of St. Nicholas, where Thomas went to Mass as a boy, had sadly neglected its educational obligations. There had been no schoolmaster at this house of Augustinian canons in 1514 and again in 1526. The grounds were surrounded by a substantial wall of red brick, not unlike the wall that surrounded his beloved Hampton Court, and there was a priory church, St. Peter's, which would serve handsomely as the chapel of the new college. The Priory was surrendered March 6, 1527, and the parishioners of the adjoining church were left to seek their religious instruction elsewhere.

My lord Cardinal was now ready to build. He must consult with divers and sundry about materials and call upon any who might aid him, be they friend or foe. Even the Duke of Norfolk, who bore him no good will, wrote in March of 1528 to depose that he can save the Cardinal large sums of money on the building. Vast quantities of stone and oak would be needed to accomplish the ambitious designs. Wolsey had hoped to build with stone from Harwich Cliff. This meant negotiations with the Dowager Countess of Oxford to the end that he be allowed to take as much stone from her cliff at Harwich as he should need. The Countess demurred, and this consumed time and called for blandishments of charm and arguments. In the end the Countess reluctantly granted his wish, saying: "Be it hurtful or otherwise, Your Grace do your pleasure." Which he did. But the stone of Harwich was not enough, and the Cardinal had to turn next to the French King, with whom Henry was fortunately on good terms at the moment, and ask for stone from the quarries of Caen.

The gateways, one of them a miniature of his gate at York Place, could be of brick, but the college itself must have massive timbers as well as massive stone. And this requirement in turn called for giant oaks. Suffolk was at this time a place of oaks. Trees could be had right readily, but specifications had to be drawn and orders placed. How much detail this phase of the task alone required may be seen from a study of a paper that survives in the Record Office, giving the number of oaks to be felled, the location of the woods and their distance from Ipswich, as well as the names of the owners to whom payment should be made.

All phases of the undertaking had to be driven forward smoothly like six white horses. For speed was of the essence. There was something frantic about the way Wolsey rushed his school to completion. The foundation stone was laid June 15, 1528, but a letter dated January 26 of that year said that Wolsey had been building "some time since." Workmen labored night and day to get it ready for the opening in September 1528.

The man named dean of St. Mary's College was William Capon, a Cambridge man, who had founded a grammar school at Southampton. Whatever his other qualifications, he knew the founder's interests and kept in unceasing touch with the affairs of the college, both great and small, reporting them with due fidelity to Wolsey. He assures the Cardinal that he has received from Mr. Dawndy 171 tons of stone and that "within a fortnight next after Michelmas . . . we shall have 100 tons more," so that "your workmen will not be unoccupied for want of stone." The same reliable Mr. Dawndy also promised that before Easter next "we shall have here ready 1000 tons more of the said stone. And thus the holy trinity preserve your grace . . ."

He is no less meticulous in acknowledging gifts, including the receipt of nine bucks, one from His Grace's servant. And at the same time the Prior of Butley gave the dean a "fatte crane." Upon the advice of Wolsey's agents, one of them being Thomas Cromwell, who were visiting at Ipswich to see how the work progressed, ten shillings was given to the town fathers "to make merry"; and money was also conveyed to the bailiffs' wives and portmen's wives that they too might make merry.

There is no reliable evidence that the busy and preoccupied Cardinal ever visited the college he caused to be built in Ipswich, though he once spoke with modest satisfaction of the college as "not inelegant." There is much to show, however, that had the native returned, he would have been received on bended knee. In January of 1529 the master of the school wrote Wolsey a flowery letter to express the gratitude of the local people for the munificence of His Grace. An official letter signed by the bailiffs and the portmen put their sentiments firmly on record: ". . . we therefore shall daily humbly pray to God to send unto your Grace in this world Life, Honour, Prosperity and Health in Body, with the accomplishment of all your noble Acts, and in the Life to come the joys of Heaven . . ." The elder Wolsey, now dead these thirty-three years, must have smiled and turned over comfortably in his grave when these words were written.

Capon writes respectfully to say that it has been necessary to add a sexton to the staff and he hopes the Cardinal will approve, pointing out that the move was sanctioned by Mr. Cromwell when he looked the situation over. The Cardinal is given to understand that one man is not able to keep the church clean, ring the bells, prepare the altar lights, see all the ornaments well and sufficiently repaired, and "set forth every day all such things as is to be occupied about God's service." Hence the selection of the new sexton, who has been named "unto the time I know farther your Grace's pleasure." Capon further says that the number of priests needed to maintain the Masses specified in Wolsey's statutes to be said every day will also need to be increased.

The father's benediction and decision are sought on all matters both great and small. Wolsey must by his nature keep in such close touch with his colleges that he requires to be consulted on the addition of a new sexton. And he welcomes news that will give him a knowledge of how the enterprise is going as well as some picture of how it appears to operate. Capon tells him of plans to hold a procession on the eighth of September, which was Our Lady's Day. But the day "brought very foul weather and it rained sore continually, so that we could not go in procession through the town to Our Lady's Chapel according to our statute by your grace made, but we made as solemn a procession in your Grace's College Church as could be devised." He tells him also that the new copes, vestments, and altar cloths which Cromwell and his companions brought had been used on the occasion, and the whole spectacle had been seen by as many people as could stand in the churchyard.[29]

The hunger of the Cardinal for these details, snug though he was in his robes and palaces, shows the unaffected character of his interest. He who could manage the King's wars and browbeat the Pope must know down to the last detail, including the gift of a fat crane, what was going on in his colleges. And the hope for these colleges, based perhaps on a touching faith in their purpose, was to endure long after other hopes had vanished.

CHAPTER XII

WHEN Wolsey assembled workmen to build at Hampton Court Manor a habitation befitting his dignity, he caused fresh water for the palace to be brought from springs three miles distant in heavy conduits laid underneath the bodies of two rivers. And the system so fashioned continued to supply the needs of the palace for over three hundred and twenty-five years after his death.

The Cardinal had taken a page from the monks' books. Not uncommonly water was brought into towns from catchment areas by open channels called leats; not often by pipes. Wolsey would not, as many people did, drink the "diluted sewage" of the Thames. Spring water was collected in standpipes on Coombe Hill, then conveyed "in a double set of strong leaden pipes from Coombe to Surbiton, under the Hogsmill River (a small tributary of the Thames), and then under the Thames above Kingston Bridge, and so through the Home Park to the palace." [1] The leaden pipes, which were among the first molded in the north of England, were laid in lengths of twenty-five feet, joined with a heavy coating of lead at the joints. The diameter of each pipe was about two and a half inches, and the pipe itself was half an inch thick. How much labor must have been involved in laying the pipes can be seen from the fact that the weight ran fifteen pounds to the lineal foot; it is reckoned that over two hundred and fifty tons were used.

One cannot discern in the Cardinal's background or schooling any factor which might account for such remarkable ability as a builder. Wolsey seems to have been a stonemason at heart, an artist who employed bricks and timbers on a lavish scale to achieve an effect. It was a natural and incurable tendency in him, and he could not pause long in any house without seeing how it could be improved or, if the opportunity allowed, without making it over.

His inner uncertainty might explain his unceasing urge to build something solid on the good earth, but it could not explain the rare and enviable talent with which he wrought his effects. This talent expressed itself not merely in design and beauty but also in attention to the householder's basic concerns. Hampton Court had great veins for carrying rain water and other refuse into the Thames. The Cardinal's foresight had seen the importance of drainage, and it was arranged that rainfall from every part of the building should be gathered in sewers three feet wide and five feet deep, made snugly of brick. He could not escape the inevitable English damp, but he would not encourage it. Although the ground floor of the building is scarcely ten feet above the average level of the river, as Law remarks, it remains wonderfully free from damp.

Proper arrangements for sewage were a part of the Cardinal's struggle for convenience. In several parts of the palace were baths and toilet facilities, all of the principal apartments having private accommodations. The area of glass in Wolsey's palace "was more than doubled . . . The windows were glazed, and no longer closed only with a shutter." [2]

In spite of the moat that surrounded it — almost for decorative purposes, one might imagine — the palace was designed primarily for residence, not for defense. Another feature was the gallery, by means of which one could move from one part of the great house to another without crossing open courts or stumbling through other rooms. Wolsey's galleries "set a fashion that was followed by nearly every great house of Tudor or Jacobean times." [3] His ambulatory spaces were long porticoes, or halls with windows on each side, looking on gardens or the rivers. They afforded him a place for exercise indoors, protected from the unscrupulous English weather.

His health, which was wondrously indifferent, occasioned much anxiety and caused him to seek, if in vain, all the means by which the ills that flesh is heir to might be held off or subdued. There is a tradition, confirmed by subsequent details, that Wolsey chose the site of Hampton Court because the physicians of the realm, aided by learned doctors from Padua, looked over the countryside at his behest and assured him that this manor was by all odds "the most healthy spot within twenty miles of London." It was declared to be a place of "extraordinary salubrity." Report has it that he suffered from a kidney stone, which may account for the colic of which he often complained. Springs in the vicinity were said to provide waters free from substances which would irritate or increase the stone. There were also recurrent attacks of ague and of quinsy, the latter being a particular hazard to orators and talkative persons. In the course of it tonsils swell to the point of bursting; the term derives from two Greek words that picture the victim as a choking dog.

Wolsey wanted Hampton Court chiefly as a suburban home. He had built York Place in London, hard by Westminster, as a kind of official residence; he had come also to own a palace known as The More near Harrow; and as one who got in his grasp the revenues of the Abbey of St. Albans he occupied occasionally the official palace of the Abbot, this being called Tittenhanger. Hampton Court, however, was to be a haven of withdrawal, a convenient seat close enough to London to give him the feeling of keeping in touch with the affairs of Church and State, yet far enough away that he might escape importunate business suitors. In the English manner his home was his castle, complete with moat; the moat that no longer served any military purpose might now serve as a defense of privacy, a protest against invasion.

Beneath the layers tht made up the public Wolsey was a householder, a person who showed a daily and painstaking interest in terracing, gardening, drainage, the color of brick, the choice of woods, and pleasing architectural effects. Even while he considered the lease of the original manor house and the demesne lands on which it stood, he invited the King and Queen to join him in an inspection of the property. He had to have the approval of friends, the nods of acceptance, as well as the sanction of his royal master. The royal couple visited the place on March 20, 1514, and on January 11, 1515, a ninety-nine-year lease was signed at a rental of fifty pounds per annum between the Knights of the Hospital of St. John of Jerusalem and "the Most Reverend Father in God Thomas Wolsey, Archbishop of York." [4]

Wolsey had his property, desirable in every respect, with a path of water that led to London. Nearby to the royal palace at Richmond, Hampton was already tinged with history. Elizabeth of York, the eighth Henry's mother, had gone there to make a retreat and pray for a happy delivery, Law declares, just a month before she died in childbirth. Henry VII had used the place as a subsidiary to his palace at Richmond. Hampton Court had, in other words, a record as a place of escape and withdrawal.

The first moves Wolsey made indicated that he hoped to keep its character private. Along with the manor house were some two thousand acres of pasture land. These he proceeded at once "to convert into two parks, fencing them partly with paling, and partly enclosing them with a stout red-brick buttressed wall." Into this wall he caused to be inserted black bricks so arranged as to form crosses at intervals and thus herald to the passerby the ecclesiastical dignity of the owner. The moat, one of the last to be dug in England, in itself announced the intended privacy. And as a further means of withdrawal the Cardinal gave immediate attention to extensive gardens and mazes. Early bills still exist in the Record Office for spades, barrows, seeds, and plants. One bill is for twigs to bind the arbor.

Another is for "four days weeding in my lord's garden and orchard at 3d the day." Another is for "a tub to water th'erbs." [5]

The Cardinal's primary work at Hampton Court, whatever turn toward public display it inevitably took later, was guided and sweetened by sentiment. He kept in touch with his former wife, Joan, and the man she married, George Legh. This couple had "issue one son and three daughters," the son named Thomas and the daughters Isabell, Margarett, and Marye. When George Legh fell into dispute over property with Sir John Stanley, natural son of the Bishop of Ely, the Cardinal right earnestly championed the cause of the Leghs, keeping Stanley in prison twelve months before he was induced to give up a contested lease. [6]

All of these sustained family loyalties and interlocking relationships furnished grist for gossip and indignation. At the same time they were signs to show a side of his nature which was balked by convention but which sought in Hampton Court to express itself all the same. Wolsey was a family man without a family. What privacy and home life he managed to eke out of his histrionic existence came to him at Hampton Court. The sharpest instances of what one writer calls his "calculated inaccessibility" are to be found in his life at Hampton Court. There is significance in the statement of the Venetian ambassador who had occasion to visit him frequently at his country residence: "One traverses eight rooms before reaching his audience chamber." [7] The rooms were in a sense inner moats. Brewer tells us that the Cardinal would slip away from London when the press of official duties became too burdensome there, have eight stout oarsmen take him to Hampton Court, and leave word that he was not to be troubled with business until he returned to town.

The importunity of one Sir T. Alen, a confidential agent of the Earl of Shrewsbury and Lord Steward of the royal household, shows the problem that both the Cardinal and those who dealt with him faced. Alen once tried vainly to get an audience with the Cardinal in London. Failing, he followed Wolsey to Hampton Court "and besought his Grace that he might know his pleasure." Wolsey refused to grant him an audience. Undismayed, Alen persisted, and the next day he sought to interview the Cardinal while he was walking in one of his gardens. This caused the Cardinal displeasure and Alen despair. Later he wrote of Wolsey: "When he walks in the Park he will suffer no suitor to come nigh unto him; but commands him away as far as a man will shoot an arrow." Alen ends his lamentation, having violated all the principles of privacy, by saying to the Earl who had sent him on his mission: "I had rather your lordship had commanded me to Rome than to deliver him letters and bring answers to the same." [8]

Such complaints were not confined to those who hounded him to his lair. Members of his own household, his agents abroad, as well as officers of the court on the King's business, found him hard to engage. Likewise dignitaries of the Church and diplomats on errands of state. For all his efforts to maneuver the world and the Pope, he longed for some semblance of solitude; he could not hope to get it anywhere save in Hampton Court and then, busy with household as well as official duties, only occasionally. And when he failed to find it there his resentment of intrusion led to rudeness of Olympian proportions.

Not even the Cardinal, who was a master of pretense, could pretend that Hampton Court was merely his home. Being but a feature of his conspicuous existence, it had to be multi-purpose — a setting for affairs of state as well as for the affairs of his own heart. He took a lively and personal interest in supervising its construction, floating back and forth in his stoutly rowed barge between the manor and Westminster on the genial waters of the Thames. It was the interest of any man who watches the building of his house day after day, winces at the delays, notes with pleasure the fulfilment of line, swears at the gaucheries of the builders, solaces his mind with imagination of the completed project.

Wolsey's concerns grew more complicated as his edifice developed before his eyes. His palace must excel. It must demonstrate, as did his offices, the rise of an Ipswich lad. Hampton Court had to be spaciously conceived and executed with some proper sense of hospitality as well as comfort. He built with a vengeance, as if to vindicate at one and the same time the class and the loins from which he had sprung and the kingdom in which he dwelt. For if this residence of the King's chief minister could dazzle the eyes of foreign ambassages accredited to it, it would argue eloquently for the state of the nation. As with men, so with nations: grandeur and magnificence, not merely military might, were becoming signs of self-esteem. The ability to build served as a token by which the rising power and selfhood of small and competitive England could assert itself. Hampton Court must stand as a tower to tell the world what tiny England, bringing men and materials together from many parts and artists from afar, could accomplish practically overnight.

The result of all this English energy directed by the Cardinal had the appearance rather of a city than a palace. The edifice being destined by its design and appeal to be tampered with and expanded by Henry VIII and successive monarchs who fancied themselves Wolseys, the size of the original structure cannot be determined. Law reckons the palace to have covered no fewer than eight acres and to have had in its vastness a thousand rooms. It was the largest building that had been erected in England since the Romans left. This was important, size being in English eyes a part of magnificence. Bigness could be seen at a glance; it afforded a canvas for the imagination.

Significant to the purpose of impressing visitors and the laying on of hospitality, the entire first court was made up entirely of rooms for guests. One French ambassador reported that there "were two hundred and four score beds, the furniture to most of them being silk, and all for the entertainment of strangers only." [9] He observes also that "the very bed chambers had hangings of wonderful value, and every place did glitter with innumerable vessels of gold and silver." The Cardinal's prodigal sense of color showed itself on every hand. His own colors were byse and gold. Byse has been described as a fierce light blue. He liked his colors strong. The inventory of his effects occupies forty folio pages, and it shows "scores upon scores of beds of red, green and russet velvet, satin and silk, with rich curtains and fringes of the same materials, and all with magnificent . . . canopies and backs."

Sheets were made of silk of Rennes. "Blankets were soft and white and furred with lamb's wool." Hundreds of counterpanes are listed, some of "tawny damask, lined with blue buckram." Others were of blue, green, and red satin; of blue and yellow silk. One was of "red satin with a great rose in the midst, wrought with needlework, and with garters. Still another had a tree in the middle "and beasts with scriptures, all wrought with needlework."

In his endeavor to beguile foreign visitors with the quality of English goods, the Cardinal had not neglected his own comfort. The inventory lists one bed, acquired not too long before his fall from the King's grace, which was "for my Lord's own lying." It had eight mattresses, each of them "stuffed with 13 pounds of carded wool." There were four pillowcases to go along with the deep mattresses, "two of them seamed with black silk and fleurs-de-lys of gold; and the other two with white silk and fleurs-de-lys of red silk." [10]

The speed with which the whole establishment of Hampton Court was brought into being, if not actually finished, was not less impressive than its size and munificence. The lease of the manor was not formalized until the early part of 1515, and by May of the following year, crews having been busy night and day, the palace was far enough along that Wolsey felt that he could appropriately entertain the King and Queen at a banquet there. Work went on steadily afterwards, of course, and it was not until four years later that Wolsey lived there for long periods of time. No record has been found of master plans for the building; and there is no record of an architect. It is not unlikely that the Cardinal laid out the plans, which appeared simple but were actually a departure from prevailing modes and foreshadowed a symmetrical treatment of buildings that were to follow. There was a succession of large courts "built on an axial line . . . through the archways between them." The gatehouses were "embellished with turrets and bay-windows, but the rest of the work, including the sides of the courts," was very plain.

There were many details which, although not novel, were relatively untried and called for close attention in construction. Bay windows had been introduced in the fifteenth century, but then they were small. Wolsey gave them a new distinction by making them more than one story high. Also the heads were squared in a firm English fashion instead of pointed after the manner of the Continent. Mullions and transoms "were much increased in number." [11] The chimneys, lofty and irregularly grouped where they were needed, were of cut and molded brick. Here English workmanship was shown at its best. Each chimney was a piece of useful art. Italians were given more decorative assignments in the courts. There was for some odd reason "a series of terra-cotta busts of four Roman emperors done in relief by the Italian artist Gian da Maiano. Still surviving, they look strange against the flat, undecorated Tudor brickwork."

Merely to build, staff, equip, and furnish such a far-flung establishment as Hampton Court might well have engaged all the faculties of a man of Wolsey's stature. He "employed some two thousand five hundred artisans and laborers, all of whom were treated in a liberal and kindly manner." [12] How many of these artisans, used on his various building enterprises, were put to work at any one time on Hampton Court it is impossible to say, but we do know the undertaking was well organized. One report has it that workmen sang while they built Hampton Court Palace, music being a ready part of the common life in those days, what with lutes being kept in barbershops to accompany any sudden outburst of song. Chalk was carried from Taplow and Windsor; timber came from Reigate. Brick kilns were kept in service at Battersea, from which bricks were bought at four shillings per thousand — the effect was all the more striking because the bricks varied in color from light red to purple-brown. A fast pace in construction was possible in part because the site was on water. Lime came from Limehouse.

Wolsey did not scruple to let diplomats know how close such matters as the furnishings of the palace lay to his bounding heart. He had an un-ashamed weakness for Damascene carpets, as the Venetian ambassador easily discovered. Venice, being a land of shrewd merchants who competed with the English, never stood in great favor with Wolsey, and he managed al-ways to keep her ambassador in a position where the Venetian might feel contrained to grant a favor. Once when some Venetian merchants had incurred his momentous displeasure, they sought to reconcile the Cardinal by the gift of carpets.

This proposal Wolsey haughtily refused, making it clear that he would have no traffic with merchants. He was by no means as coy or hard to per-suade, however, if a gift to his establishment could be made to look official. When the ambassador returned to Venice, he reported that the Cardinal wanted Venice to send him a hundred Damascene carpets. These, the am-bassador made clear, the Cardinal had asked for several times, and he had "expected to receive them by the last galleys." The ambassador strongly recommended the gift, adding that if the Venetian Signory itself should not choose to incur the expense, "the slightest hint to the London factory would induce that body to take it on themselves." If the gift were made, the ambassador felt sure it might lead the English to reduce the duties on Venetian wines. "But to discuss the matter further," he said, "until the Cardinal receives his 100 carpets would be idle." [13] The Cardinal's inven-tory notes the receipt of sixty carpets from Venice not long after.

Wolsey might thus, without troubling his roomy conscience, obtain cer-tain perquisites that came from his privileged position. But the task of managing the enormous household which he created was a task on which foreign ambassadors could not help. The duties of this management de-volved upon him and taxed any energies that remained from his other as-signments. Merely to select, recruit, and look to the welfare of a staff of five hundred household servants in various stations called for an energetic mind and rare insight. Some of these were lords and some were gentlemen, all pledged to service in the Cardinal's household, according to the custom of the day, for such political advantage or training in manners and graces as this association might afford.

In the great hall of the palace, where there was food to be had at all hours, there were three officers: the steward, who was a priest; the treasurer, who was a knight; and the comptroller, who was a squire. While some of the servants thus had dignity by virtue of birth or connec-tion, others had it by virtue of the knowledge and skills they brought to their jobs. And they all had business with my lord Cardinal and could not be ignored like so many sticks. The master cook presided over one of the two principal kitchens, the privy kitchen for the Cardinal's own table. He was a man dressed in velvet and satin, and he wore a gold chain around his neck. In the hall kitchen there were two clerks of the kitchen and a comptroller, a clerk of the spicery. Besides these valuable aides who looked after the intake and outgo of food, there were two master cooks and twelve assistant cooks "and laborers and children of the kitchen." [14] Responsibility in this division of labor was minute.

The harried master of Hampton Court had in his pay and care hundreds of other servants at lower levels of duty, all of them now and then, and often daily, on his mind. There were eighty who labored in the bakehouse, buttery, scullery, wafery, and other places connected with the preparation of food. Nearly a hundred more were employed in such places as the woodyard, laundry, and wardrobe. The Cardinal's stud and stable had sixteen grooms besides a master of the horse and various officers, together with helpers enough to attend to something like one hundred horses and mules for general use, six special horses for occasions of state, and six gray and white mules "for my Lord's own saddle." The rest of the staff included one hundred and sixty personal attendants, among them twelve gentlemen-ushers and various waiters for his privy chamber. There were sixteen doctors, or leeches, in the Cardinal's employ, two secretaries, three clerks, and four counselors learned in the law. All served the Cardinal, and in serving him were available to the household he entailed. And there had to be running footmen, messengers, and heralds to take word of my lord's bidding and to keep England and Europe at his beck.

As if this host of attendants would not suffice, there were others of a more delicate sort that required special care in selection and handling. These included sixty priests in copes, "who attended the services on great festivals and walked before the Cardinal in procession round the cloisters of Hampton Court." Every great house in those days had its choir, both for the entertainment and beguiling of visitors and members of the families and servants and for singing at other lords' manors. Even in the savage north this was so. These choirs were a matter of personal rivalry among the lords. Traill tells us that the Earl of Northumberland "was concerned to strengthen the voices of his basses, counter-tenors, standing tenors and 'tribles.' His taberett, lute and rebeck visited the houses of lords at the great feasts, as theirs visited his, and each household's minstrels received on these visits their fixed rewards." [15]

Wolsey's choir was his pride and joy, and his rivalry was spurred by King Harry's boisterous love of music. Nothing would satisfy Wolsey but to recruit a choir that would catch the King's ear and perhaps excite his envy.

In both particulars he succeeded. He had twelve singing priests, twelve singing children, and sixteen singing laymen, as well as soloists for singing parts of the Mass.

It was one of the mistakes Wolsey made, as if by compulsion, that he surpassed the King. The King told Cornish, the master of the Chapel Royal, and the judgment was duly reported to Wolsey by Richard Pace, that "your Grace's chapel is better than his, and proved the same by this reason, that if any manner of new song be brought unto both the said chapels to be sung ex proviso, the said song should be better and more surely handled by your chapel than by his Grace's."

Henry took a fancy to one of the singing boys in the Cardinal's choir and had Pace, royal secretary at the time, write and say that the King admired the boy's voice greatly and would like to have him for his own chapel. Wolsey took the hint and delivered the boy, and in acknowledgment thereof the King's secretary wrote: "My Lord, if it were not for the personal love that the King's Highness doth bear unto your Grace, surely he would have out of your chapel not children only but also men . . ." The boy was a great success, and Wolsey got the satisfaction at least of hearing the master of Henry's choir extol Mr. Pigot, Wolsey's choirmaster, for the excellent way in which the boy had been trained.[16]

All of which is to show that my lord Cardinal could not preside over a manor of the dimensions of Hampton Court, touching as it did the immediate destinies of five hundred distinct and often temperamental individuals, without involving himself in detail which he could not anticipate and complexities that would have wrecked a lesser man. Even if he had not been concerned with people, he still had the tangible and removable property to worry about. Two Venetian ambassadors at separate times independently estimated the worth of his gold and silver plate to be £150,000 — all of this under the roof of a man whose father had bought a house for £8 and some land. Giustiniani said that wherever he turned there was a sideboard of plate. And the plate on public display was not all. Cavendish tells us that every chamber had "a bason and ewer of silver, some gilt and some parcel gilt, and some two great pots of silver in like manner, and one pot at the least with wine and beer, a bowl or goblet, and a silver pot to drink beer in; a silver candlestick or two, with both white lights and yellow lights of three sizes of wax . . ."

With the growth of Wolsey's power and the multiplication of his duties, Hampton Court became more and more of a hostel and less and less of a home. Always there was the need of impressing visitors. In the total picture the outside as well as the inside had to have fastidious care. The cult of the garden had begun in England. As the houses were marked by symmetry, "so were the gardens neat and formal, the broad gravelled paths carrying on the lines of the building and flower-beds." The beds were filled with flowers "for the delectation sake unto the eye and the odoriferous savors unto the nose." These features had increasing importance as Wolsey made Hampton Court the center of the kingdom.

Henry was wont to repair to the Cardinal's house divers times in a year for his recreation. When he did, "banquets were set forth, masks and mummeries, in so gorgeous a sort and costly manner, that it was heaven to behold. There wanted no dames, nor damsels, meet or apt to dance with the maskers or to garnish the place for that time, with other goodly disports." Cavendish tells of one occasion when the King suddenly appeared in a mask, accompanied by a dozen others in masks, all dressed as shepherds. The hair and beards of the masks were made of gold wire or silver "or else of good black silk." The group was accompanied by sixteen torch-bearers.

The affair had been prearranged to look spontaneous. A banquet was in progress when, outside, cannon announced the arrival of unexpected guests. My lord Cardinal was sitting alone under the cloth of state and, at the sound of the guns, he sent a lord and a knight to see whatever it was that so disturbed their peace. They returned, after looking out upon the Thames, and reported that it must be a foreign ambassage.

At this point my lord Cardinal instructed the lord and the knight to go and greet the guests in French, finding their mission, and "desiring them to sit down with us, and to take part of our fare." The welcoming committee "went incontinent down into the hall, where they received them with twenty new torches, and conveyed them up into the chamber, with such a number of drums and fifes as I have seldom seen in one place and time." When the newcomers arrived in the chamber they went to the Cardinal, two and two together, and the Lord Chamberlain said: "Sir, forasmuch as they be strangers, and cannot speak English, they have desired me to declare unto you that they, having understanding of this your triumphant banquet, where was assembled such a number of excellent fair dames, could do no less, under the supportation of your Grace, but to repair hither to view as well their incomparable beauty . . . to dance with them and to have their acquaintance."

So the mummery went, ending right happily of course. The lord Cardinal, after further ado, bethought and said to the Lord Chamberlain that he detected "a noble man amongst them, who is more meet to occupy this seat and place than am I; to whom I would most gladly surrender the same, according to my duty , if I knew him."

This intelligence in English the Lord Chamberlain relayed to the guests in whispered French and then duly reported that the lord Cardinal had been right all along: there was such a man; and if his Grace were able to pick him out, he would be "content to disclose himself, and to take and accept your place, most worthily."

Then the Cardinal looked over the shepherds in disguise and said: "Meseemeth the gentleman with the black beard should be even he." To the rollicking delight of the assembled multitude, my lord Cardinal missed. He had fixed upon Sir Edward Neville. The King was as amused as the guests at the mistake "and could not forbear laughing." He then pulled down his own visor and showed "such a pleasant countenance and cheer" that all rejoiced. The Cardinal offered the King his seat of honor beneath the cloth of state, but the King said he would first go and change his attire. When he and his maskers had returned, "every man new appareled . . . in came a new banquet before the King's Majesty." It was made up, Cavendish estimates, of full two hundred dishes.[17]

Of such elaborate and costly nonsense and fantastic party-crashing were the King's and the Cardinal's lighter moments compounded. It was as if the whole palace with its sturdiness and its careful plan had been turned into a doll's house. No doubt these pastimes did cheer the sovereign and keep between him and his minister some camaraderie; they afforded the King the pleasure of being aggressively incognito, and there was doubtless something healthy in having both Wolsey and Henry pretend that Henry was only a rustic. It was an escape from fact — a pleasant conceit with overtones of irony.

CHAPTER XIII

Now you understand that my lord of York used the premises of Hampton Court as a spacious stage where he could play the role in which he fancied himself cast: arbiter of the destinies of Europe. Agape with admiration, his gentleman-usher records: "All ambassadors of foreign potentates were despatched by his wisdom, to whom they had continual access for their despatch. His house was always resorted to like a king's house, with noblemen and gentlemen, with coming and going in and out, feasting and banqueting these ambassadors divers times, and all other right nobly." [1]

From the moment of his rise to power, Europe held a perennial and fatal fascination for Wolsey. Its chicanery was strong drink, and he could not leave it alone or get enough of it. Its affairs had the character of mummings and disguisings, not unlike the games and pastimes with which he was wont to beguile his jaded guests. He played Europe like a game.

In this respect he was not alone, but he had to a remarkable degree that enthusiastic simplicity of mind which leads men to believe that complex problems can be settled at the summit. He saw nations in the guise of kings. It was his bent and his genius to deal with persons, not with problems, with heads of state or their pliant spokesmen, not with the clamant voice of peoples. The concern he showed in his own country for the welfare of farmers and for the administration of justice among commoners seems never to have been transferred into perception of the aspirations that might lie behind the façade of royalty abroad. Rather he behaved as if Europe were populated entirely by kings and queens and bishops, especially the Bishop of Rome, and assorted wily ambassadors. Hence my lord Cardinal's conduct of foreign affairs had the clean lines of a great epic and the poignant failure of a great drama. It was played out to its bitter end because he pitted himself blindly against crowned heads and reckoned not with forces that were more than kings and cardinals.

In what he ignored and neglected, as well as in what he did, one must assess Wolsey as the King's minister for foreign affairs. He interested himself primarily in the known, organized, tangible world, the world readily at hand and accredited, the countries more or less like England, a proper club of countries. This meant a small part of the known world.

The unspeakable Turk, while he surged ever closer to the heart of Europe, never got beyond the edge of Wolsey's calculations. The Turk was outside the rim of civilized society. His strenuous advances, of course, served as a strident warning, sounded the alarum for Europe. The threat of the Turk afforded the ever-ready means by which Christian princes could be urged to unite — in a way that Wolsey wanted them to unite. The infidel furnished the excuse for peace in Christendom; yet even after he had overthrown Hungary and stormed the very gates of Vienna, the excuse was never quite sufficient.

A sultan who came to be known as Soliman the Magnificent ascended the throne of the Turk in 1520, moving his forces all the way to the banks of the Danube, throwing the shadow of the fez across all the council tables of Europe. But with Soliman the Magnificent the magnificent

Cardinal had no diplomatic intercourse. Incurable negotiator though he was, Wolsey sought to drive no bargains with Soliman. Francis I, one of the kings Wolsey used in his games of chess and charades, was later to arrange an alliance with Soliman. Francis dealt with Soliman as a fellow king with fellow interests. The Cardinal treated him as a heathen afar. Such a sultan, enlightened in the noble arts of war and given to fits of versemaking under a nom de plume, could not be ignored by any man who looked upon Europe. But he could be kept snobbishly beyond the English pale. He was but the tocsin by which my lord of York called the kings of his day to peace and to war.

Likewise Moscow remained remote and inert in the diplomatic fancies of the Cardinal. Russ was not even a threat and consequently did not penetrate the solemnities in which England, France, and the Empire performed the ritual of diplomacy. The Kremlin kept cautiously to itself, suspicious of the rest of Europe, and it required stern initiative to enter into negotiations with those who guarded its secrets. Some fitful attempts were made, but not by Wolsey. In 1516 the Emperor Maximilian sent forward an ambassador to Moscow. His name was Sigismund von Herberstein. He had been sent on various missions in Europe, and his aim in this case was to try to fashion a peace between Russ and Poland-Lithuania.

Herberstein was received on his approach to Moscow with a combination of hospitality and suspicion. "First a courtier met him on the road with a gift of two horses, then an interpreter appeared . . . He was escorted into the Moscow gate by 15 nobles and 30 grooms, who cleared a way through the staring crowd. But when he asked questions about the Kremlin and its people out of frank curiosity, he aroused the suspicion of the guides; thereafter he got information in roundabout ways, without asking questions." [2]

If Russ was coming gradually to be a part of the outside world, it was not a part of Wolsey's world. One could not expect Wolsey to establish intercourse with a country where the Pope was held in low esteem. Indeed, Herberstein in speaking of Vasily, the reigning prince, notes that "there is no one to whom he is more obnoxious than to the Pope, whom he does not condescend to designate by any title but that of Doctor."

Nor did my lord of York pay any more heed to the lands across the turbulent Atlantic than he did to the city across the plains and rivers of Russ. Columbus died without knowing that he had discovered a new continent. Wolsey seems to have lived and died in ignorance of the significance of what Columbus discovered and of the significance of other voyages being made in distant waters. During 1519, when Henry and Wolsey were

234

zealously occupied with the election of a new emperor of that decadent vestige of medievalism known as the Holy Roman Empire, a Portuguese sailor in the hire of Spain drifted to the south of South America, sailed through "dark and forbidding" straits there and "so came into the Pacific Ocean."

A new continent, even a new nation, engaged the mind of Wolsey less than a new intrigue. There were no kings or queens or bishops or castles in the world beyond the wide seas. "His outlook was that of a man oblivious of the marvelous opening-up of the world which was going on around him and of the part which his country might play therein. Until quite the end of his ascendancy there is no authenticated voyage of discovery or attempt to penetrate new markets with the produce of industry." [3] Interest in exploration had sagged after the death of the seventh Henry, and the few projects for exploration put forward in the reign of Henry VIII died for lack of venturesome support. The City Companies in London were asked "at Wolsey's instance in 1521 to furnish ships for an expedition to the north-west, with a promise of very substantial privileges in the new trade to be opened up." [4] But Wolsey had other fish to fry, and not the expendable energy to follow through. The reply of the City Companies showed that "they were unable to envisage the meaning of the proposal and saw in it only a wanton hazarding of men's lives." [5] It was better to hazard English lives in France, where such hazarding had become a habit. What was the appeal of a land peopled with naked savages when one could play at wits with richly robed princes?

Apart from his addiction to drama and pageantry, there was another reason why Wolsey ignored the world outside his immediate ken and kept his eye on Francis instead. It was his sense of indebtedness to Pope Leo X. The red hat which Wolsey had so diligently tried to wrest from the hand of Leo had been held just beyond his grasp until Francis had routed the papal forces at Marignano. Only after events had italicized the Pope's need of Henry's help had the red hat been sent. It therefore became incumbent upon Wolsey, in exchange for the high honor conferred upon him, to acknowledge the Pope's plight and lay plans for his relief. The Turks could come later. After Marignano it was Francis who was the menace at the gates of Rome.

In this manner it came about that Wolsey was named in effect England's minister for foreign affairs by the same act that he was named Cardinal Ebor. His future course was set and determined by the circumstances in which he received the cardinalate. He was at the very beginning of the fullness of his power drawn inextricably into the dogfights of Europe, all the more so because the wishes of the papacy coincided with the wishes of the King of England. My lord of York expertly served two masters. He did it comfortably and with none of the spasms of conscience that usually come from divided loyalty. It was one of the buoyant forces in his destiny that the King of England sought the same ends as the Pope of Rome.

Certainly after Marignano Leo X did not wish Francis removed from the environs of Milan any more heartily than Henry VIII. The spectacular victory of Francis had humiliated Henry and had left him gasping. Henry's resentment of Francis was personal, the resentment of one cocky and bumptious youth for another. To make matters more acute, Francis seemed to compare favorably with the young English King in all respects and to excel him in many. Henry showed a lively and competitive curiosity about his opposite number in France. Of those who had seen the French King he asked close questions. Piero Pasqualigo, a Venetian who had accompanied Sebastian Giustiniani to London, had seen Francis in Paris. He tells of Henry's inquisitiveness: "His majesty came to me and said, 'Is the king of France as tall as I am?' I told him there was little difference. 'Is he as stout?' I told him he was not. 'What sort of legs has he?' I replied, 'Spare.' Whereupon he opened the front of his doublet, and placing his hand on his thigh, said, 'Look here: I have a good calf to my leg.' " [6] When Giustiniani told Henry that the French King was adored by his subjects, Henry ejaculated: "By God! he gives them poor reason to love him, running thus at the very commencement of his reign into the toil and charges of war!" [7]

Henry's jealousy of Francis, sharp and uncomfortable even when the two stood eying each other through the reports of ambassadors, had been increased unbearably by the seven-league stride with which the Most Christian King had crossed the Alps where no military force had crossed before. And at Marignano there had been much letting of blood upon the field, the battle having lasted eighteen hours in all and having covered two days and part of a night. Francis had been in the thick of it and at the center of danger. There was a further triumph for the French, for the Switzers had called them, harking back to the Battle of the Spurs, "hares in armor." The fierce and manly combat of the French had avenged this derisive term. The same Frenchmen who under the reign of the gouty Louis had quailed and run at the sight of Henry's forces had under Francis defeated the best fighters in the whole of Europe, defeated them decisively and in a kind of gory combat that made Henry's first military venture seem but a summer outing.

The news of Marignano stunned the English. On October 11, 1515, almost a month after the battle, Wolsey still pretended not to believe the news. Henry showed even greater signs of dazed incredulity at the unwelcome intelligence. Both Francis and his mother Louise had written directly to Henry to notify him of the victory; Henry regarded the letters as forgeries confected by the French to suit some ultimate and imagined purpose.

To convince the King of England of the victory, the King of France at last sent into England an agent named de Bapaume, armed with letters and equipped with corroborative detail. De Bapaume's meticulous report of his delivery of the letters and the incidents that followed gives a picture of the English consternation. King Henry did not "take any great pleasure" in reading the letters; "for it seemed, to look at him, as if tears would have burst from his eyes, so red were they from the pain he suffered in hearing and understanding the good news and prosperity of my master, who had advertised him thereof by his letters." [8]

Thus at last the bloody fact of Marignano was admitted. De Bapaume went next "to my lord the Cardinal of York, being at Westminster, whom likewise I informed of the good news of the king and his prosperity. He told me he rejoiced at it, and that he esteemed the victory of the king and his success as much as if they had been the king's his master, by reason of the alliance and friendship between them."

Immediately after these resounding assurances of ingenuous friendship, Henry and Wolsey launched a project designed to circumvent Francis by cunning stealth. By some testimony, the scheme was Wolsey's "own work." It is so testified by the papal chamberlain Paris de Grassis. In October of 1515 Richard Pace, a man of letters and a diplomatist of proven skill, was dispatched to Zurich to hire Swiss troops to attack Francis in Italy. It was agreed that the English would put up 120,000 crowns for the hire of 20,000 Swiss soldiers.

The scheme was known to Venice as early as December of 1515 and, as Fisher points out, once known to Venice it became the open talk of Europe. Venice being still an ally of France, its ambassador Giustiniani came hastily to Wolsey to protest the transfer of money. Wolsey denied the report with unctuous eloquence. Giustiniani reported the scene in some detail to his home government. On January 2, 1516, he wrote from London that the King had returned to Greenwich and that he had immediately gone to see the Cardinal, "who, for authority, may in point of fact be styled *ipse rex.*" He went on to say that, having paid the Cardinal the usual compliments, he commenced discussing the "affair of the moneys." The Cardinal listened to him "most attentively and patiently for the space of a quarter of an hour" — the longest recorded attention Wolsey ever gave anyone. Then he immediately set about correcting Giustiniani's misapprehensions, saying: "I will speak to you with all sincerity and truth, and will tell you what becomes a Cardinal on the honour of the Cardinalate." He went on to say: "It is true that the most serene King has remitted moneys to Flanders which will reach Germany, and perhaps Italy, for two purposes: in the first place, for the purchase of inlaid armour and other costly furniture; then again we are aware that a number of princes, whom I will not particularize to you, either in France, in Germany, in Italy, have pledged a quantity of very fine jewels, and of great value, which we hope to obtain at no great cost, and therefore thought fit to avail ourselves of this opportunity for purchasing similar things, which in other times could not be obtained at a much greater outlay . . ."

On and on went my lord of York, covering himself with a cloud of words. "No man in this kingdom," he said, "has so much as thought of waging war on the King of France, or of opposing any of his undertakings." "By the honour of the Cardinalate," he added, "what we tell you is the truth." And as for those who had told tales of England's military intent to the Venetian ambassador: "They lied in their teeth." [9]

Meanwhile Wolsey's agent in Zurich, Richard Pace, was having the devil's own time with his negotiations. The chief problem was to keep the control of the huge sum advanced out of the grasping hands of the Emperor Maximilian. The thought of so much gold all around him but not under his extravagant control almost crazed the aging Emperor, who had been too busy hunting the chamois and paying his attentions to the Princess of Hungary, a girl not yet in her teens, to halt the march of Francis when he first crossed the Alps. Now at the sight of money he became warlike and offered to lead the Swiss against the French. "He is always dunning for money," the Pope said of him.[10] And Machiavelli remarked that if the leaves on all the trees of Italy had been converted into ducats for his use, they would not have been sufficient for his need.[11] Maximilian went so far as to write his daughter Margaret in the Netherlands, asking her to seize the gold he heard the English had consigned to Antwerp and deposit it to his treasury.

It is not remarkable that the English scheme, carried out furtively and at a great distance, with many grasping hands along the route and with

Maximilian a necessary party to it, should have ended in a joke that shook the sides of Europe. Pace did a masterful job in planning the expedition against the French, handicapped by many trammels though he was. Wolsey's intructions to Pace were that he appear to be only a private citizen with no official mission and that he carry out the negotiations without reference to the ambassador regularly accredited to Maximilian. In spite of all the hazards, Pace arranged the attack, leading one column himself while Maximilian in charge of the twenty thousand Swiss led the other on the march to Milan. Revenge would be sweet.

The reasons for what happened will long remain among the abominable mysteries of history. The wily and impecunious Maximilian led his troops within nine miles of Milan and came to a stubborn halt. Pace, in an ague of bewilderment, upbraided him and laid before him in his tent all the reasons why he should leap to the attack of Milan. Pace later wrote to Wolsey of the affair: "The said Emperor could not deny that these our reasons were evident, and made this answer only, viz., that he trusted that the king's grace would not desert him. For all this yet that day he would not move, but did sit still in pensiveness, and was angry with every man that did move him to set forthward."

Not only did he sit still in pensiveness and not move forthward; he moved backward, returning to his dominions without allowing any of the troops in his command so much as to scratch a Frenchman. In the commotion and disorder that followed, the Swiss plundered and murdered, sacked villages in the route of the retreat, and their leaders fell to quarreling among themselves. All of which did not disturb the Emperor; indeed he made use of Pace's embarrassment to press for more money. Pace reported the demand to Wolsey, for the Emperor threatened that if Pace refused he would "make terms with France, and write over to England that Pace had been the cause of his defection." Pace further warns Wolsey that the Emperor is sending an agent to England and reminds Wolsey "that all money put into the Emperor's hands, or committed to any of his, shall be, in great part thereof, evil expended, as this present bearer can at large show unto the same, and declare what business and trouble I have only in resisting against this." [12]

The large ears of diplomacy caught every detail of the news quickly. These disastrous and ridiculous events in the spring of 1516 marked the first official meddling of Wolsey in his new and supreme position as Lord Chancellor of England and chief adviser to the English King. There had been nothing like it since Ferdinand, scarce four years before, had left an English force stranded and unsupplied on the shores of Spain in what was to have been a concerted attack on France. In the present case no English troops had been involved, but English honor and dignity had suffered quite as much of a defeat as in 1512. Then Wolsey had been only the King's energetic Almoner carrying out what could be construed as his Majesty's orders. In this case he was Lord Chancellor of England and generally esteemed to be responsible for the farce in which Maximilian played the doughty lead.

Nor did England's disgrace end with the fleecing by Maximilian. Other events were to increase her isolation and weaken her position in the courts of Europe despite the exertions of the Cardinal. In these events Ferdinand was to play as his last earthly act a contributing part. On January 23, 1516, "hunting and hawking to the last in fair weather and foul, and following more the counsel of his friends than his physicians," Ferdinand died. When he did, the throne of Spain passed to a solemn, spindle-legged youth of eighteen, Charles the grandson of Ferdinand. But the succession lacked the cleanness necessary to prevent trouble, and it was necessary at every turn to assure it and protect it. For Charles was master of the Netherlands and a resident there; he had never been to Spain, and there was no positive assurance that his rulership would be accepted. In fact, there was no positive assurance that he would even be able to reach Spain. Yet he must try. This child of ancient Burgundy must move on to meet his destiny, and there was suspense and a sense of that destiny in the air when in the Netherlands Charles was proclaimed King of Spain.

This solemn and dramatic moment brought into the drama of Europe one who would ultimately prove the ruin of Thomas Wolsey. But at the moment Charles was a lisping and ineffectual young man, of worth only by descent, merely a further embarrassment to be reckoned with in the threatened isolation of England. As such, he afforded bother enough. His advisers were all Flemings and inclined sentimentally and practically to France and not to England. Immediately they began maneuvers by which Charles would be encouraged to cuddle up to Francis, and by August 13, 1516, the alliance of the two had been solemnized in a pact called the Treaty of Noyon.

Again Wolsey turned with incurable hope, if not naïveté, to Maximilian. Perhaps he could be persuaded to undermine the Treaty of Noyon. He agreed to go to the Netherlands and entreat Charles to dismiss the councilors who had been responsible for the Treaty of Noyon. England advanced the money and Maximilian spent it, but instead of undermining the Treaty of Noyon he joined it himself, saying to Charles as he did: "*Mon fils, vouz alles tromper les Français et moi je vais tromper les An-*

glis." [13] All of Wolsey's attempts to circumvent the union of princes had failed; indeed Wolsey and his agents were not even consulted, for in March of 1517 Charles, Maximilian, and Francis made a fresh League of Cambrai for the partition of Italy. From this arrangement too England was excluded.

It was not a happy position for an English king and his minister who a few years before had been the talk and toast of Europe. The English had paid more than a million and a half crowns to help Maximilian rid Italy of the French, and the French were still there. England had sought to prevent the union of Charles and Francis, and the two not only were now fast in a treaty but they had extended their alliance to include Maximilian, the very man who had disgraced the English.

Having failed ingloriously through the mercurial Maximilian in an act of covert war to rescue the Pope from the Most Christian King, Wolsey now undertook to construct the kind of peace the Pope had been plaintively pleading for. Wolsey suddenly became conscious of the terrible Turk and lent his lordly ear to the solicitations of Leo that an expedition against the Sultan be organized.

Earlier both the King and Wolsey had shown a dull indifference to Leo's pleading. Wolsey himself had glibly consented to the enterprise, but Warham as Archbishop of Canterbury and head of Convocation opposed it, and Henry took the position that the prattle about the Turk was simply designed to distract him from his task of cutting Francis down to size. Henry had gone so far as to say to Giustiniani that the true Turk was the King of France. England's indifference to the danger continued through the summer and fall of 1515. Meanwhile the Turks, who had gained Syria and Egypt and were now threatening Rhodes, began actually to molest Italy. "Turkish corsairs swarmed in the Mediterranean, and swept the coast from Terracina to Pisa. On one occasion they plundered the church of Loretto; on another they sailed up the Tiber, and nearly made a prisoner of the Pope whilst he was hunting at Pali." [14] These forays were carried out by Turkish brigands and were not official; but they were painful just the same, and they served as harbingers to show what might well occur when the Sultan chose to set his face against the West.

Still the princes of Europe, busy with the excitement and dash of their own rivalries, held back. But with the shameful and at last undeniable failure of Maximilian's expedition and the drawing up of the Treaty of Noyon, England being ceremoniously ignored in the talk among Christian princes, Wolsey began to change his tune and to sing in rich tones his praises of the Pope's scheme for the union of Christendom and the repulse of the Turk. In December of 1516 Giustiniani reports that the Cardinal was much exercised. He assured the Venetian that, once other matters were settled, his King would go against the Turk. He "would perform memorable feats, and excel all others, adding *'and perhaps I myself will go in person.'* " The emphasis indicated by italics is Giustiniani's in his report of the interview to his own government. The ambassador reports also that he urged Wolsey to the cause by pointing out a number of practical considerations. "I exhorted him to the utmost, telling him that it was not merely a question of the Christian faith, and of preserving the rest of Christ's patrimony, but of obtaining two empires, five kingdoms, and so many provinces and cities now held by the Turk, but which of yore belonged to Christians." [15] He was also at pains to lay before the Cardinal the fact "that said conquests might be made with less money than would be expended for the waging of war in Italy."

This last thrust could hardly have pleased my lord Cardinal, his memory rankled as it was by Maximilian's costly perfidy. Nor is there any sign that he wanted to join in the recovery of Christian ground. It was clear to him now, however, that the time had come to unite Christendom against the infidel, obedient to the fervent and prayerful wishes of the Pope. The Pope would be the architect of the peace; the Cardinal would be the master builder who carried out the plans.

In two energetic years after the Treaty of Noyon, which was formalized in August of 1516, Thomas Wolsey changed the alignments of Europe and made England the acknowledged leader of European affairs. He did it by invoking the image of the Turk as a threat and the image of the Pope as a solution. But the deals and negotiations necessary to the accomplishment were infinite.

The arrangements which were consummated in a remarkable document known as the Treaty of London and accepted by the great powers in October of 1518 came about through Wolsey's sedulous cultivation of France. To this cultivation France yielded not unwillingly, Francis knowing that Maximilian was not long for this world and that Charles would probably succeed the old beggar. It would be as well to be on good terms with England. Hence parleying began.

One subject concerned in these talks was the return of Tournai to France for a consideration: Francis was to buy back what Louis had lost, and the Cardinal was to have from the French King a pension to replace the fees he had been supposed to receive from the diocese as its bishop. Tournai had fallen to Henry in 1513. At that time Louis Gaillart, the bishop-elect, had not been permitted by Henry to possess the temporalities of the bishopric, and the proceeds of it had been given to Wolsey. Still Gaillart had refused to budge from his claim, and Wolsey had tried in vain to get Francis to appoint him to some other position. Francis dallied and delayed. Meanwhile Gaillart secured a bull from the Pope for his settlement in the diocese.

All this had created an evil temper in my lord Cardinal, and it was at the time of his temper, whether because of it or not, that he had dispatched Pace to Zurich with gold to be spent upon ousting the French from Milan. In negotiating the Treaty of London, however, the whole moot matter of Tournai was genially disposed of. Francis agreed to pay Henry 600,000 crowns in twelve annual installments for the repossession of the city, and the Cardinal's grievous disappointment and lordly umbrage over not getting the revenues of the see had been nicely taken care of by the promise of yearly pension from Francis of 12,000 livres.

The question of Tournai having been settled, in August of 1518 a splendid French mission came to London and amid banquets, masques, processions, mummeries, and devisings the final details of an intimate alliance between England and France were sorted out and agreed upon.

But Wolsey's Peace was to be more than an alliance between England and France. It was to be a universal and permanent peace. The Treaty of London exceeded any hopes and pleas the Pope had dared express. The Pope, as Giustiniani pointed out, had labored to impose a truce of five years upon Christian princes, "whereas his lordship had made a perpetual peace." [16] The lines of the document were remarkable and new, for they were drawn to bind England and France together and yet the provisions were flexible enough to reach out and embrace all Christian countries in a great concert of powers, each country pledged to join the others in resisting an attack made upon any one of them.

It was solemnly agreed that "if the Dominions respectively then belonging to the said Confederates should be in a hostile Manner invaded by any of them, or by any other Power whatever, the Party invaded should admonish the Aggressor to desist, and to make Reparation; which if he refuse to do (within the Space of a Month) the rest of the Confederacy might declare themselves his Enemies, and in two Months after, at an equal Expence, make War upon him both by Sea and Land; That they should to this End, allow the troops of each other free Passage through their several Dominions . . ." It was further provided and consented to that "none of the Confederates should permit their Subjects to bear Arms against the Other, or should retain any Force of Strangers, to serve against

243

the said Confederates, on Pain of being interpreted to violate the League, which yet should continue in full force among the Rest . . ." [17]

Matters that troubled practical princes, such as the use of mercenaries, were thus taken care of, but a new and imaginative feature had been added: the powers that subscribed to the Treaty of London agreed to band together in force against any power that broke the peace. Far more than an alliance of great powers, Wolsey had fashioned a league of nations designed to organize peace as well as preserve it. The league was to embrace not only England and France but Spain, Denmark, Portugal, Scotland, all the Italian states, the Swiss confederation and the towns of the Hansa. It was at least universal locally, and it projected, to the astonishment of the diplomatic world, a confederacy on a vaster scale and with more adherents than the Pope or any other arbiter had dreamed of.

And the author and finisher of the league was the Cardinal of York, he who had been ignored by Charles and Francis two years before and cheated by Ferdinand and Maximilian. His name now invoked respect wherever intrigue was talked or contemplated. Men and princes must reckon with him anew. Giustiniani noted that "whereas such a union of Christian powers was usually concluded at Rome, this confederacy had been concluded in England, although the Pope was its head." [18] Fox declared that the Treaty "was the best deed ever done for England; and next to the king the praise was due to Wolsey." [19]

CHAPTER XIV

PERMANENT and universal peace having been achieved, Christian princes could now turn their energies to other matters — such as the election, for example, of a successor to the Emperor Maximilian. On January 19, 1519, the gay old pauper died; probably laughed himself to death at the kings and diplomats he had made fools of. His death left vacant the throne of the Holy Roman Empire and provided the signal for a scramble to see who might seat himself on that throne. The contest, which lay between Charles and Francis, was in essence a popularity contest with Europe as its picturesque setting. Being Emperor was in some respects like being Maypole Queen: the honor carried with it a great deal of ceremonial adulation but not much function. The title was mixed with faded glories and old lace, and one needed a good memory to appreciate the true dignity of the position. But it carried with it, by virtue of earlier associations and the idea for which the term Holy Roman Empire had once stood, a higher degree of prestige than any other royal position in Europe.

The only immediate function the Emperor would serve was that of trying to rule Germany, whatever else he might claim or attempt, and the choice of Emperor would be made by the Electors of that country, a sturdy and vigorous group of princes in whom tradition and practice had vested the right of determining who would occupy the throne.

Charles of Spain was the grandson of Maximilian and on that ground might lay special claim to preference; but actually he knew no German, had no knowledge of the country or its special problems, and was as much a foreigner there as the King of France. The King of France, being of much renown and superior in years and experience, enjoying acclaim for his victory at Marignano, believed firmly that he had a chance to be chosen king of the Germans and gave evidence of this belief by pouring unlimited funds into the contest: three million crowns, according to his testimony. His efforts and expenditures protracted and delayed the deliberations into May of 1519 and brought reports of a deadlock in the electoral college. At this point Henry sent Richard Pace forward to offer with proper blandishments the candidacy of the King of England. But Pace found that all of the Electors had made their pledges to one side or other.

The decisive factor proved to be the alliance of the Pope with Francis. Leo openly declared against Charles, and this, as Brandi puts it, "proved to be the surest means of securing the votes of the Electors for the Hapsburg dynasty." [1] The Germans had begun "to grow restive at the ostentation of French power." The marvel is that Francis ever got such serious consideration as he did. On the evening of June 27 the Electors appointed the following day as the day of decision. "At the sound of the bell every man must pray God to send down his grace on the Electors, 'that they might choose a king who would be useful to God Almighty, the Holy Roman Empire and us all.' " [2] The man who in their unanimous judgment filled these requirements was Charles, who assumed the role of Emperor under the title of Charles V.

The net effect of the election, beyond its immediate result, was to embitter the spirit of Francis irreparably and to bring him into open hostility with his rival. At the beginning of the contest for the crown of Emperor the two kings had continued their spirit of outward amiability. Francis had declared that "his brother Charles and he were, fairly and openly, suitors to the same mistress: the more fortunate, added he, will carry her; the other must rest contented." [3]

Now that the election was over, he was anything but contented. It was natural that, his hopes drawn taut by the long delay, he should be indignantly disappointed. Yet his personal disappointment afforded less concern to him and the rest of Europe than the military encirclement which his country now faced. By adding the domains of his grandfather to his own possessions, Charles now had dominions which stretched from the Netherlands through Aragon and Castile and their Italian dependencies — Naples, Sicily, and Sardinia — around France to include Germany. Moreover, Charles was lord of dominions across the sea — dominions as yet of unproven wealth, but fabulous and calculated all the more because of the uncertainty of their worth to add dimensions to his dignity. Here was an overlordship which Francis and France could not regard with equanimity. It was an empire greater and more extensive than any known in Europe since that of the Romans.

In spite of appearances on the map, Francis had of course certain advantages. His country was "compact, united, rich, populous." Further, France "being interposed between the provinces of the emperor's dominions," the French King enjoyed a strategic position which might overbalance the outward advantage given by the superior territories of Charles.[4]

Especially might this be so if Francis could stay in the good graces of the English King and the Cardinal. He had long expressed a wish to meet and discourse with Henry, and Henry himself had been pleasantly disposed to the prospect. He had not only shown a lively curiosity about the French King's appearance and qualities of build, but upon hearing that Francis had a beard he had resolved not to cut off his own beard until he should meet his brother of France. The gesture was taken in good faith by Francis. When the intelligence of King Henry's beard and resolution was conveyed to Francis by Sir Thomas Boleyn, the English ambassador, he likewise made a solemn oath that he would devote his beard to the promised meeting.

The growth of the beards was looked upon as a ratification of the agreement of the two kings. It was looked upon by the French as a solemn and religious token. But, alas, a Frenchman of repute returned to France during these days of tremulous waiting and reported that Henry had cut off his beard. This act the French regarded as breach of faith and a declaration that Henry had no real design to have the interview take place. Sir Thomas Boleyn explained the disappearance of the beard as best he could, not having firm instructions from the home government. He doubted not that the beard had been cut at the insistence of the Queen, who had "formerly made pressing instances to His Majesty, when his beard grew long and incommodious, that, to oblige her, he would cut it off." He added assurances that it "was not done with any design of frustrating the interview and that the King's mind and affection were still the same." [5]

In spite of hesitations and misgivings, plans for the majestic interview went forward. On January 10, 1520, Francis named my lord of York as his proctor for the occasion. Hall records that both kings "committed the order and manner of their meeting unto the Cardinal of York." [6] The meeting was to take place not far from Calais in a valley known as Val Doré, halfway between the towns of Guines and Ardres. In April Sir Robert Wingfield was at the Parisian court and from there wrote to Wolsey: "Sir, the king here would gladly know whether the king his brother would be content to forbear the making of rich tents and pavilions; which thing he would be well contented to forbear on his part." [7] This suggestion, so modestly and diplomatically put, must have afforded my lord of York as much amusement as it did those who later looked upon and reflected upon the magnificently tinseled meeting. For the Cardinal was not one to put a small mouth on anything, and all his preparations suggested that the occasion would be a display of English mercantile might, as the invasion of France had been eight years before. He summoned his artificers and set them to work on plans and structures no less elaborate than those required for an invasion, so that France had no choice but to compete in the display if she was not to be hopelessly outshone.

The scene of the meeting came to be known as the Field of Cloth of Gold, which Pollard says is a mistranslation of the French, *Le Camp du Drap d'Or*. At any rate, the name seemed to suit the richness and elegance of the pretensions made on both parts, and particularly by the English. Godwin says that eleven thousand artificers labored over the necessary buildings. Two Italians who later visited the lavish scene when it was complete testify that three thousand artificers were required to construct the features of the English scene alone.

Still, with all the preparations for a kind of world fair and with all the growing beards, the projected meeting was delayed. And the fault lay with the English. In the shadows beyond the council fires of all of Henry's deliberations stood the gaunt, grave figure of the new boy Emperor. If Francis needed the aid of England, Charles would need it too. It would be foolish, an act lacking in diplomatic guile, to talk with Francis until

England could determine what Charles had to offer. Henry and Charles must meet privately before Henry and Francis met publicly.

In reaching this decision it was not my lord of York but Catherine of Aragon who played the winning role. Wolsey himself was firm for the French interview, being proctor to the occasion and heavy with responsibility for the arrangements and being of course drawn toward peace with France by his pensions there. Friendship with France had been a fixed point in his scheme of things, unnatural though it was to the hatred which the English had long borne their Christian brothers beyond the Channel. His first treaty, even before he became Lord Chancellor, had been arranged through the marriage of Louis XII of France to Mary the King's sister. It lay within the logic of circumstances, seeing the Emperor's wide dominions and overweening power, that England and France should be united for everlasting peace and that the Kings of the two countries should meet and cement this union of purpose by the right hand of fellowship. To this lofty end, and with his French pensions ever on the horizon, he sought to hasten the interview.

But in his clever calculations my lord Cardinal had reckoned without the power that still resided in the Queen. He had underestimated the power of a woman, a woman of great and stern abilities in affairs of state and of great tenderness and devotion in affairs of family. Charles V was Emperor; he was also her nephew, the son of her tragic and beloved and distrait sister Joanna. And the Emperor was by her marriage nephew to the King of England her husband. It would not be amiss that Charles pay a visit to his aunt and uncle in England. Henry could not be averse to a meeting which combined the features of a family reunion with an act of homage from an Emperor to a King.

Catherine set about busily to bring Charles to England before Henry should set off for France. She moved first on the diplomatic plane and then resorted to womanhood. She let it be known in Spain that it would be well for Charles to come by way of England on a trip he planned to make to Germany. A Spanish ambassador in the person of de Mesa brought the suggestion to the English court. He elaborated it into a proposal that the Emperor and the two Kings should meet and settle all the problems of Christendom at once, with my lord of York as Cardinal and Legate *a latere* of course presiding over the conference of the princes.

The suggestion had merit, its chief merit being that it flattered the vanity of Wolsey, exalting him for at least a season above the three great rulers of the acknowledged world. But Wolsey rejected the proposal and

248

hewed to his line that Henry and Francis should meet as he had planned. Wolsey likewise stood stubbornly in the way of the more modest suggestion that Charles visit Henry. Catherine made clear and reasoned arguments against the French alliance among the King's councilors. One of her statements, carefully prepared in advance, was heard by the King and was reported later to Wolsey, who, according to de Mesa, was much shaken by it. Her ability had been demonstrated when as regent she commanded the defense of the country against the Scots at the time of Flodden; and if she had lost caste as Ferdinand's daughter and ambassador in the early days of her marriage, she had retained respect of the court and the people for her piety and her devotion to England in a moment of crisis.

The subject of the meeting now became an open contest between the Queen and the Cardinal, but it was never quite played in the open. Circumstances were on the side of the Cardinal, who had only to encourage delay until it was too late to make the proper arrangements for the entertainment of the Emperor before Henry must set off for the French interview. The Emperor himself raised many difficulties. He could not promise to reach England save at some indefinite time in the spring of 1520.

Meanwhile Wolsey went steadily forward with the plans for the Field of Cloth of Gold. And meanwhile the court and the imperial ambassadors watched Henry's beard as a sign of his wavering resolution. When it disappeared, the French looked gloomy and construed it as a sign that the Queen had won her tussle with the Cardinal. When it reappeared, the Imperialists around the court said it was because the Queen had found she liked it after all; the Venetians, being friends of the French, retorted that it was because the French had won. And the gradually increasing luxury of the King's whiskers sent the French hopes soaring.[8]

In the spring of 1520 Catherine's hopes sank very low. It was then that the strong sense of womanhood which marked all her doings came to the fore. Mattingly tells us that "in the presence of the imperial ambassadors and a number of nobles and counselors, she fell on her knees before her husband and declared that the greatest wish of her heart was to see her nephew, the successor to her father's kingdom." Henry assured her, as he raised her from her knees, that he would do everything he could to satisfy her wish. But the delay lay with Charles and not with Henry. The English King had written Charles to say that he must cross to Calais on May 31 and that unless Charles reached England by the middle of May the interview would have to be canceled. The Emperor did everything he could to hasten his passage, but the weather was against him. The middle of May came and went, and the Spanish ships had not appeared off the white cliffs of Dover.

Wolsey could now vigorously oppose further delay, and with good grace. The deadline of the visit had passed. The Channel ports were busy shipping all the paraphernalia designed to impress the French. A thousand and one details about tents and huts and palaces had to be attended to. Still the King delayed, held in check by the entreaties of his Queen. Time was running out. Mattingly believes that it was only the efforts of the Queen that made the meeting possible, and de Mesa thought that only last-minute solicitations by Catherine had kept the two from missing each other by a few hours. For it was not until the evening of May 26, 1520, that the Emperor's fleet arrived.

Meanwhile, the court had moved to Canterbury and Wolsey had gone on to Dover. When word came of the Emperor's arrival, Wolsey, whatever his views, was now the King's welcomer, and he put out in a small boat to meet the Emperor and conducted him to Dover Castle, where lodging for the night had been provided. Word of the Emperor's arrival had been conveyed to the King at Canterbury, and the King, as Godwin records it, "although it were midnight, takes horse and a little more than an hour later comes by torchlight to Dover Castle where the Emperor lay; who, sea-weary, was then asleep but being certified of the King's arrival he suddenly apparelled himself and met the King at the top of the stairs." [9]

What happened during the remaining days and nights before the English royal party left in state for Calais, no one, not even Wolsey, fully knew. Henry rode the next morning with Charles to Canterbury, where Charles met his aunt for the first time, showing her a shy and becoming deference, only to be embraced warmly and welcomed by her with unabashed tears. Henry and Catherine and Charles had breakfast together; Wolsey was not invited to the family board, nor was he bidden to be present at two long talks the three had during the remainder of the Emperor's stay. But it was plain to any observer that the family conference had worked out as Catherine had fondly hoped and fervently prayed it might. The visit of the Emperor of the Holy Roman Empire to England was unprecedented. Henry's pride had been touched as Catherine expected, and his vanity was all the more pleased and touched by the fact that this Emperor was a diffident and retiring young man of twenty-one who listened attentively to the advice and counsel he sought from the man he treated as a father. Later Charles was to complete the picture of filial fidelity by writing to thank Henry for "the advice you gave me like a good father when we were at Cantoberi." [10]

Whatever else he did at Canterbury, Charles paid Henry during his stay in England the highest compliment that can be paid even to a king: he made Henry feel needed. He came as a suppliant and a son, one who had scarcely known his own father and mother and who now at a high stage of responsibility needed the help Henry could give in the midst of all his imperial perplexities. In this role his attitude of pious deference was greatly assisted by his physical equipment and appearance. Nature had made him up for the part and left him free to operate behind a permanent mask of simple-mindedness that concealed a cunning mind. He spoke with a stammer and a pronounced lisp. His underjaw protruded so much that his teeth did not meet, and the portraits painted of him even by obsequious artists present his face and gaping mouth and vacuous eyes in a manner that suggests an overdressed dimwit, the degenerate end of a long line of illustrious sires. The impression left upon his bluff and hearty uncle, oversupplied with glandular vitality, must have been one of pathos and helpless need. Here was the Emperor of the greater part of Christendom who asked and wanted only the protection and assistance of the English King against any hostile forces that might be thrown against him.

How well Charles captured Henry's solicitude is to be noted in the fact that before his ships set sail from Dover he and the English King had arranged to meet quietly at Gravelines after the formalities of the Field of Cloth of Gold had been overpassed. And the pact of filial friendship he had established with Henry of England turned the meeting between Henry and Francis, so agreeably sought by Francis and so elaborately planned by my lord of York, into a pompous and costly farce. Even so, it must at whatever cost be carried through. Henry's bushy beard testified to that.

Henry and Francis met at last — on June 7, 1520, in the awed presence of thousands of their followers and in the sight of thousands of the common people of France who watched from the hills that created the Val Doré. They met as Wolsey had planned, despite all the delays and difficulties; they met and embraced in the presence of the multitude; and with their rich retinues they remained together for sixteen days.

Yet, oddly, they did not meet at all. Their minds remained at home or dwelt on things extraneous or afar. Henry and Francis were young and stately princes so evenly matched and endowed by nature and fortune that they spent the time preening themselves before admirers, each taking the measure of the other. There were fits and starts of friendliness, some scenes in which the two young men dropped their royal masks. But there was one occasion when the taut rivalry between them snapped in a split second of near conflict, and only the babbling intervention of their courtiers and the timely attention of their queens rescued them from the undignified spectacle of a fist fight.

It was but a moment in human history, this extravagant meeting of the two Kings, but it was one of those illumined moments when even the casual eye could see plainly at work forces usually lost in the shadows of culture or in the cushions of diplomacy. Here in the valley between Guines and Ardres these forces were not only visible but attired for their parts. History was being planned and rehearsed — demonstrated, as it were, and as it was, and evermore would be. Here were the anointed elite of two great nations, bound by a solemn treaty of friendship, meeting to sanction the future peace of the world. The author and director of the scene was a Cardinal and Legate of His Holiness. He gave the scene a religious setting and did all he could to clothe realities in magnificence; the realities were there just the same. The elite were there, with fixed schemes and purposes and a convenient sense of their own destinies. The common people were not, save those who came to serve their betters or to gape from distant hills.

The whole affair was staged and produced by my lord of York, and a study of it affords an instructive picture of the duality of his mind, part of which lingered romantically in the age of chivalry and the other part attempted, however unsuccessfully, to deal with the basic problems of government and justice. The Field of Cloth of Gold afforded the last great canvas of the Middle Ages. Such a panoplied event as he now superintended could have taken place without anomaly two hundred years before; such an event did not take place again. It marked the end of the age of chivalry and somehow prophetically dramatized the end of the age of churchmen. Particularly it adumbrated the end of an age in which a Cardinal could cloak the intrigue of princes in the vestments of his office.

From the standpoint of its effect upon witnesses, both English and French, the setting of the Field proved to be as rich and impressive as one would expect under Wolsey's diligent management. He spared no pains to make that setting colossal. Nor did he spare the nobility pains either. With the royal approval he gave them instructions, at whatever cost, to see that the wealth of England was appropriately represented there.

252

Plans in such an enterprise were subject constantly to change and often to elaboration. At first it was planned to house the English King and Queen in Guines Castle, with Francis and his queen settled in the castle at Ardres across the valley. But the castle at Guines was found to be in hopeless disrepair, its weedy moat and its keep "too ruinous to mend." So in the course of a few weeks the busy English artificers erected and decorated a summer palace, being an exact square of 328 feet, on the castle green. It was a task that called for incredibly careful workmanship and the shipping of costly materials over great distances. According to the astonished testimony of two Italian observers, the palace was "made of boards painted to look like brick, a round tower being placed at each corner. The gatehouse in the center of one quadrant had loop-holes and battlements defended by statues of armed men in the act of discharging stones and iron balls from cannons and culverins." The great hall in the palace, they said, was "as lofty as that of the Pasaro palace at San Benetto, but longer, with a ceiling of green sarcenet and gold roses, decorated with hangings of silk and gold, woven with figures and horses represented to the life." [11]

Outside this transient palace, English ingenuity and foresight had contrived a gilt fountain, said to be of antique workmanship, with a statue of Bacchus "birlying the wine." The fountain sported "three runlets, fed by secret conduits hid beneath the earth." These "spouted claret, hypocras, and water into as many silver cups, to quench the thirst of all comers." Thus the new age of inventiveness mingled with the perishing age of chivalry. Within the palace the old world held sway, as if in a citadel. Chairs were covered with "cushions of Turkey work, cloths of estate . . . overlaid with tissue and rich embroidery." The palace was "pierced on every side with oriel windows" — windows glazed in a day when glass was still a luxury — and the trimmings overlaid with gold. A French dignitary, de Fleuranges, looked upon the palace flung up with such artistry and declared that "every quarter of it, even the least, was a habitation fit for a prince."

As befitted a palace planned by my lord Cardinal, it had attached to it a spacious chapel more adorned than the palace, served by thirty-five priests and a covey of singing boys. The copes and vestments of the "officiating clergy were cloth of tissue powdered with red roses, brought from the looms of Florence, and woven in one piece, thickly studded with gold and jewelry." In the chapel stood "a beautiful silver organ with gold ornaments." And to lend further wealth and piety stood also twelve golden images of the Apostles, "as large as children of four years old." Henry

253

must move in an atmosphere of unction, and he could not visit France without the Twelve Apostles, whether they be as before in the form of cannons or now in the form of golden images.

The chapel was for the meditation and religious solace of the English royal household. For the chapel in which he would sing high Mass before the two kings and their attendants, Wolsey had brought to the Field of Cloth of Gold a chapel fabricated ahead of the sailing from England and capable of being assembled overnight. He had thought of everything.

The details were as the sands of the sea. Assembling the vast concourse of knights and nobles from all over the kingdom, scheduling their embarkation at Dover and other Channel ports, transporting them across quarrelsome waters, landing them at Calais, moving them on and lodging them in and around Guines — such an operation required at each step the precision and foresight of a military leader. The dimensions of the English party were those of an army. In the King's retinue, including dukes, earls, marquises, bishops, barons, knights, and their attendants and servants, marched 4544 persons. The Queen's contingent was smaller, but respectable, numbering 1260 persons. The Rutland Papers solemnly record that the total number of persons who came with the King and Queen was 5804. Nor was this the end. The King and his attendants had 2406 horses and the Queen and her attendants 817, making a total of 3223 horses.[12]

Orders of precedence, both in the line of march and in lodging arrangements, had to be handled with due delicacy, for there was an aristocracy among servants as rigid as among nobles. The Lord Chamberlain, the Lord Steward, the Lord Treasurer of the King's household, the comptroller, "with their numerous staffs, had to be lodged in apartments adapted to their rank and services." Lesser officers and servants formed a colony apart from the royal household but integral to the scene: 2800 tents were spread out on the barren plain that marked the English pale at Guines, each marked with a pennon or badge to show the rank or service of the occupant.

Merely to provision such a host for the duration of the meeting meant that Wolsey had to plan as shrewdly as he had in the days of 1513. It was necessary to supply and transport to the spot 340 beeves, 2200 sheep, 800 calves, 560 tuns of beer, and to provide 4000 pounds of wax for lights. Always beyond the sound of trumpets in fanfare, the ceremonial boom of cannon, the thud of hooves, and the breaking of lances in the lists could be heard the bleating of sheep and the bawling of beeves. It

254

was a sound familiar to a man who had spent his boyhood near the market place in Ipswich.

In his creative management of tangibles Wolsey's genius shone as bright as the scene he had fashioned. And if there were muttered complaints against him for the cost and inconvenience he had caused the nobles, there was ample recognition of his services by both the Kings. The vast contemporary painting depicting the arrival of the English cavalcade shows Wolsey riding at the side of Henry, the Marquis of Dorset going on before with the sword of state. And before the first meeting of the two Kings it was my lord of York who paid a ceremonial visit to the French King. The Cardinal's procession was led by a hundred archers of the guard, followed by fifty gentlemen of his household, "clothed in crimson velvet with chains of gold, bareheaded, bonnet in hand, and mounted on magnificent horses richly caparisoned. After them came 50 gentlemen ushers, also bareheaded, carrying gold maces with knobs as big as a man's head; next a cross-bearer in scarlet, supporting a crucifix adorned with precious stones." After all of these came the Cardinal Legate, in mock humility mounted on a mule "trapped in crimson velvet, with gold front-stalls, studs, buckles, and stirrups." [13]

When Wolsey with all his fancywork reached the town of Ardres and came before the French King's house, he was greeted as became his velvet virtues with the roar of cannon, the sound of drums, trumpets, and fifes. Here was a personage indeed. For the French King received him as an equal, and showed toward him the signs of greatest affection. It was Wolsey's magic hour, the height of his splendor. The great commoner had become a ruler among rulers, riding forth in conspicuous equality with his own King, being saluted bonnet in hand by another. As the indefatigable and Argus-eyed master of arrangements, he had made himself indispensable. The very eating of Kings and Queens depended on his managerial skill. And in addition to being Lord Chamberlain to the two royal households, he was, by virtue of his ecclesiastical offices, a person who could stand with kings and seem of no lesser rank. Both his ability and his dignity found their finest opportunity in the meeting of chiefs of two great nations on the Field of Cloth of Gold.

All the extravagance could not mask the suspicions and politely repressed hostility the governing classes of England and France brought with them to the Field. It was, in fact, this hostility which made the elaborate arrangements and safeguards necessary. In effect and outcome the heralded interview of the Kings and the mingling of their selected subjects was a failure, a gross and costly formality that accomplished nothing; it was as if the witnesses had been called to prove what everyone knew already: that Henry and Francis were rivals and that the daring victor of Marignano who had made Henry ridiculous by his exploits would not at this stage of the game, when he was still flushed with a sense of his own prowess, make any bid for Henry's favor. Or if the matter be put on a more diplomatic plane, Francis regarded Charles, with his encircling empire, as the real enemy he could not brook. His intent in the interview had been to woo Henry to his own support, but the futility of that purpose became plain when the interview was postponed continually in order that Henry might meet first with Charles. And the unhappy turn of events — against the wishes of Wolsey and the hopes of Francis — doomed the meeting to irrelevancy.

The meeting had been held because Wolsey's industrious preparations had made it inescapable. All the nobles and calves and beeves and knights and sheep he had set in motion could not be turned back without grave embarrassment to both countries. But these properties made the meeting all the more of a fiasco and made my lord of York, when it was clear that the meeting of Henry and Francis was but an interlude between another meeting of Henry and the Emperor, look ridiculous. In the strenuous pursuit of a thousand and one details dealing with physical comforts and rampant display, he had missed the point entirely. The same foresight which enabled him to see that there was wax for lights — four thousand pounds of it — deserted him when he looked upon the probable course of events. He had failed to calculate Catherine and the strength of family ties and the impression an Emperor in the form of a gauche and retarded youth would make on a King who had never had a son.

Of course careful efforts were made, both ahead of the event and during the course of the meeting, to insure success. Wolsey had arranged that no French ships should put out to sea until all the English party had returned. It was a daring and hazardous venture to trust the French with the cream of England, and every precaution had to be taken. The air had been poisoned by rumors. One of these, to the effect that the French were fitting out ships ready to strike England, had stopped preparations for the interview. And on the very eve of the meeting Henry is said to have "discovered that three or four thousand French troops were concealed in the neighboring country."

Further precautions had been taken in a schedule of protocol, so that each King did simultaneously what the other King did. When Henry set sail for Calais, Francis left Montreuil for Ardres. And when on June 7 the actual meeting was to take place, it was announced by a shot fired from the castle at Guines which was answered by a shot fired from the castle at Ardres.

Henry had directed Edward Hall, recorder of London, to keep a diary of the incidents, and the result is inserted in Hall's *Chronicle;* also he caused a painting to be made, which may be seen in Hampton Court. Francis ordered Monsieur Peyresc to compose a journal of the meeting, and Maréchal de Fleuranges wrote an account of it in his memoirs. The photographers were present in force.

Henry, who by the testimony of both biased chroniclers and French observers was the comeliest and most commanding prince of his age, was dressed in cloth of silver damask, thickly ribbed with cloth of gold. He rode a charger arrayed in trappings overlaid with fine gold, all topped with a red beard and ruddy countenance. Attending close upon the King was Sir Henry Guilford, who with English profligacy led a spare charger splendidly caparisoned.

On the surrounding hills was a vast cloud of witnesses — the uninvited, drawn from their dingy homes by curiosity, clinging to their bleacher seats in spite of the severity of provost-marshal and threats of chastisement. They had come from the French frontier or the populous cities of Flanders; they had come for the show and to hell with politics. When Francis set out from Montreuil, the procession drew to it a multitude of vagrants and idle followers. Accounts say that no less than ten thousand of these had been forced to turn back by "a proclamation ordering that no person, without special permission, should approach within two leagues of the King's train, 'on pain of the halter.'" Still thousands of others had gathered round to look at the Kings — among them beggars, itinerant minstrels, vendors of provisions and small luxuries to those who had been negligent in their packing, wagoners, plowmen, laborers, all proving that a cat can look at a King. Now they gazed down upon knights and ladies and Kings and Queens dressed in their finest and on parade and as if they had no higher purpose than to amuse the common people. What a setting for an opera!

They saw now the two royal parties approaching each other. Then there was a momentary pause — "a breathless silence, followed by a slight stir on both sides." Then amid the shouts of the spectators on the surrounding hills "and the shrill burst of pipes, trumpets, and clarions, two horsemen were seen to emerge, and, in the sight of both nations, slowly descend into the valley from opposite sides. These were the two sovereigns. As they approached nearer they spurred their horses to a gallop." As they reined up, they embraced first on horseback and then, dismounting, embraced again. Then in the friendliest of spirits they walked together to a pavilion that had been provided at the place of meeting and entered it to talk. No one else was allowed to enter, except Wolsey, of course, and the Admiral of France. As they entered the pavilion, the two parties attending the Kings began to intermingle awkwardly, making good cheer and toasting "each other in broken French and English: 'Bons amys, French and English!'" [14]

Inside the pavilion the French and English Kings were apparently "bons amys" too. De Fleuranges in his memoirs records a touching incident as they sat together there. Henry proposed to make some amendments to their former articles of alliance. As he began to read the draft of the new treaty, the first words he encountered were: *I Henry King.* He stopped for a moment, significantly, and then added *of England,* not adding the words *and France,* as was the usual style of English monarchs with their long and agitated pretensions to the throne of France. Francis remarked this delicacy, as Hume puts it, "and expressed by a smile his approbation of it." [15]

It was a good beginning, showing a spirit of concession that augured well. Thereafter both Henry and Francis feinted at friendship, but the days were tightly scheduled with ceremonies, and reciprocity was so minutely ordered that it was difficult for them to meet as man meets man. On the Sunday that the French King dined at Guines with the Queen of England, the English King dined with the French Queen. Catherine was gracious to Francis, having the assurance of Henry's prior meeting with Charles to comfort her. Henry on his part was treated to a bevy of French femininity; the prospect of his being entertained by the beauties of France had been one of the lures Francis had insinuated into the early negotiations for the meeting, and Henry now made the most of the fare offered. In the ruddy manner of the English, he kissed the French Queen, then kissed Louise of Savoy (the King's mother), then the Duchess of Alençon, and finally all the ladies of the company. After this example of collaboration the King sat at a great banquet until five in the evening. By the time the banquet was over, both the King and his horse were feeling their oats. "To display his skill before the ladies, he set spurs to his horse, making it bound and curvet 'as valiantly as any man could do.'"

All very pleasant, these pastimes. Still they did little to advance the purpose for which the meeting was called. The Kings were kept apart by the very ceremonies designed to bring them together. In Wolsey's Book of Ordinances the arrangements to be observed on every occasion, whether of gaiety or piety, had been meticulously set forth. Everyone, including the Kings, had his part written in the script, and he must play it accordingly. Regulation was imperative in the eyes of my lord Cardinal and Legate; his regulation and planning went far beyond the sheep and beeves; it kept the richly dressed puppets of England and the marionettes of France obedient to his strings.

The protection provided by excessive scheduling may have pleased Henry; at least he seemed content to accept it. Francis was not. He made a magnificent gesture to break through the stultifying ordinances. Being of a gallant and generous turn and given to spontaneity and trust, he grew restive under the confinement of precautions.

One morning Francis arose early and, slipping past his own guards, rode straight to Guines, accompanied only by two of his gentlemen attendants and a page. When he reached the English King's apartments there, the guards were astonied to see him and not less to hear him say, "You are all my prisoners: carry me to your master." Which they did. Henry, who had not yet risen from his couch, rubbed his eyes at the sight of the beaming French King who had come to pay him homage without benefit of protocol so early in the morning. Then he arose and threw his arms around Francis and said: "My brother, you have played me the most agreeable trick in the world and have showed me the full confidence I may place in you: I surrender myself your prisoner from this moment." He then took a collar of pearls of great price and placed it around Francis's neck, begging him to wear it for the sake of his prisoner. To this suggestion Francis assented, but only on the condition that Henry "should wear a bracelet, of which he made him a present, and which was double in value to the collar." [16]

Francis had penetrated the *cordon sanitaire* by his premeditated spontaneity. From then on there was a certain camaraderie between the two Kings; both had escaped from the governess of propriety. The next day Henry, not one to be outdone, rode to Ardres without guards or attendants. Henry and Francis were now acknowledged as individuals, not merely monarchs, and given some freedom from the abominable ordinances. Both had taken prudent steps toward each other but not enough to bring them together.

Then one day in the midst of festivities and in the presence of the two Queens, Henry, feeling jovial and playful after beating Francis at archery, seized the long-legged Frenchman by the collar, shouting, "Come, you shall wrestle with me!" It was a touch of informality Francis had not expected and he was, for a moment, caught off his guard. But he recovered quickly, and in the unpredicted struggle which followed, Francis, being released by surprise from his polite obligations as a host, threw Henry with a thud on his royal rump. If Francis had been surprised, Henry was dumfounded. This was no way to treat a pampered king. No one, certainly not since childhood, had ever laid a controlling hand on him or clipped his will or thwarted so much as one of his whims. Accounts say that he rose to his feet in a rage, squared away and muttered, "Again!" [17]

The moment was as breathless as Henry. Fortunately the Queens came forward promptly, and courtiers flocked around and smothered the crisis with a blanket of jolly palaver, all making very light of what they had beheld. They thus prevented further rounds of the wrestling match, but they could not rub out the effect of what had happened. It was not according to protocol, not in the meticulous script of ordinances my lord Cardinal had written for the occasion.

The outward relations between the two sovereigns and their attendants continued cordial to the end of the prescribed festivities. Politeness had been ordered and delivered. The royal parties behaved in a resolutely civilized way. And to smooth anything amiss, my lord Cardinal and Legate gave the great assemblage his religious benediction as the two Kings prepared to part. In a showy chapel of wood built on the Field in one night and furnished with twenty-four enormous gold candlesticks and with the golden images of the Twelve Apostles, Wolsey sang himself a high and solemn Mass before the two Kings and their Queens and pronounced sacerdotal indulgences on them and their followers. In attendance upon him were two cardinals, two legates, four archbishops and ten bishops, not to mention assorted members of the French and English nobility. The air was "perfumed with incense and flowers," and the altars were hung with cloth-of-gold tissue.

It was an inspiring moment, and the religious atmosphere brought forth the most gallant impulses of those who took part. When the Cardinal of Bourbon, "according to the usages of the time, presented the Gospel to the French King to kiss, Francis, declining, commanded it to be offered to the King of England, who was too well bred to accept the honour." Later the two Queens were equally ceremonious. After a friendly dispute as to who should kiss the Pax first, they ended by kissing each other instead.

Behind the French Queen on this vast occasion knelt a young Englishwoman, as small as a footnote on the great page of history being written there. The sister of one who had been a mistress to Henry, she was a woman of inconspicuous charm, with nothing in particular to draw sudden attention. It was said later that she had a bosom not much raised, but of her eyes men remarked that they "are black and beautiful, and take great effect." [18]

Her name was Anne Boleyn.

Book Three
(1521-1529)

Recounting the reversal of Wolsey's policy by a King who decides to manage his own affairs and the failure of the Cardinal to raise the necessary funds for a war with France; reviewing the efforts made by the Cardinal at the King's behest to secure the annulment of Henry's marriage with Catherine of Aragon, culminating in a trial of the marriage before a Roman court in England.

CHAPTER I

WHEN Henry and Francis parted, Henry, instead of going back to England, went to meet Charles in the Flemish town of Gravelines, which took its English-sounding name from the term meaning "count's canal." Gravelines was an appropriate and symbolic name, for there the King of England and the Emperor of the Holy Roman Empire began to lay grave lines of diplomacy that fitted what they considered the realities of their day and would in a few years change the destiny of the assiduous Cardinal of York.

The show at the Field of Cloth of Gold had been Wolsey's. At Gravelines it was Henry's. There was less splendor, but there was more business done. Sir Edward Belknap, General Surveyor of the Crown lands and trusted servant of Henry, had constructed in the Flemish town a huge hall of wood with a canvas roof fastened on with ropes and iron. "Within the said house was painted the heavens, with stars, sun, moon, and images." There were ships under sail "and windmills on the hills winding" and other contrivances designed to make a heavenly noise. But the wind proved to be the undoing of the brave temporary palace. For hardly had the King and Emperor met when the wind began to rise, increasing until evening. "Then on a sodaine it blew off all the canvas heaven with the planets and blew out more than 1000 torches and other lights of wax . . . The seats which were with great richness prepared for the Emperor and King were dashed and lost." [1]

The same wind blew away the canvas firmament then over Europe. Shortly after the big gale Henry took the young Emperor in train and returned with him to Calais, where for the next four days the two discussed matters of common interest and common disturbance. Meanwhile Francis, ignored and bewildered after having been courted and entertained, chafed near his own borders and hoped to be included in the interview taking place at Calais. He had even proposed that he be allowed to attend the meeting informally and without those careful details of protocol which would have been fitting. But Wolsey, knowing the mood of his master, had given him no encouragement. Two noblewomen of France, the Lady Vendôme and her daughter-in-law, managed to visit Calais on business, but they had no part in the meeting of Henry and Charles.[2] Some French nobles attended a masquerade ball Henry gave for the Emperor.[3] This was as close as the French, still fresh from being hospitable a few miles away, got to the conference.

Long before the King and Cardinal had set sail for the Field of Cloth of Gold, it had been proposed that the alliance between England and France, sealed by the betrothal of Mary to the Dauphin, be set aside and that Mary's hand be given to the Emperor.[4]

This proposal was discussed secretly at Calais. But big bargains with emperors, especially impoverished ones, take time and cannot be settled in a week. The conference there ended without being concluded. It would take a year or more before the matters that were discussed took on the firmness of agreements. The mind of the Cardinal who sailed with Catherine and Henry from Calais to Dover, however, was not the same mind that, six crowded and feverish weeks before, had sailed from Dover to Calais.

Emperor Charles V, devout and grave and pious by nature and enjoying with such good reason the noble sobriquet, His Catholic Majesty, made it plain to the Cardinal of York that he would help him gain the chair of St. Peter once it fell vacant. Here indeed was a consummation devoutly to be wished by a man approaching fifty who had reached his pinnacle as a commoner. There was no refuge for a person of his abilities save in a more exalted success; and that success he could not attain within the realm of England. He had saturated the market with his talents. There was no future and no permanence in his position. His competence was by no means a guarantee of security or a hedge against disaster. Quite the contrary. Not only did his managerial skill arouse the jealousy and irritation of his contemporaries; it might also in due course irritate the King, who had of late begun to get the impression that he might be capable of running his country, indeed might enjoy doing so. As the King learned his job, there would be less and less of a place for the Cardinal. With all his privileges and all the royal indulgence shown him, Wolsey had only one chance of achieving dignity in his own right, and that lay beyond the borders of England, beyond the quarrels of kings — in Rome. Otherwise he would remain at best enslaved by the King's kindness and at worst endangered by his ingratitude. Privy to the most intimate affairs of state, enjoying the King's confidence, wallowing in wealth, Wolsey remained in effect a subaltern living on suffrance, disposable and expendable. Only in the papal chair would he be above and beyond the slings and arrows of outrageous fortune.

Hence there were abundant reasons, if only personal and political, why Wolsey must achieve the papacy — and why his actions would be influenced by any considerations that might bring him the triple crown of Rome. Even if he did not gain the tiara himself, he would still be swayed by his sentiments toward Rome. These sentiments were part of the furniture of his mind, and they had been evident all his life. And it would appear that the Emperor rather than the King of France would be the best means both of safeguarding the integrity of the papacy and of aiding the Cardinal toward his own personal ambition. France had offered in 1520 to help him become Pope,[5] but Francis was a perennial threat to Rome and he had no great power there: he might at any moment sweep down again across the plains of Lombardy and extend his holdings, even take Rome itself. No, the future of the papacy and the future of Wolsey both lay with the Emperor.

As if to emphasize beyond misinterpretation the pivotal power of the Pope in matters of both politics and dignity, two instructive happenings took place in 1521, the year following the talks at Gravelines and Calais. First, Leo set about promulgating a secret confederation against France.[6] Second, the King of England wrote a book, and, in exchange for his handsomely bound disquisition, got for himself and his heirs and assigns the title "Defender of the Faith."

The first event had significance which it did not take a person of Wolsey's perspicacity to note. The wind was blowing against Francis and favoring the course of Charles. Other aspects of the campaign Leo launched were more subtle, but their meaning could not escape the eye of an ambitious fellow. For the duties of executing the details of the confederation were left in the ready and willing hands of one Cardinal Giulio de' Medici, the Pope's nephew. Wiseacres saw in Giulio de' Medici a potential pope; he was a favorite of Leo's, high in the councils of Rome. And Giulio de' Medici was a bastard. Certainly a man's birth was no bar to the papal throne. In the papal chair a bastard or a man descended from an innkeeper in Ipswich might attain dignity.

The deferential book by Wolsey's King and its reception in Rome provided one more sign to show the Cardinal how closely both his future and the future of his country were linked with the papacy. Henry had been engaged in writing his book for at least two years.[7] He felt obliged to get down on paper some of his theological views and lay them before the rulers of Christendom to help them in their battle against heresy and the devil, the two being incarnate in the person of Martin Luther. Credit for the document must, by the King's own hand, go to the Cardinal of York, for in a letter written by the King's secretary Wolsey was informed that the King had never intended to write against Luther's erroneous opinions "afore he was by your grace moved and led thereto. Wherefore his Highness saith that your Grace must of good congruity be partner of all the honor and glory he hath attained by that act." [8]

Wolsey may have prompted the document; he certainly did not write it. He was too wise to criticize it or edit it or accept any responsibility for its dusty and arid generalizations. He merely handled its publication in Rome, so to say, and stood back to contemplate the astonishing acclaim with which it met.

Henry might have worked indefinitely on his book, as is the way with authors, had Luther not published in 1520 his *De Captivitate Babylonica*. This book was lush with heresy. Tunstall wrote Wolsey from Worms, saying: "I pray God keep that book out of England." His prayer was not answered, for early in 1521 copies had reached England and Pace wrote to Wolsey: "At mine arrival to the King this morning, I found him looking upon a book of Luther's." [9] It was *De Captivitate*. Whether Henry read the book is not clear, but he looked upon it, and he decided that the hour had struck when he must, as he wrote the Pope, defend the Church with his pen as with his sword. Upon the receipt of this reassurance Leo rejoiced and must have felt steadier about the fate of Christendom. He said he would be very glad indeed to see the manuscript.

So Henry got out his pages and began work all over again. But it was several months before he could finish the book, being interrupted in his pious labors by the necessity of attending to the execution of the Duke of Buckingham. On August 25, 1521, however, the chef-d'oeuvre was ready, and Wolsey wrote to John Clerk, Henry's ambassador in Rome, detailed instructions of how it was to be placed before His Holiness. All told, twenty-eight copies were dispatched, but Clerk was to take a single copy covered with cloth of gold and present this copy to the Pope privately, there being two verses inserted in this copy by the King's own hand. The verses were, according to some authorities, written by Wolsey but copied out by Henry.[10]

Leo took the book in his hands and admired the binding and "the trim decking." Then, opening it, he read five leaves of the introduction without interruption. "At such places as he liked," Clerk wrote, "and that seemed to be at every second line, he made ever some demonstration." A few moments later he told Clerk that "he would not 'a thought that such a book should have come from the King's grace, who hath been occupied necessarily in other feats, seeing that other men which hath occupied themselves in study all their lives cannot bring forth the like.'"

The verses inscribed by the King were written in a small hand, and Clerk took the book from Leo and offered to read them to him. But the Pope took the book back and read the verses promptly, proving his eyesight was as good as the ambassador's.

Clerk's next move was to ask for a public consistory for a formal reception of Henry's work. This Leo refused firmly, meanwhile having had a chance to read the book. There was certainly nothing remarkable about it save that it was written by a king, and the only thing remarkable about that was that a king would write a book. As a compound of pious maxims done in prose as dressy as Henry's wardrobe, it had a certain curiosity value: it would assure the world by way of a permanent record that the King of England was eternally on the side of the Pope. It might not be a trenchant tool for the extirpation of the Lutheran heresies, but it did come to the rescue of Christian sacraments. Of marriage Henry wrote:

> The insipid water of concupiscence is turned by the hidden grace of God into the finest flavour. Whom God hath joined together let no man put asunder. O wonderful word such as no man could have uttered save the Word which was made flesh! . . . Who does not tremble when he considers how he should deal with his wife, for not only is he bound to love her, but so to live with her that he may return her to God pure and without stain, when God who gave, shall demand his own again.[11]

In gratitude for these stale sentiments the Holy Father of Christendom was supposed to laud the King of England and confer upon him some special recognition. Leo met the situation as best he could. Having refused a public consistory, he asked Clerk to meet him at a place where consistories were generally held. Then he merely called into the chamber such prelates as were loitering about the halls, "to the number of twenty." Having rounded up an audience, the Pope prepared to hear Clerk's speech. A master of ceremonies instructed Clerk to deliver it on his knees, which he did reluctantly, fearing that his heart and spirits would not be as much at liberty as they would be if he stood. But he got through the oration well enough, the Pope seated upon a dais three feet above the floor and "afore him, in a large quadrant, upon stools," the twenty prelates who had been "tarrying without." [12]

It was less of an occasion than Henry could have wished or Wolsey had planned. But it served the purpose of both, for next day the Pope issued a bull bestowing on Henry for his sturdy tilt with the devil the coveted title of *Fidei Defensor*. The lesson was plain to Wolsey, and it brought into confluence the streams of his thought and his loyalties. The King and the Pope were now even more firmly identified than ever.

In England the bull bearing the title was received with great ceremony. When a proper crowd had been assembled around the court at Greenwich, the King sat upon his throne and ordered the bull to be read. The reading must have been impressive. Leo's prose rolled on and on in waves of cadence. There was nothing casual about his style or about naming Henry his friend and brother in the Lord's work. Having reviewed the circumstances of the day in the realm of theology, Leo moved to his resonant climax:

> Considering how acceptable and welcome your gift was to Us, especially in this juncture of time, We, the true successor of St. Peter, Whom Christ before his ascension left as his vicar upon earth, and to whom he committed the care of his flock, presiding in this Holy See, from whence all dignity and titles have their source, having with our brethren maturely deliberated on these things and with one consent unanimously decreed to bestow on your Majesty this title, viz., DEFENDER OF THE FAITH. And as we have by this title honoured you, We likewise command all Christians that they name your Majesty by this title; and that, in their writings to your Majesty, immediately after the word KING, they add, DEFENDER OF THE FAITH.[13]

After the bull was read, the King repaired to his chapel. After a High Mass had been sung before the court and the foreign ambassadors, the bull was read again, following the sound of trumpets. Later when the King went to dinner, heralds in the hall where he dined proclaimed the King's new title. The whole occasion was carried out with great solemnity, the only frivolous note coming from Patch, the King's fool. Seeing his master jocund, Patch asked him the reason. The King replied that it was because of his new title. "To which the Fool made this arch reply: 'Prithee, good Harry, let thee and I defend one another and leave the Faith alone to defend itself.' "[14]

Meanwhile Francis, merely the Most Christian King, behaved in a fashion by no means calculated to set the mind of the Pope at rest and without any reference to the theoretical or political importance of the papacy. Circumstances left him little choice, for it did not take a shrewd spy to tell that Henry and Charles planned to make war on him. He knew, too, that Leo feared him and sought to unite Italian states and the Emperor against him. Surrounded by enemies, he had only one line of defense and that was his alliance with England under the Treaty of London, whereby it was provided that Henry would come to his rescue if he were attacked. He was astute enough, in the midst of the depressing combination being formed against him, to hold England to her bargain and to display toward her an attentive friendliness. He gave no outward sign that the King and the Cardinal were making preparations to turn upon him. He continued to pay his respects to the English King and declared that he would gladly ride anywhere to meet him. His respect for the Cardinal, he said, was second only to that which he entertained for the Cardinal's master.

Under the guise of unbroken friendship and unsuspecting trust, he was able to play his game, dangerous and futile though it was, with some amusement and with clever manipulations. All the French dockyards were busy hives making galleons. But could his firm and fast ally in decency object if he made himself strong? Rather Henry should rejoice! On this point he was plainspoken to the English ambassador. Indeed he added for good measure stories of three great galleons that had remarkable dimensions and principles. These were to be so constructed, he told the English, that they would draw little water — "so little water that he will bring them so near shore that he may land out of them, without a boat, 500 men . . ." They would form landing barges by means of a kind of bridge carried with them.[15]

These details being duly and credulously reported to the English court, Francis turned next to stir the kettle of trouble with a long stick, keeping the while an innocent countenance. Charles, even while he lay at Gravelines, was suffering from the rebellious spirit in Castile. Francis, knowing of this distraction, took advantage of the Emperor's embarrassment and connived to let Henry d'Albret repossess Navarre. When confronted with the news of the expedition, he blithely assured England that Henry d'Albret was only going to visit his grandfather. As for the feints and moves he himself made toward Italy, Francis handled the accusations of the English equally airily, saying that he but wished to see his duchy of Milan and visit his subjects there. However, he added in great pretended deference to the protests of the English King that he "would make no great haste thitherwards for the present." [16]

His maneuverings, in effect, were intended to goad the Emperor to attack him, so that, under the definition of aggression Wolsey had laid down lucidly in the Treaty of London, he could claim the support of the

English ally. Not that Henry or Wolsey or Charles could be deceived. Charles howled like a stuck pig when he learned of the invasion of Navarre. He howled again when Robert de la Marck, lord of Sedan and Bouillon, declared war and invaded the Emperor's kingdoms in Burgundy with a host of ragamuffins officered by French generals. Charles claimed that England must come at once to his succor, under the Treaty of London. Francis, not to be outdone, claimed that England must come to his aid when his troops, who had stirred rebellion in the Emperor's domains, were chased back across the French frontier. He claimed with rare *élan* that he had been the victim of aggression.[17]

Under these distended circumstances, Henry proposed that Wolsey be suffered to mediate the differences between the two monarchs and decide who in truth had practiced aggression. Charles, knowing from two earlier talks with Henry and his trusted minister how matters stood, agreed with blandishments of reasonableness. Francis showed an understandable reluctance. He had an army in train; his kingdom was prepared for the inevitable and would lose spirit by a postponement of hostilities. And he knew, too, of the possible outcome of any mediation in which Henry and Wolsey were the judges. But it fortuned that in the summer of 1521 his earlier successes in ruffling the Emperor's domains had come to nought, and his troops had been driven back with humiliating losses. Hence he too agreed to accept the King of England's friendly offices, and it was arranged that my lord of York as the King's agent and plenipotentiary should proceed to Calais, where he would treat with the ambassadors of Charles and Francis. Wolsey secured from both the Kings a written assurance that they would bow to his mediation, as well as the further odd promise that neither of them would attempt to be reconciled to the other until he had pronounced his sentence.[18] The contending princes must not slip around behind the Cardinal's back and make peace.

Wolsey's manner of going to Calais during this summer of 1521 was in character with his usual pomp of movement and befitting the dignity and importance of his mission. He passed through London in great state, the Great Seal of England being carried before him, and in his train were many nobles and knights, including Sir Thomas Boleyn, together with gentlemen and a proper contingent of servants.[19] On August 2 he reached Calais. He carried with him one commission to be displayed as a badge of his impartiality. This authorized him to work for closer friendship between Henry and Francis and to seek a general confederation of all the powers of Christendom, as if one did not already exist. His private instructions were to conclude a treaty of marriage between the Princess Mary and the

Emperor and arrange for military cooperation between Henry and Charles for the invasion of France.[20] His real purpose had been defined in the earlier conferences of Henry and Charles the year before, and it had been redefined at a meeting between Henry and the ambassadors of Charles on June 5.

This conference had taken place at Windsor Castle. The ambassadors were to meet with Henry between ten and eleven of the morning, but hearty Henry, after hearing Mass, had found himself in such good appetite because of his hunting the day before that he had decided to eat first. After dinner he had received the ambassadors jovially and had discussed affairs with them quite openly, saying that the Emperor should remain on the defensive in his contentions with Francis until such time as he and the Emperor might concert an attack upon Francis. The details, he added, could be arranged at their next meeting. Meanwhile he would approve sending the Cardinal to Calais under the pretense of hearing the grievances of Francis and the Emperor; once it was plain that these grievances could not be settled, the Cardinal should withdraw to the Emperor and arrange the details of the treaty both Henry and the Emperor so much desired. The heart of the strategy lay in delay, not only to prevent the advantage which Francis might have of waging a quick war, but also because the pensions from France under the earlier treaty were due in October and it would be well to postpone an open breach until these moneys arrived.

The sham negotiations at Calais were based on this secret agreement. My lord of York flashed his counterfeit commission and then carried out to the last crooked letter the private instructions given him. First he listened with solemnity to the orations of the ambassadors from Charles and Francis. Amused by the preposterous demands, Wolsey told the story of a courtier who asked his king for a forest. Confronted by his relatives for the extent of his claims and their unreasonableness, he said that actually he wanted only eight or nine trees.[21] Gattinara, the chancellor of Charles's realm, spoke of the seven reasons for peace as the seven deadly sins and of the ten reasons for war as the Ten Commandments.[22]

The proceedings wore the outer aspects of spectacular drama. The King of the French, ruler of 14,000,000 subjects, his nation the most solid and self-contained in Europe, prayed Wolsey for his judgment and, in spite of his diplomatic railleries in the past year, now seemed pathetically eager to keep England a neutral if not an ally. Not far away stood the Emperor of the Holy Roman Empire, who could boast 16,000,000 subjects in Europe alone and had as part of his prestige vast lands beyond the sea.

These two rulers were in effect suppliants to the son of Ipswich, the Lord Chancellor of a realm with only 3,500,000 people grown powerful under his tutelage and direction. And each of these two great rulers momentarily held his own destiny in check, waiting and waiting, until the Cardinal of York gave his judicial nod.

It was a scene rich in delights to a schoolmaster; he now had a class of ambassadors and courtiers; the setting was larger and packed with more atmosphere than the Star Chamber. He could not forgo lecturing the ambassadors. He told the French of the dangers of opposing the Emperor and of his wish to gain a peace acceptable to their master the French King. To the Imperialists he spoke of the importance of the good will and support of England under any and all circumstances. The French as well as the Imperialists appeared to accept his ministrations with pious expectations.

But the power actually to render judgment was not Wolsey's to employ or enjoy. If his position had been what it looked to be, with all the ceremonies of statecraft surrounding him and the minions of Kings and an Emperor attending him, he could have invoked the covenant of his league of nations and set the whole force of Europe against the aggressor. By this act he would have put into operation a principle he had conceived and stated. Actually, however, Wolsey's position at Calais was as counterfeit as the public commission he carried. Any power in his frame was bestowed by the King he served. He had gone to Calais solely as an animated detail of an elaborate conspiracy.

As such he behaved with precision and according to plan. Having listened to the complaints of both sides and found both their contentions flatulent, he discovered that the representatives of the Emperor did not have full powers to treat for a truce. As part of the subterfuge confected earlier, Wolsey indignantly refused to proceed without assurance that the Emperor's deputies would accept his decisions. There was but one thing to do and that was to go to the Emperor at Bruges and straighten the matter out. Remarkably, the French Chancellor, Duprat, accepted the proposal that the Cardinal visit the Emperor and persuade him to peace, appearing to believe that Wolsey had no other design. Charles had written to Wolsey on his arrival in Calais: "I will show you the bottom of my heart." In extending his invitation for the visit to Bruges he had dropped royal condescension and said as if to an equal: "You and I will do more in a day than my ambassadors will do in a month." [23] When Wolsey arrived, the Emperor received him with all the honor that could well be paid to a crowned head, coming out of the city to meet him and, having escorted him

274

within, making it clear that the trip to Bruges would not cost the Cardinal a farthing.

Although he was the honored guest of the Emperor and in lavish circumstances provided, Wolsey stuck to business. He got down to the real purpose that had brought him across the Channel. This purpose he achieved handsomely. He was to secure a marriage contract between Charles and the Princess Mary on terms of advantage to Henry. There was many an abatis thrown across his path. In preliminary negotiations it had been found that Charles did not know Latin, and all the documents having to do with the treaty had to be translated into French.[24] What is more, Charles was sorely impoverished and sought the alliance with England partly if not wholly because of his need for funds. He demanded a dowry of a million ducats, which could be reckoned at well over £200,000. Wolsey would offer no more than £80,000 and he stuck to his figure in spite of all efforts to dislodge him, whether by threat or cajolery.[25]

The haggling lasted two weeks, and in the end Wolsey got what he wanted. He arranged the marriage of Henry's daughter Mary on terms far lower than the Emperor demanded, bargained for the Emperor to pay England what she would lose in French pensions by a breach with France, and drew up a cooperative military program for the invasion of France. In addition, Charles promised his aid again in securing for Wolsey the papal crown.

Having these matters substantially settled, the Cardinal took his leave of the Emperor. To all appearances their amity had not been one whit disturbed by their business dealings. At his departure, however, the Emperor accompanied him only as far as the gates of the city. There Charles left the Prince of Orange and the Duke of Alva to ride with him somewhat farther on his way.

After Wolsey returned to Calais, the arguments continued and the dispatches grew sharp in tone. It looked as if the bargain for Mary's hand might not be struck after all. Margaret, the Emperor's aunt and regent of the Low Countries, who longed to see the match and fancied that she had been the originator of it, wrote: "For long enough I had good hope but now I am in despair. The Emperor has a will of his own and councillors who strengthen him in it. This very day he said openly: 'I see that the Cardinal thinks that he can treat me as he has advised my ambassadors to treat the French; he asks for things that are unreasonable and affect my honour. But he has met his match! I shall have no difficulty in finding a bride and he cannot sell me his princess so dearly.'" Then she adds words showing, as the Emperor's earlier statements had shown, how much those who ruled thought could be accomplished by personal contact with Wolsey: "I would dearly love to have two hours' talk with the Cardinal to set all right again." [26]

During the two months following his talks at Bruges, the Cardinal sought to patch up a truce between Charles and Francis. Why Francis allowed the negotiations to continue is far from plain. He lost daily by the delay, for the train of events now was plainly set. He continued to act as if Wolsey were somehow a judge and a friend and would still put matters right. Yet, when confronted with the demand for a truce, Francis accepted the advice of Duprat, the French chancellor, against further trusting M. le Médiateur. Charles, too, refused to go on with the negotiations.

Considering the climate of Calais, his incessant labors, and the anxiety induced by his position, Wolsey found it necessary with the approach of stormy weather to draw his efforts to a close. He had stayed at the job far longer than any elaborate scheme of deception would require. He had begun his conference in August. Not until November 24 did he give up and sign the agreements he had drawn with the Emperor at Bruges. In signing these agreements he covenanted for England that if Francis did not conclude peace with the Emperor Henry should declare war on him, "that the Lady Mary should be married to Charles, and that in the spring of 1523 the two sovereigns should jointly invade France, each contributing to the enterprise a land army of 40,000 horse and foot, as well as a fleet to harry the coast." [27]

Four days after the agreements were signed, my lord Cardinal sailed from Calais. A devil had troubled the waters. It took the sailing vessel which bore him fifteen tempestuous hours to cover the twenty-two miles between Calais and Dover. Nor were these the last rough waters he would pass. They but brought him back, ominously it would seem, from the vacuum of the conference table into the world of sky and land and sea, where men and women and children are harried by problems and anxieties that cannot be dissipated by polemics or wars. Much had happened that year beyond the English pale at Calais. Muskets had been invented. The people of Holland had fallen under great calamities by the overflowing of the dykes, "whereby 72 villages and 100,000 persons were drowned." England's green and merry land had been smitten by drouth, so that the price of wheat had risen and had put the people in great need. Moreover, there had been a "great decay in tillage and husbandry, owing to the vast quantity of inclosures made by the nobility and gentry, who within fifty years had kept their lands in their own hands and turned most of them into pastures." [28]

It was a disquieting world for my lord Cardinal to come back into after the prodigious labors he had performed at Calais, especially since these labors were not fully appreciated among some of the nobles at the court. There were now criticisms above a whisper, not only for the Cardinal's deceitful conduct, but also for his taking the Great Seal of England with him to Calais. It was said that justice was thereby delayed "and many English were forced to go to him to receive their dispatches." It was further charged that even "the constituting of sheriffs was suspended until his return." [29]

Wolsey exercised control over the government by keeping in his possession, or directing the use of, the actual seals by which the King's business was carried on. Among these was the Great Seal, which Henry allowed him to hold as if it were his personal property. He had taken it with him to Calais and even on his visit to the Emperor at Bruges. The King had needed it sorely and had dispatched Tunstall, Bishop of London, to bring it home so that important business could be attended to, "to the satisfaction of his subjects and the replenishing of his revenue." [30]

Besides the Great Seal there were two other stamps of authority which the Cardinal controlled. One, smaller, was known as the privy seal, entrusted to a lord in the King's court. The other was the royal signet, controlled by a secretary to the King. To see that the privy seal stayed under his hand, Wolsey in 1516 made Bishop Ruthal its keeper. As for the other seal, Wolsey found means to order it as his pleasure by appointing one of his secretaries as secretary to the King.

How fully Wolsey controlled the minor seals not actually in his possession may be seen from the fact that he trained his underlings not to use them without his sanction. While Wolsey was abroad, the King ordered the Keeper of the Privy Seal, "straitly, without any delay," to seal and deliver certain letters. Instead of obeying the King's strict command, the Keeper of the Privy Seal wrote to Wolsey as follows: "Remembering your commandment that I should advertise you before I sealed any other thing than common writs, and that John Croke, who should make the said writs, is with you, I have sent him the warrants. I desire to know your pleasure, when I receive the said letters patent, whether I shall seal them or not." [31]

If Wolsey's tight-fisted handling of the seals caused murmurs and complaints, none of these complaints had at this time any effect upon the King. He expressed unabashed satisfaction at the results of Wolsey's negotiations. He would have an imperial son-in-law at a relatively small cost; he would lose nothing from the break with France; best of all, the conquest of France was now feasibly planned. Henry commanded Richard Pace, his secretary, to express his gratitude, saying "he thanked God that he had such a chaplain by whose wisdom, fidelity and labor he could obtain greater acquisitions than all his progenitors had been able to accomplish with all their numerous wars and battles." As if this tribute would not suffice, the King directed Pace to write again and to convey "his most hearty thanks for the great pains and labors sustained by him in the bringing of his said affairs to such conclusion and end, as most redounded to his honour and surety, saying that everything in effect is finished according to his own desire." [32]

Words so full and fulsome from a prince upon whom life and career depended must have cheered the troubled mind and seasick viscera of the Cardinal as he returned to England. Let others carp and cavil; the one whose word mattered most had spoken in his behalf, and, whatever might lie ahead, this was the kind of encomium that Wolsey could cherish; it showed how diligently he had served the King.

His reward, too, had been more substantial than words. While he was away, the Abbot of St. Albans had died. The monks had called upon Henry for the necessary permission to elect a successor. Meanwhile Wolsey had written Pace, and Pace had gone straight with Wolsey's letter to the King. He reported to Wolsey later: "And I found him ready to go out shooting; notwithstanding, his grace happily commanded me to go down with him by his secret way into the park; whereby I had as good commodity as I could desire to advance your grace's permission as much as the case required. And the king read your grace's letters himself, and made me privy to the contents of the same. And the few words his Highness spoke to me in this cause were these: 'By God! my lord cardinal hath sustained many charges in this his voyage and expended £10,000,' which I did affirm and show his grace of good congruence, he oweth you some recompense. Whereupon his grace answered 'that he would rather give unto you the abbey of St. Albans than to any monk.'" [33]

CHAPTER 11

THE French War that followed failed to capture the interest of those who took their dreary parts in it. Its depredations slaughtered

French peasants and cattle, and its plunder enriched a few deadbeats; but its engagements had no traceable effect upon the map, nor was its dismal course redeemed by any encounter wherein either bravery or strategy lent color or meaning to the action.

In spite of its military insignificance, the war disturbed the atmosphere over a wide area and sent eddies whirling in many directions. It was like a storm that follows implacably its course: often the remote and distant effects, the asides spoken by the wind, bear freakishly upon men's lives and touch them more sharply than the storm itself. The asides which involved the destiny of Wolsey were of this sort. These small occurrences would have influenced him mightily even if not one English soldier had set foot on French soil.

It was, for example, the disturbance created by the French War that brought back to England from France the younger daughter of Sir Thomas Boleyn. A knight who knew the disposition and intent of his King could not leave a daughter of tender age in the French capital with war impending. Anne Boleyn had attended the French Queen Claude. She had been one of three hundred girls at the court, and it had been deemed that her association with this virtuous, chaste, and pious woman would have a beneficent effect upon her upbringing. The girls attending Claude were required to have manners suitable to their elders. They were taught, says Brantôme, to sing, dance, work, and pray. At the age of thirteen they were dressed in the costume of their elders and made to pretend that they were grown up.[1]

Anne Boleyn's father had gone to France on a mission in 1518 and at the beginning of 1519 had been made ambassador to that country. It was but natural that he give his daughter the best advantages.

How long his daughter remained with Claude in paths of rectitude is not known. There is some evidence that she went next to the Duchess of Alençon, Marguerite de Valois, sister of Francis I, a woman addicted to Lutheran heresies. In the course of her years in and about the French court Anne had picked up a speaking acquaintance with French and had learned to write it with some idiosyncratic charm. Along with certain English nationals, scholars and officials, she returned to England in the last days of 1521 and shortly thereafter appeared at the English court, where she was not long in catching the roving eye of Henry, who, having enjoyed the pleasure of her sister Mary and liking his women à la carte, took from the beginning a strong and strident fancy to her.

Indeed, Henry and his minister had been officially aware of her and familiar with her name while she was yet abroad. She had been the subject of state correspondence. The Butlers of Ireland and the Boleyns had engaged in controversy over the rights of the earldom of Ormond. The Butlers, whatever the validity of their claims to the title, had been loyal friends of Henry in a place where he could always use friends — among the savage Irish. What could be more logical than to marry a Butler to a Boleyn? With this in mind Henry had written Anne's uncle, the Earl of Surrey, who was then in Ireland, proposing that Anne be brought to the marriage bed of Sir Piers Butler and thus settle a minor succession. Surrey sounded out the prospective groom's father, the Earl of Ormond, who advanced no objection to the match, and Surrey wrote Wolsey accordingly. But by this time Wolsey was busy and weary in Calais, and the whole matter was laid away in neglect. Wolsey wrote to the King in November 1521 from Calais to say that when he returned to England he would talk with the King about the matter and, as he put it, bring the match to good effect.[2]

It was another case where the Cardinal became too busy to get anything done. After all, he was negotiating between an emperor and a king. Pressed and discouraged and driven, he would have to let something slide. Even Wolsey couldn't do everything. Some matters would have to wait until he had settled the world's affairs. Taking on all the assignments that his King burdened him with, he could but cover his confusion with gestures of abundant energy punctuated by blind weariness. Whatever the case, silence put a period to the correspondence. We hear nothing further of the projected marriage. Shortly after Wolsey returned to England, full of many postponed matters to discuss, Anne Boleyn returned also and the King caught sight of her. Then it was too late to marry her off to an Irishman.

Anne was in her sixteenth year. The first recorded appearance she made at a court revel was on March 4, 1522. The affair was held at York Place, and there is a detailed description of the festivities and of the clothes worn by the ladies.[3] There is no record of what the King thought of her, but there are other contemporary descriptions, some of them conflicting but all agreeing on certain essentials. The blood of the Ormonds ran in her veins. She had inherited "the black-blue Irish hair and Irish eyes." As Brewer describes her from contemporary documents: "She was a little, lively, sparkling brunette, with fascinating eyes and long black hair, which, contrary to the somber fashion of those days, she wore coquettishly floating loosely down her back, interlaced with jewels. The beauty of her eyes and hair struck all beholders alike — grave ecclesiastics and spruce young sprigs of nobility." An archbishop later described her as "sitting *in* her hair on a litter." She was in manner "passing sweet and cheerful." And to her other appealing qualities was added the ability to speak French at the English court and to give a French twist and accent to whatever she said. She had, in a word, learned to pass for French — at least among the English.

Wolsey was not among the grave ecclesiastics who noted the charms of Mistress Anne Boleyn or praised the effects of her vivacity. He was occupied with more momentous concerns. Even his public gaiety had some state or diplomatic function. One gets the impression that he bore his duties as a host with a gracious air but that he never lost his reserve or identity in the revels of which he was a part. He entertained with the preoccupied air of a man who thinks about the results of hospitality.

In the year 1522 it was his main obligation to ready the nation for war. The burden, added to his others, was all the more irksome because the war against France meant a complete reversal of the policy he had favored and promoted. He was asked to organize a war growing out of a line of action that went against his beliefs. These beliefs had been expressed and formalized in the Treaty of London three years before. There were no secret provisions in this treaty. It had begun with only the two high contracting parties, England and France, but it included all the Christian nations of Europe. It was directed *against no single power*. The aim of the treaty was positive and its purpose was peace. Its language had been clear and it avoided the ambiguities for which men die. It defined aggression in plain terms. What is more, it had been accepted not only by those who formally adhered to it but by minds that were cynical and critical of the old diplomacy and the shopworn treaties of the past. As Mattingly points out, every surviving document indicates that the treaty was taken in good faith and with full knowledge of the sincerity of Wolsey's intentions. "Two of the toughest-minded and most experienced working diplomats in Europe, representing the two powers most likely to be alarmed by an alliance between England and France, de Mesa for Spain and Giustiniani for Venice, although at first they entertained the gravest suspicions, ended by assuring their governments that Wolsey's treaty meant exactly what it said, and that the cardinal was sincerely and entirely behind it." [4]

It was this document of hope, this testimony to his own beliefs, that Wolsey had to forsake. In spite of all the pressure brought to bear on him by the King, he had tried to invoke the treaty with its stiff guarantees against aggression. In vain. It was to be put aside now in the memory book of diplomacy, a quaint picture of what men had once thought might be possible. And the man who had been the architect of peace must turn aside to the carpentry of preparation for war.

Wolsey had not the moral stamina to stand up to his King or sufficient influence or authority to swing the weight of England behind the treaty he had made. He had put peace on paper; he could not put it into effect. He had not been wholly callous at Calais. But with all his vaunted and vaulted power, he was impotent without the King. He might have fallen and fallen nobly instead of carrying out the King's orders at Calais, but there was no assurance in his mind, nor is there any certainty even in the backward glance of history, that his fall would have prevented the alliance or the war that followed. The King could have found then, as he did later, others who could execute his policy.

The very fact that Henry had his secretary write Wolsey on the eve of his negotiations that he wanted young men trained up for the tasks of diplomacy must have sounded a note of didactic warning to the Cardinal. The letter, written to a man old enough to be his father, had put the matter in this wise and with no due regard to the Cardinal's feelings: "Whereas old men do now decay greatly within this his realm," said the secretary, speaking for the King, "his mind is to acquaint other young men with his great affairs, and therefore he desireth your Grace to make Sir William Sandys and Sir Thomas More privy to all such matters as your Grace shall treat at Calais." [5]

As the King grew in his sense of kinghood, Wolsey shriveled in his sense of usefulness. Henry was now past thirty and feeling more and more the oats of power. The collusive alliance with the Emperor was not the first, but it was the most conspicuous, sign that he intended to run the kingdom to suit his own conceits.

It was six months after the breakdown of negotiations at Calais that war was formally declared. For the first few months Francis had kept up his charming politeness toward the English monarch and Henry had kept up his pretenses. Then Francis, convinced at last of England's hostile intentions, sent John Stewart, Duke of Albany, into Scotland, a signal always for the quarrelsome lords of that unhappy country to rally round and devil the English. The Duke was French by birth and upbringing and French in his sentiments. But, having been made regent of Scotland in 1515, he had kept close connections there, and Francis, whenever he wanted to annoy the English, loosed the Duke, who always succeeded in stealing unmolested across the waters to Scotland. Surrey wrote to Wolsey some picture of his character: "By many ways I am advertised that the Duke of Albany is a marvellous wilful man and will believe no man's counsel, but will have his own opinion followed . . . I am also advertised that he is so passionate that he be apart amongst his familiars, and doth hear anything contrarious to his mind and pleasure, his accustomed manner is to take his bonnet suddenly off his head, and to throw it in the fire, and no man dare take it out, but let it be brent. My lord Dacre doth affirm, that at his last being in Scotland he did burn above a dozen bonnets after that manner." [6]

The act of sending the tempestuous Duke to Scotland followed all the tactics Francis had pursued in his troubled relations with England. He did everything short of war, everything to provoke a war without actually starting one. Henry retorted by announcing that he would protect the Emperor's possessions in the Netherlands during the Emperor's forthcoming visit to Spain. This announcement Francis looked upon as a declaration of war, but still he pursued his policy of gifted indirection and merely seized the English wine ships at Bordeaux. He had also pardonably and frugally stopped the payment of French pensions to England.

Charles visited England again during the spring of 1522. Accompanied by a large retinue of Spanish and German nobles, he reached Dover at four in the afternoon of May 27, and there was received with great ceremony and appearances of cordiality by Wolsey, who took eight hundred lords, knights, and gentlemen down to the sands to meet the Emperor. "Taking the Cardinal's arm familiarly, Charles passed with him up to Dover castle." [7]

Next day Henry came to see Charles there. Two days were spent together at Dover, one in religious solemnities and one on Henry's good ship The Great Harry, his pride and joy, which lay with the rest of the fleet off Dover. Then the King and the Emperor and the Cardinal passed on to Canterbury, where they were met at the gates by the mayor and aldermen.

No detail of the full-throated welcome to the Emperor had been left to chance or spontaneity. An order had gone forth that all such ships as then lay in the Thames between Greenwich and Gravesend, being well garnished with streamers and banners, guns and ordnance, should fire a salute as the Emperor passed by.[8]

In this manner the three dignitaries came to the palace at Greenwich, where Catherine and the Princess Mary stood in postures of welcome. The Emperor dropped to his knee and claimed his aunt's blessing. It was all very pretty and lent a filial aspect to the meeting, in gentle contrast to all the official days spent before and after in religious services, jousting, banqueting, and treaty making. Whatever the two rulers did or wherever they went, the Cardinal was there to pronounce upon them the benediction of the Church. The concert they had made might be full of evil intent and hard bargains. But now in the confirmation of it the details of its origin were overlooked, and it was given idealized form through religious ceremonies. On Whitsunday Wolsey celebrated High Mass at St. Paul's, "at which the Emperor and the King assisted, and Dukes and other lords of the first distinction held water to him." Later when the rulers had gone by way of Hampton Court Palace to Windsor Castle and had solemnized there the covenant Wolsey had drawn at Bruges, the two submitted themselves to the jurisdiction of him as Legate *a latere* and "required him to pronounce sentence of excommunication against either of the contracting parties who should first violate the Treaty." [9] The agreements under the treaty having been concluded and arrangements made for the attack on France, the Emperor and the King received the Holy Sacrament together and swore upon the Evangelists faithfully to observe the league concluded between them.

It was fitting that a war as feudal in character and aim as the one which came out of this unholy alliance should be inaugurated by the old devices of heraldry. Heralds to announce defiance or carry unpleasant messages had long been part of the furniture of feudalism. Both kings and great noblemen had heralds in their personal service and gave them their own names or the names of their castles. Gradually heralds developed into a professional class with ranks and tabus. The assistant aspiring to the office of herald was called pursuivant; the senior herald was called King of Heralds or King of Arms.[10] In arranging truces or parleys, in the ransoming of prisoners, in summoning besieged places to surrender, the herald had his status and his etiquette and his immunities. As feudalism declined, noblemen gave up having heralds, who were then left only in the service of kings. They were chosen more for their personal qualities than for their rank or birth. "A dignified appearance at a public ceremony and firmness in making an unpleasant announcement were the most that could be expected of them." It was their business "to bear the messages of their superiors, faithfully and without softening their import." [11]

The disagreeable task of flinging defiance in the teeth of Francis fell upon a herald whose official name was Clarencieux. His private name was Thomas Benolte. He was a person of foreign extraction and doubtless employed in part for his command of languages.[12] Benolte, flanked with credentials and entertained with proper ceremonies, appeared before Francis at Lyons. There he detailed in an oration at once strident and accusing the charges Henry wanted hurled against his former brother and ally. Francis received the defiance with the grace and courtesy one would bestow upon a King's spokesman, but he flung the herald's defiance back in his teeth "with the proud assurance that if any man said the French King had failed to keep his word, he would give his maligner the lie; and if Henry took the field he was ready to meet him."

Actually the defiance, which Clarencieux had hurled at Francis while Henry and Charles were worshiping at Canterbury, was premature: Henry himself was far from ready to take the field. It was one thing to declare a war, quite another to fight it. Before it could be fought, the whole nation had to be readied for it, and the burden of execution fell upon Wolsey. To carry out the threat Clarencieux had shouted, there was one need above all others that the Cardinal had to provide:

Money.

With the growing use of cannon and heavy implements of destruction, the cost of war had increased. Early efforts to finance this war relied on old contrivances which had grown rusty and inadequate. In March 1522, two months before Henry's hollow defiance, commissioners had been sent into all the shires of England to inquire into the value of land, houses, and movables, and a loan of £20,000 had been demanded of the London merchants. Later in the same year a property tax was put forward under the name of a loan with promise of repayment. This stirred dissatisfaction, especially among the London merchants, who reminded the Cardinal that it had been scarcely two months since the King had demanded £20,000, "whereby the city is bare of money." Part of the opposition lay in the objection to having public commissioners poke into the financial affairs of men of wealth. On this point Wolsey abated his demands and graciously allowed merchants to make their own declarations.[13]

The amount procured did not suffice to finance the ambitious military program which Henry and Charles had concerted. By the early part of 1523 Henry saw that he would have to summon Parliament. The decision was an eloquent confession of extremity, for the Houses had not assembled during the past eight years.

When Parliament convened April 15, 1523, at the great hall of the Blackfriars in London, King and Cardinal and Council were present. First to enter the hall were the Lords, including bishops, mitered abbots, and priors, dressed in the habits of their callings. Then the King came among them in his royal robes and seated himself upon his throne. At his feet on the right hand sat Cardinal Wolsey and the Archbishop of Canterbury; and at the rail behind stood Dr. Tunstall, Bishop of London. With

285

the King and Lords thus in stately session, the Commons were allowed to enter the hall and array themselves deferentially, standing, at the back.

By these honored ceremonies the King identified himself with the interests of the realm, and the opening statements of the session tended to reinforce the common concerns of the ruler and his subjects. The Bishop of London dilated upon the good qualities of the King, going back to Seneca to fetch reassurance in a statement that turned out to be prophetic. The saying of Seneca, "Art thou a king and hast no time to be a king?" could in no wise, said the learned bishop, be applied to Henry.[14]

After this speech the Cardinal, in the King's name, willed the Commons to repair to their own place of meeting and choose a Speaker. They chose Sir Thomas More, who prettily disabled himself, as Hall puts it, the custom being for the Speaker to fly off into classical allusions in an attempt to show his incompetence. This rhetorical flourish being over, the King instructed the Cardinal to say that he considered More "meetest of all." For which compliment More humbly thanked His Majesty, and the Parliament was organized and ready for business.

Two weeks later the Cardinal, flanked by divers lords, as well spiritual as temporal, came before the Commons to tell them what was really expected. He set forth the necessity the King was under to enter into a war with France and assigned the causes: "That the French King had broken his promises made to England, by making war with the Emperor; notwithstanding the meeting of the two princes at Guines, where the French King had solemnly swore to keep all the articles contained in the league: that he had withholden the payment of money agreed on as to the delivering up of Tournay: that he had refused to pay the French Queen's dowry; wherefore he hoped the Commons would cheerfully assist the King in vindicating his Honours by granting the supplies necessary on this urgent occasion; which, he conceived, could not be less than £800,000." [15]

Having delivered himself of the King's request, Wolsey withdrew and left the Commons to their prerogatives and deliberations, there being the sound of not a little muttering among them. Next day Sir Thomas More sought to underline what the Cardinal had said. But his arguments did not prevail, and the Commons brought out their by no means secret weapon: endless talk. The best they could come up with was a committee to wait upon the Cardinal with the request that he prevail upon the King to accept a lower sum than had been sought of them. Wolsey said that he would rather have his tongue plucked out of his head with red-hot pincers than to induce the King to accept less.[16] Both his attitude and the figure of

286

speech he used showed where he stood and how desperately he sought from the Commons only one thing — the accommodation of the King.

The answer to the Cardinal's insistence upon the amount named was more debate. Talk spilled over into the taverns and alehouses, and it was not long before the population of London, then a city of some ninety thousand, was made privy to the matter before the House. This was the trouble with the Commons which Kings and Cardinals could not remedy. The talk could not be contained; it had happened before when the Commons debated the case of Richard Hunne, and it was happening again now. Instead of granting what the King wanted and the Cardinal requested, the Commons merely babbled, as if time did not exist and there were no war to be fought. And more, they made an affair of state a matter of gossip, being garrulous not only in the House but outside of it as well.

That the Cardinal suffered from the impatience normal to the strong executive and from the King's prodding too can readily be understood. Long accustomed to governing by decrees, he could not but regard the noisy quibbling of squires and burgesses as an irrelevant interruption. Parliament had been summoned for business, not for debate. Consequently one finds plausible the story told by Roper, Sir Thomas More's son-in-law, although it is not confirmed in other sources. According to Roper, the Cardinal could bear the babble no longer and determined to come to the House and read the members a lesson in decorum. It particularly annoyed him that the business before the House should be "blown abroad in every alehouse," that whatever the members said should immediately be echoed about among the people. Nor was he pleased with the bumbling reluctance of the House to grant the subsidy sought.

When the Cardinal advertised his intentions, the Commons had something new to talk about. The debate shifted to the question of whether he should be received with only a few lords in tow or should be allowed to bring his whole train. The debate was long. It was partly frivolous, partly in dead earnest, and in either case it delayed action on the King's request. The sense of the House appeared to be that Wolsey should be accompanied by only a small group of attendants, but, according to Roper's account, Sir Thomas More addressed the House after this fashion:

"Forasmuch as my lord Cardinal lately ye wot well laid to our charge the lightness of our tongues for things uttered out of this house, it shall not in my mind be amiss to receive him with all his pomp, with his maces, his pillars, his poleaxes, his crosses, his hat, and the great seal too . . ."

The House caught the spirit of its Speaker's proposal, and it was agreed that the Cardinal should come in all his glory and with all the reassuring accouterments of his dignity.

Wolsey had wished not only to discipline the members for their loose talk outside the House but to take vigorous part in their debates while he was there. Accordingly he came and delivered his views on the necessity of the subsidy the King wanted and then began to query various members of the House about their own views. The only response he got from any member was a stare. Like schoolboys rebelling against authority, the members had agreed that they would return no answer. Who could debate a cardinal, especially this Cardinal of York? But in the sacred confines of the House they could ignore him or treat him as an odd god out of place among mortals. No answer was the most devastating answer. The Cardinal stood like a powerful bull being baited by silence, tormented by looks that cut.

The man who had arrested foreign ambassadors, thrown detractors in jail, bellowed his wrath at papal nuncios, presided at conferences with kings and emperors — this man of competence had run now into a situation he could not understand and an atmosphere in which he could not breathe. He had risen so much beyond his own class that he had forgotten what that class was like, what ambitions and independence stirred in the breasts of men who aspired to have some part in the management of a kingdom. He forgot now the years of his youth and noted not that if he had been a member of the Commons he would have been the most assertive of the lot.

Here, as Wolsey put it, was a marvelous obstinate silence. The obstinacy was as plain and disconcerting as the silence. There was something mischievous, if not malevolent, back of a studiously silent House. It was not as if the members had nothing to say: they had much to say and they were saying it without words. They had answered his charge of talking too much by not talking at all. The Cardinal turned at last to Sir Thomas More, who excused the silence by explaining that the members had been abashed by the sublimity of the Cardinal's presence and that it was not in accordance with their privileges to debate with strangers. Upon hearing this, the Cardinal left abruptly, taking his pillars and his maces and his poleaxes and his hat.

Roper's account may be apocryphal, but if so it is a good one, illustrating dramatically the conflict between two approaches to government. In the Cardinal's robed person before the Commons the old world of kings and emperors and their thorny intrigues confronted a new world struggling to be born: a world of practical decision through debate. And the new world represented by the Commons had triumphed in this show of strength. They had stood off the most powerful man in England.

The tax bill had better advocates than the Cardinal and, "after long persuading and the privy labouring of friends," Parliament finally enacted a measure with which the Cardinal and the King professed to be pleased. It is good that they were, for no one else seems to have been pleased. The country seethed with discontent and ignorance of the details of an elaborate graduated income tax. Little understood in the provinces, this tax could but seem a general plan to confiscate all property. From the distant county of Norfolk came reports of rebellion against Henry for his highhanded measures, and in Coventry there was a plot to "seize and rob the collectors of the subsidy, and then to hold Kenilworth against the King." [17] The rumors were idle, but they spoke the private thoughts of the common people. The Cardinal with his maces and poleaxes had worked hard enough for the tax measure to be blamed for it. In making himself the King's instrument and agent, he had incurred hostility from a new source. The common people now saw him as a taxgatherer.

Wolsey lowered himself still further in public esteem by his tactless and arrogant handling of Convocation. As usual, Convocation met as a separate body at the same time as Parliament. The summons had been issued by the Archbishop of Canterbury, as was proper, and the clergy duly assembled at St. Paul's. But the Cardinal, after Mass had been said, saw fit to invoke his legatine authority and cite the clergy to appear before him at Westminster. For what reason he did this is not clear, nor was it clear to the clergy. Immediate protest was registered, but the Convocation finally held was as the Cardinal had wished and fashioned it; it comprised the two provinces of York and Canterbury, and it met under his stern auspices. But the program which he put across met with no less vigorous and outspoken opposition than it had in Parliament. Both Fox, Bishop of Winchester, and Fisher, Bishop of Rochester, energetically contended against the grant the King requested. And in the way Wolsey handled the proceedings he was suspected of trickery and undue pressure. Rowland Phillips, said to have been the most eloquent preacher of his age, showed hostility to the grant when the Convocation first debated it, but he was later induced by Wolsey to absent himself from the meetings.[18]

So again the King's chief minister, acting in the King's behalf in financing a policy which the King had conceived, won his point. Convocation granted a moiety of "one year's revenue of all benefices in England, to be levied in five years." But the Cardinal had lashed the members instead of persuading them, and the resentment they felt for his legatine hauteur was increased by its exercise in this conspicuous instance. Nor was the resentment confined to the clergy. It was noted and clucked upon by all who held the Cardinal in ill fame.

Grumblings and ambiguities had no effect on the policies or conduct of Wolsey; nor had he a mind clear or free enough of clutter to recognize the smoldering fires he had started with a graduated income tax that touched the whole populace and particularly afflicted the most powerful and wealthy of the nobles and clergy. (The charge upon himself amounted to £4000, whereas the Bishop of London, who had but recently been consecrated to his post, was to pay only £333 6s. 8d.) A busy administrator visited with painful responsibility must reckon only with palpable results; speculations on long-range epiphenomena must be left to intellectuals and bystanders. The King had asked Wolsey for money with which to fight a war; Wolsey had secured the money. What else, in the realm of practical affairs, was there to worry about?

There was the war. But in the planning and execution of a great national enterprise Wolsey had the confidence born of experience. He had managed the levying of troops, the supply of ships, and the provisioning of the army that had invaded France ten years before.

In the present war, to be sure, the complications were infinitely greater. For one thing, he was busier. During the past ten years he had added to his undertakings one duty after another in both Church and State. In the midst of the labors he had to undertake for the French War, there grew up great dissensions among the masters at Oxford over the choice of proctors. After a vain effort to settle the questions posed to them, the masters sent a deputation without notice to the Cardinal, asking him "to repair the state of the differences among them." Wolsey handled the matter in the only way he could — by evading the problem and advising postponement; but it required a thoughtful letter in which he said that he thought it advisable to defer the election of proctors for some time, "and that two persons of good reputation, who were not of turbulent, aspiring tempers, should be chosen to execute the office till Michelmas following." The two chosen should be given the functions of proctors but should not be given the impression that they had the full rights of the office. Wolsey adds that by the expiration of the Michaelmas term, he hoped he should be "more at leisure to attend the affairs of the University and to see all things settled upon so good a foundation that the state of it would be continually more splendid and flourishing."

The correspondence with Oxford continued, the university officials hand-somely excusing themselves for the frequent occasions they had of address-ing him and assuring him that they had no "prospect of relief but from his favorable interposition." Busy though he may be, they pray that he will send them "the customary form of electing proctors till he should have more respite from the greater affairs of state to regulate those of the Uni-versity." Wolsey refers them to precedent in the election of proctors but takes time to add a pious exhortation as a patron of learning and the foster father of the kingdom, urging them to "take all . . . fit precau-tions against seditions and tumultous proceedings." He also expresses the hope that "by the practise of holy discipline" they will not "from any motive of vainglory, or in pursuit of any private quarrels or animosities, suffer themselves to be diverted from opportunities of improving themselves in true and useful erudition." [19]

Upon his multifarious duties as secretary of state for culture and Lord Chancellor of England, Wolsey had to superimpose all the assignments and responsibilities of war and navy minister again. Diplomatic maneuver-ings did not end when the war began; instead they became more important, and they consumed as much time as the regulation of Oxford University. It became a matter of great urgency, for example, to detach the Venetians from the French. Their friendship with France had been of long and reliable standing, and if they could be persuaded to desert Francis, the prestige value of the change would be enormous and might have some bearing on the whole of Italy. It was part of Henry's and Wolsey's aim to harry France at every point of the map where contact could be made. Especially it seemed desirable to leave France without friends in Italy.

To bring about this end Richard Pace went to Venice to bargain and threaten. The Signory paid little attention to his blandishments. What clinched the Venetians and brought them into the confederation against France was the seizure at Southampton of the Flanders galleys, the great body of vessels which in picturesque train came once a year from Venice around the tip of Italy, laden with wines and spices and goods. Wolsey had the galleys impounded. They were seized and treated as if they be-longed to a hostile power: if Venice was not a friend of England but an ally of France, her ships would be treated as enemy ships. The Venetian ambassador made representations to the Cardinal, explaining that the crews were deserting the ships, some of them returning with Genoese mer-chants; others were perishing from hunger. Soon there would not be enough left to man the galleys. Meanwhile the ships' masters had exhausted their funds, and their goods were being infested with worms and moths. To all of which the Cardinal listened with sturdy patience. He would do nothing about the matter until Venice turned its coat for England and the Emperor. Meanwhile the galleys and crew both could rot.[20]

In accomplishing this one alienation alone the Cardinal spent hours in correspondence and conference. He might not act on the Venetian ambassador's protests; he did have to entertain them, and turning the Venetians against Francis was but one of a score of consuming tasks which Wolsey faced and, to a certain extent, carried out in these days when he was working for the vindication of the King's alliance with Charles. Everything now aimed toward the conquest of France. If the war went well . . .

But it didn't.

It went very poorly indeed, and the English performance was poorest of all in the department where Wolsey had shown his most commanding talent before: in supplying beer and victuals. During July of 1522 the Earl of Surrey crossed the Channel with a host of men to harry the French towns and villages. He captured and burnt Morlaix, to what purpose no one could say. What he did say bitterly, however, was that he had only enough beer for twelve days! [21] Wingfield wrote from Calais that there was a great scarcity there. There was even a great shortage of wood for the bakehouses and, worse still, for the brewhouses. France lay under a great drouth that summer, and Wingfield wrote that the country was ill provided with malt and water to brew. He added the comforting thought that there would be no lack of Rhenish wine and other victuals.[22] This must have been small consolation to English yeomen, accustomed to work and fight and pitch the bar and plow on beef, salt fish, and — above all — beer. Ships at sea were no better off. Surrey wrote that Fitzwilliam's ships were without either fish or flesh.

It was a wretchedly organized war. Only the destruction was methodical. In a letter to the Cardinal, Surrey wrote that "all the country we have passed through has been burnt; and all the strong places, whether castles or fortified churches, have been thrown down . . . When we have burnt Dorlance, Corby, Ancre, Bray and the neighbouring country, which I think will be in about three weeks, I cannot see that we can do much more." He reported that he had laid siege to Hesdin, which the French had abandoned because of the pestilence, adding: "The Emperor's Council are willing it shall be burned, which shall be done within three hours." He closed his letter by saying: "There is universal poverty here, and great fear of this army. I trust the King's grace and you will be content with our services here." [23]

Neither the King's grace nor the Cardinal's face could have been very much pleased with this humdrum account of the visitation of calculated brutality upon a section of France stricken by drouth and pestilence and poverty. Here was quite a comedown for the son of the victor of Flodden, who had himself played a strong part in that battle, now giving himself over to the unimaginative slaughter of French peasants. The whole enterprise wore an almost embarrassing aspect. By October 16, 1522, Surrey had withdrawn to Calais, having accomplished nothing beyond what he had written in his deadly report.

Although useless, the transport of the men under Surrey had exhausted what money had been raised for the war up to this point. Also it had left the north of England practically defenseless against the Scots. The Duke of Albany had mustered a force of 80,000 men and was marching menacingly south with them toward Carlisle, which was without defenders, while the son of the hero of Flodden, short of beer, was busy placing his heel on defenseless French villages. The Earl of Shrewsbury had been sent to assemble English defenders in the north, but again short supplies delayed him at York, and there was nothing but open country between the imperious Duke of Albany and England.

It was a moment the Scots had been waiting for. So it seemed. But even the Duke of Albany could not rally the Scottish lords into united action. With Henry's sister Margaret as Queen of Scotland and having in her care and custody a son who would one day grow to be King, Scotland had an English party of sorts — enough to divide the Duke's counsels. Hume tells us that many of the Scottish nobles were disgusted with Albany, "observing that his connexions with Scotland were feeble in comparison with those which he maintained with France." They murmured that "for the sake of foreign interests, their peace should so often be disturbed." The Scottish Earls, particularly Huntley, Argyle, and Arran, were unwilling to risk another Flodden, and the Gordons refused to advance any farther. [24]

In this manner the Scottish glacier melted away, but the crisis was not averted through any preparation on the King's or Wolsey's part. Lord Dacre, who commanded the defenses in the north, not having troops to repel the impending invasion, resorted to diplomacy, and in an act of unofficial and unauthorized audacity offered a truce to the Duke at the very moment when the Duke could have wasted the countryside. Albany, perhaps because of divisions among his followers, accepted the month's truce which

Dacre proffered. Henry and Wolsey "affected to be disappointed of a signal victory over the Scots." But both of them, no matter how little sense they displayed these days, had gumption enough to know that they had been saved by Dacre's strategy or else by English luck and Scottish arguments.

War being a seasonal affair, nothing happened during the winter of 1522-23. The treaty between Charles and Henry had set the summer of 1523 for the decisive blow against France. And so it was, but it was late summer, for delays, due partly to the difficulty in collecting the money Parliament and Convocation had granted, postponed the heralded invasion until August. Even so, the plan was elaborate and foolproof, and it would accomplish all that the union of Henry and the Emperor had designed and vindicate the tax and make satisfaction all over England for the disappointments and inconveniences and costs up to now.

Indeed, the prospect was even brighter than it had been when the Emperor and the King had formed their alliance. A new and favorable military factor had entered the scene in the person of Charles, Duke of Bourbon. This man had been made Constable of France, after his redoubtable performance as a youth at the battle of Marignano, but now he had agreed in secret notations with Wolsey to desert Francis and fight on the side of Henry and Charles. It was treason, but Wolsey decided to make the most of it. There appeared to be good cause for his desertion. He was a man at one time of great possessions, having his own court and his own parliament in the capital of his wide dominions. He was, moreover, a man of ancient family. Once when Francis accused him of jealousy, Bourbon is said to have replied: "How can your Majesty believe that I feel jealousy of a gentleman whose ancestors were only too happy to be squires of mine?" [25] As early as 1519 he had been playing the malcontent, Francis having deprived him of some of his offices, and the next year at the Field of Cloth of Gold his behavior was such that Henry told Francis that if he had a subject like Bourbon he would not long leave his head on his shoulders.[26] But Francis was more like Henry's father: he left the Duke's head and took his property instead. When Bourbon scorned the overtures of the King's mother (she was forty-five and he was thirty-one), saying that he would not marry Louise for all the riches of Christendom, she and Francis instituted lawsuits which deprived the Duke not only of his possessions but even of the sable and cloth-of-gold cloak he had worn as Constable of France.

Bitterness born of long baiting promised to make Bourbon a staunch ally, and the plan for the attack upon France in the summer of 1523 called for him to play an important part. The English under the beetle-browed Duke of Suffolk were to invade from Calais, the Emperor was to invade from the south, and Bourbon from the east. Francis was thus cornered with three lances aimed straight at his heart; and when he had been done to death, France would be partitioned and its crown pass to Henry VIII, Defender of the Faith.

The plan was laid out in this fashion, but it was sadly rumpled in the execution. Suffolk was abominably late in leaving Calais, not setting out with his army of 20,000 before September 12. Then he fell victim of a changed and confused strategy in the English high command for which Wolsey made himself responsible. Suffolk had instructions to join forces with the Burgundians from the dominions of Charles and then lay siege to Boulogne with the combined forces. But Charles objected that Boulogne was impregnable, and his councilors urged upon the English that it would be better for Suffolk to take Paris. Wolsey joined the opponents of the siege of Boulogne. There followed a weighty correspondence between him and the King, and the King at last relented to the change in plan, thanking his minister for his advice and instructing More to say to him: "His Highness esteemeth nothing in counsel more perilous than for one to persevere in the maintenance of his advice because he hath once given it. He therefore commendeth and most affectuously thanketh your faithful diligence and high wisdom in advertising him of the reasons which have moved you to change your opinion." [27]

It was a gracious and consoling letter, but it did little to cover the blunder of Wolsey's strategy. Henry had been right in not wanting to send his army upon a distant excursion where they would depend for their provisions on those of whose "slackness and hard-handling" he had already proof.[28] There was the further argument of the lateness of the season and the likelihood that Bourbon's forces would be dispersed before they could join with Suffolk's. The King proved right on all points, especially in the matter of Bourbon. The treason had been discovered and Bourbon was unable to offer effectual aid.

Suffolk got within forty miles of Paris and occasioned some alarm in the French capital. But by then it was November. Winter had set in with a vengeance. The Imperialists in Suffolk's army went home. Suffolk himself sent an emissary to the King to explain the necessity of retreating. He cited the severe frosts, the bitter winds, the wet weather, the snowy roads, the short days and long nights, "great journeys and little victuals which cause the soldiers to die daily." But Henry had appointed Lord Moulsey to relieve Suffolk with 6000 men and these would in short season be dispatched. "We wish," said the King, "that in no wise the army should break up." But (shades of the ill-fated expedition under Dorset in support of Ferdinand!) the army demanded to be led home, and led home it was. It is said that Henry, who had intended to keep up the war through the winter, was highly indignant and that for a long time he kept Suffolk and the chief captains of the army from his presence.[29]

Thus the war so carefully cooked up against France came to its ignominious end. Suffolk had failed, largely because of the strategy he had been asked to carry out against the King's advice. Bourbon had proved useless as a military factor. As for Charles, he contented himself with the conquest of Feuenterrabia and with feathering his imperial nest with English vouchers. Callous to the reproaches of his ally, he had made no move toward the conquest of France.

CHAPTER III

As A part of the festivities which had garnished the meeting of the Emperor and the King at Windsor Castle in the summer of 1522 there had been a morality play. An unruly horse was introduced upon the stage representing the person of Francis. The part of Amity was played jointly by actors representing Henry and the Emperor, whose function it was to tame the horse. Kindness and persuasion were the first order of the day, and Amity appropriately sent out messengers representing Prudence and Policy to soothe the beast in Francis. This having been accomplished, Force next appeared on the scene to bridle him and rein in his head, that he might be disciplined for the good of man.[1]

Events up to the end of 1523 had not fulfilled the naïve promise of this play in which Charles and Henry fancied themselves incarnate conceptions. As the soldiers of Suffolk, civilians all, straggled back to the shires, spreading a feeling of discontent through the countryside, taking up their plows again, the futility and cost of the imperial alliance could no longer be blinked. The invasion on which all had been staked had not added a single inch of French soil to English possessions, and Henry was as far from being King of France as ever he was. Certainly the French King had not been disciplined by Force any more than he had been tamed by Prudence and Policy.

The scene which confronted Wolsey in the grim winter of 1523-24 was dark with discouragement. The thirty months since the Field of Cloth of Gold had been a journey of error, another morality play in which Bad Advice (played by Catherine and the enemies of France in the Council) had poured mistaken sentiments and predictions into the ear of the King (played by Henry). By yielding to the blandishments of the Emperor and Catherine, even before he went to see Francis at the Field of Cloth of Gold, Henry had made a shocking mistake, as was now apparent, and his chief minister had compounded this mistake by putting it into full and detailed effect, to the sadness and disorder of the King's realm. The blunder had been Henry's; the advertisement of it, Wolsey's.

Twice since Calais the papal chair had fallen vacant, and in neither of the elections that followed had the Emperor made a genuine move in the Cardinal's behalf. Both experiences were sad and sobering. But there is no sign that Wolsey abated in the least his devotion to the papacy as an abstraction. He never let his disappointments in failing to attain the tiara impair his idealized view of the See Apostolic as the central institution of Christendom. He gave concrete evidence of this fact immediately upon the election of Clement VII. This pope showed some resolution at the outset of his reign to become head of Christendom in fact as well as in title. He busied himself with the task of the reconciliation of Christian princes and let it be known that he would not be entirely the slave of the Emperor.[2] Clement wrote Charles that his love for him had not diminished but that his hatred of others had disappeared. Hence he set about to bring about concord among Christian princes, and in the sweep of his hopes he included peace with even the Most Christian King. And as he did, Wolsey began in turn to modify England's attitude toward Francis; indeed he began secret negotiations with the French King's mother, Louise of Savoy, looking to a *rapprochement* between England and France. Considering the Emperor's attitude and his failure to live up to the arrangements made at Windsor, there were plenty of other reasons for peace with France, but the fact remains that Wolsey followed the course set by the papacy.

Outwardly the alliance between Henry and Charles continued firm. After Suffolk's profitless foray into France, however, England took no further military action. It was deemed fitting that the ally now be allowed to carry out his part of the program. The English decision to stay out of the war proved no better than the earlier decision to enter it. Although the Emperor's progress was by no means steady or untrammeled, he managed to do in the eighteen months after Suffolk's insubordinate return from

France everything that Henry had tried to do the year before, including the bridling of the unruly Francis. Where his ally had miserably failed, Charles succeeded, and without any apparent aid from Henry and the Cardinal. The turns of the wheel of Fortune, after moments of slow suspense, always stopped at a point which favored Charles.

At the commencement of the Emperor's efforts in 1524 success seemed as evasive as it had for Henry. In the councils of the imperial alliance it was settled that the Duke of Bourbon, free at last to show again the military genius of the days of his youth, would invade Provence in the south of France. Why this tough and belligerent territory was chosen is not clear, but intelligence reports indicated that the Duke's appearance there might be the signal for stirring revolt in the unhappy and debt-ridden kingdom of Francis. Accordingly Bourbon attacked Provence at the end of June. It had been agreed solemnly that the Emperor would devote 100,000 ducats to the enterprise and that England would contribute the same amount each year until the war ended.

Bourbon met with no success, and his appearance in Provence occasioned no uprising. Fascinated by Marseilles, he laid siege to that city but with such ill results that after forty days he was compelled to retire. Both his captains and his men were by this time mutinous for pay. The Emperor had sent his promised funds in driblets at irregular intervals. Of the English funds, not a penny reached the embattled Bourbon.[3]

Hopes had run high in England at the news of Bourbon's early efforts in Provence. But the hopes were not high enough to stir the King and the Cardinal to action. Henry had simply promised that he might invade from Calais. But he made no more pretense at a diversionary movement than the Emperor had in the year before. Francis, no longer molested by the threat of the English, decided that the time had come to go into Italy to recover the possessions he had lost there. Two years before, while the Cardinal conducted his tedious negotiations at Calais, the French forces in Italy found themselves hard pressed by the Emperor, one reason being that there was no money to pay the Swiss mercenaries who fought in their ranks. Marshal Lautrec, in command of these forces, had exacted of Francis a promise to send 400,000 crowns for the pay of the troops. The money had not reached him, the Swiss had deserted, and Lautrec had lost in one campaign all the conquests Francis had made in Italy. The 400,000 crowns had failed to reach Lautrec because the French treasurer, Semblancay, had paid the money instead to Louise of Savoy. The King's mother, Semblancay said, had demanded that the money be paid to her. This she had denied, and at the end of the unhappy episode Semblancay lost his foolish head. Meanwhile Francis had lost Milan, and the loss of it paved the way with bad intentions for Charles ultimately to take over Italy and the papacy.[4]

Many reasons joined to create in Francis the decision that the moment had struck when he should go into Italy. There was of course the incurable fascination the country held for him. There was also the feeling that his possessions there had been lost through treachery and inefficiency and could be recovered by military might. Bourbon's defection was also a factor: sweet could be his revenge if he pursued the fleeing Duke and his rabble. France, which a short while before had been threatened on every hand, was now free of the invader, and Francis was suddenly in command of what had seemed to be a hopeless situation. Other circumstances urged him on. The Emperor was in poor health. Advices from Spain indicated that the Emperor was "very feeble, and nothing apt for war." [5] Also he was, as always, in extreme poverty. Further, the sentiment in Spain, where the Emperor lay, had been "very desirous of peace and weary of war" since the Duke of Bourbon's defeat.

Moreover, Francis was weary of patience and defense. No sedentary peacemaker, he was a man of stubborn impulses, a personal King. Calling his officers together, he told them: "I have concluded and am resolved to pass in person into Italy; and whoever shall advise me to the contrary shall not only not be heard, but incur my displeasure . . . for God, who is a lover of justice, and the insolence and rashness of my enemies, have opened a way for me to recover that which has been unjustly taken from me." [6] Brewer says Francis was so determined on his course that he avoided talking with his mother lest she persuade him to let his army be led by his generals while he remained in France.

It would have been better if the King had talked the matter over with Mother. Five months after Bourbon's retreat from Marseilles, the fractious Francis was a captive of the Imperialist forces and a prisoner of Charles. He had left 14,000 of his army and the cream of his nobility dead on the muddy fields and in the swollen streams of northern Italy. Far from making himself master of the plains of Lombardy, he had managed to do by his own obstinacy what Charles and Henry could not do by force: he had defeated France.

Indeed the whole succession of decisions that led to the tragic battle of Pavia affords a classic study in stubbornness. Bourbon raised the siege of Marseilles in the last days of September 1524. The flight of his troops, once the siege was abandoned, was headlong. As Clerk wrote sarcastically to Wolsey: "If they had made as good speed outwards as they have made homewards, they might have been at Calais long afore this time." [7] Dispirited and disorganized, his followers threw their arms into ditches in the course of their retreat.[8] An army which had numbered 26,000 when it swung into the attack on Provence and settled before Marseilles had dwindled into a useless mob.

Instead of pursuing and destroying this mass of whilom troops, Francis headed straight for the place where his heart lay: the duchy of Milan. This he had lost and this he would now possess again. The main Imperialist defense in Italy lay at Pavia, twenty-two miles south of Milan, near the point where the Ticino joins the Po. If Francis could demolish this stronghold, he could then conquer the rest of Italy at his leisure.

By now it was already November. And, alas, the quick conquest of Pavia did not come to pass. On November 8 Francis made a feeble assault on the city to try the garrison. The following day he attacked fiercely, but his forces were repelled; over 3000 foot and 400 gentlemen were slain. Francis had no choice now but to sit down before Pavia and reduce the city by siege. He was saddled with the consequences of his own first impulsive decision, and he must face not only his foes but the horrors visited by the full onslaught of winter. A correspondent of the time wrote that the gentlemen-pensioners of the King and his captains had to send home for money. A chicken cost fifteen shillings, news which must have been received in England with horror, for there forty shillings a year was considered a good income. "All the great lords," the correspondent wrote, "are obliged to go and warm themselves in the King's kitchen. The infantry lie in the trenches and dare not leave them, lest they should die of hunger and cold." [9]

Straitened and battered though he was by his own privations, Francis continued to fondle the hope that the Imperialist forces were worse off than his own. He missed his guess about the enemy, as he had missed so many others in this luckless Italian campaign. He reckoned without the relief of Pavia, and when it hove in sight he realized for the first time the enormity of the treason of Bourbon. By January 25, 1525, the Duke had reorganized his army and, concerting with the Viceroy of Naples, he had reached Marignano of historic memory. The French King's position now appeared hopeless. Some of his officers urged him to abandon his siege and withdraw to a more defensible position. But Francis resolved to take Pavia if it meant the loss of his life. He took the advice of those who came to the support of his stubbornness and stuck with his position — a position between a large army coming to the relief of Pavia and the resolute garrison within the town.

It was not until midnight of February 23 that the relieving forces under Bourbon began their attack. The French fought well and fiercely, considering the handicaps of their position. But as the attack continued from the Imperialist forces, the garrison of Pavia sallied out and attacked the French in the rear. The result made the small territory occupied by the French, where they had been caged, into a slaughterhouse.

Francis might have escaped the melee, seeing that some of his officers did. But he fought valiantly, bringing down with his own hand one of the standard-bearers of the Imperialists. By the time he made his way toward a bridge which might have taken him to safety, he was deserted by most of his army. Then a straggling musketeer belonging to the Imperialists shot his horse, and as he fell an Imperialist man-at-arms came up and "clapping the point of his sword to his side, where his armour joined, bid him yield." Francis said, "Give me my life, for I am the King." He then added, "I yield myself up to the Emperor." One soldier took off the King's helmet. "Some took the feathers out of his crest, others cut off pieces of his coat, to carry with them as a memorial of their having been engaged in the overthrow of so renowned a prince; so that at last they left him no coat. Yet Francis, though in this condition, behaved with great trepidity and seemed to be pleased with what the soldiers did." [10]

Charles received the news of Pavia with his usual gravity and forbade any celebrations at his court; rather he expressed sympathy with the French King's misfortune. But Francis was a captive just the same, and, being captive, he had left both Italy and France at the mercy of the Emperor.

The victory had taken place on the Emperor's twenty-fifth birthday. "Never," says Brewer, "had Fortune, in whose smiles Charles at that time implicitly believed, placed the empire of the world so nearly within the grasp of so young a man. Never since the days of Charlemagne had the world witnessed so nearly a realization of its fitful dream of a real empire of the West."

The aim which Henry had so fully set his heart on, which had lured him into his alliance with Charles, had been at last accomplished, if without his help. He saw now what he had so long strained his eyes to see. His rival, the King of France, was a king without a country, stored in a respectable dungeon, his arrogance tamed by Force. The morality play at Windsor had had a happy ending at last. And the calamity had left France prostrate. The ancient enemy of the realm of England had vanished into nothingness; the nation suddenly had no sovereign, no army, no generals to organize another fighting force, no money, no nobles of consequence to provide leadership for its recovery. And to add to its contemptible position, its affairs, such as they now were, had been left in the fluttery hands of a woman. Louise of Savoy ruled as regent what was left of a once proud France.

While Charles received the news of Pavia with chaste decorum and forbade any rejoicing, Henry received it with elation and rubbed his hands together in unabashed pleasure, as excited as the courier who brought the news straight to his bedchamber. "You are as welcome as the angel Gabriel was to the Virgin Mary," he exclaimed.[11] He went at once to tell Catherine the news and then sat down to write letters congratulating his ally and the generals who commanded the assault.

Later he showed to others the face of his delight and his intentions. To the Flemish commissioners he said: "Now is the time for the emperor and myself to devise the means of getting full satisfaction from France. Not an hour is to be lost." [12]

To words, the King matched plans and deeds. Less than a month after the glad tidings of the fall of France reached the royal ears, Henry had the Cardinal dispatch an embassy to the Emperor in Madrid, there to supplement the representations of the regular ambassador, urging not only the immediate invasion of France but its dismemberment and the exclusion forevermore of Francis and his children from the throne.[13]

The move toward the Emperor was doubtless a feint, a gesture to suggest that Charles ought to pay some of his debts, debts he had incurred after the agreement at Windsor when the two had solemnly sworn to act each in the interest of the other. Sampson, the regular English ambassador at Madrid, had early given the King of England to understand that the Emperor would provide no help. "They think here," he wrote, "that the King should make the rest of any conquest at his own charge." [14]

Whatever the Emperor might decide, Henry was himself resolved upon the invasion; but with or without the putative help of his ally, the invasion required huge sums of money. The task of getting these sums into the King's money bags fell upon the already weary shoulders of Thomas Cardinal Wolsey.

How much enthusiasm Wolsey had for the project may be seen from the fact that his negotiations with Louise for a new alliance with France had now to be summarily ended, the scheme of a French alliance rudely discarded, and the residual energies of a man virtually exhausted by the machinations and double-dealings of the skinny boy who was an Emperor had to be turned to the frightful job of raising funds for another invasion of France.

302

The device hit upon for lifting money from the people's pockets was not of the Cardinal's confecting. Rather it came from a grand council of many heads consulted by the King, and the learned judges of the realm were called upon for their advice. Even in his extremities the King was legal-minded. What he needed now was money secured without commotion. The Parliament of two years before had proved obstructionist and niggardly; more, its funds had been expended on a fiasco that had gained nothing for the English and much for the Emperor. It had taken the Commons a hundred days to grant what funds they did. Time now was of the essence, with France defenseless, and even if Parliament should be willing to allow the necessary grants, the delay would be unnecessary and awkward and would postpone the invasion far beyond the royal patience. It was decided, therefore, to seek a loan from the people, or at least from the well-to-do, who were comparatively limited in number. It would not be necessary under this arrangement, perhaps, to stir the animosity of the Commons.

But if Wolsey did not contrive the idea of the loan, the details of carrying it out devolved upon him as the King's servant, and he became identified with it. Already he had established himself as the minister who put through Parliament the grant made in 1523. Now he would be held responsible for any move the King made to extract further funds. The plan of the loan was to demand a sixth from lay property and a fourth from ecclesiastical. It was to be a loan but in effect a tax, and the demand was for a prescribed amount; and the amount was not only prescribed but it was in each instance to be based on assessments made two years before when Parliament had voted a graduated income tax. In substance, the people of wealth were asked for a contribution and then told what to give. The pretense of the whole arrangement arose from an old feudal obligation of the realm to contribute aid to the King when he led an invasion in person, and Henry aimed to lead the coming invasion in his own weighty person.

Commissioners to collect the loan were appointed for the various shires, and to give the whole thing a public appeal the highest of the nobles got assignments to carry out the King's demand. Wolsey was made the King's commissioner for London, and his presentation to the town council and the leading merchants not only set the pace but showed in detail the psychology and appeal which the King would rely on. Assembling the mayor and corporation, the Cardinal made a lengthy speech, at the beginning of which he showed great tact and a fine sense of persuasion. After reviewing the list of the King of France's offenses against the English King and the necessity of a war, he paused and said with dramatic effect: "Now I ask you this question, whether you think it convenient that the King should pass the sea with an army or not; for the King will do by the advice of his subjects." There were enough scattered murmurs of approval for the Cardinal to continue: "Well, he must go like a prince, which cannot be without your aid . . . Forsooth, Sirs, I think half your substance were too little for so noble a prince — not that he means to ask so much . . ." [15] Actually the King would settle for a sixth, and by this generous-hearted concession and display of royal leniency and consideration, the King showed his friendly attitude to his subjects. What he sought was an *amicable* loan.

The term bound the whole scheme in hoops of irony. The King may have been amicable, but the people were not. Nor was the Cardinal. Charged with a superhuman task for which he had no stomach or conviction, he made the blunder of losing his temper and threatening the London merchants. When one of them weakly ventured to suggest that business had decayed and that times were hard, my lord of York cut him short with the not very inspired remark that "it were better that a few should suffer indigence than that the King at this time should lack." And he added in his best baritone: "Beware, therefore, and resist not, nor ruffle not in this case; otherwise it may fortune to cost some their heads."

The Amicable Loan very nearly cost the Cardinal his own head. The people at once saw through the thin disguise of amicability. The London merchants for the time being accepted the Cardinal's highhanded treatment, and word of their acceptance spread throughout the realm. But it created no good effect. Hall says that "the poor cursed, the rich repugned, the light wits railed; but in conclusion all people cursed the Cardinal and his co-adherents, as subvertors of the law and liberty of England." [16]

Regardless of the dignity and influence of the commissioners dispatched to the shires, these nobles met everywhere with sullen opposition. The Duke of Suffolk was sent into Suffolk and the Duke of Norfolk was sent to Norwich. The Duke of Norfolk was the son of the hero of Flodden, and from his position as Earl of Surrey he had been raised to the rank of duke upon his father's death the year before. Both Norfolk and Suffolk did their best to carry out the King's commission and kept in close touch with Wolsey over the difficulties they encountered. There was trouble in Lavenham and Sudbury particularly. The Dukes explain that they have little time to write, for they "are seven miles apart and must meet every day to determine what is to be done." One of their letters is written at midnight and after a hard day with the threat of harder ones to come. They beg Wolsey to pray the King, "if insurrection begins in other shires, which they fear more than this, that he will try to temper their madness and untruth by some dulce means . . ." The temper of the people was such that it might break out in general revolt.[17]

The Dukes made it plain to the Cardinal that the common people laid all the blame on him and that, "if any insurrection follow, the blame shall be only against him." [18] This the Cardinal understood well enough. He replied that it was the custom of the people, "when anything miscontenteth them, to blame those that be near the King." And when they dare not "use their tongues against their Sovereign, then, for colouring their malice, will not fail to give evil language" against the King's councilors. He goes on to add, with a significant *howbeit*, that he is not wholly responsible for the Amicable Loan, whatever the malicious gossip might be. Even so, he could not brush off lightly the reports that continually reached him. Menaces against his life were not uncommon. Warham wrote him from always recalcitrant Kent to say that the people spoke cursedly, saying that they "should never rest from such payments as long as *some one* was living." [19]

Word from Kent, where the shades of Wat Tyler and Jack Cade and memories of their great rebellions against the kings of England carried weight, spread to other shires and increased the prodigious labors of the commissioners. These labors would have been harrowing enough if confined to administrative detail. A letter to Wolsey from the Bishop of Ely speaks of the rumors from Kent and their disturbing effect, but it is full also of practical questions which the King's chief commissioner for the loan must decide by return messenger. Some of the inhabitants allege losses by fire and by the death of their cattle due to murrain; these stories must be investigated, and if they prove correct, what is to be done? How are those who are "utterly decayed" to be dealt with? Others in and around Ely complain to the good bishop that they over-assessed themselves in an earlier loan to make a good impression on their neighbors and raise their standing in the community. To this lament the Bishop had replied that there was no time to make fresh assessments and he had taken care of the matter by "fair words and the rough handling of one or two." But these had met his orders by much dolor and lamentation, saying that they have no money and that no man has money to lend and that they will have to sell their goods or give them to the King. This raises the urgent question of what the collectors are to do if the people have no money but offer them stuff: how can they be compelled to pay?

The only cheerful note in the Bishop's letter comes when he tells the Cardinal that the instructions he has received include Wolsey's job as

Archbishop of York and the collections from the clergy in the diocese. They have been sent in error and belong really to Wolsey. Also he notes with satisfaction that there is no mention of collecting from Cambridge University and he ventures the plaintive hope that this may mean Wolsey has reserved that job too for himself.[20]

The Bishop may well have been concerned about Cambridgeshire. At Cambridge the town and the university united in opposition, and a mob of twenty thousand milled in resistance when the commissioners sought to make their levies.[21] And the temper of East Anglia was mild when compared with the temper of the rest of England. Sir Thomas Boleyn, one of the commissioners, was treated roughly at Maidstone in Kent.[22] In Suffolk the spinners and weavers "rose in a body, rung the alarm bell, and menaced the commissioners with death." News of resistance spread as far as Lincolnshire and touched off faggots of resentment and rebellion in every town and village. In Essex the people refused to meet with the commissioners "except in the open air." The spirit of insurrection raged after the fashion of some giant contagion: there was no telling where it would strike next. Both Norfolk and Suffolk and others in the field trying to collect kept the King and the Cardinal posted daily on the temper and choler of the populace affected by the loan. In a letter on May 12, 1525, they say they think "they never saw the time so needful for the King to call his Council to determine what should be done." And they add the significant request to Wolsey that he will not send for one of them without sending for the other. It was no time for a taxgatherer to be left alone in the seething shires of England.[23]

It was not merely the extent and sweep of the resistance that disturbed the King and the Cardinal. Other factors, none of them by any means amicable, deepened its gravity. One was the virtual unanimity that prevailed. People moved in mobs and took on the spirit of a mob, so that if some agreed to pay the subsidy, their neighbors set upon them as enemies. At one place in Essex the commissioners got together "200 or 300 persons whom they could not induce to grant any money, as they said they had not enough even to pay the subsidy." More to the point, they report that "some fear to be hewn in pieces if they make any grant." They tell the Cardinal that they will suspend further proceedings until they hear the King's pleasure.[24]

Wolsey advised Warham to assemble prospective contributors in small groups and deal with them in a quiet manner, a procedure which Warham agreed with. But he felt that even this method would do little good. "One cause is the fear of the multitude, who persecute all who comply . . . As the people are obstinately resolved not to pay, it will be hard to persuade the few, and they will not think themselves kindly treated." [25]

Obviously the ferocity of the resistance sprang from more than a sense of economy and resentment of the burdens which the loan placed on business as usual, although its effects on business were not to be despised. "The gentry got no rents; the farmers sold no cattle at fairs; the clothiers and husbandmen turned off their hands . . . The citizens of Norwich declared that the prosperity of their city depended on worsted and strawmaking, and that having to pay their hands weekly, they had no coin left over for the King . . ." [26]

Thus the effects on commerce and income were in themselves bad enough to rile the English, but these effects were not in themselves sufficient to account for the bitterness. The bitterness came from the spirit and not from the pocket. It had a quality almost religious in fervor. And it was this quality that lent the resistance its cutting edge. The King and Council could not ignore the fact that the Peasant Revolt in Germany, where thousands had been stung by the heresies of Luther to rise against the state and their masters and betters, might have antiphonal response in the hearts of Englishmen. For heresies were insidious; they crept in to infect the people like the sweating sickness and with the same unaccountable suddenness and the same mysterious madness.

The dangerous similiarity between events in England and in Germany was all the greater because the resistance to the Amicable Loan was encouraged and promoted by the clergy and the religious orders. Priests denounced the loan openly and preached against it and stood forth for the rights and liberties of the people. They coupled this outspoken opposition with sturdy refusals to pay any grant demanded of them unless it was approved in Convocation. Every secular priest in the diocese of Salisbury refused to pay, and the heads of many religious houses declared that they could not pay the full amount demanded.[27] And several of them, says Grove, "did not stick to say that the Cardinal and the doers thereof were enemies to the King and Commonwealth." [28]

For the attitude of the religious, the Cardinal, to his chagrin and embarrassment, was in no small part responsible. The loan came at a time when he was most zealous in repressing some of the smaller monasteries for the building of his college at Oxford and in contemplation of his school at Ipswich. These suppressions, however justified they may have been in many instances, set a dangerous precedent of which the great religious houses and orders were acutely aware. There was no telling what my lord of York might do with his legatine authority. Resistance to the loan offered a chance for the monks and friars to thwart an effort for which the Cardinal and Legate had made himself inescapably responsible.

Whatever the true motives for resistance among lay and religious, the prospect of failure became plainer with the passing of each day. It was not a failure, either, to contemplate with any quietness of mind. It reflected seriously on the health of the kingdom and the King's position abroad. The troubles encountered in the shires were not unnoticed in the courts of Europe. Louise of Savoy, making bold plans and taking long strides to stiffen the resistance of the disorganized French people, had many spies in England, and they informed her that only 12,000 English were in marching order. She published through the whole of France that the English were in a state of mutiny and that their troubles would engage all their energies and keep them from making an invasion.[29]

Early in May 1525 it became apparent that moderation of the King's demand offered the only recourse to keep the campaign from being a complete failure. In all his dealings with the commissioners, whether because he had lacked enthusiasm for the enterprise from the beginning or for some other reason, Wolsey had counseled care and caution in dealing with recalcitrants. Warham, who had never held Wolsey in high personal esteem, wrote to compliment him on his moderation in mediating "with the King for the commons, and they are more bound to you than they have the wit to consider. The indiscreet multitude is easily moved by a very light tale." [30]

A spirit of mildness would not suffice, however. Some public move had to be made in which the King would modify his Amicable Loan. The task of making this move fell upon the Cardinal. He assembled the corporation and mayor of London and announced that the King would require no set sum but "accept from his loving subjects whatever each might be inclined to give." As Wolsey put it: "And I now ask you a Benevolence in His Majesty's name."

The show of grace from the King's grace came too late to quiet the unrest stirred by the Amicable Loan — and the form it took had unhappy memories and precedents besides. Benevolences, as they were euphemistically called, had been used by Yorkist kings, chiefly Edward IV. And when the Cardinal stood before the mayor and corporation of London and demanded a benevolence, one of the citizens was bold enough to stand up and tell him that by a statute of Richard III no benevolence could be considered legal. Unable to distinguish in his own thinking and in the stress of the circumstances between a King and Parliament, Wolsey seized only on the name of Richard. "I marvel," he said, "that you speak of Richard III, which was a usurper and a murtherer of his own nephew. Then of so evil a man, how can the acts be good? Make no such allegations; his acts be not honorable." But the citizen of London pointed out a fact which the Cardinal in his zeal had overlooked. "An't please your Grace," he said, "although he did evil, yet in his time were many good acts, made not by him only, but by the consent of the body of the whole realm, which is the Parliament." [31]

Here in a single simple statement was the answer to the mystery that had baffled the King and his Council. The loan had failed because it had been attempted without the consent of the realm. It had not been possible to by-pass Parliament after all. The Cardinal had no choice but to withdraw his request for a benevolence and merely ask each London merchant to come before him and "grant privily what he would."

From its ill-advised inception the Amicable Loan had been marked by retreat and withdrawal, and the most conspicuous figure in the whole unsatisfactory performance had been the red-robed Cardinal of York, a fair target for all barbs, both from those who sought the money and those who railed against the effort to secure it. The King, thinking he could avoid Parliament and rely in this crisis of his desire upon the strong arm of the Cardinal, had been forced to bow to the assertive will of his subjects.

It was the first time the Cardinal had failed to carry out Henry's firm wishes in ten eventful years as his chief servant — and the failure was loud and resounding; its reverberations carried all over the lovely hills and dales of England and into the gossipy courts of Europe as well. Placards and bills in taprooms had advertised the opposition, so that when the failure came, it was known that the King had been rebuffed and his minister thwarted. The Cardinal might bear the brunt of the blame, but it was the King's request which had been refused and, behind the Cardinal, it was the King who suffered the humiliation of having his announced desire publicly and flatly rejected.

To compound the King's frustration, the collapse of the Amicable Loan and the benevolence meant that, unless Henry could scurry around and get funds from some other impoverished monarch, he must abandon the invasion of France. France was to Henry as Milan was to Francis. It was part of the essence of his ego. He could not get his mind off the idea of possessing the crown of France. Now was the moment when it could be done with certainty and with the greatest ease. Henry had even hopefully had his agent Clerk make representations to the Pope in Rome, thinking that His Holiness might be willing to contribute to the cause of the invasions; but the Pope had declined, saying that "it was his duty to be a common father of Christian princes, and not to enter any league *ad offensionem alicujus . . .*" [32]

As late as June 1525, after the failure of the Amicable Loan in the middle of May, Henry had his ambassadors calling upon Charles and praying his assistance. Charles read the King's letters apart with some of his Privy Council, and then he called the ambassadors to a window and there received many messages from Henry congratulating him on the recovery of his health and the capture of the French King — at which, the ambassadors told Charles, the King rejoiced "as if he had himself been the victor." To prove the importance of their mission, they stressed the fact that the King of England "would have sent my Lord Legate to his majesty on the matter but that he was now 'so growing towards age' that so long a journey by sea and land would be dangerous to him." The ambassadors carried with them a ring as a present from the Princess Mary, "which he put on his little finger and said he would wear for her sake."

The occasion was all very homely, and it was one of many on which the ambassadors dealt with the Emperor. But their efforts to enlist his aid met with less than success. They determined that the Emperor had no money to bestow; indeed his own need for money was unfeigned, the pay of his household servants being in arrears — "some for twenty, some for twelve months, and the least for nine." They ended by saying that they "thought it needless to blow any longer at a dead coal." [33]

There was no further recourse, no other place to turn. The invasion of France, so radiantly planned when the news of Pavia reached the court of Henry, could not be accomplished. Charles had fought his own war and gained his own victory, and he had no disposition to share any advantage with his ally. And the realm of England would not provide its King with money any more than the Emperor would. It was a grave and double disappointment not calculated to improve the disposition of a King who had grown fat on success.

CHAPTER IV

IT WAS at this time that Henry's eyes began to glaze with thoughts other than those of conquest and the tedious business of government.

310

Life was not all war and taxes. Man had arms for some purpose besides wielding swords. Certainly the five turbulent years of hefting and lunging since the Field of Cloth of Gold had left him little cause for rejoicing. He had exhausted his father's treasure in fruitless war, and now in these last days his people had refused him more. He was denied by their penury and parsimony the supreme effort to claim his inheritance of the soil of France.

But the severest blow of all had been struck by the ally whose friendship he had so strenuously cultivated and innocently trusted. Charles had done nothing to redeem his promises; rather his conduct had been but a litany of excuses. Only the Emperor's pledge to marry the Princess Mary remained of a once grand alliance. This pledge was of paramount concern to Henry, and as long as it remained in force it might make up for many disappointments. Mary was nine in this year of 1525; in another five years she could be married. There were no male Tudors, but if Mary married Charles, her eldest son would inherit the crown of England, the lordship of Ireland and Wales, and the English claim on France. It meant also, as Mattingly has summarized it, that Henry's eldest grandson would also inherit Austria and the Netherlands, Naples and Sicily, the Spains and their dominions in the New World, and would wear in due course the imperial crown.[1]

Such an outcome counseled patience and fostered hope. The eventual marriage of Charles and Mary was the foundation on which the alliance made at Windsor rested. If Catherine had not been able to give Henry a son, at least she had given him a nephew who was also an Emperor. And she had brought this Emperor and her husband into a fellowship which through another marriage might be the means of carrying forward the Tudor line.

When, however, the English ambassadors pressed Charles in June of 1525 for the fulfilment of his treaty obligations in military terms, Charles not only refused to help the King but countered with a request that stunned the King's men. He wanted the Princess Mary brought into Spain at once with her dowry of £80,000. This request, though it dumfounded the ambassadors, came with a great flourish of plausible explanations. Charles said he could hardly afford to leave his territory for fear of uprisings; the presence of the Princess and "a council about her might stay the realm from such revolution as in his last absence." To this flattering conception he added his wish that he wanted my lady Princess brought up in Spain where she could learn the language and manners of the country and thus be the better prepared to rule.

It was suggested that the £80,000 Mary would bring be devoted to the common affairs of the King and the Emperor, of course, and it was further delicately proposed that the King advance an additional £40,000 to aid in the expense of the still-to-be-hoped-for invasion of France by Henry and Charles and the Duke of Bourbon.[2]

Money, money, money. Maximilian in the days of his balmiest mendicancy had not exceeded the stratagems of Charles. Following one request with another more audacious, he covered his debts with petitions for still more debts and buried any expectation of repayment under a pile of confused evasions. In this case he blithely overlooked the fact that he owed Henry £37,500 "lent him at his last transporting to Spain," not to mention the amounts he had promised to pay to indemnify Henry for losses sustained when Henry broke with France. He had fought bitterly for a larger dowry from Mary, but the Cardinal had done him in, and it was agreed by the treaty that joined the Emperor and the King that the dowry was to be paid only after her marriage — and after the amounts the Emperor owed the King had been deducted. Now the Emperor wanted the Princess Mary sent across the seas at the tender age of nine, placed in a hot climate which would endanger her health, and, above all, he wanted Henry to send her with cash on delivery.

When the King's ambassadors marshaled the reasons for rejecting so preposterous a set of ideas, and when nothing favorable was heard from letters written the King on this matter, the Emperor sadly announced that under his exigent circumstances there appeared nothing to do but to marry another cousin — Isabella of Portugal. His subjects, he explained, had long sought him to make this marriage for the good of the realm and the peace of the world. Besides, she would bring with her a dowry of not less than a million ducats. At the prevailing rate of exchange — four and a half shillings to the ducat — a million ducats amounted to almost £225,000; it was a worthy dot when measured against the £80,000 Wolsey had made Charles settle for at Bruges. Moreover, Isabella's dowry would be unencumbered by previous awkward commitments, not eaten into by debts and obligations. The Spanish nobles had offered him an additional half million ducats to complete the Portuguese marriage. All told, this would make a very considerable sum with which the Emperor hoped earnestly to set his affairs in order and be thus the better prepared to pursue his common interests with the King of England. He hoped the King of England would understand.

In this shifty manner Charles announced the intended change in his marriage plans. It could have come as no great surprise, for the Emperor himself in negotiations referred to the betrothal to Isabella as one that "hath long before mentioned, and a million ducats offered for her dote." Even so, the official confirmation of it had no less an effect than a death that is not the less real because it is expected. The news sounded the knell to Henry's fondest Tudor dreams. Henry instructed his ambassadors to say that the marriage "entirely cut away the main ground of their former alliance." [3] There was nothing of either sentiment or substance left of this alliance now, and Henry's acquiescence was cold and precise. He would, he said, consent to the Portuguese marriage on three conditions: "1, that peace shall first be treated with France so as to satisfy him, since he has had no profit as yet from the war; 2, that the Emperor shall pay all his debts to the King; and 3, that the treaties of London and Windsor shall be annulled." [4]

So the vaulted alliance conceived by the King and erected by my lord of York had proved no more permanent or protective than the tent in which the two monarchs had met at Gravelines. Its collapse might be assigned to the winds of adversity, but in Henry's experience it had been brought down by imperial treachery. The King could not have had anything but profound distaste and visceral revulsion for the whole bitter, disappointing enterprise. Thirteen years before, Ferdinand, the father of Catherine, had made a fool of him, luring him into commitments which but covered Ferdinand's own military maneuvers. Ferdinand's treachery had been so great that there had been vague rumors of Henry's divorcing Catherine. But Henry let the matter pass after his rage had cooled. He had been only a boy then and had much to learn about the nefarious minds of monarchs beyond the realm of England. Now Charles, the nephew of Catherine, had shown the same devious perfidy; but it had been more profitable to Charles and more detailed, and it had violated solemn vows. It had flouted the King's wishes and made a public fool of him again in Europe — the man who paid the piper, an easy touch, a banker for his friends. And this withdrawal of the Emperor from the marriage contract had left him with no prospect of seeing the Tudor blood flow on through an imperial union.

Henry faced the future with only a daughter and a queen who would bear him no son. The ambassadors to the Emperor had made this plain, for, as they reported to the King, they had asked the Emperor to consider what he would "do in like case; that as for my Lady Princess 'she was your only child at this time in whom your Highness put the hope of propagation of any posterity of your body, seeing the Queen's grace hath long been without child; and albeit God may send her more children, yet she was past that age in which women most commonly are wont to be fruitful and have children.' " [5] The man who rejected the proffer of Henry's only child was the nephew of Catherine, who was the daughter of Ferdinand.

Wolsey had shown none of the King's reluctance to admit the uselessness of the Emperor as an ally. He had had the advantage of direct dealings with Charles in negotiations, and he had also the knowledge that came from his two disappointments in counting on the Emperor's support for the papacy. There was, consequently, in his attitude toward Charles a great deal of personal antagonism, and even in the days when Henry and Charles were supposed to be firm friends, Wolsey did little to disguise his lack of confidence and inner feelings. It was indeed duly reported to the Emperor that Wolsey had called him a liar, his aunt Margaret a ribald, and Bourbon a traitor. He had made these statements, according to the report, when emissaries of the Emperor had asked for 200,000 ducats to support a planned invasion of Bourbon into Burgundy and Wolsey had said that the King had other things to do with his money than spend it for the pleasure of such persons. The ambassadors were hard put to mollify the Emperor when he reproached them with the report of Wolsey's demeanor. They could only say that "if such words passed privily between the Cardinal and the ambassadors, they were sure they were not spoken as reported, or else they were not reported as Wolsey's intent was . . ." The Emperor concluded the matter by saying that Wolsey must have spoken what he thought, "or else Wolsey spoke in anger, which he most believed, because he has known him in like passions." [6]

There is good reason to believe that Wolsey spoke what he thought and spoke it in anger. Early in 1525 the Cardinal had suspected the kind of reports Louis de Praet, the Emperor's ambassador in London, had been sending home. What in fact he suspected was the ambassador's suspicions of his own conduct, for at the time Wolsey had already undertaken secret negotiations looking to peace with France. To find out what de Praet was saying, Wolsey hit upon the device of seizing and opening de Praet's dispatches. It was a violation of diplomatic courtesy. As de Praet wrote later: "For a thousand years there is no instance on record of ambassadors of allied and friendly powers having their correspondence violated and divulged, much less of their being forbidden to write to their kings and masters." [7] The packet of letters, though in code, had been entrusted to the ordinary post, and Wolsey arranged to have it seized by the night watch at one of the city gates. The letters found their way into the hands of Sir Thomas More, who presented them the next morning to

Wolsey as he was sitting in Chancery at Westminster. There Wolsey examined the letters. Some of the statements they contained reflected on the King and others were aimed at the Cardinal and touched him at tender spots. He decided to confront the ambassador at once with his statements. He sent for de Praet, and in the presence of Norfolk and other members of the Council he taxed him with untruth for imputing remarks to Wolsey derogatory to the Florentines and the Pope. He objected particularly to one statement: "When matters succeed well, Wolsey knows not what to say, and when otherwise he talks wonders. I hope one day to see our master avenged, for he is the main cause of all his misfortune . . ." [8]

The statement was not only a piercing comment on the Cardinal's talkative and blustering manner; it contained a clear element of truth: the King's chief minister and servant had turned against the Emperor, and this man, lowborn though he was, had strong influence with the King. If there was any doubt on this point in the Emperor's mind, it was dispelled when Henry wrote a letter in his own hand to the Emperor, condemning the Spanish ambassador's conduct, airily overlooking any breach of etiquette Wolsey may have committed.[9] Henry not only wrote such a letter but refused to listen to any remonstrances from the Emperor. De Praet was confined to his house until his successor could be named, and Henry supported Wolsey fully in his extraordinary order that de Praet send no more dispatches. As Wolsey put it: "I ordered him to forbear writing, seeing that the King's highness and I would advertise the specialities with which the Emperor needed to be acquainted." [10]

As a hedge against the Emperor's continued failure to act to keep his agreements, Wolsey had perceived the year before that it would not be amiss to come quietly to terms with Francis. After the patent failure of the imperial alliance, which he had never advocated and had executed only as a servant of the King, he was tacitly free now to revert to the tenet that guided all his diplomacy: England and France must work together in terms of friendship. The reasons now were even more urgent than they had been in 1518 when Wolsey had made their friendship the foundation of the Treaty of London and the concert of Christian powers against the Turk. The Turk was nearer than ever to the heart of Europe, the power of Charles had grown out of all proportion to that of England, and there must now be some effort made to restore a balance against the Emperor. Only England and France could accomplish this laudable end.

Wolsey surrounded the early phases of these talks with hide-and-seek diplomacy. The agent and go-between who carried the notes and expressed the tentative resolutions and sentiments on which a peace might be based was a Genoese who rejoiced in the name of Giovanni Ciovacchino de Passano, a man of many missions and aliases, known currently as John Joachim, who was passing himself off as a merchant and an innocent bystander in the business of intrigue. Late in 1524 he took up residence in a house hard by Westminster and near to the Cardinal. His face, however, was well known in the rogues' gallery of the Imperialists, and his presence in London was enough to occasion suspicion and to cause the Emperor to demand that he be deported. It was said that "every day he spake privily with the Cardinal," but de Praet could never really be sure. It was in his effort to secure specific evidence that de Praet became conspicuously nosy and, in exchange for his prying, had his dispatches seized by the Cardinal. Up to that point Joachim had been in London eight months, and to cover his dealings with him Wolsey lied like an emperor. He protested to de Praet that Joachim had been admitted as a merchant and that as soon as he heard that the merchant's coming had a political purpose he apprised de Praet of this fact. "I have always," said the Cardinal with that histrionic disregard for the truth that he could excuse when he sought the King's interest, "made de Praet privy to the communications with Joachim."

No one would believe this kind of nonsense, least of all the Emperor; but efforts to prove the Cardinal's guilt had come to nought, and the negotiations looking to French amity had continued up to the time when the news of Pavia reached the English court. They were then suspended. Joachim was sent home. Henry hoped to invade France, and the Cardinal's plans for a French *rapprochement* had to be tucked away while Henry stormed around in a prodigious sweat and prepared to mount his courser to ride roughshod over his fallen foe. When, however, the Amicable Loan and the benevolence were smothered under public protest and the Emperor was unable or unwilling to help in the attack and, to compound his highborn felony, announced that he would back out of his agreement to marry the Princess Mary, Joachim was allowed to return, and the Cardinal was permitted to resume his efforts for peace with France. By early June of 1525 Henry had been forced to abandon his plans for the invasion of France, and he had learned the worst about his ally. On June 8 a commission was issued from Lyons by Louise of Savoy as regent of France authorizing John Brinon, president of her council, and John Joachim de Passano, to treat for peace with Henry VIII.[11]

Many of the preliminary details had already been ironed out in Wolsey's undercover palavers with Joachim, and by the end of the summer the peace had been signed, sealed, and delivered. By early July word had reached French sources in Rome that "the agreement with France was on the point of conclusion, although, to dissemble the matter, the Cardinal of York pretended that the negotiation had been interrupted." [12] Through the summer the Cardinal filled the air with prevarications and the smoke of flamboyant innocence. The imperial commissioners were still hopefully in London, and before them he put on a convincing show of heartbreak that the Emperor should think ill of him or distrust him. In July he went to the extreme of writing the Emperor expressing his "regret that the malicious reports of his enemies had supplanted him in the Emperor's favor." [13]

It was child's play to cover a man's work. For behind the transparent deceptions a treaty advantageous to England, not to mention the King and the Cardinal, was being drawn, and it would announce to the world that Charles no longer held full sway over Europe and must deal fairly with his captive French King. It was being arranged that England, while she would take no territory, would take instead two million gold crowns, of which half was to be paid in ready money and the balance in installments of 100,000 crowns a year. And the Princess Mary, she so recently rejected by Charles, bless her tender and usable young heart and hide, would be married to the Dauphin of France.[14] She would get a husband yet.

On Tuesday, August 29, the treaty which had been written out was read in the presence of the Cardinal and dignitaries of the court. It was agreed to in all points. Brinon and Joachim conveyed copies of it forthwith to Louise. They made it clear that the treaty was above all else a business deal and urged her, "for God's sake not to fail in the first payment, else all will have been done in vain." They reported that they had sought arrangements in England to get this first payment from merchants, but the King had cut the matter short, saying that "he would by no means suffer the first payment to be made in his own money, which, he said, would be a mockery." [15] As to the Cardinal, the arrears of the compensation he claimed for the surrender of the bishopric of Tournai now amounted to 130,000 crowns. There had been some stiff negotiation: "At last he let us off, and what was agreed to be paid in five years we got lengthened to seven." They end their report by saying that they are sorry they cannot bring the documents of the peace to Louise in person, but they have "pledged themselves, for her service, to Wolsey and the Council to remain until they have procured the ratification."

Wolsey's precaution in holding the Frenchmen hostages until the treaty was ratified rested on good reasons. Its terms were exacting and exorbitant, a hard bargain driven against a country impoverished by war and drouth and misfortune, a treaty as ungallant and unchivalrous as an invasion. The French King still lay captive, the Emperor having carted him to Madrid to drive a harder bargain with him than Wolsey had driven with France. Louise as regent had rallied the country magnificently during the dark hours of France after Pavia, but she lacked popularity and influence, and the good qualities she possessed were obscured by the fact that she was a woman. As one report from France at the time had it: "For all wise men think that as a woman cannot inherit the crown, neither ought she to rule."

Whatever the maneuvers employed by Louise, the treaty found French acceptance, and by the end of September the moot first payment which had so exercised the French negotiators was on its way to London. Considering the terms of the treaty and its cold and precise requirements, this was all the ratification that mattered. But meanwhile there had been decorous ceremonies of ratification, all according to procotol and including a Mass, as if nothing save the peace of the world had been touched upon in the treaty. Commands and instructions had gone out that "all the noblemen, both spiritual and temporal, now at Greenwich, London and the neighbourhood, be warned by the Vice-Chamberlain to be at Greenwich on Saturday by 1 P.M. and on Sunday by 9 A.M., to continue attending the court until all ceremonies are completed." [16] The judges and learned counsel were also ordered to be present during the same appointed hours, and they were to assemble "in their best array, with their colors about their necks." Various ambassadors were to be assigned hosts, among them somewhat ironically the Emperor's ambassador. At chapel on Sunday the Legate and prelates in pontificalibus were "to do the obsequies and sing mass," and on this occasion the French ambassador was to be placed in the lower stalls on the right side of the chapel and the Emperor's ambassador was to sit on the left.

It was fitting that a treaty which brought into being a new assortment of power should be signalized by punctilious ceremonies of Church and State. England declared by the French rapprochement her independence of the Emperor, now the most powerful prince in Christendom, and avowed by implication her will to oppose his further encroachments. The alignment which existed before the fateful meeting of Henry and Charles at Bruges was now restored — and with immediate effects in Europe. The fact that the treaty was completed before the Emperor knew of it lent a fillip of audacity to the change in England's policy and heartened states which had been wavering before the Emperor's display of strength.

It was known, too, that the author and finisher of the new arrangement was the Cardinal, he who had counseled and advocated peace with France as a makeweight against the power of the Emperor all along. Since the humiliating rejection of the Amicable Loan, when the populace showed that it did not care a tinker's damn whether the King invaded France in person, Henry had withdrawn increasingly from the tedious business of government, sulking in the tents of his pleasures, busy with hunting the stag and other kingly sports. "Everything is left," wrote the Venetian ambassador, "to Cardinal Wolsey, who keeps a great court . . ." [17] Fitzwilliam received from Wolsey a packet of letters addressed to the King; he reports that he took them to His Majesty at once. "But," adds Fitzwilliam, "as he was going out to have a shot at a stag, he asked me to keep them until evening." [18]

Not only was the Cardinal in the ascendancy again because the King was preoccupied with interests not at the moment related to politics; it was also because he had been confirmed in his judgment by a whole train of events. This confirmation, made eloquent daily by such facts as that the Emperor owed in England almost half a million crowns and had left nothing but chits of paper as security, could not fail to infect and rankle the mind of Henry. It was clear that Henry should never have rested his full confidence and policy upon so slender a reed as the impecunious Charles.

Wolsey had made many mistakes but none greater than being right. He might in the fortunes of war and peace be forgiven everything else. Friendship with France, which had been the salient tenet of his policy abroad, had been forced on the kingdom again by the mountainous weight of events. It is not without significance that Henry took no conspicuous part in the cooking of the French treaty save when there appeared a threat that he would not get his full measure of French gold. He was beginning to spend more time with dandies, engage in those chivalric fripperies that constitute the pastimes of storybook kings. Pastimes took an added appeal not only by virtue of his revulsion to the politics of defeat but also because Anne Boleyn was now a part of the court.

Not long after the French peace was drawn, the French King had been released. The terms by which he secured his release were embraced in a document called the Treaty of Madrid, and they caused consternation when they were known and before it was known that the French King had signed a secret oath that he would never carry them out. He agreed to surrender Burgundy, which was to Charles what Milan was to Francis and France to Henry; possessing Burgundy would fulfill a long dream of the young Emperor and give him access to the heart of France. It was stipulated, too, that Francis should give up his claims to Milan, to Genoa, and Naples; he was to marry Charles's sister Eleanor, the widowed Queen of Portugal. And lest he fail to keep these extraordinary promises wrung from him in the days of his captivity, he was to hand over his two sons to the Emperor as hostages.

For the Cardinal's good offices in helping effect his deliverance, Francis wrote Wolsey profuse thanks. The Cardinal by his prompt and vigorous efforts had made England again a decisive factor with which other countries must reckon. He had restored some sense of balance to the powers of Europe. He had trimmed the power of the Emperor at a time when Charles seemed the overpowering force in Christendom. And while matters were thus in this trend, he had, with the aid of circumstances, pressed forward to make the French peace into a French alliance. Not only his personal animosity toward the Emperor but the welfare of England as well demanded that this lordly beggar, successor to Maximilian in more ways than one, should not get further aid from England in building up his power.

But peace was more than a matter of paper work. As usual in all his undertakings, Wolsey erected a citadel of intentions and felt secure in it. Not by a treaty nor yet by an alliance could he set in motion enough counterforces to hold in check the momentum the Emperor had gained during the years England had been in alliance with him and had protected his flanks as well as his interests. Charles was still in command of Italy, and that meant that he was in command also of the papacy. England might announce her intention of opposing him and make him reckon with her in his future plans. But this proved to be too little too late for any genuine effect it might have on Charles.

It would not be possible, obviously, in a few short months to make up for years of wrongheaded policy. England's aid might be useful and even decisive when it came to the Emperor's designs on Burgundy, but what he did in Italy was another matter entirely. Italy was far away, and Wolsey's experience in trying to come to the aid of the Pope during the days of Maximilian had ended in wretched failure. It would be possible to do nothing but send money, and money without the control of policy and strategy might accomplish the opposite effect from what one had in mind.

Moreover, England did not have an indefinite amount of money, and

Henry VIII, for all his extravagance, had some of the parsimony in his blood that marked the calculating behavior of Henry VII. England had no generals comparable to Bourbon and those who were engaged in the warfare in Italy, and anything she did there would have to depend on mercenaries. It was a remote prospect that she could be of the slightest physical assistance to the Pope.

Elated over the descent of Francis into Italy late in 1524, the Pope and many Italian princes had welcomed the French King as a conqueror and had openly sided with him before the battle of Pavia. This Charles could never forgive, seeing that his influence had made Giulio de' Medici into Clement VII. Before the battle of Pavia Charles had said: "I shall go into Italy, and there have a fairer opportunity of obtaining my own, and taking my revenge on those who have wronged me, especially on that poltroon the Pope. Some day or other perhaps Martin Luther may become a man of worth." [19]

After Pavia the situation did not improve; it worsened. Clement VII, alarmed more than ever by the Emperor's power, tried various means, most of them devious, to concert Italy against him. Charles had not increased his popularity with the Pope by offering to absolve Francis from the oath under which he signed the Treaty of Madrid. Francis, fresh from his captivity, let it be known that he would join the Pope in opposing the Emperor, and on May 22, 1526, a Holy League was formed at Cognac, its adherents being France, Florence, Venice, and Francesco Maria Sforza, who laid claim to the duchy of Milan. Henry was named protector of the League, and it was hoped that this flattering designation would cause him to contribute actively to the defense of the Holy See.[20]

The Holy League thus ambitiously formed was enough to inspire temporarily the feeble hopes of the Pope. He wrote Henry and Wolsey to thank them for bringing France into its covenants and declared that but for their good offices that alliance would never have been made. This was true. Henry and Wolsey had been zealous to have France come to the aid of the Pope, but Henry himself was content merely to stand sponsor; he declined to join. For all the good it did, France might as well not have joined either. Francis during this period abstained from business, spent as much time in hunting as Henry did, neglected to supply or reinforce his remaining possessions in Italy.

In consequence, the League formed became too weak to offer the Emperor effective military resistance and strong enough only to irritate him. He still kept large hired forces in Italy, though the notion that he should pay them wages seems to have struck him as quaint. His poverty became both a pose and a policy. He once boasted to the English ambassadors that "ofttimes bruit runneth that men be richer than they be; howbeit," he continued, "the bruit that runneth upon him is true, for he is bruited to be poor, and is poor indeed." [21] Living as he did in ostentatious penury, with his own household servants unpaid, he left his troops in Italy largely to live on plunder and to ravage the countryside where they were stationed. Complaints of their conduct were widespread. Clerk wrote to Wolsey to say that he had reminded the Pope of the "great excesses of the Imperial army in the places where they lodge; the like whereof could scarcely be done by the Turk; and that without reformation, although thousands of complaints had been made." [22]

In effect the Pope and Italy were during these days at the mercy of bands of mercenaries without any firm command. It was an intolerable situation, and the presence of these troops — and the lack of any outside aid — understandably struck terror in the heart of the Florentine who occupied the papal throne. The Spaniards were feared and detested for their cruelty, and the Germans had imbibed just enough of the Lutheran heresies to make their brutality fanatic.

Even if the Emperor and his generals had not been hostile, Clement would have had good reason to dread the depredations of the canaille who in the guise of soldiers overran the Italian peninsula. Disappointed by Francis, who dallied; isolated from any effective English aid; confronted on all sides by enemies, and supported only by a weak alliance of states without adequate power to defend him — under these circumstances the Pope found the demands imposed by his situation greater than his abilities could match. He was a little man, a clerk by practice, training, and competence. Faithfully he had served his uncle Leo X during the days of grandeur in Rome, but he had been but a minion, exalted by virtue of his Florentine connections and not for any marked ability. Then he had been raised to the throne of St. Peter at the behest of the Emperor in the longest conclave on record and against the bitter protest of some of his fellow cardinals.

In less exigent times he might have enjoyed a placid reign. But his reach exceeded his grasp, and no sooner had he become Pope than he tried, albeit with pathetic lack of success, to give the papacy some of the dignity and independence that had been its ancient heritage. He was betrayed by his own aspirations, and in the horrors of the Italian wars he was seared by fright, so that he reached a point where he could make no decision that was not in some respects, and usually in the worst respects, political. He did not choose politics but had politics thrust upon him.

His manners belied his weakness. It was his duty to play two roles simultaneously, that of the Holy Father and that of an Italian warrior, and the fact that he was a bastard who had been given a good family name did nothing to reinforce his ego in either role. He was given over easily to weeping and to the habit of wringing his hands. His method was to contrive by persuasion, to plead and implore. He spent the summer of 1526, when, it may be said to his credit, he at least saw that disaster could not much longer be avoided, in sending out cries for help, many of them directed to the King and the Cardinal.

To the pleas of the Holy See Henry turned an inattentive ear, much to his later regret. Wolsey was full of advice and counsel and encouragement, but there was nothing of balm in England for Clement. He was left to his own pathetic devices. Having failed as a warrior, he resolved next to try his hand as a pacifist. He would purchase some measure of security on his own by making peace with one of the cardinals, Pompeio Colonna, who had taken arms against him. The treachery with which his peaceful overture was perverted did little to encourage Clement's confidence in the wisdom of turning the other cheek or in trusting the fortunes of the spirit in the presence of wolves.

Having pardoned Cardinal Colonna and his followers on condition that they make no more war on the estates of the Church, Clement dismissed most of his forces and kept only a token defense of 100 foot and 200 horse in Rome. The outward acceptance by Cardinal Colonna and the Colonnese of the Pope's pardon proved to be nothing but the smoothest ruse to disarm the Holy Father. The Colonnese did not lay down their arms at all. Far from it. Don Hugo de Moncada, imperial envoy and general, had been back of the scheme, ostensibly acting on his own responsibility but possibly with the tacit connivance of the Emperor. He had decided to teach the Pope a lesson. His bald intentions are set forth blandly in a letter preserved in Gayangos' Spanish Calendar. He wrote that, being troubled over the Emperor's affairs in Italy and especially by the fear of a French descent into the peninsula, "I have come to a resolution, with Cardinal Pompeio Colonna and the rest of the Colonnese, to help and assist the Imperial cause on our own responsibility . . . For this purpose, a truce has been concluded between the Pope and the Colonnese, that the Pope having laid down his arms may be taken unawares." [23]

The deceit worked with Spanish perfection. At daybreak on the morning of September 20, Moncada and Cardinal Colonna with their troops entered the Eternal City. Unexpected, they met only curiosity as they defiled along the streets. Lest there be commotion, Cardinal Colonna sent a trumpeter to different parts of the city — a city of 300,000 inhabitants at the time — "to proclaim that no person had the least occasion for apprehension, as the only motive of the invaders for taking arms was to deliver the Roman people from the tyranny of the Pope." [24]

It was an eerie performance in its early stages. The Pope hastily sent out two cardinals to pray the Romans to take arms in his defense, but none came to his aid save a few friends. Reduced now to his inner defense of Christian fortitude, Clement "resolved to face death in his chair, arrayed in his pontifical vestments." Meanwhile the enemy streamed through the city, meeting only slight resistance at the Porte di Santo Spirito, where one would expect resistance of the horde if anywhere. The invaders numbered 600 horse and 6000 foot, of whom four thousand were rabble and hangers-on who had joined the army for loot.

By five in the afternoon the cardinals had persuaded the Pope to withdraw from the papal palace to the Castle of St. Angelo, not far from the Vatican, a huge and virtually impregnable edifice which Hadrian had begun as a mausoleum for himself and now served as a last citadel of defense in a beleagured city. Pillage had begun in earnest. "Never was so much cruelty and sacrilege," wrote Gregory Casale, Henry's ambassador, who left his own house and went to the Castle to give what solace he could to the Pope. "The enemy attacked the church of St. Peter, spoiling everything, not sparing even the host. All the goods of the palace they carried off, spoiled the houses of the Cardinals, sparing none, not even the Venetian ambassador's . . . The persecution of the clergy and the profanation of all sacred things were unparalllelled . . . The adherents of the Pope and the Swiss saved nothing but the clothes they wore. All this plunder was carried publicly through the city to the Colonnese quarter. Two Cardinals were surrendered as hostages, and Don Hugo, the Imperialist captain, was admitted into St. Angelo to the Pope, and a treaty was arranged in which the Pope agreed to renounce the duchy of Milan, to cashier all his soldiers . . . and pay a fine of 3000 ducats . . . He binds himself to these conditions and a fine of 300,000 ducats. The army retreated at 24 o'clock to the quarters of the Colonna, returning with great booty, mules and handsome horses, such as were found in the Apostolic Palace. Those in the town were in great consternation expecting every minute to be plundered . . . No one slept a wink that night." [25]

Accompanying the desecration of the papal quarters was the suave and punctilious respect for the person of the Pope on the part of Don Hugo de

Moncada. Once in Clement's presence he assumed the mien of a good and faithful Catholic, apologized for the conduct of his soldiers, and restored the silver crucifix and pontifical miter they had stolen. Then "he besought His Holiness to renounce his opposition to the Emperor, from whose piety, justice and moderation nothing else was to be expected than the peace of Christendom and the security of the Holy See. 'His victorious arms,' quoth the Spaniard, 'neither God nor man can resist with impunity!' " [26]

This combination of filial obeisance and housebreaking, of Catholic unction and the abomination of desolation, was enough to induce nervous disorders in a man of more equable temperament than Clement. The imperial troops were withdrawn next day but not before Moncada had exacted his shameless treaty. All things considered, the Pope got off lighter than the hopeless circumstances would have led him to expect. Casale wrote later to London that "the Don wished only to frighten the Pope, but the Colonnas to take him and plunder the Church . . ."

The outcry that followed Moncada's treachery provided the Pope with a comforting display of Christian sentiment but with virtually no substantial satisfaction. Francis expressed his displeasure to the Pope's ambassadors of "the cruel and ungodly demeanor" shown the Pope, "offering to expose his person in the defence of His Holiness." [27] He even went so far as to promise to send ambassadors to England on the subject. When a secretary read Henry the Pope's report of the outrage, it "moved him to great pity and indignation that the See Apostolic should be so violated by a Cardinal's aid." Wolsey had written a letter of consolation for Henry to sign. The secretary told Wolsey that while the King liked the letter, "he desires your Grace to cancel it and write another, inserting that the King exhorteth and prayeth the Pope not to remit his courage, 'but to gather himself with wisdom,' adhere the League and not exteem his promises made to Don Hugo and Colonna, as they were extorted by violence . . . He approves of your letter advising the Pope not to quit Rome, and of your proposition to give the Pope 30,000 ducats." Henry continues with his generous advice, instructing Wolsey to tell the papal and French ambassadors "that these evils have arisen because the King's counsel was not followed, and from the negligence of the French King, and blame them sharply. He thinks the Pope should bestir himself to proclaim a general peace." [28]

The Pope's acknowledgment of the arrival of the money sent by Henry noted only 25,000 ducats and noted also that it would not go far. The 1500 Swiss, it was explained, would require "wages of five gold pieces a month each, especially at Rome where everything is dear." Even this is a bargain. "They would not serve France for less than seven gold pieces." It is to be hoped that this present to the Pope "is only the presage of greater liberality." [29] It was not. It was but a gesture — and even this gesture of help for the Holy See had been proposed not by the Defender of the Faith but by the Cardinal of York. Clement in his extremities had to face and reckon with the fact that he could expect little more than fair words and an occasional pat on the back from the King of England.

Clement was a little man caught in the vise of circumstance, and his only recourse was to cry out under the increasing pressure. And besides dealing with the foes of his own household, he had to sound ceaselessly the alarm of the ever-encroaching hordes of the Turk. Only shortly before Moncada's attack, he had received the crushing news of the defeat and death of the King of Hungary at the hands of the troops of Soliman. The battle had taken place at Mohács, and the Hungarian infantry had been slain to a man. In flight Louis, King of Hungary and brother-in-law of Charles, had fallen from his horse in a shallow swamp, and "pressed down by the weight of his armour, he was smothered in the mud." The Turk had carried away 3000 boats laden with plunder, "chiefly bells of brass and iron goods."

Upon receiving the news, Clement convoked all the cardinals and ambassadors, and, as Casale reports, "was with us more than four hours, beseeching us, with tears, to exhort our princes to make a truce." He proposed a conference in which the Emperor, Francis, and Wolsey would take part and offered to come to France to attend it in person. It was of the most urgent importance that an expedition be organized to drive the Turk out of Hungary, and he promised to go on such an expedition "in person, and make crosses and chalices and everything for the sacred enterprise." He added with a proper sense of doom but with no accuracy of detail that if the Christian princes did not unite and provide a remedy, "we shall forthwith see the Turks in Rome spoiling this palace." [30]

Clement's words came back as echoes. No one but the Pope was listening to his pleas for the concert of Christendom. Having tried truce and supplication, Clement was emboldened by desperation to address a letter to the Emperor. The letter was ill-advised, unhappy, and thoroughly justified: it explained Clement's hostility to the imperial forces on the ground of his fear that the Emperor was determined "to ruin Italy and devastate the Patrimony of the Church." Once the letter was dispatched, however, Clement began to fear its consequences, and he sent forward another and milder letter to replace it. But the nuncio who carried the luckless Pope's first letter, with the speed and diligence of a young Wolsey on his master's errand, placed it in the Emperor's hands before the milder letter arrived. Clement's forthrightness, followed by a penitent display of his hopes for a peaceful peace, did nothing to improve the attitude of Charles to "that poltroon the Pope." [31]

It was no time to be Pope. The forces marshaled against Clement were too great to be met by the ingenuity or resourcefulness of any one man, isolated from the advice and counsel of all save those who sought to flatter him and gain his favor in trifles. In the winter of 1526-27 these forces, which had been as formidable and solid as the Alps to the north, began to move against him, and his desperation and vacillation increased.

His predicament, while it might have been increased by the irresolution of his own nature, was in fact created by the situation in which he found himself. He had inherited not merely the dignity and glory of the office of the papacy but also its vexations and prejudices. The office had but the shadow of its former substance, and the voice of this particular Pope had become a pleading that merely repeated plaintively the refrain of a former greatness. Yet the man who sat in the papal chair could not for long at a time forget the ancient glories of the office and the exalted demands imposed upon him as the father image of the Church. These glimpses might be fleeting and distant and infrequent, obscured by the monstrous sight of arrogant Emperors and Kings who, for want of better pastimes, sought to overrun Italy and control the ancient dignity of the Church. Clement stood by his claims in line of apostolic succession to Peter; but he stood also and more immediately in line of apostolic succession to Alexander VI, the basest of the Borgias, and to Julius II, the first of the political Popes who had blown his trumpet and summoned Christendom to war. Clement's position was wholly untenable, but he had not assumed or created that position: he had inherited it along with the tiara, and the shilly-shallying he did arose from the fact that he tried to maintain it with dignity.

In the day-to-day politics of his position, Clement faced always the bewildering difference between profession and performance. Following Don Hugo de Moncada's seizure of the papal quarters in September of 1526, Charles had written to disavow all responsibility and to say that "the disastrous doings at Rome were unpremeditated and against the will of Don Hugo and the Colonnese." [32] Yet in November of that same year he had sent forward toward Italy an army of 6000 Spaniards, equipped with a fleet of 30 sail, and he had written to Germany and asked his brother Ferdinand "to send to Italy 8000 Germans, under the command of George Fruendsberg, notorious for his cruelty and his hatred of the Church." [33] The German and Spanish forces would be concerted in the north of Italy; their destination was Rome, and before they reached Rome they would attack Florence, the home town of Clement. Any thought that the Imperialist Huns would attack Florence seemed to distress Clement even more than the prospect of their attacking Rome, and thoughts of Florence entered into all his negotiations in the effort to stave off descending disaster.

History now repeated itself with a vengeance. But what befell Rome carried with it so many more terrors and sacrileges than the seizure of the year before that men could never quite grasp, much less coherently record, the enormities of it. Minds rejected the truth and deadened themselves with statistics and generalities.

Again the Pope made a truce, as if following fatalistically his former course. This time the truce was made with the Viceroy of Naples, one of the imperial commanders, but only one. The truce was supposed to endure for eight months, and a messenger to communicate the intelligence of it was dispatched at once to Bourbon. Again the Pope disbanded his forces, this time retaining 200 light horse and 2000 foot. The messenger who took the news to Bourbon's camp was roughly handled, and the terms of the truce rejected. Bourbon by-passed Florence, left his artillery at Siena, and headed with his undisciplined host for Rome. The men showed great skill and courage in passing mountain defiles and bridle paths and marched like a band of fanatic crusaders. Bourbon "marched by their side, singing their songs, taking their jokes, sharing their privations, and recovered a semblance of authority by fraternizing with them." But it was an army out of control, and there was none to stay its complex of passions. The soldiers "began to recognize in the Pope not only the Emperor's bitterest foe but the true originator of all their own distress and privation. The German landsknechts invested him with the face and attributes of a grasping and warlike Antichrist, living in a Roman Babel. Imperial loyalty, Spanish pride and Protestant passion, hunger and want, the sense of guilt at their own insubordination, greed and longing for plunder — all these contradictory emotions blazed up together in a frenzied hatred for the rich and vicious city of Rome." [34]

This was the horde, joined meanwhile by the Italians of villages through which it had passed, that arrived before the walls of Rome. A heavy fog shrouded the city on the morning of May 6, 1527, ominous with gloom and doom, concealing the movements of the enemy. Bourbon was killed, conspicuous in his white armor, during the first attack; his death removed the last tenuous vestige of control. The Pope had refused to leave the city, stubbornly steadfast at the moment of crisis as he had been before, and he had issued an order forbidding anyone on pain of death to take anything out of it. No order could have given greater irony to what followed.[35]

Again the Pope fled to the Castle of St. Angelo. This time it had been provisioned for a siege. He stayed until the last possible moment in the papal chair, showing the same strange and unreasoning dignity he had displayed before, and then the flight was precipitous. "The approaches were obstructed by a vast crowd of prelates, merchants, Jews and ladies, all fleeing for safety in the same direction. As the Pope and the higher ecclesiastics pressed for admittance, the hopeless fugitives of lower ranks were driven back, and, compelled to make way, were crushed to death, or forced over the bridge into the Tiber. The rusty portcullis was lowered with difficulty, and the hapless crowd without was abandoned to the rage of the infuriated foe." [36]

By two o'clock in the afternoon of the attack the soldiers and rabble began to put the city of Rome to the sack. The Prince of Orange was ostensibly in command, but he could do nothing to stay the pillage. One device used in the higher echelons of the attackers was to ask repeated ransom from the same person to assure him of protection against the mob. How this worked is described by Cardinal Como, an eyewitness. Some of the cardinals, being favorable to the Imperialists and feeling a certain security in this fact, did not escape to St. Angelo but remained in their own houses. "These houses were spared for eight days. The Spanish captains, pretending a wish for these houses to be spared, offered to protect them for a certain sum. At first they demanded for each of the Cardinals' palaces 100,000 ducats, making it a great favor to spare them on these terms. In the end the Cardinal of Cesarino was compelled to agree for 45,000 ducats, La Valla for 35,000, Enchivort for 40,000, Siena for 25,000. These sums were all paid in two days. A day or two after the captains who had received the composition money said that the lance-knights wanted to come and sack and they could not prevent them. The lanceknights accordingly attacked the palace of the Cardinal of Siena, who thought himself safe by the good cheer he had offered, and the friendly terms on which he stood with the Emperor. The fight raged in his palace for more than four hours; it was entirely gutted and the Cardinal himself made prisoner, together with all that were within. He was dragged through the streets without his biretta with a sorrowful visage and many kicks and blows, and made to pay 50,000 ducats; and after he had paid them he was tied to a stable, and his head would have been cut off if he had not paid 50,000 ducats more." [37]

Or it might have been a finger. One prelate was taken prisoner with a diamond ring on his finger. "As the soldier who was drawing it off lost patience, his corporal, seeing his embarrassment, drew his knife, cut off the prisoner's finger, and presented it to his comrade. Drawing off the ring, the soldier threw back the finger in the face of his unhappy comrade." [38]

Meanwhile the Pope remained a prisoner in the Castle of St. Angelo, and again the chiefs of the despoilers sought to make a peace with him on their own terms. The life of the city, even when it was not put upon the rack of ruin, disintegrated. One report summed up the feeling: "It is no longer Rome but Rome's grave." The Emperor remained aloof in Spain, but his real attitude may be supposed from the fact that Buonaparte wrote him: "We are expecting to hear from your Majesty whether the Holy See is to be retained or not. Some are of the opinion it should not continue in Rome, lest the French King make a patriarch in his kingdom, and deny obedience to the said See, and the King of England and all other Christian princes do the same. The Imperialists advise that the Holy See be kept so low that the Emperor will be able to dispose of it at his pleasure." [39]

It was twenty-two days after the horrors began that the first news of the sack of Rome reached London. Five days later the full particulars were noised abroad, though scarcely to be comprehended, much less believed, by the populace.[40] For the commonalty, according to the *Chronicle* of Hall, received the news with sodden indifference, saying that "the Pope was a ruffian, unworthy of his place, that he began the mischief, and that he was well served."

Not so the King and the Cardinal. Wolsey ordered prayers in every parish church "and fasting for three days for the deliverance of the Pope."

Well might he have cause to mourn. Henry had decided to terminate his marriage with Catherine of Aragon, the aunt of Charles, and Wolsey had advised him that the only way this marriage could be decently terminated was through a papal dispensation. The man who must as Pope grant that dispensation was now a prisoner of the Emperor. And the man who was charged with the responsibility of getting that dispensation was Thomas Cardinal Wolsey, who had been mainly responsible for the breakup of the imperial alliance and had incurred the hostilities of Charles.

With English understatement, to which he was not often addicted,

Wolsey wrote Henry, pending the arrival of full details of the plight of Clement: "If the Pope be slain or taken, it will hinder the King's affairs not a little, which have hitherto been going so well." [41]

CHAPTER V

A RUMOR substantial enough to make its way to Rome had been circulated as early as 1514 to the effect that "the King of England means to repudiate his present wife, the daughter of the King of Spain and his brother's widow, because he is unable to have children by her . . ." The report, given out by a Venetian writing from Rome, had it that Henry would wed a daughter of the French Duke of Bourbon, and it added that "Henry intends to annul his own marriage and will obtain what he wants from the Pope . . ." [1]

Some credence — enough for the consumption of this item in Europe at least — arose from the facts that Ferdinand had tricked and betrayed Henry on two occasions at least, that the marriage of Henry and Catherine was political to begin with, and that it had taken place in a thicket of doubts and uncertainties. The Archbishop of Canterbury had opposed it in the Council, Henry VII had cautioned his son against it, and even the Pope had been by no means casual in his decision. When asked for a dispensation which would permit Henry to marry his brother's widow, His Holiness had said that the dispensation was "a great matter; nor did he well know, prima facie, if it were competent for the Pope to dispense in such a case . . ." [2]

Whatever qualms existed had been justified during the succeeding years. The marriage had borne little fruit, at least for a King who fancied himself indispensable to his country and to Christendom. Catherine had been pregnant eight times in nine years and had nothing to show for her pains but a spindly daughter who had been offered to various crowned heads in Europe and in the bitter days of 1525 had been rejected by Catherine's nephew the Emperor. In 1517 there had been two miscarriages and in 1518 a stillborn son. [3]

For a King peculiarly fortunate in all other respects, this failure to have a son was a strange fate, and quite naturally a man of Henry's nature came earnestly to assume that the fault must lie in some circumstance and fact beyond himself. He had violated God's law and could not expect

331

to escape retribution. "To a man so prosperous, so splendid, so conscious of nobility, of rectitude, of special services to God and the Church, there seemed to be some mysterious paradox in the strange succession of calamities which had overcome the children of this dubious marriage . . . There must be some meaning in the riddle, and the meaning could only be that the marriage with Catherine was looked upon with disfavor from above, that it was no marriage, that it had never been a marriage, that the king had for 18 years been living in sin." [4]

Henry's own appraisal, written later to justify his strenuous action, is hardly less forthright than Fisher's just given. His ambassadors to the Pope were instructed to say that "whereas the King for some years past had noticed in reading the Bible the severe penalty inflicted by God on those who married the relicts of their brothers, he began to be troubled in his conscience, and to regard the sudden death of his male children as a Divine judgment. The more he studied the matter, the more clearly it appeared to him that he had broken a Divine law." [5]

It was natural that the King, once resolved upon a stern course of action, should leave the execution of the grim and unsavory details to my lord of York. Wolsey had often been tried and had only once been found wanting. He had failed to put across the Amicable Loan, but in all other respects he had succeeded in carrying out to the last detail the King's specifications.

There had been, for example, the matter of terminating an ill-advised prospect of marriage between Mistress Anne Boleyn and the young Lord Percy, wastrel son of the Earl of Northumberland. The fidelity and ruthlessness with which Wolsey had carried out the King's orders in this distasteful instance were duly noted and reported by the Cardinal's gentleman-usher, George Cavendish, and the handling left no doubt that the Cardinal, good and faithful servant, would do anything the King wanted done but didn't want to do.

Lord Percy was one of the young nobles who attended upon the Cardinal's household for his training. But there evidently was not enough to keep him engaged, for when the Cardinal chanced to be off on state affairs or busy with the King, "the Lord Percy would then resort for his pastime unto the queen's chamber, and there would fall in dalliance among the queen's maidens, being at the last more conversant with Mistress Anne Boleyn than with any other; so that there grew up such a secret love between them that, at length, they were ensured together, intending to marry. The which thing came to the king's knowledge, who was then much offended." [6]

That the King had any more than a princely and paternal interest in the affair was not at this time known. He made it clear, however, that the contract between the two young people must be terminated, that His Highness "intended to have preferred Anne Boleyn to another person." The mission was clear, and when my lord of York returned one day from court to his house in Westminster, he called young Percy before him and, in the presence of the servants of the household, began to dress him down for his dalliance. "I marvel not a little," quoth the Cardinal, "of thy peevish folly, that thou wouldst tangle and ensure thyself with a foolish girl yonder in court, I mean Anne Boleyn. Dost thou not consider the estate that God hath called thee unto in this world? For after the death of thy noble father, thou art most like to inherit and possess one of the most worthiest earldoms of this realm."

Young Percy took his discipline not well. He rose at once to the defense of Anne, not only in terms of gallantry, but also to let the Cardinal know something about her social standing and worth. In the end Wolsey decided it would be necessary to send for the young man's father. "And in the mean season," said the Cardinal, "I charge thee, and in the king's name command thee, that thou presume not once to resort to her company, as thou intendest to avoid the king's high indignation."

The bumbling old Earl of Northumberland came down from the north country and handled his young son right severely, ordering him to obey the King's command. But after he had departed and had gone his way down through the hall into his barge, there were still arguments and consultations before Lord Percy would renounce the word he had given Anne Boleyn. At last, though, it was agreed that the contract should be dissolved and that Lord Percy should marry one of the Earl of Shrewsbury's daughters. This sealed the matter neatly. Mistress Anne Boleyn was "commanded to avoid the court and sent home again to her father for a season; whereat she smoked: for all this while she knew nothing of the King's intended purpose."

Nor did my lord of York. As late as the middle of 1527 Henry said, while talking with a French ambassador about a meeting he hoped to have with Francis: "I have some things to communicate to your master, of which Wolsey knows nothing." What Wolsey did know, indeed had known months before this strange statement was made behind his back, was that Henry had fully and irrevocably decided to have his marriage with Catherine declared null and void. And the only person who could annul it in decency and order, Wolsey had insisted, was the Pope. The first approach to Rome had been made secretly in the summer of 1526. For on September 13 of that year, John Clerk, Bishop of Bath, wrote from Rome that he had seen the chief confidant of Clement VII and that the Pope could easily arrange all the various matters Wolsey had submitted but "the cursed divorce" will not be easily granted.[7]

Later, Henry explained to the Emperor that in the early stages of his efforts to satisfy his conscience "he had proceeded as secretly as possible that he might do nothing rashly." [8] Not only were the negotiations for a long while carried on through sealed documents and behind locked doors, but also the King's real reason and intent were concealed from the Cardinal.

Wolsey knew only that it was his business and his duty to obey his master's voice. This obedience had brought him to his present power and had been essential even in gaining him his papal honors. In England's court one met with a severe decorum that was in itself symbolic of the deference due the monarch at all times. Once on a mission to France an English observer had been struck by the familiarity the French King allowed to his courtiers. Divers lords and gentlemen stood about him at dinner, "some leaning upon his chair, and some upon his table, all much more familiarly than is agreeable to our English manners." [9] And on the same occasion when the French chancellor replied to the English ambassador's oration, "he never rose from his chair, nor uncovered his head, nor raised his cap, whether he named the King his master or any other prince." In reverse a French observer noted in one of his dispatches that when a bishop at the court of Henry replied to a French ambassador's oration, he "stood bareheaded at the foot of the throne."

Deference to the presence and to the person of the sovereign marked the conduct of those who attended upon the court of Henry. His decrees and edicts might water down into mildness when they reached the shires of a stubborn and independent people. But they had immense force among those near at hand, and the sense of canine loyalty characteristic of the age reached its highest expression in the man most favored by His Highness. Wolsey had that remarkable capacity of identifying himself completely with the will of a superior, of seeing by means of loyalty into another man's heart and motives, of losing his own wishes in the larger whole of the enterprise he served.

The King was still young — thirty-six when the news of the divorce began to become public. Wolsey was drifting toward age. He had consequently some of the satisfaction that comes from seeing a young man succeed and begin gradually to take over; his loyalty to the King was not lacking in the paternal, in the sad, clinging, and tenacious loyalty of age to youth.

In the sinewy personal relationship with Henry Tudor there inhered the feeling of a father for his son, a man for his friend, a child for his younger brother. In the case of Wolsey and Henry the mysterious interplay had a setting prescribed by medieval tradition. It was intensified by circumstances, but it was not created by circumstances. It might well have existed if the master of Magdalen had remained in letters and as a Fellow had rejoiced to see a pupil outstrip and surpass him in his own field of learning.

Hence one commits a blunder of interpretation if he supposes that the consuming wish of the minister to enjoy the favor and confidence of his sovereign carried with it any form of servility or abasement that reduced Wolsey to the status of a worm. Wolsey's competence made him worthy of the confidence of the King; without that competence there would have been no occasion for his singular devotion. Spineless sycophancy would not have served the purposes of Wolsey's position; these purposes were practical and all of them had to do with the administration of a growing and ever more complex kingdom.

It now became the function of the King's able servant, however, to drop adminstration and diplomacy and secure the dissolution of a royal marriage. For such a task he had neither talent nor natural bent of interest. He was engaged in a dozen and one enterprises far more entertaining to a man of his abilities. He had virtually worked out the details of a new peace with France which would strengthen the treaty drawn in 1525 and would, when ratified, constitute an alliance against the Emperor and remedy some of the sad effects of the ill-advised alliance Henry had commenced when the two rulers met at Bruges. He had his colleges and the reform of the Church to contend with, and the incessant demands of the Star Chamber and the need of the people for speedy justice. Now he must turn aside from all of this and undertake a task which he knew would be enormous and threatened at every turn in the road with unforeseeable brigands of difficulty. As a churchman and as the Pope's representative in England, he would bear the brunt not only of the task but of the responsibility; for an annulment of a marriage, royal or private, was the business of the Church and it would have to be referred to Rome.

It was one of the Cardinal's articulate superstitions that his fall would be brought about by a woman.[10] Behind Catherine and Anne Boleyn he must have caught a glimpse of the watchful figure of Nemesis. In the tracery of complexities surrounding the King's great matter it is difficult if not impossible to follow every thread of Wolsey's reluctance, but one is apparent: his respect for Catherine as an adversary. She was Queen of England, daughter of a King, and the aunt of an Emperor, and behind the mild and complaisant exterior of the woman lay a whole coastline of rocky firmness fresh in the memory of the English.

Whatever the reasons for Wolsey's reluctance about the proceedings looking to the annulment, his distaste showed itself early. He told Cavendish later, when he was free to speak his mind and memories, that he had fallen upon his knees and tried for the space of an hour or two to persuade the King "from his will and appetite." Even in his most deferential days Wolsey had not failed to speak his mind, as he did when he argued military strategy with his King over the siege of Boulogne in 1523. And to his oral protests in the privacy of the King's closet he added in July of 1527 a remarkable letter to the King, a letter still preserved among the state papers of the period.[11]

Wolsey aimed in writing this letter, which Brewer preserves in its wordy entirety, to correct an impression already conveyed to the King that the Cardinal disagreed with him on the annulment. It troubles him that the King supposed he either doubted or sought to hinder the King's cause: "For I take God to record that there is nothing earthly that I should covet so much as the advancing thereof." He goes on then to restate his position, which is simple and, if it had been adhered to, would have placed a far less intolerable burden on the Pope when he came to face the King's demand. Henry rested his case for the dissolution of his marriage with Catherine on the ground that she had carnally known his brother. This she steadfastly denied. A case resting on the disproof of a Queen's word could never stand with certainty in any court, much less one where the politics of nations were involved. Wolsey's plea was that the marriage of Catherine and Arthur had been performed in the face of the Church and had the full sanction of the ceremonies of the Church. Hence it was valid for all time and would in turn invalidate any other marriage in which Catherine might later become a partner.

It was, to be sure, a casuistical argument, but it had the merit of avoiding the disagreeable and never conclusive arguments over the sexual relations between Catherine and her first husband. It would certainly have prevented the scandalous and hearsay testimony to be offered later before the English public about the intimate affairs of a princely marriage bed. But whether it had merit or validity, the point is that the argument advanced was Wolsey's own, and it had evidently been advanced with vigor. He wrote now to reassure the King of his loyalty and of his diligent determination to do what he could to assist in the cause.

He closes his letter in a flourish of deferential rhetoric (Lord Herbert once said that Wolsey's style was ornate rather than elegant): "At the reverence of God, Sir, and most humbly prostrate at your feet, I beseech your Grace, whatsoever report shall be made unto the same, to conceive none opinion of me but that in this matter, *and in all other things that may touch your honour and surety,* I shall be as constant as any living creature . . . assuredly trusting that your Highness, of your high virtue, will defend the cause of your most humble servant and subject against all those that will anything speak or allege to the contrary . . ."

In the course of his letter, also, Wolsey tells the King that his original message had advised him to treat the Queen "both gently and doulcely" — at least "till it were known what should succeed of the Pope." The message he had thus sent the King had been verbal — conveyed by one Master Sampson. And it is not without significance that his message and charge had been given in the presence of the Dukes of Norfolk and Suffolk, the two implacable twins of opposition to the Cardinal. They stood like anxious wolves, awaiting the moment when they could attack a minister separated from his master's favor. In accomplishing this separation, one excuse would do about as well as another; and seeing the King's will and mind in his great matter, they knew that a failure to gain his object through the duplicity of his trusted servant would perhaps serve best of all.

The truth of the business is that Wolsey's life had now entered a new and bewildering phase. He was suddenly dealing with intimate personal affairs and not with the vague destiny of peoples. Here was a minister of remarkable competence, a manipulator of kings and emperors and popes, accustomed to high duties and exalted offices, with no warning at all called upon to adjust the affairs of the royal bedroom. There was an indignity about it as well as an interruption of his manifest destiny. It was as if a distinguished chef had been asked to mind the baby. And he went about it in the way he might manage a military campaign or bring a treaty to fulfillment. In doing it he put on such a show of outward earnestness that he came soon to be identified with the King's cause and, quite naturally, to be blamed for it because he worked for it.

It was Diego Hurtado de Mendoza, Spanish diplomatist, historian, scholar, and poet, who sent the Emperor the first report of the King's intention, and he assigned the blame to Wolsey. Mendoza had been sent as the ambassador of Charles to Henry. His chief mission was to prevent the closer alliance which Wolsey planned and was carrying into execution

337

between England and France in the spring of 1527. He proved to be of little use, having arrived too late. He could send no good word to the Emperor, but he did have a choice item of startling intelligence. As Mattingly describes it, a caller came to him who would not admit he came from the Queen "and begged for anonymity even in cipher. His message, couched in Mendoza's words, was brief: 'The Cardinal, to crown his iniquities, was working to separate the King and Queen . . . and the plot was so far advanced that a number of bishops and lawyers had already gathered secretly to declare her marriage null.' " [12]

At that time Catherine believed that Wolsey had put the idea into her husband's mind. On April 30, some two weeks before the messenger brought the news of the impending action to Mendoza, solemn treaties had been signed between England and France, and it was agreed that Poyntz for France and Clarencieux for England should be sent to defy the Emperor. Here was a coalition brought to fruition by my lord of York, a complete reversal of former policy, and aimed openly and plainly at Charles. Nothing could suit the policy purposes of the Cardinal better than to make the alliance unmistakably firm by the marriage of Henry with a French princess. France was the mainstay of Wolsey's policy, the one feature and line of diplomacy from which in his later years he never wavered or departed. In his consistent love of France, Catherine had consistently opposed the Cardinal and, at crucial moments before and after the Field of Cloth of Gold, with notable success. She was the Emperor's best friend in England, and it would not be amiss to replace her with a French princess who could bear Henry a male child, a child who might in easy course become what Henry had never succeeded in being — King of England and France as well. Thus ran the belief and the reports at the court and in London and among the foreign diplomatists who were resident there.

Moreover, the annulment seemed at first blush a fairly simple matter which no one could arrange better than the Cardinal of York. An ecclesiastic of Wolsey's standing, operating with hefty legatine authority, could declare the King's marriage null and void and merely have the judgment confirmed by the Pope. A procedure for relief from undesirable marriages existed in canonical practice; it was exercised every day, and by and large His Holiness in Rome could be counted on to be generous and accommodating.

The Duke of Suffolk was at the moment occupied, while married to the King's sister Mary, with cleaning up for the record a couple of untidy marriages in which he had been earlier a partner.[13] He had agreed in

338

his youth to marry the daughter of one Sir Anthony Browne; later, instead, he married one Margaret Mortimer, who was dimly related to him. A dispensation had been granted for him to marry this kinswoman. In due course the marriage became painful, and the Duke came to regard it as sinful because the woman was his kin. He appeared before the proper ecclesiastical authorities in London and made a declaration to this effect; then he married Anne Browne, his first love. After her death he married the King's sister — under circumstances by no means acceptable to the King's taste. He thought it well, in view of the awkward background and because of his royal wife, who still passed through the city as the Dowager Queen of France, to have the decision of the London court confirmed in Rome. The confirmation from Rome was duly made, and proper ecclesiastical censures were threatened if any dared call the Duke's marital status in question.

It was all neat and orderly and according to canon law, and Henry could not hope, with the invaluable aid of the Legate, for less accommodation than had been shown one of his nobles. Nor less than had been shown his hoydenish and concupiscent sister who was Queen of Scotland. In this egregious case it had been alleged that Angus, to whom she was married, had been previously contracted to marry another. Henry must have taken some lessons and consolation in the scant reasons needed in Rome, for the contract Margaret alleged was not proved; nor was her profession that she believed her husband James IV had survived Flodden three years and was alive when she married Angus. The whole case was a tissue of pretenses and flimsy allegations based on convenient fancies. Still and all, it had passed muster in Rome; and two months before Henry began his own unsettling action, Margaret had her marriage with Angus dissolved in Rome and was free to marry a lover who had had his own marriage dissolved so he could marry his Queen.[14]

Surely with annulments as common and cheap as indulgences, Henry ought to encounter no obstacle of mountainous proportions, especially seeing that he was clear in his mind and fully resolved and that the cause he pleaded touched vitally upon the succession.

The succession was the thing that caught the conscience of the King. English memory justified and supported his desperation. He must not leave a disputed inheritance and throw the realm back again into that bloody jungle of contention for the crown out of which his father Henry VII had so manfully brought it. Henry VIII knew that his father's supreme contribution had been his marriage to the daughter of the House of York and the siring of eight children, two of them male. It was this latter

339

simple peasant act that had made him a great King, for without it all of his accomplishments would have come to nought.

And now the great Tudor blood which had unquestionably saved England from continued civil strife had watered down into a simple princess. Mary might be useful for bargaining purposes, but for little else; and even as a bargain feature she had brought the throne no sure fortune. In this fateful year of 1527 she was betrothed again, this time to grace and baptize the French alliance against Charles, her former fiancé. But she left much to be desired. The French appraised her critically. She might as well have been a heifer, whose lineage and conformation both were to be judged with a shrewd trader's eye. During the ceremonies attending the peace with France she had taken part in a masque in the Queen's apartments. Together with other ladies of the court she was discovered "in a cave of cloth of gold, guarded by gentlemen wearing tall plumes, and carrying torches. Down from the cave, to the sound of trumpets, stepped the Princess, hand in hand with the Marchioness of Exeter, her hair in a gold net, a jewelled garland about her head and a velvet cap upon that." It was a pretty sight and she played her part with grace. One of the Frenchmen present admired her looks and conversation, but he remarked later with a beefeater's plain talk that she was "so thin, spare and small, as to make it impossible to be married for the next three years." [15]

And what if she had been as hale and robust as Henry? She was still a female, and a female had never ruled the English. One had lamentably tried in 1139 — some four hundred years before — but it had been an experience not to be repeated. Her name was Matilda, and she was the daughter of Henry I. The crown had gone to her head and brought with it an intolerable arrogance that led to her discard. Having a woman at the head of the government was certainly not good practice, as the Great Council of London had foreseen when her pretensions were first advanced. Her attempted reign confirmed the bitterest suspicions of the males. And if a fresher reminder happened to be needed, the carryings-on and intrigues and fierce chicanery of Margaret of Anjou might easily be beckoned as a horrid illustration of what a woman could do to a kingdom. As the aggressive wife of the pathetic Henry VI, it was she who had stirred and kept alive so much of the bitterness of the Wars of the Roses, sending the Duke of York to a chopped-up death, conspiring with Warwick the Kingmaker to put her son on the throne, and sending this son to a bootless death at the battle of Tewkesbury the year of Wolsey's birth.

340

No, the ruler of England must be a male; in this the wiseacres and longbeards agreed with Henry. And now that Catherine could bear no more children, how was a male to come from the loins of the King of England if the King did not take another wife?

There was one expedient to try, and it was but an expedient at best: Henry had a natural son, Henry Fitzroy, and the elevation of this natural son to the highest rank in the realm (save only that occupied by the Cardinal in the order of precedence) announced to the world and to the people of England the importance Henry attached to the fact of a son. The boy might be accepted, bastard though he was; if not, his elevation would at least serve to underscore the King's plight and prepare the public for still more drastic measures later. Accordingly, in the year 1525, when nature had made it plain that nothing good would come out of Catherine, the King's natural child had been brought forth before the people and, at a vast court ceremony staged in his behalf, created Duke of Richmond and Somerset. It had been established, too, that he would take precedence over all the nobility of the realm and over the Princess Mary as well. To make the distinction still more invidious, there had been set up for him a better household than Henry had provided for his legitimate daughter. The English could not miss the significance of the move or fail to interpret the details. Henry VII, before he came to the throne, had been Earl of Richmond; and Duke of Somerset had been the title of the grandfather of Henry VIII. The titles were followed spectacularly a little later by further emoluments of distinction: this lad of seven was created Lord High Admiral of England, Lord Warden of the Marches, and Lord Lieutenant of Ireland; two of these offices Henry VIII had held as a child.

The King's ambassadors were authorized to describe the Duke as one "who is near of his blood and of excellent qualities, and is already furnished to keep the state of a great prince, and yet may be easily by the King's means exalted to higher things." It was proposed that he might be married abroad and strengthen the bonds of international amity.

To all these acts revealing the King's mind on the succession, my lord of York was not only privy but a party. Indeed he was so solicitously active at every stage of the child's development that he might well have been the instigator of the patent scheme to settle the problem of the succession by settling the inheritance upon the Duke. The child made Duke had been born of Elizabeth Blount in the early summer of 1519. He was "a goodly man child, in beauty like to the father and the mother." He was christened Henry, and his godfather was none other than the Cardinal of York. The Cardinal had apparently seen to the mother's confinement at the Priory of St. Lawrence at Blackamore in Essex, and after the birth of the young Henry he set about the task of getting her well married, a task which he accomplished three years later — in the year of the return of Anne Boleyn from her sojourn in France. Elizabeth was married to Gilbert Talbois, a young man whose father had been declared lunatic and whose goods were under the guardianship of the Cardinal.[16]

Once the mother had been settled in marriage, the Cardinal kept an even more attentive eye on young Fitzroy, who seems to have been a remarkable child, amiable by nature and with a precocious aptitude for learning, suffering with natural childish indignation the restraints of luxury. Once for a trip to Yorkshire he received from his godfather a present of a horse litter, "garnished with cloth of silver and other stuffs." The boy made the trip in it, but he made it plain to his attendants, who duly reported the matter to Wolsey, that he did not like riding in a horse litter.

The care and furtherance of the child's education, once he had been created Duke, fell into the province of the Cardinal. It was during one of the busiest and most troubled periods of Wolsey's career, but the Cardinal was kept minutely informed of every occurrence and of every detail in the child's surroundings. A letter from a tutor preserved among the papers of the period shows the status of the child by referring to him quite naturally as the Prince. And it shows, too, some of the sinister influences at work and the task which the great churchman faced in directing the education of his royal charge. The tutor, one Richard Croke, complains to Wolsey that he can do nothing with the Prince unless Wolsey will restrain certain attendants, especially an usher Coton and others under Coton's influence, who make the Prince and his fellow pupils dislike literature and the clergy. Wolsey had even prescribed the hours the Prince must keep, but this devil Coton had altered the schedule and would not allow the Prince to arise at six or to attend early Mass. The tutor had expostulated with Coton and alluded pointedly to Wolsey's authority, but Coton was not impressed. The tutor appeals helplessly to Wolsey for moral assistance, meanwhile having forbidden Coton to have access to the Prince and having told the Prince that he was not to go to Coton "without definite letters from the Cardinal."

Still the matter of the influence of alien forces upon the young Duke's mind is far from solved, for Coton has encouraged "buffons to sing indecent songs before him and to abuse the clergy." Any attempt made by the tutor to punish the malefactors meets with interference by the grooms, who sweep in to rescue culprits. Coton excuses all of the Prince's faults, saying that Croke the tutor is too severe. He further demoralizes the young heir by taking him out to shoot after dinner, which "fatigues him for his lessons." In spite of all the turmoil, the Duke seems to be doing well in his study, the tutor adds, for, "although he is only eight years old, he can translate any passage of Caesar."[17]

All the detailed concern lavished by the Cardinal on the poor bright little Duke came to nought, however, as did the stately schemes promoted in the Council for visiting the inheritance upon him. The King and the Cardinal could not, try as they might, make a Prince out of a mistake. Henry's own religious scruples began to get the better of him. It would be anomalous at least for the Defender of the Faith to leave his title and his crown to a mongrel, to a child whose parenthood would always be open to question at any moment of crisis. The Defender of the Faith must have what he was entitled to: a legitimate son and heir. His conscience would settle for nothing less.

This armored conscience of the King was to baffle everyone but Henry. It was not to be penetrated by darts of doubt, and it yielded not to the corrosion of uncertainty. Once he had buckled it on, it protected him conveniently and steadfastly from the maledictions of critical ecclesiastics, the slings of gossip, and the anathemas of Rome, so that even after six years of failure to procure the annulment he sought he could still with equanimity instruct his ambassadors to say to the Emperor: "The King taketh himself to be in the right, not because so many say it, but because he, being learned, knoweth the matter to be right . . . The justice of our cause is so rooted in our breast that nothing can remove it . . ."[18] If there were inconsistencies in his conduct, there were none in his conscience. All the way along and in whatever he did, "the King taketh himself to be in the right . . ." It was that simple. The whole course of his imperious action sought but one consummation: to have his own judgment confirmed. He began and concluded every maneuver with don't-you-agree?

It was and is a mistake to speak lightly of Henry's conscience. He took it in deadly earnest. It was in some respects the conscience of a Turk clothed in the fabric of Christian theology — a firm fanaticism enforced by Scripture. The actions it fostered and justified might seem unchristian to other Christians, or even to Turks, but not to Henry. He was in his own eyes a moral man, and what he sought in the annulment did not, by all accounts, look to concubinage or promiscuity but to the dissolution of an unscriptural marriage for which the divine law had punished him. Of his own reprobate sister Margaret he spoke in terms of high moral severity. "The behavior of my sister sounds openly to her extreme reproach," he said, according to the state papers of Scotland. "She is more like an unnatural and transformed person than a noble princess or a woman with a sense of wisdom and honour." And when he learned that the annulment of her marriage had been confirmed in Rome, he instructed the Cardinal to write her "that the shameless sentence sent from Rome plainly discovereth how unlawfully it was handled." The Cardinal was also to warn her of the "inevitable damnation of adulterers." [19]

It was in the nature of Henry that whatever he did must be legal and respectable and sanctified by the sprinkling of holy water. The courtly and religious ceremonies invoked upon the creation of the Duke of Richmond in the palace at Bridewell can best be seen as a mask for his intentions, an attempt to give respectability through ritual to an act men less conscience-driven would have considered simply immoral. In its mystical aspects it was a form of expiation.

My lord Cardinal had been there that day at Bridewell, attended by the great lords of state, to be sure, but it was my lord Cardinal who as a symbol of the Church and a custodian of propriety had stood at their head. In every niche had been reminders of legitimacy, and at every turn the child had found himself in the stanchions of sanction. When he had been led from the long gallery of the palace to be created first Earl of Nottingham, he had been clad in the habit and state of an earl, "and so led between the Earl of Arundel on the right and the Earl of Oxford on the left." And before them went the Earl of Northumberland, "bearing the sword in the scabbard by the point, garnished with the girdle. The said earls were in their robes of estate. Before them went Garter, carrying the patent, and his company, and afore them lords, knights, and esquires." Both in this ceremony and in the one which followed immediately to make him a Duke after he had been made an Earl, the illegitimate child of the King had been conducted into the King's chamber, "where the king stood under the cloth of estate, well accompanied by lords spiritual and temporal and my lord Cardinal. The young lord then kneeled to the King, who commanded him to stand up." At this juncture the patent conferring the honor upon him had been read aloud in solemn voices like a Scripture before the hushed assembly by the pious Sir Thomas More, and when he had reached the words *gladii cincturam*, "the young lord kneeled down, and the King put the girdle about his neck." [20]

Thus the fruit of the King's fugitive impulses had been blessed before the whole court. Not less impressive or significant than public and ceremonious acknowledgment of the wonder of his error was the King's subsequent solicitude for the child's welfare. Toward the young Duke he behaved in a fashion and manner which was not merely moral but excessively moral, as if he meant to show the whole people how a father should treat a son, yea, even though he be a bastard.

It was the King's need of elaborate self-justification that marked every single step of his proceedings against Catherine and made him embellish his acts with legality and mummings and disguisings. His case was simple. He was, by God, a bachelor. He had not, by the laws of God, ever been married. But his case, to have validity in his own eyes and to bring him the approval which he so pathetically required, must be given the sanction and approval of the Church. Upon the already overburdened shoulders of my lord of York fell the new burden of providing his royal and stubborn master with this approval. It was Wolsey's task and it was also his opportunity — the only hold the Cardinal had over the King in the devious threadings of the King's will was Henry's sense of legality and respectability. The King's secret matter must be handled in decency and in order. And Henry's moral histrionics, his need for dramatizing the internals of his soul, had to be respected.

CHAPTER VI

THE first step toward meeting these peculiar requirements in the case was taken by my lord of York in May of 1527. It was a hearing instituted and held in great secrecy at the Cardinal's house in Westminster, and the secrecy provided only one element of the deceit with which the air of the Cardinal's house was heavy.

The occasion was a pretended and collusive suit in which the sovereign appeared before Wolsey and the Archbishop of Canterbury to lay bare his conscience and ask the guidance of the Church. As with so many men who know unshakably that they are right, Henry assumed at first the posture of an inquirer. He wanted, he said, simply to have the question of his marriage determined by a court of learned ecclesiastics.

345

The Cardinal had gone, under summons from the King, to Greenwich and in turn summoned the King to appear before him in his house at York Place. The King obediently came to answer an objection alleged against him, to wit, that he had been cohabiting with Catherine, his brother Arthur's wife, for the past eighteen years.

At this mock court the Cardinal presided, his legatine regalia serving as a kind of prodigious wig to cover both his deceit and his embarrassment. The King sat on his right hand, and to him my lord of York explained the summons. As Legate of the Holy See, he looked to His Majesty's spiritual welfare, and since it was part of his functions to correct offenses against the marriage law, he had decided to take cognizance of the King's cause. Yet he knew, Legate though he was, that he was still a subject and not fit to cite his sovereign, so "he begged to hear from the King's own lips whether he consented to these proceedings."

It should have surprised no one present that the King magnanimously consented; nor that the King listened gravely while the Cardinal informed him of the complaint made against his marriage with Catherine and noted the questions that had been raised against the dispensation under which it had been approved. The King had written his reply in advance (as well as the script for the whole act), and he said that, since he could not always appear in person before the court, he hoped the court would not mind if he were represented by a proctor in the person of one Dr. Bell. This royal request the Cardinal saw fit to grant; and, after a few further formalities, the court adjourned, and all those present took off their masks and went out.

There were further sessions in which Dr. Bell weakly justified the King's conduct, and a learned Dr. Wolman attacked it vigorously. The whole thing was a travesty, but stiffly and insistently legal, and no one could quite admit the absurdity of the proceedings, seeing that the King had fathered them. And it proved to be not only a collusive but an inconclusive suit, for even the accommodating Cardinal found the problems and arguments presented too weighty and thorny for his legatine authority, and the court petered out on May 31, with Wolsey's comment that the problem would have to be submitted to distinguished theologians and jurists.

Much more than the King's real intentions went unacknowledged in the mockery of the collusive hearing. Unacknowledged most of all were the witnesses of history who gave their testimony there. Louise of Savoy was present, hidden among the masks. She it was who in 1521, while Wolsey was at Calais, had accosted the treasurer of France for her moneys and pensions when the French King had ordered 400,000 crowns sent to his troops in Italy and the money had not arrived and the French had lost Italy to the troops of the Emperor. And it was she who had alienated the Duke of Bourbon from the French King, her son, and encouraged the Duke's treason by her legalities in seizing his property. And the ghost of the Duke of Bourbon was there, too, for he had paid his troops with the privilege of pillage, and while the dignitaries at the secret court at Westminster spoke in hushed and vapid rhetoric about the King's secret matter, the soldiers whom the dead Duke had commanded were howling through the streets of Rome.

What was really secret that fateful spring in London was the intimate effect of what appeared to be far away. It was the news that Rome had been put to the sack and the Pope made prisoner of the Queen's nephew that really adjourned the court. If the Pope had been left ostensibly a free moral agent with the power of decision in matters touching scruples of conscience, there was some reason to believe that he would confirm the findings of a court in England which might declare the King's marriage invalid. Now, alas, it seemed improbable to say the least.

As usual, Charles was vague and noncommittal, pretending at first that he did not know what had happened at Rome and saying he must await further intelligence. Lee wrote Wolsey six weeks after the sack of Rome that the Emperor claimed he had no certainty that the Pope had been taken prisoner. "After this," says Lee, "he came to his excuse, avowing, with his hands often laid upon his breast, that these things were done not only without his commission but against his will, and to his great displeasure. He said that Bourbon was compelled to go to Rome because his army was bent on it and lacked money." When he was tactlessly asked by Lee why he maintained an army he could not pay, "his defense is that he was constrained to it by the conduct of others, who would not allow him to have peace on reasonable conditions." He went on to say that if only the Pope and the Florentines had given a sum of money, they might have stopped the clamor of his army, "which only for hunger of money outraged and would go forward." He professed great sorrow for the atrocities committed "and, most of all, that there had been so little regard shown to the Pope's person, and the honor of the Cardinals." [1]

By the time of this interview — late June of 1527 — the King's secret matter was no secret whatever to the Emperor. Nor was it any longer a pretended secret in England. The advice and counsel of various assorted theologians had been solicited by the Cardinal, and on June 22

Henry broached Catherine with the dreadful news that the two had been living for, lo, these many years in mortal sin. It was the Spanish ambassador who made the report and gave the corroborative detail in a letter which has been preserved and was made public by Pascual de Gayangos y Arce in his Spanish Calendar. In May the ambassador had reported that the Cardinal's obloquy was responsible; now he speaks of how "the King and his ministers" have been trying to dissolve the royal marriage. He tells how the King had gone to the Queen and told her that "he had come to the resolution, as he was much troubled in his conscience, to separate himself from her *a mensa et thoro,* and he desired her to choose a place into which she would retire."

Catherine had been a meek and faithful consort, decorous in manner and habits, and had shown great devotion to her royal husband, even when he elevated his bastard son above their legitimate daughter. The King, seeing the scruples of his conscience and the righteousness of his biblical views, might reasonably expect the woman to take the news bravely and to cooperate in his wishes. But Catherine's obdurate nature was one of the factors which the King had not calculated properly. The Queen's answer came only in tears. Tears were more than a coldly reasoning mind could endure or deal with, and the royal countenance was covered with confusion. He told the Queen hastily "that all should be done for the best, and begged her not to divulge what he had told her." [2]

Mendoza presumes that the last injuction was added to quiet the public: "for so great is the attachment of the English people to the Queen, that some demonstration would probably take place in her household." Then he adds thoughtfully: "Not that people of England are ignorant of the King's intentions, for the affair is as notorious as if it had been proclaimed by the town crier; but they cannot believe that he will ever carry so wicked a project into effect. However this may be, and however much people may asseverate that such iniquity cannot be tolerated, I attach no faith to such assurances, as the people have no leader to guide them. If, therefore, the King should carry his design into execution, and the suit now commenced should go on, this people will probably content themselves only with grumbling."

With the Queen in tears and the Pope in captivity, the King's great matter had suddenly reached a point of vexation, with unexpected difficulties snarling at the gates of legality. Not since his friend and brother the Most Christian King had tumbled him on his royal rump at the Field of Cloth of Gold had Henry come out of his storybook and dealt with

348

anything as real as a man's aggressive muscles or a woman's defensive tears. It was exasperating, this life on a personal level. It would be well to shift the whole affair back on to the diplomatic level, where kings and cardinals lived and moved, and thus conveniently shift more of the responsibility to the shoulders of his competent minister. Wolsey would be sent to France to enlist the aid of Francis against Charles in gaining the release of the Pope.

The new alliance with France was much more important now in June of 1527 than it had been when the negotiations began in the spring of that year. The alliance had been formed and the treaties implementing it signed on April 30, but in a transaction so vast and vital there were a number of details that had yet to be ironed out. Wolsey would be the man for the mission, although during the negotiations Henry himself had expressed a cordial wish to see his brother of France again and had assured François Vicomte de Turenne, one of the French ambassadors sent to arrange the alliance, that "if their state allowed, he would not be a single day without his company." He had, he said, "an affection for the King, such as a simple gentleman might have for his friend."

Francis gave his brother of England no encouragement as far as another personal interview was concerned. The Cardinal he recognized — too conspicuously for the Cardinal's good, surely — as the author of the peace that had been brought about between him and Henry. The first thing the French ambassadors arranging the peace had done on arrival in England was to thank the Cardinal, "on the part of Francis, for being the occasion of peace with the King of England, which peace had been the means of his deliverance" from the Emperor. Wolsey in his reply thanked them for attributing their King's deliverance to him and went on to say that after seeing the French King at Ardres, "he had become his servant in consequence of his nobleness and virtues, and no subsequent circumstance had destroyed his affection, which was increased by the similarity of the two Kings in habit and person." He added pointedly that he had, in fact, endeavored to attain the French King's release "and to preserve his realm in his absence, and to dissuade Henry from invading it." [3]

Small wonder that Francis had extended a cordial invitation to Wolsey to visit France. Such a visit also served Henry's purpose well, and necessity instructed the Cardinal to go. But it was a bad time to be away. Cavendish records that the Cardinal "was commanded to prepare himself to this journey; the which he was fain to take upon him." According to the clean and simple mind of the servant, the journey was a ruse to get the Cardinal out of the country. Lords of the Council had flattered

349

him, saying "that it were more meet for his high discretion, wit, and authority, to compass and bring to pass a perfect peace among these most mighty princes of the world than any other within this realm or elsewhere." So the appeal to Wolsey went. But, his servant adds, "their intent and purpose was only but to get him out of the king's daily presence, and to convey him out of the realm, that they might have convenient leisure and opportunity to adventure their long desired enterprise, and by the aid of their chief mistress, my Lady Anne, to deprave him so unto the king in his absence, that he should be rather in his high displeasure than in his accustomed favor . . ." [4]

Documents of the period and subsequent events both support Cavendish's eloquent suspicions. From the King's point of view the trip was necessary, even imperative, seeing the urgency of his great matter and the captivity of the Pope. But it would keep the Cardinal away from the court for at least a month, and at a time when it was most important to keep the confidence of the King in the matter most stubbornly on his mind and to defend the alliance of which the Cardinal was the author.

It greatly needed defense, as did any friendly feeling toward France in England. The Cardinal had shouldered the alliance through the Council against bitter opposition. Dodieu, who kept a minute record of the transactions connected with every phase of forming the alliance, reports that Wolsey pressed the French to sign the agreement before opposition became too great to overcome. The Cardinal was "always saying that his master was continually urged to break it off by many of his Council, one of them being Norfolk, with whom Wolsey had had high words in the King's presence, which had partly caused his illness." The illness had been tertian fever, an affliction from which Charles had suffered, and it might have been tied up with an inflammation of the capacity for telling the truth. Still, he had been ill, and he had met with sour objections from the members of the Council who had always advocated an imperial alliance. The opponents of the French alliance in this instance numbered not merely the lords but the people of England whose business would be sorely affected by hostile relations with the Emperor.

Normal trade between England and the Continent was carried on at Antwerp and the Flemish ports. Wolsey, as a part of his new alliance with France, sought to divert English trade from the Emperor's dominions to Calais, but he met with little success and much opposition, the interests existing to carry out trade being vested in the Low Countries. Trade through Calais was almost as unnatural, somehow, as friendship with the French. Many of the Hanse merchants would lose their business if a change were actually brought about. And how they would suffer could be seen in the fact that there was now an enormous market for Lutheran books, all of them contraband and all of them imported through the Low Countries and sold at exorbitant prices.[5]

Opposition to the clergy, which the busy Cardinal had done so little to mitigate through his fitful efforts at reform, had not abated but had grown since the case of Richard Hunne stirred the kingdom a dozen years before. Many of those who spoke in articulate whispers against the Church envied its fabulous wealth, and many were jealous of the distinction and prestige granted to members of the clergy in the business of statecraft. Desirable diplomatic posts were held by ecclesiastics, who were versed in the English tongue as well as Latin, which was commonly used in communications, whereas the nobility and gentry around the court of Henry had no skill in either and, as Brewer puts it, "declined to qualify themselves by the necessary sacrifice of their time and amusements." [6]

Many felt, no doubt from lofty motives, that the Church ought to be disestablished as a state institution and made to serve men's spiritual needs. But those with either crass or lofty motives combined now to form an alliance as strange as the French alliance — and more powerful; and it was aimed, not against the Emperor, but, among the Cardinal's own people, against himself. As long as he remained, with his own great wealth and influence, Legate of the Pope and closest adviser to the King, the Church would remain very much as it was when he came to power. It was he who through his personal supplication in his first act as Cardinal had quieted the King in the days of Richard Hunne. But men had not forgotten the young Henry's statement at the time: "Kings of England have never had any superior but God alone. Know therefore that we will ever maintain the right of our crown and of our temporal jurisdiction." How Henry stood on the rights of the Crown and the clergy was well known. It was the Cardinal and not the King who kept the religious order stable with all the forces seething around it.

Not only those who envied the wealth of the Church and the privileges of the clergy lay in wait for my lord of York. He had interfered outrageously with the privileges and prerogatives of the clergy themselves. Beyond those who genuinely sought the reform of the Church were many who, while content to see the religious order remain substantially as it was, resented the arrogance and presumption by which the Legate had muscled in on practices usually left to the bishops and regular functionaries of the Church.[7] Among these practices was the probate of wills. By English law and custom probate was the exclusive right of ecclesiastical courts, yet Wol-

351

sey with his fictitious power derived from Rome insisted that his own legatine courts had this right — to the deprivation and profound annoyance of
the ecclesiastics who saw the revenues go into his coffers instead of their
own. And if he left the functions of the bishops undisturbed in the exercise of their jurisdiction, "it was an act of grace on his part, often qualified
by financial exaction."

Such highhandedness and greed as the Cardinal had shown derived not
merely from his legacy out of Rome but also, and perhaps chiefly, out of
his closeness to the King. And the resentment of it was not confined to
court or to a band of people known vaguely as the anticlerical party: it per-
meated many phases and territories of English life. By charging a thousand
marks for proving the will of Sir William Compton the Cardinal outraged
the laity in the exorbitance of the fee, and by proving it at all he outraged
the clergy and the ecclesiastical courts.

Warham had protested strongly in 1519 against the persistent invasion
of his own territory by the Legate, saying that, if Wolsey persisted, there
would be nothing left for him or his officers to do; that he would become
"only a shadow and image of an archbishop and legate, void of authority
and jurisdiction, which would be to me a perpetual reproach and to my
church a perpetual prejudice." But Wolsey had persisted, particularly in
the remunerative matter of wills and testaments, until, two years before
he set out on the road to France, Warham had written to him from Kent:
"I would your Grace knew what rumour and obloquy is both in these
parts and also in London that no testaments can take effect otherwise than
your Grace is content." [8]

It appeared to be to the financial and emotional interest of both the
clergy and the nobles to deprive the Cardinal of his favored position with
the King. The sentiment against the Cardinal had long been strong, but in
the summer of 1527 it gained two distinct advantages it had not enjoyed
before. The first was a topic around which a campaign of whispers could
be planned and carried on. Any and all could discuss the King's great matter. It was a good topic for sly digs and ambiguous remarks that might plant
doubts that would flower into suspicions later. The King had given Wolsey
the assignment of the annulment; the two were inextricably involved in it,
and the King had charged the Cardinal with responsibility. Hence any report of the sort that had already reached the King's ears through Master
Sampson, hinting that my lord of York lacked enthusiasm for the King's
cause, would suffice beautifully to impair the King's confidence in his servant. It required no learning, and certainly no Latin, to breed a bruit and
watch it grow.

For this purpose one man was as good as another and a woman was better than a man, and the second advantage the cause against the Cardinal now acquired was a woman near the King who could select and relay to him the best morsels of common talk. Mistress Anne Boleyn had her own grudge against the Cardinal. It was personal and intense and not tied up with such abstractions as diplomacy. He had separated her from Lord Percy, whereby, as Cavendish remarks, she "was greatly offended, saying, that if it lay ever in her power, she would work the Cardinal as much displeasure." Her father had been made a viscount, and the Duke of Norfolk was her uncle, and she was these days becoming conspicuous at court and seemed to absorb an increasing measure of the King's attention. Cheerful, pert, vivacious with her imitation French manners, she was much too insubstantial to be thought of as a leader of the opposition against the mighty Cardinal, but she made a charming and convenient vessel for gossip. There was something disquieting about her influence with the King. It boded no good for a minister who felt that he would be undone by a woman. She had, Cavendish tells us, "a very good wit, and also an inward desire to be revenged of the Cardinal."

Any misgivings my lord of York felt as he set off on his mission to France were more than amply concealed by the pomp and display with which he arrayed himself. Indeed, the excessive color and richness of the procession with which he passed through London may have been a sign that he knew this to be his final burst of glory. Or it may have been a protective measure in symbols. He had always covered an inner insecurity with outward signs of splendor. Now, referring to himself in several cases, more than was necessary, as the King's lieutenant and remarking how he must be treated as a king would be treated, he must have asserted in his pageantry more dignity and certainty than he felt.

The procession set out from the Cardinal's house at Westminster and passed over London Bridge. There were with him lords and bishops and other worthy persons "as were not privy to the conspiracy" he was leaving behind at the court. He had with him a great number of gentlemen in black livery coats, and the most part of them had great chains of gold about their necks. His yeomen were in French tawny livery coats, "having embroidered on the backs and breasts of the said coats these letters: T. and C., under the cardinal's hat. His sumpter mules, which were 20 in number and more, with his carts and other carriages of his train, were passed on before, conducted and guarded with a great number of bows and spears. He rode like a cardinal, very sumptuously, on a mule trapped with crimson velvet upon velvet, and his stirrups were of copper and gilt; and his spare mule following him with like apparel." [9]

The son of Ipswich as the Cardinal of York was in his element again, on a great embassy from one king to another, both of them his trusted friends. This was what he was fitted for. This he could understand. A special diplomatic mission belonged to a tradition of which he was a part. Such a procession as the Cardinal's brought a rustle in people's minds, reminded them of those who controlled their destiny, bathed their eyes in color, sharpened their curiosity, provided an excuse for some reciprocating ceremony.[10] In France there would be welcoming committees sallying out from the towns through which the embassy passed in its lordly state, and there might be the bark of cannons to tell of their approach.

Before he took ship for France, however, there remained one difficult task for which my lord of York had to descend from his mule and which he had to handle at a troublesomely personal level. The King wished the Cardinal to secure the views and enlist the aid of learned churchmen and theologians in the great matter nearest his heart, and the prelate whose aid might enable him to win over such a reluctant worthy as Sir Thomas More was the austere and penetrating Bishop of Rochester, John Fisher. Unless Fisher were properly handled, he might openly oppose the annulment, the King and Cardinal notwithstanding, just as he had openly opposed the subsidy sought through Convocation for the French War in 1523.

Except that Fisher and Wolsey were both members of the clergy of the same Church, and both English subjects, they had little in common. Fisher was not even from Oxford, but from "the other University." He did have some of the same love for Cambridge that Wolsey bore for Oxford, and he bestowed benefactions upon his university. But he had taught there himself, taken an active rather than a patronizing interest in its work, and all his life he had been given more to soul-searching and piety and meditation than to bricks and mortar and preferment. He was now approaching three score years and ten, and from the days of his early youth, when he had been the confessor and chaplain of Margaret Beaufort, mother of Henry VII, he had led a strict and devout life that gained him the fearful respect of his contemporaries. For twenty-two years he had remained contentedly in the minor see of Rochester, although richer sees had been offered to him.

That the King ever thought a man of Wolsey's temperament and standards could deal with a man of Fisher's godliness on a matter touching Scripture and human conduct was but another sign of how poorly Henry had assessed the difficulties that he had imposed upon the Cardinal. But then, Fisher was old and feeble and withdrawn from the busy world, and Wolsey had a ready and serviceable tongue and he might overpower the old prelate with a club of words; at least he might nullify him into neutrality. The strategy, if one is to judge by the long account of the interview Wolsey gave the King, was to leave only the impression that Henry wanted to leave and to disregard truth as unscrupulously as if the bishop had been an emperor.[11]

Wolsey started his interview by talking with Fisher about the calamities that had befallen the Church in Rome and the importance of prayer and fasting. Then he went on to find out warily how much Fisher knew: whether lately any man had been sent to him by the Queen. Writing an account of the interview to the King, Wolsey said that at this question the old bishop "somewhat stayed and paused; nevertheless, in conclusion he answered, how truth it is, that of late one was sent unto him by the Queen's Grace, who brought him a message only by mouth, without any disclosure of any particularity, that certain matters there were between your Grace and her lately chanced, wherein she would be glad to have his counsel." Fisher, however, had said that in matters touching the King and the Queen he would not give counsel without the King's pleasure and express commandment. Wolsey next inquired if the bishop knew what the affair was that had chanced between the King and Queen. He said that, on the basis of a tale brought him from a brother in London, he supposed he did. Even the secluded Bishop of Rochester had by this time heard of the King's secret matter.

What Fisher should be told — and how — had been worked out by the King and Cardinal in conference. Wolsey tells the King that he declared the whole matter to Fisher at length, "as was devised with your Highness at York." Fisher was given the distinct and wholly false impression that the King was merely troubled in his conscience and that he wished the views of learned men to satisfy his mind, but that the Queen, "being suspicious and casting further doubts than was meant or intended," had broken with the King in a very unpleasant manner "and by her manner, behavior, words, and messages, sent to divers, hath published, divulged and opened the same . . ."

A lie so fat and thick must have gagged even the Cardinal, practiced though he was in the studied prevarications of medieval diplomacy. It was not merely that it turned the facts upside down but that it shifted without apparent thought of human decency the blame for the King's cause upon an innocent woman, behind her back and to a friend. It was too much of a lie for even the aged Fisher to take calmly; he wanted to go

355

at once to the Queen and remonstrate with her and "cause her greatly to repent, humble and submit herself" to the King. This gave the Cardinal a few bad moments, but in the end he persuaded Fisher "that he will nothing speak or do therein, or anything counsel her, but as will stand with your pleasure."

Mission accomplished. When the Cardinal sought to discuss the bull granting the right of the marriage, Fisher grew silent, perhaps beginning to see through the lordly pretense of his visitor. At any rate, Wolsey had to be satisfied with having secured Fisher's alienation from Catherine for the moment. It was a sorry accomplishment, but he had acted again with success under the King's orders, being instructed not only in what his aim must be but, in this particularity, how he should attain it. If there was any doubt in the King's trust, this report of handling the most difficult prelate in the realm ought to convince the King of his servant's diligence.

What of Wolsey's own vestigial conscience after such an occasion? One finds scarcely any record of his nonpublic thoughts, of reflections that were not written for public consumption, or to impress the King, or to influence the actions of his agents or his adversaries. Wolsey lived in public and thought almost altogether in public terms. What he dealt with was either urgent or exigent: it required the use of words as weapons, not as wings. If in the midst of his labors he covenanted any time for meditation, he had none left in which to record the fruits or frustrations of his mind. State business charmed him like a serpent. What ideas he entertained beyond the range of public affairs perished before they could be even roughly shaped in the clay of essays or personal letters. Or if they did not perish before being recorded, they have been lost in the hazards of history and have not come down to us; much of what has been regarded as significant about him appears in state documents, and virtually all his letters surviving are letters of state. His diary and two or three volumes of his letters were once destroyed by a foolish parson who, according to the man who discovered this disaster, "repented his folly on learning that he might have sold them for £50." [12] What has survived of Wolsey's writing on education, a subject and field in which his mind was most alive, indicates that he had some addiction to the luxury of reflection. Certainly his mind had vast scope and range, and his imagination was virile enough that he could not have been wholly uncritical of his own conduct in certain moments when circumstances suffered him to be honest. But from documents and written sources, only the face of his ego remains.

Perhaps it is the healthy suspicion, however, that there was vastly more to the man than survives in the traces of public records that accounts for the perennial fascination Wolsey holds for us. He appeals to the strong desire in all of us to reconstruct the whole from the fragment or to know what goes on behind the façade. Even here we must be content with glimpses, but some of them are enlightening; and it must be noted that as the anesthetic of success wore off and he moved toward ruin, he became more conscious of himself as a person, more communicative in deed and word of fears and aspirations, of craven despair and lusty dreams, of the futility of striving and the infinite worth of man.

Fortunately, there had come into the household of the Cardinal about this time a man who served him as diligently as he himself had served the King. And fortunately, too, the position of George Cavendish did not require the subtleties and subterfuges Wolsey had to employ. Cavendish's devotion was untrammeled, and it brought him into daily and nightly contact with his master. No man ever had a more admiring valet or a more loyal and unshakable friend. Cavendish, like Wolsey, came from Suffolk. He was in his late twenties when he attached himself to the Cardinal, "abandoning," as Wolsey said of him, "his own country, wife and children, his house and family, his rest and quietness, only to serve me." [13] He was a shrewd and careful observer of details. His knowledge of history and of the significance of great events is scant at times and mistaken at others, but he worshiped his lord and master. From the day Cavendish came, the Cardinal was hardly out of his gentleman-usher's sight. He was in a position to see, and did see, what the Cardinal was like without the protective glory and the defensive preoccupations that kept most men at a distance.

The Cardinal reached Canterbury on Saturday, July 6, two days after his interview with Bishop Fisher. He remained in Canterbury several days, it being the time of the great jubilee in honor of the martyred Archbishop Thomas Becket, now canonized as St. Thomas of Canterbury, and with a shrine "so preciously adorned with gold and silver and stone that at midnight you might in some manner have discovered all things as well as at noon day." [14] It was a shrine for pilgrims from all over England. The jubilee and the fair and the ceremonies and the celebration would be as far removed from the fact of Thomas Becket as the jeweled shrine from the stubborn austerity of his later life. But Becket was there all the same, and the celebration could have but one purpose, and that was to remind the monks and the priests and the bishops and the Cardinal that here was a man who was honored because he had defied a King named Henry and had been done to death in his defiance.

It was a good time for Wolsey to be there. A high point of the feast day was a solemn procession within the abbey, and Cavendish tells us that

357

my lord Cardinal went presently in the same, appareled in his legatine ornaments, with his cardinal's hat on his head. Even in such a solemn moment and in the jurisdiction of Archbishop Warham and technically as a guest of the monks, he could not forbear managing the proceedings. He "commanded the monks and all their quire to sing the litany after this sort, *Sancta Maria, ora pro papa nostro Clemente.*" As the papal legate he would mourn the Pope's captivity and see that others did as well. Whatever the words, the cadence of the litany, lifted to the vaulted heights of the great cathedral, carried men's thoughts up. The rich association of song brought with it living memories, and a single act of rhythmic worship performed in unison for a moment made all men sensitively one and made all the worshipers feel at one with all men everywhere. Distinction and dignity disappeared; the cares and concerns of the world vanished, like a pain suddenly if only momentarily relieved. With the monks and all the choir standing all that while in the midst of the body of the church, the only rank left was a moral rank: every man was free to measure his conduct against his aspirations, his own behavior against the behavior of men like John Fisher and Thomas Becket; and to reckon with himself and his motives in this solemn moment, to feel his utter dependence upon something greater than kings and principalities, to shudder at his own weakness under the accusing greatness of men who had stood up against kings and had renounced principalities.

As the litany rolled on in successive waves of petition, Cavendish noticed his lord and master "kneeling at the quire door, at a form covered with carpets and cushions." But his legatine apparel and ornaments and his cardinal's hat and tassels and the carpets and cushions could no longer separate him from his inferiors or protect him from some inner convulsion. For, says Cavendish, "I saw the Lord Cardinal weep very tenderly."

It was a sight he takes pains to record, a personal glimpse in a record which at this stage concerns itself largely with the impressiveness of the Cardinal's household and train. And it was a sight which the gentleman-usher discussed with other members of the Cardinal's household. He and the other servants supposed, he says, that the Cardinal wept "for heaviness that the Pope was at that present in such calamity." In this speculation the servants of the Cardinal's house may have been right, but only if the calamity that had befallen the Pope be considered in the light of all that it revealed about a misspent life. It was not a cardinal who wept openly and unashamedly so near the shrine of St. Thomas of Canterbury. It was a man named Wolsey, a man who had shed the plumage of piety for the nakedness of spirit in the presence of God. It was a man on a mission for his

King who had turned aside to see a bush that had burned but was not consumed. The man weeping at Canterbury was man that is born of woman, that is of few days and full of trouble . . . He cometh forth like a flower, and is cut down: he fleeth also as a shadow, and continueth not.

Lying one day at the King's behest in the very teeth of the devout Bishop of Rochester.

Crying a few days later at the tomb of Thomas Becket, whose spirit was reincarnate in the body of Fisher.

This was the anomaly of Thomas Wolsey. As with so many men, including the King, his devotions had at many junctures of his life little bearing on his conduct. Yet he did not neglect those devotions, and the office which he said daily and the obeisance which he made to religion at least served to remind and accuse his soul.

The mission to France was as successful as the mission to Fisher — and in much the same way. Wolsey was in good voice during his negotiations with Francis and Louise, and he established the French alliance down to the last paltry detail. Mary was betrothed again, this time to the second son of the King of France, the young Duke of Orleans, and the allies agreed upon the demands they would make of Charles. Such an aggregate of power as the two countries concerted at Amiens might in the long run bring enough pressure to bear upon the Emperor to force him to restore the Pope. This result would, if it eventuated, make the annulment easier. But it was a long and roundabout hope, and it would call for the kind of patience which Wolsey was discovering the King lacked. As for the steps he took in helping to grant the King his immediate imperious wish, the Cardinal was doomed to a series of disappointments. And it was in France that the Cardinal was to learn for the first time the enormity of the King's intentions and the new alignment at the court which awaited him upon his return home.

He began his journey from Calais to Amiens with the talkative confidence of the Cardinal of old and in the manner that had so long charmed household servants and diplomats as well. He was in fine fettle — a minister who appeared to have no greater problem than completing an alliance which he had himself initiated and carried through in its early and difficult stages. When all his goods and train were landed at Calais and he was ready to set forth, he called together his noblemen and gentlemen and spoke with them about the respect with which he must be treated and lectured them on how they were to deal with the French.

It was a curious speech. The first part of it sounded as if it had been written by the satirist Skelton, who was forever poking fun at the Cardinal for his lofty manner and his usurpation of the King's authority. Wolsey explained that the King had assigned him to be his lieutenant-general in France. He continued: "That for my part I must, by virtue of my commission of lieutenantship, assume and take upon me, in all honours and degrees, to have all such service and reverence as to his highness' presence is meet and due: and nothing thereof is to be neglected or omitted by me that to his royal estate is appurtenant." He made it clear that he would be treated like a king and that his company would accord him the deference due his royal master if they would upon their return "avoid the king's indignation."

Then Wolsey fell into a mood of levity and talked to the assembly about a topic on which he was qualified: the loving care of the French. "Now to the point of the Frenchmen's nature," he said, "ye shall understand that their disposition is such, that they will be at the first meeting as familiar with you as they had been acquainted with you long before, and commune with you in the French tongue as though you understood every word they spake: therefore in like manner, be ye as familiar with them again as they be with you. If they speak to you in the French tongue, speak you to them in the English tongue; for if you understand not them, they shall no more understand you."

At this point Wolsey paused and spoke "merrily to one of the gentlemen there, being a Welshman. 'Rice,' quoth he, 'speak thou Welsh to him, and I am well assured that thy Welsh shall be no more diffuse to him than his French shall be to thee.'" After this detour which showed how much he enjoyed what he was saying, my lord Cardinal returned to his schoolmasterly instructions: "Let all your entertainment and behavior be according to all gentleness and humanity," he enjoined, "that it may be reported, after your departure from hence, that ye be gentlemen of right good behavior, and of much gentleness, and that ye be men who know your duty to your sovereign lord . . ." [15]

Whether the attending lords and gentlemen followed his instructions and left a poignant impression on the French is not a matter of record, but it is clear that Wolsey proceeded on his journey like a king and met everywhere the reception befitting a king. He rode out of Calais "with such a number of black velvet coats as hath not been seen with an ambassador." His gentlemen walked three abreast in rank and occupied the length of three quarters of a mile in procession. The Cardinal had "all his accustomed and glorious furniture carried before him," except the Great Seal of England, which was left behind in Calais.

Hardly had this black velvet embassy with massy gold chains set forth from Calais, however, when signs and tokens began to dim its splendor. Some of these were merely minor and inconvenient, some were disquieting reminders of danger, and some were ominous. First, it began to rain in torrents on the richly robed Cardinal and on his accustomed and glorious furniture and on the black velvet coats. It rained until the embassy reached Boulogne, miring the roads and turning the parade into a bedraggled and sorry string of men and mules and horses reduced to the quality of misery.

And once the procession had passed beyond the English pale around Calais and had entered French territory, they met there the Captain of Picardy, sent out to meet and escort them. The Captain's hosts were standing in array "in a great piece of oats, all in harness, upon light horses." Whatever they did to the oats and the countryside, the company passed "with my lord, as it were in a wing, all his journey through Picardy." Wolsey had suspected that the Emperor might lay an ambush to betray him, and the French King had ordered the Captain of Picardy to protect the Cardinal's person from enemies.

It's a wise man who knows his own enemies. In a kind of symbolic simplification, Wolsey had fancied that the Emperor would do violence to his person. The Emperor made not so much as a feint with his troops in Picardy, possibly because he could not spare the money to transport them, possibly because he knew that other forces would sooner or later dispose more easily of the Cardinal. Some of these forces were incarnate at the court back in England; others were harbingers of fate in France. For there appeared in the course of the Cardinal's journey, and in spite of the bodyguard granted by the French King, many sly signs of hostility to his mission. Wolsey had overlooked the fact that the French people might have views of his coming to stir up the country for war against the Emperor and for the recovery of distant possessions in Italy, where so many thousands of French, common as well as noble, lay in improvised graves.

The release of the Pope and the recovery of Milan — these were things that could be put into high-sounding words and made to seem pleasantly abstract when penned in treaties and confirmed by the high contracting parties. But the loss of a son on a field of battle so far from home as Milan was quite another matter, and the objection could not always be put into words. But it was there just the same, and now it began to be put into words and pictures too. The common people of France, affected no doubt by the seepage of Lutheranism, were beginning to question, no less than the English, the wishes and wisdom of their betters. Whole peoples were becoming upstarts, not just one commoner now and then who rose to power on the old ladder of privilege.

Wolsey now began to encounter signs of these upstarts in France. The weapon they used was not a spear, nor even the recently devised musket; it was something newer still: it was a book. The book dealt with the causes of Wolsey's being in France. It even touched on secret consultations about the treaty which would place the two kingdoms in alliance, and in general aired matters which should have been left to the smooth and private negotiations of diplomacy.

Many copies of the book were printed and conveyed into England while my lord Cardinal was still in France. It was a dastardly act, and "after my lord was thereof well advertised, and had perused one of the said books, he was not a little offended, and assembled all the privy council of France together, to whom he spake his mind . . ." His mind was at this point quite clear: the book gave grounds for suspecting the French, and it cast grave reflections on his own country and King. He went on to add "that if the like had been attempted in the realm of England, he doubted not to see it punished according to the traitorous demeanour and deserts." It was quite a tirade for a visiting diplomat who had lectured his entourage on the proper treatment of the French. One can almost see the French privy council listening with a Gallic sense of amusement and for an unaccustomed few moments maintaining the same obstinate silence my lord had encountered in Parliament. Cavendish admits that after the Cardinal's speech he "saw but small redress."

For the repression of a subversive book there was at least some means provided by Church and State. Wolsey had himself presided a few years before at the burning of Luther's books in St. Paul's churchyard. But there was no redress for other displeasures of which the Cardinal was a victim in France. Some were so slanderous that the gentleman-usher who attended the Cardinal would not tell them. But he did report that "some lewd person, whoever he was, had engraved in the great chamber window where my lord lay, upon the leaning stone there, a cardinal's hat with a pair of gallows over it . . ."

To a man who saw events forecast in the shadow of incidents, such occurrences had a very disquieting effect. It may have been only a coincidence that, in spite of a faithful household and the French King's protection, "there was no place where he was lodged after he entered the territory of France, but that he was robbed in his privy chamber, either of one thing or other." A boy of twelve, acting for a ruffian in Paris, was finally detected. He haunted the Cardinal's lodging without any suspicion until he was found one day under my lord's privy stairs. The boy confessed and was set in a pillory. But before that there had been those repeated and mysterious disappearances from under the Cardinal's nose.

Nor was the King's secret matter going at all well, and the responsibility of it now began to rub Wolsey's shoulders raw. Wolsey had intended to wait until the full negotiations over the treaty had been attended to before soliciting the French King's collaboration. He accomplished his aim, but on August 11 he learned that news of the impending annulment had reached Spain and had found its way from Spain to France.[16] Now that the Emperor knew of Henry's plans, there was scant chance that he would release the Pope or, even if he did, allow him to reach a decision favorable to the English King who had deserted his imperial alliance. The concert of France and England might ultimately release the Pope, but the English King in his present mood did not have years to spare. Apparently Francis and Louise, being more accustomed to regard divorce among kings as a pastime rather than an event, were not concerned with the possible effect on the Princess Mary's legitimacy. They joined the alliance and encouraged Wolsey in the resolute scheme which his mind, ever resourceful in the presence of diplomatic difficulties, now advanced. He might assemble the College of Cardinals in the territory of France and wrest from them authority by which he could act as Vice-Pope during Clement's captivity. Thus he could in person decide the King's great matter.

The scheme was so fantastic and improbable that it might work like a charm. There was little else to recommend it but the confident audacity of the man who proposed it, based on a long record of successful chicanery in negotiation. Whatever portents might dwell in his mind, Wolsey was still in many respects king of Europe. He was the one man whose favor and pleasure was sought by all. He still had the full confidence of his own King, who had not only granted him a commission to settle the French alliance but had supported him in devising that alliance and quieted opposition to it in the Council. He had been invited to France by its King, and Francis had come out to greet him a mile and a half from Amiens and had embraced him bonnet in hand.

Even the Emperor in these days of the French alliance concealed his dislike and continued to covet his friendship. Early in 1527 when the new ambassador was sent to England, it was his first object to call on the Cardinal the day after his arrival and assure him "how earnestly the Emperor wished for his prosperity and welfare, and how much indebted he was to the Cardinal for his past services." A few days later the Emperor had sent word that if the Cardinal would continue to foster the friendship between himself and the King of England, as he had in the past, the Emperor would pay all his back pensions and give him an additional pension of 6000 ducats.[17] This offer was followed, just before Wolsey left for France, with the offer of a still higher bait and a reminder of how helpful the Emperor could be in securing for him the pontificate, now that Clement was in captivity.

One can see how such a prelate, whose favor and influence were solicited by the blandishments and bribes of crowned heads, might suppose that he could manage also the Pope and the cardinals. On July 29 he wrote Henry that he had been "daily and hourly musing and thinking on your Grace's great and secret affair, and how the same may come to good effect and desired end." He repeated his conviction that the Pope's approval would be imperative and went on to say that if the Pope's deliverance could not be achieved, it would be well as an alternative to convoke the cardinals "at some convenient place in France." [18]

On August 18 the Treaty of Amiens, finishing the details of the alliance, was sealed and confirmed, and Wolsey was free to give himself over to the King's great matter. He began to solicit the Pope's approval of his scheme, supported by Francis and Louise, who suggested that all Christian princes should repudiate the authority of the Pope while he was a prisoner. Well and good, but the way of doing it offered problems. Wolsey's way of doing it at first was to seek a commission from the Pope. Such a commission would have been unlikely even if the Pope had not been closely watched in the Castle of St. Angelo. Both English agents and Italian agents in the pay of England had difficulty getting in to see him, now that the news of the annulment had reached the Emperor. The Pope under his exigencies could not issue the command Wolsey wanted. Francis wrote letters to the cardinals and offered them safe conduct and Wolsey offered them bribes, but in the end only four attended the meeting — all Frenchmen.[19]

The Pope forbade the cardinals to leave Italy, and the meeting in France ended in nothing but mild resolutions. The assembled cardinals sent word to the Pope that they had ordained prayers and fasts twice a week for his release and added that "if the Emperor proved obdurate, they would not recognize either the acts done under compulsion or the legitimacy of any new cardinals created during his imprisonment."

The Cardinal's attempt to control the Sacred College and arrogate to himself the authority of the pontiff ended, for all practical purposes, in a fizzle. But if it advertised his impotence as a member of the whole body of the Church, it likewise revealed his strict and unbending determination to go through proper ecclesiastical channels, however awkward and interminable the process and however many failures the action might encounter along the way. By the Pope's approval, tacit or expressed, the annulment must be secured, and it must be secured within the respected bounds of canon law. Wolsey might within the ample bounds of his own peculiar ethics commit perjury, bribery and simony and resort to all the evil devices used in making a treaty of peace, but the right of the Pope to decide the annulment would remain paramount in all that the Cardinal did.

Trying to assemble the cardinals under his aegis, consequently, must be looked upon as the probing reconnoiter of a strategist fighting in a difficult terrain. Already he was busy with other maneuvers toward Rome. Only a person who knew the ropes and somehow might escape suspicion could gain entrance to the Pope. Such a man, Wolsey thought, was the Italian Ghinucci, who held the bishopric of Worcester in England but who was at the time ambassador to the court of the Emperor. Wolsey had written the King, requesting that Ghinucci be dispatched to Rome to seek the same thing Wolsey had sought from the meeting of the cardinals at Compiègne: he was to obtain a general commission for the Cardinal of York to "execute plenary jurisdiction in the King's suit during the Pope's captivity." By means of this the Cardinal hoped to appoint such judges as the Queen would not refuse or appeal from. The commission was to specify that in the event of an unfortunate appeal the case was to come before the Cardinal and that "his decision as papal vice-regent should be final." [20]

But while Wolsey was occupied in France, the moles were at work at home, eating roots. Wolsey learned that the King, no longer leaving the arrangement of the annulment exclusively in the hands of the Cardinal, planned to send his own secretary, Dr. William Knight, to Rome. Wolsey wrote at once to protest the impracticality of the scheme, saying that Knight "had no colour or acquaintance there" and probably for this good reason might not even get to see the Pope. But what he wrote chiefly to protest in the King's move was the revelation it afforded of the King's mind: an impetuous independence of proper procedures and a failure to understand the labyrinth of Rome. He assured the King that he wanted to obtain the decision at the Pope's hand, and that "there is perfect hope, if your Grace will take a little patience . . ." He goes on to assure him that "by one way or other, your intent shall honorably and lawfully take the desired effect."

Henry, however, had begun to listen to other counsels, including those of his own kingly mind. He wrote Wolsey and thanked him for his diligent service, "which service cannot be by a kind master forgotten, of which fault I trust I shall never be accused, especially to you ward, which so laboriously do serve me." [21] It was an historic nod of acknowledgment, but it was a prophetic epitaph as well. For the bearer who brought this message of appreciation from the King to Wolsey at Compiègne was none other than Dr. William Knight, en route to Rome. The King had thanked the Cardinal for his advice and service. But he had ignored his advice now as he would ignore his service later. He simply explained that, since the English had not sent anyone to the Pope since his captivity and had no one resident there, Knight should be sent, "lest the Queen should anticipate us in our great matter."

That the King, against the Cardinal's pleading, would feed a feeble amateur to the lions at Rome was bad enough. But this was by no means the worst aspect of the news that smote Wolsey with Knight's coming. The King's move meant that, with Wolsey away, there were those near the throne with powers of persuasion strong enough to make Henry feel that the annulment could and should be secured without the offices of the Cardinal; indeed that it would be better if the King carried on his negotiations direct. Knight's mission betrayed not only the royal impatience but the resurgence of the royal prerogative. The specter of Richard Hunne had come with Knight to visit the Cardinal at Compiègne. The Crown was ascendant. Henry might be Defender of the Faith and fancy himself the hope of Christendom, but he was also King of England; and as King of England he sought now an accommodation of his royal wishes, not a long and tedious procession of petitions seeking to get a captive pontiff to set up the means by which his case should be tried before the eyes of men.

The King proposed to make through Knight a request, according to information which Wolsey wormed out of Knight, and by this request he removed the mask from his intentions. He intended to marry Anne Boleyn, and there now stood between him and this marriage, unless the Pope would remove it, the same impediment that stood between him and Catherine. For Henry had been intimate with Anne's sister Mary, and the fact that his relationship had been illicit made it no less of an impediment in the eyes of canon law. He was related now to Anne Boleyn in the same degree of affinity that Catherine was to him. He sought to have the dispensation on which his own marriage with Catherine was based declared invalid and another of the same sort made to enable him to marry Mistress Anne.[22]

There is no evidence that the busy Cardinal, deadened in his sensibilities by the amount of work he did and desperate to accommodate the King's technical requirements, knew before this of the King's resolve to marry Anne. Certainly he knew it now. The cat was out of the bag, and the news had come from the King's secretary and not from the King. It made clear where some of the King's ideas and independence were coming from. The slip of a girl he had separated from Lord Percy at the King's command, a girl whose lineage he had told Percy was not worthy of a future earl, might be Queen of England.

On September 17, a week after Knight arrived at Compiègne, Wolsey started for Calais. He crossed from there to Dover at the end of the month. The homecoming was a disappointment. A subtle change had crept into the atmosphere. "It was supposed among us," said Cavendish, "that the Cardinal would be joyfully received at his homecoming, as well of the King as of all other noblemen; but we were deceived in our expectation." According to the report of Mendoza, the Spanish ambassador, the Cardinal and his train rode straight to Richmond, where the King was staying. He sent word to the King of his return and asked him at what place he might see him, "it being the custom, whenever the Legate has affairs of State to communicate, for the King to retire with him to a private closet." But it happened on this occasion that the Lady Anne Boleyn was in the room with the King when the messenger from the Cardinal arrived, "and before his Majesty could reply, she exclaimed, 'Where else should the Cardinal come? Tell him he may come here, where the King is.' " [23]

Notwithstanding the fact that Anne's retort boded him no good, the Cardinal had a long talk with the King and continued at court two or three days. After all, he had just brought to fullness a firm alliance with a nation that had four times as many subjects as his own — a country "almost equal in population and resources to the next three European powers combined." With the French alliance the King of England had an instrument by which he could reasonably hope to set the Pope at liberty.

CHAPTER VII

HENRY had good cause to be pleased with the Cardinal at this juncture, but he had lost his mind in his own thoughts. He must have his annulment. His conscience ran rampant. If he had not been married to Catherine, then he had not committed adultery in his relations with

Mary Boleyn and Elizabeth Blount and he was free to point out the errors in his sister Margaret. The whole matter needed to be sorted out quickly and neatly, and upon his return from France Wolsey began a cannonade of the Pope with all the learned arguments he could forge in the foundry of his resourceful mind. Now, of course, if he succeeded, his success would be less than perfect, for the woman who would replace Catherine had good reason to hate him, and she was manifestly the center of a faction which sought the properties of the Church and would unseat him.

If Wolsey was shaken by the knowledge that Henry intended to marry Anne, no note of equivocation crept into his petitions. He was writing for the eyes of the King as well as for the Pope. If he could but lead the King along the canonical course, he would at least postpone and delay disaster; procrastination is the hope of a badgered mind.

Late in 1527 he began his petitions to the Pope, having meanwhile entertained, as if without a care, a de luxe French embassy that had come across the Channel to confirm the Treaty of Amiens. All things done and said at Rome during the next harrowing year were variations on a theme by Wolsey. His letter of December 5, 1527, to Sir Gregory Casale, then in Venice but ready to go to Rome, followed by a more informal one the next day, instructively set the tone and tempo.

The Cardinal was subsequently to maneuver and temporize and repeat and reiterate, but the position taken in these letters is one he maintained against all odds to the bitter end. Whether the Pope was free or captive, Wolsey sought a commission authorizing him to decide the case in England, backed by written assurance that the decision he reached would be supported and sustained by the Pope. There were letters and papers and bills and bulls to be thrust under Clement's nose for his signature; there were minutes and briefs and arguments arrayed like wooden soldiers. But all the notes of the King's great matter put together made a kind of fugue in which the English agents fumed and the Pope and his falsetto advisers answered in counterpoint. The case must be decided by the Cardinal of York. Yet it must be pre-decided by the Pope.

The Cardinal begins his instructions to Casale, who has only a thin, hearsay background of the annulment plan, with a cogent summary of the King's public relations line. The King, "partly by his assiduous study and learning, and partly by conference with theologians, has found his conscience somewhat burthened with his present marriage; and out of regard to the quiet of his soul, and next to the security of his succession, and the great mischiefs like to arise, considers it would be offensive to God and man if he were to persist in it, and with great remorse of conscience has for a long time felt that he is living under the offence of the Almighty, whom in all his efforts and his actions he always sets before him. He has made diligent inquiry whether the dispensation granted for himself and the Queen as his brother's wife is valid and sufficient, and he is told that it is not.

"The bull of dispensation is founded on certain false suggestions," Wolsey continued, "as that his Majesty desired the marriage for the good understanding between Henry VII, Ferdinand and Isabella; whereas there was no suspicion of misunderstanding between them. And, secondly, he never assented or knew anything of this bull, nor wished for the marriage. On these grounds it is judged inefficacious. Next, when the King reached the age of fourteen, the contract was revoked and Henry VII objected to the marriage. To this the King attributes the death of all his male children, and dreads the heavy wrath of God if he persists. Notwithstanding his scruples of conscience, he is resolved to apply to The Holy See, trusting that, out of consideration of his services to the Church, the Pope will not refuse to remove this scruple out of the King's mind, and discover a method whereby he may take another wife, and, God willing, have male children." [1]

Knowing that the naïve Knight, who had left London three months before, had not been able even to get a passport into Rome, much less an audience with the Pope, the Cardinal next directs Casale in the necessary subterfuges: "You should change your dress, and, as if you were in some other person's employ, or had some commission from the Duke of Ferrara, obtain a secret interview with the Pope." Arranging the interview will of course call for money, and the Cardinal has arranged that 10,000 ducats will be deposited to Casale's credit with bankers in Venice. He tells Casale that he "shall promise to those who have the management of these matters any sums of money requisite for the purpose." Bribes may be necessary beyond the Pope's household, for the Cardinal thoughtfully adds that money is to be paid "to any person whatever that can secure you the interview."

When Casale gains admittance, he is to show the King's letter of credence, which has "an energetic paragraph written by the King's own hand." He is to lament the plight of the Pope and the cardinals and to assure His Holiness how eager the King and Wolsey are to remedy the evils that now beset them. He is to dwell on the insufficiency of the King's marriage and the sufficiency of the King's scruples. Then Casale, being far from England's verdant land and with no one to check his reporting, is to stress "the vehement desire of the whole nation and nobility, without any exception, that the King should have an heir; that the more thoughtful consider that God has refused us so great a blessing, from the legality of the marriage . . ." By this wily skew, the King's desire was to be made to appear in Rome an obedient response to public clamor, whereas any detectable sentiment in England at the time was a growing resentment of the Cardinal and a strong sympathy for Catherine.

After this detour of the facts, Casale was to set before the Pope a circumstance which was regrettably true and was to sound out like a dirge through all the letters and solicitations the Cardinal addressed to His Holiness. The status of the Church in England was such that the Church and the Pope's authority would be ruined if the Pope did not accede to the King's demand. Nothing was to be said about the fact that my lord of York, through his neglect of the serious business of reform, was responsible for this bitter circumstance. It did no good to dwell on spilt opportunity. The point to stress was that the Cardinal's authority and the Pope's authority were inextricably tied up with a favorable decision on the King's secret matter.

Casale is to picture to the Pope, as if he needed a reminder, "the evils of the Church at the present moment, the contempt for its authority, the avowed purpose of extinguishing the dignity of the See Apostolic; and you shall urge that there is no prince on whom so much reliance can be placed for refuge and defence against these evils than on the king of England, who has hitherto shown himself so good a friend of the Pope." It is really ridiculous to have to argue the matter at all: "when the Pope knows the insufficiency of the dispensation, he ought to offer, unsolicited, some relief for the King's conscience." But if the Pope shows any unaccountable doubt, he is requested to "consider the infinite advantages which are likely to arise to the Apostolic See" if he will forward a special commission, says Wolsey, "in form of a brief directed to me, granting me a faculty to summon whom I please to inquire into the efficiency of the dispensation according to the tenor of a bill enclosed . . ."

The idea was to make the whole business as easy and painless for the Pope as possible. He would not even have to go to the trouble of writing the desired commission. Being accustomed to writing important documents for the King to sign, the Cardinal provided a brief "so written and arranged as not to require transcription or occasion any delay if the Pope's officials are to take a copy of it. But to avoid all peril on that behalf, the Pope may affix his signature and seal, thus openly testifying that it is his mere will and pleasure, and then I can proceed to take cognizance of the cause."

The Cardinal even sent a dispensation for the King's second marriage "to be expedited by his Holiness affixing his signature and seal." And, anticipating even the danger that the pontiff might consult some of those near him in the matter, Casale is directed to "obtain their good graces by promises and remuneration." He is reminded again that he can use the money sent him in Venice at his discretion.

By the end of the letter the King's conscience, which loomed so large at the outset, was significantly lost to sight in a haze of intrigue. The whole arrangement for dealing with the annulment at the Court of St. Peter was put on a bread-and-butter basis, with side orders of *quid pro quo*. No argument is too flimsy to use as a threat or a promise if the Pope shows obstinacy. Casale is instructed to remind the Pope that he granted the Emperor dispensation from his oath for his marriage with the Princess Mary and to urge that he ought to do more for the King of England. And in case the Pope demurs to leaving the decision in the annulment to Wolsey as one of the King's subjects, my lord of York tells Casale to tell the Pope "that I will do nothing foreign to my duty as a Christian and a Cardinal."

What it was that possessed a person of Wolsey's perspicacity to approach the Pope with a miscellany of threats and cajoleries must be left to analysis and speculation. Was this the man and the mind that wrote the Treaty of London and a percipient preface on education? It was the man but not the mind. Anxiety had fostered in him an extravagant resourcefulness. Baited by fears and doubts, he lunged first one way and then another, bellowing. Not only his position and his houses and his plate and ornaments, but his colleges also were at stake. All the acquisitions with which he had buttressed his insecure being through the years would be lost, leaving him naked to his enemies, if he failed the King. A strong premonition of disaster unhinged him, and his desperation to stay the hand of fate with words made him contrive and fashion all possible arguments, good and bad, on the theory that one could never tell which argument might win the day.

The day after he indited his instructions to Casale, Wolsey wrote another letter, more personal; it was a kind of postscript in which, as is so often the case, the hidden agenda of the mind appears. He cites now his personal reasons why the Pope must accede. "Among all the arguments I can think of," he says, "none is stronger than the friendship with which I have inspired the King toward His Holiness — a friendship which will be permanent, unless some occasion should be offered for alienating the King's mind, in which event it will never be in my power to serve his Holiness."

371

He repeats some of the rhetoric of his earlier letter, makes an ungenerous and unsupported reference to the Queen's health, then comes back to his own great matter: "If the Pope is not compliant my own life will be shortened, and I dread to anticipate the consequences. I am the more urgent as the King is absolutely resolved to satisfy his conscience; and if this cannot be done, he will of two evils choose the least, and the disregard of the Papacy must grow daily, especially in these dangerous times . . . I am a humble suitor to the Pope to grant this request, not so much as an English subject, as one who has certain knowledge of what the result must be . . ."[2]

Before Casale could present his letters of credence and begin his bombardment, Clement had escaped from the Castle of St. Angelo. As dusk fell on the evening of December 9, 1527, disguised as one of the domestics of the Castle, he passed unchallenged through the gates, wearing a blouse and a long false beard, a slouched and tattered hat, carrying a basket on his arm and an empty bag — probably the only empty bag that left Rome in those parlous days — on his back. It was a curious disguise, but not inappropriate for the Vicar of Christ, and it worked: no one suspected the Pope in such an attire. The Emperor had arranged to let Clement escape the next day, but Clement did not trust the arrangements. A cart had been provided for him, and, with a solitary peasant as a companion, Clement took short cuts through the night and the next morning arrived at the dismal town of Orvieto, where a shabby and dilapidated Vatican awaited him in the palace of the bishop of the area.[3]

Clement had escaped like a bird from a cage; all the hazards remained, indeed were multiplied; and he seemed more than ever aware, far from the papal palace and in the chilly freedom of Orvieto, of his difficulties. He could still use friends and relish the thought of deliverance, but, being so manifestly at the mercy of the Emperor and with the hideous days of the sack of Rome so fresh in his memory, he was incapable of resolute action. In the same manner as a distinguished and astute churchman in the kingdom of England, Clement was caught by circumstances of his own making in the snare of politics. What good qualities and marked abilities he might possess did him little good now. As an aid to his uncle Leo X, he had been conscientious, efficient, hard-working, faithful at official chores, comfortable in the routine of responsibility. It had been part of his job to supervise the government of Florence, and this he had done well. He liked an assigned task, respectable drudgery, and ecclesiastical duties where he knew what was expected of him.[4] The very trait of hesitancy and caution, which would have served him so admirably as a scholar or a judge or a teacher of inquiring minds, took on now the color of cowardice.

It was at Orvieto that the battle of wits was fought over the King's great matter. Knight reached the Pope a few days after the escape, carrying a request for a commission which would permit the annulment to be decided in England. He carried also, and in spite of the King's apparent withdrawal of them after Knight's visit to Wolsey in Compiègne, secret instructions to secure an unlimited and open dispensation which would give Henry carte blanche to do anything he pleased. Knight got nowhere with the King's secret instructions about his secret matter. As for the commission, Clement showed some hesitant interest, but he suggested that the commission be framed and drawn by Cardinal St. Quatuor, who was expert in such matters. St. Quatuor proved expert enough to revise the draft brought by Knight to a point where it lost all meaning. Late in December the commission was approved, and Knight, overjoyed, rushed home from Rome with it. Where were all the difficulties the Cardinal had prated about? Knight had secured all the King wanted in a short time and without the help of devious Italian interlocutors. Or so it seemed, but once he arrived with the instruments in England it took only a glance to see that they were "of no effect or authority." St. Quatuor had done his job too well; Knight in his sublime innocence had offered him a fee of two thousand crowns for his services and thirty crowns to his secretary, but the cardinal-canonist had had the good grace not to accept it.[5]

With Knight's mission such a transparent failure, it was well that Sir Gregory Casale had been so elaborately instructed and could proceed to Orvieto. But before his presentation of the King's case, another move had been determined upon and he was sent further instructions: he was to seek now a commission from the Pope in which the Cardinal of York would be joined by a cardinal from Rome and the two would, with the Pope's approval, have full permission to settle the King's great matter. The negotiations now entered a stage where they made up a kind of dance of irresponsibility, each person involved seeking to put off part of the task on the others. The Cardinal of York wanted to have the responsibility shared by the Pope, the Pope wanted the Cardinal of York to have it, and now the Cardinal of York wanted it shared with another cardinal from Rome. Wolsey was conscious of the increasing unpopularity of his role and of the Queen's determination to make the validity of the marriage an issue which she would take to Rome. In asking for another cardinal to be joined with him in the commission he asks that it be done so that "all objection which might be urged by the Queen against me as the King's subject, and all evil surmises, might be avoided." [6]

With all his coaching and all his experience, Casale failed to get the kind of commission that would satisfy the Cardinal and the King. It too had been amended by the fine Italian hand of St. Quatuor, and when it arrived in England it too was declared for one reason and another insufficient. Two further agents must be sent to the Pope to get exactly what the King wanted. It was high time. Delay aggravated all of the problems in England and did nothing for the King's patience, which was never one of his durable qualities. It had been eight months since the Cardinal of York and the Archbishop of Canterbury had in their secret court first given ear to the King's conscience. And Henry was now no nearer the fulfillment of his one purpose through proper ecclesiastical channels than he had been then.

The two men chosen for the new mission were Edward Foxe, the King's Almoner, and Dr. Stephen Gardiner, the latter being Wolsey's competent secretary, whose services he reluctantly gave up as a further mark of his esteem for his royal master. The agents were properly indoctrinated and their baggage packed with instructions. More delays conspired to hold their departure from Dover until February 12, 1528. The elements joined in the further postponement of their mission, for when they set out for Calais they found a contrary wind and had to put back to Dover until two o'clock the next morning. At that hour they set out across the dark waters of the Channel but could not reach their destination, so that they were at sea all that day and the night following. Then they came within a few miles of Calais, where they were visited by a tempest. They reached Calais eight days after they had left Dover, twenty-two miles distant. They did not reach Orvieto until March 21, "with no garments but the coats they rode in, which were much worn, and defaced by the foul weather." At Orvieto they had to postpone their audience until their wardrobe was mended. They could borrow nothing; few men in Orvieto had "more garments than one." [7]

It was an odd place the Pope had chosen, an unhealthy and impoverished town. Prices were extraordinarily dear, as the King's agents noted at once, commodities being conveyed into the town by asses and mules. "I cannot tell," wrote Gardiner, "how the Pope should be described as being at liberty here, where hunger, scarcity, bad lodgings, and ill air keep him as much confined as he was in the Castle Angelo." His Holiness could not deny that "captivity in Rome was better than liberty here." Before reaching the Pope in the palace of the bishop, they passed through three rooms, "all naked and unhanged, the roofs fallen down, and, as we can guess, 30 persons, riffraff and other, standing in the chamber for a garnishment."

Wretched though his conditions were, here was the man whose judgment would decide the King's cause and the Cardinal's fate. At least, the conditions provided a setting for intimate if not altogether pleasant conversation. After dinner on the Monday after their arrival Foxe and Gardiner were admitted to the Pope's bedchamber and stated the cause of their coming. The conversation turned in part on Mistress Anne Boleyn. Wolsey had told Foxe and Gardiner in their marching orders of a report from Rome which had caused the Pope to labor under some misapprehension, "as if the King had set on foot this cause, not from fear of his succession, but out of a vain affection or undue love to a gentlewoman of not so excellent qualities as she is here esteemed." The agents are to assure the Pope that Wolsey would not for any affection to his prince or for any reward engage in dissimulation; nor would he have reported to His Holiness "otherwise than his conviction, which was the insufficiency of the marriage." Once having assured the Pope on this point of his detachment, the agents were to stress the many excellent qualities of the said gentlewoman, among them the "purity of her life, her constant virginity, her maidenly and womanly pudicity, her soberness, chasteness, humility, wisdom . . . and her apparent aptness to procreate children." [8]

The encomium to Anne Boleyn got solidly into the recorded instructions, where it could be seen by the King, but it proved to be wholly superfluous. Clement graciously brushed aside any thought that Henry might be led by improper affection.

Next day the agents presented the Pope with some written matter, which he read in part and said he would like to keep and read more at leisure. That evening they spent with St. Quatuor, seeking to persuade him that the commission they wanted was no violation of canon law. The next day St. Quatuor was not well, and the Pope refused to talk with the Englishmen until he had recovered. The next time they met, the Pope had some little stools brought to his sleeping chamber, and he and St. Quatuor and the agents sat around discussing the commission for four solid hours, Gardiner answering all questions extempore in Latin.

Day after day and often night after night the discussions hummed on in the presence of the Pope and his advisers. One gets the feeling from the documents that a great part of the energies of the Holy Catholic Church as well as of the realm of England were consumed by Henry VIII's domestic difficulties. Such items as this appear in the report Gardiner and Casale gave Wolsey: "Discussed the matter warmly for five hours until

1 A.M., when we departed with no other answer but that we should have a definite reply the next day before dinner." On another occasion a troublesome point came up on which the advice of the cardinals must be sought. The night being then far past, the Pope sent a canonist and his prothonotary, Gambara, out to the cardinals' houses for a speedy judgment; but they got nothing from the sleepy cardinals but the answer that they would look up their books on the morrow.[9]

Other signs indicate that those surrounding His Holiness must have been bored out of all reason when they were not actively irritated by the persistent English agents who never relented their attack. As for Clement, he showed an indomitable endurance, doubtless because annoyance had become a steady and reliable routine. He knew what to expect with each return of the assault party. It was Gardiner who led this attack, with no noticeable respect for the position or person of the Holy Father. He pressed his case with increasing roughness and vigor, but he found Clement as hard to argue with as an apparition. He had a wispy and impenetrable strength that was stronger than noise. A good deal of the self-effacing ignorance he displayed at crucial points in the discussions was as false as the beard he wore when he escaped from the Castle of St. Angelo. He found modesty useful as a means of postponement and delay, and in a like manner his pathetic remarks that he was not a canonist made it possible for him to put off any flat commitment on the ground that he must consult his advisers.

Once after a particularly stormy session His Holiness said that he was not learned, and to say truth, "albeit it were a saying in the law that the Pope had all laws locked up in a cabinet in his heart, yet God never gave him the key to open it." As for the point thrust at him on this occasion, he merely sighed and wiped his eyes and said he would consult with the cardinals.

By using the very opposite of the English tactics, Clement in his papal meekness helped to unnerve his adversaries. He sighed often and wiped his eyes and showed signs of torment, but Gardiner came to regard his weakness as a pose. He complained that the Pope "sees all that is spoken sooner and better than any other, but no man is so slow to give an answer." And an answer, the right answer, was what the English wanted.

Wolsey's agents had brought with them to Orvieto a whole arsenal of arguments designed to pulverize every form of opposition. They knew what they wanted. It was a case where beggars would be choosers. They were prepared for opposition but not for attrition and quibbling. Toward the end the sessions turned into conferences over the phrasing of the commission from the Pope, and the Pope's advisers kept changing their copy — making only a few discreet alterations, of course, but subtly enervating the document. After one particularly exasperating set of alterations, Gardiner told the Pope that the men who had tampered with Wolsey's copy had shown no learning, but only ignorance, in their corrections, "fearing a scorpion under every word." But in reporting the matter to Wolsey the agents add: "We believe, however, that this is all done by the Pope's order . . ." [10]

It was hand-to-hand fighting — this wording of the commission. The agents report: "On Tuesday after Palm Sunday, about two hours before night, the Pope showed us a draft commission, corrected and signed . . . but when we saw the amount of correction in it, Gardiner accused the Pope of a breach of his promise in choosing such men as instruments; that his Holiness first protested that he cared nothing about style, but only for justice; and when the question of justice was set at rest, difficulties were raised about the style." Again the agents repaired to the Pope before Mass, argued with the canonists until two in the afternoon, and left with the assurance that they should have the commission before night, "clearly finished to our satisfaction." But on visiting the Pope again that evening, they found it altered from what was agreed on.

Finally the controversy was narrowed down to two words, and here the Pope's advisers stood fast. By now Dr. Gardiner, whose manners were not as good as his Latin, became thoroughly if pardonably vexed, and after expostulating with one of the Pope's chief councilors for luring them "as men do hawks to the fist," he turned to the Pope and taxed him with ingratitude. "The Pope said nothing, and sighed, and wiped his eyes." Then Gardiner went on to say it was God's will that when the agents would report what sort of men they had had to deal with, the favor of the prince who was their only friend would be taken away and that the Apostolic See would fall to pieces with the consent and applause of everybody.

This straw, not as heavy as other maledictions Gardiner had called down, broke Clement's outward resistance. "At these words the Pope's Holiness, casting his arms abroad, bade us put in the words we varied for, and therewith walked up and down the chamber, casting now and then his arms abroad, we standing in a great silence." [11]

Clement had capitulated with a great show of being overpowered, but the commission he granted after all these tempestuous scenes left much to be desired, and Gardiner in sending it to London says he waits to see how Wolsey is satisfied with it. The commission empowers the Cardinal of York

377

to hear the King's case and determine his cause, and in the hearing he is to be joined by a cardinal from Rome. "There is no cardinal here, except Campeggio, fit for this legation," Gardiner says. But of the only clauses in the commission that vitally mattered — those touching the question of whether the Pope would confirm the decision of a legatine court in London and agree not to revoke the powers granted — Gardiner has written his opinion in the margin. But the Pope had promised that he would confirm the sentence and not revoke the right of the two cardinals to decide the case — even if he had not allowed his promise to be written into the commission.

Foxe carried the commission back to London. With it he took also a dispensation authorizing the King to marry whom he pleased, but only after the nullification of his present marriage. Foxe reached England at the end of April 1528 and went at once to Greenwich, where he expected to find Wolsey with the King. The Cardinal had left two hours before. When the King heard Foxe had arrived, he commanded that Foxe be taken to Mistress Anne's chamber, where he would come and join them shortly. The Princess Mary and other maidens at the court were sick of the smallpox at the time, so Anne lay in the gallery in the tiltyard. Foxe found her there and told her about Stephen Gardiner's diligence and the commission, for which, Foxe says, she seemed to be most grateful. But it was obvious that she was vague about the import of the whole transaction and not even clear in her mind about the identity of the man she was talking to. In the course of their talk she kept calling Foxe "Master Stephens." She knew there was a Stephen involved somewhere.[12]

When the King joined them, Anne left; Foxe told him of the long debate at Orvieto and of the results. The King took the news "marvelously thankfully, and made marvelous demonstrations of joy and gladness." Then the King called Anne back and had Foxe repeat the story again for her benefit, filling in such details as needed to be explained to her. Foxe, with a generosity that marked all he did, gave full credit to Wolsey's letters for what they had accomplished. The Pope had been falsely told long before their arrival at Orvieto, Foxe said frankly, that Anne was with child and of "no such qualities as should be worthy of his Majesty." But Wolsey's letters had proved so effectual that the Pope afterwards "leaned to justice, and showed himself marvelous prone and glad to satisfy the King's requests . . ."

By the time Foxe found the Cardinal it was ten o'clock at night. Wolsey was at Durham Place. His great hall of York Place was being "sumptuously and gorgeously" extended and repaired: no great crisis, even if it

threatened his future and menaced his life, could deter him from his favorite pastime of building and repairing and renovating.

The Cardinal was in bed when Foxe arrived, but he commanded that
the returned ambassador be brought to his chamber. My lord of York, his
neck being at stake, examined the tidings of Foxe more critically than had
the King and Mistress Anne. His first impression was that the commission
was hardly better than the one Casale had brought. Later he talked it
over with Dr. Bell and, in the presence of Anne's father, professed himself better contented.

During the year after the Cardinal summoned the King to explain why he had been living in sin, the King's secret matter became his
great matter and then a public matter. In houses and alehouses talk
touched upon the problems of marriage and the rights of parties, both
male and female, in the marriage contract. That a King who was one of
the most envied and powerful princes of Christendom could not do as he
pleased about his marriage had a sobering effect on the whole populace
and led many to reflect and ponder. Clement's obstinacy, advertised by the
delay, made men reckon anew with marriage.

The point involved might affect any marriage in England. Consanguin-
ity, or affinity between two persons, had come to be looked upon as the
devil's handiwork. The most carefully arranged marriage, celebrated with
every precaution in the face of the Church, might be invalidated by the
discovery of this impediment. "If the parties were related within the fourth
degree — that is, if they had a common great-great-grandparent — then
their union was null or void, unless a papal dispensation could be secured."
And this was only the beginning of the complications, for a husband was
related to all his wife's relations and a wife to all her husband's. "The liai-
sons of unmarried persons engendered affinity just as if they had been man
and wife, and untold misery must have been caused by them, as well as by
clandestine marriages, to the unsuspecting relatives of the parties concerned, who were unaware of the impediments thus created for them.
This multiplication of impediments 'made the formation of a valid marriage a matter of chance.'" Parish registers offer many references, says
Abram, to persons who had married in ignorance of the fact that they were
related within the prohibited degree. And in some cases a husband might

379

merely weary of his wife, and then suddenly discover that the two were related and that their marriage ought to be dissolved.[1]

For the most part, litigation over marriage involved the nobility and the gentry. Between villagers, as Coulton observes, it was seldom sufficiently to anyone's interest to upset a marriage and transfer an inheritance. But with the rise of the merchants and the general increase of wealth, more and more families were emerging into the propertied class, or else hopefully thought that soon they might do so. There was, in consequence, a real basis for widespread dissatisfaction with untrustworthy marriage arrangements. The interest the public showed was more than the interest of idle spectators and gossips. And in this respect the preoccupation of the King and the Cardinal with the validity of the royal marriage was a preoccupation with the validity of marriage as an institution. The strenuous course the King pursued made up a kind of morality play in which such abstract terms as Affinity and Dispensation came alive and took on roles and no longer slumbered harmlessly in ecclesiastical documents.

Henry was not content to settle his difficulty by concubinage. He was the Defender of the Faith, who insisted that the highest ecclesiastical authority give full sanction to his plea for a new wife. In an odd, twisted, and by no means intentional way, Henry's pursuit of respectability called attention to the fact that all marriage needed to become more respectable. Marriage was beginning to emerge from the casual into the solid, and men and women were thinking about its problems and its improvement.

Among a boisterous, lusty, undisciplined people, whose dances included the brawl and whose pastimes were notoriously amorous, the lines of marriage were by no means firm. One of the practices that had most beguiled Erasmus on his first coming to England was the free and easy kissing among the English. "Whenever you come you are received with a kiss by all," he wrote. "When you take your leave you are dismissed with kisses; you return, kisses are repeated. They come to visit you, kisses again; they leave you, you kiss them all around. Should they meet you anywhere, kisses in abundance; in fine, wherever you move, there is nothing but kisses." [2] This same practice had been noted and recorded earlier by a Greek traveler, Nicondes Nucium. He pointed out that the English displayed great familiarity "in their usage toward females. For not only do those who are in the same family and house kiss them on the mouth and embrace, but even those who have never seen them. And to them this appears by no means indiscreet." A Venetian ambassador, writing to his home government on the odd nature of the English a year or so before Wolsey came to power, notes the affectionate freedom of the English women: "When they meet friends in the street, they shake hands, and kiss on the mouth and go to some tavern to regale their relatives, not taking this amiss, such is the custom." [3]

Weddings and the festivities attending them had begun also to come in for the kind of critical comment that often shows impending change. Erasmus wrote with undisguised horror of "the ceremonies that precede our weddings," where, he noted, "the mass of Christians sin almost more grievously than any pagans ever did or do." What end is served, he asks, "by wanton dances from dinnertime to supper, wherein the tender maiden may not refuse any man, but the house is free and open to the whole city? There the wretched maiden is forced to clasp hands (and in Britain even to exchange kisses) with drunken men, with others infected with loathsome diseases, and sometimes even with ruffians who have come rather inclined to theft than to dancing. Then comes a tumultuous supper, then dancing again . . . We call a wedding honorable when vast sums have been wasted on it, when many guests have surfeited even to vomiting or fallen into fevers through their intemperance and weariness; a carouse in which the greatest license of filthy speech and folly have been permitted . . . Is this the proper fashion to enter upon a Sacrament of the Church?" [4]

In spite of stern ecclesiastical safeguards against even remote incest, and beyond bargain marriages arranged in the market place and among crowned heads, a vast number of marriages began informally, to say the least. "We find men and women at any time, and in any place, without the assistance of a priest, and without any religious ceremony, marrying simply by making a mutual declaration that they take each other as man and wife, now, at this very minute." [5] Such marriages could be dissolved only by papal dispensation or by taking religious vows.

It was a time of swirling factors and invisible currents, when things less conspicuous but more important than a Cardinal's robe and train were passing through the realm. It was still impossible to sort out all the forces that gave public interest to the King's great matter, but one was the increasing recognition of the dignity of woman and with it a common concern for the dignity of marriage. Theoretically, the lordship of a house was still vested in the male, "and when he asserted it by fist or stick he was seldom blamed by public opinion." [6] But here was a case where even the King could not dispose of his wife without endless trouble and where his wife showed resolution to defend her rights and the rights of her daughter. It was an unequal struggle but it was a struggle just the same, and it marked a moment of change in the traditional liberties of the husband.

Already English women enjoyed a freedom which was the marvel of foreign visitors. No one seems to have raised serious eyebrows over their conduct in public or their practice of going where they wanted and doing what they pleased. "Married women especially, either alone or with a female companion, would accept invitations to dine, not only from an Englishman but from a foreigner as well. It was said to be the custom, after having spoken once or twice to any woman, on meeting her again in the street 'to take her to a tavern where all persons go without any reserve, or some other place, the husband not taking it amiss but remaining obliged to you and always thanking you, and if he sees you with her he departs.' " [7]

Perhaps all this might serve further to show the looseness of marriage, but it also showed the independence and self-reliance of English women. General agreement among visitors was to be found on their attractiveness, their complexions, and their ready wit; and it was said that "in no respect were they inferior to the women of Siena or any of the most esteemed in Italy" and that "only at Augsburg were their equals to be seen." The women of England could not be ignored as women, and circumstances now demanded that men regard them as something more than inferior creatures. Arguments even began to be advanced for their education. Women managed great households and handled household accounts, all of which made it worth while to improve their minds and skills. If they were educated, they could not only do their chores well but could write their husbands without the aid of a secretary. References began to appear in the writings of the day to the "new woman," and, as usual, her cause was both advanced and retarded by those who asserted and proved that a woman could do anything a man could do, and often do it better. One writer reports that he had known the records of "more than a thousand women who have been excellently seen in divinity, in philosophy, in physics, in music, in painting and in all sciences." Another spoke of women who could "play at tennis, practise feats of arms, ride, hunt, and do (in a manner) all the exercises besides that a gentleman can do." [8]

With woman ascendant and struggling to release herself still further from old tyrannies, it is not surprising that a great deal of the weight of public opinion sided now with the woman who was Queen and was also a wife who showed that she intended to stick by her canons. From the standpoint of the vigorous and assertive women of England, Catherine was to be thought of not merely as Henry's queen but also as Mrs. Tudor.

In the circumstances, the zeal which Wolsey displayed in the King's cause served to inflame the people all the more against him. For at this stage Catherine still considered the Cardinal the author of the King's conscience and the goad in the proceedings against her. The Cardinal faced, on the one hand, the wrath of his King if it were suspected for one moment that his efforts were halfhearted or slack, and, on the other hand, the resentment of countryfolk and housewives if he pushed the King's cause with his accustomed earnestness. Regarded as responsible for the King's action, he would be visited with blame one way or another, however matters went.

Tied in with the obloquy of the Cardinal for his labors to gain the King's objective was the further obloquy of the treaty with France; and for this he was responsible too. He had made peace with England's natural foe and, to compound the felony of judgment, had now linked England in an unholy alliance with France against the Emperor. He became identified in the popular mind with two causes that riled the English. And the English when riled, either as a nation dealing with a recalcitrant Pope or as individual villagers and artisans resisting an unpopular government, were not to be regarded without caution.

Recollection of the insurrections against the Amicable Loan still remained fresh among governors and governed. There was always a chance, which had to be reckoned with, that a people which produced Wat Tyler and Jack Cade and had spent thirty-five years out of the past hundred fighting among themselves, would flair into revolt. The Spanish ambassador, Mendoza, wrote to his government that the King's cause was so unpopular that "if six or seven thousand men were to land on the coast of Cornwall, prepared to espouse Catherine's cause, they would be joined at once by 40,000 Englishmen." [9]

These words may have been written with more hope than reason, but Mendoza's feeling for English sentiment was shared by other foreign observers. The Milanese ambassador wrote his government that if the King's cause succeeded and Henry married Anne Boleyn, "the population here will rebel." [10] The Cardinal had to face the fact that Catherine's cause enjoyed wide popular support and that this support might at any time become violent.

Part of the English esteem for Catherine, to be sure, came from the reflected glory of her nephew the Emperor — from the fact that the English sold their goods abroad to the Emperor's dominions. It is hard to tell where trade left off and affection began, but there is much to show that the English also loved and respected Catherine as a person. When she had first arrived in England, the common people had taken her to their unaffected hearts long before there was any economic reason to champion her cause. Mattingly tells how they received her when she came to marry Prince Arthur: "Here and there knots of yokels lined the road, staring fixedly, shouting cheerful, incomprehensible greetings; at every stage the local magnates rode in . . . beefy, red-necked, self-important squires with voices like Andalusian bulls, and weather-beaten, long-toothed wives, as assured and nearly as aggressively masculine as their husbands, a boisterous, excitable, demonstrative people, given to loud laughter and bellowing rages and much promiscuous kissing, but, for all their queer manners and appearances, genuinely eager to make a foreign Princess feel at home." [11]

As a wife Catherine had been no less dutiful than as a regent and ruler. She had sought always the happiness and pleasure of the King, bearing him children like a peasant, attending his every need, comporting herself with dignity, and engaging in those activities of the home which made her exemplary and, somehow, thoroughly English. Devout and given to pious practices, she too had a conscience, though of a more conventional sort than her husband's.

If more than Catherine's conduct were needed to imbed her firmly in the hearts of the English, it was provided now by her wretchedness. Outwardly the King, following the Cardinal's advice, continued to treat her with ceremonious courtesy. And she continued to dissemble her discouragement and to cover her heartbreak. The loneliness which had been her appointed lot during the dismal years after Prince Arthur's death returned to isolate her from all that lent meaning to her life as a woman. She would never bear another child, and she had missed fulfillment by failing to give her husband his expected heir. It was a disappointment which the times would not let her forget and her husband would not forgive. She had been forced to observe dutifully the ceremonies by which her husband's bastard son, Henry Fitzroy, was made Duke of Richmond. She had not possessed her husband to the exclusion of other women. His eye had wandered, she being eight years older and never competitively attractive. As early as 1515 a Venetian had described her as "rather ugly than otherwise." And the King of France had brutally remarked: "My brother of England has no son because, although a young and handsome man, he keeps an old and ugly wife." [12]

Prematurely old, her figure loosened and splayed by frequent pregnancies, ever crowded aside as her husband's adviser in statecraft by Wolsey with his French addiction, Catherine had only one possession as a wife and mother — and that was the Princess Mary. On her she lavished her affection, and in training her she showed her power and skill as a mother. Mary was a slender child with a profusion of flaxen ringlets. At ten she could converse fluently in French, Italian, Spanish, and Latin. Her father admired the child, which afforded the mother some satisfaction, and he had been able, in lieu of a male child, to offer her here and there as a marriage hostage for the good of England. Thus she was not without usefulness in the royal scheme of things, but to her mother she was the center of all living and affection; the two were constantly together.

Near the time of Catherine's disappointment, even the Princess Mary was taken from her. It was a political custom for the Princess of Wales to hold a kind of toy court at Ludlow, and in the year 1526 the child had been sent there. Catherine was left alone at the moment she needed companionship most. Even the Emperor her nephew had neglected her for affairs of state; late in 1526 she wrote him plaintively: "For upwards of two years I have had no letters from Spain. And yet I am sure I deserve not this treatment . . ." [13]

In brilliant contrast to the drab and somber figure of the King's discarded wife, who possessed only the virtues taught by the Church and admired by the State, was the flashing figure of the other woman seen more and more often with the King — Anne Boleyn. What she possessed, Henry knew best; but she had one quality above all that had struck others before she smote the King: her gaiety. She appears to have been gay rather than vivacious, for her cheerfulness had vitality that came from roots and was not merely the kind that awaits a royal audience or a command performance. A French writer speaks of her later, and perhaps with the reminiscent vitality of an old man, as "the fairest and most bewitching of all the lovely dames at the French court in my time. She possessed a great talent for poetry, and when she sang, like a second Orpheus, she would have made bears and wolves attentive. She likewise danced the English dances, leaping and gliding with infinite grace and agility . . . She harped better than King David and handled cleverly both lute and rebec. She dressed with marvellous taste and devised new modes . . ." [14]

Anne might keep herself in ignorance about bothersome affairs of state and in conversation with him refer to a man who had been to Rome with Stephen Gardiner as "Master Stephens," but possibly her very distaste for business added to her appeal. She was friendly enough to brighten any gathering and, as one writer puts it, "in the sparkle of her talk the old of heart felt young and fresh." [15]

Such a creature would naturally have appealed to Henry as a part of his court, even if she had not struck a personal nerve in the royal heart. When she returned from France and came to court, Henry had completed thirteen years of married life with a woman of almost forbidding virtue and, with all this virtue, no communicable vitality. True, Henry had had his excursions, one of them with Anne's sister Mary; at the moment he had just finished off another mistress, Elizabeth Blount, and he was free to look around with a quick and appraising eye, his scruples of conscience not at this time being conspicuous.

Oddly, though, Anne Boleyn had scruples of her own, already strong and conventional. She had spent some six years at an impressionable period of her life with the good Queen Claude of France, a woman as pious and domestic as Queen Catherine of England. Queen Claude, it is recorded, "was always surrounded by a number of young ladies who walked in procession with her to Mass and formed part of her State whenever she appeared in public. In private life she directed their labors at the loom or in the embroidery frame, and endeavored by every means in her power to give a virtuous and devotional bias to their thoughts and conversation." To stress the strictness of the regimen, "the society of gentlemen was forbidden to these maidens." [16]

Anne had fitted into the rigid and pious scheme at Claude's court without protest; indeed she seems to have been strongly influenced by Claude's devoutness. Francis wrote his ambassador in London that she was a credit to her father, adding: "She is discreet and modest; and it is hinted amongst the court ladies that she desires above all things to be a nun. This I should regret." [17] Coming from a busy judge of womanflesh, this last sentence was a tribute.

Henry was later to urge Catherine to enter a religious house for the good of her soul and his own, but there is no record that he gave Anne Boleyn any encouragement to become a nun. If she dropped her desire to become a nun, she at least kept her sense of basic decorum amid the pleasures of the English court. There was more than a touch of the "new woman" in her, an eagerness to be free and at the same time to choose among the acts that freedom allowed. She was content with the frivolities of the court as long as these did not interfere with the serious business of getting a husband; she carried around in her not too remarkable mind the romantic notion that love and marriage should go together, a notion that in her day was not old enough to have become quaint. The plan to assign her to a practical and political marriage with the Earl of Ormond, which Henry and Wolsey had discussed before they ever saw her, came to nought. That this kind of marriage, designed for some end of use to the State rather than the contracting parties, did not appeal to her is indicated by the fact that she formed a deep attachment to the young Lord Percy and her marriage agreement with him was broken only by the King's command.

Both her charm and her strict ideas about marriage combined to lure her into a situation from which she could extricate herself only by becoming Queen of England. It was not a situation she contrived or created but one into which she was drawn — and chiefly by the King. His ardent attention at first disturbed her, and her resistance sorely disturbed him. Her audacity in refusing his amorous advances bewildered Henry and fascinated him like a fire. In her reply to one of the first of a series of letters he wrote her, she told him: "Your wife I cannot be because you have a queen already. Your mistress I will not be."

It was not easy to stand off an imperious prince without insulting him and involving herself and her family in the wake of his wrath. The history of the period would have been much simpler if she had accepted the favor of the royal bedfellow and left the King's conscience untroubled. But Anne, for all her irrepressible gaiety, was a strict and proper person and she could only say to the King: "I beseech your Highness to desist in writing to me . . . I will rather lose my life than my virtue, which will be the greatest and best part of the dowry I shall bring to my husband . . ." [18]

Henry was not one to be brushed aside by contrary sentiments. His ardor grew. The possession of Anne Boleyn became the main object of his life. The extent of his passion and of his commitment to her may be seen in the following letter: "I have been in great agony about the contents of your letters, not knowing whether to construe them to my disadvantage . . . or to my advantage. I beg to know expressly your intentions touching the love between us. Necessity compels me to obtain this answer, having been more than a year wounded by the dart of love, and not sure whether I shall fail or find a place in your affection. This has prevented me naming you my mistress; for if you love me with no more than ordinary love, the name is not appropriate to you, for it denotes a singularity far from the common. But if it pleases you to do the office of a true, loyal mistress, and give yourself body and heart, to me, who have been and mean to be your loyal servant, I promise you not only the name but that I shall make you my sole mistress, remove all others from my affection, and serve you only. Give me a full answer on which I can rely; and if you do not answer by letter, appoint some place where I can have it by word of mouth." [19]

Not exactly a king speaking to a subject. Nor is this: "I and my heart put ourselves in your hands. Let not absence lessen your affection, for it causes us more pain than ever I should have thought, reminding us of a point of astronomy that the longer the days are, the further off is the sun, and yet the heat is all the greater. So it is with our love, which keeps its fervour in absence, at least on our side. Prolonged absence would be intolerable, but for my firm hope of your indissoluble affection. As I cannot be with you in person, I send you my picture set in bracelets." [20]

C H A P T E R   I X

DELAY had withered Henry's first robust hope of a prompt annulment. But in the spring of 1528 his affairs appeared at last to be in good train, for the competent Cardinal of York had wrung from the Pope, captive of the Emperor though he still was in effect, a commission for the hearing of the cause in England. Joined with Wolsey in a legatine court to decide the King's request would be another cardinal thoroughly acceptable to the King. He was Cardinal Lorenzo Campeggio, a great canonist who knew the insides of the law.

An Italian, Campeggio was nonetheless acquainted with the English landscape from a sojourn as papal Legate to Henry ten years before. He was also acquainted with Henry VIII, Catherine, and Wolsey. He had himself enjoyed a fruitful marriage before he became Cardinal, and he would not rattle the dry leaves of ecclesiastical righteousness without some concern with the human factors involved. Henry had conferred upon him the bishopric of Salisbury in 1524, and it might well be thought that the temporalities and revenues derived therefrom, enjoyed during the past four years which had been so lean in Rome, would attach him with vines of obligation to the King. Certainly he had no occasion to bear the Emperor or his vandal associates any good will. In the sack of the Eternal City his own house had been plundered, all his possessions taken, and he had been forced to redeem his life with a large sum of money.[1]

Wolsey, in his choice of a fellow judge tacitly obliged to render a predetermined judgment, had apparently done well. Indeed, the qualities that made Campeggio lean toward the King might well make up for some of the shortcomings of the commission under which the Pope sent him. Wolsey had expressed himself, after some sagacious reluctance, as satisfied with this commission. It authorized the two Legates to try the case and pronounce sentence.[2] Either Legate might in fact pronounce sentence

388

if the other declined, and no appeal was to be allowed from the jurisdiction of this legatine court.³ What more could the King or his obedient servant want? The commission looked as solid as a castle. But what Wolsey had sought through his agents was a decision made in the King's favor by the Pope and a commission which required that the Legates ostensibly arrive at a decision which had already been made by the Pope. There was nothing in the commission which had been granted to keep the Pope from recalling the case to Rome before a decision should be reached; nothing to show publicly where the Pope stood.

To be sure, Clement did reinforce the open commission with a decretal commission saying that he would not recall the case, but this instrument was to be shown only to Henry and Wolsey and not to the court. Likewise in secret the Pope gave Wolsey a written promise "that he would not revoke, or do anything to invalidate, the commission, but would confirm the cardinals' decision." ⁴

In point of fact, there was nothing certain or trustworthy about the whole elaborate arrangement. It was a trellis for the King's and the Cardinal's hopes; that was all. So it was that in the ominous spring of 1528, when even the weather appeared to be hostile, Wolsey found himself actually no nearer the satisfaction of his King's aching conscience than he had been a year before. He was living on appearances, living beyond his means of power, outwardly as glorious and successful as ever, yet with no staff or rod to comfort him in the murky course he had to follow.

A man less accustomed to living off the fat of his confidence, less sustained by the power of positive thinking, would have shown signs of sheepishness at a paper that gave no more promise than the commission. Not Wolsey. He sought instead to act on it, to make it suffice. Whatever Wolsey's theology, he had a profound religious belief in assiduity, especially letter writing. If only he wrote enough letters to enough people about enough things, all matters would be set right, whether they concerned his colleges or the tragedy of enclosures or the King. Such activity showed the strange and urgent need of a man isolated from normal communication and thrown back on the device of one-way communication with his subalterns. Letters to him were reports; letters from him were instructions.

Thus Wolsey's first industrious move when Clement promised to designate Campeggio in May of 1528 was to write his fellow Legate a letter. It urged haste. And, as usual, the Cardinal was ready with a plan to implement his request. Horses, mules, and money for the journey would be waiting in France and it would be well if Campeggio started at once. To cheer his prospect, Wolsey even offered to meet him in France and accompany him on the rest of the journey.[5] But Campeggio had his own problems. His affairs were still in poor order as a result of the sack of Rome. Besides, he was ill and in no condition to undertake an arduous journey. He was gnarled by gout, suffering great pain even under the best of circumstances, and his progress once begun would be as slow as growth.

Again it was a case where the King's great matter wore the aspect of order but seethed underneath with problems. A commission had been granted, the proper Legate named to sit with Wolsey, this Legate was en route to London. But the Legate was ill, and his delay would serve the suspected purposes of the Pope to postpone judgment as long as possible and thwart the avowed purpose of the King to get justice speedily.

Solutions had a way now of begetting illegitimate minor problems for which no provision had been made. One of these appeared when the reliable Campeggio, even before he left on his tedious journey, began to display a gilt-edged independence.[6] When Wolsey had his agents press upon the Cardinal of San Tommaso a sum of expense money to make the trip more commodious, he kindly refused the offer, saying that he would take no more than he needed for horses and mules and the modest outlay the trip required. And when Clerk, the English agent involved in the transaction in Italy, explained that such a refusal would not be understood by the King and that the obloquy of it would be visited upon the King's messenger, Campeggio still refused, saying that he had quite enough. Apparently six hundred ducats meant nothing to him. Such irregular and unexpected behavior in a cardinal might be an unaccountable peculiarity of which no serious notice should be taken; or it might, if one thought about it hard, augur ill for the King's cause.

No single incident was an omen, but the year which had begun so wretchedly for Wolsey worsened as the days wore on. It had been agreed, as a part of the alliance with France, that war be made on the Emperor and that he be given proper defiance. In January of 1528 the clarion-voiced Clarencieux was sent forward on this mission, joined by the herald of France. Arriving at the Emperor's court, the two demanded an audience. They found His Imperial Majesty seated "with great solemnity on his Throne, attended by all his Grandees." In his harangue Clarencieux recited the reasons why Henry had chosen the path of war, including the Emperor's failure to pay his debts. At the end of his stern rebuke in the King's behalf, he gave notice that Henry would make war on land and sea against the dominions of the Emperor.[7]

It was all done according to accepted form and in proper style. Yet, oddly, no one took the matter seriously, and no one seemed inclined to care whether there was a war. Indeed the whole affair was tinged with the comic, and the comic with the improbable. His Imperial Majesty received the oration of Clarencieux with appropriate decorum, saying that he disliked having the King of England as an enemy and being at pains to lay the blame for the unhappy rupture between him and Henry on Cardinal Wolsey. To the French herald, however, the Emperor showed no politeness, taxing Francis with the charge that the French King had dealt with him falsely and basely. This charge the French herald carried to his master, and Francis in turn sent the herald back again, this time with a paper containing a written challenge, "wherein the King of France gave the Emperor the Lie, and demanded the field of battle to fight him hand to hand." The herald continued to pass back and forth for an interval, carrying charges and challenges, and thunderous threats sheathed in technicalities. The war of heraldic words went on for months, but the King of France and the Emperor of the Romans never came to blows.

Nor did the English and the Imperialists. War might be all right as a part of a diplomatic game, but business was business, and a war against the dominions of the Emperor in the Low Countries would be war against England's best customers. Merchants refused to buy wool, hoping to stir the wool-gatherers to an insurrection. Wolsey called some of them before him, saying that he knew what they conspired to do and that they knew where the Tower was. They cried for mercy, says du Bellay, and promised that at the next Wednesday's market they would buy — whatever the price demanded. Apparently the conspiracy had been nipped. "But," du Bellay adds, "you may be sure Wolsey is playing a terrible game, for I believe he is the only Englishman that wishes a war with Flanders." [8]

Trade was paralyzed. By March, conditions had reached a point of panic. Large stocks of cloth in search of a market piled up in Blackwell Hall.[9] Back along the line, like blocks being toppled over, went the effects of lost outlets. Workmen were discharged in Norfolk, and clothiers closed their shops. London merchants refused to buy wool they could not sell to clothiers who could not sell cloth. Wolsey tried to meet the crisis by decree. He sent down orders that no clothier should discharge his workmen. But it was a case where the magic of words would not work its spell. More than the cloth trade was disturbed. Eastern county farmers who sold their butter and cheese, their red herrings and sprats, had lost their foreign markets too — and at the very time when prices were high.[10]

And who had started all this creeping paralysis of trade? The Cardinal of York, who had sent the English master-at-arms to fling defiance at the

Emperor. The Cardinal was the maker of the mischief that affected every home. A small revolt broke out in Kent, where one would expect it. A rising of the clothiers was reported in Wiltshire. The Cardinal was the target of all the hostility, and there was rumor of a plot to seize him and turn him adrift in a boat with holes bored in it.[11]

Against threats both real and idle the Cardinal found it expedient to yield. It became necessary to quiet the murmurs of the people, and this was done by an agreement strange in the annals of war: trade with Flanders would go on as usual and as if there were no war. Under such genial and businesslike circumstances hostilities were out of the question, and by summer the Cardinal's war had been patched up with a truce and the defiance of the Emperor withdrawn.

But the country could not be as easily patched up as a truce. Mere withdrawal of an ill-advised defiance would not halt the discontents it had either started or accelerated. By association now, all misfortunes visited upon the realm were seen to be the fault of the government, which is to say, the Cardinal. Acts of nature past and present came to be construed to be a part of the diabolical intent of the man who had roped England to the court of France and was now busy, men said, trying to separate England's king and queen and make a bastard of the Princess Mary. Men in hardship and misery, short of corn, could cry out bitterly against English weather, but it was an old and futile cry against something high and far away. It did little good to shake a fist at a cloud. It was more of a release to blame in loud talk an arrogant politician and prelate whose life was so cushioned that he could not share the fare of the common man. In this frightful summer of 1528 the Cardinal got the blame for the shortage of corn, for the facts that the bread carts had to be guarded, that hunger stalked the roads, that commissioners had to be sent out to determine the amount of grain every man possessed, that vagabonds increased.

For six gruesome years the weather had withdrawn its favor from the English, as if by intent, and the sadness of those years now contributed to the plight of the people — and by indirection to the plight of the Cardinal. What was a government for if not to bear the sins of nature and the complaints of the populace? Years of drouth had stricken the land. In those implacable years cattle had been driven as far as fifteen miles to water. They had died by the score, and the breeding stock left was poor and scrawny. Ponds had shriveled to caked mud, and the fish had perished along with the water fowl, so that the national diet lost its supplement as well as much of its substance. Then when these years of black drouth had taken their toll, there came a year when the land was drenched with floods. In the winter of 1526-27 it had rained from November through January; there followed a reminder of drouth until April, and then rains came again and did not let up for eight weeks. Grains rotted in the fields and fodder spoiled, and the animals that survived the drouth now fell victim to a cattle plague called murrain.[12]

There was a creepy, invisible terror about murrain, a term made up of earlier words suggesting *death* and *murder*. It was more than a plague that struck oxen, and occasionally sheep, with sudden ferocity. It carried with it the suggestion of demons at work in the countryside, and its effects were enough to dismay the strongest. Beasts affected had sunken eyes and a discharge from nose, mouth, and eyes. They were given to shivering fits which recorded their inner misery and sense of death, as if they shuddered. Breathing was labored from the onset of the disease, and generally animals stricken with it were dead in a few days. The breath was bad, and sores appeared around the mouth. The course of murrain was accompanied by a dry, harsh cough that would not let men forget suffering. The sight and sound of death coming from the fields and sheds spread a kind of terror. Murrain seemed somehow to dramatize mortality and to show man at the mercy of the animal, his dependence on the beast.

The growing season of 1528 showed no better promise than the year before, for the rains came again in too much abundance, and there was now an accumulation of evils to make hunger as familiar a figure as the vagabonds along the road. A kingdom usually rich and verdant and teeming with animal life ached from repeated afflictions and suffered the justice of extremes, and the people who had confidently drawn their plenty from a beneficent land looked bitterly at the one who might be held accountable for prices and shortages.

The government's measures for dealing with the effects of dislocations caused by drouth and flood could not have added to the popularity of the Cardinal. Laws against regrating — hoarding for resale — were fiercely enforced. Forestalling animals — selling through several hands at increasing profits — brought sharp action from the law. Severe measures, together with the work of the commissioners who pried into the amount of grain a man had, brought home to the people the punitive and regulatory power of the government. And the man in the red hat who had painstakingly identified himself with the government paid the penalty of assumed and flaunted responsibility.

That murmurings would rise against Wolsey as the man who stood between the people and the King was natural. He must receive and absorb their complaints now, their railing against misfortune. It was part of his function as Lord Chancellor to serve as a kind of effigy for the King, sparing the King actual contact with the populace and keeping the royal person sacrosanct.

Yet the mutterings now had in them a tone not proper to be directed at a dignitary of government; they seemed to be directed at a person and not an office, at a man who strutted about in the flamboyant finery of a prelate and the glaring red of a prince of Rome while corn was dear and money hard to come by and vagabonds stalked the roads and infested the alehouses and poverty became the captain of men's thoughts. Suddenly the son of an innkeeper and grazier, who had risen to be the shield of the King, began to seem personally as well as officially offensive: the very manner of his living implied a disregard for the common lot, and the splendor of his palaces and the stateliness with which he moved through London or across to Calais, acceptable in better times as a part of the show that was part of the dazzle of the court, now offered an affront to a public suffering from diminished prosperity in some ranks and from actual hunger in others.

The temper of the people had altered while the Cardinal was too energetically engaged in administering the regime to revise his values or see the changed look in men's eyes as he passed through the smells of the crowd, his protective orange stuffed with spices held beneath his nostrils. He refused to smell, thus deadening a sense that might have told him much. His eyes were busy with paper and his ears with the sound of his own voice. The man from Ipswich had in effect forsaken the woolsack of his father; he had risen too high to see what went on below, to observe that a "more frugal, prosaic and commercial element was daily gathering strength and ascendancy" and that this element "found itself more in conformity with the severe, rigid, and economic spirit of Protestantism than with the sumptuous ritual of the ancient Church, or the dazzling amusements of the court." [13]

In this summer of discontent, while Campeggio tarried on his way and cattle sickened and died and bread carts had to be guarded and the rains came malignantly again, a new evil appeared to tower over all the others. The sweat returned. There is no record that the people blamed the Cardinal for that, but it added horribly to the confusion of living, a confusion for which he was blamed.

There were bewildering similarities between murrain among the cattle and the sweating sickness among those to whom God had given dominion over the beasts of the field. It was as if the piteous affliction of animals had prophesied the coming plight of man. As in the case of murrain, the sweat spread terror and dismay by the peculiar behavior it induced in its victims. It was brief and violent, and its severity this time was greater than it had been twelve years before, when, according to du Bellay, ten thousand persons had died in ten or twelve days.[14] Again it seemed to pass over the poor and lowly in hovels and garrets and fetch out the well-to-do and those about the court. This time it confined itself to the counties near London, and it did not appear to spread, for merchants did not carry it with them when they went abroad, and Englishmen afflicted in Calais did not carry the infection to Gravelines, a dozen miles away. Known in France and Flanders as the King of England's Sickness, it was accepted abroad and in the King's dominions as a peculiarly English affliction. And therein lay the enervating horror of it. It was a disease of threat and terror, a plague visited on England as specifically and locally and with as much clean accuracy as any of those the Lord had visited upon Pharaoh. The fact that it would not yield reliably to any known medication or treatment gave it more than ever the aspects of something supernatural. One man's remedy was another man's death. There was no defense save in the minds of men, and its devastation was greatest where men, hearing of its onslaught, died from the fear of fear.

What part fear played in the spread and effects of the sweating sickness is told by Brian Tuke, the King's secretary at the time. Tuke said that the disease was spread mainly by report, "for when a whole man comes from London and talks of the sweat, the same night all the town is full of it, and thus it spreads as the fame runs. It came in this way from Sussex to London, and a thousand fell ill in a night after the news was spread." Children, lacking the terror of it, did not get the disease.[15]

The sweat struck London in June at the time when the truce was drawn with Flanders, so that a problem more terrible almost to the day replaced one that had been solved. The French ambassador, du Bellay, wrote on June 18: "Yesterday going to swear the truce, we saw them as thick as flies rushing from the streets and shops into their houses to take the sweat, whenever they felt ill. I found the Ambassador of Milan leaving his lodgings in great haste because two or three had been suddenly attacked." At the time he wrote only two thousand in London were said to be ill of the sweat, but a few days later du Bellay reports that the number had grown to forty thousand. Of these but two thousand had died, but many had died in three or four hours, and even if the disease carried with it no high incidence of mortality it wrought the devastation of impending disaster.[16] The notaries had a fine time of it. One observer said he thought a hundred thousand wills had been made, "for those who were dying became quite foolish the moment they fell ill." [17]

Public assemblies were out of the question. Wolsey came to Westminster to open a term of his Court in the Star Chamber, but the sweat had lessened the demand for justice, and men's quarrels seemed prosaic in the presence of the great affliction. It was said that the Legate "immediately bridled his horses again; there will be no term, everyone is terribly amazed." [18]

Henry, frightened out of his wits but not out of his purpose, moved from place to place, fleeing the King of England's Sickness. His Council was dispersed; only the Cardinal remained at his post, dispatching such business as he could, trying to cope with the problems of a lingering war and a hasty truce, and all the while waiting for Campeggio.

Campeggio's arrival, bringing with it the resolution of the King's difficulty, was to be longed for more devoutly every day, now that Englishmen were dropping down all around in the undignified death of the sweat. There prevailed a mood of mortality and a dread uncertainty about the future. The plague brought a stern reminder, too, that the King was still without an heir and could hope for one only through a new queen. The King himself remained unsullied by the sickness, but he was never more tenderly conscious of his royal person and its value to the kingdom. He escaped in no small part through evasive action, moving restlessly from manor to manor, having dismissed most of his entourage, keeping only a few servants. His concern calls in question Brian Tuke's plausible theory that the sweat was spread by terror: if fear had been a ruling factor in susceptibility, Henry would surely have been attacked. The very name and view of the sweat was so "terrible and fearful to his Highness' ears that he dare in no wise approach unto the place where it is noised to have been . . ." [19]

The King at last came to rest twenty miles from London "at a house built by Wolsey, finding removals useless. I hear he has made his will, and taken the sacraments, for fear of sudden death. However, he is not ill." The house where he settled was Tittenhanger, and here Henry established himself with some apparent sense of security and satisfaction, writing to commend Wolsey on the state of the house and the wholesomeness of the air there and remarking on "how commodious it is for such a time of sickness as this is." Yet he still took no chances with the royal body, keeping great fires roaring to hold back the infection, although it was technically summer, and taking many of his meals apart in a tower of the house with his favorite doctor.[20]

In general, Henry presented a good many of the aspects of a fugitive. In spite of his flight and stately precautions, he showed withal a sturdy and cheerful countenance in his hideout, sustained by abundant vitality. Withdrawn from the court and the frivolities of courtiers' chatter, he spent a great deal of time in religious observance, hearing three Masses daily, assessing his soul and readying it for eternity, and working on revisions of revisions of what his secretary refers to as "the book of his will." His behavior suggests a conviction that preparedness for death is the best guarantee of life, for he went through all the elaborate purification of a man who is about to take his spirit and leave his carcass. Certainly no man ever fitted himself more studiously for the last journey; nor did Henry again. There was something positive and forthright about the way he faced death, as if to stare it down.

His last will and testament became a kind of icon, and he was before it unceasingly. He proposed to send Wolsey a copy of his will, and one of the men working with him on it wrote that when Wolsey saw it His Grace would "see and perceive the trusty and hearty mind that he hath unto you, above all men living . . ." [21]

As the days passed and the King did not get the sweat, he became more confident of his health, and before long he was recommending royal home remedies. In particular he was solicitous of the Cardinal's health, as well he might be, the whole burden of public business in an hour of panic having fallen upon Wolsey's shoulders. Henry begged him to stay out of the air, keep only a small and clean company near him, "use small suppers, drink little wine, and take once a week the pills of Rasis . . ." He accompanied his advice with drugs, herbs, and preservatives, and he urged my lord of York to "put apart fear and fantasies" and make as merry as the contagion would allow.[22]

So it was that while Wolsey was waiting for Campeggio and trying to carry on the manifold duties of his offices, he had at least the firm consolation of the King's faith. He needed it. Wolsey himself had been racked by the sweat in 1517; and now that the pestilence stalked again, he could not but feel anxiety when he heard reports of this swift devastation. At the residence of the Archbishop of Canterbury eighteen persons died in four hours. Wolsey was a man whose energy appears to have been created by exigent circumstances rather than supplied by good health. Even some of the King's kindest inquiries after his health and some of the gentlest expressions of interest were so conveyed as to remind the Cardinal of his frailty. Once Henry instructed Dr. Bell to say to him: "The King often wishes your heart were as good as his is." [23]

Wolsey tried to carry on the increasingly complicated business of the government from his residence at York Place near Westminster, receiving and sending dispatches, keeping the King informed, talking with foreign diplomats, who, being un-English, had no fear of the sweat. Once when the French ambassador was walking with Wolsey in his garden there, word was brought that five of the Cardinal's household had taken the sweat.[24] The interview ended abruptly; even business of state could not divert the Cardinal from the care of his servants. It was reported later that only four men in Wolsey's great household remained well, and at last Wolsey sought sanctuary at Hampton Court, taking with him only a few attendants and fortifying the walls and the gardens against intruders. He became so inaccessible now that du Bellay suggested in his reports that he might have to speak to the Cardinal through a trumpet.

In one minor respect the sweat brought a good effect. It offered at least temporary distraction from the other great problem that rent the Cardinal's mind. There was something almost clean and comforting about a simple problem of life and death. Temporarily at least the question of survival took possession of men's minds in and around London, and the King's great matter and the Cardinal's great mistake in starting a war were swallowed up by a sea of common misery. But the sweat passed as mysteriously as it came; by mid-July its worst ravages were over, the quick had buried the dead, and a populace, albeit shaken, was ready to resume its normal worries. The Cardinal had had a strange interlude of new problems and frustrations, but now the old ones were rudely back.

Nothing had been changed, and much had been intensified. The land was alive and working with the lice of unrest and discontent. Conditions as well as alien books had infested men's minds with unhealthy ideas and brought distemper to their spirits. A period of convulsive mortality had served to show all the more forcibly the threat of a disputed succession and a renewal of the Wars of the Roses. But most important of all, the Cardinal faced the fact that the problem of Henry's annulment had not changed in the least. Henry's conscience, far from showing any remorse around the edges or any wear and tear in the middle, had become all the more groomed and sanctified while he dodged death.

Further, all the principals were still alive. Death had feinted at Anne Boleyn, but that was all. She had been one of the first to be stricken at the time Henry broke up his court. Henry wrote her at once to acknowledge "the most afflicting news possible" and to say that he was grieved "to hear of my mistress's sickness, whose health I desire as my own." It distressed him that under the circumstances he might have to

398

"suffer longer that absence which has already given me so much pain." [25] With this letter he sent his personal physician, "praying God he may soon make you well, and I shall love him the better." A few days later he wrote that his doubts of her health had troubled him extremely, adding, "I should scarcely have had any quiet had I not received some news of you." He then goes on to offer her the consoling thought that few women have suffered from the sweat; "what is more, none of our Court, and few elsewhere, have died of it." [26]

Anne was spared. But another woman died, and her death was to create an effect which my lord of York, with all his capacity for anticipating troubles, had not expected. The woman who died was the abbess of a nunnery of Benedictine sisters near the market town of Wilton, seventy miles from London. Her death vacated a position which the brother of Mary Boleyn's husband sought for his sister, Elinor Carey, one of the nuns. Anne promoted the matter with the King. But an inquiry held at Wilton uncovered the fact that Dame Elinor was not fit on grounds of turpitude, being by her own confession the mother of two children born out of wedlock. The details of the woman's character were reported to Henry, who immediately wrote Mistress Anne a letter, showing a mind as pure as the snow on a convent roof. "I would not for all the gold in the world cloak your conscience nor mine," he said, "to make her ruler of a house which is of so ungodly demeanor." And he is sure that Anne would not want him to "distain mine honour" by such an appointment.[27]

Wolsey proposed that the election fall upon the prioress, Dame Isabel Jordon, who, as one writer puts it, was at least advanced in years. Anne and her kinsmen put forth charges against Dame Isabel and so persuaded the King that he finally wrote Anne that, to do her pleasure, neither candidate would have the appointment.

Of this promise my lord of York apparently was unaware. For he went ahead and nominated Isabel Jordon, being assured that most of the convent favored the prioress and that she was well connected. When her name went to the King for confirmation, Wolsey got the first intimation of the royal displeasure. He began at once to make excuses and to plead ignorance of the King's intentions. It was a most unhappy tactic. It opened the sluice gates of Henry's mind, and much that had been pent up there for a long time now came out in a rhetorical torrent. Fresh from his escape from the sweat, confident in his own righteousness, Henry wrote Wolsey a letter such as no man had ever written the Cardinal before. It was a letter lecturing him as he had lectured Anne on the principles of upright conduct, and it contained a summary passage that would have crushed a bolder spirit than Wolsey's: "Ah! my lord, it is a double offense, both to do ill and color it too; but with men that have wit it cannot be accepted so. Wherefore, good my Lord, use that way no more with me, for there is no man living that more hateth it." [28]

These severe words were part of a long letter, a king-size letter, in fact. The letter was inlaid with kindly terms and assurances that it carried no displeasure. But it did. This the King anticipated by going over it carefully, before it was sent, with John Hennege, a gentleman of his household and a friend of Wolsey's. After this talk it was the King's considered opinion that it was a proper letter from "a friend and master" and ought to be delivered. Hennege warned Wolsey and sought to prepare his mind for the rebuke, but neither the warning nor the loving words in the letter could prepare Wolsey. Indeed, the loving words made the force and severity all the greater. Here was a letter from a King who had at last come of age, who knew his mind as well as his will. It was written in the vigor of confidence from a young prince to an old man.

The letter reached Wolsey at a moment of despondency, when he was himself dispirited by the threat and reminders of the sweat, when he was exhausted by the grueling task of carrying on the business of the kingdom while the King himself had barricaded himself in the privacy of one of Wolsey's houses. The letter followed hard upon the heels of manifold expressions of solicitude and spoke of failings that involved his whole conduct. It was a letter written by a man who felt he had earned through long kindness the right to be stern and enjoyed that right by virtue of his position. Wolsey, who had so long listened to his master's voice, now heard it for the first time in harsh and humiliating terms.

An unforeseen trifle, an administrative error, a slip in process, had provoked the King to reveal his mind. The occasional assertiveness of the minister, where he had spoken his mind clearly, as in the case of the question of strategy over the siege of Boulogne or where he had sought to persuade the King against the annulment — these courageous stands had provoked nothing in the way of displeasure. But now, as is so often the case, the mistake he didn't realize he had made was the one that rose to smite him.

The real subject of the letter was not Wolsey's act in filling the vacancy created by the death of the Abbess of Wilton but Wolsey's busy presumption in dealing with the monasteries. The King's letter went on to a further section, which appeared almost in the nature of a postscript. It had the tone of while-I-am-about-it. This section of the letter showed how deeply in Henry's mind still rankled the rejection of the Amicable Loan and the part the religious houses played in that rejection; and it brought forth in accusing terms the one subject which was closest to Wolsey's heart: his colleges.

Word had reached the King's ear of contributions made by various religious houses to the founding of Cardinal College at Oxford. By this report, according to those who mumbled it abroad, Wolsey had granted houses that favored his enterprise special privileges and certain immunities to which they were not entitled. They had paid fees to agents sent to conduct a visitation under Wolsey's legatine authority. As Henry phrased the matter: "Surely this can hardly be with good conscience. For, and they were good, why should you take money? and if they were ill, it were a sinful act."

Henry apparently accepted the reports at face value: he was not asking for an explanation but delivering a sermon. The conscience of the Defender of the Faith had been touched to the quick of his pride. Wolsey had been able to extract money from monasteries that had stood out against the royal request for an Amicable Loan that might have enabled Henry to invade France. The King's letter goes on: "These same religious houses would not grant to their sovereign, in his necessity, not by a great deal, so much as they have done for the building of your college. These things bear shrewd appearance." The King instructs Wolsey to look to his agents who are "meddling with religious houses," as though Henry VIII could not endure the thought that anyone might mistreat a monastery.[29]

The letter ended with a flourish of genial terms, a bit of cheery personal news, a reminder that the Cardinal could set all matters right if he managed the King's great matter, and its last sentence read: "Written with the hand of him that is and shall be your loving sovereign lord, and friend, Henry R."

Wolsey's house had been disorganized by the sweat, his servants had been ill, the Council had been dispersed. The King had taken Brian Tuke to help with the drafting and redrafting of his will, leaving Wolsey with inferior and amateur assistants at a time when he most needed a competent staff. His best secretary, Stephen Gardiner, was still abroad, on loan in the King's service. The King kept himself at considerable distance from London and the difficulty of getting messengers back and forth involved delay and added immensely to the burdens and the confusion of the Cardinal's efforts to carry on the business of both State and Church.

Some of these extenuating circumstances were presented to the King in Wolsey's letter of reply; and the King was gracious enough to acknowledge them. "As touching the matter of Wilton," he said, "I marvel not that it overslipped you, as it did. But it is no great matter, standing the case as it doth. For it is yet in my hand, as I perceive by your letter . . ." The Cardinal had merely nominated an abbess, and he had sent his nomination to the King. He had made no appointment, had not in fact overstepped what a subject or a minister might be allowed to do. Henry admitted now that the fault "was not so great, seeing the election was but conditional."

The King's outburst had been out of all proportion to the provocation. Yet this was the alarming part of the whole affair. It was not that the Cardinal had made a great mistake, but that the King had taken him violently to task for a small one. Here was a warning that even a wayfaring man, a man without Wolsey's sensitiveness, might well have winced to see.

If the King had moderated his tone about the matter of Wilton, he had not abated one jot in his expressions about the use of monastery funds for Wolsey's educational enterprises. He reminds Wolsey that "there is a great murmuring of it throughout all the realm. They say," he goes on, "not that all that is ill gotten is bestowed on the College, but that the College is the cloak for covering all mischiefs. This grieveth me, I assure you, to hear it spoken of him, which I so entirely love. Wherefore methought I could do no less than thus friendly to admonish you." [30] He went on pointedly to admonish him against taking any further contributions from religious houses for the building of his college.

In one single deft stroke Henry had managed to demolish Wolsey's sanctuary, the inner citadel where, for all his public flamboyance, he kept himself. Wolsey's college at Oxford and the feeder college now abuilding night and day in his native Ipswich represented the carpentry of his noblest dreams. It is perhaps for this reason rather than for acquisitiveness that the deeds and charters were made to him and not to a corporation or a board. In all other departments of his life he was the servant of the King and he had surrendered his identity to the State; even his palaces were places for display and entertainment. He owed his positions and offices to the power of the King and the authority of the Pope. In both cases his worth came from being a part of something more worthy than he. His colleges, however, were to be the personal expression of his personal views, to show his mind rather than his influence, to reveal the man of affairs as an honorable intellectual. Thus they belonged to a part of his life and integrity which he had not surrendered either to His Highness or His Holiness.

Wolsey wrote an abject and submissive letter to the King, but for all its submissiveness it did point out that the reports of his exactions from religious houses were greatly exaggerated and that nothing corrupt had been done with his knowledge. He had, although he did not say it at the time, highhanded and unscrupulous agents who called on the religious houses, and the chances are that if the whole matter had been examined it would have been found that the rumors against the Cardinal carried a great deal of truth. Whatever the facts, Wolsey assured the King that there would be no further occasion "for ill speech, untrue report or judgment." To this end he wrote: "I promise to your Majesty that from henceforth, though I should be compelled to sell that I have and to live very straitly and barely, I, ne none other by my consent or knowledge, though the same be never so clearly, frankly, or friendly offered towards the building of the said college, or to any other mine use, shall take any-thing of any religious person, being exempt or not exempt . . . so that your poor Cardinal's conscience shall not be spotted, encumbered, or entangled . . ." [31]

The affair passed, and the King appeared to be appeased, but the rebuke had hurt Wolsey to the marrow. He was despondent long afterward and yielded little to the reassurance of friends that he still stood high in the royal favor. Nor did he take their advice that he seek a personal interview with Henry. The sweat lingered, though it was less severe in July, and Wolsey stayed busy with the business of his offices while the King re-mained at a distance. The old daily or frequent talks which had been the heart and soul of their relationship had passed, and the separation caused by the prevalence of the sweat made it impractical to renew former practices. There had come about an estrangement which made easy give-and-take impossible and the normal gestures of friendship awkward. Up to now Wolsey had paid homage to the King willingly and with cheer; now the King had reminded Wolsey sharply of the homage due. This made a world of difference.

Wolsey went on with outward energy, but he seemed now for the first time to be sluggish, to perform by rote and role, though as he shook himself and went through the motions he seemed to be pushing away from his mind the thought that his strength had departed from him. But his talk indicated, as it had not before, a sense of new values which his public character had not displayed, save in the founding of his colleges. He began to question whether a life that had been so energetically and respectably spent had been spent well.

Some of these plaintive hankerings of his spirit he confided to du Bellay, whom he trusted enough to be honest with, and the French ambassador put them into a masterful letter that has been preserved. Here was an old man and a new Wolsey as du Bellay reports: "Sometimes in walking with me, while speaking of his affairs, and the course of his life up to that time, he has said to me, that if God permitted him to see the hatred of these two nations (France and England) extinguished, and firm amity established, as he hopes it will shortly be, with a reform of the laws and the customs of the country, and the succession of the kingdom assured, especially if this marriage took place, and an heir male were born to it, he would at once retire, and serve God the rest of his life; and that, without any doubt, on the first honorable occasion he could find, he would give up politics." [32]

Any man surfeited with problems and restricted by responsibilities might talk in a similar manner; but it is significant that the talk du Bellay reported came after the King's rebukes and while Wolsey was waiting for Campeggio. Such talk was more than a luxury that goes along with a favored position. It struck a note that had not been heard before in the remarks of a man wholly committed to the King and his wishes. In addressing Wolsey on the business of his colleges Henry had with unerring insight detected the Cardinal's first alien interest, the first interest not immediately related to the King's welfare. Wolsey's devotion to education revealed *not so much a disloyalty but an unloyalty,* a divided allegiance, a great fraction of energy and concern taken from the King's business. And the King, having been the one who placed Wolsey in a position where he could afford to build colleges, naturally resented the turn the Cardinal's mind had taken.

By the time Wolsey talked with du Bellay his words could form only a lament and a longing, not an expression of intent. He had overextended his commitments in so many directions and with indiscriminate enthusiasm had involved himself in so many enterprises that required his presence or official action that a kind of automatic momentum kept him going from morning until night.

The aggregate of these activities might have had a deadening quality that helped to numb his anxiety while waiting for Campeggio to make his interminable, gouty way across France. Yet many of these activities sharpened the agony of waiting, for some of the demands made upon him were urgent, and some of them were touching, and nearly all of them were irrelevant to the King's great purpose and by their very irrelevancy reminded him of important unfinished business.

There were such things to cope with as the appealing letter from the child Henry Fitzroy, Duke of Richmond, still his charge, esteemed by those who observed him to be "a child of excellent wisdom and towardness," so that it would be hard "to find any creature living twice his age worthy to be compared to him." And now to my lord of York in his misery and waiting came the request of this child, isolated by titles and honors from the normal loves of childhood, for his help in getting a manly plaything. "In most humble wise I desire your Grace of your daily blessing," he wrote to Wolsey, "advertising the same that I have written unto the King's Highness, making my most humble intercession unto the same for an harness to exercise myself in arms according to my erudition in the Commentaries of Caesar. In most humble wise beseeching your said Grace to be means for me unto the King's Highness in this behalf . . ." [33] Whatever business lay on a Lord Chancellor's table or on the King's conscience, such a petition as this could not be airily dismissed. But the miniature Duke of Richmond was in less pious favor now than he had been two years before; for if the King could get his way, he would have a true heir and not have to settle for a substitute. The Duke had become a problem child: how to treat him was a problem, and a problem took time.

Likewise the loving letters from Wolsey's own son, known as Thomas Wynter, brought requests that could not be ignored or else had to be deliberately ignored. These might be tucked between the lines of an account of his enthusiasm for a new teacher or for some course of reading on which he was launched. For Thomas Wynter was a student in European universities, a proper intellectual who spent all his time in the pursuit of learning, unhampered by official duties, and in due time he might fulfill the vaulted dreams of his father. It was important to hedge against misfortunes which might befall the young man if the father came to evil days. Those who were kind to him must in turn be treated well. Once he wrote from Paris, sending the letter by a man who had received him kindly and who now desired Wolsey's favor. In this letter Wolsey's son tells of another man who is "not only a most diligent teacher but a most dear friend." The young man reports that this teacher instructs him by his readings and delights him by his conversation. He has been with him daily for twelve months, reading Mela or Pliny. During this time the teacher has not taken any pay, but the son knows he wishes to finish his life in England where he spent his youth. Wolsey's son writes that he is sure the teacher would not refuse a benefice if it were offered.[34] The son writes later to the father to say that he ought always to be thanking him for his never-ceasing kindness.

Requests and importunities that reached the spacious ears of the Cardinal — whether it was the Duke of Norfolk's desire that cheese have preferential export treatment[35] or an Observant Friar's desire for an appointment when he might speak about various people and discuss his own personal difficulties[36] — took extensive time and care. It took time to say No and more to say Yes; it took time to postpone and to regurgitate; and it took energy to pretend and to promise, with no immediate prospect of fulfillment. The Cardinal had sedulously made himself arbiter of Europe, so that no prince or diplomat would make a move without habitually consulting or cultivating him. Now the need was to work out a peace that would release the Pope from further threats and menaces by the Emperor, and it was important that my lord of York be the author of this peace and duly rewarded. To this end Wolsey grappled with the problem and instructed Knight in Rome to suggest that the Pope meet him in Nice and that the King of France and the Emperor both come to their frontiers, there to do business as the Pope and Cardinal should instruct. Again the Pope proposed that the cardinals be sent for to help him restore a general peace. On another occasion the Pope told Gregory Casale that he was sure no peace could be concluded unless he and Wolsey went to the Emperor in Spain, which he would be ready to do if Wolsey would go also.[37]

Having made himself arbiter of England as well as Europe, the Cardinal clutched all the strings of government in his skilled and restless hands. In a day of confidence this was good and gave him some of the comforts of security. In a day of shattered confidence, when only one task mattered, it added to his weariness and frustration. And of course nothing ever got thoroughly and satisfactorily done. The Cardinal had it in mind to reduce the immoderate expenditure of the King's household and had instructed the comptroller, Sir William Fitzwilliam, to look to this end. But the comptroller had reported the year before that the King was "keeping a very great and expensive house" and that he had with him various nobles and their families and he did not see how the expenses could be reduced.[38] What was a Lord Chancellor to do in a case of this sort? A Lord Chancellor who had been rebuked for his own financial ethics by a King with a bulbous conscience who wanted nothing from his Lord Chancellor at this moment save the hastening of Campeggio and the settlement of his painful marriage?

CHAPTER X

CAMPEGGIO had left Rome in June. The journey from Rome to London required less than six weeks even in the unfriendly midst of winter. Yet by August 22 he was no farther than Lyons and it took him three weeks more to reach Paris, a distance of 315 miles. All the while Wolsey had sent him urgent entreaties to hasten. He had left Paris on September 18, but he had to be carried in a litter because his hands would not hold a bridle and his feet would not stand the squeeze of stirrups. Weather joined the gout to keep him at Calais until September 29, and he did not reach Canterbury until October 1. His journey in a season generally favored by weather had taken more than twice as long as an urgent trip over the same distance in winter.

The prelate whom Wolsey had selected as a safe associate in the speedy dispatch of business had made a mockery of time, and in doing so he made a mockery of business that had nonetheless to be gravely conducted while he plodded toward London. There was no outward change in the status of Wolsey, no diminution in the demands made upon him. He must transact the duties and look after the concerns with which he had surrounded himself. He was still a man of dignity and high standing, and his motions must not betray what emotions did not fit appearances. Oxford, ever deferential, had written the spring before that it would defer its commencement until he might be able to attend and that it looked to him now for his usual fatherly guidance.[1] Wolsey might of necessity accept the King's wish that he accept no more moneys from religious houses for his colleges, but he could not suspend the work on these colleges any more than he could stop his breathing. They were his breathing. Perhaps he could find help elsewhere, even in France. He took time to write to the Grand Master of France, saying that there was not the abundance of stone in England that there was in France, continuing: "I pray you very earnestly to be the means with the King your master that he will do me the honour to assign me a quarry at Caen in Lower Normandy" in order that he might import stone "without paying any duty thereupon." [2]

Colleges, cheese, diminutive Dukes, Observant Friars, his own son — all required time and energy and all would come to nought if Campeggio did not suit the King's desire. And there was a growing suspicion in the Cardinal's mind that Campeggio had some indirect purpose in his coming. For in France Campeggio talked for two hours with the French King, and the report Wolsey got of the interview indicated that Campeggio's purpose in coming to London was to reconcile the King and the Queen and not proceed to sentence until he had a new and explicit commission from Rome.

The news was made more plausible by the sad state of military affairs now in Italy. The French, who had shown some signs of equalizing Charles, had lost ground and face. Sorest blow of all had been the decision of Andrea Doria, the famous Genoese soldier of fortune, to shift his influence and forces to Charles. Francis had been niggardly in his pay and had not kept his promise to hand back Savona to the Genoese.[3] As Wolsey remarked, Doria was worth a dozen Savonas, but it was too late. The Emperor was once more in firm command of Italy. Was it not likely that Giulio de' Medici, who loved his native Florence above all else, might in these circumstances behave more like a Florentine than like the Vicar of Christ?

Wolsey's first sessions with Campeggio did nothing to reassure him or to assuage his acute doubts. Campeggio had come by slow and painful stages from Canterbury; nor had he been well received. At one point a press of two thousand women made their appearance, as if the Italian did not have torments enough already, and began to shout acclamations for Queen Catherine. "No Nan Boleyn for us!" they called. One of the nobles accompanying Campeggio waved his hand disapprovingly, but the cries were renewed: "No Nan Boleyn for us!"[4] Campeggio was supposed to enter London in state with Wolsey, but as he approached the suburbs he found that he could travel no farther, either on a litter or on horseback. He stopped at a house owned by the Duke of Suffolk, and the next day Wolsey came and conveyed him by river to a place called Bath House, where Campeggio immediately took to bed again.[5]

But his bed was no protection against the Cardinal of York, who came to see him the day after and every day thereafter, arguing the King's case with him for hours and with such desperation and vehemence that Campeggio was taken aback. There was no resourcefulness in Wolsey's arguments, no persuasion, but there was heat and the zest of a man determined. He was a man, as he had so often been, acting under orders. He told Campeggio that if the King's desire was not complied with, "total ruin would specially ensue of the kingdom, of himself, of the Church's influence." Campeggio tried to present the Pope's point of view and enlist

Wolsey's aid in reconciling the King and Queen, but, as he was to write Rome, "I have no more success in persuading the Cardinal than if I had spoken to a rock."

He was speaking to a rock, a graven image carved to the King's taste and miraculously animated to say what it was told. The words of Wolsey were a litany. They had meaning only because they had been spoken often before, and their recurrence carried with them the overtones of conviction only because they were rhythmically repeated. "His objections," reported Campeggio to the Pope, "are founded on the invalidity of the marriage, the instability of the realm and the succession." The King and the Cardinal of York, he went on to say, were so wedded to their opinion that "they not only solicit my compliance with them, but the expediting of this business with all possible despatch . . . They will endure no procrastination, alleging that the affairs of the kingdom are at a standstill, and that if the cause remains undetermined it will give rise to infinite and imminent perils." [6] These were the same cries Wolsey's stentors had sounded in Rome and Orvieto. Nothing new had been added.

Nor was the King content with Wolsey's bedside treatment of Campeggio. Henry's impatience grew. He moved to his palace near Bath House and let it be known that he would give an audience. "Although I could neither ride nor walk, and could not sit without discomfort," Campeggio said, "I was compelled on the 22nd (Tuesday) to go for my first audience." The next day he saw the King again and tried to talk with him, but the King listened patiently and, in what Campeggio called a premeditated reply, used the very same arguments Wolsey had used. It was no marvel, for the arguments were Henry's to begin with.

Only when Campeggio suggested that the Queen might be persuaded to enter a religious house did the King show a cheerful countenance. The thought pleased him highly, and he felt sure that the Queen might agree, seeing that for two years he had ceased cohabiting with her and would not return to her bed whatever the decision of the legatine court might be. So, deprived of his amorous attentions, why should not a woman want to get her to a nunnery? The King would be generous with her. Indeed he would even settle the succession on her daughter if he failed to have male issue by another marriage. Accordingly Wolsey and Campeggio were appointed to speak with the Queen on this convenient arrangement the very next day.

The two Cardinals repaired to the Queen and were alone with her for two hours. But they found her the daughter of Isabella, devout and stern, with a conscience as firm as her husband's. She listened prudently and with

409

dignity and would say little save that she "was resolved to die in the Faith, and in obedience to God and His Holy Church." She told them she had heard that they were to induce her to enter a religious house. Campeggio did not deny it and immediately set upon her with all the persuasions which would show her the advantages, including the fact that she would keep her dower and the guardianship of her Princess. She merely listened. Campeggio having dwelt as long as his breath and gout permitted on the beauties of life in a nunnery, Wolsey then urged her with the same arguments and begged her to ponder them well.[7]

It was a lame seconding by my lord of York of the arguments advanced by the man who had now become the chief hope of the King. Campeggio had the center of attention these days. He was not only an experienced canonist but the only new element in what had become a tiresome situation at best. Ten years earlier, Wolsey had been strong enough to hold Campeggio in Calais during a detestable summer before giving him permission to cross to Dover, and then only on the condition that the Cardinal of York be joined with him in the legateship. This time he had offered to go to France and meet him, and he had written often to hasten his coming. On the previous visit Wolsey had by assertiveness and a quick command of circumstances made himself first Legate; now, although he had back of him all the assurance of an experienced diplomat, he had been subtly and imperceptibly forced into a subordinate position, almost a lieutenant, who went about with Campeggio as if to reinforce and italicize what he had to say. Suddenly Wolsey found himself in second place on a vital mission that concerned the King; and Wolsey in second place was not Wolsey at all.

It was to Campeggio and not to Wolsey that Catherine asked leave to confess. Wolsey brought the news of her request to Campeggio one morning at break of day while he was still in bed and not a little tormented by the gout. She came privately at nine o'clock and was with Campeggio for a long space. What she told him was under the seal of confession, but she not only gave the Cardinal of San Tommaso permission to reveal it but urged him "to write to the Pope certain resolutions." Her confession covered her life from the time of her arrival in England. To Campeggio "she affirmed on her conscience that from her marriage with Prince Arthur, on the 14th of November, until his death on the 2nd of April, she had not slept in the same bed with him more than seven nights, and that he had left her as he had found her — a virgin." Her attitude about entering a religious house was as painful to Campeggio as the gout. She said that "she intended to live and die in the estate of matrimony, to which God had called her; that she would always remain of that opinion and never change it." [8]

On the next visit to the Queen, Wolsey accompanied Campeggio. This time they found her flanked by advisers. Campeggio reiterated the arguments he had used before, and my lord of York got down on his knees before the Queen, supplicating her long and earnestly to follow the advice they had given her.[9] To the kneeling Cardinal she merely replied that she would do nothing to the condemnation of her soul or the violation of God's laws.

Shortly after Campeggio's arrival, Wolsey renewed his entreaties to the Pope for a more explicit commission with a command to proceed at once with the trial. He had taken the initiative again, comfortable once more in the medium of letters, and this time it was Campeggio who seconded the request he made.

But nothing came of Wolsey's new plea to the Pope. In fact, nothing promised to come of anything. Meanwhile, the sentiment of the commonalty, kept at a distance and fed only on surmises and speculations, had taken a turn which made Henry feel that the time had come to make a statement. Campeggio was lampooned in ballads and "uncomplimentary remarks about his master were everywhere scrawled on the walls." Henry summoned the Lord Mayor and Corporation of London to his palace at Bridewell, told them about the scruples of his conscience, especially as they touched the matter of the succession. He reminded them of the Wars of the Roses when the succession was in dispute and drew a favorable contrast with the twenty years of peace and prosperity in his own reign. He praised Catherine's many fine qualities and bemoaned the fact that God's law stood in the way of continuing to live with so good a wife. Having summed the matter up to his own satisfaction, "with a feeling compounded of majesty and pathos, as a Christian bachelor manhandled by fate," he urged his audience to declare the case to the people of England. He would like the affair handled amicably, but if "he found anyone, whoever he was, who spoke in any terms than he ought to do of his Prince, he would let him know that he was his master." [10] One report had it that he said "there was never a head so dignified but that he would make it fly."

Meanwhile the King had lodged Anne in a fine house close to his own. Greater court was paid to her than had been paid to the Queen for a very long time. "I see," wrote du Bellay, "that they mean to accustom the people by degrees to endure her, so that when the great blow comes it may not be thought strange. However, the people remain quite hardened and I think they would do more if they had more power; but great order is continually taken . . . There has been a search for hackbutts and cross-bows, so that no worse weapon remains than the tongue." Throughout the country also a continual watch was kept, and the French ambassador did not think there would be an uprising. Henry had been aroused to irritated caution not merely by the gossip of the people but by the threat that the Imperialists might stir his subjects to revolt against him in Catherine's behalf.[11]

For whatever reason, Henry made clear to the English public what had been long and painfully clear to the Cardinal. Henry would countenance no opposition, however mild and trifling. Even the wrong attitude might fortune to cost some their heads. At any point that touched the Tudor succession the King was merciless and swift to anger. The headless Buckingham stalked back of his words. He had resolved, as Wolsey knew and the populace was now made to understand, to dissolve his marriage and take another wife. Any who assisted his cause would incur his gratitude; any who stood in his way would be trampled.

It was well that he served this public notice, posted his one thesis on the door of the cathedral. It helped to make somewhat comprehensible if not popular or acceptable the stark procession of events that slowly followed. And it might well have helped to explain to the talkative English the behavior of Thomas Cardinal Wolsey — behavior that could not be defended but could be speculated on charitably and pityingly in the light of the toils of circumstances which held him in their tightening grip.

A course of action which had seemed to him simple and right — the annulment of the King's marriage through the orderly processes of a legatine court and with the permission of the Father of Christendom — had turned out to be grievously wrong. Far from being simple, the course he chose had led into an ambush of complexities. As Sanga, the Pope's secretary, wrote to Campeggio: "Would God the Cardinal had allowed the matter to take its course; for if the King had decided for himself, rightly or wrongly, without reference to his Holiness it would have been without blame or prejudice to his Holiness." Wolsey's recommendation had involved all of Christendom, siphoned off energy that could have been better used, and embarrassed and embittered not only His Holiness but the King and the Emperor and everybody involved. The protracted delay and the canonical contentions engendered made a public spectacle and a European scandal of an affair which might have been settled neatly and quietly, without commotion and the need of Henry's explaining his conduct to his subjects, if only "the Cardinal had allowed the matter to take its course." [12]

But no. The Cardinal had influenced the King to lay his great matter in the lap of the Pope, who would in turn be influenced by the Cardinal. From then on the forces of fate, operating through such apparently extraneous media as the drunken Lutheranism of the unpaid troops of Bourbon, had conspired against him.

Yet at every point Wolsey had solid reasons to suppose that he would succeed. When these reasons began to shrivel, he conjured them back with his strong and imaginative mind; when they began to vanish, he grew desperate, lunging toward any possible escape from his tragic impotence. He made no attempt to escape from his own responsibility; on the contrary, his whole sense of self was inextricably tied up with his ability to serve in the King's great matter.

In his desperation the Cardinal's attitude toward the Queen, the innocent and injured person in the whole tumultuous mess, lacked not only a priestly demeanor but even the gallantry one might expect of an oaf. For the most part she was regarded as a disagreeable cipher in a nasty problem; and when she was treated as a person she was mistreated, spied on, intimidated, her interests, rights, and wishes either ignored or subverted.

Perhaps what lay at the heart of the incredible series of rebukes to be visited upon Catherine was the complaint that "she ought to have informed the King of the brief, which she pretends to have had for a long time, and not to have kept it close, for the exhibition thereof might have given much ease." [13]

The brief . . .

Here was a document that threw consternation into the King's camp when a copy of it was presented to Campeggio not long after his arrival. It was, in effect, a second dispensation from Julius II, who had granted the original dispensation for the marriage of Henry and Catherine. Upon the imperfections of this original dispensation Henry and the Cardinal had rested their whole case. But the supplementary and amplifying dispensation from Julius in the form of a brief carefully remedied the imperfections of the bull which Henry's conscience so canonically criticized. Thus the marriage was valid. Henry, who suffered only to know the truth, now had his answer, and he need not belabor his soul longer in the sight of God. One would think that a royal sigh of Christian relief might have been heard as far as Rome.

Instead, the possession of the brief was numbered among the items for which the Queen was to be chastened. There was no copy of it in England and no record of it in Rome. It was said to have been procured by wily Ferdinand the Catholic at the time of Henry VII's parsimonious arrangement for the marriage of Catherine to his second son in order that he might keep her dowry. A dispensation, which gave precise papal permission for the marriage, was said to have been given to the devout Isabella to quiet the scruples she felt toward this non-Levitical union of her daughter with Prince Henry. The brief was found, so the report ran, among the papers of Roderigo de Puebla, long since dead. He had been the Spanish ambassador to England who in 1503 had negotiated the marriage of Catherine and Prince Arthur.[14]

Wolsey had advised Henry at the beginning of his action not to rely entirely on the invalidity of the bull Julius had granted. Instead he should urge that Arthur and Catherine had been married in the sight of the Church and that this marriage constituted a public impediment which had not been removed by the dispensation of Julius for the simple reason that, while accepted as an impediment by canon law, it was not mentioned at all in the dispensation. It was an error of omission — safe to quarrel with. But the Defender of the Faith had rejected this course as insufficient to satisfy the theological cravings of his soul. The dispensation itself must be declared invalid on grounds that it was improperly drawn and issued under false representations. But the brief in Catherine's possession, if it were genuine, could prove the dispensation valid. If the Queen produced it in evidence at the trial, the King would have no case at all.

No doubt the brief was a forgery, for it had been discovered and put forward at a suspiciously convenient time for the Queen. Whatever the case, it had to be secured. A decisive document of this sort could not be left floating around, and the Cardinal now took upon himself the task of securing it, or, failing that, having the Pope declare it a forgery. Wolsey's plan was to make Catherine herself implore the Emperor to send it forth out of Spain and merely keep a copy of it, which, as the instructions to Catherine put it, "would equally serve his purpose but not yours." Under the King's and Wolsey's orders, deceit as black as a London fog was to be practiced. In an astonishing document,[15] which Brewer summarizes, Catherine is told that when the trial begins "the copy will not help you. As the King, therefore, cannot and ought not to be satisfied with the said copy, you must endeavor for his satisfaction, the advancement of your cause, and as ye tender the continuance of love between you, to obtain the original, now in the Emperor's hands." She is reminded that the failure to obtain the original "might be the extreme ruin of your affairs, and no little danger to the inheritance of your child." If the Emperor refuses her request, she must protest that it is her own and say that she will sue the Pope to make the Emperor give up the brief.

Catherine obeyed.[16] She sent the letter by her chaplain Thomas Abell, but he conveyed to the Emperor the intelligence that she had written under pressure and that her request was to be ignored. The Emperor's reply, delivered in due course, was that he would take the brief to Italy and deliver it to the Pope in person. English agents examined the original in Spain and came away convinced that it was not genuine.[17] Still the fact remained that the opinion of English agents could not be regarded as either judicial or final. Wolsey turned to the Pope again and began through a series of letters and instructions dispatched to English agents in Rome a bastinado aimed at making Clement declare the brief a forgery before he had seen it.

Wolsey, harried by Campeggio's evasiveness and deviation from the Pope's commission, found his desperation mounting with each failure. Yet it was mainly in the moves he made that he betrayed this desperation. He was still blind to defeat and heedless of the warning and still apparently convinced that by prodigious diligence he could overcome all obstacles, including the brief.

In the early days of 1529 a meteor of hope flashed across his sky. Clement was reported dead. Henry wrote with indecent haste to express the grief that racked the royal frame at the news and to say in the same letter that he would be deprived of the remedy which he had expected of the Head of the Church "if the future Pope be not a person of whom he is perfectly assured." The King's letter reminds the English agents that he is "loath to recur any remedy except the authority of the See Apostolic." It is thus imperative that the Pope chosen to succeed Clement shall be first of all favorable to the King's cause.

Of all the cardinals, none meets all the requisites "except Wolsey himself." He has zeal for the tranquillity of Christendom and for other matters of great import, "and also for the perfection of the King's cause." The agents are to use every means to advance Wolsey's election, "for upon it depends the making or marring of the King's cause." The means to advance Wolsey's election included promises of money and offices and dignities. The cardinals were to be reminded, "since human fragility suffers not all things to be weighed in just balances," that Wolsey's election would vacate many valuable posts, and that these posts, not to mention other large rewards, would be given to the King's friends.[18]

Again my lord of York had taken his virtues out of storage and paraded them before the cardinals. But the plans so carefully labored were labored in vain, and, in spite of Wolsey's willingness "to enter into this dangerous storm and troublous tempest for the relief of the Church," the whole scheme was defeated, as so many others had been, by the perversity of Clement. He got inscrutably better and slowly recovered his health after months of being a part-time Pope. Death was no ally. The proper people would not die for the Cardinal. The Abbess of Wilton had died, but Anne Boleyn and Clement lived on. All the sprites of fortune which had aided Wolsey in his ascendancy had turned to imps now, and at a moment when he had never needed the aid of mysterious forces more.

Yet the Cardinal of York, who had risen to the heights and maintained himself there on grandiloquence, still kept his touching faith in the power of argument and persuasion. But now his arguments were connected less and less with reality. He came forward with the prayerful proposal that the Pope be provided with a bodyguard of two thousand men.[19] It was Wolsey's thought that this cordon would bring the Pope to have "as much fear and respect towards the King's highness as he now hath towards the Emperor, and consequently be the gladder to grant and condescend unto the King's desire." Wolsey, having become obsessed with one idea, reckoned superficially with all problems connected with it. He oversimplified the difficulties to endure them. He displayed only the faintest understanding of Clement's position and the content of the Pope's mind. What Clement wanted in Italy could not be secured by a bodyguard. He wanted his native Florence, now transformed into a noisy republic, restored to the house of the Medicis. And he wanted the papal cities of Cervia and Ravenna, now in the possession of the Venetians, restored to the Holy See. Clement had said: "Rely on it, though the Venetians retain what belongs to me, I shall get the cities back. Either I shall ruin myself utterly, or I shall ruin them." [20]

Wolsey, of course, was aware of this attitude, but the awkward part of it was that the Venetians were allied with France and England against the Emperor. How contrive to make an ally surrender valuble possessions and prestige just to please the King of England? Wolsey's scheme was to put Cervia and Ravenna under the joint custody of France and England, but it was a feeble scheme at best and met no response in Paris. To the Venetians it must have seemed preposterous to go to such lengths, for the King's great matter was far enough away to seem no matter at all among these practical merchants of the seas.

Several causes occurred in the first four fateful months of 1529 to make Wolsey more desperate with every lunge toward the improbable. One was the King's boiling impatience and the increased urgency of his demands.

416

No longer outwardly content to rely on Wolsey's direction of strategy, he sent successive ambassadors to the Pope. Sir Francis Bryan arrived there in January along with Peter Vannes. Sir Gregory Casale was already there, as was Knight, the agent Henry had sent with secret instructions at the time Wolsey was in France. And hardly had Bryan and Vannes arrived when the King sent forward Stephen Gardiner, the young lawyer who with his brilliant talk and rough manners had wrested the commission from the Pope the year before. Gardiner had stood high in the estimation of the King since his return, and Henry had even stated publicly that he was "the very pearl of our realm." [21] He had been Wolsey's secretary, and now he was the King's instrument and, ominously, a favorite of Mistress Anne. The King who at the time of the conference at Calais had counseled Wolsey to choose young men and post them on affairs of state now followed his own advice.

With five English ambassadors harrying the Pope, there was competition in absurdity as well as competition for the King's good will by the display of imaginative suggestions and demands. Wolsey still directed the strategy, though it was impossible to tell what was Henry's idea and what was Wolsey's. Knight, along with still another ambassador, Dr. William Benet, was sent to ask the Pope to secure the brief from the Emperor: "considering how many persons are implicated in this forgery, it would be well to put an end to the scandal." Let the Pope, in view of the signs of its falsity, "write peremptorily to the Emperor to send the brief within three months," and let the Pope forward it to England. Or let the Pope give the Legates in England a commission to declare it a forgery. If the Pope will take neither course, let him command that the brief be sent to Rome where he can himself declare it fraudulent: but let the Pope promise in writing that he will give sentence on the brief in the King's favor.[22]

There was still a lingering hope that Catherine might be induced to enter a nunnery; but even if high-policy pressure persuaded her to this course, it was anticipated that she might ask the King also to take the vow of chastity! It was part of the assignment given the ambassadors to find out whether the Pope would in this unhappy contingency agree to release Henry from his vow, "discharging him clearly of the same, and thereupon allow him to proceed to a second marriage with the legitimation of the children." And, "to provide for everything," as the instructions unnecessarily put the matter, they were to find out if the Pope, failing to release Henry from his vow and hold Catherine to hers, would allow Henry to have two wives, "making the children of the second marriage legitimate, as well as those of the first." Wolsey, the incurable writer, drafted a bull to relieve the Pope of the labor of writing it, instancing in behalf of the proposal "great reasons and precedents, especially in the Old Testament."[23]

To the tough and able Gardiner, Wolsey gave the most arduous if not the most ridiculous task. Wolsey, despite Campeggio's delay and dallying and palaver, had not lost hope that the commission under which the two Legates acted could be strengthened before they proceeded to the trial. He wanted permission from the Pope to compel even princes, if need be, to produce "whatever documents might be required." Any possibility that the decision reached in England might be appealed to Rome must be obviated. Gardiner did well, as usual, but Wolsey saw certain flaws in the supplementary document which were better remedied. Accordingly he returned it with the necessary revisions to Gardiner. The problem was to get the Pope to accept the revisions placidly. His suspicions of the changes must not be aroused. Gardiner was directed to say to the Pope, after studying the changes Wolsey had made in the document, *that the original had been injured by the wet weather in its passage to England* and that another must be secured in its place. To save the Pope trouble, Gardiner was to say that he would be glad to write it out fresh from memory. In doing so, he would, of course, put in the words Wolsey wanted inserted.[24]

Such prestidigitation did little to advance the King's cause and less to improve the disposition of an ailing Pope. Signs showed themselves that the pontiff's boredom and longsuffering were changing to irritation and might mount to fury, and the fury of a mild man was not to be lightly regarded. When John Casale delivered a message to the Pope for his brother Sir Gregory, who was absent at the time it arrived, he encountered a worm in the process of turning and, quite taken aback, reported to Westminster that "his Holiness laid his hand upon my arm with expressions of anger, forbidding me to proceed." Later at the same meeting "he grew more angry and more excited" and said that he would make no further concessions.[25]

At times the Pope expressed indirectly his resentment of the unceasing intrusion of the King's great matter upon his person. Not being able openly to blame the Cardinal and the King, he blamed Catherine's obstinacy, her chaste refusal to enter a convent, for his misery and desolation. Gardiner reported to Henry that Clement wished the Queen in her grave, saying also that he thought, like as the Emperor had destroyed the temporalities of the Church, so shall she be the cause of the destruction of the spiritualities.[26]

Wolsey, in turn, living in a shell of words and sustained by the nostalgia of power, continued to believe that the Pope would yield. None of the mules on which the Cardinal rode was ever more stubborn than he. But while Wolsey would not admit defeat, there were others near the Pope and in the confidence of the King who saw that Wolsey's tactics were doomed. They would lead only to delay — a more vigorous and active delay than Campeggio's — but delay all the same. Wolsey might sit busily in one of his palaces and indite long letters of inspired instructions, but the men who daily besieged the Pope and his counselors and sought to carry out these instructions came to the firm conclusion that their efforts would not fructify. Sir Gregory Casale, one of the most able and devoted of the English emissaries to the Pope, wrote his brother Vincent, then in England: "I think his Holiness will do nothing; and you may tell Wolsey so, in the event of his desiring my opinion." Sir Gregory goes on to his brother: "If you remember, one of my reasons for sending you to England was to tell the King and Wolsey that they should make some other arrangement, because, if the Pope's fears were entirely removed, he will never do what we want . . ." The Pope had said that he would do all that could be done, but there are many things, Sir Gregory observes, that the Pope could not do. He could not declare against a brief "emanating from Pope Julius, in the event of its being brought from Spain, without examination." Other ambassadors reported in the same vein: the Pope would do nothing, for "though it might well be in his Pater Noster, it was nothing in his Creed." [27]

One of the men Henry had sent to Rome, Sir Francis Bryan, a personal friend and a cousin of Anne Boleyn, was to report directly to him. He wrote Wolsey, but he also wrote the King what he had told the Cardinal. He reminds the King of a letter written the Cardinal, "whereby ye shall perceive that plainly the Pope will do nothing for your Grace." He continues: "There is not one of us but that hath essayed him by fair means and foul, but nothing will serve. And whosoever hath made your Grace believe that he would do for you in this cause, hath not, I think, done your Grace the best service." He ends his letter by saying, "Sir, I write a letter to my cousin Anne, but I dare not write her the truth of this . . ." [28]

In early May of 1529 the English delegation, in a charge led by the redoubtable Dr. Stephen Gardiner, made a final attack on the Pope. By all reports, Gardiner used His Holiness roughly and made him ashamed of his deeds. But, although tearful, Clement merely said again that he could not declare the brief a forgery. Now Gardiner admitted defeat and reported to England that not only had the Pope refused to yield but that there was talk in Rome of recalling the commission of the Legates. Any hope that remained would have to be carried out in England — and promptly, before the Pope could interfere.

419

It was now clear by the command of dictatorial events that the great matter of the King of England would have to be decided in England, where it might well have been decided in the first place. Let England decide and the Pope confirm.

But, alas, the problem was not this clean or simple now. It was festered over with ill will and irritated by long negotiations. It could hardly be said at this late date that the matter would be decided in England if the court before which it came was a legatine court of Rome, presided over by an Italian acting under instructions from the Pope. Thanks to the Cardinal of York, it was too late to act without reference, direct or indirect, to the Holy See and the Emperor. Wolsey's long detour by way of Rome had complicated the problem irretrievably. And if it had done nothing else it had incurred the suspicion of the King. The mind of Henry was quick to detect, and his soul was loath to forgive, any divided loyalty.

There were not lacking significant signs of the King's altered attitude toward his servant, and this altered attitude was reflected, of course, by those around the court. Indeed it was magnified. With the King fevered by impatience, any sign or rumor unfavorable to the faltering favorite could be enlarged and distorted. As the cause dragged on without visible results, the King's suspicions increased. Du Bellay reported in one of his dispatches: "Wolsey is in the greatest difficulty, for matters have gone so far that if the divorce do not take effect the King will lay the blame of it on him." With a fine sense of reporting, the French ambassador cites an incident which showed how Anne Boleyn had begun to have her way with the King's mind. A gentleman named Cheyney had offended the Legate and had been put out of court. But, says du Bellay, the lady had put him in again — and not without using rude words to Wolsey.[29]

A report touching the same change in attitude was written by Mendoza, the Spanish ambassador. "The lady who is the cause of all this disorder, finding her marriage delayed that she thought herself so secure of, greatly suspects that the Cardinal puts impediments in her way, from a belief that if she were Queen his power would decline. In this suspicion she is joined by her father, and the two dukes, Suffolk and Norfolk, who have combined to overthrow him. As yet they have made no impression on the King, except that he does not show the Cardinal in court so fair a countenance as he did, and it is said that he has had some bitter words with him."[30]

Most noteworthy of all the subtle signs of Wolsey's impending rejection was the desertion of some of his household servants. Those capricious minions who derived their sense of status from the status of the man they

420

worked for and had previously prayed the Cardinal for positions in his service now prophetically began to fall away from him and find employment with those who were ascendant. Such servants were the true soothsayers; they knew what the human weather would be. Day in and day out, night in and night out (if they ever had a night out), they saw and savored the signs of royal esteem, and they felt and quaked at the first hints of royal displeasure toward their masters. They were the ignored intimates of every great household before whom all details were bared; the ears in the walls. Another Lord Chancellor at the court of Henry later learned of his loss of favor one day as he rode to court. His hat blew off in the wind as he entered the palace yard, and none stooped to pick it up. It was the sign of doom. That day he lost his hat; not long after he lost his head.[31]

All occurrences now bore the aspect of evil omen and pitiless fate, as if they expressed the punitive measures of Nemesis, at last ready to trim the Cardinal down. His haughtiness would be humbled, his wealth would decay, and his red glory would fade. The lowborn priest would return to the obscurity from which he had been conjured up by the King. It had been written that pride goeth before a fall, and so it would be now.

The forces that were carrying the Cardinal to his fall in the reluctant spring of 1529 were political as well as moral, the result of reasoned policies undertaken in good faith as much as of personality and behavior offensive alike to the nobles and the commons. These policies, in which he steadfastly if wrongheadedly believed, had been ambushed by events which none had foreseen. He had advised and insisted upon recourse to Rome in the King's great matter; the sack of Rome and the capture of Clement and the failure of the French to counter the supremacy of the Emperor in Italy had made this course disastrous; and its failure had alienated the King. His policy of an alliance with France aimed at the Emperor, a policy he had carried through almost singlehandedly, had alienated the people through the interruption of trade. For all its unpopularity, this alliance of England and France offered the one hope of denying to Charles the control of Italy and the Pope. This policy, too, had come to nought through the failure of French arms in Italy, the transfer of the Genoese admiral Andrea Doria to the imperial side. None of these grisly happenings could have been predicted. Nor could the final and fantastic end of the policy back of the French alliance which made itself known with the suddenness of an unexpected blow:

Francis was preparing to make peace, behind England's back, with Charles, leaving Charles in untrammeled control of Italy.

The news from Gardiner that the Pope would do nothing for the King and the news from Paris that peace would be negotiated between Francis and Charles at Cambrai reached England only weeks apart, and it meant that the two policies pursued with such vigor by the Cardinal of York had failed almost simultaneously.

There might still have been a chance to see that England's interests were respected in the negotiations of the peace between Francis and Charles if my lord of York had been free to go to the conference at Cambrai in all his accustomed glory and confidence. But the King kept him pointedly at home. The affairs of Europe, which Henry had let Wolsey manipulate for so long, had sunk into a place of secondary importance, and plans must be moved forward for the hearing of his cause before the legatine court.

The very origin and arrangement of the conference at Cambrai bore an odd aspect. England was simply *invited* to attend — and after the main details had been fixed. The insult was hardly more than implicit, but it was there: the insult of neglect. The whole affair had at first a seemingly trifling quality, as if to disguise its true nature. It was not only the result of petticoat influence in the two courts of Francis and Charles, but it was to be carried out in detail behind the ample skirts of the ladies who dreamed it up: Louise of Savoy, the dominant mother of the King of France, and Margaret of Austria, aunt of Emperor Charles V.

Obviously these two women had power. They also had in their plans another quality — and that was prudent informality. The conference was said to have originated at an evening party given in Paris by the French King's mother. Someone mentioned peace to Margaret's ambassador, and suggested that Margaret might be persuaded to make it. At first Margaret showed reluctance and put the burden of argument on the side of the French. But she gradually allowed herself to be argued into what she had been going to do in the first place. There followed an abundant correspondence between Margaret and Louise, the contents of most of it known to the English court. The women kept the initiative and the details strictly in their own hands. As Guizot puts it, they did not seek to give one another mutual surprises and play off one another.[32] They worked with feminine directness, and their methods differed at every point from the elaborate deceptiveness of the old diplomacy. Ambassadors and advisers were relegated to secondary places. They even planned to reside in adjoining houses connected by a gallery, so that they could meet privately and talk over the progress of the negotiations.

How seriously such diplomatic dalliance was to be taken by England could not be determined, but both Henry and Wolsey, having dealt with a woman as an adversary, knew that the ladies meant business and that a peace would be made. Certainly Wolsey knew it. He wanted to go immediately to Cambrai, and, according to du Bellay, when he saw that the King objected he was deeply vexed.[33] Here was a chance of surcease, an opportunity to shake free of the intolerable burden of the King's great matter, and resume the role in which he had so often demonstrated his fitness: that of a conference diplomat. It was the one chance he had to stay the forces turning against him, to save the peace he had made with France. Moreover, it was highly embarrassing, if nothing else, for him to remain away. He had repeatedly assured the King, "both in public and private," that the King of France would do nothing without the consent of the King and himself. Now he saw the peace forming and he was forced to stay home like a bad boy. It was said that the ladies had matters so arranged that when they came together for their interview all would be concluded in two days.

The prospect was almost more than Wolsey could endure. The French ambassador had to bear the fury of his disappointment as news of the impending peace reached the Cardinal's ears. "I assure you," du Bellay wrote his government, "that Wolsey is in terrible pain . . . I defend myself with beak and claws, yet in the end he will come at me again." [34] The Cardinal had counted strongly on the friendship of the King of France. Formalizing this friendship had been the crowning act of his diplomacy. And now Francis was being led blindfolded into a dishonorable peace with Charles, the ruler who from the start had been Wolsey's treacherous enemy, the deceiver of Henry, the Hun who had desecrated Rome.

Yet Henry would not let Wolsey go. There were many discussions with Henry about going, according to a postscript in one of Campeggio's letters to Salviati, but the King was adamant. Henry made it plain that he would be willing for Wolsey to go, but not until his great cause was terminated. Wolsey could not believe his ears as he heard the decision, or his eyes as he saw the lines of peace forming not two hundred miles from Westminster. He had written his agents to inform the Pope that he would be with the ladies at Cambrai and to assure the Pope that, whatever reports might be to the contrary, no universal peace would be concluded without him.

These professions of certainty and intent only added to his humiliation over being fettered at home. Francis and his mother expected that he would come. So did all the others. But the conference was poorly timed. It was to take place when the trial of the King's cause, so long and infuriatingly postponed, was to take place in England. The King made it plain that Wolsey would not go by designating the Bishop of London and Sir Thomas More to go instead.

CHAPTER XI

THE trial to determine the validity of the marriage of Henry VIII began with spectacular formality on May 31, 1529, in the great hall of the Dominican monastery of the Blackfriars. There a court had been ordered and furnished befitting the momentous matter to be decided and the distinguished company called to decide it. There was "a solemn place for the two legates to sit in, with two chairs covered with cloth of gold, and cushions of the same and a dormant table railed before, covered with carpets and tapestry." [1] On the right side of the court was a cloth of estate and under it a chair and cushions for the King; on the left a chair for the Queen. Immediately in front of the judges sat officers of the court. The Archbishop of Canterbury and all the bishops of the realm were arrayed in a semicircle before the Legates. Both Campeggio and Wolsey entered with "crosses, pillars, axes, and all ceremonies belonging to their degree." The lords temporal were in attendance, too, as well as ladies and friends of the court, many of whom would serve as witnesses. Counsel for the King and for the Queen were arrayed on opposite sides of the hall, with a bar made for them.

In this stately setting, surrounded by the costumes of history, my lord of York was to play out the last act of his career. It was appropriate that he should do so under these implausible circumstances. The rise and power of this talkative fellow, sitting here in judgment on the King and the Queen, had been incredible, and the court itself was sheer fantasy. The fact that it was actually held and that it continued in session for two months taxes human credulity, and its proceedings would be dismissed as legend if they were not a matter of explicit record.

The air was filled with make-believe, and most of the chief characters moved behind masks of pious pretense. And they exchanged masks and switched roles until it was impossible to tell who was coming and who was going.

For example, the day before the court opened the King issued a license under the Great Seal of England,[2] which was in the possession of Wolsey as Lord Chancellor, to allow the Legates of the Holy See, one of whom was Wolsey, to act on the commission which the ambassadors of the King under the instructions of the Cardinal had wrung from a captive Pope. Without this legal double-dealing the court theoretically could not have met at all. In such fatiguing and spangled conditions the King must have seen his conscience through the looking glass and met himself coming out of court as he entered in.

For enter he did. He had himself summoned. The business of the court on the first day was to issue citations. One of the King's subjects and a foreign prelate, constituting together a legatine commission, commanded him and the Queen to appear. Nor did the pretense of the court stop with the split roles of the actors. For all its conspicuous ceremony and color, which surely could be seen at a great distance and would attract the eye of the curious, the King and the Cardinal pretended that the court was not being held at all. The English agents around the Pope were ordered to desist from their efforts to wrest the original of the brief from the Emperor; instead they were to distract His Holiness until the trial in England was over and the Pope could be presented with the verdict in the hope that he would confirm it. One of the agents dispatched to Clement on this mission did his job perhaps too well, but he revealed the English strategy: a month after the trial had actually commenced, he kept assuring Clement that it was not in progress and that "the King was looking for a quieter way" out of his difficulties.[3]

Charles had demanded that Clement recall the commission. There remained now only one remote chance of achieving the King's wish, and that was to hasten the trial and annul the marriage in England before the Pope interfered. Wolsey expressed his anxiety of the outcome to Campeggio in the days between the opening of the court May 31 and the date set for the first appearance of the King and Queen — June 18. He continued his letters in the same refrain, telling his ambassadors in Rome that if the case is called back to Rome, Clement "will lose the devotion of the King of England to the See Apostolic"; and that he himself would be utterly destroyed. But Campeggio could only remind him of all the difficulties and of the various interests involved in the suit. "And so I left him," Campeggio writes, "between hope and fear."[4]

There Wolsey remained while the trial dragged out its bitter length. Though it was too slow for him, it was too fast for Campeggio, with his incessant gout and his deliberative manner. A canonical expert in delaying action, Campeggio did everything in his power to protract the trial. A desperate minister, with fate looking over his shoulder, Wolsey did everything he could to hasten its progress. To the Cardinal of York time was of the essence, and the delays of the hearing at Blackfriars chafed him unconscionably. Not only his plight but his past experience in legal procedures disposed him to haste. In the Star Chamber where he sat for the King he had been used to making swift, informal, and often arbitrary judgments; and in his system of legatine courts he had been the supreme judge. Now he sat in a complicated and cumbersome court with a colleague who knew all the curvatures of canon law and meticulously followed them. It was justice with gout. It took Campeggio as excruciatingly long to get from point to point in the procedure as it had taken to get him from town to town in his journey.

The Queen answered the citation to appear between nine and ten o'clock in the morning on June 18. She answered it in person, the King by proxy. Her coming caused a rustle and flurry in the court, for many thought that she would not come at all, being only the injured party in the suit and knowing that the commission was designed to separate her from the King. She knew it, too, and she came only to protest the jurisdiction of the court and to have this protest registered and acknowledged. She read a carefully prepared statement to make it clear that her coming must not be regarded as an act of recognition: the case was pending in Rome, where it belonged, and should not be tried in England. She further requested that the Legates give their opinion on the points she raised and make this opinion a matter of record.

All of which meant immediate further delay. The Legates appointed the following Monday, June 21, as the time she must return to hear their opinion and, with no more business than that, the court adjourned for a long week end. Monday came, and on this day both the King and the Queen appeared before the Legates. The Queen entered the great hall first and took her seat under a canopy of cloth of gold on the left of the judges, placed on a lower level than a similar chair occupied by the King. It was a tense and dramatic moment, and the King was not one to miss an occasion for oratory. He arose and harangued the court, saying that he was determined to live no longer in sin with his wife the Queen. The legality of the marriage which pained his conscience must be decided speedily; therefore he required the Legates to proceed at once. Wolsey himself now added a further delay, for he also could not miss a chance to make a speech. He told the assembled dignitaries that he had received many favors of the King and that, therefore, his impartiality had been and was suspected, but he reminded them that the case had been committed to him and his colleague by the Pope and that he would therefore render judgment to the best of his poor ability and "omit nothing that the justice of the case required." [5]

Now the Queen arose. But she did not address the court; she addressed the King. Because of the crowded arrangements she could not go directly to His Majesty, so, as Cavendish describes the scene, "she took pain to go about unto the king, kneeling down at his feet in the sight of all the court and assembly." And when she had knelt down before him, she poured out in broken English all the things she had wanted to say to him and all that she wanted the people to know. She alone among the principals had only one role to play, and she played it straight. If the court offered her no justice, at least it offered her an audience, this woman who had been guarded and spied upon, her own cause held in neglect and contempt.

The words she spoke as she knelt before the King brought forth the fact which all those assembled needed to be reminded of: that behind the sumptuous deceit of the court lay the simple human problem of the right of a woman to her husband and child and her inheritance. That this woman kneeling in the great hall happened to be a queen and her husband a ruler and her daughter a princess — all these things were incidental; or if they mattered at all, it was to intensify the salient fact that she was a woman in trouble, that she was Everywoman. She spoke as a woman to Henry as a man.

"Sir," she began, "I beseech you for all the loves that hath been between us, and for the love of God, let me have justice and right, take of me some pity and compassion, for I am a poor woman and a stranger born out of your dominion, I have here no assured friend, and much less indifferent counsel; I flee to you as to the head of justice within this realm." She went on to say: "I take God and all the world to witness, that I have been to you a true, humble and obedient wife, ever conformable to your will and pleasure, that never said or did anything to the contrary thereof . . ." Next she reminded Henry that she had loved those he loved for his sake — "whether I had cause or no; and whether they were my friends or my enemies." The painful subject of the loss of her children through death she touched on with dignity and stressed the fact that "although it hath pleased God to call them out of this world," it had been no fault of hers and nothing on which the King could lay the blame. Then, in the presence of all nobles and the ecclesiastical dignitaries of the realm, she went boldly to what Henry had made the heart of the King's great matter: "And when ye had me at the first, I take God to be my judge, I was a true maid without touch of man; and whether it be true or no, I put it to your conscience." [6]

The remainder of her remarks, eloquent with devout conviction in the justice of her cause, called into question the validity of the court. She begged the King to spare her the "extremity of this new court. And if you will not extend to me so much indifferent favor, your pleasure then be fulfilled, and to God I commit my cause!"

With these words she rose up, made a low curtsy to the King, and departed. It was supposed that she would resume her seat in the court, "but she took her way straight out of the house. And the King being advertised of her departure, commanded the crier to call her again, who called her by the name, 'Catherine Queen of England, come into court!'" She ignored the crier and, leaning on the arm of an attendant, "departed out of that court, without any farther answer at that time, or any other time, nor would ever appear at any other court after." The judges then ponderously overruled her objections to their right to hear the case, and after she had been summoned three more times and failed to appear, they put the seal of ecclesiastical disapproval upon her by pronouncing her contumacious.

Catherine may have failed to impress the judges with her plea, but she had impressed the women of England. They saw the justice of her cause and the wisdom of her defiance. Du Bellay reports that as she entered the court and departed from it, the women encouraged her with their cries, telling her to care for nothing and not to give in to her enemies. If the matter were to be decided by the women, he added, the King would lose the battle.[7]

Catherine had left in stately protest and with profound contempt for the court. She was well out of it. Not only did she feel the chill of the Legates' hostility and abominate the sacrilege of their using an ecclesiastical court to carry out the King's intent; there was another reason why she as a woman of propriety and decorum would not want to attend the trial, much less submit herself to an active part in it. The King's whole case was to be rested on the claim that Catherine was not a virgin when she came to his bed.

The testimony in the days that followed turned on the connubial delicacies of her first marriage to Prince Arthur. The prying eyes of the legatine court were turned on the carnal pastimes of a marriage that had terminated twenty-five years before, and the ears of the court were filled with the tales of aging witnesses rejuvenated by salacious memories — all done with the King's excuse to build a case on inference.

Judging by the testimony, Catherine and Arthur had no more privacy in bed than their marriage had now in court. The Duchess of Norfolk said she was present at the marriage, that the age of Prince Arthur at the time of the marriage was about fifteen, and that she saw the two "alone in bed together the next night after their marriage." This was about as far as the testimony got toward conclusiveness. The male witnesses put on a reminiscent parade of their own youthful virility and reasoned from their reassuring recollections to the belief that Arthur must have known Catherine. The Earl of Shrewsbury said he believed "the Prince knew his Lady carnally, because he might be able so to do, as he himself had been, who knew his wife before he was 16." The great Duke of Norfolk, ranking head of the nobility, deposed that since Arthur was of good complexion and nature and above fifteen he believed that he carnally knew his lady, "because himself at the same age did know and carnally use a Woman." He believed it all the more because "he heard, from credible persons, that the said Prince Arthur did lay with the said Lady Catherine five or six nights after."

Even some of Arthur's manly statements on which a bawdy interpretation could be put were now brought forward in depositions. Viscount Fitz-Walters said that he once served breakfast to the Prince, assisted by one Maurice St. John, "at which time Maurice St. John demanding of the Prince what he had done that night to make him so dry? the Prince answered, 'I have been in Spain this night.'" Again Sir Anthony Willoughby deposed that, being in Arthur's privy chamber the morning after his marriage, "the said Prince spoke before divers witnesses these words, 'Willoughby, give me a cup of ale, for I have been this night in the midst of Spain.' After which he said, 'It is good pastime to have a wife'; which words he repeated divers other times." Willoughby added the further intelligence that "he had heard say, they lay at Ludlow together the Shrove-tide next following." [8]

These farfetched hearsay items, dredged up by reminiscence and preposterously admitted as evidence, came out chiefly in depositions solicited by the scurrying counsel of the King, who "alleged the marriage not good from the beginning, because of the carnal knowledge committed between Prince Arthur her first husband, the king's brother and her." As Cavendish puts it, the matter was "very sore touched and maintained by the king's counsel . . . and to prove the same carnal copulation they alleged many coloured reasons and similitudes of truth."

Repeated sittings led gout-crippled Campeggio to protest that there was no breathing time and that it was "impossible to act according to the evidence, except after their fashion." Four days later he wrote again to Rome: "They are proceeding with inconceivable anxiety in the King's cause . . . The Queen, since she presented her appeals, has appeared no more; consequently they have a wide field for action, and entirely clear, so that they

429

may do whatever they like, and conduct the trial with all those arts which can influence the results in their favor." [9]

Speed was part of the strategy carried out by Wolsey. The cushions and coverings of his chair in the legatine court could not make it comfortable; he was sitting on the anxious seat, and history was breathing down his neck. Beyond the obvious reasons that urged Wolsey as the King's corporeal shadow to hasten the case, there were others that must have stirred the fires of impatience in a man of Wolsey's energy and restless temperament. The twenty years of his life at court had been marked by a baffling variety of activities touching every phase of the life of the kingdom. Now he sat day after day on a trifle, entertaining evidence and arguments touching the sexual relationship of a boy and a girl who had slept together before he ever came to court. This relationship had now become of transcendent importance. But the matter was dull and trifling all the same, and the only thing interesting about it was the irony: a man upon whom rested the whole responsibility of the government of the kingdom of England sitting day after day in judgment on the adolescent sex life of England's Queen.

What a waste of manpower! By his sedulous labors when the court was not in session, Wolsey might keep abreast of the routine demands of an office made burdensome by the fact that he had consistently arrogated to himself all the reins of responsibility in Church and State. But all the larger affairs were in suspense or relegated to insignificance.

Meanwhile the forces that would shape and determine the future continued as busily at work as ever, and the Cardinal of York had no part in regulating them. While the fate of one woman in England required most of his time and energy, two other women were meeting in Cambrai to decide the immediate fate of Europe. The Turk, ever menacing, hovered near the borders of Christendom. Russ slumbered on in its prodigious isolation, standing for all that was unknown in the world that was known. The Emperor's explorers continued to thread their way through perilous climes which men said were friendly and to treasures which men said were fabulous. In England enclosures went on unmolested, and men of wealth abused men of modest means, and the Cardinal's court of conscience could do little to arrest injustice because the Cardinal was taken up with the King's court of conscience.

Even dreams hung in suspense. Wolsey's great college at Oxford and the school at Ipswich might well have their fate determined by the legatine court sitting in the great hall at Blackfriars. St. Mary's at Ipswich was designed to fetch out of obscurity boys of talent and train them for leadership, and who could reckon or measure the potential of that? Cardinal College at Oxford was to bring to students of alert and eager mind a world of new ideas and spread the contagion of learning, and who could deny the good of that to England's sturdy heart? But whatever the strength of the invisible and the unpredictable, the King had no stomach for it and the Cardinal had no time for it.

In Henry's view, there was only one problem in the whole wide world. And the legatine court, to which he required the Cardinal to give the full measure of his attention, was only one means of solving it. Even while the court was sitting, he continued unrelentingly to hound Wolsey and Campeggio to hound Catherine. The King's impatience waxed as the court passed from session to session without appearing to accomplish anything, and Cavendish tells us that after one futile morning session the King sent word for my lord of York to come to him, the King being then at his nearby palace of Bridewell. Wolsey went and was there in communication with the King from eleven until past noon. Then he came out and took his barge at Blackfriars for his house in Westminster. "The Bishop of Carlisle being with him in his barge said unto him, (wiping the sweat from his face), 'Sir,' quoth he, 'it is a very hot day.' 'Yea,' quoth my lord Cardinal, 'and if ye had been as well chafed as I have been within this hour, ye would say it were very hot.' " [10]

When he reached his house at Westminster, Wolsey, worn out and ill from the lashing he had received, took off all his billowing red robes "and went incontinent to his naked bed." But after he had been there only a short time, Anne Boleyn's father, now my lord of Wiltshire, came to him with a message from the King. Wolsey was to take the other Cardinal and go back to the palace at Bridewell to speak to the Queen in her chamber "to persuade her by their wisdoms, advising her to surrender the whole matter unto the King's hands by her own will and consent." Wolsey heard the message while still in bed. He said he would go, of course, but he gave my lord of Wiltshire an unforgettable piece of his mind, saying, among other things: "Ye and other my lords of the council, which be near unto the king, are not a little to blame and misadvised to put any such fantasies into his head." He added "many other vehement words and sentences, which caused my lord of Wiltshire to water his eyes, kneeling all this while by my lord's bedside."

Having expressed his views, Wolsey got up incontinent from his naked bed, donned his hot and cumbersome robes and gear again, took to his barge, and went by Bath Place for Campeggio. Together they entered the chamber of presence of the Queen's lodgings in Bridewell and announced themselves there to the gentleman-usher, who advertised the Queen that they were there. She, being busy with the domestic duties that engaged much of her time and not expecting their coming, came out of her privy chamber with a skein of white thread about her neck. Wolsey asked if they might speak with her in her privy chamber. At this Catherine demurred, saying: "My lord, if you have anything to say, speak it openly before all these folks . . ." Whereupon Wolsey began to speak to her in Latin. "Nay, my good lord," quoth she, "speak to me in English, I beseech you; although I understand Latin."

Wolsey explained that they had come to counsel her, "to declare secretly our opinions and our counsel unto you," and this, strangely, Catherine believed. She told the Legates that she had been sitting among her maidens at work, thinking little of the matter the Legates wished to discuss, but she would be glad to hear them, "for I am a simple woman and barren of friendship and counsel here in a foreign region." Then she took Wolsey by the hand and led him, accompanied by the other Cardinal, into her privy chamber. Cavendish reports that they were there in long communication. He could not hear what was said; he could occasionally hear the Queen speak very loud, but he could not make out the words.

The visit was as futile as Wolsey knew it would be. The two Legates went from the Queen to the King and reported the interview, but nothing came of it. In the end the Legates resorted to my lord of York's barge again and went home to their houses for supper.

The trial went on — at a snail's pace for the King and "always faster than a trot" for Campeggio. Nor did it go entirely well, in spite of the King's great precaution and the care of the Cardinal of York in steering the proceedings. One incident in particular upset the decorum of the court and set off reverberations that were heard in Rome and Spain. One of the Queen's counsel spoke out in open court against the King's cause. Moreover, the man who gave this unhappy turn to affairs had the unqualified respect of the whole realm. John Fisher, Bishop of Rochester, was the one prelate whose recalcitrance in the King's great matter had been feared and on whom Wolsey had made the special call to silence him if possible. But when he stood up one day in the legatine court, he showed that this effort, along with all of Wolsey's other efforts made at the behest of the King, had been in vain.

Apart from his formidable reputation for piety and righteousness, Fisher had another quality which lent prophetic drama to his address before the

432

court: his appearance was that of an accusing apparition. His body was "so bare of flesh as is almost incredible, which came by the great abstinence and penance he used upon himself for many years, even from his youth." He was "to the quantity of six feet in height; and being very slender and lean was nevertheless upright and well formed, straight backed, with big jaws, and strongly sinewed." His forehead was large and smooth and the veins stood out on his face.[11]

Campeggio reported the substance and the fact of Fisher's speech to the Pope. Since the King had sought to know the truth, said Fisher, he would be glad to tell him.[12] He "presented himself before their reverend lordships to assert and demonstrate with cogent reasons that this marriage of the King and Queen could not be dissolved by any power, divine or human. He declared that in maintenance of this opinion he was willing to lay down his life." He ended his remarks by saying that he had written a book on the subject, and he presented the Legates with a copy.

It was a brilliant and tactless tactic, and it stunned the court. Wolsey, chafed by many irritations, protested against what he called the bishop's attack on the Legates. The court had been called, he said, to hear the case and render judgment "in whatever way divine wisdom should inspire them to do." But, said Wolsey, the Bishop of Rochester had taken upon himself by the positiveness and vigor of his utterance to preempt the prerogative of the court and pronounce judgment himself.

So he had. The King was furious and penned a violent reply in the form of an address to the Legates. A copy of this reply, with Fisher's notes in the margin, is preserved. One of these notes concerned the hapless interview Wolsey had had with Fisher on the way to Canterbury and Calais in 1527. The King alleged that Rochester had approved his scruples and had said that he could not recover his tranquillity of mind without consulting the Pope. To this Fisher replied in his commentary: "I did not say so; but the Cardinal would have been glad if I had said so." [13]

Fisher's audacity lent the one touch of magnificence that redeemed the trial at Blackfriars from legal immorality. Its effect was more than dramatic. It seemed to give Campeggio some reason and courage for carrying out the Pope's private instructions that he settle the case without pronouncing sentence. The change in him was noted by all, especially by the Cardinal of York. On July 13, two weeks after Fisher's appearance in court, du Bellay wrote that those who favored the annulment were extremely troubled, "finding Campeggio not so favorable as they expected. I think he is inclined to remit the matter to the Pope." [14]

Even so, the King's counsel pressed for decision. On Friday, July 23, the sentence was expected. On this day the King himself appeared, "sitting within a gallery against the door" that "looked unto the judges where they sat, whom he might both see and hear speak, to hear what judgment they would give in his suit." Still the suspense continued while "all their proceedings were first openly read in Latin." Following this tedium, the King's learned counsel at the bar called fast for judgment.

Campeggio stood up. He was the canonist, the man acquainted with the technicalities of the law. In a fluent Latin speech he explained that it was the custom of the court in Rome to "suspend all legal proceedings from the end of July until the commencement of October." He said also, according to Cavendish, that he "would wade no farther in this matter, unless I have the just opinion and judgment, with the assent of the pope, of such other of his counsel as hath more experience and learning in such doubtful laws as I have. Wherefore," Campeggio continued with words that fell like a knell on the ears of the King and the Cardinal of York, "I will adjourn this court for this time, according to the order of the court in Rome, from whence this court and jurisdiction is derived."

It was now the King's turn to stride contemptuously from the great hall of the monastery. For two years the Defender of the Faith had sought the aid of the Pope in the matter of his conscience and with no result but one subterfuge after another. And now another two months' delay. This was all the King of England could expect from Rome.

The meaning was clear. The King left, but the Duke of Suffolk, who had been sitting with the King, came forward, and, giving a great slap on the table, spoke the sentiments that were plain to all: "By the mass! now I see that the old-said saw is true, that there was never legate nor cardinal that did good in England." [15]

He went on, speaking "in great dispight" and with a vehement countenance. But it was the old saw that stuck in Wolsey's craw. He took Suffolk's words not as an assertion of long-standing grievances against Rome but as a personal insult from one whom he had befriended with the King. Twice in the days of Wolsey's power Suffolk had been nearer losing the King's favor than Wolsey was now — once when he married the King's sister secretly, and again when in 1524 he allowed his army to mutiny and return from France. It was with a bitter realization of his ingratitude, representing the ingratitude of all men, that Wolsey now spoke to the Duke. "Sir, of all men within this realm," he said, "ye have the least cause to dispraise or be offended with cardinals; for if I, simple cardinal, had not been, you should have had at this present no head upon your shoulders, wherein you should have a tongue to make any such report in despite of us . . .

Ye know best what friendship ye have received at my hands, the which I have never revealed to no person alive before now, neither to my glory, nor to your dishonour." [16]

So spoke Thomas Wolsey of Ipswich, by the King's grace lord of York, to Charles Brandon, by the King's grace Duke of Suffolk. The Cardinal for a moment had become a person. But he spoke other words also to Suffolk in the closing moments of the trial at Blackfriars, and these words revealed that he was still a cardinal of Rome and still consistent in his conviction that the King's cause could be decided only by the Holy See. He defended the commission and reminded Suffolk "that we be but commissioners for a time, and can, nor may not, by virtue of our commission proceed to judgment, without the knowledge and consent of the chief head of our authority, and having his consent to the same; which is the pope."

Wolsey's hour of decision had struck, and the sound of it reverberated with tones of doom. The failure of the legatine court to grant the King's wish would mean the end of Wolsey's power. Yet the court need not have failed, for under the commission wrung from the Pope Thomas Cardinal Wolsey had the full right to pronounce judgment himself; he could have pronounced it, if he had had a mind to, in favor of the King. If he had done so, he might have saved his station and his powers. In an atmosphere crackling with hostility and before an audience expecting a verdict favorable to the royal will, Wolsey had spoken plainly and he had spoken in defense of Rome. He had made his choice, and what so many had suspected and alleged now proved to be true: when the chips were down, the Cardinal was playing against the King.

What led to this concurrent decision, wherein the Lord Chancellor of England joined an Italian canonist against the English King's wish for speedy compliance, no one can say or gainsay. His action at the end of the trial at Blackfriars must remain a part of the magnificent mystery of Wolsey. On the day of choice he had taken the course which was sure to be freighted with costs. What had made it so? Was it the steady association with the incorruptible Campeggio and the environment provided by that man's character? Was it the accusing worth and dignity of Catherine of Aragon and the sure knowledge that she was a woman wronged? Was it the sinewy tradition of Thomas Becket, living still in the bones of John Fisher of Rochester, that decisions of conscience must never be finally made by a king? Was it a sudden and unadmitted disgust, growing out of boredom, with a prince who had neglected subjects and responsibilities and honor in the vain pursuit of a selfish object? Was it all of these or most of these or none?

Whatever the reason or the compound of reasons, Wolsey made his decision. He might regret it, he might rue it, but he made it.

Actually it was a decision he had made long before. Through the years of his power, amid all the distractions of diplomacy, Wolsey had remained steadfast to the ideal represented by the Holy See. During those years, however, the idea had been a convenience. Now it was a test. What mattered at Blackfriars was that, in a moment of supreme crisis, when he had to choose between the King's wishes and continued devotion to that ideal, he chose the thing called Rome. The ideal of a kingdom above kingdoms, of a united Christendom over and beyond the state and the individual, was an ideal tarnished and corroded by practices as evil as many of his own. Still, it was there, a distant star for the imagination.

A good name for Christendom was rather to be chosen than great riches. There must be some tribunal above peoples to which matters of faith and conduct could be referred. Without the deterrent of this touching faith, a man of Wolsey's resourcefulness could have found a dozen solutions to the King's problem. But not in the trial at Blackfriars, nor in the bitter and futile effort to redeem himself with the King later, did Wolsey propose or attempt a settlement of Henry's problem on his own responsibility or without reference to the See Apostolic. In the vicissitudes and vexations of politics which he knew so well his great illusion sustained him. Rome was Christendom, a symbol of universality and integration. His actions were ruled by what Rome adumbrated and stood for, not by what it was. He never acknowledged in the hard realities of the day that Rome was but another kingdom, a minor one at that, and the Pope a petty Italian prince. Wolsey's belief that Rome was something more than a state lured him to his ruin as a politician, but at the same time his belief made him, for once, more than a politician.

Book Four
(1529-1530)

Describing the banishment of Wolsey from the King's presence for his failure to secure the annulment; the loss of his palaces and colleges and most of his offices; his constant hope of being recalled by the King; his life as a priest in the north of England; the intrigues, fostered by Anne Boleyn and his enemies, that brought about his arrest; his death and burial; and a brief note about events that followed.

NOT until seventy harrowing days after the adjournment at Black-friars did Wolsey learn the consequences of his decision. Meanwhile he carried about with him all the luggage of dignity, his crosses and his pillars and his maces and even the Great Seal of England. The King had withdrawn to lick his wounds and to spend his fury in hunting, shooting the stag instead of the Pope, and he left the dreary routine of government business in the hands of the shattered Cardinal. Wolsey went through the motions of his office like a sleepwalker, agitated by bad dreams he could not communicate, sternly keeping up appearances, still pretending fiercely that he was Lord Chancellor of England, not knowing from day to day when the axe might fall.

Only by the jagged edge of signs and tokens was Wolsey warned — by small hints of royal disfavor that increased his anxiety. In the weeks that followed the trial these hints had the character of indirect cruelty and aggression. Henry made no forthright disavowal of his minister. He continued to use him on menial tasks and on some that were delicate and required shrewd negotiation. But in the main he ignored him conspicuously and shut off all direct personal contact with him, either by conversation or by letter. Stephen Gardiner was now back in England and very much the up-and-coming young man about the court. He had been made the King's chief secretary, and Wolsey's only communication with the King was through his own former secretary, who now conveyed the King's sentiments, such as they were, to the Cardinal.

Once after Wolsey had quashed the threat that the King and the Queen should be summoned personally to appear before the Pope for the continuation of their cause, Wolsey wrote Gardiner and asked for an interview with Henry. Gardiner's reply was devastating. Not only did Henry tell his secretary to deny the interview as an experience too painful for his nerves; he asked Gardiner to add another insult for good measure, and one that would gouge the Cardinal. At the end of his letter Wolsey had mentioned that he would like to talk with Henry about certain things he could not put in writing. The King asked Gardiner to inquire what in heaven's name it was that Wolsey would not find convenient to put in writing. His Highness marveled at this, said Gardiner, especially since the King knew "right well that your Grace is not wont to spare any labors or pains in writing." What a blow to a man who had lived by letters and had thought any problem could be solved by letters. Then Gardiner required that the Cardinal let the King know "incontinently, by letters of your own hand," what matters he referred to. And, added Gardiner, do it in the fewest possible words.[1]

The King's coldness chilled the Cardinal with an ague of suspense and uncertainty. Without assurance in office and without his wholesome official preoccupations, he became more sensitively personal in his reactions. The quick was exposed, the shell of his ego being gone. And in his shaken condition he seems to have lost sight entirely of the political factors working to accomplish his isolation and deprive him of his usefulness. He who had had so little privacy in the glare of public affairs, and so little time for personal affairs, now became almost wholly personal. He was famished for affection, having postponed until the end of his life the day when men and women were no longer to be regarded as means to some end but as creatures possessed of hands and feet and blood.

To be sure, the renewal of the King's favor would in turn restore his political personality, make him again a statue who towered above the heads of nobles and commons alike. The nature of the Tudor monarchy was such that he could do nothing without the royal pleasure. But it must be noted that in all his petitions to the King and in all his supplications after the trial, there were always the recognizable signs of deep craving for friendship and acceptance and the anguish and agony of personal rejection. In these dark days it was not my lord of York addressing His Majesty the King, but Thomas Wolsey crying out to Henry Tudor. A man of fifty-nine called to one who was dear to him and yet young; and he could get no reply. An old man who had spent his energies lavishly in the service of one young enough to be his son now faced the mystery of that strange reversal of roles wherein the child is father to the man and the man feels left behind by one he nurtured and loved. There was a rending now of a tie that had held Wolsey and Tudor together for more than twenty years. Something good had come to an end, and the end was not good.

All through the years of Wolsey's connection with the court there had been many small acts of unnecessary kindness and recognition on the part of the King to keep their relationship from being coldly official. Henry was accessible, even to bores, and he delighted in good talk. He stood with his feet apart on his prerogatives, defiantly, but he stood not on ceremony. He was a personal king, not simply a figurehead under a crown. His reign from first to last involved strong attachments. He was attentive to all Wolsey said and did, and he was especially attentive to his letters and dispatches. As befitted a King's position, it was Henry and not Wolsey who took the initiative in condescending but unpatronizing acts of thoughtfulness that gave the Cardinal a warmth of mind that all his offices could not have bestowed.

Even after the first frost fell between them, these trifling but tremendous acts continued. Once after the arrival of Campeggio, a letter was sent by Wolsey to the King. Word came back from Brian Tuke, Henry's secretary: "In reading your Grace's letter, his Highness said, 'This is of my Cardinal's own hand,' and I said yes, which seemed very much to please him." [2] Up to the time of the trial, the dealings of the King and the Cardinal had been enlivened by such condiments of kindness. And Henry, who had added the spices, now by merely withholding them changed and allowed to spoil the whole relationship between them. It was almost as if he sought to prove that the greatest unkindness of all is the absence of any kindness at all.

Thus while Wolsey waited for impending penalties which everyone knew would eventually fall, he suffered all the torments and showed all the symptoms of a man who has lost his best friend. When he received Gardiner's curt letter announcing the King's refusal to see him, the Cardinal crawled on his belly toward his master — a mastiff converted into a cur by harshness and seeking to ingratiate himself again through misery. He signs his letter, "Your Grace's most prostrated, poor chaplain, creature and bedesman, T. Card. Ebor, *Miserrimus*." [3] All the words he uses are designed to humble himself beyond recognition and thus gain reinstatement, a device more touching than effective, as is true of many a device used by those who seek to recapture affection. He begins by referring to himself as "your poor, heavy, and wretched priest" and goes on to say, "I do daily pursue, cry, and call upon your Royal Majesty for grace, mercy, remission, and pardon . . ." He assures the King "that, next unto God, I desire nor covet any thing in this world but the attaining of your gracious favor and forgiveness of my trespass . . ."

The man whose tongue once ruled Europe had now been reduced to obsequious gibberish. Starved as he was for companionship, peered at from behind masks by both supercilious and sniveling enemies, he could construe his desolation as due to the King who had withdrawn his coun-

441

tenance. He gave no signs of discerning that it was the flood of history that isolated him, that the King himself was but a creature caught in a tide moving to its fullness. For during the days when the Cardinal so pathetically sought the King's friendship, happenings in England and Europe went forward with the steady rapidity of men hammering at the building of a gallows. Each event seemed of relentless intent.

Louise of Savoy and Margaret of Burgundy in adjoining houses had been conferring at Cambrai during the trial at Blackfriars; two weeks after the sudden adjournment of the trial the peace they had supervised was formally signed. The peace thus made was known with a mixture of contempt and respect as the Ladies' Peace. It was the work of gifted amateurs, and the hardened professionals had been kept out of it. For the first time in fifteen years the Cardinal had not been consulted in the realignments of power known as peace. There would be no immediate future for the gifts and talents he had so long displayed. Francis had turned his back on the alliance with England that Wolsey had fashioned and had made terms with Charles, who owed Henry endless money and held the Pope captive. By the terms of the Ladies' Peace Francis went so far as to renounce his claims to Milan and to withdraw from Italy.

Nor was his withdrawal a mere polite concession of territory. While the trial was in progress at Blackfriars, Francis had lost his army in the battle of Landriano, fought five miles from the field of ill memory at Pavia. This battle left Charles master of Italy, and the first person to recognize this potent fact was Giulio de' Medici of Florence. With a good sense of weather, Clement had already sent his nuncio to Barcelona to negotiate an alliance with the Emperor, and five days after the French forces were annihilated at Landriano, the Treaty of Barcelona was signed. Its provisions were many but some of them significantly affected the Cardinal. The Pope got what he wanted most of all: the government of his beloved Florence was taken out of the clutches of the populace, who had audaciously sought to establish a republic, and the house of Medici was restored to glory. Henry and Wolsey could not have given Clement that gift; nor could they have returned, as Charles did, Ravenna and Cervia. In exchange for favors received, Clement was to crown Charles with the imperial crown and, most amicable and remarkable of all, he was to "absolve from ecclesiastical censures all those who were present at, or consented to, the sack of Rome." [4]

The face of Europe had been changed behind his back while the Cardinal sat on a cushioned chair in the great hall at Blackfriars and moved about in the haze of his vanished glory. There was suddenly a new Europe, and to this new Europe the Cardinal of York, old and weary in Henry's service, was a stranger. The dumfounding changes made him seem out of date. The whole concept of Rome as an ideal had vanished in the smoke and tumult of battles. The Pope was more of a captive of the Emperor than ever now. The King's cause now would have to be decided not only by Rome but in Rome. There was nothing else for it. The English agents had written in July that the cause would be taken to Rome and the commission revoked.

The face of England was changing, too, and even the myopic Cardinal of York could see that some of the changes would sorely affect him. He had consistently resisted the King's impulse to assemble Parliament. But three days after the peace of Cambrai was signed in early August, writs were issued to assemble the Commons for November. In this matter Wolsey was not consulted, merely instructed. As Lord Chancellor he handled the clerical detail, and there is a letter from Gardiner saying that the King wanted certain of the writs sent to him so that His Highness could see that they are delivered "by the hands and advice of Norfolk." [5] The Parliament was to be an assembly that carried out the King's wishes better than any legatine court.

To these stark events of the summer of 1529 my lord of York was a remote and unwitting party, executing the orders of destiny like a clerk, without any apparent perception of their meaning. Only the King and his mercy had meaning. A soul in the torment of happenings he could neither control nor measure, he must simplify his complexities by one clear, vital hope, must have one object of steadfast faith, must feel that if one matter is settled all others can be put right. Dazed and numbed by circumstances, Wolsey turned to the one problem he might personally solve — his relation with the King.

Not until September 14, almost two months after Campeggio adjourned the hearings, did Wolsey get to see the King. The experience on this occasion tantalized his hopes for part of a day and then left him in more desperate uncertainty than ever. The setting and the conditions of the meeting were awkward, to say the least. Campeggio wished to return to Rome but he must first have the leave of the King. Dr. Stephen Gardiner arranged that he should resort to the King at Grafton, where Henry and Anne Boleyn had gone in pursuit of the stag and other pleasures. Wolsey was to accompany Campeggio, as was fitting their joint legateship under the commission, but it is far from clear whether the invitation came from the King or his secretary; nor is it clear whether it was extended in good faith or as a means of publicly humiliating Wolsey with reminders of his changed status. Among the lords of the court, says Cavendish, were laid many great wagers that the King would not speak with my lord Cardinal.

The Legates made the journey to Grafton from The More, one of Wolsey's houses near Harrow. They arrived at the lodgings of the King on a Sunday morning and expected to be received with the dignities usually accorded them. Campeggio was. He was conducted to quarters prepared for him, and Wolsey accompanied him to get him established there, expecting then to go on to his own rooms. It was only after he left Campeggio that he was told that he had no lodging appointed for him in the court. My lord Cardinal was astonished to hear this, and the news also caused some consternation among the officers of the house. In the emergency Sir Henry Norris, Groom of the Stole to the King, came forward, full of apologies for the smallness of the house, and begged Wolsey to take his own chamber until some lodging could be found for him in a house not far distant. Wolsey accepted and, having shifted his riding apparel, now entertained various friends of the court who came by to see him and tell him various details of the King's displeasure; all of which, says his gentleman-usher, the lord Cardinal was glad to hear, that he might better prepare his defenses.[6]

These defenses, however, were not on this occasion needed. Master Norris came to notify Wolsey that he should now "prepare himself to give attendance in the chamber of presence against the king's coming thither." Campeggio came by and the two went into the chamber of presence, where the lords of the Council stood waiting in a row and in the order of their ranks.

It was a moment dramatic with doubt, this first appearance of Wolsey at court since the failure of the legatine court to accommodate the King. Henry went around the chamber, making his salutations to the lords, "putting off his cap to every one of them most gently, and so did they no less to him." The atmosphere was tense with politeness, and all waited expectantly to see what countenance the King would show Wolsey.

They had not long to wait. The King placed himself under the cloth of estate. Both Cardinals knelt before him, and he took each by the hand as a signal to rise. This ceremony ended, he took Wolsey by "both arms and caused him to stand up." Then a moment later he called him aside and led him by the hand to a great window and began talking with him, and with his old amiable condescension caused him to dispense with deference due a monarch and put his cap back on his head.

Henry and Wolsey continued standing apart in long and earnest conversation, ignoring the rest of the company. "To behold the countenance of those that had made their wagers to the contrary," Cavendish remarks, "it would have made you smile." The gentleman-usher who furnishes the account could not overhear what they said. The King did pluck out of his bosom a paper and ask the Cardinal of York if it was not signed in his own hand. The Cardinal admitted that it was, and with that the King suggested that the Cardinal go to dinner with the lords, who would keep him company, adding that after dinner "we will commune further with you in this matter."

The table was then spread in the chamber of presence, and Wolsey dined with the lords of the Council. There was an exchange, amiable in appearance but pointed, between Wolsey and Norfolk, in which the Duke suggested that the Archbishop should go to his province. It was far from court. After the lords had been served, the waiters dined and Cavendish with them, and among them were the servants who had waited on the King and Anne Boleyn at their private dinner in her chamber. These servants reported that she was much offended because the King had dealt so gently with my lord of York. She reminded him of the "things he hath wrought within this realm to your great slander and dishonour," including the Amicable Loan. The King, according to the report of the waiters, defended the Cardinal genially, but Anne persisted in her criticisms until the waiters ended the conversation by coming in to take up the table.

After dinner in midafternoon the King returned to the lords, taking the Cardinal of York back to the great window again and talking with him there secretly for a while and then retiring with him and no other into his privy chamber, there to talk with him until it was night. This confidential treatment of one the lords had expected to see humbled and insulted "blanked his enemies very sore, and made them stir the coals." Meanwhile Cavendish had scoured the countryside for a place where his Cardinal might be lodged and had found one at a house called Euston, three miles from Grafton. To this place Wolsey and his gentleman-usher and other servants now departed, but the King had commanded him as they left to resort to him again the next morning that they might finish their talk.

What Wolsey and Henry discussed so energetically in these private talks, no one, not even the servants, knew or reported. Since there was only one subject on Henry's mind, it is easy to suppose that they talked about the annulment and that Henry still thought the Cardinal could serve as the hammer for his purpose. Surely he would not otherwise have paid him such conspicuous attention or singled him out from among his councilors. Henry was not one to reject a person he could use, and the wild hopes held by Wolsey seemed now by no means extravagant. His petitions had not been in vain, for not only had the King received him but embraced him, and on this historic Sunday evening in September it looked for all the world as if the King's old and trusted minister would be restored to a place of intimacy and favor.

So it seemed as Wolsey left that night. In a genial, confident, and expectant mood, he rode to Euston, where he had supper and fell into talk with divers of his friends of the court. But there was no escape from odd signs and omens — little untoward incidents such as the failure to provide lodging for him at court. For hardly had the party settled at supper when in came Stephen Gardiner, who had grown lately like a beanstalk and waxed strong in the favor of the King, being a young man with a future and, above all, a man who knew how to wield words. His vigorous tongue and pen could put sentiments and sentences in Henry's letters that would keep the monarch in the intellectual state of mind to which he had under Wolsey become accustomed. He was, moreover, a young man willing to do the King's instant bidding, and it was for that reason, Wolsey surmised, he had come to visit. He had come, Wolsey took it, "to dissemble a certain obedience and love towards him, or else to espy his behavior and to hear his communication at supper."

The feints in their conversation had all the characteristics of remarks men use to avoid mental contact. Wolsey bade his young rival welcome, asked him to sit down at the table with the others, inquired after his health, and asked him when he came from Rome and what he had been doing since his return. Gardiner explained that he had been following the court on its present progress, which no one knew better than Wolsey. Then talk turned to hunting and included such colloquy as this: "What greyhounds have ye?" quoth my lord. "I have some, sir," quoth he. Thus went their guarded conversation at supper. After supper, says Cavendish, "my lord and he talked secretly together, till it was midnight or they departed."

The next morning Wolsey rose early and rode the three miles back to court. He could have saved himself the trouble. Change had stalked in the night. He found Henry ready to ride off with Anne Boleyn to inspect the ground of a new park. The trip would take a long while, and Henry explained that he could not tarry and talk with him. Instead he suggested that the Cardinal of York resort to the lords of the Council in his absence, but he also made it plain that Wolsey was to return to London with Cardinal Campeggio, who had taken his leave already and would be ready to go to London before the King would return.

It was a scene obviously staged, with all the actors speaking their parts in character, and it had the abruptness and the cold, impersonal quality of a Gardiner letter. Wolsey, his expectations still buoyed by the events of the day before, had no choice but to obey the King's command. He therefore took his formal leave before the King rode off, and if there was any consolation to assuage the Cardinal's chagrin it was in the fact that the King departed from him "amiably in the sight of all men."

It was hardly more than a month after this amiable parting in the sight of all men that the Dukes of Norfolk and Suffolk took from Wolsey the Great Seal of England; took from him the emblem and stamp of his authority, the amulet of his ambition: took the Great Seal in its white leather bag, enclosed in another of crimson velvet,[7] leaving him naked of power and bereft of function.

Meanwhile the King had kept him turning on the spit of uncertainty. Wolsey and Campeggio had ridden from Grafton back to The More and then on to London with proper legatine dignity, their trains and robes and pillars and maces a signal to the countryside of Rome's closeness to the throne and life of England. They had come from the King. Campeggio had gone on to Dover, arriving there October 10 en route to Rome. There had been an ominous delay in his passage to Calais. It had been said that ships were short and wanting, but two persons close to Wolsey's household heard that Campeggio had been detained by the King's messengers and his baggage searched by the King's warrant; for the King had been informed that the Legate took with him large sums of silver and gold belonging to the Cardinal of York. These, it had been said, he was transporting to Rome, "whither," says Cavendish, "they surmised my lord would secretly convey himself out of this realm."

Instead of Wolsey's treasure they had found many chests filled with "old hosen, old coats, and such vile stuff as no honest man would care to have it." [8] But if a report that Wolsey planned to flee to Rome could be credited and acted upon by the King, there was no telling what the King could believe next. Still Wolsey had fresh in his mind the remembrance of those long talks with the King at Grafton, when some had wagered that Henry would not converse with him at all. He had thus, upon his return to London, gone about the business of government with preoccupied zeal, and he had sat with the lords of the Council at Westminster. One chronicler said that he "showed himself much more humblier than he was wont to be, and the lords showed themselves more higher and stranger." [9] If this is true rather than fancied, it was the only circumstance in which the Cardinal had ever shown humbleness to any other than the King. Having lived for the past twenty years mostly in public and being accustomed to putting on a noble front, he had given no inkling or outward sign that he had felt the King's displeasure. Nay, rather, he had gone to the opening of his court "in such like sort and gesture as he was wont most commonly to do." He had let it be known with his usual train that he was still Lord Chancellor of England, qualified to hear common complaints in the name of his King.

It had been a strange and sparsely attended court, and he had not sat there after that one day. For while he had sat as a judge in one court, he had become a culprit in another court. The lords of the Council had gone to the King, who lay then at Windsor, and had persuaded him to have his attorney, Christopher Hales, sue out a writ in the Court of King's Bench, charging that Wolsey had by the exercise of his legatine authority violated the Statute of Praemunire. It was an old and thorny word, having acquired, for all its simplicity and cadence, the sound of treason through two hundred years of unpleasant history. A charge of praemunire was enough to condemn a man, at least to isolate and smear him. Indictment carried tacit judgment and condemnation.

Wolsey had been a consistent advocate of papal authority in England. In the crucial affair of the King's great matter he had turned to Rome for the right to act. He had "drawn out of the realm in plea." The court at Blackfriars was a papal court trying an English matter involving the English succession and hence the peace and quiet of the English people.

Perhaps it was not without significance that the Statute of Praemunire took its name from a harmless Latin term that acquired its ominous connotation through use. The opening words of the writ were, *Praemunire facias* Thomas Wolsey, meaning, "Cause Thomas Wolsey to be forewarned . . ."

But we are never sufficiently forewarned of what we most dread. Wrapping himself in sentiments of personal devotion, Wolsey had failed to see the motion of facts. Fresh from the long and earnest conversations with the King at Grafton, he had sat in the Council again, and he had sat in Chancery, too, as one of the great of England. Then as he had sat there, listening as he so long had to other men's problems and miseries, there had been that same day and not far away sued out against him a charge that amounted to treason. While looking piously in one direc-

448

tion, he had been struck from another. And what must have stunned him most this fateful October 9 was the fact that the blow had not come directly from the King but from the King's Bench; not from Henry but from an act of an ancient Parliament. It had been an impersonal thing like a Gardiner letter.

Again the King had withdrawn into the fastness of royal privacy and left the fate of his aged minister to the operation of implacable forces — and it was these forces that my lord of York in his present overwhelming bewilderment could not sort out or understand. Not the King but law had turned against him. Behind the law lurked enemies who sought his undoing, and these his gentleman-usher could see. But behind the enemies moved, no less stealthily, the creatures and abstractions of history, and these no man could be expected to see.

Wolsey had returned with his train to his house, York Place, after that first brave day in the Star Chamber. Other lords, many of them, would now do the work of administering justice he had done. He had not gone back the next day or any day thereafter to the room with the stars in its ceiling. In fact, he had not gone out. He had tarried at home, knowing that soon there would come to him lords who had always wanted to show him haughtiness and would show it now and would take from him the Great Seal of England. A prisoner incarcerated by dread and embarrassment, he had tarried in the great house that his skill had caused to be built and expanded and stuffed and stacked with treasures of silver and gold and silk and velvet and fine linens. He might as well have been in a cell awaiting the steps of the turnkey. He had known that before long the Dukes of Norfolk and Suffolk would ride from the King. But they had waited, and the waiting had deepened his dejection.

In this state he was visited by the French ambassador, du Bellay, who still paid him court and who remained now his only friend with status. To him as a friend Wolsey felt free to talk — too free, in fact. Into his diplomatic ear the Cardinal poured all the laments of his misery, official and personal. Du Bellay found him the saddest example of fortune a man could witness, he reported later. "He represented his case to me in the worst rhetoric I ever saw, for heart and words entirely failed him. He wept much," said du Bellay, and he could not "say anything more expressive than his countenance, which is deprived of half its animation." Indeed, exclaimed the Frenchman, Wolsey's "misfortunes are such that his enemies, even though they were Englishmen, could not fail to pity him." [10]

Wolsey's incoherence and tearful pleading had been remarkable enough on this occasion, but the full extent of his desperation could only be

449

judged by the requests he made of du Bellay. The Cardinal had come to his present pass by favoring the transcendent importance of Rome; now in his straits he had sought aid from another foreign power, praying du Bellay that he would intercede with Francis and the French King's mother that they might in turn intercede with the King of England. A course of action so improbable could not have occurred to a great mind unless it had been staggered and unhinged. How little he knew the King he had served so long! And to make this felony of judgment a felony of conduct he had sent later to du Bellay an Italian servant in whom he had reposed his confidence with the request that du Bellay ask the French King to write Henry;[11] and as in the case of devising the bulls he wanted the Pope to sign, Wolsey had virtually written the letter for Francis to sign.

It had been shortly after the Cardinal had tearfully broken down in the presence of the French ambassador and made his wild pleas for deliverance that the messengers of the King had arrived at York Place amid a great clatter of hooves in the courtyard. They had brought the message he had expected: he was to deliver up the Great Seal into their hands; he was to deliver up also his great house and move at once to a smaller palace known as Esher, belonging to the bishopric of Winchester, and lying near Hampton Court, which now also was to be occupied by the King. He had listened patiently to the message carried by the gaunt Norfolk and the fat Suffolk. In this case they had ridden straight from the King, and the message they bore was devastating in the main; but it had left a strange ray of light and hope. The King had not shut him off entirely; he had not consigned him to the Tower. He had banished him but had not demolished him.

To my lord of Norfolk and my lord of Suffolk, my lord of York, still Cardinal and still by a hair's breadth Lord Chancellor of England, had not shown the countenance he had shown du Bellay. Instead he demanded to see their commission. They had answered that they had the King's commission by his mouth, and to this my lord of York had replied: "That is not sufficient for me, not without further commandment of the king's pleasure; for the great seal of England was delivered unto me by the king's own person, to enjoy during my life, with the ministration of the office and high room of chancellorship of England: for my surety whereof, I have the king's letters patent to show." [12]

So he had spoken to the lofty Dukes, his rhetoric back in his mouth again and his countenance firm to them. Many stout words, says his gentleman-usher, passed between him and them. But in this encounter my lord of York held his ground and held his house, and the Dukes, seeing him determined, as ever he had been with them, "were fain to depart again without their purpose at that present." He had gained the small moral victory of postponement, and he had held for another twenty-four hours the weapons of authority in the State.

It was odd how, for all his deference and suppliance toward Rome, he had held fiercely to his position as Lord Chancellor. It was the last official tie that held him to the King, and he had no intention of letting it be severed without the express command of the King's hand. The duality which he had lived and acted threatened now to deprive him at one and the same time of both the objects of his loyalty. He had lost his power with the Pope, and now he had seen that he must lose it also with the King. Only a small graven image in a white leather bag and a red velvet bag remained to him who loved possessions and reverenced acquisitions. He would not give it over, this symbol of the whole physical world, to any man, not even to the ranking nobles of the realm. The more the mind is shaken, the more the hand must have something to hold in its grasp. As long as Wolsey had something in his hand to give the stamp of authority, the King might relent.[13]

Next day the Dukes came riding back from the King, accompanied this time by Fitzwilliam, Dr. Taylor, Master of the Rolls, and, of course, the ubiquitous Dr. Stephen Gardiner. The party arrived at six in the evening, and Wolsey received them in the gallery of his great house. This time they brought with them letters from the King, and, while the lords and officers and their attendants and those of the Cardinal stood awkwardly and tensely about, Wolsey took the letters. He read them, Cavendish noted, with much reverence. His final hope perished in the lines of the familiar handwriting, and, without a further murmur, he gave over to his enemies the Great Seal of England.

He gave over also to the custody of his enemies for transfer to the King's use all his properties. About this transfer there would be many a murmur later, but for the moment he appeared content to pay the toll exacted by the law and the King. The law carried with it the penalty of imprisonment as well as the loss of goods, but the King had already given him assurance that he would retire to Esher.

Two days after he surrendered the instruments of his office he signed an indenture acknowledging his guilt in the charge of praemunire by virtue of having exercised his legatine authority in England.[14] This indenture signed and delivered to the King with a prayer of penitence, my lord of York called together the officers of his great household at York

Place and ordered them to put on tables for public display like so much merchandise all such stuff as they had in their charge. It was to be drawn up for the inspection of the King. All of it was classified and marshaled by the officers, and by each display were books in which the officers listed the weight and value of every item. Under the tables were baskets of old plate, "not worthy to be occupied," but showing that the Cardinal held nothing back.

It was a dumfounding display when all this slowly accumulated wealth was laid out on tables, and the sight of it smote the eye of the Cardinal's gentleman-usher, who had thought up to that time that he knew the house fairly well. What had been stored in closets now took on life. Apart from plate of silver and gold were rich cloths in all colors, including a thousand pieces of fine holland cloth and, as Cavendish notes with particular interest, the richest suits of copes he had ever seen in England. These copes the Cardinal had caused to be made for his colleges at Oxford and Ipswich. He had made the copes, like the colleges, his personal possessions. And like the copes, the colleges now would be transferred to the King, unless he could yet find some way to prevent it. As long as he had his life and freedom left there might still be some way to mitigate the penalty which he at that present accepted. One needing sustenance of encouragement could at least gnaw the rinds. In a few swift days my lord of York had been banished from the Council, deprived of his position as chief dispenser of the King's justice, charged with treasonable procedures, stripped of the badge of his office as Lord Chancellor, required to surrender his property, forced to vacate his house near the seat of government, and retire from all his activities in government. But he was not to go to prison, and this one concession took on a glowing importance, like a secret that might one day become an announcement.

Indeed, when all the goods were arrayed for the King and the time came for my lord of York to leave his great house in Westminster, there seemed to be in him almost a note of gaiety, as if he privately knew more than those who were ranged against him. His treasurer, Sir William Gascoigne, said to him: "Sir, I am sorry for your grace, for I understand ye shall go straightway to the Tower." To which Wolsey replied: "It hath always been your natural inclination to be very light of credit; and much more lighter in reporting false news. I would ye should know, Sir William, and all other such blasphemers, that it is nothing more false than that, for I never (thanks be God) deserved by no ways to come there under any arrest . . ."

Claims of innocence and independence were beginning to assert themselves — and not without some reason provided by his circumstances, for after these words all his gentlemen and yeomen, making a considerable entourage, went out by his privy stairs to take barges. Wolsey's attitude, as made plain to Gascoigne in his further and parting remarks, was simply that the King wanted the house and he would be glad to let him have it, "else I were an unkind servant."

Once in his barge at the foot of his privy stairs Wolsey had another grim negative satisfaction, the kind the imagination can lick its chops over. Word of the Cardinal's fall had spread through London like the plague, and multitudes assembled now to see his disgrace, which, they knew, like everything else about him, would be a display. More than a thousand boats full of men and women of the city of London were congregated in the Thames.[15] They, like Gascoigne, thought he would go to the Tower; and, although, as Cavendish remarks, they had never received damage at his hands and had no cause to triumph at his fall, they rejoiced that he should go to the Tower. But as the Cardinal's barge moved out from shore, it headed in the opposite direction, leaving the multitudes cheated of the spectacle which, out of curiosity if not out of malice, they had come to see. The man who had so often paraded through London with his train had had borne before him as he entered his barge only one cross, that of York; but he was still Cardinal, and he still had others to bear his cross.

At Putney town the Cardinal left his barge to travel the remaining distance by land to Esher. Horses had been provided for his attendants and a mule for him. Hardly had the party set out when the Cardinal "espied a man coming riding empost down the hill, in Putney town." As the rider overtook them, Wolsey saw that it was Sir Henry Norris, who had so thoughtfully given up his chamber at Grafton. He had come from the King, and the message he brought amplified Wolsey's childish hopes of restoration into ecstasy. The King had sent Sir Henry to say that he was "as much in his highness's favor as ever he was, and so shall be." He went on to say "that the King commanded him to be of good cheer, and take no thought, for he should not lack. And although the king hath dealt with you unkindly as you suppose, he saith that it is for no displeasure he beareth you, but only to satisfy more the minds of some (which he knoweth be not your friends), than for any indignation; and also ye know right well, that he is able to recompense you with twice as much as your goods amounteth to; and all this he bade me, that I should show you; therefore, Sir, take patience."

Sir Henry brought not only words but a token from the King, a seal, as it were. It was a ring of gold with a rich stone. Wolsey knew the ring well, "for it was always the privy token between the king and him whensoever the king would have any special matter dispatched at his hands."

The message and the ring together were too much for the Cardinal to bear with any composure or control. They confirmed every hope he had nurtured since the trial and the first signs of the King's personal rejection. He was back now in the warm symbiosis of friendship that had sustained him so long. This relationship he could understand and surrender to and warm his heart on. Popes, emperors, conferences, commissions, trials, wars, parliaments, taxes, copes, enclosures, velvets, maces, mules, houses, gardens — all had their place; but they were specters of unreality now, for the King had taken him back. This one thing he knew.

Wolsey's response was that of a child unexpectedly restored to parental acceptance. As he put it later to Sir Henry, "the sudden joy surmounted my memory." He lighted off his mule, Cavendish reports, "all alone, as though he had been the youngest person amongst us, and incontinent kneeled down in the dirt upon both his knees, holding up his hands for joy." Nonplused by this humbleness of gesture, Sir Henry knelt by his side and embraced him. Next Wolsey tried to get off his under cap of velvet so that he might kneel bareheaded. But it was tied in a knot under his chin, which he could not undo in his impatience. Violently he broke the laces and tore the cap from his head, uncovered in the sight of God and in memory of his King. The two were indistinguishable in his mind, and in this posture and in the dirt not far from Putney he rendered thanks "to God my maker and to the king my sovereign lord and master."

This done, he covered his head again and got up. Then he and the others realized how much the news had rejuvenated him, for he now could not get back on his mule "with such agility as he had lighted before." His footmen set about helping him mount, and they "had as much ado to set him in his saddle as they could have." The Cardinal and his party rode up the hill into Putney town and on to Putney Heath, where Sir Henry Norris took his leave, the Cardinal making him a present of a small gold chain. It was all he could do, the Cardinal explained, seeing that "I have nothing left but my clothes on my back." But the chain had appended to it a piece of the Holy Cross, and it was one that he wore continually about his neck, next to his skin. Norris was to wear it and think of him.

Any gift he made now must be personal and out of what remained to him. Norris had started on his return journey when the Cardinal suddenly called to him. He must bear a gift to the King. The Cardinal prayed him to take with him his Fool, "for surely for a nobleman's pleasure he is worth a thousand pounds." Norris accepted the gift but he could not take it. So attached was the Fool to the Cardinal that he fell into a rage upon the prospect of leaving him, and the Cardinal had to detach six tall yeomen to convey him back to court. Now these yeomen went off with the Fool, he all the while kicking and struggling at the separation from the household of which he was a part.

It was an occasion turgid with the symbols of tragedy, recalling and anticipating so much of Wolsey's own personal suffering. Distraught with sudden reassurance from his own lord and master, the Cardinal now was taking a Fool no less devoted and attached to him than he himself was to the King and commanding that the poor fellow's closest personal ties be severed and that the Fool too be sent to a place where he did not want to go.

CHAPTER II

THUS passed my lord of York to Esher, a more modest mansion than any to which he had been accustomed, but at least an appointed habitation granted specifically for his use by the King. It was a plain house of only two wings stretching away from the central portion marked by four towers. The west front was severe in line, with no ins and outs to the design save those made by the towers, but on the east front the wings bulged and bayed, so that the windows let in light from three sides.

Esher Palace had belonged to the see of Winchester, but Bishop Fox had granted it to the Cardinal in 1519 as a subsidiary house to Hampton Court. Henry VII had used the smaller dwelling at Hampton Court as a cell to Richmond; it had been the intention of Fox that Wolsey use Esher as a cell to Hampton Court. "Use it all ways," he had written, "as often and as long as it shall please you, right as your own . . ."[1] Technically it had gone to the King with all of the Cardinal's other property a few days before, but the King was pleased and disposed to let Wolsey occupy it in his adversity. Might not this roundabout pattern of accommodation set the design for future living?

To be sure, living arrangements at Esher left something to be desired.

When the Cardinal arrived he found the place without beds, sheets, tablecloths, cups, or dishes. Either the Cardinal had not properly foreseen his use of the place, or there had been an administrative slip in the amenities. It would have embarrassed a lesser householder and housekeeper than Wolsey. But there were "all kinds of victuals, and of drink, both beer and wine, whereof there was sufficient and plenty." Not one to be flustered by a practical emergency, the Cardinal borrowed dishes and cups and sheets from both the Bishop of Carlisle and Sir Thomas Arundel.

On borrowed linen in a palace that was but an annex to one he had formerly owned, but with plenty of victuals in his larder and beer and wine in his cellar, Thomas Wolsey, late of York Place, settled down somewhat to await the future. The future was closer than he knew, but there was nothing in his background or temperament to help him recognize it, nothing to help him look beyond the periphery of his own immediate concern. Sheets and tablecloths and cups and dishes served as the symbols of this concern: the full restoration of his property and power through the kindness of the King. This was his aim. He pursued it with unflagging monotony through all his negotiations, petitions, and maneuvers.

Meanwhile, beyond the narrow confines of Esher other men with other views stirred as restlessly as the Cardinal. The whole kingdom of England was shifting its weight to move in new directions. When Dr. John Taylor, Master of the Rolls, had carried the Great Seal from York Place to the King at Windsor, Henry himself, glad to have it back in his hands, had affixed it personally to the documents that then required it. Nor had the King been in any hurry to bestow the seal.[2] It had been clear in the reports of all his deliberations with the lords of the Council that it would not go to a man of the cloth. And when, on October 25, the Great Seal was delivered to Wolsey's successor as Lord Chancellor, it was placed in the hands of Sir Thomas More, no priest and no lord but a layman and a lawyer.

A week later Parliament met, with the new Lord Chancellor on the woolsack. It was a king's parliament, its mood and membership set by Henry, who had shown great care in handling the writs for the election of members to the lower House. It was to be a time of sounding off, of making an expressive record of what was in the air. Hardly had the Lords met when they fell to considering a bill against the Cardinal based on certain articles that had been drawn up four months before, framed by the hand of Lord Darcy, who had once been deprived of valuable of-

456

fices by Wolsey. The aim of the bill was to make the Cardinal's restoration impossible, and to the end that he might be permanently disqualified the Lords cited no fewer than forty-four charges against him.[3] They scraped the bottom of the slough in their diligence and dredged up for public inspection everything that might cut or hurt or cast mire upon the Cardinal. Having exhausted all epithets and terms of opprobrium by the time the forty-fourth article was reached, the Lords, some of them with the haughtiest snouts in Christendom, could only allege that the Cardinal "by his outrageous pride had greatly shadowed for a long time the King's honour."

Wrapped in layers of respectable legal verbiage, the assorted charges, ranging from the obvious to the frivolous, made up a bill which was solemnly passed by the Lords on December 1 and sent to the Commons. There the articles were read, and it might have been expected that they would have been the signal for commotion, seeing how often and in how many ways the Cardinal had vexed the lower House.

The bill requested that "he be so provided for that he never have any power, jurisdiction, or authority hereafter . . ." But in the Commons the charges met with no less obstinate silence than the Cardinal himself had encountered on his last visit there. The bill had served its purpose by being drawn; it had provided a public rostrum for a verbal airing of the heats and hates of Wolsey's enemies, and there is no record that any questions were raised about it or action taken on it. And the fact that it died on the table afforded Wolsey further cheerful proof that the lances of legal opposition directed against him could be parried or broken. He could take solid consolation in the fact that neither in the charge levied against him in the Court of King's Bench nor in the charges brought by hostile nobles had the King suffered his enemies to have full rein. Plainly the mumbled menaces of a lot of nobles known to be his foes would not have any effect or bearing on his future. That he still had every chance to return to power was shown plainly by the fact that the King would not sanction or even encourage a bill expressly designed to keep him from power.

Thus in spite of his comparative poverty, of being down to his last palace, the Cardinal could assume, from viewing the scene through the turrets of Esher, that his affairs might yet be in good train. At the highest level he still had a rope to hold to, and on it he kept a firm and unrelenting grip. His eyes, as well as his heart, were trained to follow the King, to study the royal countenance for a smile or a grimace. Parliament he must have regarded as a royal appendage. There is little indication

457

that he paid any heed to the acts of the Commons that did not touch directly on his own future. Yet the same Commons which disdainfully ignored the charges the Lords handed down against him enacted legislation aimed at correcting abuses he had neglected, and while the sentiments expressed in this legislation were not directed pointedly against the Cardinal by name, they formed an indictment more severe than the outburst against him in the forty-four charges. The acts the Commons brought to pass were aimed at the system of which Wolsey had been an unprotesting part.

In the best English tradition, the Parliament of 1529 provided a time for grievances, and the grievances were against the priests and the monks. One knight told of paying a thousand marks sterling for the probate of a will. Others told of high funeral fees exacted by priests not only from fathers but from wives, servants, and children. It was reported that "if a man died in one parish and had a household in another, a mortuary would be claimed in both places, and until the mortuary was paid the curate would decline to bury the body." Others told what was already known, namely, that many clergy held many benefices and drew their fees from all. And that the monks would farm out land for profit.[4]

The stories told were old, but the Commons now set to work to redress these oft-repeated grievances. It was enacted that no mortuary should be taken in more places than one and that a fee should not be paid at all if a person at the time of his death had less than ten marks in movables. The amount of the duty, moreover, was defined, and it was graduated according to the wealth of the deceased. A further act defined and moderated and standardized fees for the probate of wills. A third prohibited a person from holding a benefice and not living in it, and it imposed a fine of £10 upon a cleric who was absent one continuous month or an aggregate of two months from his living.[5]

The legislation passed was mild, certainly not revolutionary and not accompanied by heroics. In particular, the act against clergy holding more than one living was vitiated by generous exceptions, such as the allowance that members of the Council could purchase the right to hold three benefices at once. Modulated though its voice was, however, the secular government had spoken out now against the jurisdiction of the Church, had dared by acts of Parliament to define the practices and regulate the conduct of the clergy. The lay worm had turned. The same Commons which passed an act "limiting the price of woollen hats made beyond sea" considered it within its proper province also to decide that it was lawful for a great monastic house to sell corn or cattle to maintain its standards

458

of hospitality but unlawful for this house to sell corn or cattle for profit.[6] Parliament, in a word, had poked its meddlesome nose into the sacred secrets of Church business. The government would tell the Church in detail what it could and could not do.

In these acts of the new Parliament was a forward thrust of forces my lord of York had long held at bay. The bills that grew into laws were worked out in committees made up of members of both Houses; and the Lords in each case approved the anticlerical sentiments of the Commons. The King, far from being a judicious bystander, took actual part in the deliberations of both Houses, arguing for hours at a time with the members.[7] On one occasion the whole Parliament spent three hours with the King at York Place. Far from attempting to browbeat or intimidate the Commons as his Lord Chancellor had in 1523, Henry respectfully reasoned with the members, often knowing and calling them by name and encouraging the candor of those who opposed the measures introduced at his instigation. One John Petit, a member from London, stood out against a bill releasing Henry from his debts to his people. This the King took in good stride; and often thereafter he "would ask in Parliament time if Petit were on his side." [8]

Times and places had changed, what with the whole body of Parliament mingling together to fashion anticlerical legislation with his Majesty at the former house of the Cardinal of York. But there is scant trace in the letters and papers of the period to show that Wolsey took any profound notice of the changes or that he had any ear for the grumble of distant thunder that might presage a storm. He was sealed off from new enemies by old scenes that lingered on in memory. Indeed, the King's indecisive kindness mixed with calculated deprivation kept him in a state of aggravated nostalgia, too hopeful of a world he had known to prepare himself for a world he knew nothing about, peopled with strange new faces.

There was no telling what hour of the day or night the King might send some consoling or stirring message. On Halloween my lord of York and all his household went to bed early, spirits being awalk that night. At midnight there was a great commotion at the gate of Esher Palace, and one of the porters came to Cavendish to say that, if one could judge by his voice, Sir John Russell was come from the King and sought admittance. The gentleman-usher ordered the porter to build a great fire while he put on his nightgown and went to the gates. Cavendish recognized Russell's voice, whereupon he commanded the porter to open the gates and let Russell and the horsemen in, all of them being wet to the skin. Russell assured Cavendish that he had come from the King, and while Sir John dried himself by the fire, Cavendish went to wake his lord and tell him that news had been brought that would make him rejoice. Whereupon my lord of York arose hurriedly and put on his nightgown while Cavendish went back to the lodge to fetch the knight.

Russell, coming into Wolsey's presence, knelt like a good courtier in simple reverence; and when Wolsey had raised him up, he delivered another ring as a token from the King, who wanted Wolsey to be of good cheer. He "loveth you as well as ever he did," Russell assured Wolsey, "and is not a little disquieted for your troubles, whose mind is full of your remembrance."

It was the old personal touch again, accompanied by something tangible. Russell explained that the King, before he sat down to supper, had sent for him and asked him to make the journey secretly to Wolsey, in spite of the vileness of the night, to comfort him as best he could. The affair had a somewhat bewildering and spooky quality about it, and the conspicuous emphasis upon secrecy lent a conspiratorial touch which Wolsey might interpret as a sign that he and the King were leagued against his enemies. Wolsey wanted to make his guest comfortable for the remainder of the night, but Russell said he would "tarry but a while, for he would, God willing, be at the court at Greenwich again before day, for he would not for anything that it were known, his being with my lord that night." So he rested while his servants dried themselves before the fire and supped, and then he rode away with speed back to court.[9]

Shortly after this midnight ride of Sir John Russell, Wolsey received from the King a goodly shipment of household goods, including plate and vessels. He received some of everything he needed, although not as much as the King would have wanted him to have, his gentleman-usher felt. This was the fault of the officers and those charged with deliveries. These had fouled up the royal generosity, but at least my lord's circumstances were greatly improved, and Wolsey rejoiced even in the little he had now in comparison with what he had before. Whatever happened, it was not the King's fault. The loyalty of the Cardinal and his gentleman-usher did not waver. There were repeated signs and tokens that Henry would yet take Wolsey and raise him up again. When Wolsey dismissed a great many of his servants for want of money to pay them with, he told them, so certain was he of restoration, merely to take their pleasures for a month, "and then ye may come again unto me, and I trust by that time the king's majesty will extend his clemency upon me." [10]

It ill became Wolsey to divulge his expectations to his household attendants, but certainly he had many reminders if not reasons for his presumption. Not only the King but those close to the throne joined in watching Wolsey perform the task of Tantalus. Even my lord of Norfolk came calling at Esher, he who had been the Cardinal's high adversary in the Council, and he was all smiles and charm, commending the servants of the palace for their faithfulness and urging them to remain steadfast. When water was brought to Wolsey and Norfolk for them to wash before dinner, the Cardinal invited Norfolk to wash with him, but the Duke refused the courtesy, saying "that it became him not to presume to wash with him any more now, than it did in his glory." Wolsey remarked with a sigh that his legatine authority and dignity were gone and that nothing of his high honor remained. "A straw," quoth my lord of Norfolk, "for your legacy. I never esteemed your honor the more or higher for that. But I regard your honor for that ye were Archbishop of York and a cardinal, whose estate of honor surmounteth any duke now being in this realm; and so will I honor you and acknowledge the same, and bear you reverence accordingly. Therefore, I beseech you, content yourself, for I will not presume to wash with you; and therefore I pray you, hold me excused." Nor would my lord of Norfolk sit down on the inner side of the table with the prelate at dinner. He refused the invitation humbly and kept his inferior station in a chair opposite and on the outside of the table.

It could occasion no surprise that the Cardinal fattened on hope and oily words and began to show in his royal prison some of the traits and mannerisms which had marked him among men in the days of his unquestioned power. Not having felt the full lash of the law, he could not be expected to show signs of having been punished. On the contrary, he was assertively impenitent and at times indignant at his treatment. If there had been plainly no chance of reinstatement in the King's favor and in the excitement of the court, he might have felt some of the humbleness befitting his position. Confidence that his plight was a temporary one, however, gave him a kind of indignation and even an appearance of outraged virtue. He wrote Gardiner words that could not have set well with the King, saying that he had not deserved to lose the bishopric of Winchester and the abbotship of St. Albans, "having done no offense to the king." [11] He even showed some signs of resistance. Lord Chief Justice Shelley came to see him about the formal details of the transfer of his house, York Place, to the Crown. Henry proposed to make a royal palace out of it and call it Whitehall. Wolsey took the position that the house belonged in reality to the province of York and was not his to give — an odd view because of the close personal grasp with which he held everything, and an ignorant view because he seems to have understood little of the King's determination, shown in so many ways, to assert the supremacy of the Crown. It summed up sentiments that would have had a better tone if they had come from a prelate who had given his whole life to the Church. He said he would accede to the royal commandment. "Howbeit, I pray you," he added, "show his majesty from me, that I most humbly desire his highness to call to his most gracious remembrance, that there is both heaven and hell." [12]

Strong words from a fallen official, whose every syllable would be duly reported to the King and would doubtless be amplified in the process. Wolsey was not behaving well in retirement. It was almost as if he were baited to speak lines which could be advertised against him. His gentleman-usher felt that his enemies missed no opportunity of poisoning the King's sentiments, "perceiving the great affection the king bare always toward him." They "feared him more after his fall than they did before in his prosperity . . ." If he were readopted by the King, Cavendish felt, his enemies, now known and active, would be in danger of losing their estates. It was very important to many persons, including Anne Boleyn, that the Cardinal not rise again. He remained a threat, even in his reduced and dubious state, and his enemies set about to complete the King's alienation.

Not all the messages that came from the court were good. Intermingled with the King's secret assurances were petty annoyances which reminded the Cardinal of his helplessness. One day the King would send for four or five of his gentlemen to come and serve at court. Messengers would arrive with rumors which he must either deny or verify. Another time the King took sixteen of Wolsey's yeomen and pressed them into service in his guard. So it went. Cavendish says that "there was no one day but, or ever he went to bed, he had an occasion greatly to chafe or fret the heart out of his belly."

Compounded frustration and suspense took their toll of the Cardinal's health, and by Christmas he fell so sick that his life was despaired of. When the King heard the news, he sent immediately his personal physician, Dr. Butts, to Esher. Dr. Butts took one look at the Cardinal and returned to the King. The Cardinal, he said, would be dead in four days if he did not receive at once some comfort from the King and Mistress Anne. "Marry," quoth the King, "God forbid that he should die. I pray you, good Master Butts, go again unto him, and do your cure upon him; for I would not lose him for twenty thousand pounds."

It was a high value — twenty times the price Wolsey had placed on the Fool he had given to his King. Butts agreed to go at once but only if the King would send some comfortable message. Again the King sent a ring — "a token of our good will and favor." It was a ring with the King's face engraved within a ruby. "This ring he knoweth very well," Henry told Dr. Butts, "for he gave me the same; and tell him that I am not offended with him in my heart nothing at all, and that shall he perceive, and God send him life, very shortly." He charged his physician not to return until Wolsey was out of danger. Then the King turned to Anne Boleyn and said, "Good sweetheart, I pray you at this my instance, as ye love us, to send the Cardinal a token with comfortable words; and in so doing ye shall do us a loving pleasure." Anne obeyed, making up a pretty message for the doctor and taking a tablet of gold from her girdle to put into his hands.

With Dr. Butts the King sent three other court physicians for good measure, one being Dr. Cromer, a Scot who struck Wolsey's fancy particularly, for Wolsey had once been the patron responsible for getting Cromer to practice in England. So much solicitude revived the Cardinal almost immediately. He heard the messages gladly and then sat up in bed and debated his case learnedly with the doctors, showing that he knew a thing or two about medicine. For a moment, if only on a bed of pain, he was back at the center of things, where men paid some attention to his views and judgments. The experience had a revivifying effect. Four days later, instead of his being dead, the doctors had Wolsey on his feet again and had "got him a good stomach to his meat." To cap the occasion with satisfaction, the doctors refused his reward when they prepared to leave, saying that the King had commanded them to take nothing from him for their ministrations.[13]

On such morsels of mercy can a famished man's satisfaction feed. The King's physicians brought the Cardinal no change of status. They brought only another earnest at best. But they bestowed upon him something rather to be chosen than riches: an audience. Here was a man of abundant and vocal energy, well used to sitting day after day at the very center of the kingdom, and busy there with enough detail to engage the talents of a score of men. And now this man had suddenly been retired. One day he had ruled England and worried Europe. The next day he had nothing to rule but a small palace. He had been sentenced not to forced labor but to what for him was infinitely worse: forced idleness. The gravest loss of all had been a loss of function. Physically, temperamentally, and in abilities, he was the one and the same man who had thundered his way to greatness and authority. Yet now he was useless and unemployed, cut off from the tumult and the shouting, and the sweat and the swearing, and the ceremony and the symbolism that had been a part of his daily life for so long. The man who had been sought was now forgotten. So it was a blessing and a joy when, propped up by pillows, he could argue with the King's physicians.

The anomaly and humiliation of his position at Esher was increased by the fact that he was a prisoner. He could not leave the place without express permission. Rings and tokens and carts full of goods from the King and the visit of the royal physicians did not disguise this fact. As Godwin puts it: "The King had marked him out for destruction, yet permitted him to live but so, as that he could never escape, and yet never despair of his escaping." [14] All the while, his energies coursed through like waters of a torrent, churning and white with frustration. With no proper outlet for these energies, he could devote himself only to his reinstatement and to the protection of those dignities and promotions that might remain to him in a reduced state. In a word, he had nothing to look after but his own interests. Shut off by temperament and circumstances alike from the new and surging stream of English life, he lived on in a twilight of intrigue, his actions guided by reminiscence, looking backward until he became as strange as a statue of salt.

Wolsey's one channel to the court in these days was through the shrewd and cunning young lawyer Thomas Cromwell who for the past six years had been in the Cardinal's employ, engaged chiefly in looking after the legal business conducted with the dissolution of the monasteries out of which Wolsey had built and endowed his colleges. A thousand and one details connected with the transfer of vast properties and the building of two new institutions had afforded Cromwell rich opportunities for commissions and exactions and fees. In the course of his work he had incurred the enmity of many, and outcries against him as an agent of the Cardinal had long reached the ears of the King. My lord of York, however, being too busy with affairs of state to scrutinize the labors of his subordinates and too convinced of the value of his colleges to question the methods by which they were built, held Cromwell in high esteem. He was witty, persuasive, a gifted talker, widely traveled, smooth in manner, and ingratiating because he was able to disarm enemies with some words and stir the confidence of friends with other words.

Of the competent secretariat and corps of agents Wolsey had had in his heyday, only Thomas Cromwell stuck prominently by him in the time of his banishment to Esher. He became the go-between. While he enjoyed as yet no great favor at the court, he did have access to the nerve center of affairs, being a member of the new Parliament and a man of many obligated connections because of his ability to lend money. As a wool stapler and merchant he had built up a small amount of capital, and he was able to make loans to the scions of the nobility in a day when extravagance around the court made it imperative to get money at any cost and from any source.

Cromwell championed Wolsey's cause openly and well and thus placed his former master under everlasting and tearful obligation to him. When efforts were made to introduce a bill of attainder in the House of Commons at the opening of Parliament, it was Cromwell who opposed it.[15]

His defense of Wolsey was rhetorical, but it was enough to establish him with the Cardinal as a faithful and trustworthy servant. And it was not long before this ostensible servant became Wolsey's real master, having freedom to move about, access to those near the throne, and a mind that could disentangle the complications of the Cardinal's bankruptcy. In due course the fallen Cardinal wrote to Cromwell in the same abject manner he had written to the King, apologizing for incurring his displeasure and saying that he would perish if Cromwell did not help him.

In effect Cromwell became only another jailer who kept the Cardinal confined to a world of intrigue and favor that was gone but not forgotten. Now Wolsey had his own shabby Orvieto. He was another Clement who thought mainly of recovering those physical possessions that lent his office greatness. In his efforts, Cromwell helped a little and got much credit. But nothing and no one helped much. The King had promised to make definite arrangements for the Cardinal's future after the prorogation of Parliament December 17, but he became too entranced with the property he had taken from the Cardinal to follow through.[16] The King's cheering message at Christmas and the visit of the physicians brought hope again, but shortly thereafter the King expressed a desire for a gallery that had been erected in Esher Palace. He had been persuaded that it would grace York Place, as if that house were not already well appointed, and the gallery was torn out and taken away.

By now it had become clear that all would be confusing. Any act of generosity would be followed by some withdrawal or modification or neglect. On February 2, 1530, the King sent him four cartloads of stuff, most of it locked in great standards to prevent pilferage. It included beds and kitchen equipment and dishes and hangings for the chapel of Esher Palace. The gift was all to the good, as Cavendish pointed out, but it could have been better, and he was sure that it was not as good or as rich as the King had intended.

But my lord of York professed to be well contented withal. Matters appeared at last to be looking up. Ten days later he received from the King a full pardon for his offense in exercising legatine authority in England. It referred to him as "alias late Chancellor of England . . . formerly called Thos. Wolsey." The phrasing lacked dignity, but it was a pardon just the same.[17] In another two days he had restored to him the archbishopric of York, save for the house of the see in Westminster, this being York Place and its two gardens and three acres of land, with which the King was by now right well pleased.[18]

In the act of the King's pardon, of course, lay some hope. The pardon was accompanied with no invitation to resume any of the activities that had been his joy, but it was a gesture, and Wolsey, waiting, made the most of it. When the servants opened the great crates that came from the King and remarked that the stuff in them might have been better appointed, my lord of York chastened them with a few well-chosen words that revealed his own tempered spirit and at the same time showed his incurable expectations. To his servants Wolsey said: "He that hath nothing is glad of somewhat, though it be never so little, and though it be in comparison half so much and good as we had before, yet we rejoice more of this little than we did of the great abundance that we then had." To this sober comment on the psychology of the consumer he added these significant words: "We thank the king very much for the same, trusting after this to have much more."

There were now rumors as well as signs that the Cardinal might return to power. The new imperial ambassador, Eustache Chapuys, was a man who reported to his government more than official business. He had a sense of public opinion, and he garnered his impressions from talks with persons not always in official posts of high importance. He lacked accuracy, but he did not lack reporting skill. He wrote along about this time to his government that the King was not thought to entertain any ill will toward the Cardinal. "To reinstate him in the King's favour would not be difficult, if it were not for the lady (Anne Boleyn). His only wish is for the Cardinal's goods . . . As a proof that the King has no ill will to him, I am told that he did not wish the Cardinal's case to be determined by Parliament; for if it had been decided against him, the King could not have pardoned him." [19] Chapuys adds other bits of revealing court gossip, one of them being that John Russell had spoken favorably of the Cardinal to the King and Anne Boleyn had been very angry and had refused to speak to Russell at all. The same lady, according to what Norfolk told Chapuys, had been irritated with Norfolk because "he had not done against the Cardinal as much as he might."

It was not long after his pardon that the Cardinal asked Cromwell to sue the King for license to move from Esher to Richmond. Cromwell was to explain that the Cardinal was weary of "that house at Esher: for with continual use thereof the house waxed unsavoury." He wrote also to the King's secretary, urging the matter, begging him at the reverence of God to hasten his suits. He could not, he said, live in the moist and corrupt air of Esher, "being entered into the passion of dropsy," attended by loss of appetite and lack of sleep.

His appeal brought him license to move. It was a victory that rumbled with implications. Not only did the move mean an escape from the house to which he had been confined at the time of the loss of the Great Seal; more significant still, Richmond was five miles closer than Esher to Westminster, and it was hard by the royal palace at Greenwich. Shortly before the license was granted, the Duke of Norfolk had sworn very loud when John Russell had told of the Cardinal's ambition to return to favor and had said that "rather than suffer this, he would eat him up alive." The Cardinal had been forbidden to come within ten miles of the court.[20]

Now after all these months he was on the move — and in the right direction. He wrote to Cromwell with a touch of elation and even a whiff of levity, referring to the money he needed for the move as the wholesome medicine Cromwell must bring to him.[21] His fortunes appeared to be on the mend, and with the prospect of greatly improved conditions at Richmond in sight he "made haste to prepare him thitherward."

The house in Richmond Park was one that my lord of York had himself repaired and put into order before his fall and at considerable cost. It was a small house, and Wolsey would be able to use only a few of his servants there. What he called "the rest of his family" would have to be put out to work for their board elsewhere. But it was "a very pretty house and neat, lacking no necessary rooms that to so small a house was convenient and necessary." There was also a "very proper garden garnished with divers pleasant walks and alleys."

License for the move to Richmond had been granted at Cromwell's suit to the King's own person, and the move was made without the knowledge of the Council. When they learned of it, they were sore vexed and in their minds much disturbed. It was now the middle of February — hardly four months after the King had charged the Cardinal with exercising the authority of Rome in the realm of England, dismissed him from the Council, deprived him of the Great Seal, seized his property, and banished him to the damp of Esher. In the past two weeks Henry had granted Wolsey full pardon, restored to him the archbishopric of York, delivered to him goods and furnishings for his house and chapel, and now, without the consent or knowledge of the Council, the King had released the Cardinal from the dingy palace of Esher and allowed him to move not only into better quarters but nigh unto the court. Something must be done at once, lest "the King might at length some one time resort to him, and so call him home again." 22

The stratagem chosen was wise and plausible. It had a good many advantages but the chief of them was distance: the Cardinal must be sent a great way off and given a task that would put him out of the King's mind. It was proposed to the King that the Cardinal go to York and assume his official duties there; it was about as far away as one could get and still stay in the kingdom and thus convenient to the purposes of those in the Council who opposed the Cardinal's efforts to rise again. Moreover, the assignment was not unreasonable, seeing that Wolsey had been appointed to the see of York not less than fifteen years before and had never so much as deigned to set foot within the territories of it. It was further represented to the King that the Cardinal would in the north, always a troubled part of the kingdom, wield a right good influence for law and order and bring the distant people closer to the throne.

It was an odd piece of legerdemain, this business of turning a prelate into a curate. Here indeed was poetic justice put into action, that the nobles so long ruled by a titular priest now required that he become a priest in fact. They would dispose of him by insisting not unreasonably that he do what he ought to have done fifteen years before.

The King agreed to the arrangement. How now would Wolsey feel about it? At first he took the news calmly because he misunderstood it. The Duke of Norfolk, who saw Cromwell every day, told him to tell Wolsey it was the King's pleasure "that he should go with speed to his benefice." To which my lord of York replied: "Well then, Thomas, seeing there is no other remedy, I do intend to go to my benefice of Winchester, and I pray you, Thomas, so show my Lord of Norfolk." He still had hopes that Winchester might be restored to him, and perhaps this was the sign of it. Accordingly Thomas Cromwell carried the message back to Norfolk, but the Duke made it abundantly clear that he meant York, which was nearly two hundred miles away, and not Winchester, which was hardly seventy miles distant from court.

If Wolsey's offer to go to Winchester was a ruse, it failed. The strategy in the Council had been carried out with consummate skill. The Cardinal had assented to the idea of assuming a religious role, and it had been arranged with the King before Wolsey knew fully what was going on that he would be sent to his province and required to carry out the duties of a shepherd. The dignitary who had so long been called my lord of York and had so consistently signed himself T. *Cardinalis Ebor* without so much as going near unto York must now be lord of York in fact and justify the Ebor. The Archbishop had been tricked by the temporal lords into piety.

Seeing there was no other remedy, Wolsey accepted the plans with good grace. He would depart for the north as soon as the roads, then clogged with February snow, were passable, and as soon as he could make the proper plans for travel. Meanwhile, as he lay at Richmond, the very prospect of performing religious duties had a notable and sobering effect on him. By nature, gifts, and practice an actor, his long career at court had never before called for straight lines and simple acts, for a performance that was primarily religious, that dealt with the deeper and inner reckonings of man and his destiny. His religious life had been almost wholly histrionic. While he appears to have been punctual and consistent in his daily devotions, his religious interest even in private seems to have been public, looking to form and ceremony rather than to meditation and conduct.

The theory and structure of the Church aroused in Wolsey the great conviction that had led to his loss of power. He saw the Church as the firmament of Christendom, above countries and princes. He stuck stubbornly to his conviction through the trial of the King's great matter; and when the trial was over, he made no effort to compromise a point which could have brought him swiftly back to power. But the supremacy of the Church was a political theory as well as a religious belief, and Wolsey's faith in the Church threw little light on the character of his inner being. There is scarcely any indication, from the unhappy days of his first parish at Limington to the time he was ordered to go to York, that Wolsey had any personal religious conviction or that he felt himself a priest. He was an official in shepherd's clothing.

The reasons for his neglect of his religious functions were many, but the chief of them was that he had no time to be a priest. Apparently the role simply did not occur to him. But with enforced leisure and with the assignment to go north and perform the duties of his office, there came a change. How profound this change was, only Wolsey knew.

But at any rate, he now began to reckon with and conduct himself in a world he had not seriously noted before.

At the beginning of Lent, Wolsey moved from the house which the King's license had granted him in Richmond Park. He moved of his own volition to a lesser lodging that had been built by Dean Colet of St. Paul's. It was Colet, now dead, who had preached with such tactless reference to the Christian virtues of service and humility at the time of Wolsey's reception of the hat. The house which Wolsey now occupied adjoined a monastery of the Carthusian Order and was connected by a secret passage with the church of the monastery, known as the Charterhouse. It had been built by Colet, a man of severe disciplines in his personal life, that he might commune with the monks and gain from them even stronger disciplines for himself. The Carthusians were high in the admiration of the people, above reproach, "never reformed because never deformed," strict beyond belief, giving all their time to praying, reading, and hard labor.[23] The monks not only kept themselves shut off from the world, but each monk lived alone in a separate hermitage within the enclosure; there was a meal for all the monks in the refectory once a week, otherwise they ate and dwelt alone, each a hermit with a monastery for a habitat.

The Charterhouse at Richmond was one of nine within the realm of England, and it was to this settlement of monks, so conveniently located for his purposes, that my lord of York now repaired in his extremity and in the newness of his resolution. The shade of Colet must have been with him, smiling. The poles of the Church had bent and met, for surely there was never greater contrast than the Cardinal of York, long arrayed like Solomon in all his glory, and the meek and lowly Carthusians. Their dress was the meanest and poorest among the monastic orders, "so short and scanty and so rough, that the very sight affrights one." They wore coarse hairshirts next to their skin, fasted almost perpetually, and ate only bean bread. Whether sick or well they would never touch flesh.

Every day now Wolsey slipped into the services of the Charterhouse, and every afternoon he sat in contemplation with one of the monks in his hermitage. He who had set out to reform the monastic orders and had told them how to sing and comport themselves had got around at last to the business of reforming himself. By the counsel of the monks he was persuaded "from the vainglory of this world." And in token of the new life of self-abnegation he had determined to lead, he got from the monks divers shirts of hair which, as his gentleman-usher was prepared to testify, he now began to wear.

At the Charterhouse of the Carthusians Wolsey had turned aside for the first time to see a burning bush. He had put off the shoes from his feet in the land of the Pharaohs and stood on bleak but holy ground, watching the bush that was burned but not consumed, the fire that burned the dross but left the man. In the house where John Colet, who hated the worldliness of churchmen, had lived his last days and died, Thomas Cardinal Wolsey came to reckon, at least for a moment, with the world of the spirit, foreign and incomprehensible to a secular ecclesiastic. It was a new and profound experience for him. He who had thought so much about what lay ahead and what lay behind thought now about what lay within. He continued, as Cavendish tells us, for the time of his abode among the Carthusians, "in godly contemplation."

But the time was short, possibly three weeks. The experience was too little and too late. Jesus might spend forty days in the wilderness, but Wolsey could spare only twenty. Daily contact with men of another philosophy, holy men who had renounced all semblance of the world, the flesh, and the devil, might quicken his spirit but it could not change his course. He was too involved with political forces to surrender his will. The momentum of old habits would carry him on. Colet might die a monk, for he had lived a saint. It was inconceivable that the "proudest prelate that ever breathed" should suddenly become a Carthusian hermit-monk.

At least, so it seemed to those of the Council who thought as much in political terms as my lord of York had always thought. One day my lord of Norfolk accosted Thomas Cromwell at the court and said to him: "Sir, me thinketh that the cardinal your master maketh no haste northward; show him, that if he go not away shortly, I will, rather than he should tarry still, tear him with my teeth."

These words, when delivered to Wolsey, brought him back to the world of practical reality with a snap. He was in business again, and godly contemplation would have to wait. There was no escape from a misspent past gilded with success. Can the leopard change its spots? No one who had watched the Cardinal stage-manage the meeting of two Kings and the nobility of two kingdoms at the Field of Cloth of Gold could ever believe that this man of restless ability would be long content in a Carthusian monastery. So the Cardinal who had caught a glimpse but not a vision in the barren huts of the Charterhouse remained a Cardinal, touched but not transformed. The King had ordered him north, and north he would go.

And if he was to go at the behest of the King and Council, he would go as nearly as possible in the manner to which he had been accustomed. Somewhat under the spell of the Carthusians, he reduced the number of his attendants to 160. His household goods went mainly in a convoy of vessels, but he had also twelve carts in his train to carry his own personal belongings and sixty carts to carry north with him items he had managed to save from his college at Oxford.[24] Cavendish had been sent to London to buy new livery for his servants and hangings of arras and masses of plate for his household.

Wolsey set out for York at the beginning of Passion Week. Ahead of him had gone letters from the King — at least one of them corrected by the hand of Wolsey, as in days agone — asking for the Cardinal "the loving and favourable assistance of noblemen and others" in northern parts.[25]

CHAPTER III

My lord of York was back in the workaday world of cardinals and kings. Managing an expedition of this sort was almost enough to revive the spirits of the old statesman and engage his neglected capacities. But trouble and depression hovered over his train. The Cardinal who rode north in this stately procession carried more problems than luggage. He was a beggar harried by debtors — in spite of all the new livery on his servants and the heraldic letters from the King. Having surrendered all his goods to the King, he had been forced to send Cromwell to the Council for funds necessary for the trip and for the repair of his manor houses in the see of York. The Council had granted him 1000 marks, which was equal to £600. To this the King had added £1000 from the revenues of properties he had seized.

Most of the marks had gone to satisfy claimants who came forward now to present old bills. The King had agreed to liquidate Wolsey's debts at the time he took his property, but the complexities of Wolsey's finances were many, and there is no sign that he had any clear notion of the state of his affairs. A messenger sent Wolsey from Gardiner was told to remind the Cardinal that he did not confess all his debts, "but concealed very many, so as the King has paid four times more than it was thought he should have done." [1]

Too, many of Wolsey's transactions were casual, and the King refused to honor them, passing the responsibility back to Wolsey. One Laurence Bonwys wrote to Wolsey to remind him that when he was last at York Place the Cardinal told him that a piece of cloth of gold provided by the partner of Bonwys was not properly cut and it was to be taken back, "but the cloth of gold I provided for you was cut, and I should be paid for it . . . Now the King will have none of it." The matter has cost the man and his partner £1000, but he says: "I shall be content if you will pay me £100 for it." He adds a personal touch: "I would have visited you, but have been ill with the gout for three months." He closes by beseeching my lord of York to make amends, "as I am old and in debt . . ." [2]

Claims good and bad, indefinite and specific, from persons involved in the building or furnishing of his houses or colleges, absorbed most of the grant Wolsey had from the Council for his journey to York. What he had not been able to beg he now sought to borrow. He turned to every possible source, borrowing £124 from Robert Browne of Newark and £100 from Sir W. Paulet, who had done some overseeing work for him, and an equal amount from the master of the Savoy.[3] With an improvident faith in Providence, as if the Lord would be bound to pay for so worthy a journey, he scraped together all he could assemble from all touchable quarters, and rode off in a cloud of dust and debt. Money now joined the ranks of his enemies. It would plague him to the end.

That he had any money at all was enough to provoke bitter comment at the court. A week after he had left and word had drifted back, Sir John Gage, a friend of Norfolk's, wrote bitterly to Cromwell: "It has been reported in the court that he rode in such sumptuous fashion that some men thought he was of as good courage as in times past, and that there was no impediment but lack of authority." [4] His every move was watched and studied like a symptom, and there was much to show that my lord of York, with all his goods and his 160 servants in new livery and his workmen to repair his places in the north, was unchastened and given as much to splendor as ever. He had reached Peterborough on Palm Sunday, and on Easter Sunday he rode to service of the Resurrection in the Abbey in his cardinal's vesture, "with his hat and hood on his head."

Still the showman of religion. But there were other signs and tokens, not as clearly reported to the court, for they were new and they might indicate strange change in the Cardinal and make him into an unfamiliar figure. They were not political signs for the gossips at court to read but

473

for men in the north to shake their heads and speculate on. On Maundy Thursday, he had taken an intimate and personal part in the services as befitted a day which celebrated the mandate "that ye love one another; as I have loved you." To show his obedience to this new commandment, he had washed and wiped and kissed the feet of fifty-nine poor men, one for each year of his life, and he had given each of them twelve pence in money, canvas with which to make them shirts, a pair of shoes, three red herrings, and three white herrings.[5]

This too had been a performance in symbols, but it had directly touched human life. It was something more than a religious parade. It marked the beginning of a course of conduct which, with all its variations and undulations, established the Cardinal with the people of the north as a man worthy of his office. Talk among those at the court who opposed him and feared his return was one thing; his acceptance in the province of York told a different story. When he had actually reached his see and lay at Southwell on the edge of it, he assumed with grace the role of shepherd. "He used much charity and pity among his poor tenants and other . . . He made many agreements and concords between gentleman and gentleman, and between some gentlemen and their wives that had been long asunder and in great trouble, and divers other agreements between other persons." He used his palace at Southwell, once it was renovated and put into order for him, as a meeting place for reconciliation. For this purpose he brought people together in assemblies and feasts within his house, using some of the money he had begged and borrowed to spread peace and amity in a neighborhood given to feuds and brawls. The fame he gained in these endeavors "was no pleasant sound in the ears of his enemies and of such as bare him no good will," but the common people, his gentleman-usher reports proudly, bore him much love and friendship.

Wolsey lay at Southwell until the end of grease time — which meant the end of the hunting season — the beginning of September. Then he prepared to move on to Scrooby and on toward York. On the road he would pass through a park of the Earl of Shrewsbury, and in this park was much fine game. Divers gentlemen of the household of the Earl extended the Cardinal a hearty invitation to hunt on the Earl's preserves, but Wolsey, wearing now a hair shirt beneath the familiar robes, refused them kindly. They entreated him but they could in no wise persuade him. He told them he had not come into the north country "to frequent or follow any such pleasures or pastimes, but only to attend to a greater care that he had in hand, which was his duty, study, and pleasure." As he rode through the park the gentlemen tried again, but he made as much speed as he could and refused to turn aside for the sport he had once enjoyed. Twice again on the same journey he refused the invitation. It was an odd and severe gesture; his replies, for all his train, were spoken like a Carthusian.

At Scrooby, where he had another house belonging to York, he continued for several weeks the charitable ministrations he had commenced at Southwell. A pamphlet published not long after gives a vivid and lasting picture of the work Wolsey did at Scrooby. It shows among other things the remarkable change that came over the people of the north when they had some direct contact with the Cardinal and indicates the impression his presence made on the commoners. "Who was less beloved in the North," the author asks, "than my lord Cardinal before he was amongst them? Who better loved after he had been there a while? We hate oftimes whom we have good cause to love. It is a wonder to see how they were turned, how of utter enemies they became his dear friends."

What had impressed the people of the north was the conduct and demeanor of the man who was now among them on a mission of good. Of the Cardinal who had neglected the Church for the things of Caesar and, busy with the affairs of the King, had not set foot in his enormous parish, the author wrote: "He gave bishops a right good example how they might win men's hearts. There were few holy days but he would ride five or six miles from his house, now to this parish church, now to that, and there cause one or other of his doctors to make a sermon unto the people. He sat amongst them, and said mass before all the parish; he saw why churches were made. He began to restore them to their right and proper use. He brought his dinner with him, and bade divers of the parish to it. He inquired whether there was any debate or grudge between any of them. If there were, after dinner he sent for the parties to the church, and made them all one. Men say well that do well . . ." [6]

Sloughing gradually the skin of fame he had brought from London, Wolsey came to be regarded as a priest diligent in the service of the Church. People sought his ministrations as a man of God rather than as a man of distinction. When, toward the first of October, he moved from Scrooby toward York and lay two nights and a day at St. Oswald's Abbey, he found his progress halted and his path clogged with parents from miles around who had brought their children to him to be confirmed. From eight o'clock in the morning until twelve noon he confirmed children. Then he took a short dinner, went back immediately to the church of the Abbey and confirmed more children until four of the clock. Finally from weariness he had to stop, resting a while before his evensong and supper. The next morning he could not leave the Abbey until he had confirmed a hundred children more. This done, he rode on his journey, but he had not gone far when he "found assembled at a stone cross upon a green, within a quarter of a mile of Ferrybridge, about the number of two hundred children, to confirm; where he alighted and confirmed them all; and then he took his mule again and rode to Cawood . . ."

He was now within sight of York. Cawood Castle was to be his last stop before his installation, and he would arrange all the details of the ceremony from here. It was therefore meet and fitting that the Castle should be put in a good state of repair, and Wolsey set about the job with the compulsive drive that had made him build and repair wherever he went. It was interesting to see him repeat in what was almost a new incarnation the patterned activities that had marked his whole life. No new guise could still the hammer of habit. Wherever he went, he built. His palaces at Hampton Court and York Place had outshone the royal palaces at Greenwich and Windsor, and the King had paid him the compliment of taking them over for himself. His smaller houses, The More and Tittenhanger, were no less desired by the King. His colleges at Ipswich and Oxford were things of beauty.

All along the journey to York, Wolsey, living on borrowed time and money, built and built again and thought in terms of building. He lived in three dimensions, and the avarice and acquisitiveness which men laid against him in their gossip and their charges arose in part at least from the fact that he thought with sticks and stones and saw in paradigms and expressed in all he did a sublime consciousness of the physical world. This consciousness at times approached reverence, and at all times it bordered on preoccupation. A wall had for him some of the sacredness that a conviction had for a saint or a postulate had for a philosopher.

Those who did not understand this three-dimensional mind of Wolsey, recurrently expressing itself in houses and in renovations and repairs, found his activities in the north incomprehensible. Cromwell wrote to Wolsey with great satisfaction to say that his modest behavior and humility had gained him the love and good report of the north country and that his reputation was now growing in the court. But, Cromwell warned, his enemies found much to criticize, adding that many criticized him because he was "continually abuilding. I beseech you, as I have often done before, to consider the times and refrain from all building more than necessity requires." [7]

To this advice Wolsey paid little heed. He was too busy listening to the sound of building. At Cawood he had "a great multitude of artificers and laborers, above the number of 300 persons, daily in wages." Much of what his enemies called building actually involved only repairs to make the places of his see habitable, nothing but the stopping of holes where it rained in the windows and doors. So unskilled were the local workmen, it was reported, that not a man could be found who could plaster the walls with lime and hair.[8] But with three hundred daily in wages and with Wolsey's ineradicable reputation as a master builder, these unceasing activities in the north could easily be construed as the sign of an unchanged cardinal.

Whatever he did, there were many who saw in his deeds only the repetitious pattern of the haughty Cardinal of yore. There was no allowance in many men's minds for the fact of change. Even his labors of charity and reconciliation might appear to be merely the old Wolsey sitting in a rural, informal, and ecclesiastical Star Chamber. Much could be found to support this opinion. Wolsey was curiously preoccupied in these days with breaking up feuds and causing enemies to strike the posture of friendship. The work of amity which he had carried on at Southwell and Scrooby he continued with redoubled vigor at Cawood, as if he had transferred the drama of his own life to the lives of others. He sought out and tackled the toughest problems of the neighborhood.

One case in particular showed his methods of operation. At Cawood he learned of a "great variance and deadly hate between Sir Richard Tempest and Mr. Brian Hastings." The promise, by all reports, was murder unless the two could be brought to terms with each other. Wolsey got them to agree to come to his castle and talk the problem over. They came, but each brought a great band of retainers, spoiling for a fight. Wolsey's first move was to get the two gentlemen to admit only six of their menial servants into the castle. The others were to disperse into the town. This agreed to, Wolsey went out and addressed the retainers of both of them and urged them to keep the King's peace and go away, "without either bragging or quarreling either with other." He then told them, with an odd notion of what makes for peace, that he would send beer and wine into the town for them.

Having delivered himself of his speech to the bands outside the castle, he went back in and settled down to the business of bringing Tempest and Hastings to a point where they would not cut each other's throats but agree to have dinner with him. He began his persuasions at nine in the morning. For a long while the case looked hopeless. But by four o'clock in the afternoon the parties to the feud had shaken hands and were willing to go arm in arm to dinner. It was a very late dinner by the custom of the times, "yet notwithstanding they dined together with the other gentlemen at my Lord's table, where they drank lovingly one to the other, with countenance of great amity." After dinner Wolsey persuaded the two gentlemen to discharge their small armies and ride home with no more servants than they were used to. It was a remarkable performance. Unable to silence his own enemies, he would at least settle the quarrels of others.

Wolsey showed in these last days an outward modesty as great as his outward arrogance had been before. If the modesty of the Cardinal was a pose, it was a good one. When the dean of the church at York came to welcome him, bringing the chief officers to plan for Wolsey's installation, he told them that he hoped "not only to be among you for a time, but also to spend my life with you as a very father, and as a mutual brother." He determined that he would be installed more quietly than his predecessors. One of the officers suggested that he ought at the time of his installation to go from St. James's Chapel, standing outside the gates of the city of York, all the way to the minster on cloth. To this Wolsey replied: "Although that our predecessors went upon cloth right sumptuously, we do intend, God willing, to go afoot from thence without any such glory, in the vamps of our hosen." He made it clear also that he would command his servants to go humbly and in apparel that was comely. It was a point of view that would have pleased the monks of Charterhouse, if indeed they would have been pleased with the ceremonies for the installation of an archbishop.

This of course was the anomaly of Wolsey's position, that he tried to continue into the elaborate and dramatic ceremonials of the Church a kind of Christian humility acquired late and inadequately from Carthusian hermits. His acts thus appeared to be mere affectations of simplicity: he would walk in his stocking feet to the minster, not on cloth, although tradition had it that the cloth so used would be cut up later and given to the poor.

Wolsey, in a word, was carrying the whole intolerable burden of his past and trying to live as if he were a new man. But he had given too many hostages to fortune. He could not disentangle himself from old concerns and worries. Not that all of these worries were worldly, save that they were tied up with the world of which he had so long been a part.

Chiefly and painfully on his mind were his colleges. Nothing was closer to his heart, nothing more in line with the natural bent of his interests than the future of these institutions. In all else he might be guilty of pretense; in the founding of his colleges he was sincere. If there was any secondary or ulterior motive, it was a lofty one — that he might live in the awakening minds of future generations and gain from posterity the pardon his contemporaries had refused. If all else failed or faded, his luster would linger and be ever renewed in the young. It was an old man's dream of recurrent spring.

But his dream had been too personal and his hopes too acquisitive. He had made his colleges his personal property, and at his fall he faced the loss of these colleges, whatever their intent and ideals, along with all other property. When charged with having exercised in England the authority of a foreign power under his legatine office, he had pleaded guilty and thrown himself upon the mercy of the King. This mercy had been niggardly, but the operation of the law had been inexorable. The judges of the Court of the King's Bench had been unanimous in their ruling that, since the donations of the property to his colleges had been made after his use of his legatine authority, "all such donations were void, and were now at the King's pleasure." [9] Unless he could be restored to favor and his property restored to him, he would have no claim over his colleges.

It had become evident even at Esher that the King was resolved upon taking his colleges as if they were so many chattels. William Capon, dean of the college at Ipswich, wrote early to express his sorrow at the founder's heaviness and to say that all the company of the college prayed daily that he might be restored to his prince's favor. Already trouble with the tenants of the lands of the college had begun to show itself. Capon reported to Cromwell that one Vesey, a villainous fellow near Ipswich, had distressed the tenants by taking their cattle, and when the sheriff recovered them, Vesey got twelve men with bows and arrows and took them back again. This Vesey had taken advantage of the Cardinal's disgrace and had said that "my Lord Cardinal was not worthy to wipe his horses' feet, with other opprobrious words." [10]

As the days passed, Capon's agony and alarm grew. He had no instructions from Wolsey what he should do and no counsel from friends, "of whom he has few in these parts." He wanted to know whether he should come to London to talk with Wolsey or sue directly to the King. Wolsey was in no position to advise him, and it was too late for advice besides. Hardly a month after Wolsey's loss of the Great Seal, commissioners from the King, accompanied by sixteen yeomen of the guard and their servants, arrived at St. Mary's in Ipswich and began to make an inventory of all plate and of building materials. Capon entertained the commissioners as well as he could, at a cost of twenty marks from his depleted treasury. But they stayed five days and carted off a vast amount of valuables, including twenty-four copes, a silver-gilt ship, three silver-gilt chalices, and all the greater and smaller crosses of the college. They insisted that the King merely wanted to see the stuff, and they implied that they would return it.[11]

By early July, while Wolsey lay at Southwell, hopelessly out of touch with the court, Capon had gone to London and retained the best counsel he could find. The advice of counsel had been in key with the decision of the judges: because Wolsey had incurred the praemunire, his lands would go to the King. "We have no remedy," Capon had written, "except to petition the King; which we have done, but with little comfort." [12] It was plain, he wrote July 20, that the King would dissolve the college by September 29. He would take all the rents of the property on which the college kept tenants for its support. And, ever with an envious eye on Wolsey's choirs, he would even take the children of the chapel and put them into his own service.

About the time Wolsey left Scrooby for Cawood, he learned from Capon that the college at Ipswich, erected with such expense and hope, would be no more. Capon had had commandment from the King to dissolve the college. He had written to Wolsey: "I paid the singing men and the choristers, with all their necessary apparel, as I trust shall stand with your honor . . . My payments for the college exceed the receipts by £100, by which I was compelled to pawn my plate." [13] The King had ridden roughshod over an ideal, his yeomen and commissioners had been entertained at college expense, college treasures appropriated for royal favorites, and the final cost of the dismemberment borne by the college dean. The buildings would be pulled down, only a gateway unaccountably remaining as a kind of shard to remind men that here was once a great vessel for the containment of learning.

It was such grievous tidings as those touching his colleges that reached the stricken Cardinal on his journey north and took their toll of his hopes as he lay at Cawood. He might wear a hair shirt, strike the posture of Christian modesty, declare that his enthronement in the see of York would not be sumptuous. He might reconcile men who were at enmity one with the other and lay his hands in priestly benediction upon little children brought to him. But he could not commit himself wholly to piety while he felt his colleges being dismembered. The power he needed now was the kind of power he had once enjoyed.

There still might be a remote chance that he could save his college at

Oxford. Cromwell had done stout service in its behalf. Gardiner had made his petitions to the King. More astonishing still, the Duke of Norfolk had shown an accommodating mien. When the dean of the college and Robert Carter went to call upon my lord of Norfolk, while the court was at Windsor, my lord told them that the college would be dissolved, but when they made their representations to him, "he mused awhile, and then went straight to the King." While the dean and Carter awaited the results of Norfolk's talk, Sir John Russell advised them to tarry at the door of the King's closet and accost Henry as he went to Mass. This they did, and the informal device worked. The King saw them and drew them aside to talk privately. He assured them that he proposed to have a college at Oxford, "but not so great and of such magnificence as my lord Cardinal intended to have, for it is not thought meet for the common weal of our realm . . . Yet we will have a college honorably to maintain the service of God and literature." [14]

These were fair words lined with promise, but at best Henry's statement meant that Cardinal College might continue on a scale suited to the King's pleasure; the decision and control would be vested in the King; and my lord of York must keep his distance. Wolsey had not seen the King since their hasty leave-taking at Grafton. Communication afterwards had been indirect, by courtier, so to say, through messages relayed and ricocheted. Now in the matter of most vital concern to the Cardinal he had not even had the courtesy of a courtier. He had simply heard what the King had said, the cold statement of his intent, and the passing side reference to "my lord Cardinal," as if he belonged to the dead past.

All that summer and into the melancholy days of the fall Wolsey clutched like a beggar at every sleeve which might have an arm that could help save his college at Oxford. He wrote to the King, "humbly and on my knees with weeping eyes to recommend unto your excellent charity and goodness the poor college at Oxford." He entreated Cromwell to make suit that the college be preserved. Cromwell, growing now like a beanstalk, was his chiefest hope, and when enemies began to sow variance between them, the whispering campaign was effective. Wolsey implied that Cromwell was not doing all he could. Cromwell spoke sharply to his old master: "I reckoned your Grace would have written plainly unto me of such a thing, rather than secretly to have misreported me." Wolsey wrote back abjectly to say that reports had reached him that Cromwell "hath not done him so good offices as he might concerning his colleges," but he had not believed these reports and he besought Cromwell to give no credit to false suggestions "and so leave me destitute of all help." [15]

Desperate, not willing to relinquish any line that might save him, he even wrote to Gardiner. He wrote also to the Lord Chief Justice and, being both desperate and convinced of the righteousness of his cause, a note of indignation and protest crept into his letter. He pointed out that he was the first prominent prelate ever convicted in the praemunire "for using the authority of the legate de latere within this realm." He goes on to say, "I never never used the said authority contemptuously or maliciously, intending to do thereby anything that should be either to the derogation of the King's dignity or laws." [16] And it seems to him a great pity that it is to his students at Oxford that the sharpness and rigor of the law must be administered. In another letter he points out that the college had been erected with the full approval of the King and the Pope, and the laws drawn accordingly, so that if there has been any offense against the law the King and the judges are no less guilty than he.

For all his professions of pious humility of late, Wolsey's return to power was watched and dreaded by those who considered his leaving a good riddance. When in the middle of October Thomas Arundel delivered some letters at Wolsey's request to the Duke of Norfolk and declared to him Wolsey's "good fashions and manner of living" and went on to say that the Cardinal no longer aspired to authority, the Duke said flatly that no man could believe that. And, Arundel adds: "The more I spake to the contrary, the more out of frame I found him . . . He showed me, though I list to be blinded, I should blind no man here; for, he said, he had both your Grace's hand to the contrary, and knew three messages sent by three divers persons of your Grace to the King, whereby it might well appear that ye desired as much authority as ever ye did." [17]

The fear of Norfolk and the Boleyn faction that the Cardinal would return to power was matched by the hope of others around the court that he would return. A sympathizer wrote from London to one of Wolsey's chaplains that "my lord Cardinal is communed of, and among lords of the council specially. They fear that they shall of necessity be compelled to call for my lord cardinal's grace again. God continue their minds in that behalf." [18] And as late as the last days of October the imperial ambassador passed along to his government a report that not long before "the King was complaining to his Council of something that was not done according to his liking, and said in a rage that the Cardinal was a better man than any of them for managing matters; and, repeating this twice, he left them." [19]

Since this scene, according to the ambassador, the Duke of Norfolk and

Lady Anne Boleyn and her father "have not ceased to plot against the Cardinal, especially the lady, who does not cease to weep and regret her lost time and her honor, threatening the King that she will leave him, in such sort that the King has much trouble to appease her . . ."

My lord of York, banished to the north, was still ominous as a thunder-head, a granite face chiseled in far-off clouds. It had been a year since they took from him the Great Seal in its white leather bag, and still Henry cited him as an example and held his name like a lash over the heads of his Council.

Furthermore, the exile of the Cardinal had not proved as sore a punish-ment as some had expected. It was thought at one time that he would be murdered by the people of his province and that "he was quite afraid of going thither; but it appears on the contrary that he was quite well received in York." [20] Later it was reported that "he was showing great hospitality and leading so religious, quiet, and humble a life among those with whom he now is, that he is wonderfully loved and respected and is beginning to win universal praise."

The Cardinal had elected November 7, this being the Monday follow-ing Halloween, as the appropriate time for his installation as Archbishop of York. He had previously issued a call for a Convocation to meet at York on that same day, and he had not stayed his invitation to wait for the formality of securing a royal mandate. The proposed Convocation had been frowned upon by Tunstall, then Bishop of Durham and chief of the King's Council in the north parts.[21] But the clergy of the area would assemble just the same for the installation; it would not greatly matter whether the assembly was called a Convocation or not. Obviously the Cardinal, even if he dispensed with the cloth proposed for his path to the minster and walked in his hosen, planned to make the enthronement a demonstration of his power in the north. Indeed the unconscionable delay in the installation arose out of the fact that he must wait until the rents had been collected from his tenants so that he could put on an installation feast worthy of his fame and dignity.

At least, the facts could be interpreted this way to the King. The Cardi-nal might be planning a return to power by means other than the King. He had developed a miniature kingdom of his own in the north during a sojourn of barely six months. Who knows what he might do next? And it further must be noted that he had never altered by word or deed his insistence, so long and tediously maintained, that the King's great matter must be referred to Rome. Already other novel and effective devices had been advanced to help the King gain his freedom from Catherine. A young man named Thomas Cranmer, from the other university, had suggested the year before that it might be expedient to get the judgment of leading canonists in the universities on the validity of Henry's marriage. With their judgment in hand it would be possible for ordinary ecclesiastical courts to declare the marriage null — without appeal to Rome.

In the midst of all the resulting bustle my lord of York had remained conspicuously silent. Once in the dead of night at Southwell, when Cavendish was "scantly asleep and warm" in his bed, two messengers came from the King and said they must speak with the Cardinal at once. They exhibited to Wolsey a great document with many seals and put his own seal upon it and went out again into the night, complaining later, Cavendish learned from other servants, that they should have had a better reward. It was a memorial to the Pope, signed by prelates and temporal peers, urging him to accede without further delay to the King's wishes.

Signing the document had been the extent of Wolsey's efforts since the close of the trial at Blackfriars. This and nothing more he had done to help the determined King reach the goal he would not relinquish.

If this was so, might not other matters be true as well? Might the Cardinal not be now more than ever on Catherine's side and making representations to Rome in her behalf and against Anne Boleyn?

News of Wolsey's unauthorized Convocation in the north and of a papal bull issued against Henry from Bologna reached Henry at about the same time — during the closing week of October. If the right use could be made of these two occurrences, even though the bull was mild and of no great consequence, the Cardinal might be brought to his long-postponed day of judgment.

CHAPTER XV

On Allhallows day my lord of York sat at dinner with divers chaplains and worthies of his household in the castle at Cawood. The meal passed quietly. All was in order and dignity, the great silver cross of York standing at one end of the table against one of the heavy curtains of the dining chamber. The meal over, those at the table arose and came to take their leave of the Cardinal with a curtsy, he sitting apart at another table. It chanced that Dr. Augustine, his physician, wore a "boisterous black gown of velvet," and as he passed the great silver cross, the gown swept against it and overthrew the cross. And as it fell, it struck the head of Dr. Bonner, who was Wolsey's personal chaplain, as he stood ready to take his leave. It was a glancing blow, but the blood ran down.

The accident froze for a moment those who saw it. Wolsey asked Cavendish, who was seated near him, what had happened. The gentleman-usher explained that the cross had struck Dr. Bonner's head.

"Hath it drawn any blood?" Wolsey asked.

"Yea, forsooth, my lord," Cavendish answered, "as it seemeth to me."

At that Wolsey looked very soberly at his servant for a long while without speaking, and then he said, shaking his head, *"Malum omen."* Then he said grace and got up from the table. He went forthwith to his bedchamber, heavy with foreboding, and made his prayers.[1]

On the following Friday, before the installation that was to take place on Monday, Cavendish heard a commotion of many horses in the courtyard at Cawood. Wolsey was sitting at dinner, being at his fruits, when one of his servants, going to see what caused the commotion, saw the Earl of Northumberland with a group of attendants coming up the stairs. He went at once and told his lord and master. Wolsey rose from the table and went to meet the Earl on the stairs. It was an odd and unannounced visit, and Wolsey, taking in at a glance the great company with the Earl, must have felt a coldness in his spine. This young man on the stairs had once been in his own service, learning manners and decorum, when he was merely Lord Percy.

The Cardinal put off his cap and embraced the Earl, took him by the hand and led him into the chamber where he had been dining. He was not able to forgo saying to the young man that he should have let him know of his coming. But in all other respects Wolsey was the host for which he had just fame.

Only in his talkativeness and excessive hospitality did my lord of York betray his uneasiness at the unexpected visit. All of the Earl's servants crowded into the dining chamber, but Wolsey, not at all nonplused by this, went around and shook each by the hand and commended the Earl on keeping in his service so many of his father's old retainers. Then he took the Earl by the hand and led him into his bedchamber that he might shift his apparel. The gentleman-usher went along with them to keep the door. Now the two lords were alone and they did not talk. They walked to the window by the chimney, the Earl trembling. Then the gentleman-usher heard the Earl say, laying his hand upon the Cardinal's arm and speaking in a faint and soft voice:

"My lord, I arrest you of high treason."

It was a moment when emotion conquered drama. With all his clamoring attendants who had come along for the excitement, and armed though he was by the King's authority, the Earl gave way to embarrassment. He had entered the house unannounced and climbed the stairs unbidden, but my lord of York by his hospitality had placed him in the guise of a guest and forced him, to whatever purpose, to confront his host. Whatever enmity stirred him or whatever memory stirred in him a sense of poetic justice, when he came face to face with the Cardinal of York, his former master, he could only lay a trembling hand on the old man's sleeve and speak his imperious lines in a whisper.

Wolsey's long and stony silence added to the young man's discomfort. At last, though, Wolsey asked, as he had when Norfolk and Suffolk came to take the Great Seal, by what authority the Earl acted. When he found that Northumberland would not show him his commission, he said stoutly that he would not obey him, seeing that there had long been contentions between the house of Percy and the province of York. But as the two stood debating the matter, Cavendish heard words at the door he was keeping. Someone was saying, "Go in then, traitor, or I shall make thee." With that Cavendish opened the door, and someone thrust Dr. Augustine into the room. The man who followed was Walter Walsh, who plucked off his hood and fell on his knees before the Cardinal. He too refused to show his commission, saying that it had appended to it certain instructions which could not be seen. But to him Wolsey was content to yield, inasmuch as he was one of the King's privy chamber. "For the worst person there is a sufficient warrant to arrest the greatest peer of this realm, by the King's only commandment, without any commission. Therefore," Wolsey added, "I am ready to be ordered and disposed at your will."

On Sunday, the day before the appointed time of his installation, my lord of York was commanded to leave Cawood with his captors. Five servants were to accompany him — Cavendish, a chaplain, his barber, and two grooms of his chamber. When he was ready to go down out of his chamber, he asked the Earl where the rest of his servants were. They were not far away, the Earl explained. They had been shut up in the chapel of the castle so that they would not cause disturbance at the time of his departure.

"Sir," said Wolsey, "I pray you let me see them or ever I depart, or else I will never go out of this house."

The Earl explained that they would merely trouble him. Wolsey made it plain that he would not leave even the chamber until he had said farewell to them. At this point the servants in the chapel set up such a noise that the commissioners feared a tumult and let them pass before their master in farewell. They came, and each knelt down before him, and to each he gave comfortable words and the assurance that he was a true man and not guilty of the treason which had been charged. He shook each by the hand and among all of them "was not one dry eye."

My lord's mule had been brought to the inner court; there he mounted and rode to the gates of the castle, where the horsemen to conduct him were ready. As the gates swung open, a noisy crowd of not less than three thousand persons, having heard of his arrest, stood without, and when they caught sight of the Cardinal many of them began chanting: "God save your Grace, God save your Grace." Others shouted: "The foul evil take all them that hath thus taken you from us! We pray God that a very vengeance may light upon them!" And Cavendish says that the crowd ran after him all through the town of Cawood, crying out words of encouragement to him and calling down maledictions upon his enemies and detractors.

In these circumstances the great party of horse accompanying the Cardinal on his mule set forth. And when they had gone but a short way, my lord of York called Cavendish to ride near him and asked him if he could get permission to send back to Cawood. "I have left a thing behind me that I would fain have," he said. It was a red buckram bag, lying in his almonry in his chamber, sealed with his seal. The permission was granted, and so quickly did the messenger sent back to Cawood do his errand that the red buckram bag arrived and was delivered to Wolsey that very night as he lay at Pomfret Abbey. In the red buckram bag, sealed with the Cardinal's seal, was nothing but three shirts of hair which he had forgotten. These he gave, very secretly, to his chaplain.

That night the Cardinal expounded to his gentleman-usher the significance of the incident of the falling cross. He saw the future now in retrospect; all had been adumbrated in the scene. The cross, he explained, belonged to York, and he understood this cross to be the symbol of himself. Augustine, who knocked the cross over, "he understood to be he that should accuse him, by means whereof he should be overthrown." Dr. Bonner was master of his spiritual jurisdictions, and the drawing of blood betokened death. The last observation was a bit confused, but what lent the misshapen incident such meaning was the fact that at the very moment of its occurrence, Wolsey now knew, Master Walsh had taken horse at the court near London and had started out to exercise the commission of his arrest.

The Cardinal might well have understood that Augustine would be

487

the one who would accuse him.[2] At the time of his loss of the Great Seal he had sent Augustine, whom he trusted, to du Bellay with a request that the French King and his mother aid the Cardinal in recovering his offices and powers. He had used him, too, on other confidential missions. And now Walsh had sent Augustine to London, his legs tied to the belly of his horse in token of the fact that he was a traitor. With Augustine in the hands of those about the court who sought the Cardinal's ruin and death, the master was at the mercy of his servants. Almost anything might pass for truth.

With these meditations my lord of York lay all night at Pomfret Abbey, still not knowing his destination, much less his destiny, or the specific nature of the charges against him. The next day the party moved toward Doncaster, planning their journey so that he might be brought there at night and thus cause less mumbling and demonstration among the people. But word of their coming went ahead of them, and by the time the procession had reached Doncaster by torchlight the people were there to meet the Cardinal, running before him with candles and shouting: "God save your Grace, God save your Grace, my good lord Cardinal." Cavendish rode hard by his mule to protect him from the press and the candles, but the people saw the Cardinal, cheering him as they did and cursing his enemies. The demonstrations continued along the road the next day as the party moved to Sheffield Park, where Wolsey had conscientiously refused to hunt on his journey north.

Sheffield Park, apparently, was to be his destination. For once the Earl of Northumberland and Master Walsh had delivered him into the hands of the gracious Earl of Shrewsbury, who received him as an honored guest, they rode off with all their horsemen, as if their mission had been accomplished. With his wife and all her gentlewomen, the Earl had come out to meet the Cardinal, who had embraced the Earl and kissed the Lady Shrewsbury and all her gentlewomen bareheaded, and had shaken all the servants, both gentlemen and yeomen, by the hand. Then the Earl had escorted his guest to the lodge, the two going arm in arm. The two were to stay there together, Wolsey being lodged in a new part of the building at the end of a goodly gallery by which he could repair to the Earl whenever he wished.

For eighteen days Cardinal Wolsey remained in the lodge with the Earl of Shrewsbury, without visible guard to detain him, ostensibly a guest whiling away a holiday. But the pleasant circumstances only sharpened the irony that tore at his vitals. He refused all efforts made to entertain him, "all manner of earthly pleasures and disports either in hunting or other games, but applied his prayers continually very devoutly." Once a day the Earl would come to visit him, and together they would sit on a bench near a great window of the gallery near Wolsey's rooms. The Earl did in all ways the best he could to comfort him, assuring him that the trial to which he would yet be taken had been planned more with a view to satisfying some persons than because of the King's distrust. Being one who had signed the forty-four articles of complaint against the Cardinal at the time of his first fall, the Earl was in a position to speak on this point. Complaints must not be taken too seriously.

But Wolsey was inconsolable. It was not the fear of the outcome of the trial that sickened his spirit, for he was sure he could establish his innocence. The wormwood and gall he drank came from knowing that the King had been persuaded to accuse him of treason, of disloyalty to the royal person he loved with the love of a dog. He had been cuffed by the one person to whom he was wholly devoted. This was the bitterness. "I have no assured friend in all the world," he told the Earl during one of their talks, "in whom I put my trust but only in his grace." He had, he lamented, "none other refuge to flee to for defense or succor, in all adversity, but under the shadow of his majesty's wing."

The King was still his god, and Wolsey was still the psalmist of his earthly friend. In his deepest grief he thought only of his friend, and his friend was his god; but his god had hidden his face and left him no one to pray to. If only his accusers could be made to confront him in the King's presence, he doubted not that he would confound them utterly. They would never be able to prove a case against him. "But I fear me," he said with more than a trace of memory of the case of Buckingham, "that they do intend rather to dispatch me than I should come before him in his presence." Whatever fate lay ahead of him, the worst fate had already been visited upon him: "The loss of goods, the slander of my name, nor yet all my trouble grieveth me nothing so much as the loss of the king's favor."

Insulated as he was by the Earl's hospitality, it is doubtful that Wolsey heard any of the bruits current in London during these dreary days. It was said around the court that the Cardinal was to be lodged in the same chamber of the Tower of London where the Duke of Buckingham had been detained. It was said that the Cardinal had been returning to his ancient pomp and corrupting the people of the north and that he had written to Rome to be reinstated in his possessions. And the case against him had gained force and detail since the return of his physician, Dr. Augustine. The doctor's testimony would give Wolsey's enemies what they had been looking for. Augustine, brought back as a traitor, had been living in the Duke of Norfolk's house like a prince, and, as Chapuys reported to the imperial court, "He is singing the tune as they wished him." [3]

If Wolsey did not know these putative details, he certainly perceived from experience how matters were arrayed against him. For two weeks he became more and more depressed with the prospect ahead. Then one night at dinner Cavendish, ever solicitous of his lord's welfare even in his misery, noticed at the end of the meal that his color changed several times. He was eating roasted Warden pears. Cavendish was standing at the table dressing the pears for him when he noted his color, and he leaned over the table, saying softly: "Sir, me seemeth your Grace is not well at ease."

The Cardinal admitted he had been taken suddenly about the stomach "with a thing that lieth overthwart my breast as cold as a whetstone." He asked his gentleman-usher to take away the table and, after he had had his own dinner, to come to him again. When Cavendish had seen to it that the waiters were properly at dinner, he came again and found Wolsey sitting where he had left him, very ill at ease but still talking with those who remained about him.

Meanwhile the veteran amateur doctor, who had sat up in bed at Esher and lectured the physicians who attended him, had diagnosed his own ailment to his own satisfaction. It was nothing but wind. So he sent his gentleman-usher to the apothecary of the household "to inquire of him if he had anything that would break wind upward."

It was a simple and human request, but the faithful servant could not execute it without protocol. It now became clear how much of a prisoner Wolsey was, for Master Walsh had exacted of Cavendish the promise that he would allow the Cardinal no drug which might enable him to escape this life. So Cavendish had first to go to the Earl of Shrewsbury for permission and then to the apothecary and get the powder and have it assayed and then take it back to the Earl for approval. Henry intended to see to it that the Cardinal would arrive at the Tower intact, on the theory that a man's life is more sacred to the State which would take it than to the man who possesses it.

Once the careful instructions and precautions were duly carried out, my lord of York got his powder. It proved to be what he needed, for immediately he took it, "surely he voided exceeding much wind upward." He was eased, and he said to Cavendish, "Lo, now you may see that it was but wind." He got up from the table and went to his prayers, as

490

his custom was after his dinner. But even while he was at his prayers, a seizure of the bowels came upon him and he was forced to go incontinent to his stool. It was while he was there that the Earl of Shrewsbury called Cavendish to him and gave him the news which would seal the Cardinal's doom: Sir William Kingston, Constable of the Tower of London, had arrived at Sheffield Park, accompanied by twenty-four yeomen of the guard.

The matter was not put thus bluntly by the Earl to Wolsey's servant. Still resolved upon hospitality, and apparently acting on the belief that a sick man must be spared the truth that is known to everyone else, the Earl asked Cavendish to dissemble the telling of Kingston's arrival by a long and fulsome contrivance. Cavendish was to "break first this matter unto him so wittily, and in such sort, that he might take it quietly in good part." The story to be told was that the Earl had written the King — as he had — to ask that the Cardinal be allowed to answer in the King's presence the accusations laid against him. This day he had received the answer, and it had been brought by Sir William Kingston, who was here at Sheffield to escort him to London for the answer the Cardinal so much wanted to give. Kingston's arrival, in effect, was to be made to sound like a cheerful bit of news and the escort of the twenty-four yeomen a guard of honor.

Cavendish shook his head in doubt, but he promised the Earl to do what he could. In his eagerness he overplayed his part and put on layers of sugary deceit that even the Earl had not ordered. Wolsey was sitting at the upper end of the gallery of the lodge, "upon a trussing chest of his own, with his beads and staff in his hands." Seeing his gentleman-usher coming, he asked what news he brought. "Forsooth, sir," Cavendish replied, "the best news that ever came to you; if your grace can take it well." He then told the story of the honor that had been paid him by the King's sending Kingston.

There is no good way to tell bad news. Wolsey's ear caught only one word. Kingston. Master Kingston. He repeated the name over once or twice, clapped his hand on his thigh, and sighed. Cavendish launched into a long and encouraging speech to his master, who listened and mused. When it was finished, he answered it with but a few words: "Well, well, I perceive more than ye can imagine or do know. Experience of old hath taught me." With that he got up and went to his room and to his stool again, for by now the flux had begun to trouble him sorely.

After he came out of his room, the Earl of Shrewsbury joined him in the gallery and the two sat down together on a bench in front of a great window, the Earl inquiring gently after his health and then repeating the story Cavendish had told: representations had been made to the King by letter for a hearing of the Cardinal's cause in Henry's presence, and the answer had been sent by Sir William Kingston, who now stood ready to take him honorably to his trial. Kingston was not referred to as Constable of the Tower but as "that worshipful knight Master Kingston." A further alluring touch was added by the fact that the twenty-four yeomen of the guard who accompanied him were all Wolsey's old servants, thoughtfully commanded by the King for the journey "to defend you against your unknown enemies, to the intent that ye may safely come unto his majesty."

Wolsey had only one comment to make: Master Kingston was Constable of the Tower.

"Yea, what of that?" said the Earl. "I assure you he is only appointed by the King for one of your friends . . ."

It was the kind of story he had heard so often in various forms since the loss of the Great Seal, a deadly kind because it was remotely plausible.

"Where is Master Kingston?" Wolsey asked. The Earl said he would be glad to send for him. Evidently Kingston waited nearby, for when a messenger went to fetch him he came at once to the gallery. Wolsey got up and went to meet him, but Kingston came forward and knelt down to salute him in the King's behalf. The Cardinal took off his cap and tried to raise Kingston up, but still he refused to rise. At last Wolsey said, "Good Master Kingston, stand up, or I will myself kneel down by you."

Kingston stood up then, and he delivered in convincing terms the message he said he had brought from the King. It was in substance the same message that Sir Henry Norris had brought him at Putney town on the way to Esher. "He commanded me," said Kingston, "to say first unto you that he beareth you as much good will and favor as ever he did; and willeth you to be of good cheer." The King thinks the reports of Wolsey's crimes are untrue but, to avoid the appearance of partiality, he must ask the Cardinal to stand trial. The Cardinal is to take his journey toward the King at his own pleasure, and Kingston has been sent merely to preserve his person from damage and inconvenience.

A year before, such a message had caused the Cardinal to tear off his hat and grovel with thanksgiving in the dust. But it had not been brought by the Constable of the Tower. It was the same King and the same message, but not the same messenger and not the same Cardinal. Wolsey listened attentively and respectfully to Kingston, thanked him for what he called his good news, and then said: "But, Master Kingston, all these comfortable

492

words which ye have spoken be but for a purpose to bring me into a fool's paradise: I know what is provided for me." He said that he would be ready to ride with Kingston on the morrow, and the three men sitting in the gallery of the lodge fell to talking about other matters while Cavendish went off to truss things up and make ready for the journey.

Wolsey was not ready to ride the next day. He had no stomach left. That night the sickness tore at his bowels so grievously that he had fifty stools. The night left him pitiably weak, but he would have ridden with Kingston if the Earl of Shrewsbury had not forbidden it. Wolsey tarried all that day, but the day following he mounted on his mule and prepared to join Master Kingston and the guard. It was late November. The weather in those parts at that season was foul and damp and an imposition on those in the best of health. But it would get worse, and for all his courtesy and his kindly messages from the King, the Constable of the Tower did not offer to delay his journey until the Cardinal was better.

There was only one ray of warmth when Wolsey set out in the November chill: the yeomen the King had sent to bring him to the Tower were indeed his friends, and when they saw their old master, sick and in disgrace, they showed their affection with unabashed tears. He took them all solemnly by the hands, inquiring after them and exchanging memories. And as he rode along, he talked with them, first with one and then with another, until he had a sense of companionship that cheered him in his infirmity.

Something must have cheered him and sustained him, for the party rode all that day and lodged in a house belonging to the Earl of Shrewsbury in Nottinghamshire. There the Cardinal spent a miserable night, but he rode again the next day to Nottingham. There his condition grew worse, but late the next morning, which was Saturday, the party set out for Leicester. On the way, says Cavendish, the Cardinal "waxed so sick that he was divers times likely to have fallen from his mule."

Thus they approached by very slow stages the Abbey of St. Mary of the Meadows, which lay but a short way north of Leicester. To the broken Cardinal, the Abbey of St. Mary of the Meadows was a fitting destination, either for the night or for eternity. He was spent and could go no farther; his exhausted body must use it as a stopping place. But there was more. In the cycle of history to which he belonged, Leicester had been the beginning and now it would be the end. From Leicester Richard III had ridden forth to meet Henry Tudor in the fields not far away, and to Leicester the broken body of Richard had been returned, there to be buried, after days of neglect, in the monastery of the Gray Friars.

To Leicester Henry VII had come in triumph after Bosworth, and here, it might be said, had begun the whole Tudor reign of which the Cardinal with his abundant talent had been such a luminous part. Leicester was near the center and heart of England. It was not without significance that a man whose whole destiny had been inextricably tied up with a tapestry of events that began at Leicester should, after all his wanderings, come to Leicester at the end of his fortune — should with the last of his strength manage to reach Leicester, as if led and supported by some inscrutable force.

There is a fog in history that lends strange shapes to men and events, that shrouds the commonplace and the familiar with mystery, that slows the pace of the mind down to meditation. Without this softening mist to ennoble men and motives, Wolsey's approach to the Abbey of St. Mary of the Meadows can be seen only as one more incident in a dramatic story. Another stopover on the road to London. Nothing more. But the Cardinal's approach was rich in symbols and imagery. In the days of his prosperity Wolsey had become a member of the Canons Regular of the Order of St. Augustine, to which the Abbey north of Leicester belonged. But his connection with the Order had been merely honorary and nominal. What had been an adminstrative detail in his legateship became a haven in his rejection, and what he had neglected most in the days of his prosperity he needed most in the last hours of his adversity.

Wolsey knew that the great Abbey would receive him hospitably, but it would be the hospitality of the tomb. What lay beyond would not belong to the world in which he had lived with such furious energy. When the whole convent came with many torches to meet him at the gates of the Abbey grounds and crowded around in the ghostly light to do him reverence, the Cardinal said simply: "Father Abbot, I am come hither to leave my bones among you."

He had little else to leave. All that Wolsey had so sedulously coveted had turned to dust before his eyes. His wealth and estates were gone, the architecture of his dreams torn down. The man in whom he had put his trust above all else had suffered his enemies to arrest him of high treason. Only his gentleman-usher and the yeomen of the guard sent to escort him to his doom could be counted as his friends. His confessor and confidant, Thomas Larke, a boon companion over the years, had died at Southwell four months before. His daughter had been consigned to a nunnery; his son, Thomas Wynter, upon whom he had lavished so many honors and for whom he had begged so many preferments, was traveling in France, living beyond the means his father had provided, a perennial scholar too busy with learning to come near the dying Cardinal.

Too weak to walk the distance from the gate, the Cardinal rode on to the massive doors of the Abbey, and those attending him led his mule into the great hall and to the foot of the stairs that would lead to his chamber. There he dismounted, and Master Kingston supported him as he climbed the stairs. Afterwards Kingston told Cavendish that he had never carried so heavy a burden in all his life.

CHAPTER V

THE complicated life of the Cardinal of York had now reduced itself to the simple matter of death. Yet for one who had been intricately involved in the affairs of a whole generation of turbulent Englishmen and in the convulsions of Europe, death could not be simple. The peace and privacy of dying must be left to lesser men. There would be buried with him the properties of an immense institution. This man had stayed history. By the sheer force and weight of his personal influence he had countered a revolution. Now it awaited only the signal of his death.

Nor could Wolsey die unmolested by the man whose wish he had failed to satisfy. Even as he lay ill in the Abbey, the long arm of the King reached out and shook him a final time. It shook him and it searched him. An account book found in Cawood Castle by the Earl of Northumberland showed that Wolsey had in his possession fifteen hundred pounds. Word of this discovered scent had reached Henry, but no trace of the money itself could be found. One David Vincent, who had been a groom in Wolsey's privy chamber, had been suspected of hiding the money. He had been taken to London and imprisoned in the Tower but later released with the order that he go to meet the returning Cardinal, find the money and, if he succeeded, bring it to the King.[1]

Wolsey arrived at the Abbey of St. Mary of the Meadows on Saturday night. On Monday afternoon Vincent arrived there with the King's commission. Kingston sent for Cavendish and asked him how he thought the matter might be broached. Cavendish said he thought Kingston should ask the Cardinal directly and without reference to Vincent. The approach was made to Wolsey with as much delicacy as possible. Kingston explained that the money had simply disappeared: the King thought it a pity that both he and the Cardinal should be embezzled by its loss. Then Kingston demanded in the King's name that Wolsey tell him where the money could be found.

It was a sad and bitter moment. Wolsey could tell by the very nature of it that it was the last message from his King. And what did it concern? Was there a touch of gratitude or blessing in it? Solicitude? No; all that was past. Wolsey paused before he replied to Kingston, and then he said: "Ah, good Lord! how much doth it grieve me that the King should think in me such deceit, wherein I should deceive him of any one penny that I have." Rather than embezzle the King of one mite, he said, he would rather it were put in his mouth while it was molten. These last words he repeated vehemently. He had never had any goods that he did not consider belonged to the King and that he had not intended to leave him after his death. "And for this money that ye demand of me," he went on to Kingston, "I assure you it is none of mine; for I borrowed it of divers of my friends to bury me, and to bestow among my servants, who have taken great pains about me, like true and faithful men."

When Kingston asked the names of those from whom the money had been borrowed, Wolsey reeled off the names and the amounts, including "a hundred pounds of my steward, whose name I have forgotten." Then Kingston asked quietly, like a good servant of the King merely eager to get the facts: "But, sir, I pray you, where is the money?" To which the Cardinal replied: "I will not conceal it from the King. I will declare it to you, or I die, by the grace of God. Take a little patience with me, I pray you." He added that the money was in an honest man's keeping, who would not hold back one penny of it from the King.

Grieved though he was by the King's hounding him on his deathbed for the last remnant of his borrowed wealth, Wolsey showed an element of disdain in his attitude. He had at last slipped beyond the temptation of any return to favor. With this final bitter reminder, Wolsey accepted rejection. His fatal illness gave him a kind of franchise and privilege he could not enjoy in good health. If his hours were numbered, it did not greatly matter what the King thought or sought; there might even be a grim and malicious satisfaction in holding out against Henry's last request.

Besides, the Cardinal was busy dying. He played out the role of his death as he had played out all the others. He would make an event of it. He planned his last hours with the same attention to schedule he had shown in his most active days. He had it in mind to die at eight o'clock. He would die at eight o'clock, but he was not sure, under the distractions of fever, what day it would be. On Monday morning his gentleman-usher approached his bedside. The Cardinal, seeing his shadow, asked his servant how he was and what hour it was of the clock. When Cavendish told him it was past eight, the Cardinal shook his head, repeating the hour several times. "Eight of the clock, eight of the clock, nay, nay, it cannot be eight of the clock, for by eight of the clock you will lose your master . . ."

The figure eight seems to have been fixed in his mind by his illness. He had been in continual fever for eight days, he told Kingston in an analysis of his disease; now the eighth day had come and there was bound to follow excoriation of the entrails or frenzy or else death: and the best thereof was death.

Scorched inside and out by unrelenting fever, the Cardinal slipped now and then into a querulous delirium. On Monday Dr. Palmes, the Cardinal's chaplain and ghostly father, was standing near his bed and, thinking the end near, bade Cavendish ask if his master wanted to be shriven and put in readiness towards God. The question angered Wolsey, and he protested so strongly the presumption of it that Dr. Palmes had to take the servant's part. He came forward to the bed "and talked with him in Latin and so pacified him."

Monday night, after his talk with Kingston about the missing money, Wolsey waxed sicker and sicker. The flux was still upon him and he swooned often. At four o'clock the next morning, however, he asked for meat, saying to his gentleman-usher: "I intend this day, God willing, to make me strong, to the intent that I may occupy myself in confession, and make me ready to God." Cavendish went at once to rouse the cook that he might prepare some meat, then called Dr. Palmes that he might attend the Cardinal in confession. He went also to awake Kingston, who was much put out over being called at such an ungodly hour. By the time Cavendish returned to the Cardinal's chamber, the soup he had ordered from the cook had arrived. Wolsey took a spoonful or two of it and asked whereof it was made. When he found that it was made of chicken he refused to eat more, being suddenly indignant that they had given him meat on a fast day. The fever exaggerated both the present and the past, and his mind flitted back among old memories and resolutions. The Cardinal of York was with the Carthusians again, firm in his austerity. His chaplain tried to console his conscience, saying that his sickness entitled him to meat. To which Wolsey merely replied, "I will eat no more."

At six he made his confession for the space of a whole hour. And when

497

he had finished, Master Kingston came to him again, returning, as he had promised, to find out more about the missing money. But Kingston did not mention the money again. Instead he set about to cheer the Cardinal with assurances that he would live and do very well.

It was too late. Wolsey explained the course of his disease. There was no chance to live; and if there was no chance to live, there was no need to feign. He could speak plainly now. When Kingston told him again what he had heard so often of late, that he had nothing to fear, Wolsey replied:

"I see the matter against me how it is framed." Then he added: "But if I had served God as diligently as I have done the King, He would not have given me over in my grey hairs." [2]

A distinction, subtle and dim but there all the same, had grown up in his mind between God and the King. It was too late for anything now but the experience of remorse, a vision of a life that could have been better spent. Yet even in his eloquent statement of remorse the image of God was very close to the image of the King. Even in his last feverish hour it was the King's good will he sought. With a candor made possible by death but with a pleading that marked the tenor of his life, Wolsey went on to Kingston:

"I pray you, with all my heart, to have me most humbly commended unto his royal majesty; beseeching him in my behalf to call to his most gracious remembrance all matters proceeding between him and me from the beginning of the world unto this day, and the progress of the same: and most chiefly in the weighty matter yet depending . . . then shall his conscience declare whether I have offended him or no . . ."

Wolsey continued to talk to Kingston and to those assembled about his bedside until his tongue began to fail. And when his tongue began to fail, his gentleman-usher knew that the end was near. Cavendish, ever attentive to detail, sent at once for the Abbot, who came and anointed him. And the servant called also the guard to stand by and to hear him talk before his death and to witness it. There was an awed silence in the chamber. The voice of the great Cardinal was still; the man of many words was quiet. And at that moment the clock began to strike the hour of eight. The day was Tuesday, November 29, 1530.

It was important to have witnesses "to see him personally dead, in avoiding of false rumors that might hap to say that he was not dead, but still living." Accordingly, the mayor of Leicester, together with dignitaries of the town, was sent for to bear official witness. The body of the Cardinal was placed in a coffin of plain boards, being stripped and prepared for interment. Under his outer garments the attendants found a shirt of very fine holland cloth; and underneath that, next to his body, a shirt of hair.

All the rest of the day the body lay open and barefaced, "that all men might see him there dead without feigning." When the mayor and his brethren had satisfied himself that the Cardinal was quite definitely dead, the Abbot and the monks followed the body down into the church. The corpse was set in the Lady Chapel, and tapers of wax were placed near it, and many poor men sat around with torches in their hands, watching the dead body all night. All night, too, the canons sang dirges and orisons. And about four o'clock in the morning they sang Mass and the body of Thomas Wolsey was laid to rest.

Cavendish carried the news of Wolsey's last hours to the King. He found Henry shooting rounds in a park in the Cardinal's old home at Hampton Court. He asked the gentleman-usher to wait until he had finished his game, then he gave his bow to the yeoman of bows and invited Cavendish into the palace. There he talked with him for an hour and more. "During this time," says Cavendish, "he examined me of divers weighty matters concerning my lord, wishing that liever than twenty thousand pounds he had lived. Then he asked me for the fifteen hundred pounds . . ." [3]

Thus passed the Cardinal of York from the stage of history under a cloud of vague suspicion that left people greedy for any report. With no particulars established in the charges against him, rumors prevailed until they hardened into the semblance of fact. Chapuys, the imperial ambassador, wrote his government: "The Cardinal of York died on St. Andrew's Day at a place where King Richard was killed. They were both buried in the same church, which people call *The Tyrants' Sepulchre* . . ." [4]

It was an error of fact, for Richard was buried in the monastery of the Gray Friars. But nobody cared. It would suit the Tudor purpose well to associate the dead Cardinal with the detested Richard. And the error, being in an ambassador's letter, got potted and transplanted and, like other errors about Wolsey, was destined to live for centuries.

Yet one must admit that the man will outlive the errors about him. Witnesses could testify that he was dead, and the mayor and the mayor's brethren at Leicester could guarantee that he was dead. But no one could guarantee that he would not rise to haunt history and to appeal to men's fancy in generations to come.

On many an evening in late November a chill mist from the River Soar creeps in over the walls still surrounding the spacious grounds of the Abbey of St. Mary of the Meadows. No trace of the old Abbey remains above the earth today. Within ten years after the death of Thomas Cardinal Wolsey virtually all the monasteries and nunneries of England had been razed, their lands and holdings and works of art and herds appropriated by the Crown or distributed by Henry to his favorites. The jeweled shrine of St. Thomas of Canterbury was cast down, a fragment of it having been made into a ring for Henry's thumb; St. Thomas was declared a traitor, his images and pictures ordered out of the churches, his bones disinterred and burned in the middle of Canterbury, and his ashes fired from a cannon.[5]

From the fury of the dissolution of the monasteries that went on during the period of 1536-1540, the Abbey of St. Mary of the Meadows did not escape. The agent sent to find some excuse for destroying the Abbey admitted that the Abbot was an honest man, adding "but he hath here the most obstinate and fractious canons that ever I knew." [6] Petitions that the Abbey might be spared were made to Thomas Cromwell, who, as the King's henchman, presided over the whole spoliation. The Abbot, seeing that bribery was the only hope, sent Cromwell a present of forty pounds to be used at his pleasure, and his successor, after paying a special annual tax of two hundred and forty pounds, sent "a brace of fat oxen and a score of fat wethers." [7]

Nothing availed. The Abbot and canons had buried the Cardinal in the full robes and regalia of his office; and when they had done this, they had buried the office. They had buried Rome in Leicester.

For in the turbulent decade that followed the death of Wolsey, Henry VIII made himself, through successive acts of a suppliant Parliament and Convocation, supreme head of the Church in England. By his guidance and maneuvering, the clergy rebelled against the Pope only to surrender to the King, and the Church became an obedient appendage of the royal frame. The one ideal for which Wolsey consistently stood, however abominably he failed to implement it, was destroyed as definitely as the religious houses: a Christendom unified by conscience above crowns.

Henry the King and the Crown and the State had won, and the Cardinal had lost, and never was a kingly triumph more complete. Upon the death of the decrepit Warham, Henry had named young Thomas Cranmer Archbishop of Canterbury. Cranmer declared the marriage of Catherine and Henry null and void. Henry secretly married Anne Boleyn late in January of 1533. In June of that year she got her crown, after Cranmer had certified the earlier marriage, and in early September a child was born to their union — a daughter. She was named for Henry's mother: Elizabeth.

Catherine had been deprived of her rights and title as Queen, separated from her daughter Mary, and imprisoned in Kimbolton Castle. There had been talk that a conspiracy and revolt would form around her, but on January 8, 1536, she died. With her last energy she wrote to Henry, urging that he look to his soul and beseeching him in behalf of her daughter and her servants and ending the letter with these words: "Lastly, I make this vow, that mine eyes desire you above all things." [8]

Henry and Anne received the news of Catherine's death with joy and celebrated it with revelry. Yet four months after Catherine's death, Anne was charged with adultery and with incest. She was ostensibly tried, and her head was cut off on Tower green by the executioner imported from Calais. Two days before the execution Cranmer had conveniently pronounced the marriage of Henry and Anne null and void, Anne having been allegedly pre-contracted to the Earl of Northumberland and Henry having had Anne's sister as his mistress. While Anne lay awaiting execution in the Tower, Henry held a series of nocturnal water parties on his barges in the Thames. Ten days after Anne was executed he married Jane Seymour.

By then Henry had destroyed practically every vestige of the regime in which the Cardinal had played a leading part. The King had renamed Cardinal College for himself, and later he was to refound it as Christ Church. And he destroyed Wolsey's last resting place so completely that only a few foundation stones were left to guide future inquirers. From these shards of history enterprising citizens have managed to reconstruct the foundations. The Abbey no longer towers above the earth, but lies there, a dignified skeleton of its former greatness.

Today one can find his way to a slab lying within the ghostly foundations. It marks, as well as historians can mark, the grave of Cardinal Wolsey. Underneath the name is a deeply carved inscription from the play *King Henry VIII*. It is from a speech the dramatist put into the Cardinal's mouth when, describing himself to the Abbot as "an old man, broken with the storms of State," he came to leave his bones in the Abbey. His petition to the Abbot, the last public request the Cardinal ever made, forms a fitting epitaph:

GIVE HIM A LITTLE EARTH FOR CHARITY

Reference Notes

The following book will be of particular value to the reader whose interest may be stirred to a point where he will want to read further in the period covered:

Conyers Read, ed., *Bibliography of British History, Tudor Period, 1485-1603* (Oxford, 1933). Issued under the direction of the American Historical Association and the Royal Historical Society of Great Britain.

Certain abbreviations of titles will be found in the Notes as follows:
L. & P.

> *Letters and Papers, Foreign and Domestic, of the Reign of Henry VIII, Preserved in the Public Record Office, the British Museum, and Elsewhere in England* . . . arranged and catalogued by J. S. Brewer (London, 1876). The Roman numeral designates the volume, and the numbers following, unless specified as pages, designate the documents in the volume.

State Papers

> *State Papers* published under the authority of His Majesty's Commission, King Henry VIII, Volumes I and II (London, 1830-1852). Of this collection the historian Read says: "Contains only material in the P. R. O. Correspondence printed *in extenso*. Superseded by *Letters and Papers* except where full text of letter is needed."

Spanish Calendar

> *Calendar of State Papers, Spanish.* Vols. I, II, and Supplementary Volume, 1485-1525, by G. A. Bergenroth; Vols. III-VII, 1524-1544, by Pascual de Gayangos y Arce.

Venetian Calendar

> *Calendar of State Papers, Venetian.* Vols. I-IX, 1202-1603. By Rowdon Brown, Cavendish Bentinck and Horatio Brown.

BOOK I

CHAPTER I
[1] Arthur Mee, ed., *The King's England: Suffolk* (London, 1941), p. 79; for details of early Ipswich, John Wodderspoon, *Memorials of the Ancient Town*

of Ipswich in the County of Suffolk (London, 1950) and G. R. Clarke, *The History and Description of the Town and Borough of Ipswich* (London, 1830).

2 J. Bohn, ed., *Chronicles of the White Rose of York* (London, 1945), "Warkworth's Chronicle." References in order of material quoted: pp. 109, 115, 132, 133, 38.

3 James Gairdner, ed., *The Paston Letters 1422-1509 A.D.* (London, 1872), Vol. III, p. 15.

4 Augustus Jessopp, *The Coming of the Friars and Other Historical Essays* (New York, 1895), p. 172, quoting Villani. Contains much valuable data on the Black Death, especially in East Anglia.

5 G. M. Trevelyan, *English Social History: A Survey of Six Centuries —* Chaucer to Queen Victoria (London, 1942), pp. 10, 11.

6 *Ibid.*, p. 23.

7 S. T. Bindoff, *Tudor England* (Harmondsworth, 1950), p. 12.

8 Edward P. Cheyney, *Social Changes in England in the 16th Century as Reflected in Contemporary Literature* (Boston, 1895), pp. 27, 28.

9 S. H. Burke, *Historical Portraits of the Tudor Dynasty* (London, 1893), Vol. I, pp. 102, 103.

10 Cheyney, *op. cit.*, p. 36.

11 L. F. Salzman, *England in Tudor Times* (London, 1926), p. 8.

12 Eileen Power, *Medieval People* (Boston, 1935), p. 131.

13 Sir Walter Besant, *London in the Time of the Tudors* (London, 1904), Vol. I, p. 275.

14 Trevelyan, *op. cit.*, p. 71.

15 Frederick Chamberlin, *The Private Character of Henry the Eighth* (New York, 1931), p. 82.

16 Philip Lindsay, *The Tragic King, Richard III* (New York, 1934), pp. 50, 51.

17 *The Annalls of Ipswiche, The Lawes and Customes and Government of the Same.* By Nathaniel Bacon, Serving as Recorder and Town Clark in that Towne (Ipswich, 1654). Edited by W. H. Richardson (Ipswich, 1884), pp. 131, 134, 147.

18 *Ibid.*, pp. 137, 139.

19 Vincent R. Redstone, "Social Condition of England During the Wars of the Roses," *Transactions of the Royal Historical Society*, Vol. XVI (1902), Appendix, pp. 199, 200.

20 James Gairdner, *History of the Life and Reign of Richard the Third* (Cambridge, 1898), pp. 16, 17.

CHAPTER II

1 Dorothy Hartley and Margaret M. Elliot, *Life and Work of the People of England* (New York, 1926), Vol. II, p. 35.

2 Thomas Wright, *Homes of Other Days,* A History of Domestic Manners and Sentiments in England From the Earliest Known Period to Modern Times (London and New York, 1871), p. 425.

[8] Frederick J. Furnivall, ed., *Early English Meals and Manners* (Oxford, 1868), pp. 46, 47.
[4] Eileen Power, *Medieval People* (Boston, 1935), p. 163, quoting Thomas Deloney's works.
[5] James Gairdner, ed., *The Paston Letters 1422-1509 A.D.* (London, 1872), Vol. III, p. 481.
[6] Christina Hole, *English Home Life 1500-1800* (London, 1947), p. 41 ff.
[7] H. F. M. Prescott, *Mary Tudor* (New York, 1953), p. 26.
[8] G. Laurence and Alice Bertha Gomme, *The Traditional Games of England, Scotland and Ireland* (London, 1894-1898), Vol. I, p. 234.
[9] J. Brand, *Observations on the Popular Antiquities of Great Britain. Chiefly Illustrating the Origin of Our Vulgar Customs, Ceremonies and Superstitions.* (London, 1900), p. 229.
[10] *The Annalls of Ipswiche, The Lawes and Customes and Government of the Same.* By Nathaniel Bacon. Edited by W. H. Richardson (Ipswich, 1884), pp. 140, 147.
[11] Alice Stopford Green, *Town Life in the Fifteenth Century* (London, 1907), Vol. II, pp. 22, 23, 16.
[12] Furnivall, *op. cit.*, pp. 18-20, 179, quoting John Russell's *Boke of Nurture.*
[13] *Ibid.*, pp. 201-202, quoting *The Boke of Curtsaye.*
[14] *Ibid.*, p. 66.
[15] *Ibid.*, p. 7.
[16] *Ibid.*, pp. 63, 64, 66.
[17] *Ibid.*, pp. 128, 129.

CHAPTER III
[1] Descriptions of early butchering practices are posted in modern Ipswich.
[2] Hastings Rashdall, *The Universities of Europe in the Middle Ages.* Edited by F. M. Powicke and A. B. Emden (Oxford, 1936), Vol. III, p. 362.
[3] *Ibid.*, p. 371.
[4] Charles Edward Mallet, *A History of the University of Oxford* (London, 1924), Vol. I, p. 389.
[5] Rashdall, *op. cit.*, p. 417.
[6] Rashdall, *op. cit.*, p. 432.
[7] Mallet, *op. cit.*, p. 389.
[8] H. C. Maxwell Lyte, *A History of the University of Oxford from the Earliest Times to the Year 1530* (New York, 1886), p. 208.
[9] *Ibid.*, p. 209.
[10] Gladys Temperly, *Henry VII* (Boston, 1914), p. 308, citing Wilkins' *Concilia*, iii, 618, 619, 620.
[11] Richard Henry Gretton, *The English Middle Class* (London, 1917), p. 78.
[12] James Gairdner, *Henry the Seventh* (London, 1899), p. 6.
[13] James Gairdner, *History of the Life and Reign of Richard the Third* (Cambridge, 1898), p. 185.
[14] *Ibid.*, p. 206, quoting Croyland's *Chronicle.*
[15] For an excellent account of the battle of Bosworth, see Alfred H. Burne, *The Battlefields of England* (London, 1950), p. 137 ff.

[16] H. A. L. Fisher, *The History of England from the Accession of Henry VII to the Death of Henry VIII (1485-1547)* (London, New York and Toronto, 1934), p. 10. (Vol. V in *The Political History of England,* edited by William Hunt and Reginald L. Poole.)

[17] Sharon F. S. A. Turner, *The History of England* (London, 1823-1826), Vol. III, p. 551, quoting Drake's *Ebor,* p. 121, note.

[18] Matthias A. Shaaber, *Some Forerunners of the Newspaper in England* (University of Pennsylvania, 1939), p. 39.

[19] James Gairdner, *Henry the Seventh,* p. 90.

[20] Details of the story of Lambert Simnel may be found in Fisher, *op. cit.,* and other standard reference works of the period.

[21] Fisher, *op. cit.,* pp. 1, 2.

CHAPTER IV

[1] G. M. Trevelyan, *English Social History* (London, 1942), p. 75.

[2] W. W. Copes, *The English Church in the Fourteenth and Fifteenth Centuries* (London, 1900), p. 363.

[3] Anthony Wood, *The History and Antiquities of the University of Oxford* (Oxford, 1792-1796), Vol. I, p. 648.

[4] H. D. Traill and J. S. Mann, eds., *Social England: A Record of the Progress of the People in Religion, Laws, Art, Industry, Commerce, Science, Literature and Manners from the Earliest Times to the Present Day* (London, 1903), Vol. III, p. 240.

[5] William Dunn Macray, *A Register of the Members of St. Mary Magdalen College Oxford from the Foundation of the College* (London, 1894), New Series, Vol. I, pp. 14, 15.

[6] Wood, *op. cit.,* p. 651.

[7] Macray, *op. cit.,* p. 26.

[8] S. T. Bindoff, *Tudor England* (Harmondsworth, 1950), p. 29.

[9] Alice Stopford Green, *Town Life in the Fifteenth Century* (London, 1907), Vol. I, pp. 52, 53.

[10] H. C. Maxwell Lyte, *A History of the University of Oxford from the Earliest Times to the Year 1530* (New York, 1886), p. 213.

[11] *Ibid.,* pp. 214-215.

[12] Charles Edward Mallet, *A History of the University of Oxford* (London, 1924), Vol. I, p. 392.

[13] George Cavendish, *The Life of Cardinal Wolsey* (London and New York, 1885), p. 14.

[14] Thomas Wright, *Homes of Other Days* (London and New York, 1871), pp. 373, 384.

[15] Dorothy Hartley and Margaret M. Elliott, *Life and Work of the People of England* (New York, 1926), Vol. II, p. 51.

[16] Hartley and Elliott, *op. cit.*

CHAPTER V

[1] Ethelred L. Taunton, *Thomas Wolsey: Legate and Reformer* (London, 1902), p. 19.

[2] A. F. Pollard, *Wolsey* (London, 1929), p. 13, note 5.
[3] H. A. Wilson, *University of Oxford* (London, 1899), p. 56.
[4] Taunton, *op. cit.*, p. 17.
[5] George Cavendish, *The Life of Cardinal Wolsey* (London and New York, 1885), p. 14.
[6] Taunton, *op. cit.*, p. 20.
[7] George Baskerville, "The Secular Clergy," *Mediaeval England* (a new edition of Barnard, *Companion to English History*). Edited by H. W. C. Davis (London, 1924), p. 412.
[8] *Ibid.*, p. 422.
[9] Charles Earle Funk, *Thereby Hangs a Tale* (New York, 1950), p. 60.
[10] *A Relation or Rather a True Account of the Island of England With Sundry Particulars of the Customes of These People, and of the Royal Revenues Under King Henry VII. About the Year 1500.* Translated from the Italian, with notes, by Charlotte Augusta Sneyd (London, Camden Society, 1847), p. 30.
[11] Arthur P. Stanley, *Historical Memorials of Canterbury* (London, 1885), p. 46.
[12] *Ibid.*, p. 48.
[13] *Ibid.*, p. 88 ff.
[14] *Dictionary of National Biography*, Vol. V, p. 704.

CHAPTER VI
[1] Robert Bell Calton, *Annals and Legends of Calais* (London, 1852), p. 56.
[2] *Ibid.*, p. 55.
[3] T. W. Cameron, "Wolsey's Early Life," *English Historical Review*, Vol. III (1886), p. 469.
[4] S. H. Burke, *Historical Portraits of the Tudor Dynasty* (London, 1893), Vol. I, p. 45.
[5] Garrett Mattingly, *Catherine of Aragon* (Boston, 1941), p. 25.
[6] Frank Arthur Mumby, *The Youth of Henry VIII, A Narrative in Contemporary Letters* (Boston, 1913), p. 9.
[7] *Ibid.*
[8] George G. Coulton, ed., *Life in the Middle Ages* (New York, 1930), Vol. III, pp. 155-164.
[9] Wilhelm Busch, *England Under the Tudors.* Translated under the supervision of the Rev. A. H. Johnson and Alice M. Todd (London, 1895), Vol. I, pp. 236-237.
[10] George Cavendish, *The Life of Cardinal Wolsey* (London and New York, 1885), p. 20 ff.
[11] Ethelred L. Taunton, *Thomas Wolsey: Legate and Reformer* (London, 1902), p. 32, referring to Weaver's *Somerset Incumbents*.
[12] Busch, *op. cit.*, p. 311.
[13] Arthur D. Innes, *England Under the Tudors* (New York, 1926), p. 19.

BOOK II

CHAPTER I
[1] Sebastian Giustiniani, *Four Years at the Court of Henry VIII. Selection of Despatches Written by the Venetian Ambassador, July 12th, 1515, to July 26th, 1519.* Translated by Rawdon Brown. (London, 1854), Vol. I, p. 27.
[2] A. F. Pollard, *Henry VIII* (London, 1951), p. 19.
[3] *Leviticus* 20:21.
[4] S. H. Burke, *Historical Portraits of the Tudor Dynasty* (London, 1893), Vol. I, p. 67.
[5] Garrett Mattingly, *Catherine of Aragon* (Boston, 1941), p. 125.
[6] Iris Brooke, "Dress," *Life Under the Tudors*. Edited by J. E. Morpurgo (London, 1950), pp. 201-202.
[7] A. Hartshorne, "Costume Civil," *Mediaeval England*. Edited by H. W. C. Davis (London, 1924), p. 166.
[8] H. A. L. Fisher, *The History of England from the Accession of Henry VII to the Death of Henry VIII* (London, New York and Toronto, 1934), p. 167.
[9] Rose Graham, "Monasteries," *Mediaeval England*. Edited by H. W. C. Davis (London, 1924), pp. 373-374.
[10] E. L. Cutts, *Parish Priests and Their People in the Middle Ages in England* (London, 1898), p. 268.
[11] Edward Geoffrey O'Donoghue, *Bridewell Hospital, Palace, Prison, Schools from the Earliest Times to the Reign of Elizabeth* (London, 1923), p. 37.
[12] George Ormerod, *The History of the County Palatine and the City of Cheshire* (London, 1819), Vol. III, p. 332.
[13] A. F. Pollard, *Wolsey* (London, 1929), p. 14.
[14] *Ibid.*, p. 15.
[15] *Ibid.*, p. 16.
[16] Fisher, *op. cit.*, p. 164, quoting *Discorsi*, iii, 31.
[17] J. D. Mackie, *The Earlier Tudors 1485-1558* (Oxford, 1952), p. 271.

CHAPTER II
[1] Francis Godwin, *Annales of England* (London, 1630), p. 29.
[2] George Cavendish, *The Life of Cardinal Wolsey* (London and New York, 1885), pp. 24, 25.
[3] J. D. Mackie, *The Earlier Tudors 1485-1558* (Oxford, 1952), p. 270.
[4] H. A. L. Fisher, *The History of England from the Accession of Henry VII to the Death of Henry VIII* (London, New York and Toronto, 1934), p. 168. See note same page, citing Vergil's *History*, lib. xxvii, 623.
[5] A. F. Pollard, *Henry VIII* (London, 1951), p. 140.
[6] Garrett Mattingly, *Catherine of Aragon* (Boston, 1941), p. 143.
[7] *Ibid.*
[8] A. F. Pollard, *Wolsey* (London, 1929), p. 17.
[9] Fisher, *op. cit.*, p. 173.
[10] *Ibid.*, p. 174.
[11] *L. & P.*, I, 3355.

[12] Ernest Law, *England's First Great War Minister* (London, 1916), p. 9.
[13] Mattingly, *op. cit.*, p. 151.
[14] L. & P., I, 3555.
[15] *Ibid.*, 3469.
[16] Law, *op. cit.*, p. 19.
[17] *Ibid.*, p. 28.
[18] *Ibid.*, p. 69, citing de Favri, attaché of the Venetian Embassy.
[19] *Ibid.*, p. 68.
[20] L. & P., I, 3820.
[21] *Ibid.*, 3877.
[22] *Ibid.*, 4005.

CHAPTER III

[1] H. A. L. Fisher, *The History of England from the Accession of Henry VII to the Death of Henry VIII* (London, New York and Toronto, 1934), p. 181, citing *Archaeologia*, Vol. XXVI, p. 395.
[2] *Ibid.*
[3] C. W. C. Oman, "The Art of War," *Social England*. Edited by H. D. Traill and J. S. Mann (London, 1903), Vol. III, Section I, p. 94.
[4] Ernest Law, *England's First Great War Minister* (London, 1916), p. 99.
[5] *Ibid.*, pp. 97, 98.
[6] *Ibid.*, p. 207.
[7] Fisher, *op. cit.*, p. 182.
[8] Sir Charles Oman, *The Sixteenth Century* (London, 1936), p. 106.
[9] Law, *op cit.*, p. 218.
[10] Garrett Mattingly, *Catherine of Aragon* (Boston, 1941), p. 160.
[11] S. H. Burke, *Historical Portraits of the Tudor Dynasty* (London, 1893), Vol. I, p. 119.
[12] Law, *op. cit.*, p. 221.
[13] J. D. Mackie, *The Earlier Tudors 1485-1558* (Oxford, 1952), p. 281.
[14] Mattingly, *op. cit.*, pp. 157-158.
[15] *Original Letters Illustrative of English History, Including Numerous Royal Letters from Autographs in the British Museum.* Edited by Henry Ellis, Keeper of the Manuscripts in the British Museum. (London, 1825), Series I, Vol. I, Letter XXVIII, pp. 78-81.
[16] *Ibid.*, Letter XXIX, pp. 82-84.
[17] *Ibid.*, Letter XXX, pp. 84-85.
[18] *Ibid.*, Letter XXIX, p. 83.
[19] J. S. Brewer, *The Reign of Henry VIII From His Accession to the Death of Wolsey* (London, 1884), Vol. I, p. 30.
[20] James Gairdner, *Henry the Seventh* (London, 1899), p. 165.
[21] For a vivid account of the battle, see Alfred H. Burne, *The Battlefields of England* (London, 1950), p. 156 ff.
[22] Francis Godwin, *Annales of England* (London, 1630), p. 12.
[23] Mackie, *op. cit.*, p. 282.
[24] Frank Arthur Mumby, *The Youth of Henry VIII, A Narrative in Contemporary Letters* (Boston, 1913), p. 219.

CHAPTER IV

[1] Ethelred L. Taunton, *Thomas Wolsey: Legate and Reformer* (London, 1902), p. 38, citing *L. & P.*, I, 4747.

[2] Richard Fiddes, *The Life of Cardinal Wolsey* (London, 1726), p. 40.

[3] *Ibid.*

[4] A. F. Pollard, *Wolsey* (London, 1929), p. 22.

[5] Taunton, *op. cit.*, p. 37, quoting Matthew Paris, *Chronica Majora* (Roll Series), IV, pp. 546-547.

[6] Pollard, *op. cit.*

[7] *Ibid.*, p. 23.

[8] Taunton, *op. cit.*, p. 42, quoting Creighton's *Wolsey*, pp. 34-40.

[9] George Cavendish, *The Life of Cardinal Wolsey* (London and New York, 1885), p. 87.

[10] A. F. Pollard, *Henry VIII* (London, 1951), p. 121.

[11] Garrett Mattingly, *Catherine of Aragon* (Boston, 1941), p. 167.

[12] Pollard, *Wolsey*, p. 32, note 3.

[13] H. A. L. Fisher, *The History of England from the Accession of Henry VII to the Death of Henry VIII* (London, New York and Toronto, 1934), p. 209.

[14] Pollard, *Wolsey*, pp. 34-35.

[15] Fisher, *op. cit.*, p. 209.

[16] Pollard, *Wolsey*, p. 37.

[17] *L. & P.*, II, 2.

[18] Edward Hall, *Hall's Chronicle; Containing the History of England, During the Reign of Henry the Fourth, And the Succeeding Monarchs, To the End of the Reign of Henry the Eighth. In Which are Particularly Described the Manners and Customs of Those Periods. Carefully Collated with the Editions of 1548 and 1550.* (London, 1809), p. 579.

[19] Pollard, *Wolsey*, p. 30.

[20] *Ibid.*, pp. 44-45.

[21] *Ibid.*, p. 42.

[22] Fisher, *op. cit.*, p. 195.

[23] David Hume, *The History of England from the Invasion of Julius Caesar to the Revolution of 1688* (London, 1810), p. 494.

[24] S. H. Burke, *Historical Portraits of the Tudor Dynasty* (London, 1893), Vol. I, p. 130.

[25] J. S. Brewer, *The Reign of Henry VIII from His Accession to the Death of Wolsey* (London, 1884), Vol. I, p. 40.

[26] *L. & P.*, II, 209.

[27] *Ibid.*, 224; Brewer, *op. cit.*, p. 90.

[28] *L. & P.*, IV, 227, 229.

CHAPTER V

[1] Sebastian Giustiniani, *Four Years at the Court of Henry VIII* (London, 1854), Vol. I, p. 100 ff; J. S. Brewer, *The Reign of Henry VIII from His Accession to the Death of Wolsey* (London, 1884), Vol. I, p. 99.

[2] Brewer, *op. cit.*, p. 100.

[3] A. F. Pollard, *Wolsey* (London, 1929), p. 55.

[4] *Ibid.*
[5] Giustiniani, *op. cit.*, p. 128.
[6] Ernest Law, *England's First Great War Minister* (London, 1916), p. 100.
[7] E L. Cutts, *Scenes and Characters of the Middle Ages* (London, 1930), p. 234.
[8] Pollard, *op. cit.*, p. 56; *L. & P.*, I, 1153; Edward Hall, *Hall's Chronicle* (London, 1809), p. 583.
[9] J. H. Lupton, *Colet* (London, 1887), p. 194.
[10] Frederic Seebohm, *The Oxford Reformers, John Colet, Erasmus and Thomas More* (London, 1887), p. 84.
[11] Lupton, *op. cit.*, p. 197.
[12] *L. & P.*, II, 1315.
[13] H. A. L. Fisher, *The History of England from the Accession of Henry VII to the Death of Henry VIII* (London, New York and Toronto, 1934), p. 213.
[14] Pollard, *op. cit.*, p. 48.
[15] Fisher, *op. cit.*, p. 215.

CHAPTER VI
[1] G. M. Trevelyan, *English Social History* (London, 1942), p. 37.
[2] A. F. Pollard, *Wolsey* (London, 1929), p. 71.
[3] Lucy Toulmin Smith, "Town Life," *Mediaeval England*. Edited by H. W. C. Davis (London, 1924), p. 314.
[4] L. M. Larson, *History of England and the British Commonwealth* (New York, 1924), p. 247.
[5] Pollard, *op. cit.*, p. 96.
[6] George Cavendish, *The Life of Cardinal Wolsey* (London and New York, 1885), p. 39.
[7] J. D. Mackie, *The Earlier Tudors 1485-1558* (Oxford, 1952), p. 296.
[8] Sebastian Giustiniani, *Four Years at the Court of Henry VIII* (London, 1854), Vol. II, p. 315.
[9] *L. & P.*, II, 1552, 1814.
[10] Pollard, *op. cit.*, p. 74.
[11] *Ibid.*, p. 60.
[12] Alice Stopford Green, *Town Life in the Fifteenth Century* (London, 1907), Vol. I, p. 212 ff.
[13] Pollard, *op. cit.*, citing Pollock and Maitland, ii, 436.
[14] *L. & P.*, III, 608.
[15] L. F. Salzman, *England in Tudor Times* (London, 1926), p. 89.
[16] *L. & P.*, III, 1070.
[17] Mackie, *op. cit.*, p. 297, quoting Edward Hall, *Hall's Chronicle* (London, 1809), Vol. I, 227, p. 585.
[18] Pollard, *op. cit.*, p. 78.
[19] *Ibid.*, p. 77.
[20] A. F. Pollard, *Henry VIII* (London, 1951), p. 88.

CHAPTER VII

[1] Garrett Mattingly, *Catherine of Aragon* (Boston, 1941), pp. 38-39.
[2] A. T. Thomson, *Memoirs of the Court of Henry the Eighth* (London, 1826), Vol. I, p. 312. Various accounts are given of this incident.
[3] J. S. Brewer, *The Reign of Henry VIII from His Accession to the Death of Wolsey* (London, 1884), Vol. I, p. 385.
[4] *Ibid.*
[5] H. A. L. Fisher, *The History of England from the Accession of Henry VII to the Death of Henry VIII* (London, New York and Toronto, 1934), p. 237.
[6] Thomson, *op. cit.*, p. 316.
[7] *Ibid.*, pp. 316-317.
[8] George Lyman Kittredge, *Witchcraft in Old and New England* (Cambridge, 1929), p. 109.
[9] Brewer, *op. cit.*, p. 238, quoting "A Boke or Counseill Against the Sweate," note 9.
[10] *Ibid.*
[11] Francis Bacon, *History of the Reign of King Henry VII.* Edited by J. Rawson Lumby (Cambridge University Press, 1902), pp. 12-13.
[12] David Riseman, *The Story of Medicine in the Middle Ages* (New York, 1935), p. 241.
[13] Brewer, *op. cit.*, p. 241, citing *L. & P.*, II, 3645.
[14] *Ibid.*, pp. 240-241, citing *L. & P.*, II, 4125.
[15] *Ibid.*, p. 243.
[16] *A Relation or Rather a True Account of the Island of England With Sundry Particulars of the Customes of These People, and of the Royal Revenues Under King Henry VII. About the Year 1500.* Translated from the Italian, with notes, by Charlotte Augusta Sneyd (London, Camden Society, 1847), pp. 20-21.
[17] *Ibid.*, p. 20.
[18] Edward Hall, *Hall's Chronicle* (London, 1809), p. 586 ff. This gives a full account of the riots.

CHAPTER VIII

[1] Ernest Law, *England's First Great War Minister* (London, 1916), p. 33.
[2] W. C. Richardson, *Tudor Chamber Administration* (Baton Rouge, 1952), pp. 236, 237.
[3] Frederick J. Furnivall, ed., *Early English Meals and Manners* (Oxford, 1868), p. 46.
[4] A. F. Pollard, *Evolution of Parliament* (London, 1926), p. 264.
[5] Richard Henry Gretton, *The English Middle Class* (London, 1917), p. 112.
[6] Sir Walter Besant, *London in the Time of the Tudors* (London, 1904), Vol. I, pp. 36, 37.
[7] G. M. Trevelyan, *English Social History* (London, 1942), p. 117.
[8] George Ralston, "Country Life," *Mediaeval England.* Edited by H. W. C. Davis (London, 1924), p. 334.

[9] W. J. Corbett, "Agriculture," *Social England*. Edited by H. D. Traill and J. S. Mann (London, 1903), Vol. III, p. 152.
[10] A. F. Pollard, *Wolsey* (London, 1929), p. 86.
[11] Lord Ernle, *English Farming, Past and Present* (London, 1927), p. 60.

CHAPTER IX
[1] John H. Harvey, "The Building Works and Architects of Cardinal Wolsey," *British Archaeological Association Journal*, Series 3, Vol. VIII (1943), pp. 50-59.
[2] John Heneage Jessee, *London: Its Celebrated Characters and Remarkable Places* (London, 1871), p. 2.
[3] *A Relation or Rather a True Account of the Island of England With Sundry Particulars of the Customes of These People, and of the Royal Revenues Under King Henry VII. About the Year 1500*. Translated from the Italian, with notes, by Charlotte Augusta Sneyd (London, Camden Society, 1847), p. 78, note 41.
[4] Gladys Temperly, *Henry VII* (Boston, 1914), p. 309.
[5] G. M. Trevelyan, *English Social History* (London, 1942), p. 46.
[6] A. F. Pollard, *Henry VIII* (London, 1951), p. 271, citing L. & P., II, 1733.
[7] Paul Van Dyke, *Renascence Portraits* (New York, 1905), pp. 208-209.
[8] *Ibid.*, p. 209.
[9] G. M. Trevelyan, *England in the Age of Wycliffe* (London, 1920), pp. 328-329.
[10] H. S. Bennett, *The Pastons and Their England — Studies in an Age of Transition* (Cambridge, 1932), p. 144.
[11] J. J. Jusserand, *England Wayfaring Life in the Middle Ages (XIVth Century)* (New York, 1925), p. 312.
[12] Trevelyan, *English Social History*, p. 44.
[13] A. Abram, *Social England in the Fifteenth Century* (London, 1909), p. 50.
[14] L. & P., II, 2492.
[15] Sharon F. S. A. Turner, *The History of England* (London, 1823-1826), Vol. IV, p. 571.
[16] James Gairdner, *History of the Life and Reign of Richard the Third* (Cambridge, 1898), p. 163.
[17] Francis Aidan Gasquet, *Henry VIII and the English Monasteries* (London, 1889), p. 13.
[18] *Ibid.*, p. 14.
[19] Edward Hall, *Hall's Chronicle* (London, 1809), p. 593.
[20] A. F. Pollard, *Wolsey* (London, 1929), p. 179.
[21] Gasquet, *op. cit.*, p. 15.
[22] Ethelred L. Taunton, *Thomas Wolsey: Legate and Reformer* (London, 1902), p. 73.
[23] *Ibid.*, p. 77.
[24] *Ibid.*, p. 90.
[25] *Ibid.*, p. 91.
[26] Hall, *op. cit.*, p. 657.
[27] Pollard, *op. cit.*, p. 192.

CHAPTER X

1 E. L. Cutts, *Parish Priests and Their People in the Middle Ages in England* (London, 1898), p. 371.
2 Edward Hall, *Hall's Chronicle* (London, 1809), p. 691.
3 Ethelred L. Taunton, *Thomas Wolsey: Legate and Reformer* (London, 1902), p. 87, citing L. & P., IV, 478.
4 Cutts, *op. cit.*, p. 374.
5 A. L. Rowse, *Tudor Cornwall, Portrait of a Society* (London, 1941), p. 165.
6 *Ibid.*, p. 166.
7 *A Relation or Rather a True Account of the Island of England With Sundry Particulars of the Customes of These People, and of the Royal Revenues Under King Henry VII. About the Year 1500.* Translated from the Italian, with notes, by Charlotte Augusta Sneyd (London, Camden Society, 1847), p. 51.
8 Rose Graham, "Monasticism," *Mediaeval England.* Edited by H. W. C. Davis (London, 1924), p. 373.
9 *Italian Relation* (see note 7 above), p. 79, note 41.
10 Graham, *op. cit.*
11 Paul Van Dyke, *Renascence Portraits* (New York, 1905), p. 210.
12 G. M. Trevelyan, *English Social History* (London, 1942), p. 72.
13 Philip Hughes, *The Reformation in England* (London, 1954), Vol. I, p. 67.
14 Francis Aidan Gasquet, *Henry VIII and the English Monasteries* (London, 1889), p. 19.
15 *Ibid.*, p. 20, quoting Hall, *op. cit.*
16 Hall, *op. cit.*, p. 694.
17 Richard Fiddes, *The Life of Cardinal Wolsey* (London, 1726), p. 351.
18 J. S. Brewer, *The Reign of Henry VIII from His Accession to the Death of Wolsey* (London, 1884), Vol. II, p. 394, as quoted in Gasquet, *op. cit.*, p. 22.
19 A. Abram, *Social England in the Fifteenth Century* (London, 1909), p. 58.
20 Brewer, *op. cit.*, Vol. I, p. 443.
21 Ralph Roeder, *The Man of the Renaissance. Four Lawgivers: Savonarola, Machiavelli, Castiglione, Aretino* (New York, 1933), p. 418.
22 Brewer, *op. cit.*, p. 576.
23 Taunton, *op. cit.*, p. 144, quoting Bergenroth, *Spanish Calendar* Vol. II, No. 370.
24 A. F. Pollard, *Wolsey* (London, 1929), p. 169, and note 3, same page.

CHAPTER XI

1 Richard Fiddes, *The Life of Cardinal Wolsey* (London, 1726), p. 177.
2 *Ibid.*, p. 175.
3 Ethelred L. Taunton, *Thomas Wolsey: Legate and Reformer* (London, 1902), p. 103.
4 Fiddes, *op. cit.*, p. 168.
5 *Ibid.*
6 *Ibid.*, p. 292.
7 *Ibid.*
8 Charles W. Boase, *Oxford* (London, 1890), p. 102.

[9] Fiddes, *op. cit.*, p. 172.
[10] George G. Coulton, ed., *Medieval Panorama* (New York, 1944), p. 662.
[11] Frederick J. Furnivall, ed., *Early English Meals and Manners* (Oxford, 1868), p. 13.
[12] A. Abram, *Social England in the Fifteenth Century* (London, 1909), p. 219.
[13] Fiddes, *op. cit.*, p. 202.
[14] Taunton, *op. cit.*, p. 85; *L. & P.*, IV, 15.
[15] Francis Aidan Gasquet, *Henry VIII and the English Monasteries* (London, 1889), p. 17.
[16] A. F. Pollard, *Wolsey* (London, 1929), p. 326.
[17] Fiddes, *op. cit.*, p. 293.
[18] John H. Harvey, "The Building Works and Architects of Cardinal Wolsey," *British Archaeological Association Journal*, Series 3, Vol. VIII (1943), p. 55.
[19] Fiddes, *op. cit.*, p. 287.
[20] John J. Lingard, *The History of England from the First Invasion by the Romans to the Accession of William and Mary in 1688* (London, 1883), Vol. IV, p. 395.
[21] Lewis Einstein, *The Italian Renaissance in England* (New York, 1902), p. 55.
[22] S. H. Burke, *Historical Portraits of the Tudor Dynasty* (London, 1893), Vol. I, p. 231.
[23] T. L. Jarman, "Education," *Life Under the Tudors*. Edited by J. E. Morpurgo (London, 1950), p. 79.
[24] Frederic Seebohm, *The Oxford Reformers, John Colet, Erasmus and Thomas More* (London, 1887), p. 120.
[25] *Ibid.*, p. 130.
[26] Caesar Caine, "Cardinal Wolsey's College, Ipswich," *British Archaeological Association Journal*, New Series 20 (1914), pp. 91-106 and 225-241.
[27] *Ibid.*, p. 231; Foster Watson, *The English Grammar Schools to 1660* (Cambridge, 1906), p. 16 ff.
[28] T. Corcoran, "Thomas Cardinal Wolsey, Educator," *Studies*, Vol. XX (1931), pp. 30-33.
[29] Fiddes, *op. cit.*, Collections, pp. 103-104.

CHAPTER XII
[1] Ernest Law, *The History of Hampton Court Palace in Tudor Times* (London, 1885), pp. 23-24.
[2] J. A. Gotch, "Domestic Architecture," *Mediaeval England*. Edited by H. W. C. Davis (London, 1924), p. 81.
[3] James Lees-Milne, *Tudor Renaissance* (London, 1951), p. 44.
[4] Law, *op. cit.*, p. 16.
[5] *Ibid.*, p. 22.
[6] Edward Geoffrey O'Donoghue, *Bridewell Hospital, Palace, Prison, Schools from the Earliest Times to the Reign of Elizabeth* (London, 1923), p. 38.

[7] Sebastian Giustiniani, *Four Years at the Court of Henry VIII* (London, 1854), Vol. II, p. 314.
[8] A. F. Pollard, *Wolsey* (London, 1929), note p. 318.
[9] Law, *op. cit.*, p. 72.
[10] *Ibid.*, p. 74.
[11] Gotch, *op. cit.*, pp. 80-81.
[12] S. H. Burke, *Historical Portraits of the Tudor Dynasty* (London, 1893), p. 230.
[13] Giustiniani, *op. cit.*, p. 315.
[14] Law, *op. cit.*, p. 84.
[15] H. D. Traill and J. S. Mann, eds., *Social England* (London, 1903), Vol. III, p. 147.
[16] L. & P., II, 4024.
[17] George Cavendish, *The Life of Cardinal Wolsey* (London and New York, 1885), p. 41 ff.

CHAPTER XIII
[1] George Cavendish, *The Life of Cardinal Wolsey* (London and New York, 1885), p. 41.
[2] Harold Lamb, *The March of Muscovy* (New York, 1948), p. 96.
[3] James A. Williamson, *Maritime Enterprise 1485-1558* (Oxford, 1913), p. 21; *An Historical Geography of England Before A.D. 1800.* Edited by H. C. Darby (Cambridge, 1936).
[4] Williamson, *op. cit.*
[5] James A. Williamson, *Voyages of the Cabots* (London, 1929), p. 97.
[6] Sebastian Giustiniani, *Four Years at the Court of Henry VIII* (London, 1854), Vol. I, p. 90.
[7] J. S. Brewer, *The Reign of Henry VIII from His Accession to the Death of Wolsey* (London, 1884), Vol. II, p. 99.
[8] Brewer, *op. cit.*, Vol. I, p. 106 ff. Quoted in full.
[9] Giustiniani, *op. cit.*, pp. 156-157.
[10] L. & P., II, 1877.
[11] Giustiniani, *op. cit.*, p. 160, note 1.
[12] Brewer, *op. cit.*, Vol. I, p. 124 ff.
[13] L. & P., II, 2930.
[14] *Ibid.*, 2017.
[15] Giustiniani, *op. cit.*, Vol. II, p. 16.
[16] *Ibid.*, p. 219.
[17] Richard Fiddes, *The Life of Cardinal Wolsey* (London, 1726), p. 207.
[18] Giustiniani, *op. cit.*, p. 219.
[19] L. & P., 4540.

CHAPTER XIV
[1] Karl Brandi, *The Emperor Charles V: The Growth and Destiny of a Man and a World-Empire.* Translated from the German by C. V. Wedgwood (New York, 1939), p. 60.

[2] *Ibid.*, p. 61.
[3] David Hume, *The History of England from the Invasion of Julius Caesar to the Revolution of 1688* (London, 1810), p. 500.
[4] *Ibid.*, p. 501.
[5] Richard Fiddes, *The Life of Cardinal Wolsey* (London, 1726), p. 218.
[6] Edward Hall, *Hall's Chronicle* (London, 1809), p. 601.
[7] Sharon F. S. A. Turner, *The History of England* (London, 1823-1826), Vol. IV, p. 174.
[8] Garrett Mattingly, *Catherine of Aragon* (Boston, 1941), p. 207.
[9] Francis Godwin, *Annales of England* (London, 1630), p. 39.
[10] Mattingly, *op. cit.*, p. 211.
[11] James Lees-Milne, *Tudor Renaissance* (London, 1951), p. 24.
[12] *Rutland Papers: Original Documents of the Courts and Times of Henry VII and Henry VIII Selected from the Archives of the Duke of Rutland,* edited by Will. Jordan (London, Camden Society, 1842), pp. 28-49.
[13] J. S. Brewer, *The Reign of Henry VIII from His Accession to the Death of Wolsey* (London, 1884), Vol. I, p. 351. For further details on the meeting of Henry and Francis and Wolsey's management of it, see Edward Hall, *Hall's Chronicle* (London, 1809), p. 601 ff.
[14] Brewer, *op. cit.*, p. 354.
[15] Hume, *op. cit.*, p. 502.
[16] *Ibid.*
[17] Mattingly, *op. cit.*, p. 213.
[18] S. H. Burke, *Historical Portraits of the Tudor Dynasty* (London, 1893), Vol. I, p. 113.

BOOK III

CHAPTER I

[1] *Rutland Papers,* edited by Will. Jordan (London, Camden Society, 1842), p. 55, quoting Stowe, *Annals of London* (Howes edition), p. 507.
[2] J. S. Brewer, *The Reign of Henry VIII from His Accession to the Death of Wolsey* (London, 1884), Vol. I, p. 357.
[3] Francis Hackett, *Francis the First* (New York, 1935), p. 218.
[4] Brewer, *op. cit.*, p. 359.
[5] J. D. Mackie, *The Earlier Tudors 1485-1558* (Oxford, 1952), p. 310.
[6] H. A. L. Fisher, *The History of England from the Accession of Henry VII to the Death of Henry VIII* (London, New York and Toronto, 1934), p. 239.
[7] Brewer, *op. cit.*, p. 601, citing L. & P., II, 4257.
[8] L. & P., III, 1772.
[9] Brewer, *op. cit.*, p. 602, quoting a manuscript in the Society of Jesus College, Oxford.
[10] L. & P., III, 1574.
[11] Fisher, *op. cit.*, p. 256.
[12] L. & P., III, 1656.

[13] J. Grove, *The History of the Life and Times of Cardinal Wolsey* (London, 1746), Vol. III, pp. 141-145.

[14] *Ibid.*, p. 146, quoting Fuller's *Church History*.

[15] *L. & P.*, III, 1198.

[16] Brewer, *op. cit.*, p. 407.

[17] Garrett Mattingly, *Renaissance Diplomacy* (New York, 1955), p. 168.

[18] *L. & P.*, III, 1340, 1383.

[19] Grove, *op. cit.*, p. 176.

[20] Brewer, *op. cit.*, p. 417.

[21] *L. & P.*, III, 1622.

[22] Fisher, *op. cit.*, p. 231.

[23] *L. & P.*, III, 1475.

[24] Brewer, *op. cit.*, p. 372.

[25] *Ibid.*, p. 420.

[26] Karl Brandi, *The Emperor Charles V: The Growth and Destiny of a Man and a World-Empire.* Translated from the German by C. V. Wedgwood (New York, 1939), p. 164.

[27] Fisher, *op. cit.*, p. 232.

[28] Grove, *op. cit.*, pp. 194, 193.

[29] *Ibid.*, p. 192.

[30] A. F. Pollard, *Wolsey* (London, 1929), p. 92.

[31] *Ibid.*, p. 93, citing *L. & P.*, IV, p. 2560.

[32] *L. & P.*, III, 1539.

[33] Brewer, *op. cit.*, p. 428. A fragment of the letter appears in *L. & P.*, III, 1759.

CHAPTER II

[1] Elizabeth Ogilvy Benger, *Memories of the Life of Anne Boleyn* (London, 1821), p. 85 ff.

[2] Philip Walsingham Sergeant, *Anne Boleyn: A Study* (London, 1934), p. 36; J. S. Brewer, *The Reign of Henry VIII from His Accession to the Death of Wolsey* (London, 1884), Vol. II, pp. 173-174.

[3] Sergeant, *op. cit.*, p. 25, citing *L. & P.*, III, pp. 1558-1559.

[4] Garrett Mattingly, *Renaissance Diplomacy* (New York, 1955), p. 167.

[5] R. W. Chambers, *Sir Thomas More* (New York, 1935), p. 167, citing *L. & P.*, III, 1437.

[6] *L. & P.*, III, 3405.

[7] J. S. Brewer, *The Reign of Henry VIII from His Accession to the Death of Wolsey* (London, 1884), Vol. I, p. 452.

[8] Dorothy Hartley and Margaret M. Elliott, *Life and Work of the People of England* (New York, 1926), Vol. III, pp. 6-7.

[9] J. Grove, *The History of the Life and Times of Cardinal Wolsey* (London, 1746), Vol. III, pp. 228-229.

[10] *Boutell's Heraldry.* Revised by C. W. Scott-Giles (London, 1950), p. 246.

[11] Mattingly, *op. cit.*, p. 31.

[12] Mark Noble, *A History of the College of Arms and the Lives of All the Kings, Heralds and Pursuivants from the Reign of Richard III, Founder of the College* (London, 1804), p. 111.

[13] H. A. L. Fisher, *The History of England from the Accession of Henry VII to the Death of Henry VIII* (London, New York and Toronto, 1934), p. 241.

[14] Grove, *op. cit.*, p. 247.

[15] *Ibid.*, pp. 248-249.

[16] Brewer, *op. cit.*, p. 475.

[17] Fisher, *op. cit.*, p. 247.

[18] Brewer, *op. cit.*, p. 493.

[19] Grove, *op. cit.*, p. 240 ff.

[20] Brewer, *op. cit.*, pp. 501-502; L. & P., III, 2863.

[21] A. F. Pollard, *Henry VIII* (London, 1951), p. 126.

[22] L. & P., III, 2454 and 2456.

[23] *Ibid.*, 2459.

[24] David Hume, *The History of England from the Invasion of Julius Caesar to the Revolution of 1688* (London, 1810), p. 508.

[25] Marian Andrews, *Charles de Bourbon* (London, 1911), p. 98.

[26] *Ibid.*, p. vi.

[27] L. & P., II, 3346.

[28] Fisher, *op. cit.*, p. 250.

[29] Sharon F. S. A. Turner, *The History of England* (London, 1823-1826), Vol. IV, p. 196.

CHAPTER III

[1] Edward Hall, *Hall's Chronicle* (London, 1809), p. 641.

[2] A. F. Pollard, *Henry VIII* (London, 1951), p. 135.

[3] J. S. Brewer, *The Reign of Henry VIII from His Accession to the Death of Wolsey* (London, 1884), Vol. II, p. 13, quoting *Venetian Calendar*, Vol. III, p. 388.

[4] J. Grove, *The History of the Life and Times of Cardinal Wolsey* (London, 1746), Vol. III, p. 212 ff; M. Guizot, *History of France* (London, 1881), Part I, p. 38.

[5] L. & P., IV, 780.

[6] Brewer, *op. cit.*, pp. 116-117.

[7] *Ibid.*, p. 16, note 1.

[8] *Ibid.*, p. 18, note 2.

[9] L. & P., IV, 1053.

[10] Grove, *op. cit.*, p. 369.

[11] Garrett Mattingly, *Catherine of Aragon* (Boston, 1941), p. 225.

[12] H. A. L. Fisher, *The History of England from the Accession of Henry VII to the Death of Henry VIII* (London, New York and Toronto, 1934), p. 254.

[13] J. D. Mackie, *The Earlier Tudors 1485-1558* (Oxford, 1952), p. 315.

[14] L. & P., IV, p. 543.

[15] Brewer, *op. cit.*, p. 49.

[16] R. W. Chambers, *Sir Thomas More* (New York, 1935), p. 212, quoting from Hall, *op. cit.*

[17] L. & P., IV, 1319.

[18] *Ibid.*, 1318.

[19] *Ibid.*, 1243.
[20] *Ibid.*, 1272.
[21] *Ibid.*, 1323.
[22] Fisher, *op. cit.*, p. 255.
[23] L. & P., IV, 1529.
[24] *Ibid.*, 1321.
[25] *Ibid.*, 1332.
[26] Fisher, *op. cit.*, p. 255.
[27] *Ibid.*, p. 254.
[28] Grove, *op. cit.*, p. 352.
[29] L. & P., IV, 1401 and 1464.
[30] *Ibid.*, 1332.
[31] Hall, *op. cit.*, p. 698.
[32] L. & P., IV, 1336.
[33] *Ibid.*, 1378.

CHAPTER IV
[1] Garrett Mattingly, *Catherine of Aragon* (Boston, 1941), p. 226.
[2] L. & P., IV, 1378.
[3] *Ibid.*, 1628.
[4] *Ibid.*, 1409.
[5] *Ibid.*, 1484.
[6] *Ibid.*, 1379.
[7] J. S. Brewer, *The Reign of Henry VIII from His Accession to the Death of Wolsey* (London, 1884), Vol. II, p. 34, quoting Gayangos, *Spanish Calendar*, Vol. III, p. 53.
[8] L. & P., IV, 1083.
[9] Brewer, *op. cit.*, quoting Gayangos, *op. cit.*, p. 74.
[10] L. & P., IV, 1083.
[11] *Ibid.*, 1398.
[12] *Ibid.*, 1522.
[13] Brewer, *op. cit.*, p. 67, quoting Gayangos, *op. cit.*, pp. 222, 221, 227.
[14] L. & P., IV, 1522.
[15] *Ibid.*, 1557.
[16] *Ibid.*, 1633.
[17] Brewer, *op. cit.*, p. 101.
[18] L. & P., IV, 1049.
[19] Brewer, *op. cit.*, p. 26.
[20] H. A. L. Fisher, *The History of England from the Accession of Henry VII to the Death of Henry VIII* (London, New York and Toronto, 1934), p. 259.
[21] L. & P., IV, 1484.
[22] *Ibid.*, 1443.
[23] Brewer, *op. cit.*, p. 95, quoting Gayangos, *op. cit.*, p. 859.
[24] *Ibid.*, p. 96.
[25] L. & P., IV, 2543.
[26] Brewer, *op. cit.*, p. 97, quoting Buonaparte, *Il Sacco di Roma*, p. 190.
[27] L. & P., IV, 2557.

[28] *Ibid.*, 2558.
[29] *Ibid.*, 2629.
[30] *Ibid.*, 2510.
[31] Brewer, *op. cit.*, p. 111.
[32] *Ibid.*, p. 99, quoting Gayangos, *op. cit.*, p. 1004.
[33] *Ibid.*, p. 100.
[34] Karl Brandi, *The Emperor Charles V: The Growth and Destiny of a Man and a World-Empire.* Translated from the German by C. V. Wedgwood (New York, 1939), p. 252.
[35] *L. & P.*, IV, 3122.
[36] Brewer, *op. cit.*, p. 116.
[37] *Ibid.*, pp. 124-125.
[38] *Ibid.*, p. 118.
[39] *Ibid.*, p. 123.
[40] Ralph Roeder, *The Man of the Renaissance. Four Lawgivers: Savonarola, Machiavelli, Castiglione, Aretino* (New York, 1933), p. 413.
[41] *L. & P.*, IV, 3147.

CHAPTER V
[1] A. F. Pollard, *Henry VIII* (London, 1951), p. 141, quoting *Venetian Calendar*, Vol. III, p. 479.
[2] *L. & P.*, IV, 5773.
[3] Pollard, *op. cit.*, p. 142; Philip Marshall Dale, *Medical Biographies: The Ailments of Thirty-three Famous Persons* (University of Oklahoma Press, 1952), p. 23.
[4] H. A. L. Fisher, *The History of England from the Accession of Henry VII to the Death of Henry VIII* (London, New York and Toronto, 1934), p. 266.
[5] *L. & P.*, IV, 5156.
[6] George Cavendish, *The Life of Cardinal Wolsey* (London and New York, 1885), p. 48 ff.
[7] *L. & P.*, IV, 2482.
[8] *Ibid.*, 5156.
[9] *Ibid.*, 3173.
[10] A. F. Pollard, *Wolsey* (London, 1929), p. 283, quoting R. Hall, *Fisher*, p. 51.
[11] J. S. Brewer, *The Reign of Henry VIII from His Accession to the Death of Wolsey* (London, 1884), Vol. II, p. 180; *State Papers*, Vol. I, p. 194.
[12] Garrett Mattingly, *Catherine of Aragon* (Boston, 1941), p. 241, citing Gayangos, *Spanish Calendar*, Vol. III, ii, pp. 193-194.
[13] *L. & P.*, IV, 5859.
[14] Pollard, *Henry VIII*, p. 161.
[15] H. F. M. Prescott, *Mary Tudor* (New York, 1953), pp. 29-30.
[16] William S. Childe-Pemberton, *Elizabeth Blount and Henry the Eighth* (London, 1913), pp. 116, 141, 153.
[17] *L. & P.*, IV, 3155.
[18] Pollard, *Henry VIII*, p. 155.

[19] S. H. Burke, *Historical Portraits of the Tudor Dynasty* (London, 1893), Vol. I, p. 162.
[20] L. & P., IV, 1431.

CHAPTER VI
[1] L. & P., IV, 3201.
[2] J. S. Brewer, *The Reign of Henry VIII from His Accession to the Death of Wolsey* (London, 1884), Vol. II, pp. 202-203, quoting Gayangos, *Spanish Calendar*, Vol. III, p. 276.
[3] L. & P., IV, 3105, pp. 1397, 1400.
[4] George Cavendish, *The Life of Cardinal Wolsey* (London and New York, 1885), p. 67 ff.
[5] Brewer, *op. cit.*, p. 157.
[6] *Ibid.*, p. 158.
[7] A. F. Pollard, *Wolsey* (London, 1929), pp. 194, 193.
[8] L. & P., IV, 1118.
[9] Cavendish, *op. cit.*, p. 67.
[10] Garrett Mattingly, *Renaissance Diplomacy* (New York, 1955), p. 36.
[11] Brewer, *op. cit.*, p. 194 ff., quoting *State Papers*, Vol. I, p. 196.
[12] Pollard, *op. cit.*, p. 6.
[13] Cavendish, *op. cit.*, Introduction by Henry Morley, p. 9.
[14] Frederick C. Dietz, *A Political and Social History of England* (New York, 1937), p. 178.
[15] Cavendish, *op. cit.*, pp. 72-73.
[16] H. A. L. Fisher, *The History of England from the Accession of Henry VII to the Death of Henry VIII* (London, New York and Toronto, 1934), p. 271.
[17] Brewer, *op. cit.*, p. 210, quoting Gayangos, *Spanish Calendar*, Vol. III, ii, p. 17.
[18] *Ibid.*, p. 208, quoting *State Papers*, Vol. I, p. 230.
[19] Fisher, *op. cit.*; Ethelred L. Taunton, *Thomas Wolsey: Legate and Reformer* (London, 1902), p. 161.
[20] Brewer, *op. cit.*, p. 221, quoting *State Papers*, Vol. I, p. 270.
[21] L. & P., IV, 3419.
[22] Pollard, *Henry VIII* (London, 1951), p. 167.
[23] Brewer, *op. cit.*, p. 226.

CHAPTER VII
[1] L. & P., IV, 3641.
[2] *Ibid.*, 3644.
[3] J. S. Brewer, *The Reign of Henry VIII from His Accession to the Death of Wolsey* (London, 1884), Vol. II, p. 229, quoting Buonaparte, *Il Sacco di Roma*, p. 214.
[4] Ralph Roeder, *The Man of the Renaissance. Four Lawgivers: Savonarola, Machiavelli, Castiglione, Aretino* (New York, 1933), p. 405.
[5] L. & P., IV, 3751.
[6] *Ibid.*, 3693.

[7] *Ibid.*, 4090.
[8] *Ibid.*, 3913.
[9] *Ibid.*, 4167, p. 1841.
[10] *Ibid.*
[11] *Ibid.*
[12] *Ibid.*, 4251.

CHAPTER VIII
[1] A. Abram, *Social England in the Fifteenth Century* (London, 1909), p. 119.
[2] Sir Walter Besant, *London in the Time of the Tudors* (London, 1904), Vol. I, p. 286.
[3] Frank Arthur Mumby, *The Youth of Henry VIII, A Narrative in Contemporary Letters* (Boston, 1913), p. 160.
[4] George G. Coulton, ed., *Social Life in Britain from the Conquest to the Reformation* (Cambridge, 1938), pp. 439-440.
[5] Abram, *op. cit.*, p. 118.
[6] G. M. Trevelyan, *English Social History* (London, 1942), p. 65.
[7] Lewis Einstein, *The Italian Renaissance in England* (New York, 1902), p. 223.
[8] *Ibid.*, p. 86.
[9] J. S. Brewer, *The Reign of Henry VIII from His Accession to the Death of Wolsey* (London, 1884), Vol. II, p. 205.
[10] *Ibid.*, p. 275, note 1.
[11] Garrett Mattingly, *Catherine of Aragon* (Boston, 1941), p. 34.
[12] William Hepworth Dixon, *History of Two Queens* (London, 1873), p. 266.
[13] Brewer, *op. cit.*, pp. 103-104, quoting Gayangos, *Spanish Calendar,* Vol. III, p. 1018.
[14] S. H. Burke, *Historical Portraits of the Tudor Dynasty* (London, 1893), Vol. I, p. 149.
[15] Dixon, *op. cit.*, p. 282.
[16] Burke, *op. cit.*, p. 94.
[17] *Ibid.*
[18] Sharon F. S. A. Turner, *The History of England* (London, 1823-1826), Vol. III, p. 183.
[19] L. & P., IV, 3218.
[20] *Ibid.*, 3221.

CHAPTER IX
[1] L. & P., IV, 3160.
[2] *Ibid.*, 4345.
[3] A. F. Pollard, *Henry VIII* (London, 1951), p. 172.
[4] *Ibid.*, p. 173, citing Stephan Ehses, *Römische Dokumente zur Geschichte der Ehescheidung Heinrichs VIII von England, 1527-1534* (Paderhorn, 1893). See James Gairdner, "New Lights on the Divorce of Henry VIII," *English Historical Review,* Vol. XI (1896), pp. 673-702; Vol. XII (1897), pp. 237-253.

[5] *L. & P.*, IV, 4286.
[6] *Ibid.*, 4733.
[7] *Ibid.*, 4564.
[8] *Ibid.*, 3930.
[9] James A. Williamson, *Maritime Enterprise 1485-1558* (Oxford, 1913), p. 186.
[10] H. A. L. Fisher, *The History of England from the Accession of Henry VII to the Death of Henry VIII* (London, New York and Toronto, 1934), p. 277.
[11] *L. & P.*, IV, 4310.
[12] *Ibid.*, 3761.
[13] J. S. Brewer, *The Reign of Henry VIII from His Accession to the Death of Wolsey* (London, 1884), Vol. II, p. 268.
[14] *L. & P.*, IV, 4391.
[15] *Ibid.*, 4510.
[16] *Ibid.*, 4391 and 4440.
[17] *Ibid.*, 4542.
[18] *Ibid.*, 4391.
[19] *Ibid.*, 5825.
[20] Charles Creighton, *A History of Epidemics in Britain from A. D. to the Extinction of the Plague* (Cambridge, 1891), Vol. I, p. 252; *L. & P.*, IV, 4409.
[21] Brewer, *op. cit.*, p. 274, quoting *State Papers*, Vol. I, p. 31.
[22] *L. & P.*, IV, 4476.
[23] *Ibid.*, 4478.
[24] Creighton, *op. cit.*
[25] *L. & P.*, IV, 4383.
[26] *Ibid.*, 4403.
[27] *Ibid.*, 4477.
[28] *Ibid.*, 4507.
[29] Brewer, *op. cit.*, p. 284.
[30] *L. & P.*, IV, 4509.
[31] Brewer, *op. cit.*, p. 286; *State Papers*, Vol. I, p. 317.
[32] *L. & P.*, IV, 4649.
[33] *Original Letters.* Edited by Henry Ellis (London, 1825), Series III, Vol. II, Letter CLXIII, p. 117. Certainly one of the most touching documents of the period.
[34] *L. & P.*, IV, 5382.
[35] *Ibid.*, 3649.
[36] *Ibid.*, 5642.
[37] *Ibid.*, 5138, 5222, 5387.
[38] *Ibid.*, 3318.

CHAPTER X
[1] *L. & P.*, IV, 5189.
[2] *Ibid.*, 5212.
[3] *Ibid.*, 4426.
[4] S. H. Burke, *Historical Portraits of the Tudor Dynasty* (London, 1893), Vol. I, p. 198.

[5] L. & P., IV, 4857.
[6] Ibid., 4881.
[7] Ibid., 4858.
[8] Ibid., 4875.
[9] Ibid., 4880.
[10] Ibid., 4892.
[11] Ibid., 5016.
[12] Ibid., 5072.
[13] J. S. Brewer, The Reign of Henry VIII from His Accession to the Death of Wolsey (London, 1884), Vol. II, p. 316.
[14] Philip Hughes, The Reformation in England (London, 1954), Vol. I, p. 177.
[15] Brewer, op. cit., p. 308.
[16] L. & P., IV, 5154.
[17] A. F. Pollard, Henry VIII (London, 1951), p. 176.
[18] L. & P., IV, 5270.
[19] H. A. L. Fisher, The History of England from the Accession of Henry VII to the Death of Henry VIII (London, New York and Toronto, 1934), p. 283.
[20] Brewer, op. cit., p. 320.
[21] L. & P., IV, 4251.
[22] Ibid., 4978.
[23] Ibid., 2977, p. 2158.
[24] Ibid., 5523.
[25] Ibid., 5038.
[26] Ibid., 5518.
[27] Ibid., p. 2370.
[28] Brewer, op. cit., p. 334.
[29] L. & P., IV, 5210.
[30] Ibid., p. 2317.
[31] Lewis Einstein, Tudor Ideals (New York, 1921), p. 39.
[32] M. Guizot, History of France (London, 1881), Part I, p. 103.
[33] L. & P., IV, 5742.
[34] Ibid., 5700.

CHAPTER XI
[1] J. S. Brewer, The Reign of Henry VIII from His Accession to the Death of Wolsey (London, 1884), Vol. II, p. 338; Edward Hall, Hall's Chronicle (London, 1809), p. 756 ff., gives an account of the trial and details of the setting.
[2] L. & P., IV, 5611.
[3] Philip Hughes, The Reformation in England (London, 1954), Vol. I, p. 189.
[4] Ibid., p. 187, citing Stephan Ehses, Römische Dokumente zur Geschichte der Ehescheidung Heinrichs VIII von England (Paderhorn, 1893), p. 99.
[5] Brewer, op. cit., p. 342.
[6] George Cavendish, The Life of Cardinal Wolsey (London and New York, 1885), p. 116.
[7] L. & P., IV, 5702.

[8] J. Grove, *The History of the Life and Times of Cardinal Wolsey* (London, 1746), Vol. III, p. 233.

[9] L. & P., IV, 5733.

[10] Cavendish, *op. cit.*, p. 124.

[11] S. H. Burke, *Historical Portraits of the Tudor Dynasty* (London, 1893), Vol. I, p. 325.

[12] L. & P., IV, 5732.

[13] Brewer, *op. cit.*, p. 340.

[14] L. & P., IV, 5789.

[15] Edward Hall, *Hall's Chronicle* (London, 1809), p. 758.

[16] Cavendish, *op. cit.*, p. 131.

BOOK IV

CHAPTER I

[1] J. S. Brewer, *The Reign of Henry VIII from His Accession to the Death of Wolsey* (London, 1884), Vol. II, p. 368, citing *State Papers*, Vol. I, p. 344.

[2] L. & P., IV, 5403.

[3] *State Papers*, Vol. I, p. 347; L. & P., IV, 5999.

[4] A. F. Pollard, *Henry VIII* (London, 1951), pp. 181-182.

[5] L.& P., IV, 5993.

[6] George Cavendish, *The Life of Cardinal Wolsey* (London and New York, 1885), p. 132 ff.

[7] E. M. G. Routh, *Sir Thomas More and His Friends* (London, 1934), p. 184.

[8] Edward Hall, *Hall's Chronicle* (London, 1809), p. 759.

[9] *Ibid.*, p. 760.

[10] L. & P., IV, 6011.

[11] *Ibid.*, 6018.

[12] Cavendish, *op. cit.*, p. 140.

[13] L. & P., IV, 6025.

[14] *Ibid.*

[15] Cavendish, *op. cit.*, p. 143.

CHAPTER II

[1] A. F. Pollard, *Wolsey* (London, 1929), p. 253, note 2, quoting L. & P., III, 414.

[2] L. & P., IV, 6025.

[3] *Ibid.*, 5749, p. 2554. For a statement of the charges, see Richard Fiddes, *The Life of Cardinal Wolsey* (London, 1726), Collections, pp. 172-179.

[4] H. A. L. Fisher, *The History of England from the Accession of Henry VII to the Death of Henry VIII* (London, New York and Toronto, 1934), pp. 297, 293.

[5] *Ibid.*, p. 298.

[6] L. & P., IV, 6043.

[7] *Ibid.*, V, 120.

[8] A. F. Pollard, *Henry VIII* (London, 1951), p. 209.

[9] George Cavendish, *The Life of Cardinal Wolsey* (London and New York, 1885), p. 159.

[10] *Ibid.*, p. 155.

[11] *L. & P.*, IV, 6182.

[12] Cavendish, *op. cit.*, p. 168.

[13] *Ibid.*, p. 170 ff.

[14] Francis Godwin, *Annales of England* (London, 1630), p. 108.

[15] A. F. Pollard, *Wolsey* (London, 1939), p. 223.

[16] J. S. Brewer, *The Reign of Henry VIII from His Accession to the Death of Wolsey* (London, 1884), Vol. II, p. 404.

[17] *L. & P.*, IV, 6213.

[18] *Ibid.*, 6214.

[19] *Ibid.*, 6199.

[20] *Ibid.*, 6199, p. 2781.

[21] *Ibid.*, 6249.

[22] Cavendish, *op. cit.*, p. 175.

[23] F. H. Crossley, *The English Abbey, Its Life and Work in the Middle Ages* (New York, 1949), p. 5.

[24] Cavendish, *op. cit.*, p. 187.

[25] *Original Letters.* Edited by Henry Ellis (London, 1825), Series II, Vol. II, Letter CLXXXVI, pp. 172-173.

CHAPTER III

[1] *L. & P.*, IV, 2946.

[2] *Ibid.*, 6302.

[3] A. F. Pollard, *Wolsey* (London, 1929), p. 273.

[4] *L. & P.*, IV, 6335.

[5] George Cavendish, *The Life of Cardinal Wolsey* (London and New York, 1885), p. 187.

[6] *A Remedy for Sedition, Wherin Are Conteyned Many Thynges Concerning the True and Loyall Obeysance that Commes Owe Unto Their Prince and Soverayne Lord the King* (London, 1536).

[7] *Original Letters.* Edited by Henry Ellis (London, 1825), Series III, Vol. II, Letter CXC, pp. 181-188.

[8] *L. & P.*, IV, 6329.

[9] J. S. Brewer, *The Reign of Henry VIII from His Accession to the Death of Wolsey* (London, 1884), Vol. II, p. 424.

[10] *L. & P.*, IV, 6034.

[11] *Ibid.*, 6055.

[12] *Ibid.*, 6510.

[13] *Ibid.*, 6663.

[14] *Ibid.*, 6572.

[15] *Ibid.*, 6076.

[16] *Ibid.*, 6575.

[17] *Ibid.*, 6688.

[18] *Ibid.*, 6411.
[19] *Ibid.*, 6738.
[20] A. F. Pollard, *op. cit.*, p. 286.
[21] L. & P., IV, 6687.

CHAPTER IV
[1] George Cavendish, *The Life of Cardinal Wolsey* (London and New York, 1885), p. 211 ff.
[2] L. & P., IV, 6018.
[3] *Ibid.*, 6738.

CHAPTER V
[1] A. F. Pollard, *Wolsey* (London, 1929), p. 299.
[2] This phrasing of Wolsey's statement comes from George Cavendish, *The Life of Cardinal Wolsey* (New York, 1885), p. 250. It was rephrased as spoken by the character Wolsey in Act III, Scene 2, of the Shakespearean play *King Henry VIII*. Parts of the play dealing with Wolsey and the annulment derive from Cavendish, whose book was circulating in manuscript, if not in printed form, at the time the piece was written.
[3] Cavendish, *op. cit.*, p. 257.
[4] L. & P., IV, p. 6757.
[5] Francis Aidan Gasquet, *Henry VIII and the English Monasteries* (London, 1889), pp. 408-410.
[6] *Ibid.*, pp. 120-121.
[7] *Ibid.*, p. 149.
[8] Garrett Mattingly, *Catherine of Aragon* (Boston, 1941), p. 430 and note 16, p. 463.

Acknowledgment

ONE who fashions a modern biography of Wolsey must rely at every turn upon the work of scores of persons who have examined with skill and patience hundreds of musty muniments, burrowed into archives, classified and codified the documents of the period covered by the Cardinal's life. Living as we do now in an age when information is almost inescapable, we can hardly imagine the labor and pains spent to give some semblance of order to the records of early Tudor times. Those who for three hundred years after Wolsey's death ferreted out materials did so by firsthand examination of such original documents as they were lucky enough to uncover in scattered places. There are of course values in this kind of research, but the values are limited to scholars and privileged specialists.

In the past hundred years a remarkable change has come to pass: many of the actual materials of sixteenth-century history have appeared in printed form and are, within reason, available to the nonprofessional student. By having access to the slow accretion of data made possible by scholars, the modern writer has a distinct advantage in both breadth of view and perspective.

An example — and perhaps the best example — of the prodigious work performed by collators is to be found in the labors during the middle part of the nineteenth century by J. S. Brewer, then professor of English literature and history at King's College, London. It was Mr. Brewer who smelled out, dusted off, and placed in reasonable sequence — often dating from internal evidence — the letters and papers of the years when Wolsey served Henry VIII. The dimensions of the task may be guessed from the fact that the letters and papers were strewn around half a dozen repositories; and the scope and inclusiveness of the job may be seen from the fact that "no letter written by or to an Englishman at this period, or even by a foreigner if it contained news about English affairs escaped Mr. Brewer's researches." No fewer than 24,000 papers were selected, collated, and legibly published (with modern spelling) in a colossal work entitled *Letters and Papers, Foreign and Domestic, of the Reign of Henry VIII* . . . This work appeared in four volumes, each volume with several parts, in 1876. And as if this were not service enough, friends and beneficiaries of Mr. Brewer brought together the prefaces he had written for the four volumes of the *Letters and Papers,* and these prefaces were published in 1884 in two sizable volumes under the title *The Reign of Henry VIII From His Accession to the Death of Wolsey.*

In a word, thanks to these and other collections, the events of the period of Wolsey's public life are a matter of convenient record. To be sure, the interpretation of the documents must be left to the individual writer, and this interpretation will be influenced both by the writer's training and by his perception. A mere slavish addiction to documents will not suffice. The glaring error that Wolsey was buried at Leicester in the same monastery as Richard III comes from the uncritical acceptance and ready transcription of an official paper. It has been perpetuated by writers who did not take the pains either to visit Leicester or to read books about Leicester.

But the use of the materials of history is one thing; their availability quite another. Today more and more readers can check materials for themselves. In the course of preparing this book I have had an occasional chance to work in the British Museum, the Library of Congress, and the New York Public Library. But, more to the point, I have been able through a small-town library to inspect in my own home the contents of sixteenth-century documents, not to mention scores of other source books from which this book was drawn.

During five years of active research I had the gifted assistance of Mrs. Genevieve Egerton, then living in Chappaqua, New York. Without her enthusiasm for the period under study, her percipience in selecting pertinent material, and her energy in transcribing lengthy passages for close consideration, this book would probably not have appeared for another ten years. And her own work would have been sorely handicapped without the diligence and imaginative cooperation of Mrs. Margaret Handley and the staff of the Chappaqua Library. Resourceful and determined in their willingness to help, members of the staff met virtually every request for books through the facilities of the inter-library loan service of Westchester County and the New York State Library at Albany. To be sure, the combined resources of libraries in Westchester are exceptional, but inter-library loan arrangements are widespread, and my experience suggests that any serious interest, even if it appears to be obscure or remote, can today be pursued through a local library.

Hence the thanks I express involve more than polite acknowledgment. I admit my indebtedness in the reference notes, but my obligations go far beyond my sources. My thanks must be diffuse because my benefactors are many. And they include all those who have made books and materials available.

CHARLES W. FERGUSON

Index

Index

533

534

City Companies in London, 235
Clarencieux (Thomas Benolte), 284, 338, 390-391
Claude, Queen of France, 279, 386
Clement VII, Pope (Giulio de' Medici), 267, 442; elected Pope, 203; urges reconciliation of Christian princes, 242, 297, 326; Holy League of Cognac against Charles V, 321; pleas for aid ignored, 323-324; prisoner of Imperialists, 323-324, 328-330; escapes to Orvieto, 372; receives English agents seeking commission, 333-334, 373-378, 388-390, 411-421, 424-425, 432-433; alliance with Charles V, 442
Clergy, under Henry VII, 38-39; opposition to, 76, 351; controversy over rights of, 139-141; rebelled against Pope, 500. *See also* Church *and* Church reform
Clerical privileges, controversy over, 126-129; Wolsey's neglect of the problem, 197-198
Clerk, John, Bishop of Bath, 268-269, 309, 334
Cloth manufacture, 29, 49
Coinage, 172
Colet, John, Dean of St. Paul's, 137-138, 148, 470
Colleges of the universities, 23, 25
Collis, Boniface, 136
Columbus, Bartholomew, 43-44
Columbus, Christophorus, 43
Combes, Robert Wolsey's native town, 14
Common law courts, 150, 151
Commons, assert themselves, 41, 88
Compiègne, 366
Compton, Sir William, 352
Convocation, 139-151, 289-290
Corpus Christi, College of (Oxford), 43, 209, 211
Court of Piepowder, 145
Courts, system and practices, 146-152. *See also* Star Chamber, Court of
Cranmer, Thomas, Archbishop of Canterbury, 484, 500, 501
Crécy, battle of, 65
Crime and lawlessness, under Henry VII, 40-41
Croke, Richard, royal tutor to Henry Fitzroy, 342
Cromer, Dr., 463

Cromwell, Thomas, 197, 219; championed Wolsey's cause openly, 464-465, 467; effort to save Cardinal College, 481; with Wolsey in last days, 481-482
Crown gold, 172

Dacre, Lord, 293-294
Danes, 7-8
Darcy, Lord Thomas, of Templehurst, 66, 456-457
Dawndy, Mr., 219
Deane, Henry, Archbishop of Canterbury, 59, 61, 64
Derby, Earl of. *See* Stanley, Thomas
Dictes and Sayings of the Philosophers, 28
Discoveries, 43-45
Dominicans (Black Friars), 190
Doria, Andrea, 408
Dorothy, Wolsey's daughter, 87, 494
Dorset, Marquis of. *See* Grey, Thomas I *and* II
Dover Castle, 250
Dress, regulations in, 144
du Bellay, French ambassador, 395; Wolsey's talk with, 403-404, 449-450
Duprat, Antoine, 274

Education, awakening of interest in, 20; crisis in, 207-208; Wolsey's devotion to, 216-217, 403-404
Edward, Earl of Warwick, 13-15, 31; rumors regarding, 35-36; lineage and claims to throne, 68; hanged, 68
Edward III, King of England, 65, 68
Edward IV, King of England, 12-16, 26, 56
Edward V, King of England, 26
Eleanor, sister of Charles V, 320
Elizabeth of England, daughter of Henry VIII, 500
Elizabeth of York, wife of Henry VII, 33, 64, 223
Ely, Bishop of. *See* Alcock, John
Enclosure system, 10, 173-175
England, parlous times in, 8-14; the monarchy, 12; lack of stability in, 30; discontent in, 39-40; time of opportunity, 49-50; years of drouth and flood, 392-393; murrain, 393; plague, 394-395; changing face of, 443
English Merchant Adventurers, 49

535

536

Henry VII, King of England, 32; marriage to Elizabeth of York, 33; character of reign, 33-40; position as King secured, 34; birth of son Arthur, 35; plot to unseat, 36; description, 37-38; complexion of court, 39-40, 66; interest in explorations, 43-45; question of succession, 67-68; marriage schemes, 71-77; attitude toward old nobility, 75-76; last days and death, 77-78; urged Henry's marriage to Catherine, 83; contrasted with Henry VIII, 84-85, 113-114; relations with Scots, 113-114; Wolsey's debt to, 171; replaces monasteries with hospitals, 196. *See also* Henry Tudor

Henry VIII, King of England, 3, 69, 78; a dilettante, 80-82; marriage to Catherine of Aragon, 80-84; protests against validity, 83; gaiety and extravagance, 84-85; contrasted with Henry VII, 84-85, 113-114; summons Parliament, 88; lacks interest in explorations, 92; policy toward Scotland, 92, 113-114; joins Holy League against France, 93, 99; plans to conquer France, 93-113, 130, 270-296, 302, 309-310; hears controversy over clerical rights, 140-141; dissolves Parliament, 142; makes Wolsey Lord Chancellor of England, 142-143; resentment of Francis I, 236; meetings with Francis I at Field of Cloth of Gold, 247-251; receives visits from Charles, 248-251, 283-284; deferential book, 267-269; receives from Pope Leo X title *Fidei Defensor*, 267-269; on marriage, 269; relations with Emperor, 272-276, 313; Anne Boleyn, 279, 280, 366-367, 387-388; *The Great Harry*, 283; summons Parliament for subsidy, 285-287; receives news of Francis I's defeat at Pavia, 301-302; protector of Holy League (1526) against Emperor, 321; decision to terminate marriage, 330-347, 363; Henry Fitzroy, 345; tells Catherine about annulment, 348; seeks annulment through Pope's approval, 373-390; withdrawal during plague, 396-397; solicitous of Wolsey's health, 397; on confiscation of religious houses, 400; bitter over rejection of

Amicable Loan, 400-401; estrangement from Wolsey, 403-421, 439-441; resentment of Wolsey's devotion to education, 404; session with Campeggio, 409; statement to people on annulment, 411-412; trial at Blackfriars, 425-434; warm relationship with Wolsey over years, 440-441; private talks with Wolsey at Grafton, 444-445; kindness shown Wolsey in last days, 453-454, 460-462; marriage to Catherine declared null and void, 500; supreme head of Church in England, 500

Henry Tudor, 30; a threat to reigning monarch, 28, 31; proclaimed Henry VII, King of England, 32. *See also* Henry VII, King of England

Heraldry, 284

Heresy, Wolsey's leniency toward, 198-199

Holy League (*1511*) formed against France, 90, 93; (*1526*) against Emperor, 321

Holy Roman Empire, 111, 244-246

Holy See, sack of, 324

Horsey, Dr., 124-125

Howard, Sir Edward, killed Andrew Barton, 92; Admiral of the Fleet, 104-105; death, 106

Howard, John, Duke of Norfolk, 32

Howard, Thomas I, Earl of Surrey, second Duke of Norfolk, 32, 75, 88-89, 105, 171, 481-483; antipathy toward Wolsey, 337, 350, 352, 467, 468, 471; Wolsey surrenders Great Seal to, 447-451

Howard, Thomas II, Earl of Surrey, third Duke of Norfolk, 106, 165, 167, 292-293

Hundred Years' War, effects on England, 11

Hunne, Richard, 123-129

INDULGENCES, 181-182

Innocent VIII, Pope, criticism of Church in England, 178

Ipswich, 7, 14, 16

Ipswich Grammar School, 18, 22

Isabella, Queen of Castile. *See* Ferdinand the Catholic, and Isabella

Isabella of Portugal, 312-313

Italy, influence felt in England, 20; French campaigns in, 134, 135, 235-237, 298-299; threat of Turk in, 241; Emperor in command of, 319-328, 347, 408, 442

JAMES IV OF SCOTLAND, description, 114-115; death, 116; married to Margaret, daughter of Henry VII, 399
Jasper, uncle of Henry VII, 33
Jesus College, Cambridge University, 196
Joanna, Queen of Castile, 112
Jordon, Dame Isabel, 399
Joseph, Charles, 124-125
Judicial system, Henry VII strengthens, 40-41
Julius II, Pope, issues bull sanctioning Henry's marriage to Catherine, 69-70; doubts about validity, 82-83; aggressiveness, 89-90; forms Holy League, 90; death, 99; second dispensation, 413
Justices of the Peace, 41

KENT, THOMAS, 46
Kidderminster, Richard, Abbot of Winchcombe, 127
King, enlargement of the concept of, 170
King of England's Sickness, 394-396
King's College, Cambridge University, 196
King's Council, 38-39, 40-41, 145-146, 171-172
Kingston, Sir William, Constable of the Tower of London, 491-498
Knight, Dr. William, 365-366, 369
Knights, 11
Kremlin, 234

LABOR UNREST, 144
Laborers, 9
Ladies' Peace, 442
La Maison curiale, 86
Lambeth Palace, 61, 177
Lancaster, House of, 11, 12, 13, 15
Landless laborers, 9
Landriano, battle of, 442
Larke, Joan, Wolsey's noncanonical marriage to, 86-87, 224; later married to George Legh, 87
Larke, Peter, father and grandfather of Joan, 87
Larke, Thomas, brother of Joan, 57
Larke, Thomas, kinsman of Joan's father, 87; Wolsey's confessor, 87, 494
Lateran Council, 90
Latin versus Greek conflict, 42-43
Lautrec, Marshal, 298
Legateship, Wolsey's efforts to secure, 120, 177, 185, 211
Legatine courts, Wolsey's creation of, 198
Legh, George, married Joan Larke, 87, 224; children, 224-225
Legh, Thomas, son of George and Joan, 224
Leicester, 493-494
Leo X, Pope (Giovanni de' Medici), Holy League, 99; creates Wolsey Cardinal, 119, 121, 135; grants legateship, 184-185; death, 199; Wolsey's indebtedness to, 235; secret confederation against France, 267; in constant fear of Francis, 271
Levies, for King's war, 103-104
Limington, 54-55, 75
Livery and maintenance, 29; under Henry VII, 33-34, 40, 152
Local administration, 150
Lollards, 180-181
Lollards' Tower of St. Paul's, 123
London, Bishop of. See FitzJames, Richard
Lord Chancellor of England, office of, 143-145
Louis XII, King of France, threat to Pope's peace of mind, 90, 93; schismatic scheme, 90, 93; death, 129-130; marriage to Mary (sister of Henry VIII), 130-131
Louise of Savoy, mother of Francis I, 237, 297, 298; rules as regent, 302, 346-347; treats for peace with Henry VIII, 316-317; peace at Cambrai, 422-423, 442
Lovell, Sir Thomas, 72
Low Countries, 391
Lower classes, rise of, 14; emulating upper classes, 20
Lower schools, 215-216
Luther, Martin, 181-182, 268

538

Lutheranism, effect on common people, 361-362
Lydd, Kent, 75

MACHIAVELLI, NICCOLÒ, *The Prince*, 170-171
Madrid, Treaty of, 319
Magdalen College, Oxford, 23-26, 35-37, 42-43, 47-48, 56
Maiano, Gian da, 227
Manorial courts, 151
March, Robert de la, 272
Margaret, Queen of James IV of Scotland, 114, 166, 293, 339, 344
Margaret of Anjou, Queen of Henry VI of England, 15-16, 340
Margaret of Austria (also called Margaret of Savoy), daughter of the Emperor Maximilian and regent of the Netherlands, 71-77, 111-112; aunt of Charles V, 275, 422, 423
Margaret of Burgundy, 99, 442
Marguerite de Valois, Duchess of Alençon, sister of Francis I, 279
Marmelanius, Peter, lutanist, 107
Marriage, Henry VIII on, 269; problems and improvement as an institution, 379-381
Marseilles, 298
Mary (daughter of Henry VII), Queen of Louis XII of France, 129, 166, 339; contract of marriage to Charles V, 76-77, 272-276, 311, 312; married Charles Brandon (Duke of Suffolk), 129-133
Mary, Princess (daughter of Henry VIII and Catherine), 157, 283; plan to marry Dauphin of France, 317, 340; betrothed to Duke of Orleans, 359; Catherine's devotion to, 384-385
Master of Arts, Oxford, 50-51
Masters, Wolsey's instructions to, 217
Matilda, daughter of Henry I, 340
Maximilian, Emperor (Holy Roman Empire), 52; Wolsey's mission to, 71-72, 76-77; homage to Henry VIII, 111-112; treacherousness, 130; Maximilian farce, 238-239; League of Cambrai, 241; death and election of successor, 244-245
Mayhew, Richard, Bishop of Hereford, 47, 56, 74
Medici, Giovanni de'. *See* Leo X, Pope

Medici, Giulio de'. *See* Clement VII, Pope
Mendoza, Diego Hurtado, 337
Merchants, growing class of, 11, 14
Merchants of the Staple, 49
Mesa, Bernardino de, 249, 281
Milan, Duchy of, 298-299, 320, 321, 324, 442
Milan, Duke of. *See* Sforza, Francesco Maria
Milford Haven, 32
Monasteries, wealth and power, 179-180; problem of immovability of, 192; hospitality of, 192-194; dissolution, 195-197, 218, 500
Moncada, Don Hugo, 323-325, 327
Monus Christi, 163
More, The (Wolsey's palace), 223
More, Thomas, 315, 354, 424; Speaker of Commons, 286-288; Great Seal delivered to, 456
Mortimer, Margaret, marriage to Duke of Suffolk, 339
Morton, John Cardinal, Archbishop of Canterbury, 38, 178
Mortuaries, 123
Moscow, 234
Murrain, 393

NANFAN, SIR RICHARD, 65-66, 67
Naples, 71, 320
Nationhood, growing consciousness of, 168, 170-173
Navarre, 271, 272
Netherlands, 71-73, 76-77, 240, 350-351
Neville, Sir Edward, 232
New Learning, 208-210
New World, 234
Nobles, under Henry VII, 33, 75-76
Norfolk, Duke of. *See* Howard, John; Thomas I; Thomas II
Norris, Sir Henry, 444, 453-454
Northumberland, Earl. *See* Percy, Henry
Nunneries, 194, 196, 500

OBSERVANT FRIARS, 190-191; chapel of the, 83-84
Orleans, Duke of, betrothal to Princess Mary, 359
Orvieto, Pope Clement's escape to, 372-375

539

541

543